Visual
InterDev™ 6

Paul Thurrott, et al.

SAMS

201 West 103rd Street,
Indianapolis, Indiana 46290

Unleashed

Visual InterDev™ 6 Unleashed

Copyright © 1999 by Sams Publishing

International Standard Book Number: 0-672-31262-x

Library of Congress Catalog Card Number: 98-84681

Printed in the United States of America

First Printing: April 1999

01   00   99   4   3   2   1

Trademarks

Warning and Disclaimer

EXECUTIVE EDITOR
Bradley L. Jones

ACQUISITION EDITOR
Chris Webb

DEVELOPMENT EDITOR
Matt Purcell

MANAGING EDITOR
Jodi Jensen

PROJECT EDITOR
Tonya Simpson

COPY EDITOR
Kate Talbot

INDEXER
Erika Millen

PROOFREADERS
Ben Berg
Billy Fields
Mary Lagu
Eddie Lushbaugh

TECHNICAL EDITOR
Glenn Fincher

SOFTWARE DEVELOPMENT SPECIALIST
Andrea Duvall

TEAM COORDINATOR
Carol Ackerman

INTERIOR DESIGN
Gary Adair

COVER DESIGN
Aren Howell

LAYOUT TECHNICIANS
Brandon Allen
Tim Osborn
Staci Somers

Contents at a Glance

Contents

About the Authors

Paul Thurrott is a Web developer and the publisher of WinInfo, the Windows news and information mailing list. Through this newsletter and his other online affiliations, such as WUGNET, the SiteBuilder Network,and ClubWin, Paul advocates the use of Windows as a general computing and development platform. Paul has been nominated by Microsoft as a MVP twice for his contributions to the Windows community. He spent over a year creating some of the first dynamic Web sites on the Internet as the Webmaster at Big Tent Media Labs before cutting back to spend more time at home with his first child. Paul has been involved with Visual InterDev since the first beta of what was then called Internet Studio. He has championed the product ever since.

The author of over a dozen books about Windows and Web development, Paul lives in Phoenix with his wife Stephanie, their son Mark, and two bilingual cats. When not writing about Windows, Paul roots for the Arizona Cardinals and just wishes they'd win once every once in a while. Paul can be reached at `thurrott@wugnet.com`.

Ken Cox is a Web applications programmer and information developer for Nortel Networks in Toronto, Canada. He is a Microsoft Most Valuable Professional (MVP) in the Visual InterDev and Active Server Pages groups. Ken has been involved with VI and ASP from the earliest betas and continues to contribute to books and magazines. He has a degree in Radio and Television Arts, and spent over 20 years as a broadcast journalist in Toronto and Quebec City. You can reach Ken at `kenc@corinet.com`.

Steven Banick has been a lead and contributing author for several Macmillan publications and is currently a development manager for the consumer Internet division of TELUS Advanced Communications in Alberta, Canada. Steve can be reached at `http://www.banick.com`. Steve likes warm socks.

Brian M. Fino is a Web developer at Cyberian Outpost. Previously, Brian worked for the University of Dayton Research Institute, where he built sites exculsively in ASP using Microsoft Visual InterDev and Microsoft Site Server Commerce. He can be reached at `bfino@outpost.com`.

James Kindred is the director of development at Cyberian Outpost. Prior to developing `http://www.outpost.com`, James was a senior engineer with LEXIS-NEXIS, where he worked extensively with COM/DCOM and other Microsoft Web-based technologies. James can be reached at `james@outpost.com`.

Michael Marsh earned his B.A. in Aquatic Biology at the University of California at Santa Barbara in 1984. He quit graduate school in San Diego to become a professional programmer in 1984. He began programming in 1978 when his organic chemistry teacher let him fool around with an Apple II in the lab. At that point, he was hooked. Michael can be reached at mmarsh@stellcom.com.

Doug Mitchell is a senior principal for American Management Systems, Inc., where he has spent the last nine years developing custom client/server and Web business applications for a variety of clients. More recently, he has focused his efforts on leveraging Microsoft technology to develop n-tier business applications. Doug is a graduate of Carnegie Mellon with a degree in Information and Decision Systems and is a Visual Basic and InterDev MCP. He can be reached at doug_mitchell@mail.amsinc.com.

Michael R. Starkenberg is the chief technology officer at Cyberian Outpost, a leading e-commerce site. Prior to building http://www.outpost.com, he was the manager of Internet integration at America Online, where he built some of the largest sites on the Internet. He can be reached at stark@outpost.com.

Dedication

This book is lovingly dedicated to my beautiful son, Mark. I love ya, poops.

—*Paul Thurrott*

Acknowledgments

It's been said so many times that it's almost a cliché, but no book is the work of one person. I'd like to thank all my co-authors and the wonderful staff at Macmillan Publishing for making this the best Visual InterDev book on the market. I certainly couldn't have done it without all of you. Special thanks to Chris Webb for not unleashing Bruno on me, despite a couple of late deliveries. Thanks, Chris. You're the best.

As always, thanks to Stephanie for giving me that most precious gift of time so that I could complete this manuscript on schedule. Only a handful of people understand what I do for a living, but Stephanie has always understood the time and dedication it takes to make this happen. Thanks, babe.

And that wasn't Stephanie's only gift for me last year. Together, we celebrated the birth of our first child, Mark Andrew, in April 1998. People think the world of their own children, but let's be honest. Mark is just the cutest kid in the world, no contest, and I love him very much. This one's for you, little buddy.

I'd also like to thank the dedicated readers of *WinInfo*, my daily Windows news and information email newsletter. *WinInfo* has developed into a lively community that encompasses everyone from computer industry insiders to students just getting their first break in this exciting and dynamic field. It wouldn't be worth writing if it weren't for the wonderful people I correspond with every week.

Thanks, finally, to the great guys at WUGNET: Joel Diamond, Larry McJunkin, Howard Sobel, and my good friend, Keith Furman. They've given me a home on the Web and some great times at trade shows and other events around the country. I look forward to working with you further in 1999.

Tell Us What You Think!

As the reader of this book, *you* are our most important critic and commentator. We value your opinion and want to know what we're doing right, what we could do better, what areas you'd like to see us publish in, and any other words of wisdom you're willing to pass our way.

As Associate Publisher for Sams Publishing, I welcome your comments. You can fax, email, or write me directly to let me know what you did or didn't like about this book— as well as what we can do to make our books stronger.

Please note that I cannot help you with technical problems related to the topic of this book, and that due to the high volume of mail I receive, I might not be able to reply to every message.

When you write, please be sure to include this book's title and author as well as your name and phone or fax number. I will carefully review your comments and share them with the author and editors who worked on the book.

Fax: 317-817-7070

Email: adv_prog@mcp.com

Mail: Bradley L. Jones
            Sams Publishing
            201 West 103rd Street
            Indianapolis, IN 46290 USA

Introduction

In February 1998, I found myself sitting in on the first public demonstration of what would become Visual InterDev 6. I was in Los Angeles for a weeklong SQL Server 7.0 Sphinx workshop that Microsoft was holding as part of an early information release program. Although we were still bound at the time by a nondisclosure agreement (NDA) for the SQL Server information, InterDev Product Manager Garth Fort told me that anything and everything he demonstrated that day was for public consumption. Microsoft really wanted to get the word out.

And for good reason. Visual InterDev 6 represents a major leap forward over its predecessor. I'd always wondered when a truly visual tool would arrive that would be good enough to make me leave behind hand editing. Although products such as Microsoft FrontPage, NetObjects Fusion, and even the venerable Allaire Homesite have offered varying degrees of visual Web development, these products have always left me cold. The first version of InterDev, although a throwback visually, offered up the excellent Visual C++ code editor, a boon to hand coders such as myself.

Still, I knew that the technology was changing and that it was only a matter of time before a tool would arrive that would change everything.

Yes, Visual InterDev 6 is that tool.

As I watched Fort manipulate recordsets visually in the beta InterDev, I saw my whole world crumbling. Here, finally, was the tool that would take dinosaur hand coders such as myself into the brave new world of visual editing. What I didn't realize at the time, however, was just how much of InterDev 6 was brand new. The company had re-architected the product from the ground up, while adding support for a host of new and exciting technologies. When I finally got my hands on InterDev 6 during the early days of the beta, I quickly realized that I had no idea where to begin.

Is this starting to sound familiar?

At its most basic level, Visual InterDev 6 is all about choice. Indeed, one could effectively argue that there's too much to choose from this time around. For example, your options for adding live data to Web applications are almost limitless. InterDev 6 builds on the primary strength of the old product—programmable access to Web/database integration—and enhances it with a heady and often confusing array of options, leaving the Web developer to decide which path to take.

Of course, that's where this book comes in. Written by a team of experts—Visual InterDev masters, all—*Visual InterDev 6 Unleashed* gives you the answers you need in order to take your Web applications to the next level. Yes, we assume you have a basic understanding of the product. Perhaps you're an old hand at Visual InterDev 1.0, confused by all the new options and capabilities (don't be ashamed, it's a natural reaction). Perhaps 6 is the first version of InterDev you've tried to experiment with, and you're not sure where its true powers lie.

Welcome. We're all friends here.

We won't insult your intelligence. You're no dummy. You know where the File menu is, and you can work the mouse and chew gum at the same time. You have work to do, a boss to please, and maybe clients to blow away. The Web sits still for no one.

For the professional Web developer, Visual InterDev is the right tool, and this book is its perfect companion. Unlike many rush-to-market books (that is, every InterDev 6 book published in 1998), we've actually worked with this product on production Web sites, and we've used the final release version, not an early beta, to write the book.

You say you're looking for answers? You're holding them in your hands. We not only have the answers, but we'd also love to share them with you. As with every book I'm involved in, our relationship doesn't end at the bookstore checkout line. Please visit my Web site for the latest InterDev information, sample code, and errata from the book (sure, we're human). See you on the other side.

Paul Thurrott
Boston, Massachusetts
January 1999

Visit *Visual InterDev 6 Unleashed* on the Web at `http://www.internet-nexus.com`.

Creating Web Applications

PART

I

Creating Crossbrowser Web Applications

by Michael Starkenburg

IN THIS CHAPTER

CHAPTER 1

Introduction: What Ever Happened to Standards?

In the beginning, there was the HTML standard, and it was good. One reason for the Web's amazing growth is the medium's capability to show the same information on any platform, using any browser. HTML 2.0 was implemented across the board in a standard manner so that any message you tried to get across would be presented consistently. The limitation was that most HTML pages were pretty simple, mostly just simple text and embedded images. As HTML coders demanded more sophisticated features, the standards process started to break down.

The first problem was the standards process itself. Requirements were changing in "Internet time," and the standards bodies couldn't keep up. HTML 3.0, for example, was implemented in the Netscape browser months before the standard was finalized by the W3C.

In fact, Netscape turned out to have a far better capability of responding to HTML programmers' feature requests than the standards body, and the balance of power began to change. People began to design pages that were "optimized for Netscape," ignoring the not-ready-for-primetime HTML standard.

As Microsoft and Netscape fought to win a bigger share of the browser market, they continually released new features designed to win the hearts of the Web developer. Because of this, we have a wide variety of capabilities in our browsers, but only a shell of an HTML standard that we can follow.

This leaves the Web developer with some tough choices to make. Do you require your visitors to use a specific browser? If you're building a corporate intranet, you might be able to set the official browser. However, in most Web applications you don't have much control over the browser choice of your visitors.

Coding for the Lowest Common Denominator

Do you code to the lowest common denominator? This can greatly limit your ability to present information. Depending on your application, you might have lots of visitors using older browsers, which don't support the latest features. The audience might be using 14.4K modems and old, slow computers. However, in some applications, such as e-commerce sites, you don't have a choice. The site's success depends on allowing access to the widest number of users, no matter how behind they are in technology.

Internet Browser Resources

New browsers are coming out at an amazing rate, and new ways to work with current browsers are continually being discovered. Keep an eye on these sites to get the latest data on Internet clients:

- `http://www.microsoft.com/ie`—The home page for Microsoft's Internet Explorer. Download the latest release or beta versions of Internet Explorer, and see the Microsoft Knowledge Base and a host of links to other Internet Explorer–related sites.

- `http://www.clubie.com`—A community site of developers who have collected examples, tutorials, and discussion groups on Internet Explorer–related topics.

- `http://www.netscape.com`—A home page for Netscape's Navigator products. Now that Netscape's home page is primarily the Portal site Netcenter, it is harder to find the software information. It's there, and plentiful.

- `http://developer.netscape.com`—To bypass the Netcenter and get straight to the good stuff, try Devedge Online. Here you will find articles, book excerpts, documentation, newsgroups, and examples about Netscape and JavaScript.

- `http://browserwatch.internet.com`—A good source for keeping tabs on who's winning the browser wars. This contains links to lots of information on browser statistics, plug-ins, and a complete (and scary) list of all browsers out there.

- `http://www.zdnet.com/products/internetuser/browsers.html`—Zdnet's version of BrowserWatch. It isn't as information rich, but sometimes has a good article.

- `http://webmaster.info.aol.com`—AOL always does things a little differently. If more people knew about this site, we'd have a lot fewer `AOL users click here` warnings. The site has information on AOL's propriety browsers, caching system, and image compression.

- `http://www.delorie.com/web/wpbcv.html`—The Backward Compatibility Page by Delorie Software, a cool little Perl tool that lets you see what your page will look like without certain functionality. Source code is available.

Things to Watch Out For

What does it mean *to code to the lowest common denominator*? If you're a fanatical purist, it means giving up using anything above, say, the HTML 2.0 standard. Obviously, that would be a little extreme, but you have to consider what percentage of your audience will be eliminated if you use any features released since then.

The good news? Tables have been around for a while, and the vast majority of users are using table-capable browsers. The bad news? They aren't all capable of advanced features such as background cell colors and background cell images. This can have a dramatically negative effect on your user interface (UI) if you don't plan for it.

Although the frames tag has a built-in handler for non–frames-compatible browsers, several advanced features aren't cleanly implemented across browsers. You have to check for the visitor's capability to handle floating frames and borderless frames.

Because many earlier browsers don't support client-side imagemaps, you have to back them up with a server-side imagemap handler, just in case.

Does the browser support Java applets? Because Microsoft and Netscape have different object models, you need to check for JavaScript, VBScript, or JScript support. Also, some browsers offer pluggable script engines so that additional languages can be interpreted.

Table 1.1 lists the capabilities for some common browsers.

TABLE 1.1   COMMON BROWSER CAPABILITIES

Browser	Frames	Tables	Cookies	Java Applets	ActiveX Controls	Java-Script	VB-Script
Internet Explorer 2.0	No	Yes	Yes	No	No	No	No
Internet Explorer 3.0	Yes	Yes	Yes	Yes	Yes	Yes	Yes
Internet Explorer 4.0	Yes	Yes	Yes	Yes	Yes	Yes	Yes
Internet Explorer 5.0	Yes	Yes	Yes	Yes	Yes	Yes	Yes
Pocket Internet Explorer	No	Yes	Yes	No	No	No	No
Netscape 2.0	Yes	Yes	Yes	Yes	No	Yes	No
Netscape 3.0	Yes	Yes	Yes	Yes	No	Yes	No
Netscape 4.0	Yes	Yes	Yes	Yes	No	Yes	No
Oracle 1.5	Yes	Yes	Yes	Yes	No	Yes	No
Opera	Yes	Yes	Yes	Yes	No	No	No
WebTV	No	Yes	Yes	No	No	No	No

One More Possibility

If you can't proclaim a specific browser type for your audience, and you want to use some of the more advanced browser functionality, you have one more option. You can split your audience into groups, based on browser capabilities, and create separate HTML pages for each group. For example, you might have one set of pages for version 4 browsers and later, using all the technologies available to you. You might pull out DHTML and layers functionality for your version 3 visitors. You might have a text-only version of your site for the unlucky few who can't handle frames or tables.

The rest of this chapter focuses on this method of handling visitors' browser differences. First, you will walk through several methods of determining browser types and capabilities. Then, you will look at some third-party technologies that make this process easier.

Determining the User's Browser

The first step in writing a crossbrowser Web application is to figure out your visitor's limitations. There are several ways to do this, some of which run on the client side and some on the server side. They provide varying levels of information, but you can determine browser manufacturer, major version, and platform, at a minimum.

The specific method you use depends on your application, but before you choose, ask yourself the following:

- Will I use the information in server-side or client-side scripting? (You should gather the information in the same kind of script you will use it in.)

- What exactly do I have to know about the visitor? Which method collects that data?

- What does my audience primarily use? Will most of them have JavaScript-capable browsers? Will they send unusual headers that I might want to collect?

The following examples give you a good start on gathering some basic client information and provide a choice of doing it on the client side or the server side.

A Simple Client-Side JavaScript

The simplest method of finding a user's browser information is to use a simple client-side JavaScript. This first example interrogates a variety of properties of the Navigator document object to gather information. Depending on how your visitor's browser handles this object, you can obtain the following information using this method:

- appCodeName
- appMinorVersion
- appName
- appVersion
- browserLanguage
- connectionSpeed
- cookieEnabled
- cpuClass
- onLine
- platform
- systemLanguage
- userAgent
- userLanguage
- userProfile

In this example, you get only the appName, appVersion, and platform properties, which work well across all JavaScript-capable browsers. I have found that the other properties are poorly handled by some browsers. If you want to gather any of this additional information, be prepared to handle the undefined case. Here's the code:

```
<HTML>
<HEAD>
<TITLE></TITLE>
</HEAD>
<BODY>
This page shows some basic client info, using a simple
JavaScript to grab the client's data and stick it in the
html page.
<p>
<SCRIPT Language=Javascript>
document.write("You are using " + navigator.appName + ",
 Version " + navigator.appVersion + " on a " +
navigator.platform + " machine.")
</SCRIPT>
</BODY>
</HTML>
```

Here's the output for a Microsoft Internet Explorer browser:

```
This page shows some basic client info, using a simple
JavaScript to grab the client's data and stick it in
the html page.
```

```
You are using Microsoft Internet Explorer, Version 4.0

(compatible; MSIE 4.01; Windows 95) on a Win32 machine.
```

And the output for a Netscape browser:

```
This page shows some basic client info, using a simple
JavaScript to grab the client's data and stick it in
the html page.

You are using Netscape, Version 4.04 -

(Win95; I) on a Win32 machine.
```

A Simple Server-Side VBScript

There are several situations in which you wouldn't want to do your detection on the client side. The audience might be using non–JavaScript-capable browsers, or you might not want them to know that you are making a browser-dependent decision. In these cases, you can use server-side scripting to accomplish the same thing.

In this example, you create an ASP page in which you pull the HTTP_USER_AGENT from the Request object and display it to the user:

```
<%@ Language=Vbscript>
<HTML>
<HEAD>
<% browser = Request.ServerVariables("HTTP_USER_AGENT")%>
</HEAD>
<BODY>
This page shows some basic client info, using a simple VBScript
 (evaluated on the server side) to grab the client's data and
stick it in the html page.
<p>
You are using <%=browser%>.
</BODY>
</HTML>
```

You can't achieve the same level of granularity as with the client-side script because the properties aren't neatly broken out for you. Instead of the nice little sentence from JavaScript, you only get the User_Agent displayed as it is sent from the browser.

The output from an Microsoft Internet Explorer browser:

```
This page shows some basic client info, using a simple VBScript
 (evaluated on the server side) to grab the client's data and
stick it in the html page.

You are using Mozilla/4.0 (compatible; MSIE 4.01; Windows 95)
```

The output from a Netscape browser:

```
This page shows some basic client info, using a simple VBScript
 (evaluated on the server side) to grab the client's data and stick it in
the html page.

You are using Mozilla/4.04 - (Win95; I)
```

Both the next two examples show how you can parse through the User_Agent to get a more usable form of data out of it.

A Powerful Client-Side JavaScript

The first examples show simple ways to grab the general information about the visitor. The simplicity lies in the way the returned values are handled: You don't attempt to interpret them at all, but just to display them or use them in simple If statements.

To get more in-depth information, you have to put some more logic into the client-side script. First, you create a new function with properties that can be tested to find browser manufacturer, version, and platform. You use the same Navigation object to pull the data from the browser, but you then parse the returned values to set a True/False property:

```
<script language=javascript>
function BrowsType ()
{    // Get rawAgent from Navigator object and force lowercase
     var rawAgent=navigator.userAgent.toLowerCase()

     // Parse rawAgent for Browser Manufacturer.
     this.netscape  = ((rawAgent.indexOf('mozilla')!=-1)
     && (rawAgent.indexOf('compatible') == -1))
     this.ie   = (rawAgent.indexOf("msie") != -1)
     this.opera = (rawAgent.indexOf("opera") != -1)

     // Parse rawAgent for Platform.
     this.win    = ((rawAgent.indexOf("win")!=-1) ||
                    (rawAgent.indexOf("16bit")!=-1) ||
                    (rawAgent.indexOf("win16")!=-1) ||
                    (rawAgent.indexOf("windows 3.1")!=-1) ||
                    (rawAgent.indexOf("windows 16-bit")!=-1)
                   )
     this.win95 = ((rawAgent.indexOf("win95")!=-1) ||
                   (rawAgent.indexOf("windows 95")!=-1)
                  )
     this.win98 = ((rawAgent.indexOf("win98")!=-1)
     ||(rawAgent.indexOf("windows 98")!=-1))
     this.winnt = ((rawAgent.indexOf("winnt")!=-1)
     ||(rawAgent.indexOf("windows nt")!=-1))
     this.mac    = (rawAgent.indexOf("mac")!=-1)
```

```
    // Parse Browser Version from Navigator object.
    this.major = parseInt(navigator.appVersion)
    this.minor = parseFloat(navigator.appVersion)
}
</script>
```

When you define the browstype function, you have basically re-created the functionality of the first example. You can now determine a visitor's browser manufacturer, version, and platform. Although it takes a few more lines of code, you are now in a good position to add a second layer of logic.

Now, you have to use what you know about specific browsers to test against the gathered information. Say you want to create a page in which you use DHTML or layers to implement some UI features. You know that Microsoft Internet Explorer 4 supports DHTML and that Netscape 4 supports layers. If you add the following code to the page, you can display the appropriate markup for the browser you're using:

Here's the code:

```
<script language=javascript>
browstype= new BrowsType
if (browstype.ie && (browstype.major=4))
     document.write("This browser is MSIE4.
        Insert DHTML Code Here")
  else if (browstype.netscape &&
     (browstype.major=4))
     document.write("This browser is Netscape 4.
     Insert Netscape Layers HTML Code Here")
  else
     document.write("This browser is Not MSIE4
     or Netscape 4.  Better use static HTML")
</script>
```

Of course, this could be tedious to implement across an entire site because each decision requires new code. The next section explains a couple of detection methods that use server-side reusable code to make this less painful.

Advanced Browser Detection

It didn't take long for Web developers to realize that browser detection is useful in many places on their sites and worthy of some well-developed routines. Several groups have built these browser detection components, but they all have the following in common:

- Easier management of many User_Agents
- An extendable list of browser properties
- A centralized store of browser property values
- Server-side solutions, relieving the need for client-side scripting

Both of the two most popular solutions, Microsoft's Browser Capabilities Component and cyScape's BrowserHawk, create objects that you can access from within an ASP page. Let's take an in-depth look at these two solutions.

Detecting Browser Capabilities with Microsoft's Component

Microsoft ships the Browser Capabilities ActiveX Component with the Internet Information Server (IIS) ASP package. Microsoft uses this component on `http://www.microsoft.com` to provide one set of pages for ActiveX-capable browsers, one set for frames-capable browsers, and one set for everyone else.

The Browser Capabilities Component creates an object of type BrowserType whose properties can be interrogated to find a wide array of browser information. The object gets it properties and values from a text file called browscap.ini, which contains a series of browser definitions. I will discuss the browscap.ini in depth later in this chapter.

When a browser makes a request of the server, the BrowserType object attempts to match the contents of the incoming HTTP_USER_AGENT header against a browser definition in the browscap.ini.

When a match is found, the object's properties and values are set, using the entries for that browser definition. If no match is found, the object will fall back on the default browser definition. If no default browser definition exists, all properties will be set to unknown. Also, if you query the object for a property that has not been set in the matching browser definition, that property will return an unknown.

By default, the Browser Capabilities Component supports 17 properties. All properties will not be defined for every possible browser. The default properties include

- Browser—Returns the browser type, generally IE or Netscape
- Version—Returns the full version, including major and minor version numbers
- Majorver—Returns just the major version number
- Minorver—Returns just the minor version number
- Platform—Returns the visitor's operating system
- Frames—Returns True or False for the visitor's frames capability
- Tables—Returns True or False for the visitor's tables capability
- Cookies—Returns True or False for the visitor's cookie-handling capability
- Vbscript—Returns True or False for VBScript support
- Javascript—Returns True or False for JavaScript support

- Jscript—Returns True or False for JScript support
- Javaapplets—Returns True or False for Java Applet support
- Activexcontrols—Returns True or False for ActiveX support
- Backgroundsounds—Returns True or False for sound support
- Beta—Returns True if the visitor is using a beta version
- AOL—Returns True if the visitor is using an AOL-specific version
- Cdf—Returns True if the visitor is capable of handling the Channel Definition Format

The following code implements a simple example of the Browser Capabilities Component:

```
<%@ Language=VBScript %>
<HTML>
<HEAD>
<% Set bc = Server.CreateObject("MSWC.BrowserType") %>

</HEAD>
<BODY>
Browser: <%=bc.browser %><BR>
Version: <%=bc.Version %><BR>
Major Version: <%=bc.majorver %><BR>
Minor Version: <%=bc.minorver %><BR>
Platform: <%=bc.platform %><BR>
Supports frames?
   <% If (bc.frames = "True") then %>       Yes<BR>
      <% Else %>        No<BR>
   <% End If %>
Supports tables?
   <% If (bc.tables = "True") then %>       Yes<BR>
      <% Else %>        No<BR>
   <% End If %>
Supports Cookies?
   <% If (bc.cookies = "True") then %>      Yes<BR>
      <% Else %>        No<BR>
   <% End If %>
Supports VBScript?
   <% If (bc.vbscript = "True") then %>      Yes<BR>
      <% Else %>        No<BR>
   <%    End If %>
Supports JavaScript?
   <% If (bc.javascript = "True") then %>      Yes<BR>
      <% Else %>        No<BR>
   <%    End If %>
Supports Jscript?
   <% If (bc.jscript = "True") then %>      Yes<BR>
      <% Else %>        No<BR>
```

```
<%   End If %>
Supports Javaapplets?
   <% If (bc.javaapplets = "True") then %>        Yes<BR>
      <% Else %>        No<BR>
   <%   End If %>
Supports ActiveX?
   <% If (bc.activexcontrols = "True") then %>        Yes<BR>
      <% Else %>        No<BR>
   <%   End If %>
Supports background sounds?
   <% If (bc.BackgroundSounds = "True") then %>        Yes<BR>
      <% Else %>        No<BR>
   <%   End If %>
Supports Beta?
   <% If (bc.Beta = "True") then %>        Yes<BR>
      <% Else %>        No<BR>
   <%   End If %>
Supports AOL?
   <% If (bc.AOL = "True") then %>        Yes<BR>
      <% Else %>        No<BR>
   <%   End If %>
Supports CDF?
   <% If (bc.cdf = "True") then %>        Yes<BR>
      <% Else %>        No<BR>
   <%   End If %>

</BODY>
</HTML>
```

Here's the output for a Microsoft Internet Explorer browser:

```
Browser: IE
Version: 4.0
Major Version: 4
Minor Version: 0
Platform: Unknown
Supports frames? Yes
Supports tables? Yes
Supports Cookies? Yes
Supports VBScript? Yes
Supports JavaScript? Yes
Supports Jscript? No
Supports Javaapplets? Yes
Supports ActiveX? Yes
Supports background sounds? Yes
Supports Beta? No
Supports AOL? No
Supports CDF? Yes
```

And for a Netscape browser:

```
Browser: Netscape
```

```
Version: 4.00
Major Version: 4
Minor Version: 00
Platform: Win95
Supports frames? Yes
Supports tables? Yes
Supports Cookies? Yes
Supports VBScript? No
Supports JavaScript? Yes
Supports Jscript? No
Supports Javaapplets? Yes
Supports ActiveX? No
Supports background sounds? No
Supports Beta? Yes
Supports AOL? No
Supports CDF? No
```

Enhancing the Browser Capabilities Component

The core of the Browser Capabilities Component is the browscap.ini configuration file. The browscap.ini file consists of a listing of HTTP_User_Agent strings. Each User_Agent section is followed by any number of name-value pairs. These name-value pairs define the properties of the BrowserType object created by the Browser Capabilities Component. A browser can have any number of properties. A minimal browscap.ini file will contain several parent definitions, several child definitions, some wildcard definitions, and a default definition.

A *parent definition* is used to minimize entry and increase accuracy. You can set the base name-value pairs for an entire family of browsers in this one definition. The following sample entry is the base for all the Internet Explorer 4.x browsers:

```
;;;;;;;;;;;;;;;;;;;;;;;;;;;;;;;;;;;;;;;;; IE 4.x
[IE 4.0]
browser=IE
Version=4.0
majorver=4
minorver=0
frames=TRUE
tables=TRUE
cookies=TRUE
backgroundsounds=TRUE
vbscript=TRUE
javascript=TRUE
javaapplets=TRUE
ActiveXControls=TRUE
Win16=False
beta=False
AK=False
```

```
SK=False
AOL=False
crawler=False
cdf=True
```

Notice that the section head, [IE 4.0], is not a valid HTTP_USER_AGENT and therefore will never match directly against a user's browser. It is still useful, however, because the Browser Capabilities Component supports a simple form of inheritance. A special property name, parent, lets you pick a parent definition. The child definition will then inherit all the properties of the parent, while overwriting any that are explicitly defined in the child definition.

For example, if you are using Internet Explorer 4.0 final release, on a Windows 95, your browser would match the following definition:

```
;;ie 4 final release
[Mozilla/4.0 (compatible; MSIE 4.0; Windows 95)]
parent=IE 4.0
platform=Win95
beta=False
```

The object created by the Browser Capabilities Component would then have the properties and values declared in the preceding code, as well as those of the parent definition in the preceding code.

TIP

cyScape, Inc., the maker of BrowserHawk, maintains one of the most comprehensive and up-to-date browscap.ini files available. This is a free public service. cyScape modestly requests that those who use the file also help one another by contributing to its maintenance. Get the file at `http://www.cyscape.com/asp/browscap/`.

The component will look for the first matching HTTP_USER_AGENT in the file. You can create catchall entries to handle groups of browsers or future browsers by using a simple wildcard. An asterisk (*) can take the place of zero or more characters anywhere in the HTTP_USER_AGENT entry. The following example is the catchall for the Internet Explorer 4 family of browsers. This entry will catch all browsers that aren't specifically defined before this in the browscap.ini file and assign them the values of the Internet Explorer 4.0 parent:

```
;;;;;;;;;;IE 4.x WILDCARD (IF ALL ABOVE FAIL)
[Mozilla/4.0 (compatible; MSIE 4.*)]
parent=IE 4.0
```

If the component scans all the way to the end of the file and doesn't find a match, it will use the default browser definition, if one exists. The default definition that ships with the IIS server looks like this:

```
;;;;;;;;;;;;;;;;;;;;;;;;;;;
;;; Default Browser    ;;;
;;;;;;;;;;;;;;;;;;;;;;;;;;;
[Default Browser Capability Settings]
browser=Default
Version=0.0
majorver=#0
minorver=#0
frames=False
tables=True
cookies=False
backgroundsounds=False
vbscript=False
javascript=False
javaapplets=False
activexcontrols=False
AK=False
SK=False
AOL=False
beta=False
Win16=False
Crawler=False
CDF=False
AuthenticodeUpdate=
```

Detecting Capabilities with BrowserHawk

An alternative to Microsoft's Browser Compatibilities Component is the BrowserHawk application by cyScape. BrowserHawk is a DLL that, like Microsoft's solution, creates an object that can carry properties and values for specific browsers.

BrowserHawk does a few things better, however. Instead of you manually editing a text file to change or add browser definitions, BrowserHawk includes the Visual Definition Editor. The editor enables you to easily create groups or families of browsers. The editor produces a binary definition file, which is read and cached by the BrowserHawk DLL. You then implement the BrowserHawk component in your pages in a manner similar to the Browser Capabilities Component.

Some other features of the BrowserHawk component include

- Better Matching—BrowserHawk allows significantly more complex pattern matching against HTTP_USER_AGENT strings. Besides the asterisk wildcard, you can use other regular expression wildcards to fine-tune your definition matching.

- Automatic Updates—The system comes with an NT service that can be programmed to automatically download definition updates from the cyScape Web site. The system can notify you via email when new definitions are imported.

- Browser Filters—Filters enable you to dynamically override an assigned property value with a new value, based on keywords or characters that occur within user agent strings.

Using BrowserHawk

BrowserHawk can be downloaded for evaluation or purchased from cyScape's Web site at `http://www.cyScape.com/browserhawk`. The download (which at the time of this writing is about 3.6MB) is a self-executing zip file containing all the necessary files to install the application.

After downloading the file, run the executable. You will have to be logged in as the system administrator to properly install the product. The installation takes only a few moments.

After the product is installed, you will be asked to import an activation key. If you purchased the program, you will receive a license key via mail. If you are evaluating, you can download a limited-time evaluation key. To import the license key, simply start the BrowserHawk editor, select Import, and point the editor at the license file. The license file will have a `.lic` extension.

The data files that cyScape maintains are incredibly complete. It's very possible that you will use their definition file as is and never have to add a definition yourself. The editor will be familiar to Visual Interdev users: Its interface is very similar to a Microsoft Internet Explorer interface.

From within the Visual Definition Editor, you can do the following:

- Add, change, or delete browser definitions.
- Add, change, or delete browser properties.
- Add, change, or delete browser filters.

Referencing the BrowserHawk Component in Your Code

The syntax to create a BrowserHawk object is exactly like that used for the Microsoft Browser Capabilities Component, except for one line. Where you would have used

```
<% Set bc = Server.CreateObject("MSWC.BrowseType") %>
```

you would now use

```
<% Set bc = Server.CreateObject("cyScape.browserObj") %>
```

A more complete example would look like this:

```
<%@ Language=VBScript %>
<HTML>
<HEAD>
<% Set bc = Server.CreateObject("cyScape.browserObj") %>
</HEAD>
<BODY>
Browser: <%=bc.browser %><BR>
Version: <%=bc.Version %><BR>
Major Version: <%=bc.majorver %><BR>
Minor Version: <%=bc.minorver %><BR>
</BODY>
</HTML>
```

Because of this similarity, conversion from the Microsoft component to the
BrowserHawk component is simple. All you have to do is move through your ASP pages,
switching out the CreateObject references.

Summary

The failure of browser manufacturers to stay within any published standards has caused a
wealth of problems for Web developers. Browser capabilities vary widely across any
Internet audience, which leaves you with a tough choice. Either you code to the lowest
common denominator, which means not using some of the advanced features of newer
browsers, or you build sites that intelligently present content differently for each browser.

The first step in presenting disparate content for different browsers is detecting which
browser is in use and determining that browser's capabilities. There are several methods
of determining this information.

On the client side, you can use JavaScript to (a) simply display browser information or
(b) create variables that can be tested in other JavaScript logic. On the server-side, you
can parse through the HTTP_USER_AGENT header to achieve the same effect, without
relying on JavaScript-enabled browsers or alerting the user to your browser snooping.

At least two companies have come out with ActiveX components that make this effort
significantly easier. Microsoft's Browser Compatibilities Component uses a flexible
definition file to assign properties and values to specific browsers. cyScape's
BrowserHawk goes a step further with the Visual Definition Editor and advanced detection features. The two products are implemented in ASP pages in a very similar manner,
which makes it easy to switch between them.

As you continue to build more complex Web applications and take full advantage of advanced Web technologies, it becomes more important to have a backward compatibility solution. Going forward, easy browser capabilities detection are the key to this.

Using Dynamic HTML

by Ken Cox

IN THIS CHAPTER

In this chapter, you will look at the most important features of Dynamic HTML (DHTML), focusing on Microsoft Internet Explorer 4 and higher.

What Is Dynamic HTML?

Dynamic HTML is a way of manipulating HTML codes to create Web pages that have rich visual content, speed, and interactivity. For the most part, a Web browser that supports DHTML can duplicate the look and functionality of compiled standalone programs such as those found in the Windows environment or even a multimedia CD-ROM application.

The *dynamic* in DHTML is the capability to interact with virtually every HTML tag and attribute by using program code. In a trivial example, your program code can change the size of all text tagged as <H1> whenever the user passes the mouse over a certain region. For a more advanced example, your program could enable the user to drag an image icon around the screen and then, depending on where the image was dropped, load related information into the page from a database. By allowing the browser to revise its content on the fly, DHTML relies less on the Web server and network traffic to refresh and reformat the text and images. That makes it fast and flexible.

The Document Object Model (DOM) is the path by which you get to all the tags and attributes on a Web page. The DOM includes a hierarchy of objects that exposes the properties you can change. The DOM also enables you to detect events such as mouse movements so that your Web page can react to the user's actions. The DOM includes various methods that send instructions to the browser, such as indicating that it should navigate to a different HTML page.

Scripting languages, such as VBScript or JavaScript, provide the programming commands and logic you use to manipulate all the components that go into an HTML page.

DHTML and the World Wide Web Consortium

As one wag put it, "The nice thing about standards is that there are so many to choose from." Unfortunately, when it comes to DHTML and Web browsers, true words were spoken in jest. The latest versions of Internet Explorer and Netscape Navigator support Dynamic HTML, but they aren't based on the same standard. For example, Netscape uses <LAYER> tags to position objects, although Microsoft puts its positioning capability in CSS styles.

The World Wide Web Consortium (W3C) has not endorsed Dynamic HTML as a standard, as it did with HTML 4.0. However, it has issued a standard for the DOM. In the *Document Object Model (DOM) Level 1 Specification Version 1.0,*

(`http://www.w3.org/TR/1998/REC-DOM-Level-1-19981001/cover.html`) released in
October 1998, the W3C notes that Dynamic HTML was the immediate ancestor of the
DOM.

Writing CrossBrowser DHTML

The DOM recommendation from the W3C leaves room for hope that the major browsers
will eventually support the same standard. In the meantime, Web developers have choices
and compromises to make if they want their DHTML pages to look good in the competing products. One approach is to use script to detect the user's browser type and then display the page's content in a way the detected browser respects. This approach works best
if there are relatively few incompatible segments in each page.

A second approach is to detect the browser type and then redirect the user to a Web page
specifically designed for that version. This method requires extra effort to maintain separate pages, but it enables you to produce pages that take advantage of the specific
browser's strengths.

Some Web authoring packages maintain external libraries of JavaScript that are included
or not, depending on the browser. Visual InterDev, a Microsoft product, is definitely
biased toward Microsoft's brand of DHTML. The Visual InterDev Design view makes it
relatively easy to create DHTML pages that look fine in Internet Explorer. All bets are
off when it comes to the rival Netscape Navigator.

Because this book is about Visual InterDev 6, and the sample code has been developed in
the VI environment, the target browser is Internet Explorer 4.01. In fact, some of the
pages, such as those that use data binding, depend on technology only Microsoft offers.

Scripting the Document Object Model

The Document Object Model (DOM) describes a hierarchy of objects within a DHTML
page. The objects, such as the Document object, have their own methods, properties, and
collections. To drill down to a specific part of the DOM, you "walk" the hierarchy. For
example, if you wanted to change the value of the third text box in the second form on
the page, you would use the special dotted syntax to reach the object. In this case, it
would help to work backward through the hierarchy, using the following analysis.

The third text box is part of the Elements collection. The Elements collection is in the
second form. The form is part of the Forms collection. The Forms collection is part of

the Document object. The Document object belongs to the Window object. Retracing your steps you can walk the value "A value" into the third text box with this code:

```
window.document.forms[1].elements[2].value="A value"
```

Notice that the digits 1 and 2 are an offset. When you deal with collections, the members start at zero, so 2 means the third item.

Actually, there's a much simpler way in DHTML to reference elements. The Document object includes an extremely handy collection called All. All includes all the objects found on the page. You can make a beeline for the one you want, as long as you make sure that the tag includes a unique ID such as the following:

```
<input id="textbox3">
```

To manipulate the value of textbox3, you just have to reference it in script as part of the All collection, as in the following:

```
document.all.textbox3.value="A value"
```

Figure 2.1 shows the DOM for Internet Explorer. It is interesting to note that a new object has been inserted called clientInformation. It functions like the navigator object without reminding you of the days when Netscape Navigator was winning the browser war. Visual InterDev's autocompletion feature recognizes this object.

Choosing a Language

The scripting language you use in Visual InterDev depends on your target browser and your comfort level. Many programmers versed in Visual Basic prefer to use VBScript on the server, but find themselves using JavaScript inside the browser client in order not to exclude Netscape. Internet Explorer supports both languages, whereas Netscape supports JavaScript. Be aware that older browsers that support JavaScript might not recognize recent versions of the same language.

Dynamic Styles

DHTML achieves much of its speed and visual appeal by the capability to change the appearance of text without refreshing the entire HTML file. You can change the style, color, and size of text dynamically, based on events. Listing 2.1 shows a simple example of this power. Notice that the check boxes and the nonbreaking (<nobr>) text have unique identifiers (using the id attribute). Using the DOM, the JavaScript determines the state (checked or not) of each check box. If a box is not checked, the script changes the style of its adjacent text from ordinary script to strikethrough text. This example uses the OK button's onclick event to initiate the checking. It also uses the <nobr> tag to hold the ID of the text. This shows you have access to every element on the page. When a user clicks OK, there's no need to contact the Web server to send out new formatting information. The text's style is changed on the fly, dynamically. Figure 2.2 shows the strikethrough effect that results from clicking OK with one or more check boxes unchecked. A similar technique is commonly used with the onmouseover event to change the color of text as the user passes the mouse over it.

FIGURE 2.1

The DOM for Internet Explorer now includes the All collection. Also, the navigator object can be referenced as clientInformation.

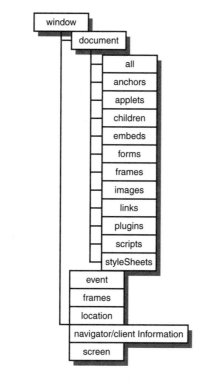

LISTING 2.1   CH2-01.HTM—DYNAMIC HTML ENABLES YOU TO CHANGE THE APPEARANCE OF TEXT WITHOUT RELOADING THE PAGE

```html
<html>
<head>
<title>Dynamic Changes</title>
<script language="JavaScript">
function changeitem() {
```

continues

LISTING 2.1   CONTINUED

```
document.all.oilchange.style.textDecorationLineThrough=
  !document.all.checkbox1.checked;
document.all.tuneup.style.textDecorationLineThrough=
  !document.all.checkbox2.checked;
document.all.rotatetires.style.textDecorationLineThrough=
  !document.all.checkbox3.checked;
}
</script>
</head>
<body>
<p>
<form>
<input id="checkbox1" name="checkbox1" type="checkbox">
<nobr id="oilchange">Oil
change</nobr><br>
<input id="checkbox2" name="checkbox2" type="checkbox">
<nobr id="tuneup">Tune-up</nobr><br>
<input id="checkbox3" name="checkbox3" type="checkbox">
<nobr id="rotatetires">Rotate tires</nobr> <br>
<input type="button" onclick="changeitem();" value=" OK "> </p>
</form>
</body>
</html>
```

FIGURE 2.2

The onclick *event of the button triggers code that turns regular text into strikethrough text.*

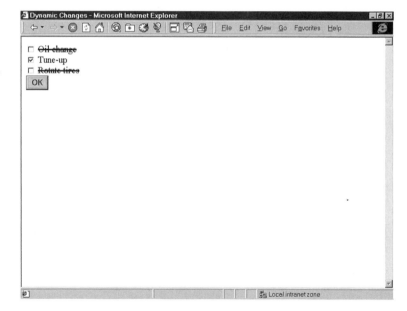

> **CAUTION**
>
> Make sure you have a backup if you are using Visual InterDev to rework DHTML
> files that have been created in other authoring tools. Visual InterDev might con-
> vert the code to its preferred syntax. That code could be totally at odds with
> the original tool's parsing approach and end up looking dreadful in the
> browser. Before doing any substantial work on a file, save it in Visual InterDev
> and view the page in your target browsers. You will find out whether the
> authoring tools are compatible.

X and Y Positioning

With regular HTML, authors have very limited control over where images and text
appear on the browser window. Many people use the cells inside an HTML table to keep
objects in position relative to one another. With DHTML, you can put an image or text
segment precisely where you want it with confidence that your carefully crafted layout
won't fall apart the moment the user resizes the window. Furthermore, you can change
the position of an object on the fly by resetting its screen coordinates.

Listing 2.2 shows how a click of the button changes the positions of three images. In
each case, the script updates the image's left coordinate (`pixelLeft`) and top edge
(`pixelTop`) relative to the document window's upper-left corner (which is at 0 pixels).

Figure 2.3 shows the graphics in their absolute positions. Figure 2.4 demonstrates that
even when the user resizes the browser window, the fruit images keep their absolute positions.

LISTING 2.2   CH2-02.HTM—YOU CAN SET THE ABSOLUTE POSITION OF IMAGES AND
OTHER SCREEN OBJECTS

```
<html>
<head>
<meta NAME="GENERATOR" Content="Microsoft Visual Studio 6.0">
<title>Position</title>
<script language="JavaScript">
function gomotion() {
document.all.pear.style.pixelLeft=168;
document.all.pear.style.pixelTop=73;
document.all.orange.style.pixelLeft=47;
document.all.orange.style.pixelTop=250;
document.all.apple.style.pixelLeft=277;
```

continues

LISTING 2.2   CONTINUED

```
document.all.apple.style.pixelTop=177;
document.all.mover.value="Done";
}
</script>
</head>
<body>
<p><img src="apple.jpg" id="apple"
    style="LEFT: 47px; POSITION: absolute; TOP: 169px;
    Z-INDEX: 100" WIDTH="100" HEIGHT="118">
<img src="pear.jpg" id="pear"
    style="LEFT: 277px; POSITION: absolute; TOP: 177px;
    Z-INDEX: 101" WIDTH="100" HEIGHT="145">
<img height="95" src="orange.jpg" id="orange"
    style="HEIGHT: 95px; LEFT: 168px; POSITION: absolute;
    TOP: 67px; WIDTH: 100px;
    Z-INDEX: 102" WIDTH="100"></p>
<form>
<input type="button" id="mover" value="Move" onclick="gomotion();"
    style="LEFT: 201px; POSITION: absolute; TOP: 196px; Z-INDEX: 200">
</form>
</body>
</html>
```

FIGURE 2.3

The images change places with the click of the Move button. This effect is created by updating the LEFT and TOP coordinates.

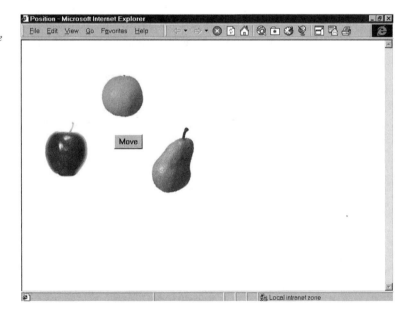

FIGURE 2.4

Absolute positioning prevents objects from shifting on the page even if the user resizes the pane.

VISUAL INTERDEV AS A DESIGN TOOL

Visual InterDev's strength is in database-driven Web pages, not in page design. There are much better tools on the market for creating sophisticated DHTML layouts, including Macromedia DreamWeaver and Elemental Software's Drumbeat. With that said, VI does a creditable job with absolute positioning in a WYSIWYG mode.

To position objects, display the Design toolbar: from the View menu, click Toolbars and then make sure Design is checked (it toggles, so watch that you aren't turning it off). Open or create an HTML file and go into Design view. Drop a graphic or other object on the page. Select the object and click the Absolute Positioning button on. At this point, you can move the object around the page. When you check the source code, you will notice that VI has added position information such as the following:

```
<INPUT id=button1 name=button1
style="LEFT: 137px; POSITION: absolute; TOP: 228px;
Z-INDEX: 100" type=button value=Button></P>
```

When your object is where you want it, lock it into position. Select the object and then click the Lock icon on the Design toolbar. If you must move the object later, select it and click the Lock icon again.

Z Positioning

Not only can you move objects around the page as x and y coordinates, but you can also dynamically set the Z order of the objects. *Z positioning* describes the front-to-back order. Objects with higher Z-INDEX values appear on the screen in front of objects with lower Z-INDEX values. For example, an image with its Z-INDEX property set to 101 will block from view a button with a Z-INDEX value of 100. At design time, you can control the Z-INDEX by setting a value such as 120 in the object's properties, or you can use the Z order item from Visual InterDev's Format menu to move the object's Z position toward the front or back of the pack. At runtime, you can use code to adjust the positions. In Listing 2.3, a click of the Start button changes the zIndex value of button2 to 99 from 101. Because button1's Z-INDEX value is 100, button2 immediately drops to the background, and button1 takes the foreground. Figure 2.5 shows the visual result of switching the zIndex.

LISTING 2.3   CH2-03.HTM—BY CHANGING THE Z ORDER PROPERTIES, YOU CAN MOVE SCREEN OBJECTS FORWARD OR BACKWARD

```
<HTML>
<HEAD>
<META NAME="GENERATOR" Content="Microsoft Visual Studio 6.0">
<TITLE>Z-Order</TITLE>
<SCRIPT language="JavaScript">
function changez() {
document.all.button2.style.zIndex=99
}
</SCRIPT>
</HEAD>
<BODY>
<P>
<INPUT id=button1 name=button1 style="LEFT: 79px; POSITION: absolute;
  TOP: 137px; Z-INDEX: 100" type=button value="Button Number 1">
<INPUT id=button2 name=button2 style="LEFT: 95px; POSITION: absolute;
  TOP: 146px; Z-INDEX: 101" type=button value="Button Number 2">
<INPUT id=button3 name=button3 style="LEFT: 135px; POSITION: absolute;
  TOP: 282px; Z-INDEX: 102" type=button value=Start
    onclick="changez();"></P>
</BODY>
</HTML>
```

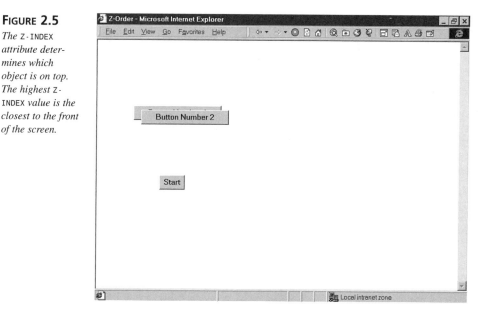

FIGURE 2.5

The Z-INDEX attribute determines which object is on top. The highest Z-INDEX value is the closest to the front of the screen.

Animation with DHTML

With the ability to set the x, y, and z positions of screen objects, it's easy to see how you can do animation with DHTML. It's a matter of putting the objects into position on the browser window and establishing their Z order so that the objects mask one another whenever they share the same screen space.

In Listing 2.4 and Figure 2.6, you can see how to create simple animation. When the page loads, the animation sequence starts. The chopsticks draw a candlestick out of the boot. Notice that the Z-ORDER values put the boot at the very front, with the candlestick behind it and the hand that holds the chopsticks at the back. The result is that you can't see the candlestick at the beginning of the animation. The JavaScript decrements the top position of both the candlestick and the chopstick images at the same rate, so the chopstick appears to be pulling the candlestick.

ANIMATION TIMING WITH setTimeout()

Dynamic HTML provides a handy method that creates the short pauses required for smooth animation. When you call setTimeout(), you pass it at least two parameters: the function you want to execute and the number of milliseconds to wait before proceeding. In Listing 2.4, look at the script for the gomove()

function. The function starts by calling `dopull()`, which gets the motion sequence underway. Then `gomove()` calls `setTimeout("gomove()",21)`. This line instructs the processor to wait 21 milliseconds and then run `gomove()`. After the brief pause, `gomove()` runs, the image moves another pixel, and the brief wait happens again. By using `setTimeout()` for the animation, you rely on a time value instead of the computer's processing speed to control your object's motion.

LISTING 2.4 CH2-04.HTM—USE THE `setTimeout()` FUNCTION AND DECREMENT THE OBJECT'S TOP POSITION FOR UPWARD ANIMATION

```
<html>
<head>
<meta NAME="GENERATOR" Content="Microsoft Visual Studio 6.0">
<title>Animation</title>
<script language="JavaScript">
var tmid;
function resetit() {
document.all.boot.style.top=158;
document.all.boot.style.left=79;
document.all.canstck.style.top=155;
document.all.canstck.style.left=144;
document.all.chopstck.style.top=84;
document.all.chopstck.style.left=149;
}
function gomove() {
dopull();
tmid=setTimeout("gomove()",21);
}
function dopull() {
if (document.all.chopstck.style.posTop > -25) {
document.all.chopstck.style.posTop=
➥document.all.chopstck.style.posTop-1;
document.all.canstck.style.posTop=document.all.canstck.style.posTop-1;
} else {
clearTimeout(tmid);
}
}
</script>
</head>
<body onload="gomove();">
<p>
<img src="boot.gif" id="boot" style="LEFT: 79px;
   POSITION: absolute;
   TOP: 158px; Z-INDEX: 103" WIDTH="141" HEIGHT="149">
```

```
<img src="candlstick.gif" id="canstck"
    style="LEFT: 144px; POSITION: absolute;
    TOP: 155px; Z-INDEX: 102" WIDTH="35" HEIGHT="99">
<img src="chopsticks.gif" id="chopstck"
    style="LEFT: 149px; POSITION: absolute;
    TOP: 73px; Z-INDEX: 101" WIDTH="105" HEIGHT="85">
<input id="button2" name="button2"
    style="LEFT: 46px; POSITION: absolute;
    TOP: 211px; Z-INDEX: 105" type="button"
    value="Again" onclick="resetit();"></p>
</body>
</html>
```

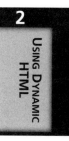

FIGURE 2.6

*You can do simple
animation with
DHTML. Here,
the chopsticks
pull a candlestick
out of the boot.*

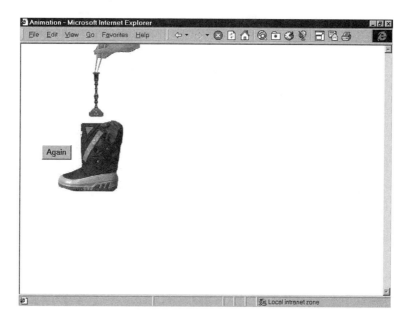

About Filters and Transitions

Microsoft's DHTML includes some built-in multimedia effects collectively known as
filters. There's a wide array of effects, ranging from blurs to dissolves to shadows. You
can apply filters to the following elements: BODY, BUTTON, IMG, INPUT, MARQUEE, TABLE,
TD, TEXTAREA, TFOOT, TH, THEAD, and TR. You can also apply filters to SPAN and DIV if you
define a height and width or if you use absolute positioning in the style attribute
(POSITION: absolute;).

> ## GO EASY ON THE EFFECTS
>
> A little flash goes a long way on a Web page. Unless you're creating a video game, don't assume that every visitor to the page appreciates the jazzy effects as much as you do.

Transition Effects

Transitions are filters that change an object's appearance over time; for example, an image that takes four seconds to dissolve into a second image. Likewise, a horizontal blind effect that lasts one second can reveal an entire Web page.

The special effects `blendTrans` and `revealTrans` are members of the special `filters` collection. They appear in the style attribute of the element to which they apply. In general, you must pass parameters to the filters. The parameters describe the effect you want to see, the objects that take part in the effect, and how long you want the effect to last. Because filters expose properties and methods, you can manipulate them quite readily with a little script.

Listing 2.5 shows how to use the `revealTrans` filter. By clicking the button, you cycle through all the 24 transition types. (Actually, there aren't 24 transitions because one of the allowable values, 23, just selects one of the effects at random. See Table 2.1 for the complete list of transitions and their values.) The script increases the value of the transition parameter while the duration parameter remains at one second.

In Listing 2.5, note the use of `Onfilterchange`:

```
<img Onfilterchange="reshow();"
```

`Onfilterchange` is an event that fires when a transition has finished. If you don't track the state of transitions, your script might catch a transition during execution, causing an error. That's why the sample code hides the button until the `Onfilterchange` event confirms that the transition is complete and it's safe to click the button again. Figure 2.7 shows a box transition in progress. Notice that the button is hidden.

LISTING 2.5 CH2-05.HTM—THIS CODE STEPS THROUGH ALL THE AVAILABLE TRANSITIONS (NOTICE THAT THE SCRIPT HIDES THE BUTTON DURING A TRANSITION)

```
<html>
<head>
<title>Using revealTrans()</title>
<script LANGUAGE="JavaScript">
var tnum=0;
```

```
function revealit(){
kimage.src="cntower.gif";
document.all.gobutton.style.visibility='hidden';
kimage.filters.item(0).transition=tnum
kimage.filters.item(0).apply();
kimage.src="sunset.gif";
kimage.filters.item(0).play();
}
function reshow() {
tnum ++
if (tnum>23){
  tnum=0;
  }
document.all.gobutton.value='Play revealTrans ' + tnum;
document.all.gobutton.style.visibility='visible';
}
</script>
</head>
<body bgcolor="white">
<br>
<input id="gobutton" type="button"
   value="Play revealTrans 0" onclick="revealit()"
   style="LEFT: 138px; POSITION: absolute;  TOP: 315px; Z-INDEX: 100">
<img Onfilterchange="reshow();" ID="kimage" src="cntower.gif"
   style="FILTER: revealTrans(transition=0, duration=1, );
   HEIGHT: 218px; LEFT: 83px; POSITION: absolute; TOP: 40px;
   WIDTH: 269px; Z-INDEX: 101" WIDTH="269" HEIGHT="218">
</body>
</html>
```

FIGURE 2.7

The box in transition hides one image as it reveals the other. DHTML offers more than 20 transitions.

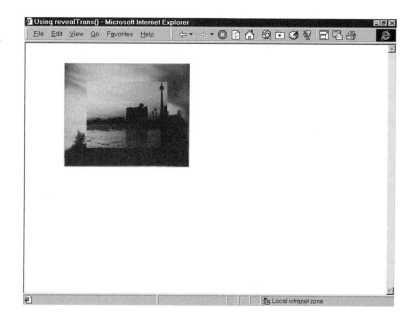

TABLE 2.1 TRANSITION TYPES AND VALUES FOR THE revealTrans() FILTER

Transition Name	*Value*
Box in	0
Box out	1
Checkerboard across	10
Checkerboard down	11
Circle in	2
Circle out	3
Dissolve	12
Horizontal blinds	9
Random transition	23
Random horizontal bars	21
Random vertical bars	22
Split horizontal in	15
Split horizontal out	16
Split vertical in	13
Split vertical out	14
Strips left down	17
Strips left up	18
Strips right down	19
Strips right up	20
Vertical blinds	8
Wipe down	5
Wipe left	7
Wipe right	6
Wipe up	4

The blend transition filter, blendTrans(), fades an image in or out over the number of seconds you provide in the duration parameter. The most frequent use for blendTrans() is to create a smooth cross fade between two images. You might find that some fades aren't as smooth as you expect if the images have different color palettes. Listing 2.6 creates a cross fade between two images that lasts five seconds; you set the length of the fade in seconds with the duration parameter.

LISTING 2.6 CH2-06.HTM—THE blendTrans() FILTER IS HANDY FOR CREATING A CROSS FADE BETWEEN TWO IMAGES

```
<html>
<head>
<title>Using blendTrans()</title>
<script LANGUAGE="JavaScript">
function revealit(){
document.all.gobutton.style.visibility='hidden';
kimage.filters.item(0).apply();
kimage.src="apple.jpg";
kimage.filters.item(0).play();
}
function reshow() {
document.all.gobutton.value="Done"
document.all.gobutton.style.visibility='visible';
}
</script>
</head>
<body bgcolor="white">
<br>
<input id="gobutton" type="button" value="Do blendTrans"
   onclick="revealit()"
   style="LEFT: 69px; POSITION: absolute;  TOP: 167px">
<img Onfilterchange="reshow();" ID="kimage" src="pear.jpg"
   style="FILTER: blendTrans(duration=5,); LEFT: 83px;
   POSITION: absolute; TOP: 40px">
</body>
</html>
```

2

USING DYNAMIC HTML

Filter Effects

Although transitions animate an object, filters without added scripting tend to be static effects. Examples of filter effects are shadows, upside-down text, monochrome images, and blurring. You apply DHTML filters within the object's style attribute. Within the attribute, you provide the name of the effect and any parameters the filter takes, such as a color or offset values. As with any screen object, DHTML enables you to change the style with script. This means that you can animate objects by changing their filters.

Table 2.2 shows the available filters and the effect you achieve.

TABLE 2.2 FILTERS AND THEIR EFFECTS

Use This Filter	*To Achieve This Effect*
Alpha	Set a transparency level
Blur	Appear as if moving at high speed

continues

TABLE 2.2 CONTINUED

Use This Filter	*To Achieve This Effect*
Chroma	Make the stated color transparent
DropShadow	Create an offset solid silhouette
FlipH	Flip the object on the horizontal
FlipV	Flip the object on the vertical
Glow	Add radiance to the outside edges
Grayscale	Make the object monochrome
Invert	Reverse the hue, saturation, and brightness values
Light	Project light sources onto an object
Mask	Create a transparent mask from an object
Shadow	Create a solid shadow
Wave	Warp the object along a sine wave
XRay	Show only the edges of the object

Listing 2.7 shows how to apply filters to an image. Notice that some filters, such as flipH() and invert() don't take any parameters, whereas others such as glow() must have a color or other value supplied.

In Figure 2.8, you can see the results of displaying Listing 2.7 in Internet Explorer 4.01. All the filters are applied to the same image, even though it might appear as though the HTML uses different graphics. You can see how using filters can keep your HTML light. You can get a lot of mileage out of very few files.s

Please note that some of the visual effects are subtle and depend on color. To appreciate the differences between the filters, you will want to view them on your monitor.

LISTING 2.7 CH2-07.HTM—YOU CAN ADD FILTERS TO TEXT OR IMAGES

```
<html>
<head>
<title>Filter Effects</title>
<body bgcolor="white">
<div style="FILTER:
 shadow(color=magenta); HEIGHT: 34px; LEFT: 607px;
 POSITION: absolute; TOP: 359px; WIDTH: 150px; Z-INDEX: 100">
<h2>Filter Effects</h2>
</div>
<img src="boot.gif" style="FILTER: alpha(opacity=10)" >
<img src="boot.gif" style="FILTER: blur()" >
<img src="boot.gif" style="FILTER: chroma(white)" >
```

```
<img src="boot.gif" style="FILTER: dropshadow(color=gray)" >
<img src="boot.gif" style="FILTER: flipH()" >
<img src="boot.gif" style="FILTER: flipV()" >
<img src="boot.gif" style="FILTER: glow(Color=yellow)" >
<img src="boot.gif" style="FILTER: gray()" >
<img src="boot.gif" style="FILTER: invert()" >
<img src="boot.gif" style="FILTER: light" >
<img src="boot.gif" style="FILTER: shadow(color=gray)" >
<img src="boot.gif" style="FILTER: mask(color=red)" >
<img src="boot.gif" style="FILTER: wave(strength=7, freq=5,
  lightstrength=30, add=0, phase=90)" >
<img src="boot.gif" style="FILTER: xray" >
</body>
</html>
```

FIGURE 2.8

*A sample of some
of the filter effects
included in Listing
2.7, best viewed
on a color monitor*

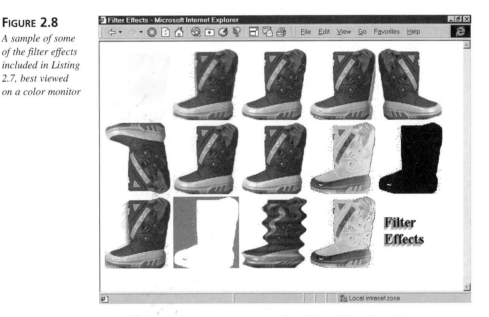

DEBUGGING AND onmousemove EVENTS

When you are debugging scripts that use onmousemove and then check the page in Quick view, you might be caught in what appears to be an endless loop. As soon as you clear the dialog box that tells you there's a syntax error, the dialog box pops up again. The trick is to move the dialog box away from the Quick view pane. Dismiss it and then carefully move your mouse around the outside edges of your Visual InterDev environment, avoiding the Quick view area. After you make it back to the Source View tab, you can fix the error.

Manipulating Text

You've seen how you can change the appearance of text with DHTML. In fact, after the document is loaded, you can change the words themselves by using the innerHTML and innerText properties.

The innerText property sets or retrieves the text between the start and end tags of the current element. In Listing 2.8, you can see that on loading, the paragraph tag (<p>) contains the text Starter text, and the button tag (<button>) contains the text Pass your mouse here. Each element has its own ID—alsomytext and mytext, respectively. The JavaScript triggered by the onmouseover event changes the text between the start and end tags. The rollover() function accepts the value of the replacement text, whereas window.event.srcElement.id provides the ID of the calling tag. The function then changes the innerText property to update the text. Notice that the tags themselves are not changed.

LISTING 2.8   CH2-08.HTM—THE innerText PROPERTY CHANGES THE TEXT INSIDE A TAG.

```
<HTML>
<HEAD>
<TITLE>innerText Example</TITLE>
<SCRIPT language="JavaScript">
function rollover(strProvided) {
theid=window.event.srcElement.id
document.all(theid).innerText=strProvided;
}
function rolloff(strProvided2) {
theid=window.event.srcElement.id
document.all(theid).innerText=strProvided2;
}
</SCRIPT>
</HEAD>
<BODY>
<FONT style="BACKGROUND-COLOR: moccasin">
<p id="alsomytext" onmouseover="rollover('You are here.');"
   onmouseout="rolloff('Mouse moved off.');">Starter text</p>
<button id="mytext" onmouseover="rollover('Mouse is over');"
   onmouseout="rolloff('You can still click');">
   Pass your mouse here</button>
</BODY>
</HTML>
```

The outerText property lets you change the HTML tags, as well as the text. Listing 2.9 shows how you can use outerText to remove the <Button> tag and its contained text. The replacement text has no tag at all.

> **TIP**
>
> Be careful with the `outerText` property. Because it removes the tag, any script-
> ed references to the removed tag or its ID will fail.

LISTING 2.9 CH2-09.HTM—THE `outerText` PROPERTY CHANGES THE TEXT INSIDE A TAG
AND THE TAG ITSELF

```
<HTML>
<HEAD>
<TITLE>outerText Example</TITLE>
<SCRIPT language="JavaScript">
function rollover(strProvided) {
theid=window.event.srcElement.id
document.all(theid).outerText=strProvided;
}
</SCRIPT>
</HEAD>
<BODY>
<button id="mytext"
 onclick="rollover('The button tag and inline script are gone.');">
Click to remove the button
</button>
</BODY>
</HTML>
```

The `innerHTML` property retrieves or applies any HTML tags included with the text.
When you run Listing 2.10, you see that the initial button is rendered with its text in
italic. However, after the `onclick` event, the script inserts replacement text that no longer
includes the <I> tag. The <BUTTON> tag remains, but everything inside it changes. The
replacement text includes bold and font tags rendered as HTML markup. Figure 2.9
shows this.

LISTING 2.10 CH2-10.HTM—THE `innerHTML` PROPERTY RENDERS ADDED TAGS WHILE
MAINTAINING THE OBJECT'S TAG

```
<HTML>
<HEAD>
<TITLE>innerHTML Example</TITLE>
<SCRIPT language="JavaScript">
function doclick(strProvided) {
theid=window.event.srcElement.id
alert('The innerHTML text is: ' + document.all(theid).innerHTML);
```

continues

LISTING 2.10   CONTINUED

```
document.all(theid).innerHTML=strProvided;
}
</SCRIPT>
</HEAD>
<BODY>
<BUTTON id="mybutton"
 onclick="doclick('<Font color=red><B>The bold and font tags
 are applied. Click again.</B></FONT>');">
<I>Click to make bold and red</I>
</BUTTON>
</BODY>
</HTML>
```

FIGURE 2.9

Use innerHTML *to set or return HTML markup within, but not including, the object you reference.*

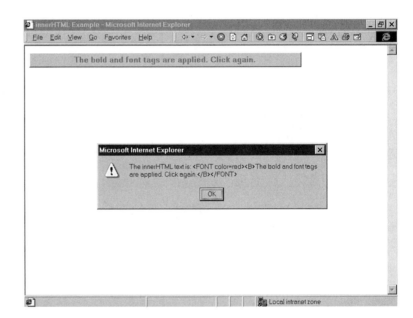

The outerHTML property retrieves or applies the tags contained within the object that is being referenced and then goes farther afield to take in the referenced tag itself.

LISTING 2.11   CH2-11.HTM—THE outerHTML PROPERTY RENDERS THE REPLACEMENT TAGS AND TEXT BUT REMOVES THE ORIGINAL HTML TAG

```
<HTML>
<HEAD>
<TITLE>outerHTML Example</TITLE>
```

```
<SCRIPT language="JavaScript">
function doclick(strProvided) {
theid=window.event.srcElement.id
document.all(theid).outerHTML=strProvided;
}
</SCRIPT>
</HEAD>
<BODY>
<BUTTON id="mybutton"
 onclick="doclick('<P><Font color=red>
<B>The button tag is gone.</B></FONT><P>');">
<I>Click to replace with bold and red text</I>
</BUTTON>
</BODY>
</HTML>
```

Using TextRange

The TextRange object gives you access to all the HTML text on the page or a particular range of text. You use the createTextRange method to zero in on the portion of the text you want to deal with. For example, in Listing 2.12, the JavaScript line

```
rangeobject=document.body.createTextRange()
```

returns a text range object covering the entire <BODY> element, except for <BUTTON> text. (Although not included in this example, please note that text inside a <TEXTAREA> element is not returned as part of the body text either.)

By using the TextRange object's text property, you can retrieve the text from the page, minus the HTML tags:

```
alert("The BODY text range content is: " + rangeobject.text);
```

As you might expect, the htmlText property gives you access to the same range of text, but it includes the HTML tags.

The preceding example took in all the body text. To drill down to a particular element, you must reference the element. For example, to retrieve the text and HTML markup from within the <BUTTON> element, you reference the element's ID (mybutton) as the range and retrieve it with the htmlText property.

Figure 2.10 shows the text from Listing 2.12 as it appears in the browser. Figure 2.11 shows what is returned by using the text property, and Figure 2.12 shows the same range as returned by the htmlText property.

LISTING 2.12   CH2-12.HTM—THE text PROPERTY OF THE TextRange OBJECT HOLDS TEXT WITHIN TAGS BUT NOT THE HTML MARKUP

```
<html>
<head>
<title>TextRange object example</title>
<script>
function checkit() {
rangeobject=document.body.createTextRange()
alert("The BODY text range content is: " + rangeobject.text);
rangeobject=document.all.mybutton.createTextRange();
alert("The mybutton text range content is: " + rangeobject.text);
rangeobject=document.body.createTextRange()
alert("The BODY htmlText range content is: " + rangeobject.htmlText);
rangeobject=document.all.mybutton.createTextRange();
alert("The mybutton htmlText range content: "
➥ + rangeobject.htmlText);
}
</script>
</head>

<body><p><EM>This text is on the page.</EM></p>
<p><BUTTON id="mybutton" onclick="checkit();" name="button1"
 type=button>
 This button's <b>id</b> is 'mybutton'.</BUTTON> </p>

<p><b>And there's more text down
here.</b></p>
<div id="mydiv"><p>There's DIV content too.</p></div>
</body>
</html>
```

After you capture a range of text within the document, you can manipulate it in several ways. You can search for text within the range, highlight or remove words, or substitute the existing content with something completely different.

FIGURE 2.10

The DHTML page produced by Listing 2.12 on loading.

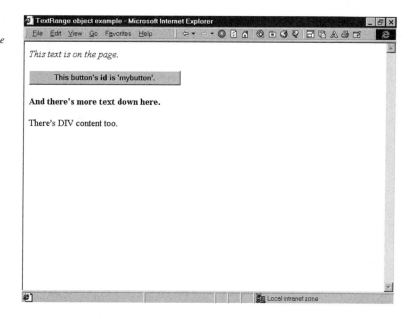

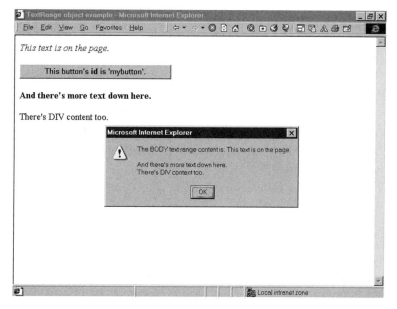

FIGURE 2.11

An alert box showing the text returned from Figure 2.10 by `rangeobject.text` *in Listing 2.12. The* text *property returns text without tags*

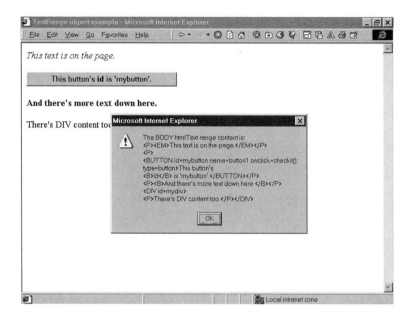

Data Binding

DHTML enables you to take much of the data-handling burden off the server and place it on the client. The technology, known as *data binding*, binds individual fields in a Web page to corresponding fields in a database. Rather than hard-code data in your HTML files, you can retrieve the data at runtime and update the database at will.

Consider the case of a Web surfer who is stepping through database records without DHTML. Each time the browser needs new data, it must make a trip to the Web server, retrieve the formatted Web page, and re-render the content. By using data binding and a data source object (DSO), you can cut the round trips dramatically and boost the responsiveness of the page. Because the DSO can be cached on the client computer, access to the data is very fast.

Visual InterDev's design-time controls (DTCs) make extensive use of DSO. Although the DTCs speed the creation of pages, the best way to understand data binding is to bypass the tool's handholding features and dig into the code. This example uses JavaScript, the Tabular Data Control (TDC), and ordinary HTML to assemble a data-driven page. Figure 2.13 shows the end result of the page you are creating.

FIGURE 2.13

A data-bound Web page in which the user can page through the records without contacting the Web server for each change.

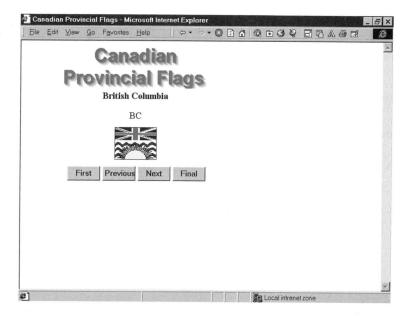

2

USING DYNAMIC
HTML

TIP

The Design view of Visual InterDev 6 can destroy hand-built code by reformatting it according to its own criteria. Make sure you have a safety copy. Because files with the .HTM extension default to opening in Design view, you might want to give them an .ASP extension to be safe.

This example builds a data-bound Web page based on a list of comma-separated values (CSV). Although you can create these data files in Notepad, it's easier to use data from an Excel spreadsheet and save the file as a *.CSV. The file provs.csv contains a title for each column (the first line) and then a series of records (the name of the province, its usual abbreviation, and the name of the graphics file for its flag). Listing 2.13 shows the entire contents of provs.csv.

LISTING 2.13 PROVS.CSV—CONTAINS THE COMMA-SEPARATED VALUES USED WITH A DATA-BOUND CONTROL

```
Province,Abbr.,Graphic
British Columbia,BC,britcolm.gif
Alberta,AB,alberta.gif
```

continues

LISTING 2.13   CONTINUED

```
Saskatchewan,SK,saskatch.gif
Manitoba,MB,manitoba.gif
Ontario,ON,ontario.gif
Quebec,QC,quebec.gif
New Brunswick,NB,newbrun.gif
Nova Scotia,NS,novascot.gif
Prince Edward Island,PE,pei.gif
Newfoundland,NF,newfound.gif
```

Now that you have the raw data, you need a way to connect the data source to your Web page. This is handled by an embedded ActiveX control called the Tabular Data Control (TDC). Listing 2.14 shows the use of the TDC, including the Object tag and its parameters. Notice the ID of the object kimages. You will use that ID later to reference this control. The key parameters for your purposes are FieldDelim, which indicates that a comma separates the fields; UseHeader, which tells the control that your column of data has a title; and DataURL, which points to the data source, provs.csv.

LISTING 2.14   THE TABULAR DATA CONTROL IS AN ACTIVEX CONTROL EMBEDDED AS AN OBJECT IN THE HTML PAGE

```
<OBJECT classid="clsid:333C7BC4-460F-11D0-BC04-0080C7055A83"
    height=1 id=kimages style="LEFT: 0px; TOP: 0px"    width=1>
    <PARAM NAME="RowDelim" VALUE="">
    <PARAM NAME="FieldDelim" VALUE=",">
    <PARAM NAME="TextQualifier" VALUE='"'>
    <PARAM NAME="EscapeChar" VALUE="">
    <PARAM NAME="UseHeader" VALUE="-1">
    <PARAM NAME="SortAscending" VALUE="-1">
    <PARAM NAME="SortColumn" VALUE="">
    <PARAM NAME="FilterValue" VALUE="">
    <PARAM NAME="FilterCriterion" VALUE="??">
    <PARAM NAME="FilterColumn" VALUE="">
    <PARAM NAME="CharSet" VALUE="iso-8859-1">
    <PARAM NAME="Language" VALUE="en-us">
    <PARAM NAME="CaseSensitive" VALUE="-1">
    <PARAM NAME="Sort" VALUE="">
    <PARAM NAME="Filter" VALUE="">
    <PARAM NAME="AppendData" VALUE="0">
    <PARAM NAME="DataURL" VALUE="provs.csv">
    <PARAM NAME="ReadyState" VALUE="4">
</OBJECT>
```

DISAPPEARING ACTIVEX CONTROLS

If you paste the TDC's Object tag and classid value into your page in Visual InterDev's Source view, the control's data might disappear from view. Actually, it is still there as a small point—a control with no interface. To see the code, from the View menu, click View Controls as Text.

At this point, you have the raw data and a connection between the data and the Web page. The next step is to create the normal HTML code to display the data. For example, the HTML markup that displays the flag graphic looks like this:

```
<IMG DATASRC=#kimages DATAFLD=Graphic style="LEFT: 200px;
POSITION: absolute; TOP: 180px;" >
```

Note that the DATASRC attribute references kimages prefixed with a # sign. The DATAFLD attribute indicates that the value for this image comes from the Graphic column in the CSV file. Similar HTML markup uses DATASRC and DATAFLD to display the province's name and abbreviation.

With the data, the control, and the display in place, you must give the user a way to navigate through the records. This requires some HTML input buttons, inline onclick events, and some JavaScript. On the click of a button, the JavaScript uses the familiar database methods MoveFirst(), MovePrevious(), MoveNext(), and MoveLast() to move forward and backward through the recordset.

Listing 2.15 shows the complete source code for a Web page that could potentially display huge amounts of data, one record at a time. By using DHTML and a data source object, your HTML is lighter and easier to maintain. You avoid hard-coded data that makes pages difficult to update. For example, if one of Canada's territories achieves provincial status, a quick update to provs.csv adds the new province to the Web page without you even dealing with HTML.

LISTING 2.15 CH2-15.HTM—A DEMONSTRATION OF DATA-BOUND CONTROLS WITHIN A DHTML PAGE

```
<HTML>
<TITLE>Canadian Provincial Flags</TITLE>
<HEAD>
<SCRIPT language="JavaScript">
function donav(myRS) {
```

continues

2

USING DYNAMIC HTML

LISTING 2.15   CONTINUED

```
theid = window.event.srcElement.id;
if (theid == "first")  {
   myRS.recordset.MoveFirst();
   }
   else if (theid == "prev") {
      myRS.recordset.MovePrevious();
      if (myRS.recordset.BOF) {
         myRS.recordset.MoveFirst();
      }
      }
   else if (theid == "next")  {
      myRS.recordset.MoveNext();
      if (myRS.recordset.EOF) {
         myRS.recordset.MoveLast();
         }
      }
   else if (theid == "final") {
      myRS.recordset.MoveLast();
         }
}
</SCRIPT>
</HEAD>
<BODY>
<OBJECT classid="clsid:333C7BC4-460F-11D0-BC04-0080C7055A83"
      height=1 id=kimages style="LEFT: 0px; TOP: 0px"
      width=1>
      <PARAM NAME="RowDelim" VALUE="">
      <PARAM NAME="FieldDelim" VALUE=",">
      <PARAM NAME="TextQualifier" VALUE="'">
      <PARAM NAME="EscapeChar" VALUE="">
      <PARAM NAME="UseHeader" VALUE="-1">
      <PARAM NAME="SortAscending" VALUE="-1">
      <PARAM NAME="SortColumn" VALUE="">
      <PARAM NAME="FilterValue" VALUE="">
      <PARAM NAME="FilterCriterion" VALUE="??">
      <PARAM NAME="FilterColumn" VALUE="">
      <PARAM NAME="CharSet" VALUE="iso-8859-1">
      <PARAM NAME="Language" VALUE="en-us">
      <PARAM NAME="CaseSensitive" VALUE="-1">
      <PARAM NAME="Sort" VALUE="">
      <PARAM NAME="Filter" VALUE="">
      <PARAM NAME="AppendData" VALUE="0">
      <PARAM NAME="DataURL" VALUE="provs.csv">
      <PARAM NAME="ReadyState" VALUE="4">
</OBJECT>
<DIV style="FILTER: shadow(color=gray,direction=135); HEIGHT: 76px;
   LEFT: 60px; POSITION: absolute; TOP: 7px; WIDTH: 361px;">
<DIV align=center> <STRONG>
<FONT color=red face=Arial size=6>Canadian Provincial
```

```
Flags</FONT></STRONG></DIV></DIV>
<form>
<INPUT ID="first" TYPE=button VALUE="First" onclick="donav(kimages)"
 style="LEFT: 100px; POSITION: absolute;TOP: 262px; width: 70;">
<INPUT ID="prev" TYPE=button VALUE=Previous" onclick="donav(kimages)"
 style="LEFT: 175px; POSITION: absolute; TOP: 262px;width: 70;">
<INPUT ID="next" TYPE=button VALUE="Next"onclick="donav(kimages)"
 style="LEFT: 250px; POSITION: absolute; TOP:262px; width: 70;">
<INPUT ID="final" TYPE=button VALUE="Final"onclick ="donav(kimages)"
 style="LEFT: 325px; POSITION: absolute; TOP:262px; width: 70;">
</form>
<DIV align=center DATASRC=#kimages DATAFLD=Province
 STYLE="FONT-WEIGHT: bold; HEIGHT: 61px; LEFT: 160px;
 POSITION: absolute;TOP: 103px; WIDTH: 168px;">
</DIV>
<DIV align=center DATASRC=#kimages DATAFLD=Abbr.
 STYLE="HEIGHT: 61px;LEFT: 160px; POSITION: absolute;
 TOP: 145px; WIDTH: 168px;">
</DIV>
<DIV align=center>
<IMG DATASRC=#kimages DATAFLD=Graphic style="LEFT: 200px;
POSITION: absolute; TOP: 180px;" >
</DIV>

</BODY>
</HTML>
```

2

USING DYNAMIC
HTML

A DHTML Case Study: An Interactive Quiz

Nothing demonstrates the *dynamic* in DHTML better than the capability to move objects around on the Web page. Whereas regular HTML is static, DHTML is truly interactive. In the DHTML case study, you create a game in which the player matches the name of a Canadian province to the provincial flag. The source code for the game is in file Ch2-15.htm on the CD-ROM. Figure 2.14 shows how the game looks in the Web browser. Here are some of the features of the Canadian Provincial Flag game:

- Users drag and drop a flag onto the name of the province.
- A flag that is close to its target snaps to the exact position.
- When there's a match, the code dims the flag by changing the graphic's opacity value.
- The province's name disappears when its flag is in position.
- The title uses the drop shadow filter.

FIGURE 2.14

The DHTML Case Study. An interactive quiz in which players learn by moving flags around the browser window.

Summary

You've seen how DHTML adds a richness to the browser environment that closely resembles the speed and interactivity of compiled programs. Filters enable you to apply dramatic effects without any scripting. The capability to manipulate virtually any element via the DOM means fewer trips to the Web server and lower bandwidth. With data binding, the browser can be an effective front end to a database application. On the downside, the major browsers handle DTHML differently. Without care, the exciting page you create for one browser can collapse when displayed in another.

Programming the Scripting Object Model

by Ken Cox

IN THIS CHAPTER

CHAPTER 3

Introducing the Visual InterDev 6 Scripting Object Model

The Scripting Object Model (SOM) is a framework that provides an easy-to-use package of HTML elements, frequently used routines, and database functions. The SOM exposes properties, methods, and events for key components of an HTML page, such as boxes, buttons, and tables.

Because it is built to be object oriented and event driven, the SOM makes it easy to link objects and events with your own script. SOM is especially helpful with the creation of database-driven applications for Internet Information Server (IIS). In many cases, you can handle events such as mouse clicks through server-side processing as simply as you would script them with Dynamic HTML (DHTML). Granted, the requirement for round trips to the server won't give you anywhere near the same responsiveness.

The SOM in Visual InterDev 6 (VI 6) simplifies the development of Web applications by creating a familiar model and environment for programmers. The SOM more closely resembles the object-oriented design used in Visual Basic and other popular software tools.

Scripting and the Scripting Object Model

Scripting the SOM goes hand in hand with the use of design-time controls (DTCs). Usually, the programming code takes over where the DTC leaves off. Here's a common sequence for using the SOM within the Visual InterDev environment:

1. Drag a script object from the Design-Time Controls toolbox onto your Web page. You might start with a text box DTC.

2. Enable the SOM that supplies the background functionality to link script objects to one another. Usually, the VI 6 environment prompts you to add the SOM whenever you start using a control that requires it.

3. Using the script object DTC's property pages, set the object's initial values, such as text, color, and size.

4. Use Script Outline view to add a skeleton event handler for the object. For instance, with a `Textbox` script object, you might want something to happen when the `onchange` event fires, meaning the user has changed the text.

5. Add script that changes the properties of an object. For instance, you might increase the height of a `Textbox` script object if the user has entered more than 200 characters of text.

NOTE

Most of the samples in this chapter use server-side scripting. Although this method puts the processing burden on the Web server and takes more time and resources, it is still the best way to make sophisticated, interactive, and generic pages available to the most browsers. To follow the examples and run the code, you need Personal Web Server or Internet Information Server. Both are included with Visual InterDev 6.

Starting the SOM

If the SOM isn't already enabled on a page, you can enable it manually. In the VI environment, go into Source view and click in an area of whitespace on the page. Right-click to open the Properties page. As shown in Figure 3.1, the scripting settings are enabled in the lower area of the page. Make sure Enable Scripting Object Model is checked.

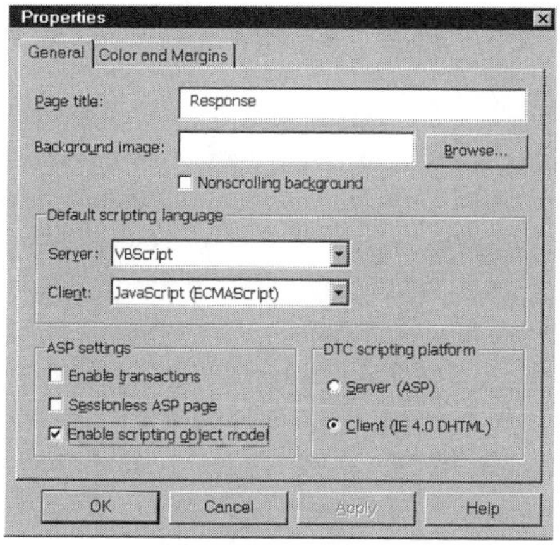

FIGURE 3.1

Enable the SOM on the Properties page for each HTML page.

When the SOM is enabled, you will see gray portions of text at the start and end of your script (see Figure 3.2). This text, which cannot be edited, adds powerful JavaScript routines to the page and wraps all the page's content in its own type of HTML form. This way, the SOM has a degree of control over events within the page, interactions with the server, and code contained in other pages.

FIGURE 3.2

The Script Library is included in the page with the HTML `#include file` *directive.*

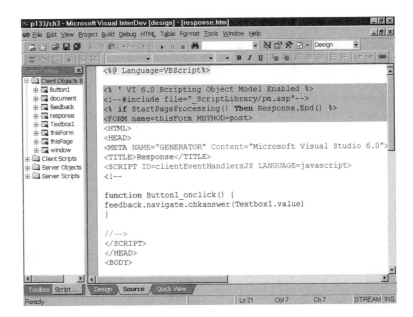

Script Objects as Starting Points

The key to scripting the SOM is in knowing what objects are available, what characteristics they can have, and what events they can trigger. Like other object-oriented environments, VI 6 provides a range of built-in objects and capabilities for you to harness. In Appendix G, "Scripting Object Model Quick Reference," you will find lots of code and examples for all the properties, methods, and events used in the SOM. This chapter focuses on some of the problems that programmers have run into as they move into this new environment. The VI 6 design-time controls (DTCs) themselves provide many examples. One of the best ways to see how things are done is to go into the VI editor's Source view, select an object that was created with a DTC, right-click, and click Show Run-Time Text. Keep in mind that a DTC is really just a type of wizard that gathers information about how a script object should look and then writes code based on your choices.

Although there's a downside to converting script objects to text permanently, don't be afraid to do so when you have to add some custom code to script that the DTC has created. Sometimes that's the fastest way to get the job done. There's no law against customizing. That said, except in extreme cases you should not edit the Script Library files in your project. The kludge you make to solve one issue will almost certainly come back to haunt you or whoever follows you. Consider the Script Library files as untouchable as compiled DLLs.

Navigating from One Page to Another Page, Using Script

If you are accustomed to using HTML forms and buttons to submit data and navigate, the SOM can be confusing. When you look at the source code of a page that has the SOM enabled, you notice that the whole page is set up as a form. For instance, in the following snippet, you see that the form called `thisForm` actually comes before the opening HTML tag. Even before all that is an `include file` that inserts much of the JavaScript where the SOM's magic hides.

```
<% ' VI 6.0 Scripting Object Model Enabled %>
<!--#include file="_ScriptLibrary/pm.asp"-->
<% if StartPageProcessing() Then Response.End() %>
<FORM name=thisForm METHOD=post>
<HTML>
```

If the whole page is a form, you can understand how adding more forms within it is a recipe for trouble. When you submit a form inside a form, what part is processed? The simple answer is that you make do with the form that is already there. The SOM gives you several other ways to accomplish navigation to other pages and submission of data to a server.

Simple Page Navigation

Let's start with a navigation example. In your VI 6 project, add an HTML page called `nav.htm` to your project and enable the SOM. An easy way to enable the SOM is to view the page in Source view, put your cursor just after the `<BODY>` tag, and right-click. This opens the Properties page. On the General tab, you find the check box you need in the bottom-left corner. After enabling the SOM, close the Properties page. In Design view, go to the Design-Time Controls toolbox (watch that you're not using the HTML list), and drag a `Listbox` script object, a `Button` script object, and a `PageObject` script object onto your page.

You are using the list box to give a Web surfer a choice of sites to visit. In Source view, select Listbox1 and open its Properties page. On the Lookup tab, enter some data for the list box. Put a URL such as www.microsoft.com in the Bound Value column and a friendly name for the site, for example, Microsoft, in the Display column. Add two or three sets of data to make the Listbox Properties page look like Figure 3.3. When you have finished entering data, click OK to return to your source code.

FIGURE 3.3

A view of the data used for navigation to a URL.

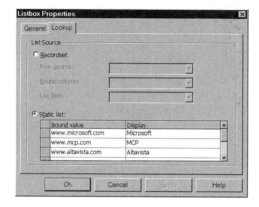

On your page, you want the user to select the site from the list box and click the button to go there. You might want to change the caption for Button1 to Go.

Web pages are event oriented. Generally, nothing new happens on a page until someone or something triggers an event. Your navigation page is no exception. You have to tap into the onclick event of the Go button to make the navigation happen. Make sure you are in the VI editor's Source view, and then click the Script Outline tab. (If the Script Outline window isn't showing, you have to go to View>Other Windows>Script Outline to get it.) Expand the Client Objects & Events node, and then expand the Button1 node. To start a skeleton handler for the onclick event, double-click the little lightning bolt next to the word *onclick*. You will notice that VI creates some starter script for you in the language that you have chosen for client-side scripting. The default language for client-side script is JavaScript.

WHICH SCRIPTING LANGUAGE?

VI offers VBScript and JavaScript as scripting languages. Many programmers who already know Visual Basic prefer to use VBScript for server-side code. They can write faster, and because the browser never sees server-side code, compatibility isn't an issue. For the client, it is almost imperative to use JavaScript. Unless you know that your only target browser will be Internet Explorer, you have to work in JavaScript.

If you don't know either language, the choice is simple: JavaScript for both server and client. JavaScript/ECMAScript is becoming a standard, and it will serve you well. You will notice that Microsoft's Script Library files are all in JavaScript, even those that run on the server. That's a pretty good hint from the people who introduced VBScript to the world that the rival JavaScript is here to stay.

Insert a line above the closing brace of the `Button1_onclick()` function, and add the following two lines of code. Notice that IntelliSense shows you the choice each time you type a dot or opening bracket.

```
url='http://' + Listbox1.getValue(Listbox1.selectedIndex);
thisPage.navigateURL(url);
```

The first line uses the `getValue()` method to fetch the URL data that the user has selected in the `Listbox1`. The `selectedIndex` property tells us which item number was selected, starting at zero for the first item (zero-based). You concatenate the complete URL by adding the prefix `http://`, and then the complete string is stored in the variable `url`.

The second line uses the `navigateURL()` method, which belongs to the `PageObject` script object, to carry out the navigation. The `navigateURL` method takes the address as a target. If you look in the Script Outline window, you will notice that the `PageObject` actually has two identities. It can be used as `thisPage` as you've done here, or as `nav`, the default name given to the `PageObject` when you dropped it on the page.

After saving your work, right-click on the page and click View in Browser. The page should look like Figure 3.4. When you select a name and click the button, you should navigate to the requested site. The source code for this example is on the CD-ROM as `nav.htm`.

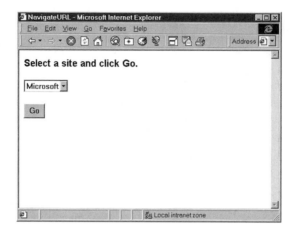

FIGURE 3.4

A navigation page created with script objects and JavaScript.

SOM's Version of an HTML Form

In the next example, you will create the SOM equivalent of a form that includes a text box and a submit button. If this were regular HTML, you would be using syntax such as the following lines:

```
<form action="feedback.asp" method="post">
<input type=submit>
</form>
```

In the first line, `feedback.asp` evaluates the data sent from the form and gives the user some feedback. Let's put this together using the SOM.

In your VI 6 project, add an HTML file called `response.htm` to act as the "form" page. This is the page on which the user will type the answer to a question and click a button to submit the answer. Add `Textbox`, `Button`, and `PageObject` script objects to your page and enable the SOM as you did in the preceding example. Save `response.htm`. You aren't finished with it, but you have to create the target file before going further.

Add another page to your project, called `feedback.asp`. You're now working with server-side code in Active Server Pages (ASP). Drop a `Label` script object and a `PageObject` script object onto the page. This is the page that evaluates the answer given in `response.htm`. You're going to add a sub procedure in this file and make the procedure available to the previous file. Open `feedback.asp` in Source view and put your cursor after the HTML `</TITLE>` tag. From the HTML menu, click Script Block and then Server. This creates the starter space for some VBScript code that runs on the server. Between the `SCRIPT` tags, type the following code:

```
Sub chkanswer(ans)
if ucase(ans)="INTERNET STUDIO" then
   Label1.setCaption "Correct!"
else
   Label1.setCaption "Sorry, that's wrong."
end if
End Sub
```

The sub procedure `chkanswer` accepts the person's answer as a parameter. In the second line, the code evaluates an uppercase version of the answer. If the answer is correct, the code sets the caption of `Label1` to `Correct!`; otherwise, it is `Sorry`.

Now that you have a procedure, you have to "advertise" it to any other pages that might want to use it. The way you advertise is through the `PageObject`. Open the Properties page of the `PageObject` script object, and on the Methods tab, click the drop-down button in the Navigate methods list. Notice that your `chkanswer()` routine is available for other pages to use as they "navigate" in. Select `chkanswer` and click Close. Save your work and return to `response.htm`.

You have a target HTML page and an evaluation subroutine embedded in it, so you just have to navigate to it. Although `feedback.asp` has made a method available in the environment, your page, `response.htm`, needs a way to tune in to the advertisement. To do that, open the Properties page of the `PageObject` script object. On the References tab, click the button with the three dots (...) to open a list of files in your Web. Click `feedback.asp` and then click OK. Notice that the target page is now available as a `PageObject` script object. Close the Properties page, make sure you are in the editor's Script view, and display the Script Outline window.

Because you're going to use `Button1`'s `onclick` event to submit the answer, you need an event handler. Double-click the `onclick` node to create a skeleton handler. In the line above the closing brace of the JavaScript code, type the following code. Notice, as you type, that IntelliSense knows about the `feedback` object and prompts you not only for its `navigate` child object but also for the `chkanswer` method and its parameter `ans`! It can be eerie, the first time, to realize how much the SOM is tracking in your files.

```
feedback.navigate.chkanswer(Textbox1.value)
```

What you've done in the preceding line of code is to grab the page as an object and use its child object to make your method available. You get the parameter from `Textbox1` on the current page. View the page, shown in Figure 3.5, type `internet studio` in the text box, and click the button. The page navigates to `feedback.asp`, where the answer is evaluated and the response appears.

FIGURE 3.5

Using the SOM, you create a form-less HTML form.

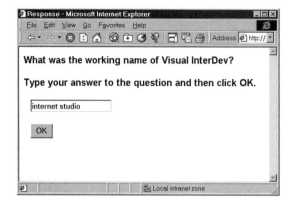

Using Remote Scripting

One of the handy features of VI 6 is remote scripting. Sometimes you don't have to navigate to another page, but you do want to use routines contained in it. Imagine the case in which many pages use the same mathematical formula, but the calculation changes from time to time according to market fluctuations. Rather than dig through all the HTML pages in your Web, you can keep the formula in one script and simply execute the routine that you need remotely. You don't navigate to the page that contains the code you are using.

In this example, your goal is to strip the spaces out of whatever text the user types in the box and then redisplay the "spaceless" code in the same text box. You need two files, one to act as the interface or front end and another in the back end to store the working code.

Add an ASP file to your project, called execute.asp. Add Textbox and Button script objects as you have done in previous examples, except make sure that their Scripting Platform property is set as Client. Add a PageObject object and change its name to myexe. Changing the name can be a little tricky. You have to do it within the Name box of the DTC. After saving execute.asp, start a new ASP page called stripspaces.asp. Add a PageObject script object and name the object myfunctions. This page is where you store the "brains" called on by your preceding page.

Open stripspaces.asp in Source view and enter (or paste from the CD-ROM) the following script. This function simply accepts a string, parses out the spaces, and returns the string to the caller. Notice that this code is running on the server. If you have formulas or algorithms that you don't want to share with the world, you can keep them on the server side.

```
<SCRIPT LANGUAGE=vbscript RUNAT = Server>
Function StripSpaces(thestring)
phraselength=len(thestring)
for counter=1 to phraselength
  if mid(thestring,counter,1) <> chr(32) then
    tempstr=tempstr & mid(thestring,counter,1)
  end if
next
StripSpaces=tempstr
Textbox1.value=StripSpaces
end function
</SCRIPT>
```

Now that you have a function called StripSpaces, you have to let the other pages know about it. Open the PageObject properties page, and on the Methods tab, move to the Execute Methods area and select the function name StripSpaces. Recall that in a previous example, you made a method available for navigate. You're finished with stripspaces.asp, so save your work and return to execute.asp.

To initiate the action, you need an event and a handler. Open the Script Outline window, and in the Client Objects & Events node, expand Button1 to find its onclick event. You will recall that this button was set to use the Client scripting platform, even though it is an ASP page.

Enter the following code inside the Button1_onclick() handler. This script reaches across the Web to the myfunctions object (also known as stripspaces.asp) and taps into that object's function. As it goes, it passes the value that the user typed in the text box. When it gets a return value, it puts the return value back into Textbox1. As you see when you view the page, the return value is the string minus spaces that the remote script has massaged.

```
function Button1_onclick() {
callobject= myfunctions.execute.StripSpaces(Textbox1.value);
Textbox1.value=callobject.return_value
}
```

The resulting page should look like Figure 3.6.

3

PROGRAMMING
THE SCRIPT
OBJECT MODEL

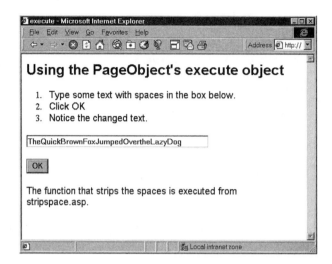

Passing Values Among Pages

If you are accustomed to scripting in ASP, you are probably familiar with the Session object to store variables. Session values don't disappear on each change of page. Although you can still use that technique, the SOM offers other ways to share scripted values among pages.

Let's start by adding an ASP page called start.asp to our project. This is the page that initiates a variable and passes it to a second page, called endpoint.asp. Drop a Button script object and a PageObject script object onto start.asp. Open the PageObject's property page and go to the Properties tab. This is where you can add your own variables, which, in SOM parlance, are considered defined properties of the page. In the Name column, type the variable name kjc (or you can use your own initials). Set the lifetime of this variable/property to Session. Make it Read/Write for both Client and Server platforms. The properties page should look like Figure 3.7. Click Close and return to the VI editor's Source view.

Because you are planning to pass a value from one page to another, you need an event to initiate the navigation. From the Script Outline, double-click Button1's onclick event to generate a skeleton script handler. Back in the editor's Source view, add the following code inside the handler. Watch carefully as you type the dot after thisPage. Notice that setkjc appears as an option in the IntelliSense window, as shown in Figure 3.8.

```
thisPage.setkjc("myvalue")
thisPage.navigateURL("endpoint.asp")
```

FIGURE 3.7

In the SOM, variables appear as defined properties of the PageObject.

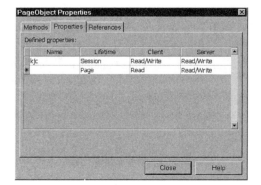

In effect, you've created a new method named setkjc whose job is to assign a value to the variable kjc. The rest of the first line assigns the string "myvalue" to kjc. This can be confusing when you realize that your variable is considered a property, but it shows up as a method to be assigned a value. What you're using is the SOM's set*property* method, where *property* is user-defined.

The second line uses the navigateURL method to navigate to the next page. Save your work and create a new ASP page called endpoint.asp.

FIGURE 3.8

PageObject *defined properties appear in IntelliSense as* methods.

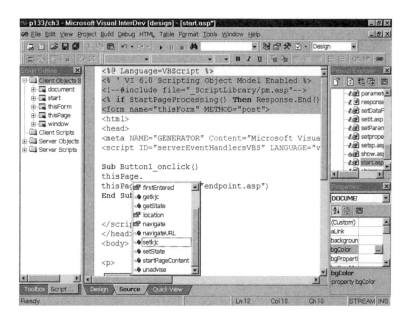

3

PROGRAMMING THE SCRIPT OBJECT MODEL

The sole purpose of endpoint.asp is to prove that you have passed a value across pages. You have to drop two objects onto endpoint.asp: a Label script object and a PageObject script object. Because this page is sharing data with start.asp, it has to reference that page. To create the reference, select the PageObject, open its properties, and go to its References tab. Click the button with the three dots (...), create a reference to start.asp, and click Close.

You want to display the value of kjc that is being passed from start.asp. An easy way to do this is with the PageObject's onenter event. With the editor in Source view and the Script Outline window showing, expand the Server Objects & Events node and then expand the thisPage node. Double-click onenter to create a skeleton handler. Type the following line of code inside the handler:

```
Label1.setCaption start.getkjc()
```

The preceding line uses set*property*'s counterpart, named get*property*. In this case, because your user-defined property/variable was kjc, start.asp is making available a method called getkjc that lets you retrieve the value. Once again, you see the user-defined method as an option as you type the code. The first part of the line assigns the returned value to Label1 for display on the page.

After saving your project, view start.asp in your browser and click the button. The page navigates to endpoint.asp, which displays the value that you set in the preceding page.

You won't deal with them here, but you should know that there's another pair of methods for passing values, called setState() and getState(). Look for examples in Appendix G.

Scripting and Events

The SOM supports the usual events such as onclick and onchange. However, the designers of the SOM have included the advise method, which lets you expand event trapping. In this section, you use the advise method to create something unusual—a server-side onmouseover event.

A Server-Side onmouseover Event

Start by creating an ASP page called newevent.asp. Drop the following script objects on it: a Button (name the button B1), a Label, and a PageObject. Put the following code inside the HTML <HEAD> tags:

```
<script ID="serverEventHandlersVBS"
        LANGUAGE="vbscript" RUNAT="Server">
Sub thisPage_onenter()
myhandle=B1.advise("onmouseover", "B1_onmouseover()")
End Sub

Sub B1_onmouseover()
Label1.setCaption "Mouseover event at " & time()
end sub
</script>
```

The SOM's `advise` method registers an object to be notified when the stated event fires, and then calls a function that you provide.

When the page loads, the `PageObject`'s `onenter` event fires. That executes the line that contains the `advise()` method. `B1` is the name of the `Button` script object. The `advise` method dictates that when `B1` gets an `onmouseover` event, the script should run the sub procedure called `B1_onmouseover()`. For its part, the routine called `B1_onmouseover()` sets the `Label1` caption to a string that includes the time—a way of showing that the `onmouseover` event is actually firing. Figure 3.9 shows the browser page in action. Try it for yourself and notice that you have a server-side `onmouseover` event that could really hammer a Web site with repeat requests.

Notice that the script captures a value from the `advise()` method into the `myhandle` variable. To turn off the `advise()` action, you need the handle as a parameter for the `unadvise()` method. The `unadvise()` method is included in Appendix G.

3

PROGRAMMING
THE SCRIPT
OBJECT MODEL

FIGURE 3.9

Using the Advise method, you can expand the SOM's events.

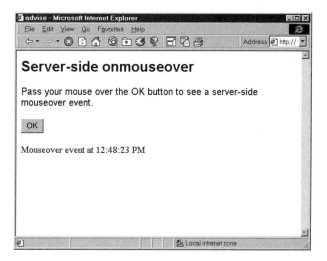

Trapping Client-Side Events

Even when you are using server-side script, you might want to trap client-side events. Validating data or a user's choice is more efficient when done on the client. It saves a round trip to the server. The SOM offers a handy event called onbeforeserverevent that gives you a chance to intervene before a page submits data or moves on. For this example, add an ASP page to your project, called trapit.asp, and add Button (name this one mySubmit) and PageObject script objects. Put the following code inside the HTML <HEAD> area:

```
<SCRIPT ID=clientEventHandlersJS LANGUAGE=javascript>
<!--
function thisPage_onbeforeserverevent( obj, event){
    if (obj=="mySubmit"){
        if(event=="onclick"){
          if (confirm("Do you really want to go there today?")){
              alert("Okay, here we go!");
          }
           else {
             alert("Staying put!");
             thisPage.cancelEvent = true;
           }
        }
    }
}
//-->
</SCRIPT>

<SCRIPT ID=serverEventHandlersVBS
    LANGUAGE=vbscript RUNAT=Server>

Sub mySubmit_onclick()
    thisPage.navigateURL("http://www.microsoft.com")
End Sub

</SCRIPT>
```

The onbeforeserverevent fires just as a page is about to submit data or navigate away. When it fires, the event supplies two key pieces of information that you can use: the name of the object that fired the submit (or other) event and the type of event that the object fired. With these two pieces of information you can use script to determine whether you want to intervene. As you see in the preceding code, an onclick event from the mySubmit button starts a navigation sequence to the Microsoft Web site. But because you trap the onbeforeserverevent, the routine finds out what button is trying to navigate and launches a JavaScript confirmation box, as shown in Figure 3.10. If the user clicks OK, the navigation proceeds. If the user clicks Cancel, the page's cancelEvent property is set to True and the navigation never happens.

FIGURE **3.10**

By using
onbeforeserverev
ent, *a script can
evaluate what is
submitted.*

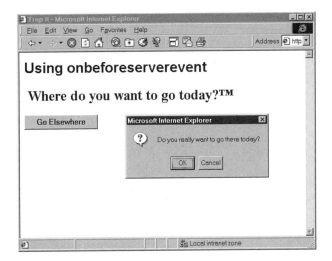

Changing the Appearance of Script Objects

By using the SOM, you can hide, disable, show, or resize script objects with the click of a button. Not only are the pages interactive, but also the coding time and maintenance are dramatically reduced. In the first example of changing objects on-the-fly, I will show how to change the state of familiar controls.

Hiding, Showing, and Disabling Objects

Start a new ASP page called hsd.asp. The HTML page will look like Figure 3.11. Add Listbox, Button, and Textbox script objects across the top. These are the controls that you are going to manipulate. Include a horizontal rule to separate the sections.

At the bottom of the page, drop an OptionGroup script object and a Button script object. As shown in Figure 3.12, configure the OptionGroup object's properties to use the bound values 0–3 and the Display values Hide, Show, Disabled, and Enabled, respectively.

Insert the code shown in Listing 3.1. (The complete script is included on the CD-ROM). You might have to adjust the names of your script objects. This code assumes that the top three objects are Listbox1, Button1, and Textbox1.

3

PROGRAMMING
THE SCRIPT
OBJECT MODEL

FIGURE 3.11

The page called hsd.asp *demonstrates changing the state of objects.*

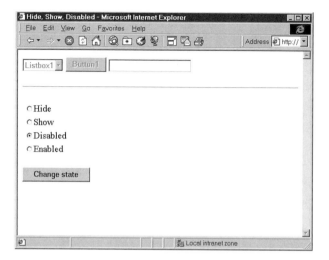

FIGURE 3.12

Adding static values to the OptionGroup *object.*

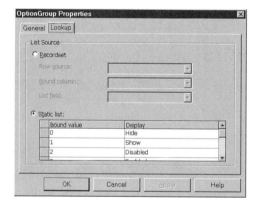

LISTING 3.1 THE CODE IN hsd.asp HIDES, SHOWS, AND DISABLES SCRIPT OBJECTS

```
<SCRIPT ID=serverEventHandlersVBS LANGUAGE=vbscript RUNAT=Server>

Sub Button2_onclick()
a= OptionGroup1.getSelectedIndex()
Select Case a
 case 0
  Listbox1.hide()
  Textbox1.hide()
  Button1.hide()
 case 1
```

```
   Listbox1.show()
   Textbox1.show()
   Button1.show()
 case 2
   Listbox1.show()
   Textbox1.show()
   Button1.show()
   Listbox1.disabled=true
   Textbox1.disabled=true
   Button1.disabled=true
 case 3
   Listbox1.show()
   Textbox1.show()
   Button1.show()
   Listbox1.disabled=false
   Textbox1.disabled=false
   Button1.disabled=false
End Select
End Sub

</SCRIPT>
```

The code in Listing 3.1 executes when the user clicks `Button2`. It fetches the selected index of the option buttons (zero-based) and uses a series of `Case` statements to determine what should be done. For instance, if the option button for Disabled (value is 2) is selected, the script ensures that each script object is showing and then sets each object's `disabled` property to `true`. If you have to find out whether an object is hidden, you can test it with the `isVisible()` method, described in Appendix G.

Changing the Alignment and Style of Script Objects

There are many properties of script objects that you can change on-the-fly. In this example, you show how to change the appearance of the `OptionGroup`, `Button`, `RecordsetNavbar`, and `Textbox` script objects.

Start a new page called `obrt.asp`, and drop the four script objects mentioned in the preceding paragraph on the page. Add another button to use for initiating the changes. You will have to add some static lookup data to make the `OptionGroup` script object appear on the screen.

Add the script in Listing 3.2 to your page.

LISTING 3.2   THE SOM PROVIDES METHODS FOR CHANGING THE OBJECTS' APPEARANCE

```
<SCRIPT ID=serverEventHandlersVBS
    LANGUAGE=vbscript RUNAT=Server>
Sub Button2_onclick()
OptionGroup1.setBorder(true)
OptionGroup1.setAlignment(1)
Button1.setStyle(1)
Button1.src="button1.gif"
RecordsetNavbar1.setAlignment(0)
Textbox1.setStyle(1)
Textbox1.setRowCount(4)
End Sub
</SCRIPT>
```

Here's a rundown of what the script in Listing 3.2 does. By default, the option group has no border. The `setBorder(true)` statement adds a border. By using `setAlignment(1)`, the layout of the option group moves from the default vertical to horizontal. For `Button1`, the script sets the button style to the value `1`, which is an image. Having done that, you provide the `Button1.src` property with the name of the graphic to display. The `RecordsetNavbar` script object is horizontal by default. Using `setAlignment(0)`, you make it vertical. Finally, the original text box turns into a text area when you use `setStyle(1)`. To increase the size, you pass the number of rows (4) to the `setRowCount()` method. All these methods and properties are shown in Appendix G. Figure 3.13 shows the page before the button click starts the script. Figure 3.14 shows the result of the changes to the objects.

> **TIP**
>
> Most of the set methods have a corresponding get method that you can use to determine the current state of the object.

Applying HTML Markup to the `Label` Script Object

For the last example of manipulating script objects, you will deal with text information on a `Label` script object. This script object can handle and render HTML markup, which means you can change the size, font, and color of the text. However, you have to tell the object to expect HTML coding. Otherwise, it displays the markup without rendering it (not a pretty sight). The key method is `setDataFormatAs()`. Pass it the value `html` if you want rendering or `text` if you don't.

FIGURE 3.13

The script objects before executing the code in Listing 3.2.

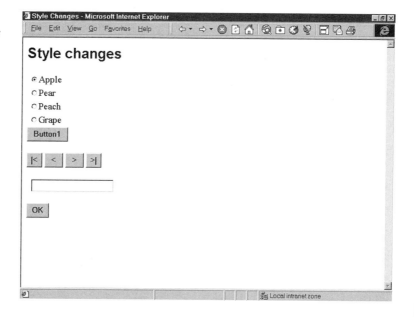

FIGURE 3.14

The Web page in Figure 3.13 after executing the script in Listing 3.2.

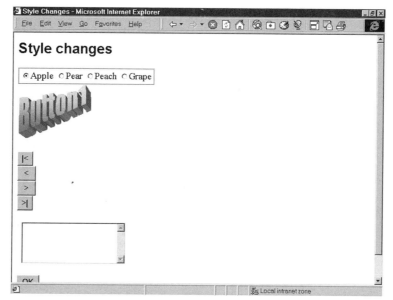

Start an ASP page called `labut.asp`, and drop `Label` and `Button` script objects on it. Add the following code in the HTML `<HEAD>` area:

```
<SCRIPT ID=serverEventHandlersVBS
    LANGUAGE=vbscript RUNAT=Server>
Sub Button1_onclick()
Label1.setDataFormatAs "html"
captext="<H2><FONT color=red face='Comic Sans MS'>"
captext=captext & "The snazzy new text!</FONT></H2>"
Label1.setCaption captext
End Sub
</SCRIPT>
```

Figure 3.15 shows what the page looks like in the browser. Just for fun, try substituting the value `text` in the `setDataFormatAs` method to see what the unrendered HTML looks like.

FIGURE 3.15

Use the `setDataFormatAs` *method to tell the* `Label` *script object what text to expect.*

Custom Queries and Interactivity

The `Grid` and `RecordSetNavbar` design-time controls do a great job of putting a basic database onto a Web page. To enhance the usefulness of the information, you have to let the user choose or zoom in on the data he or she wants to see. In this example, I will show how very few lines of script can dramatically increase the usability of a page.

Scripting Updates for SQL Queries

This example assumes that you have the Adventure Works database (advworks.mdb) in your project and can create a data connection to it. You can find lots of information on data connections in this book, so there's no need to repeat it here.

You are building a data-driven page in which the user can filter the records according to employee number. Start by adding an ASP page to your project and name the file datasql.asp. From the DTC window, drop a Listbox script object, two Recordset objects, and a Grid onto your page. Configure the objects as follows:

- Recordset1 uses Connection1. The source of its data is the Orders table.
- Recordset2 uses Connection1. The source of its data is the Employees table.
- Listbox1 looks up its data from Recordset2, with the Bound Column and List field both set to EmployeeID.
- Grid1 gets its data from Recordset1 and displays two fields, EmployeeID and PurchaseOrderNumber.

If you need help with the configuration, the source code is on the CD-ROM in the file datasql.asp.

Rather than use a button to initiate an event, this page uses a change in the choice in the list box. Insert the code from Listing 3.3 into the HTML <HEAD> area of your page.

LISTING 3.3 USING THE onchange EVENT TO UPDATE A SQL QUERY

```
<SCRIPT ID=serverEventHandlersVBS
    LANGUAGE=vbscript RUNAT=Server>
Sub Listbox1_onchange()
empnum=Listbox1.getValue(Listbox1.selectedIndex)
Recordset1.close
sql="select * from `Orders` where EmployeeID=" & empnum
Recordset1.setSQLText sql
Recordset1.open
End Sub
</SCRIPT>
```

Let's look at what the code in Listing 3.3 is doing. It is triggered by the onchange event of Listbox1. Using the variable empnum to hold the value, the script finds out what item number is selected and correlates that index number to the value of the item. Don't forget that Listbox1 gets its data from the database, so you don't necessarily know how many items there will be. Next, you close the recordset. This is a safety precaution because in MS Access, if you try to open a recordset that is already open you could get a nasty crash. The following line assembles a SQL query by concatenating a hard-coded portion of the string with the variable empnum. From there, you use the Recordset script object's setSQLText method to update the database query. Finally, you open the recordset with the new SQL statement.

3

PROGRAMMING
THE SCRIPT
OBJECT MODEL

When you view the page in your browser, try selecting Employee ID 5. As you see in Figure 3.16, the page refreshes, with the table showing only the purchase order numbers associated with Employee ID 5. You could expand on this example by including more list boxes in which users could further narrow their queries.

FIGURE 3.16

The records returned, based on the user's choice of employee ID in datasql.asp.

Passing Parameters to a Stored Procedure

Sophisticated database applications often use stored procedures where the logic for retrieving records resides in the SQL Server database. This increases speed because it cuts the amount of information sent to the SQL Server and puts the processing close to the action. In this example, you pass a value (a parameter) to a stored procedure. This example requires the pubs database that comes with Microsoft SQL Server. Once again, you assume that you can create a data connection or can find the information you need elsewhere in the book.

The pubs database has a built-in stored procedure that returns the records for authors whose royalties match a given percentage. You don't have to write a query, because it is already in the stored procedure. However, the stored procedure needs a parameter: the author's royalty percentage. Start an ASP file called setsp.asp, and drop Recordset and Grid objects on the page. Configure Recordset1 to use the data connection to the pubs database (for instance, Connection3). Its database object is Stored Procedures, and the stored procedure you need is byroyalty. Set the Grid script object to get its data from Recordset1 and display the available field.

You're now ready to add some script that provides the parameter to the stored procedure. To generate an event handler, view your page in Script view and open the Script Outline window. Expand the Server Objects & Events node, and then expand the Recordset1 node to reveal the available events. Double-click the onbeforeopen event to create the skeleton code for a handler. What you have to do is pass your parameter to the stored procedure before any records are retrieved from the database. Inside the handler procedure, insert the following line of script:

```
Recordset1.setParameter 1, 50
```

The setParameter method takes two values. The first value (1) is the index of the stored procedure that you are using. You can't reference the stored procedure by its name (byroyalty), so you have to know what order it is in. Watch out for some confusion here. In script, the parameters passed to these stored procedures are one-based instead of zero-based. The second parameter is the value that the byroyalty stored procedure expects. In this case, you are looking for authors who earn 50%, as shown in Figure 3.17. Try a value of 25. Notice that if you provide a value for which there are no records, the table doesn't appear on the browser page.

FIGURE 3.17

Use the SetParameter *method to pass data to stored procedures.*

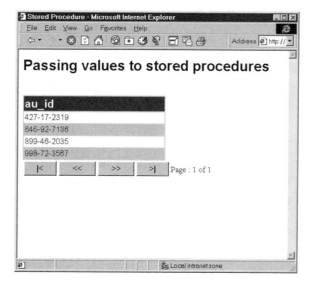

Scripting with Script Objects Versus Regular HTML

There's a learning curve as you move from coding in regular HTML to the object-oriented approach of the SOM. Be careful that you don't try to switch to the SOM for your first big project. Ramp up on small projects like those in this chapter before diving into the deep end. The newsgroups are full of pleas from drowning Web developers who are on tight deadlines and desperately trying to figure out how to accomplish a task, using the SOM. Often the obstacles are tasks that they could code by hand in a matter of minutes in the old-fashioned HTML way. Just because the SOM is there doesn't mean you have to take a sink-or-swim approach and lose valuable time.

There are other considerations. Make sure that you know your target browser when you start using the script objects. The JavaScript magic that makes them work might not be compatible with older browsers or even newer browsers on platforms other than Windows 9x or Windows NT. Imagine the horrible feeling of showing your scripted pages to a client, only to find that they crash with JavaScript errors on his Mac. Test the code on every browser that you intend to support. It is quite legitimate to declare that you are writing for a 4.x or higher browser on the Windows platform. Just make sure the client or boss agrees.

The SOM requires a great deal of overhead. When you start looking at the JavaScript `#include` files, you realize that a penalty exists for the functionality. In many cases, it is worth the extra baggage. However, if you're just putting a small form with a text box and button on a page, you might decide to stay with the light version in regular HTML than the heavy-duty SOM.

Although clearly an innovation, the SOM has a fairly high percentage of bugs and quirks. Many of these are documented in Appendix G, "Scripting Object Model Reference", right with the method, property, or event to which the bug applies. If you are banging your head against code that *should* work but won't, take a minute to check in Appendix G or the Microsoft Web site Knowledge Base for a known problem or bug. If you don't find the bug reported in the usual places, ask about it on a VI newsgroup. Chances are, somebody has already discovered it. Even if there's no fix or workaround, at least you can stop wasting time and losing sleep.

> **TIP**
>
> To check for acknowledged bugs in VI 6, go to
> http://support.microsoft.com/support and use the keyword kbVisID600bug.
> Another useful keyword for Web programmers is kbDSIASPGrp.

Summary

In this chapter, you have taken a first look at a new feature of Visual InterDev, the SOM. It presents an environment and techniques that are more familiar to Visual Basic programmers than to traditional HTML coders. You've seen how the SOM requires different methods for submitting data, passing values from one page to another, and changing the appearance of a page on-the-fly. By using events that the SOM makes available, you can query a database and pass parameters to a stored procedure with very little code. Several references to Appendix G contain a description and sample code for each of the events, methods, and properties that the SOM makes available. Finally, you've seen that programming the SOM might not be the best approach for all Web projects because of its learning curve, overhead, and browser incompatibilities.

3

PROGRAMMING
THE SCRIPT
OBJECT MODEL

Creating Web Sites with Style

by Steven Banick

CHAPTER 4

In this chapter you will experiment with Cascading Style Sheets (CSS) to create complex and attractive layouts for your Web site. Cascading Style Sheets offer you a great deal of flexibility and precise control over your site's appearance.

Separating Form from Function

Since their inception, Web pages have lacked the finer control of layout, typography, and presentation that their print brethren have taken advantage of. Traditionally, the formatting of Web pages relied on using a combination of the intrinsic HTML tags provided by a Web browser and using intricate graphics arranged to create a pleasing appearance. With the introduction of *Cascading Style Sheets* (CSS), a new level of control over appearance has been provided to Web designers that, in many ways, exceeds the control found in print and other electronic media.

Cascading Style Sheets, or simply *style sheets*, empower you with the ability to control the appearance and layout of your Web pages, independently of your raw HTML code. Style sheets don't replace standard HTML formatting, however. Instead, they complement this formatting by adding a new level of control.

Style Sheets and the Web

Introduced several years ago, style sheets establish a method for describing how documents are presented onscreen (and even in print). The essential advantage to style sheets is their flexibility: You can attach a style sheet to a document to influence its appearance without sacrificing device independence or adding new HTML tags. Style sheets are formed through a simple styling language that can be "embedded" in or attached to a Web page. This styling language enables you to affix formatting instructions to HTML elements, margins, and positioning. The beauty of style sheets is their "graceful degradation" within Web browsers that do not support CSS. When a Web browser does not understand CSS or a particular formatting instruction, the Web browser ignores it and displays the page with its own formatting knowledge, based on intrinsic HTML.

> **NOTE**
>
> The key thing to keep in mind when you are working with feature degradation and CSS is that it is graceful, but not elegant. If your page relies immensely on CSS to deliver its appearance, a Web browser that does not support CSS (or at least the CSS formatting your page uses) will ignore it entirely. This could translate into a page that is, for all intents and purposes, unreadable and distinctly unusable. Later in the chapter, this is covered in more detail in the section "Handling Cross-Browser Incompatibilities."

Using a combination of traditional formatting through graphics and CSS, you can achieve spectacular page layouts and functional control over your Web pages. Figures 4.1 and 4.2 illustrate a comparison of the same page; the first is without CSS formatting, whereas the second relies on it almost exclusively.

FIGURE 4.1

A Web page without using style sheets. Notice how some items are difficult to see.

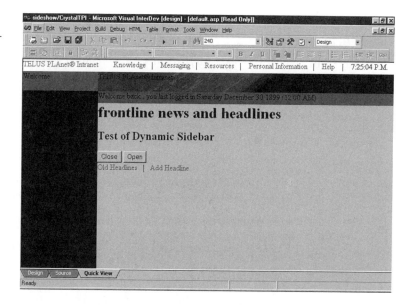

FIGURE 4.2

Notice how formatting was defined through style sheets to enhance the page's appearance.

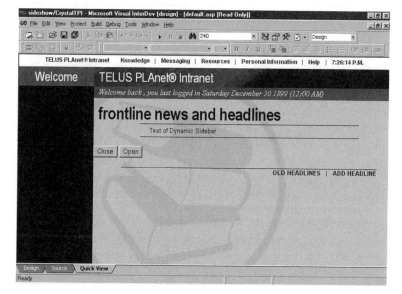

Style sheets can be used to define (or redefine) the formatting and layout information for intrinsic HTML tags (such as the <B> or <H1> tags). They can also be used to create new formatting tags exclusively for your own page finessing. Let's use the examples shown in Figures 4.1 and 4.2. In the main window area, a single frame, the HTML code in Listing 4.1 is used.

LISTING 4.1 THE HTML CODE FOR MAIN-WELCOME.ASP IN FIGURE 4.1

```
1 <!DOCTYPE HTML PUBLIC "-//W3C//DTD HTML 4.0 Transitional//EN">
2 <html>
3 <head>
4    <title>Main: Welcome</title>
5    <link rel="stylesheet" type="text/css" href="resource/main.css">
6 </head>
7 <body BGCOLOR="#c6c7c6" CLASS="Knowledge">
8 <h1>frontline news and headlines</h1>
9 <h2>Test of Dynamic Sidebar</h2>
10 <INPUT type="button" value="Close" id=closebutton name=closebutton>
11 <INPUT type="button" value="Open" id=openbutton name=openbutton>
12 <div CLASS="BottomButton">
13     <a HREF="main-oldheadline.asp" TITLE="View old and expired
       ➥headlines from the past.">Old Headlines</a>  
14     ¦   <a HREF="administration/main-createarticle.asp" TARGET=
       ➥"Main" TITLE="Add a new article headline for others
       ➥to view.">Add Headline</a>
15 </div>
16 </body>
```

In Listing 4.1, on lines 8 and 9, you can see the use of the standard HTML <H1> and <H2> tags for the page titles. However, the appearance of the text in Figure 4.2 differs greatly from that in Figure 4.1. In Figure 4.2, you can also see that the text generated from lines 13 and 14 differs greatly from that in Figure 4.1.

This listing demonstrates two key concepts behind CSS. In lines 8 and 9, CSS is used to redefine the formatting attached to the intrinsic HTML elements (in fact, several other intrinsic elements are modified, but more on that in a moment). In lines 13 and 14, a new style of formatting is applied to the text, using information defined in a style sheet file. Later in the chapter, in the section "Using Style Sheets in Your Web Applications," you explore how this is done.

At the heart of this magical transformation between the two displays is a style sheet file. This file contains the formatting instructions used by the page shown in Figure 4.2. Listing 4.2 displays several style sheet formatting instructions used for this page.

LISTING 4.2   AN EXCERPT FROM THE EXTERNALLY REFERENCED MAIN.CSS STYLE SHEET FILE

```
1  BODY
2  {
3      FONT-FAMILY: Arial, Helvetica, Sans-Serif;
4      FONT-SIZE: 10pt
5  }
6  BODY.Knowledge
7  {
8      BACKGROUND: url("../images/watermarks/knowledge.gif") fixed
       ➥no-repeat left top
9  }
10 H1
11 {
12     COLOR: black;
13     FONT-FAMILY: Arial Narrow, Arial, Helvetica, Sans-Serif;
14     FONT-SIZE: 28pt;
15     LETTER-SPACING: -1pt;
16     MARGIN-TOP: 10px;
17     TEXT-ALIGN: left;
18     TEXT-INDENT: 10px
19 }
20 H2
21 {
22     BORDER-BOTTOM: black solid 1px;
23     BORDER-LEFT: thin;
24     BORDER-RIGHT: 1px;
25     BORDER-TOP: black solid 1px;
26     COLOR: black;
27     FONT-FAMILY: Arial, 'Arial Narrow', Helvetica, Sans-Serif;
28     FONT-SIZE: 10pt;
29     FONT-WEIGHT: 100;
30     MARGIN-LEFT: 100px;
31     MARGIN-RIGHT: 50px;
32     MARGIN-TOP: -20px;
33     PADDING-BOTTOM: 5px;
34     PADDING-TOP: 5px;
35     TEXT-ALIGN: left;
36     TEXT-INDENT: 20px
37 }
38 .IndentedBodyText
39 {
40     MARGIN-LEFT: 100px;
41     MARGIN-RIGHT: 50px;
42     PADDING-BOTTOM: 5px;
43     PADDING-TOP: 5px;
44     TEXT-ALIGN: left
45 }
46 .BottomButton
```

4

CREATING WEB
SITES WITH STYLE

continues

LISTING 4.2   CONTINUED

```
47 {
48     BORDER-TOP: black solid 1px;
49     COLOR: black;
50     FONT-FAMILY: Arial, Helvetica, Sans-Serif;
51     FONT-SIZE: 10pt;
52     FONT-VARIANT: small-caps;
53     FONT-WEIGHT: bold;
54     MARGIN-LEFT: 60px;
55     MARGIN-RIGHT: 10px;
56     MARGIN-TOP: 20px;
57     TEXT-ALIGN: right
58 }
```

As you can see from Listing 4.2, style sheets follow a simple but regimented syntax for defining formatting. In lines 10–19 of Listing 4.2, the formatting definition for the <H1> tag (used in line 8 of Listing 4.1) can be found. The instructions specify a font, color, size, and margins for any text using the <H1> tag within that page. The same occurs for the <H2> tag in lines 20–37, with the addition of a border above and below the text.

Lines 46–58 in Listing 4.2 display the formatting instructions for the text found in lines 13 and 14 of Listing 4.1, the bottom "buttons" of the screen. You might also notice additional formatting within Listing 4.2, including a formatting definition for the page's <BODY> and background image. This segues nicely into the topic of *selectors*.

Understanding CSS Selectors

In style sheet parlance, a *selector* is the equivalent of an HTML tag. It is an identifying string that corresponds to the formatting declaration within the style sheet. Put another way, a selector is a means of naming and referencing your formatting instructions, much as you use intrinsic HTML formatting tags (such as <B> for bold text). The following four kinds of selectors are in use with style sheets:

- Type
- Class
- ID
- Contextual

> **NOTE**
>
> The CSS 2.0 standard has introduced two new selectors, the Attribute and Parent-Child. CSS 2.0 is briefly discussed under the heading "An Introduction to the CSS 2.0 Specification."

Type Selectors

The Type selector is the most basic and common kind of selector used in style sheets. The Type selector is the direct counterpart to the intrinsic HTML formatting tags. *Type selectors* are used to redefine the formatting attached to an HTML element or tag. For example, in Listing 4.2, the <H1> tag was reformatted using the <H1> Type selector on line 10.

Class Selectors

A *Class selector* is a standalone formatting instruction, typically applying style to multiple HTML elements. Class selectors are used to create new kinds of formatting, free from the conventional HTML tags or even the styles of those tags. In Listing 4.2, line 46 defines a new Class selector for the BottomButton. This formatting is used for several elements within Listing 4.1 to create the desired layout.

> **TIP**
>
> You can use Class selectors to create unique "subsets" of existing Type selectors. This is demonstrated in line 6 of Listing 4.2, where a new subset of the <BODY> tag is created to add a background to the page. These subsets inherit the properties of the parent Type selector and can be used to create complex formatting.

ID Selectors

ID selectors are used to create individually defined styles to be used by only one HTML element per document. Within the HTML document, an ID tag is associated with an HTML element. You first learned of using IDs for HTML elements in Chapter 2, "Using Dynamic HTML." The same ID you assigned to an HTML element for use in scripting is used by the ID selector to assign a style. For example, on line 10 of Listing 4.1, the Close button is displayed with an ID of closebutton. A style could be attached to this button, and only this button, using this ID. The formatting could be created in the style sheet by referencing the ID with a # symbol preceding it. Listing 4.3 demonstrates an example of an ID selector.

LISTING 4.3   AN EXAMPLE OF AN ID SELECTOR USING THE closebutton ID

```
1 #closebutton
2 {
3    MARGIN-LEFT: 80px;
4 }
```

This would give a wide margin to the Close button, and only that button.

Contextual Selectors

A *contextual selector* is a selector that addresses the specific occurrence of an element in a page. Using a string of individual selectors as a search pattern, only items that match the specific context will be formatted with the specified style. For example, if you wanted to apply a specific set of formatting instructions to any hyperlink contained within a table, but not those residing outside the table, you could use the following code:

```
TD A { color: red }
```

This would format any hyperlink within a <TD> element the color red, while leaving alone hyperlinks outside a <TD> element.

> **TIP**
>
> You can use contextual selectors to create elaborate and intricate formatting for your pages. You can embed contextual selector restrictions within multiple elements, such as format all <A> records within a <TD> that is also contained within a <CENTER> tag.

Defining Styles to Selectors

Obviously, there is more to style sheets than merely defining a selector. Listing 4.2 displays several properties that are assigned values. *Properties* define the attributes of a style, ranging from the type of font being used to the margins placed on the style. A property's setting is defined through a value that relates to the property. Before stepping into the types of properties you can manipulate, take a look at how values are treated in style sheets.

You can think of *values* as the physical characteristic behind a property. Every property you specify in your style sheet must have one or more values specified. The kinds of values assigned to a property depend on the kind of property you are manipulating. There are a few kinds of values:

- Size

- Characteristic

- Attribute

Size Values

When you are working with a property that involves size, such as a margin or the size of text in the style, you are working with a size value. Traditionally, HTML supports two kinds of size values: absolute and relative. Style sheets are much the same, but they provide greater flexibility when you are defining values. With style sheet size values, you can define a size as the following:

- Pixels—Using a `px` unit, you can define size as an absolute number of pixels.

- Points—For typography, you can use `pt` units to specify the size of a font, for example. Points are based on the size of a font in relation to the user's display.

- Percentage—A relative value based on a percentage, such as 60%.

- Pica—For typography, you can use `pc` units to specify the size of a font, for example. *Pica* refers to a unit of measurement equal to 1/6 of an inch or 12 points.

- Em—For typography, you can use the `em` unit to specify the size of a font, for example. The `em` defines the point size of a font.

- Millimeters, Centimeters, and Inches—Absolute measurements can be defined using the `mm`, `cm`, or `in` units.

- Ex—For typography, you can use the `ex` unit to specify the size of a font, for example. The `ex` unit represents the size of the font as a percentage of the system default font's cell height.

Characteristic Values

A *characteristic value* defines the characteristic of a property. Good examples of characteristic values are those for font alignment, such as center, left, right, or full justification. You can think of characteristic values as defining the behavior of a style's property. Another example is font face names—for example:

```
font-family: arial, helvetica, sans-serif;
```

Multiple characteristic values can be defined for some properties by separating the values with a comma.

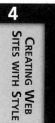

Attribute Values

What qualifies as an attribute value and not a characteristic value? It is somewhat of a judgement call. You can look at an attribute value as the value defining a singular attribute to a property. For example, the color of a font or the font weighting (boldface text) could be considered an attribute value, like the following:

```
font-color: red;
```

CSS 1.0 Properties

With an understanding of values behind properties, you can now look at the individual properties that can be manipulated within your style sheets. Table 4.1 lists the standard properties.

> **CAUTION**
>
> Be careful! Not all properties are supported by all CSS-supporting Web browsers. Often, if a property is supported, it might be supported slightly differently than in another browser. Experimentation is the key. All the properties defined in Table 4.1 are supported in Microsoft Internet Explorer 4.0 and higher.

TABLE 4.1 CSS 1.0 PROPERTIES

Property	Description
Font and Text Properties	
font-family	Specifies the typeface name for the text used in the style.
font-style	Sets the font style: normal, italic, oblique.
font-variant	Sets the font variation to small caps in the current font family: normal, small-caps.
font-weight	Sets the weight (boldness) of the font: normal, bold, bolder, light, lighter, *100... 900*.
font-size	Specifies the size of font to be used when rendering text in this style. Sizes can be absolute-size, relative-size, *length*, *percentage*.
@font-face	Specifies a font to be embedded in your HTML document (for download).
letter-spacing	Specifies the additional space between letters: normal, *length*.
line-height	Specifies how far apart the lines in a paragraph of text are: normal, *number*, *length*, *percentage*.

Property	Description
	Font and Text Properties
text-decoration	Specifies the decorations that are added to text within this style: none, underline, overline, line-through, blink.
text-transform	Changes the rendering of the text in this style: capitalize, uppercase, lowercase, none.
text-align	Describes how the text in this style will be aligned: left, right, center, justify.
text-indent	Specifies the indentation for the first line of text in a paragraph: *length*, *percentage*.
vertical-align	Specifies the vertical positioning (subscript or superscript) of the text in the style: sub, super.
	Color and Background Properties
color	Describes the foreground color of an element. The color can be specified by name (such as *red*) or with a standard HTML #RRGGBB value.
background-color	Describes the background color of an element. The color can be specified by name (such as *red*) or with a standard HTML #RRGGBB value.
background-image	Describes the background image of an element. It is specified using url(*URL*).
background-repeat	Determines how the background image of an element is repeated: repeat, repeat-x, repeat-y, no-repeat.
background-attachment	Determines whether the background image of an element scrolls with the content or is a fixed watermark: scroll, fixed.
background-position	Specifies the initial position for the background image of an element: *percentage* of width/height, *length* of width/height, top, center, bottom, left, center, right.
	Layout Properties
margin-top	Specifies the top margin of the element: *length*, *percentage*, auto. Margins can specify a negative value.
margin-right	Specifies the right margin of the element: *length*, *percentage*, auto. Margins can specify a negative value.
margin-bottom	Specifies the bottom margin of the element: *length*, *percentage*, auto. Margins can specify a negative value.

continues

4

CREATING WEB SITES WITH STYLE

TABLE 4.1 CONTINUED

Property	Description
	Layout Properties
margin-left	Specifies the left margin of the element: *length*, *percentage*, auto. Margins can specify a negative value.
padding-top	Specifies the spacing for the top of the element: *length*, *percentage*.
padding-right	Specifies the spacing for the right side of the element: *length*, *percentage*.
padding-bottom	Specifies the spacing for the bottom of the element: *length*, *percentage*.
padding-left	Specifies the spacing for the left side of the element: *length*, *percentage*.
border-top-width	Sets the width of an element's top border: thin, medium, thick, *length*.
border-right-width	Sets the width of an element's right border: thin, medium, thick, *length*.
border-bottom-width	Sets the width of an element's bottom border: thin, medium, thick, *length*.
border-left-width	Sets the width of an element's left border: thin, medium, thick, *length*.
border-width	Sets the overall width of an element's border: thin, medium, thick, *length*.
border-top-color	Sets the color of an element's top border: *border-color*. The color can be specified by name (such as *red*) or with a standard HTML #RRGGBB value.
border-right-color	Sets the color of an element's right border: *border-color*. The color can be specified by name (such as *red*) or with a standard HTML #RRGGBB value.
border-bottom-color	Sets the color of an element's bottom border: *border-color*. The color can be specified by name (such as *red*) or with a standard HTML #RRGGBB value.
border-left-color	Sets the color of an element's left border: *border-color*. The color can be specified by name (such as *red*) or with a standard HTML #RRGGBB value.
border-color	Sets the overall color of an element's border: *border-color*. The color can be specified by name (such as *red*) or with a standard HTML #RRGGBB value.

Property	*Description*
	Layout Properties
border-top-style	Sets the style of an element's top border: none, dotted, dashed, solid, double, groove, ridge, inset, outset.
border-right-style	Sets the style of an element's right border: none, dotted, dashed, solid, double, groove, ridge, inset, outset.
border-bottom-style	Sets the style of an element's bottom border: none, dotted, dashed, solid, double, groove, ridge, inset, outset.
border-left-style	Sets the style of an element's left border: none, dotted, dashed, solid, double, groove, ridge, inset, outset.
border-style	Sets the overall style of an element's border: none, dotted, dashed, solid, double, groove, ridge, inset, outset.
float	Specifies whether the element floats, causing text to flow around it: left, right, none.
clear	Specifies whether the element allows floating elements (normally images) to the left or right: none, left, right, both.
	Classification Properties
display	Specifies whether an element is rendered onscreen: none, block, inline, list-item. By specifying a value other than none, the space is reserved onscreen for the item, but not displayed.
list-style-type	Specifies an item marker for lists: disc, circle, square, decimal, lower-roman, upper-roman, lower-alpha, upper-alpha, none.
list-style-image	Specifies an image to be used as a list item marker: none or url(*URL*).
list-style-position	Determines how the list item marker is rendered in relation to the content: inside, outside.
	Positioning Properties
clip	Defines the clipping region for the element. This is used to define the part of the element that is visible, where any part of the element outside the clipping region is transparent. The value can be *shape* or auto. A sample shape can be defined as: *shape*:rect(*top, right, bottom, left*).
height	Specifies the height of the style's element: *length*, *percentage*, auto.
left	Specifies the position of the element in relation to the left side of the document: *length*, *percentage*, auto.

continues

4

CREATING WEB SITES WITH STYLE

TABLE 4.1 CONTINUED

Property	Description
	Positioning Properties
overflow	Determines what to do when an element's content exceeds the height and width of the element: scroll, hidden, visible, auto.
position	Specifies the type of positioning to use for the element: absolute, relative, static. The default is static.
top	Specifies the position of the element in relation to the top of the document: *length*, *percentage*, auto.
visibility	Indicates whether the content of a style's element is displayed: visible, hidden, inherit.
width	Specifies the width of the style's element: *length*, *percentage*, auto.
z-index	Specifies the stacking order of elements on the screen; the higher the value, the closer to the top: *integer*, auto.
	Printing Properties
page-break-before	Indicates where to set a page break and on which page (left or right) the subsequent content should resume: auto, always, left, right.
page-break-after	Indicates where to set a page break and on which page (left or right) the subsequent content should resume: auto, always, left, right.
	Pseudo Classes and Other Properties
cursor	Specifies the type of cursor to be displayed for the mouse pointer over the element: auto, crosshair, default, hand, move, e-resize, ne-resize, nw-resize, n-resize, se-resize, sw-resize, s-resize, w-resize, text, wait, help.

An Introduction to the CSS 2.0 Specification

The new Cascading Style Sheets 2.0 specification introduces considerable extensions to the CSS 1.0 specification. Unfortunately, full support for CSS 1.0 is not found in the two leading browsers (Microsoft Internet Explorer and Netscape Communicator). Both vendors have promised complete support for CSS 2.0 in their 5.0 release browsers. However, time will tell how closely they adhere to the specification. The following are the CSS 2.0 design principles:

- Forward and backward compatibility with other CSS specifications.
- A complement to structured documents (HTML and XML), to change style sheets without affecting the markup.
- Vendor, platform, and device independence.
- Maintainability through referenced style sheet files.
- Simplicity. Although more complicated than CSS 1.0, CSS 2.0 remains a simple style language that is human readable.
- Network performance improvements through compact encoding of presentation information.
- Flexibility, due to the way CSS can be applied to documents.
- Richness, by providing authors with a rich set of rendering effects to improve the presentation capabilities of the Web.
- Alternative language bindings to support a consistent formatting model for visual and aural presentations.
- Accessibility for users with challenges, who might have difficulty with inaccessible bitmap text and layout.

Although CSS 2.0 is not directly supported in Visual InterDev, you should begin to experiment with CSS 2.0 features for your applications. This enables you to keep current and adapt your existing style sheets to suit the new standard.

TIP

For current information on CSS 2.0, you should pop over to http://www.w3.org/TR/REC-CSS2, maintained by the W3C. Microsoft's SiteBuilder Network (http://www.microsoft.com/sitebuilder) also maintains a workshop (http://www.microsoft.com/workshop) with information on CSS. Keep in mind, however, that the SiteBuilder Network is consolidating with Microsoft's Developer Network (MSDN) at http://msdn.microsoft.com, and the information might move in the future.

4

CREATING WEB SITES WITH STYLE

Using Style Sheets in Your Web Applications

So, that's all well and good. You understand the concept of selectors, properties, and values. You've seen an example of how style sheets can be used to radically enhance a page's appearance, and you've also seen a list of the basic CSS 1.0 properties available to you. Where to now? Visual InterDev, of course! It's time to start using style sheets in your own pages and applications to simplify your formatting. For this section of the chapter, you're going to create a new project to work with for experimentation. To create this project, follow these steps:

1. Open Visual InterDev 6.0.

2. If the New Project dialog box shown in Figure 4.3 does not appear, choose File, New Project.

FIGURE 4.3

The New Project dialog box should be familiar by now.

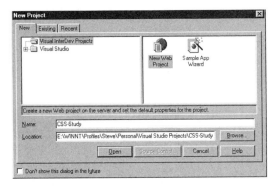

3. Make sure that the New Web Project icon is selected in the top-right pane of the window.

4. In the Name text box, enter the name for your new project: CSS-Study.

5. Click the Open button to move to the Web Project Wizard dialog box, shown in Figure 4.4.

FIGURE 4.4

Choose Connect Using Secure Sockets Layer only if your Web server is config-ured to support SSL.

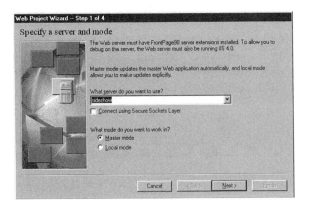

6. Specify your Web server's address in the What Server Do You Want to Use? text box.

7. Click the Next button to proceed to Step 2 of the wizard, shown in Figure 4.5.

FIGURE 4.5

Make sure that you are creating a new project at this step.

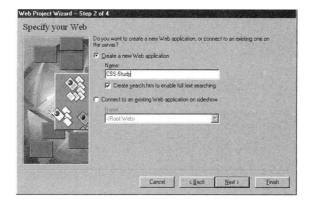

8. Click the Finish button to accept the defaults on this page: Create a new Web application with the name CSS-Study.

> **NOTE**
>
> Feel free to replace this project with your own if you would prefer to work with your own pages during this chapter. Make sure to account for any differences in the file references, however.

Embedded Styles Versus Inline Styles Versus Style References

Before stepping into the creation of your style sheets, let's first discuss how style sheets are used within a Web page. When you want to add style sheets to your Web pages, there are three methods for doing so:

- Embedded styles
- Inline styles
- External style references

4

CREATING WEB SITES WITH STYLE

Embedded Styles

The first method for incorporating style sheets into your pages is by embedding the style sheet information directly into your Web page. This method enables you to take advantage of all the CSS properties. However, it forces you to open each Web page and use embedded styles for modification whenever you have to change a property. Embedded styles are specified as content within the <HEAD> element of your Web page and apply throughout that single Web page. Listing 4.4 demonstrates an embedded style.

LISTING 4.4   THE CODE USED IN A WEB PAGE TO ADD AN EMBEDDED STYLE

```
1 <HEAD>
2       <TITLE>My Web Page</TITLE>
3       <STYLE TYPE="text/css">
4       <!--
5       P { text-indent: 10pt }
6       -->
7       </STYLE>
8 </HEAD>
```

The code contained within the <STYLE></STYLE> tags marks the content as style sheet information to CSS-supporting Web browsers. The inclusion of the <!-- and --> comment tags hides the style sheet information from browsers that do not support the <STYLE> tag. You might also have noticed on line 3 that the <STYLE> tag includes an attribute of TYPE="text/css". This is used as a safeguard to ensure that the Web browser will understand that the information is style sheet information.

- The advantage to embedded styles—Simplicity. It's easy to add the style sheet information for one-off formatting.

- The disadvantage to embedded styles—Maintainability. Complexity increases if you use embedded styles in more than one page. Each time you have to change a style's properties, you must edit each page that includes that style.

Inline Styles

Inline styles are closely related to embedded styles and, in fact, can be considered a "shorthand" embedded style. Like embedded styles, inline styles are located within the Web page itself. Unlike embedded styles, however, inline styles are specified throughout the document, rather than in one central <STYLE> tag. You can use inline styles to apply formatting to any element on a Web page. Listing 4.5 illustrates inline styles in use.

LISTING 4.5 THE CODE USED IN A WEB PAGE TO ADD AN INLINE STYLE

```
1 <HEAD>
2     <TITLE>My Web Page</TITLE>
3 </HEAD>
4 <BODY>
5 <P STYLE="text-indent: 10pt">Indented paragraph</P>
6 </BODY>
7 </HTML>
```

Line 5 of Listing 4.5 demonstrates how an inline style was applied to one instance of the
<P> tag. The inline style is used for a single element only (however, it might affect other
elements that inherit properties below it). In most cases, inline styles should be avoided
for one simple reason: maintainability.

- The advantage to inline styles—Simplicity. Like embedded styles, it's easy to add
  the style sheet information for one-off formatting. In the case of inline styles, however, the one-off formatting is for a single element, as opposed to all recurrences of
  the element on the page.

- The disadvantage to embedded styles—Maintainability. As with embedded styles,
  complexity increases if you use inline styles in more than one page. Each time you
  have to change a style's properties, you must edit each page that includes that style.
  To complicate things further, you might have multiple inline styles to a page that
  require modification.

External Style References

External style references is really where Cascading Style Sheets earned their name.
Throughout all three methods of using style sheets, the style sheet information itself
remains the same. What changes is how a Web page uses that information. With external
style references, a separate file is used to store the style sheet information used in Web
pages. That file can be updated and modified as many times as you need. To use the
external style sheet information in your Web pages, a simple reference is added to your
Web page within the <HEAD> element. Listing 4.6 illustrates referencing an external style
sheet file, and Listing 4.7 lists the style sheet file itself.

LISTING 4.6 THE CODE USED IN A WEB PAGE TO REFERENCE AN EXTERNAL STYLE SHEET

```
1 <HEAD>
2     <TITLE>My Web Page</TITLE>
3     <LINK REL=Stylesheet HREF="style.css" TYPE="text/css">
4 </HEAD>
5 <BODY>
6 <P>Indented paragraph</P>
7 </BODY>
8 </HTML>
```

4

CREATING WEB
SITES WITH STYLE

LISTING 4.7 THE EXTERNAL STYLE SHEET (STYLE.CSS) REFERENCED IN LISTING 4.6

```
1 P {
2          text-indent: 10pt
3 }
```

In line 3 of Listing 4.6, a reference is made to the external style sheet file, style.css, shown in Listing 4.7. Multiple Web pages could contain the same reference, all sharing the same CSS information. The key advantage to this is maintainability: Changes can be made to the external style sheet file (in this case, style.css) without requiring changes to each individual page that references it.

- The advantage to external style references—Maintainability. The same style information can be extended to multiple Web pages within your site (or even from another site) with only one file to maintain. You can make sitewide changes to your styles and formatting without modifying each Web page.

- The disadvantage to external style references—Complexity. Because multiple pages can use the same style sheet information, unwanted changes could cascade throughout your site if you're not careful. Rather than change the style on just one page, you could propagate the change through all pages.

TIP

You can add an external style reference quickly and easily to your Web pages without manually coding the reference in the Source editor. With the Source editor open, locate your style sheet file in the Project Explorer. Select and drag the style sheet file between the <HEAD> and </HEAD> tags of your page. Visual InterDev will automatically create the appropriate link to the style sheet file. Nifty!

Each of these methods illustrates the same simple style sheet in action, creating a 10-point indentation for a paragraph. The difference lies in the scope of the style. In the first example (the embedded style), every instance of the <P> tag on that page would share the indentation. The second example (the inline style) would indent only the single <P> tag that used the inline style. Other <P> tags would require their own inline style to have the same indentation. Finally, the third example (the external style reference) demonstrates how the indentation would be applied to any and all <P> tags in all pages that use this style sheet.

Using the Visual InterDev CSS Editor

Now that you have a strong understanding of what a style sheet comprises and how to add one to your Web page, you can set about creating a sample site using style sheets. For this example, you are going to create four files:

- default.htm—The first page of your sample site
- news.htm—A second page, which will share your style sheet information with the home page
- style.css—The external style sheet file, which will contain your style sheet formatting information
- style2.css—A second external style sheet file, which will demonstrate how multiple styles can be shared on a page

After the pages have been created, you will use the Visual InterDev CSS editor to define the properties for your style sheet files. The CSS editor provides you with a GUI interface for creating style sheets and previewing their appearance. You can also create and edit CSS files using the standard Visual InterDev Source editor. However, you will use the GUI editor in this chapter.

Creating the Sample Pages

You will begin by creating the two sample pages. These pages will be very simple in appearance and will not include any graphics, unless you want to include them on your own. To begin, follow these steps:

1. Right-click your project name (CSS-Study) in the Project Explorer. From the context menu, choose Add, HTML Page. The Add Item dialog box shown in Figure 4.6 appears.
2. In the Name text box, enter the name for this page: `default.htm`.
3. Click the Open button to create the page, add the page to your project, and open it in the Visual InterDev editor.
4. Switch to the Source editor and replace the default.htm file with the contents of Listing 4.8.

FIGURE 4.6

*After you have
created the two
sample pages, you
create the style
sheet files.*

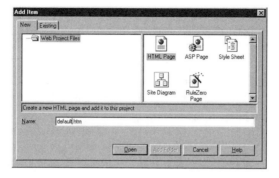

LISTING 4.8   DEFAULT.HTM—THE HOME PAGE TO YOUR SAMPLE SITE

```
1 <HTML>
2 <HEAD>
3 <TITLE>CSS-Study Site</TITLE>
4 </HEAD>
5 <BODY>
6 <H1>The CSS-Study Site</H1>
7 <P>This page is the first page of the CSS-Study Site. This page
8 will reference one external style sheet file that will alter its
9 appearance.</P>
10 <P>Visit the <A HREF="news.htm">News</A> page to see multiple
11 style sheets in use on the same page.</A></P>
12 </BODY>
13 </HTML>
```

5. Save the page by choosing File, Save default.htm from the menu bar.

Repeat steps 1–5 to create the news.htm file, replacing the contents of the file with the code in Listing 4.9.

LISTING 4.9   NEWS.HTM—THE SECOND PAGE OF YOUR SAMPLE SITE

```
1 <HTML>
2 <HEAD>
3      <TITLE>CSS-Study Site News</TITLE>
4 </HEAD>
5 <BODY>
6 <H1>News Flash!</H1>
7 <P>This page, unlike the first, uses two external reference
8 style sheet files. This demonstrates how you can use multiple
9 files to control your site's appearance.</P>
10 <P>Return to the <A HREF="default.htm">First</A> page to see
11 a single style sheet in use on a page.</A></P>
12 </BODY>
13</HTML>
```

You will add the style sheet references after you have created the individual style sheet files.

Creating the External Style Sheet Files

Before you can add the style sheet references to the sample pages, you must create the style sheet files that will be used. For this example, you will be creating two style sheet files. The first page of your CSS-Study project site will use the first style-sheet file, and the second page (news.htm) will use both files. You can use multiple style-sheet files to create a cumulative effect when applying formatting. Multiple files also give you more flexibility to create a series of styles that will be used only by certain pages, without affecting others.

To create the style sheet files, follow these steps:

1. Right-click your project name (CSS-Study) in the Project Explorer. From the context menu, choose Add, Style Sheet. This opens the Add Item dialog box shown in Figure 4.6.

2. In the Name text box, enter the name for this CSS file: style.css.

3. Click the Open button to create the style sheet file, and open it in the Visual InterDev CSS editor, shown in Figure 4.7.

FIGURE 4.7

The Visual InterDev CSS editor enables you to create and modify selector properties.

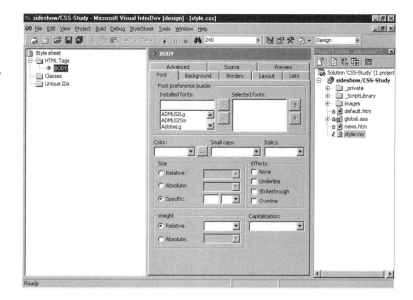

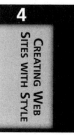

4. On the right of the CSS editor, a hierarchical tree is displayed. Right-click the HTML Tags folder in the list and choose Insert HTML Tag from the context menu.

5. The Insert New HTML Tag dialog box appears, shown in Figure 4.8. From the HTML Tag drop-down list, choose H1.

FIGURE 4.8

The Insert New HTML Tag dialog box.

6. Click OK to close the dialog box, and confirm your selection. Below the HTML Tags folder in the tree, the H1 tag appears with the BODY tag.

7. On the right of the CSS editor, the multi-tabbed editing panel gives you access to the element properties. You begin with the Font tab. In the Installed Fonts list box, select Arial and click the right-arrow button.

8. From the Color drop-down list, choose Silver.

9. In the Size panel, enter a specific size of 16 and choose pt from the drop-down list beside the size.

10. From the Capitalization drop-down list, choose All Caps.

11. Click the Borders tab to switch to the page shown in Figure 4.9.

FIGURE 4.9

The Borders tab is used not only for an element border but also for margins and padding.

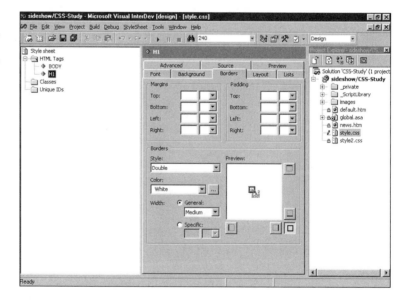

12. In the Borders panel, choose `Double` from the Style drop-down list.

13. For the color of the border, choose `White`.

14. Click the Layout tab to switch to the page shown in Figure 4.10.

FIGURE **4.10**

The Layout tab controls the text layout of your element.

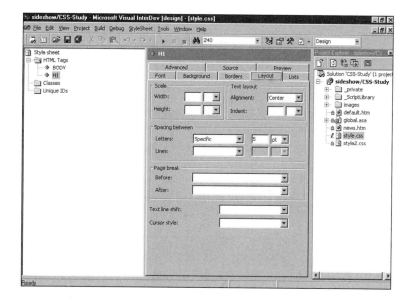

15. In the Text Layout pane, choose an alignment of Center from the drop-down list.

16. In the Spacing Between pane, choose Specific from the Letters drop-down list. Specify a value of 5 pt in the text boxes beside the drop-down list.

17. In the hierarchical tree on the left of the CSS editor, select the `BODY` tag from the HTML Tags folder.

18. Click the Background tab on the right of the multitabbed panel. This displays the page shown in Figure 4.11.

19. Select Black from the Background Color drop-down list.

20. Click the Font tab (refer to Figure 4.7).

21. Select White from the Color drop-down list.

22. Click the Preview tab to display a preview of your style sheet settings. Figure 4.12 shows the preview of this style.

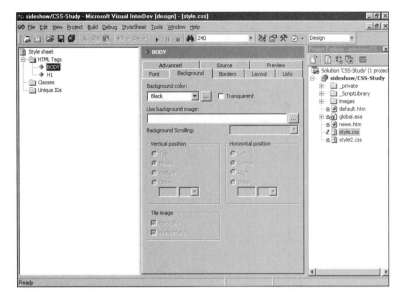

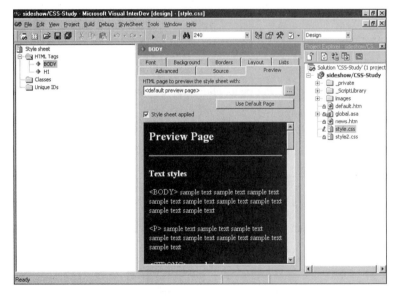

23. Save the style.css style sheet by choosing File, Save style.css from the menu bar.

Now, create the second style sheet, style2.css, by following these steps:

1. Right-click your project name (CSS-Study) in the Project Explorer. From the context menu, choose Add, Style Sheet. This opens the Add Item dialog box (refer to Figure 4.6).

2. In the Name text box, enter the name for this CSS file: `style2.css`.

3. Click the Open button to create the style sheet file, and open it in the Visual InterDev CSS editor (refer to Figure 4.7).

4. Right-click the HTML Tags folder in the list and choose Insert HTML Tag from the context menu.

5. The Insert New HTML Tag dialog box appears (refer to Figure 4.8). From the HTML Tag drop-down list, choose P.

6. Click OK to close the dialog box, and confirm your selection. Below the HTML Tags folder in the tree, the `P` tag appears with the `BODY` tag.

7. In the multitabbed panel, click the Background tab. Here you will create a different background color for the <P> element for this style sheet.

8. From the Background Color drop-down list, choose Olive.

9. Click the Borders tab.

10. In the Margins pane, specify a left margin of 50 px.

11. Right-click the Classes folder in the hierarchical list and choose Insert Class from the context menu. This opens the Insert New Class dialog box, shown in Figure 4.13.

FIGURE 4.13

You can tie a class to a specific HTML tag, restricting its application.

12. Under Class Name, enter `.BottomLine` (note the preceding period).

13. Click OK to add this new Class selector.

14. Click the Font tab.

15. From the Small Caps drop-down list, choose Yes.

16. Click the Layout tab.

17. In the Text Layout pane, choose Right for the alignment.

18. From the Cursor Style drop-down list, choose Wait.

19. Save the style2.css style sheet by choosing File, Save style2.css from the menu bar.

Good job! Now your two style sheet files have been created and saved to your project.

Applying Styles to Elements

With the exception of inline styles, merely providing the style sheet information does not necessarily apply the style to your page's elements. When you are applying styles to Type selectors, the style information is automatically applied to the element (in the preceding examples, the indentation for the <P> tag). However, if you are using Class selectors, you need some method for applying the style information to the HTML element. To begin, link the style sheets to your sample pages:

1. Open the default.htm page into the Visual InterDev Source editor, if it isn't already open.

2. Locate and select the style.css style sheet file in the Project Explorer.

3. Drag the style.css file from the Project Explorer to the Source editor, between the <HEAD> and </HEAD> tags in the default.htm file. This should add a line to your page like the following:

   ```
   <LINK rel="stylesheet" type="text/css" href="style.css">
   ```

4. Save your changes by choosing File, Save default.htm from the menu bar.

5. Open the news.htm page in the Visual InterDev Source editor.

6. Locate and select the style.css style sheet file in the Project Explorer.

7. Drag the style.css file from the Project Explorer to the Source editor, between the <HEAD> and </HEAD> tags in the news.htm file. This should add a line to your page like the following:

   ```
   <LINK rel="stylesheet" type="text/css" href="style.css">
   ```

8. Repeat the process by selecting style2.css from the Project Explorer and dragging it from the Project Explorer to the Source editor, between the <HEAD> and </HEAD> tags in the news.htm file. This should add a line to your page like the following:

   ```
   <LINK rel="stylesheet" type="text/css" href="style2.css">
   ```

9. Move to line 10 of the news.htm file. This line reads
   ```
   <P>Return to the <A HREF="default.htm">First</A> page to see a
   ➥single style
   ```

10. Change line 10 to read
    ```
    <P CLASS="BottomLink">Return to the <A HREF="default.htm">First
    ➥</A> page to see a single style
    ```

11. Save your changes by choosing File, Save news.htm from the menu bar.

Now, if you preview your default.htm page by right-clicking it and choosing View in Browser from the context menu, you should see a page similar to the one shown in Figure 4.14.

FIGURE 4.14

The external style sheet information is used to redefine the <BODY> and <H1> tags for this page.

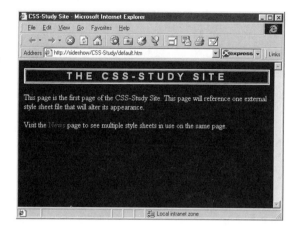

Clicking the News page link opens the screen shown in Figure 4.15.

FIGURE 4.15

The news.htm file combines style information from the two style sheet files to create this page.

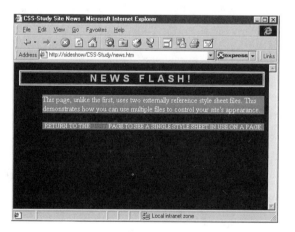

In the news.htm file, the definitions for the <BODY> and <H1> tags are being used from the style.css style sheet file, and the <P> tag is redefined through the style2.css file. Notice how the properties are combined to create one style, particularly in the case of the olive-colored background for the <P> tag. The style.css file defines white as the text color, and the style2.css file defines the olive color background, in addition to the left margin of 50 pixels.

The bottom link, to return to the first page, uses a Class selector, which is specified in the <P> tag of the file. You can specify a Class selector for any element by including the attribute CLASS="*Class*". You might also want to apply a Class selector across multiple elements. Rather than apply the Class to each element, you can use the <DIV> and <SPAN>tags.

Using <DIV>

The <DIV> tag is used to apply a style to a complete block of elements. Multiple HTML elements can be included within the <DIV> tag to share the properties. The <DIV> tag is used as follows:

```
<DIV CLASS="CLASSName">Your block of HTML code goes here,
including <B>Other HTML Tags</B></DIV>
```

Because the <DIV> tag treats the area as a block, margins and padding are supported.

Using <SPAN>

When you are working with only a selection of elements, as opposed to a complete block, the <SPAN> tag is ideal. Like the <DIV> tag, multiple HTML elements can be included within the <SPAN> tag to share the properties. Unlike the <DIV> tag, however, the contents of the <SPAN> tag are not treated as a block and do not support block functions, such as margins and padding. The <SPAN> tag is used as follows:

```
<SPAN CLASS="CLASSName">Your nonblock HTML code goes here,
including <B>Other HTML Tags</B></SPAN>
```

Handling CrossBrowser Incompatibilities

As with all Web development, cross-browser incompatibilities are a fact of life with style sheets. When developing with style sheets, you will have to contend with two types of incompatibility problems:

- Browsers that do not support CSS
- Browsers that interpret CSS differently

Browsers That Do Not Support CSS

When you are dealing with public sites on the Internet, you are dealing with a large number of users who still use "outdated" Web browsers. Most users continue to use older browsers because they do not know any better, their computer is incapable of supporting the newer browsers, or they are content and not ready to change. When you are designing sites that will likely be accessed by users who have a Web browser that does not support CSS, you are faced with a dilemma: How do you maintain a functional site for users who don't have CSS-capable browsers, while creating the richest experience for those who do?

There are a few tactics you can use to address this dilemma. The first is to use CSS to enhance standard Type selectors for HTML tags. You can use formatting and styles to enrich the standard HTML formatting tags, such as <H1>, <I>, <B>, and so on. Using this tactic, you can be confident that at the most basic level, your formatting using the HTML tags is supported by the lower-end Web browsers. Those users that support CSS will then experience a more graphically rich extension to those tags.

The second option is to create two versions of your pages: one for CSS-capable browsers and one for browsers that do not support CSS. For non-CSS browsers, you might have to fall back on the traditional techniques of using graphics to control your layout. The key problem with this approach is maintenance. This forces you to maintain two distinct copies of your site and content to support lower-end users.

Finally, you can opt out of supporting one group of users or the other. If you are keen on using CSS to control your site, you might choose to draw that line in the sand: CSS browsers only! This will prevent non-CSS browsers from functionally interacting with your site, if you use CSS in such a way that it does not gracefully degrade. The other tactic is to fall back on the traditional techniques of using graphics throughout your site to control layout, opting out of using CSS entirely.

Cascading Style Sheets 1.0 is supported in Microsoft Internet Explorer 3.0 and higher, as well as Netscape Communicator 4.0 and higher. Each browser might not adhere 100% to the standard, as the next section explains.

Browsers That Interpret CSS Differently

Web developers are all too familiar with incompatibilities between the major Web browsers. Each browser formats HTML slightly differently than the other, which is a never-ending headache for designers who create complex and layout-intensive Web sites. Unfortunately, CSS is not much different. Although CSS establishes more of a "base line" of compatibility between the browsers, each browser interprets CSS slightly differently. Additionally, Netscape Communicator supports less of the CSS specification than Microsoft Internet Explorer, which in turn also does not support 100% of the specification.

It's very important that you test your style sheet–based pages in all the Web browsers your audience might be using. Ensure that your style sheets conform well in both the major Web browsers. Some areas where compatibility problems exist between the two browsers are

- Borders
- Margins and padding
- Line and character spacing
- Positioning

> **NOTE**
>
> The next release (5.0) of both major browsers, Microsoft Internet Explorer and Netscape Communicator, promises greater support for CSS 1.0 and 2.0. Be sure to keep current on these browsers and plan your development accordingly.

A CSS Case Study

The Banick.com Web site (`http://www.banick.com`) is a site that I developed and maintained . The site is used as a starting point and home for several friends and acquaintances, as well as a developer's resource. When redesigning the Web site, I made a conscious choice to move more toward the newer Web technologies, such as CSS, to deliver an attractive and fast-loading experience. The site relies heavily on server-side scripting and database interaction, allowing CSS to format the returned data without expending overhead on the server for formatting.

Figure 4.16 illustrates the welcome screen to Banick.com. This page uses a background image, inserted with style sheets, as its only image. The rest of the page is built around text and style sheet–formatted elements.

Listing 4.10 displays the raw HTML code behind the page, and Listing 4.11 shows the style sheet used to create this appearance.

FIGURE **4.16**

*Only one graphi-
cal image is on
this page. The rest
is text using CSS.*

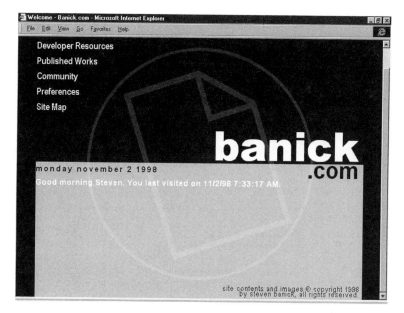

LISTING **4.10**   THE SERVER-GENERATED DEFAULT.ASP FILE USED AS THE STARTING PAGE

```
<!DOCTYPE HTML PUBLIC "-//W3C//DTD HTML 4.0 Transitional//EN">
<HTML>
<HEAD>
    <TITLE>Welcome - Banick.com</TITLE>
    <LINK REL="stylesheet" TYPE="text/css" HREF="front.css">
</HEAD>

<BODY BGCOLOR="#000000" LEFTMARGIN=0 TOPMARGIN=0 BGPROPERTIES="FIXED">
<CENTER>
<TABLE WIDTH="90%" BORDER="0" CELLSPACING="0" CELLPADDING="0" NOWRAP>
<TR>
<TD CLASS="TableTopBG">
<TABLE BORDER=0 CELLPADDING=0 CELLSPACING=0 WIDTH="100%">
<TR>
<TD>
<DIV ALIGN="LEFT" CLASS="menuitem">
<A HREF="News/">Headlines</A><BR>
<A HREF="Developer/">Developer Resources</A><BR>
<A HREF="Works/">Published Works</A><BR>
<A HREF="Community/">Community</A><BR>
<A HREF="preferences.asp">Preferences</A><BR>
<A HREF="map.asp">Site Map</A>
</DIV>
</TD>
```

4

CREATING WEB
SITES WITH STYLE

continues

LISTING 4.10   CONTINUED

```
</TR>
</TABLE>
<DIV ALIGN="right" CLASS="sitename">
banick
</DIV>
</TD>
</TR>
<TR>
<TD BGCOLOR="FFCF00" ALIGN="LEFT" VALIGN="TOP" CLASS="TableBottomBG">
<TABLE BORDER=0 CELLPADDING=0 CELLSPACING=0 WIDTH="100%">
<TR>
<TD>
<DIV  ALIGN="left" CLASS="datelarge">
sunday november 1 1998
</DIV>
<DIV ALIGN="LEFT" CLASS="welcometext">
Good afternoon, Steven. You last visited on 11/1/98 4:26:09 PM.
</DIV>
</TD>
<TD ALIGN="RIGHT" VALIGN="TOP">
<DIV ALIGN="right" CLASS="subsitename">
.com
</DIV>
</TD>
</TR>
<TR>
<TD COLSPAN="2" ALIGN="RIGHT" VALIGN="BOTTOM">
<IMG SRC="images/layout/shim-yellow.gif" WIDTH=1 HEIGHT=200 ALT=""
➥BORDER="0">
<DIV ALIGN="RIGHT" CLASS="copyright">
site contents and images &copy; copyright 1998<BR>
by steven banick, all rights reserved.
</DIV>
</TD>
</TR>
</TABLE>
</TD>
</TR>
</TABLE>
</CENTER>
</BODY>
</HTML>
```

LISTING 4.11 THE FRONT.CSS STYLE SHEET USED BY THE DEFAULT.ASP PAGE

```
.sitename
{
    COLOR: #ffffff;
    FONT-FAMILY: Arial Black, Arial, Helvetica, sans-serif;
    FONT-SIZE: 64pt;
    FONT-STYLE: normal;
    FONT-WEIGHT: normal;
    LINE-HEIGHT: normal;
    MARGIN-BOTTOM: -20px;
    PADDING-RIGHT: 10px;
    TEXT-TRANSFORM: lowercase;
    VERTICAL-ALIGN: text-bottom
}
.subsitename
{
    COLOR: #000000;
    FONT-FAMILY: Arial, Helvetica, sans-serif;
    FONT-SIZE: 36pt;
    FONT-STYLE: normal;
    FONT-WEIGHT: bold;
    MARGIN-TOP: -15px;
    PADDING-RIGHT: 10px;
    TEXT-TRANSFORM: lowercase
}
.datelarge
{
    COLOR: #000000;
    FONT-FAMILY: Arial, Helvetica, sans-serif;
    FONT-SIZE: 12pt;
    FONT-WEIGHT: bold;
    LETTER-SPACING: 2pt;
    MARGIN-TOP: 5px;
    TEXT-ALIGN: left;
    TEXT-TRANSFORM: lowercase;
    VERTICAL-ALIGN: top
}
.copyright
{
    COLOR: black;
    FONT-FAMILY: Arial Narrow, Arial, Helvetica, Sans-Serif;
    FONT-SIZE: 12pt;
    LETTER-SPACING: 1pt;
    LINE-HEIGHT: 8pt;
    MARGIN-BOTTOM: 5px;
    MARGIN-RIGHT: 5px
}
.menuitem
```

4

CREATING WEB
SITES WITH STYLE

continues

LISTING 4.11 CONTINUED

```
{
    COLOR: white;
    CURSOR: hand;
    FONT-FAMILY: Arial Narrow, Arial, Helvetica, Sans-Serif;
    FONT-SIZE: 14pt;
    FONT-WEIGHT: bolder;
    LETTER-SPACING: 0.1pt;
    LINE-HEIGHT: 24pt;
    MARGIN-TOP: 15px
}
A
{
    COLOR: white
}
A:active
{
    COLOR: yellow
}
A:visited
{
    COLOR: white
}
A:link
{
    COLOR: white
}
.title
{
    COLOR: #ffff62;
    FONT-FAMILY: Arial, Helvetica, Sans-Serif;
    FONT-SIZE: 18pt;
    MARGIN-TOP: 10px
}
.username
{
    COLOR: yellow;
    FONT-FAMILY: Arial, Helvetica, Sans-Serif;
    FONT-SIZE: 10pt;
    MARGIN-TOP: 5px
}
```

This page uses a relatively complex nesting of tables and CSS to create the layout shown in Figure 4.16.

Summary

By separating form from function, Cascading Style Sheets provide the flexibility to create your Web application independently of its appearance. Using CSS, you can choose to revamp and change your site's visual appearance without reworking your code. In using CSS, you are splitting your Web application into two unique segments: application logic and visual appearance. With the growing adoption of CSS, you should consider using Cascading Style Sheets throughout your Web applications.

Debugging Web Applications

by Doug Mitchell

IN THIS CHAPTER

CHAPTER 5

Introduction and Background

If debugging is an art, Microsoft has just given us one heck of a brush with its latest version of InterDev. One of the greatest weaknesses of the preceding version was its poor debugging support. Here is a quick history lesson so that you can appreciate the new debugging environment that InterDev 6 now provides.

With the preceding version of InterDev, you had two unsatisfactory methods for debugging. In the first method, you had to resort to opening message boxes or using `Response.Write` to display debug information. From a productivity prospective, this method of debugging brought you back to the Stone Age days of computing. The second method involved the use of the Microsoft Script Debugger. Note that this utility was not released until well after InterDev 1 was released and therefore was not integrated into the InterDev Integrated Development Environment (IDE) nor discussed in its online help. After you discovered its existence, and configured, it did provide some powerful debugging features for client-side scripting. Unfortunately, it did not support debugging of server-side scripting, which, at least in my applications, is where the real complexity resides.

Debugging Setup

My debugging nirvana for Web applications is a powerful and integrated debugging environment such as the one found in Visual Basic. With the new version of InterDev, Microsoft almost delivered it. The most obvious exception has to do with the overly complex configuration. In particular, debugging server-side script on a remote server can be problematic. This section focuses on techniques and considerations for setting up the debugging environment correctly.

Web applications pose significant challenges for debugging server-side scripts because these scripts are interpreted on a Web server rather than within the InterDev process. Therefore, what you have is cross process debugging. Cross process debugging is a complex task that requires tight interaction between the Web server process and InterDev development process. This complex task becomes even more complicated when the Web server process is on a remote machine.

Because of the complexity, Microsoft has released an article on Microsoft Developer Network (MSDN) that should be required reading for anyone serious about debugging InterDev applications.

> **NOTE**
>
> Consider the following MSDN article required reading for debugging Web applications. It is likely that Microsoft will continue to update and improve this document, so be sure to check out the latest version on Microsoft's Web site for the most up-to-date information.
>
> "Microsoft Visual InterDev 6.0 Debugging"
>
> `http://msdn.microsoft.com/developer/news/feature/visep98/videbug.htm`
>
> Furthermore, *Microsoft Internet Developer* magazine has been posting article after article dealing with the complexities of remote machine debugging configuration. For additional information, consider these articles:
>
> - Michael Corning's FAQ Column, "Remote Machine Debugging", *Microsoft Internet Developer*, January 1999
> - Ken Spencer's Beyond The Browser Column, "Debugging with Visual InterDev 6.0", *Microsoft Internet Developer*, February 1999
>
> Unfortunately, the complete text is not available online, but reprints can be ordered from the magazine's Web site at `www.microsoft.com/mind`.

Rather than regurgitate the content of this lengthy (currently more than 40 pages) but critical article on debugging, I will highlight its key points and add some commentary to help maximize its value to you.

The first important point to understand is that InterDev 6 has quite a number of issues with debugging Web applications because of the existing Internet Information Server (IIS) problems. To begin with, server-side debugging requires IIS 4.0. Microsoft makes it very clear that to make server-side debugging work, you should have either Windows NT Service Pack 4 or, at the very least, the ASP hotfix provided with InterDev 6 as a stopgap measure. Making sure that you have the latest Visual Studio Service Pack doesn't hurt either. Even after applying these service packs, and following the guidance detailed in the MSDN debugging article, you will still find that server-side debugging can be problematic when using a remote Web server because of the many configuration considerations.

> **TIP**
>
> If you are planning to take advantage of InterDev 6's debugging capabilities, in particular, server-side script debugging, you should have Windows NT Service Pack 4 applied to the machine running your Internet Information Server 4.0 Web server.

As a result of all the complex configuration considerations necessary to configure debugging properly, Microsoft discusses three separate modes for debugging in its MSDN debugging article: client-side debugging, local server debugging, and remote debugging. Table 5.1 gives a summary.

TABLE 5.1 DEBUGGING MODES

Debugging Modes	*Description*
Client-side debugging	This mode supports client-side script debugging only. Consider this mode if you do not use server-side scripting or if you cannot get local or remote server debugging working because of Microsoft's special considerations, discussed in the MSDN debugging article.
Local server debugging	This mode supports the debugging of both client-side and server-side scripts. Both the Web sever and development environment must be running on the same NT server or workstation. This mode is useful if the Web application is being developed by a single person or if the Web application components can be developed in isolation from one another. This works only under Windows NT (Workstation or Server).
Remote debugging	This mode supports the debugging of both client-side and server-side scripts. The Web server and development environments must be physically running on different machines. If your client machines are running Windows 95 or 98 instead of Windows NT, remote debugging is your only hope when you want server-side debugging. Note that the client machines running InterDev can be Windows 95 or 98, but must have DCOM support installed, and your Web server must be running on Windows NT.

If your Web server is not running under Windows NT (that is, your computing environment consists of only Windows 95 or 98), server-side debugging is not currently possible. Remote debugging can be used by only one developer at a time, which can cause problems if too many developers are debugging Web applications using the same Web server. Local server debugging is Microsoft's recommended debugging configuration with InterDev 6.

> **TIP**
>
> Before you dismiss the development model in which each developer constructs his or her portions of the Web application in isolation, using local Web servers, you should read Chapter 6, "Team Development." InterDev 6 has made this type of development model a viable, if not a desirable, alternative.

The remaining sections of this chapter assume that you have both client-side and server-side debugging properly configured.

Debugging Environment Basics

InterDev 6 now sports a modern and powerful debugging environment that is integrated into the product. If you have used any of Microsoft Visual Studio's other development environments, such as Visual Basic, C++, or J++, you are already familiar with the debugging basics. This is because Microsoft has made a concerted effort to have a common look and feel among its products' debugging environments.

Before going into the details of the various InterDev debugging components, you should keep in mind the typical flow involved in debugging scripts. The flow includes these common steps:

- Enabling server-side script debugging
- Invoking the debugger
- Breaking, continuing, and ending script execution
- Controlling the script execution flow
- Viewing and manipulating script variables and objects

When you understand the debugging basics, you will easily be able to follow the case study presented later in this chapter. This case study ties together the more important debug features to help reinforce the debugging concepts discussed in this section.

Enabling Server-Side Script Debugging

For InterDev to start debugging server-side script, it has to be enabled. You can configure InterDev to do this automatically, whenever a debug session is started or simply on demand.

Automatic Enabling

InterDev can be configured to automatically enable server-side debugging whenever a debugging session is started. This is particularly useful when you are using a local Web server and you don't have to be concerned about affecting other developers. (Remember that remote debugging is currently limited to only one developer using it at a time.)

CAUTION

If Automatically Enable ASP Server-Side Script Debugging on Launch is not available (grayed out), your Web server is not running on Windows NT. Furthermore, you will not be prompted to enable this feature when you begin a debug session. Again, server-side debugging is available only when the Web server is on Windows NT.

To automatically enable server-side debugging, follow these steps:

1. In InterDev's Project Explorer, right-click the project and select Properties.
2. From the Launch tab, verify that the Automatically Enable ASP Server-Side Script Debugging on Launch is checked (see Figure 5.1).

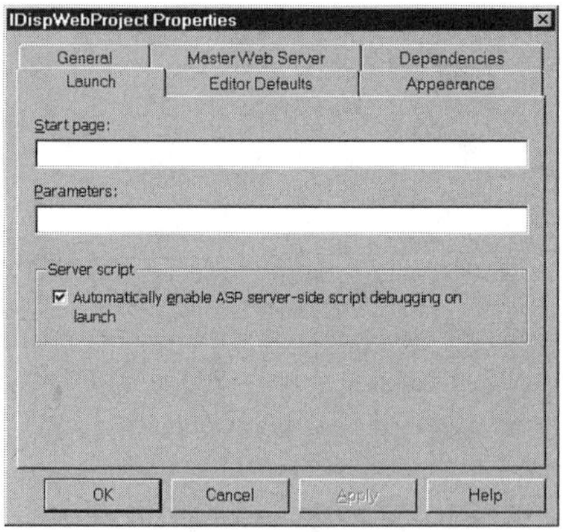

FIGURE 5.1

The Web project's launch properties.

If server-side debugging is enabled for the Web application on the Web server, InterDev performs the following tasks for each debugging session:

- Directs the Web application to be run in its own memory space on the Web server. This is required so that Microsoft Transaction Server (MTS) can be configured to allow users to attach to the process for debug purposes. If you are not familiar with MTS and how it is involved with InterDev, refer to Chapter 19, "Programming Microsoft Transaction Server."

- Enables, if necessary, the Web application's debugging options (server-side and client-side script debugging flags). This means that even if your Web application on your Web server is configured not to debug server-side script, the debug session initiated by InterDev will override the original configuration.

- Configures an MTS package to allow you to attach the debugger to the Web application. You will be prompted for a user ID and password when you first start the debugging session. MTS will run the package under the specified account.

When you have ended the debugging session, InterDev restores the Web server to its previous state.

> ## CAUTION
>
> Setting the server to debug is not a simple matter, especially when you are using a remote Web server. If you encounter problems when InterDev attempts to set the server for debugging, review the Debugging Setup topic discussed earlier in this chapter before proceeding.

> ## TIP
>
> During development, if you configure your Web application to run in a separate memory space (isolated process) using Microsoft Management Console (MMC), a debug session will be faster to launch because it will not be necessary to switch in and out of its own memory space each time.

Manual Enabling (On Demand)

Just because you do not have your Web project configured to automatically enable ASP server-side script debugging does not mean you can't do it. If the option is available, but not checked, you will be prompted each time you start a debugging session from within

5

DEBUGGING WEB APPLICATIONS

InterDev, as in Figure 5.2. Choosing Yes permits you to debug the ASP code that is executing on the server; choosing No results in only client-side script (JScript or VBScript) being debugged.

FIGURE 5.2

*A prompt to
enable server-side
ASP debugging.*

In fact, not setting it can have its advantages. For example, if you are developing your Web application using a remote Web server shared by other developers, it might be better not to have InterDev automatically enable server-side debugging because of the current limitation that only one developer can use remote debugging at a time.

Invoking the Debugger

Before debugging can begin, the debugger has to be started. The method used to start the debugger depends on the circumstances, as discussed here:

- Explicitly entering debugging mode when starting the Web application from InterDev's IDE—This can be accomplished using the Debug menu's Start option. This method requires that a page be designated as the start page within your solution so that InterDev knows what page to launch first. The start page can be specified by right-clicking on the desired page within the Project Explorer and selecting Set as Start Page from the shortcut menu. This method is most commonly used when a Web application is under active development.

- Launching the debugger in response to an error or an explicit statement encountered in the script—This is known as Just-in-Time (JIT) debugging, which is discussed in the next section. This method is often used during unit testing when your Web application encounters an unexpected error at runtime.

- Attaching to an already running document by selecting Internet Explorer's View/Script Debugger menu option or InterDev's Debug/Process menu option— This can be used when you did not start out in debug mode but later decided you wanted to perform some debugging. Note that it will allow you to perform only client-side debugging.

Just-In-Time Debugging

Just-in-time debugging has two requirements before it can be used. First, on the client machine, JIT debugging must be specifically enabled within InterDev. This can be enabled within InterDev by selecting Options from the Tools menu, shown in Figure 5.3.

FIGURE 5.3

Visual InterDev's debugger options.

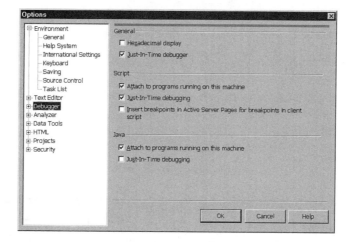

Second, on the Web server, the Web application must be configured to enable the debugging of ASP server-side scripts. You can enable this by using Microsoft Management Console (MMC), as detailed in the MSDN debugging article discussed in the Debugging Setup section of this chapter. Figure 5.4 shows the Web application's configuration screen, where debugging server-side scripts is enabled.

After JIT debugging is properly configured and enabled, a message box will prompt you with the option to debug the Web application when a runtime script error or debug statement is encountered. If you select Yes, a new instance of InterDev will be launched, and you will be prompted to open the project that contains your Web application for debugging. Select your project, and the page that produced the error will be loaded into the Source window with the problematic line highlighted and the script execution halted.

FIGURE 5.4

*The Web applica-
tion's debugging
configuration
options.*

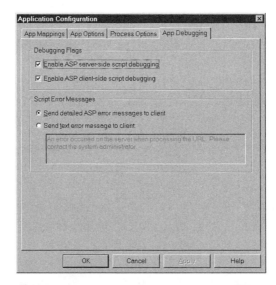

CAUTION

When you choose to debug an application in response to a runtime error, a second, new instance of InterDev is always loaded if InterDev is already running. Unfortunately, if the project you want to debug is already open in the first instance of InterDev, the second InterDev instance will encounter an error opening the file. The error states that the process cannot access the file because it is being used by another process. After clicking OK, the page (not the project) is loaded with the error highlighted and is ready to be debugged. However, the page is read-only. Therefore, if you encounter a runtime error and you have the project already loaded, switch to InterDev and close all files before selecting the project to open.

If JIT debugging is not enabled, your script might simply ignore the error and produce incomplete pages for the browser, with little or no clue indicating that a problem exists.

You can also induce the JIT debugger to activate by inserting into your server-side script either a Stop statement in the case of VBScript or a debugger statement in the case of JScript. Of course, if JIT debugging is not enabled, or the Web application is not configured to debug server-side scripts, these statements will be ignored just like runtime errors.

> **TIP**
>
> Enable JIT debugging during development to ensure that you can identify and debug all the runtime errors you encounter during your testing (refer to Figures 5.3 and 5.4).

Breaking and Continuing Script Execution

Just because the debugger is started does not mean you have control of the script execution (except in the case of JIT debugging, which both starts the debugger and breaks the execution). To gain control over the script execution, you have to break the script execution. When a break occurs, the script execution halts, and the developer can control the script execution flow or take advantage of the various debug windows discussed later in this chapter. A break in script execution can occur for a number of reasons:

- You set an explicit breakpoint. (Breakpoints are the next topic discussed.)

- You manually break the execution using Break from either the Debug menu or toolbar. (Note that the project must have been started with debugging.)

- In response to an error or an explicit Stop or debugger statement encountered in the script. (The JIT debugger must be enabled.)

Setting a Breakpoint

You can set a breakpoint at either runtime or design time (using Source view) by clicking in the margin to the left of the code line. Alternatively, you can use the Insert Breakpoint option from the Debug menu or toolbar. If this is successful, a red dot will appear in the left margin. Again, breakpoints break script execution only when the Web application is being debugged. Otherwise, they are ignored.

Disabling Breakpoints

Using the Debug menu or toolbar, it is possible to remove or to temporarily disable a breakpoint. A disabled breakpoint is indicated by a white dot in the left margin of the source. Considering how easy it is to insert and remove breakpoints, you might wonder why anyone would bother disabling them rather than removing them. This is a good question and one that leads us to the next topic, conditional breakpoints, which require more effort to set up.

Conditional Breakpoints

One powerful yet often overlooked debug feature is the capability to specify conditional breakpoints. These are breakpoints that will be ignored unless a specific condition is fulfilled. To use conditional breakpoints, simply specify a normal breakpoint, and enter a conditional expression (for example, `OverdrawnFlag = true`) into the breakpoint properties, as shown in Figure 5.5. Unfortunately, no visual cue indicates that a breakpoint is conditional.

FIGURE 5.5

Setting conditional breakpoints in the Breakpoint properties window.

Breakpoint properties can be accessed from the Breakpoints window discussed next. A quicker way to access a breakpoint line's properties is to select Breakpoint Properties from the shortcut menu.

Breakpoints Window

When you are dealing with a complex Web application, the management of all breakpoints can sometimes become unwieldy. The Breakpoints window, which can be accessed from either the Debug menu or toolbar, is a perfect way to handle these situations (see Figure 5.6). This window lists all the breakpoints in your current project, not just those in the current file. This gives you an easy way to jump to, disable/enable, and remove breakpoint in code.

5

DEBUGGING WEB
APPLICATIONS

FIGURE 5.6

The Breakpoints window.

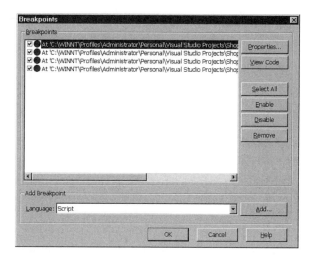

Continuing and Ending Script Execution

After you have completed your debugging at a particular breakpoint, you will want to continue script execution. Select Continue from the Debug menu (or use the Debug toolbar) to resume execution. When you have completed all debugging, you will have to stop the debug session explicitly. Exiting the Web browser is not sufficient. Select End from the Debug menu or toolbar.

> **TIP**
>
> Remember that the current version of IIS can support only one debug session at a time. Therefore, make sure that you explicitly end your debug session when multiple developers are sharing the same remote Web server.

Controlling the Script Execution Flow

Script execution flow is controlled from either the Debug menu or toolbar. When a breakpoint is encountered, the script execution is halted until you manually continue, stop, or step through the remaining code. Stepping through your code is a very powerful debugging technique that lets you move line by line. InterDev provides several stepping variants to maximize your productivity. These are summarized in Table 5.2.

TABLE 5.2 STEP OPTIONS

Toolbar Icon	Name	Description
	Step Into	Executes the next line regardless of where it is located. This includes following execution into function calls. This is the most common step action.
	Step Over	Executes the next line at the current call stack level but does not follow execution into procedure calls. If the next line is a procedure call, all its code will be executed, and control will break following the return from it. This variant is handy when your next line is a procedure that you have already debugged.
	Step Out	Executes the remaining lines in the current call stack level and breaks again when the stack is popped. It will execute all the remaining lines in the current procedure and will break when the procedure returns execution back to where it was called. I find this variant useful when I accidentally step into a procedure I really didn't want to debug, rather than step over it.
	Run to Cursor	Executes the lines from the current breakpoint to where the cursor is presently located in the Source window.

Controlling the execution flow is demonstrated later in this chapter during the sample debugging case study.

Viewing and Manipulating Script Variables and Objects

The final common debug step involves viewing and manipulating variables and objects within your scripts. InterDev's debugging environment provides a large degree of control over script variables and objects. In fact, its numerous debug windows are almost exclusively devoted to this task. These various debug windows are detailed in the next several sections.

Debug Windows

Visual Studio's powerful debugging environment is now fully leveraged in this version of InterDev. For those of you who have not encountered the debugging environment, the number of features and windows can be overwhelming at first.

Because the debugging environment is common across the tools contained in Visual Studio, some of the debug windows included have little or no relevance when it comes to debugging using InterDev. Although I list all the debug windows available in Table 5.3 for completeness, additional detail for the more relevant windows can be found after the summary table.

TABLE 5.3 INTERDEV DEBUG WINDOWS

Toolbar Icon	Relevant to InterDev	Window Name	Description
	Yes	Breakpoints	Lists all breakpoints defined in the current project. This window was detailed during the preceding discussion on breakpoints.
	Yes	Immediate	Used to evaluate expressions or execute statements on-the-fly.
	Yes	Locals	Displays the values of all variables currently in scope. It also permits a user to change the value of any variable listed. The main difference between the Locals and the Autos window is that the Autos window shows variables for all threads.
	Yes	Watch	The Watch window is also used to display the value of user-specified variables or expressions.
	Yes	Call Stack	Lists all active procedures (or stack frames) for the current thread of execution.

continues

5

DEBUGGING WEB
APPLICATIONS

TABLE 5.3 CONTINUED

Toolbar Icon	Relevant to InterDev	Window Name	Description
	Yes	Running Documents	Lists all documents currently loaded to any attached process. Double-clicking any document will open it in the Source window.
	Sometimes	Processes	Lists all out-of-process components and allows you to debug them by attaching to them. If server-side script debugging is enabled, this attach process occurs automatically. Therefore, you do not have to access this dialog as a normal course of action.
		Autos	Same as Locals except it shows variables for all threads. Because InterDev Web applications are not normally concerned with threads, the Locals window is more relevant.
		Threads	Lists all the threads for the current process and some basic information about them, such as ID, name, state, and location. Because InterDev Web applications are not typically concerned with threads, this window is not relevant.
		Output	Displays status messages at runtime. Doesn't seem to be used significantly by InterDev.
		Java Exceptions	This feature is enabled only if you have a Java project, but it still appears on the default InterDev toolbar.

TIP

Customize the Debug toolbar and remove the debug windows that you don't frequently use. You can still access the removed items through the Debug menu, if necessary.

The Immediate Window

Essentially, the Immediate window is a free-form, multiline textbox that enables you to execute and evaluate expressions while the script execution is halted. An *expression* can be as simple as a variable or as complex as you can imagine, as long as it can be completely expressed in a single line of code.

The Immediate window use is surprisingly simple. During a script execution, break, type, drag and drop, or paste an expression into the Immediate window, and press Enter (see Figure 5.7). If you are concerned with the return value of the expression, precede the expression with a question mark. The return value appears after the line it follows. Values of variables can also be changed just as easily by typing the assignment and pressing Enter.

FIGURE 5.7
The Immediate window.

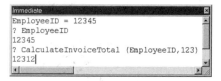

Evaluating and setting expressions and variables on-the-fly is useful, but the Locals and Watch windows can often help you accomplish this more easily. However, unlike the other windows, the Immediate window can execute procedures using different argument values for testing purposes.

TIP

The content of the Immediate window is not preserved when InterDev is closed. If you want to retain the contents for future use, you have to make your own provisions. For example, I sometimes copy my test code and paste it into the ASP file as server-side script comments for later use.

The Locals Window

The Locals window is a good place to start if you are interested in viewing or setting the value of a simple variable within the current scope. It displays all variables that are in scope at the current breakpoint by default, shown in Figure 5.8. However, you can also examine the variables in scope for any stack frame listed in the Call Stack window by selecting a different frame from the context list. You can change the value of a variable by double-clicking the value and typing a new one. If you attempt to change the value to something not allowed by the type, it will ignore your change and revert back to the preceding value.

FIGURE 5.8

The Locals window.

The Locals window also displays more complex objects, although not always in a useful fashion. For example, if you are debugging server-side script, you will see ASP objects, such as Response, Request, Server, and Session. Unfortunately, you cannot view the content of some of the collections contained in these objects, using this window. For example, using the Locals window, you cannot view a list of all the Session variables in the Contents collection of the Session object. Viewing collections is better done by using either the Watch or Immediate window.

TIP

For both the Locals and Watch windows, the values of the variables that have been changed since the last breakpoint are highlighted in red.

The Watch Window

The Watch window combines features of the Locals and Immediate windows. Like the Locals windows, it displays variables and their values. However, the variables displayed are only those that you have specified (see Figure 5.9). Also, like the Locals window, the value of the variable can be modified. Like the Immediate window, you can evaluate more complex expressions, as well as simple variables. To watch any expression, select it in the script source window, and use the shortcut menu to add Watch.

FIGURE 5.9

The Watch window.

ToolTips: A Quicker Way to Watch

One less obvious debugging feature that people accidentally stumble across is the capability to use the ToolTips to display the values of variables while script execution is broken. When you break, pause the mouse pointer over a variable in scope that you are interested in. A ToolTip will reveal the variable's current value, as shown in Figure 5.10.

FIGURE 5.10

The Tooltip watch value.

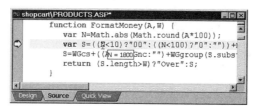

If you are more interested in evaluating complex expressions, highlight the expression you are interested in evaluating, and pause the mouse pointer over the expression to see its evaluation (see Figure 5.11).

FIGURE 5.11

The Tooltip watch expression.

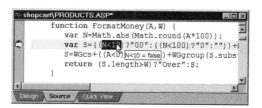

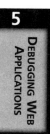

The Call Stack Window

If your application has many nested procedures, the Call Stack window might be useful for identifying your current context. Each level listed in the Call Stack window is referred to as a *stack frame* (see Figure 5.12). By double-clicking a stack frame listed in the window, the insertion cursor in the Source window will move it to where the procedure that changed the stack frame was called and will highlight the line in green.

FIGURE 5.12

The Call Stack window.

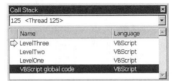

The Running Documents Window

The Running Documents window displays all running documents. Double-click a document to load it into the InterDev Source window. Notice that when you are debugging both client-side and server-side scripts, you will often see the same page twice. For example, in Figure 5.13, Products.asp appears under Microsoft Active Server Pages and under Microsoft Internet Explorer. In fact, these two running documents represent two perspectives of the same file. Files listed under Active Server Pages are considered server-side scripts. If you examine a file by double-clicking it, you will see the ASP file that you normally see in InterDev.

FIGURE 5.13

The Running Documents window.

Files listed under the browser are client-side scripts. If you double-click a file, you will see the file as it appears to browser after the Web server has processed it. All the server-side script will be gone, and any HTML dynamically generated will be in its place. This provides an interesting opportunity to see an ASP page before and after the Web server has processed it.

Debugging a Global.asa File

With the prior version of InterDev, debugging the Global.asa file was problematic because its procedures were triggered indirectly by a Web application. However, with the new debugging environment, you can treat it like any other page and place a breakpoint or use the Stop or debugger statement in any of its procedures. Keep this in mind when the procedure you are trying to debug is triggered. For example, to debug the Application_OnStart procedure, you might have to stop and restart the Web server to trigger the event again.

A Sample Debugging Case Study

This sample debugging session uses the Visual InterDev Samples Gallery provided with the InterDev 6 product. This sample is a collection of mini Web applications that showcase typical design patterns encountered on the Web. To follow along with the case study, you must have the Visual InterDev Samples Gallery already installed on your Web server. To perform the install, all you have to do is create a new project, select the Sample App Wizard (rather than use New Web Project) and follow the directions.

The objective of this debugging case study is to demonstrate how the more important components in the new debugging environment work together. One obvious use of a debugging environment is to debug buggy applications. To make this a bit more interesting, I will use the debugging environment in a less orthodox manner. Rather than debug a buggy application, I will use the debugging environment to help you understand a moderately complex Web application: the Visual InterDev Samples Gallery.

A Case Study Scenario

Imagine that your hotshot Web developer, Marcia, just got a new job, and now her application is your sole responsibility starting yesterday. How would you go about learning how it works? Sure, you've used the Web application before, but how exactly does it generate the HTML you see as a user? You could just print out all the scripts and pore over them, hoping the Web application is relatively simple and well commented. However, after reality sets in and you realize that the application is not simple or commented, you decide that the debugger should do the stepping....

Case Study Scope

The Visual InterDev Samples Gallery, shown in Figure 5.14, is an extensive Web application. To keep this case study focused, you will concentrate your efforts on one of the mini applications: Shopping Cart. In this application, a user can select from a list of products and add them to a virtual shopping cart. You will further refine your focus to the particular ASP file (Products.asp) that generates a list of products from which the user can choose. If you haven't tried this particular application already, I recommend that you give it a quick test drive before proceeding.

FIGURE 5.14

The Visual InterDev Samples Gallery Web application.

CAUTION

If you are following along online with the case study, it is likely that your application will timeout because of extended pauses. If this occurs, you might encounter unpredictable behavior while debugging the application. Therefore, in the case of a timeout, you should stop and restart the debugging session and return to where you left off.

Getting Started: Debugging Global.asa

Thereare two objectives for this first part of the case study. The first is to practice setting a breakpoint. The second is to note when Application_OnStart procedure is triggered. You will begin the case study with the Application_OnStart procedure in Global.asa. This procedure triggers only when the Web server first loads a Web application.

1. Open the Samples Gallery project in InterDev.
2. Open Global.asa in the Source window.

3. Place a breakpoint on the Application(Gallery_ConnectionString) line in the Application_OnStart procedure.

Observe that database-related information is being set to application variables in this procedure. It is common practice to set variables that have to be persistent during the time the application is running.

4. Verify that the Start Page is specified as Default.htm.

5. Start a debugging session using the Debug menu.

6. Under the Scripting Samples section in the left frame, click the Shopping Cart link.

InterDev will pop to the foreground with the global.asa script loaded and the line you breakpointed earlier highlighted in yellow. Script execution is now broken and the debugging environment is available for your commands.

> **NOTE**
>
> Notice that the Application_OnStart was not triggered until you clicked the Shopping Cart link. This is because the shopping cart page was the first ASP encountered in the Gallery application. This illustrates an important concept: Until the first ASP file is processed, the Web application is not considered started.

7. Continue script execution using the Debug menu to return to the Gallery application in the browser.

8. If you have not done so before, click the Behind the Scenes link (in the right frame) to see an overview of the Shopping Cart Sample application.

9. Click the Run Sample link in the right frame.

10. Before proceeding, switch to InterDev and load Product.asp from the shopcart subdirectory.

11. Set a breakpoint on the first var declaration in the FormatMoney function, shown in Figure 5.15.

Notice that the breakpoint includes a question mark. This indicates that the breakpoint will not be hit because the file is currently not loaded on the Web server. When the file is actually loaded, the question mark will disappear, and the breakpoint will trigger as normal.

FIGURE 5.15

*The breakpoint on
the first variable
declaration.*

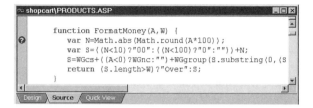

12. Return to the Gallery application, and click the Search button. This loads and executes the Products.asp file. When FormatMoney is executed, the breakpoint is triggered, and the script execution is halted.

BEHIND THE SCENES OF PRODUCT.ASP

The Products.asp file contains a design-time grid control to display the products and prices in an HTML table. The prices are formatted using a function in Products.asp called FormatMoney. This function is called for every row in the recordset displayed in the HTML table. This is accomplished by specifying an expression for the desired grid column on the Data tab under the Grid Properties as shown in Figure 5.16.

FIGURE 5.16

Grid properties.

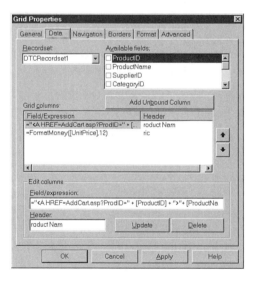

FormatMoney is a good illustration of how the debugging environment can be used to understand complex code written by someone else (see Figure 5.17). However, it is a nightmare to deal with from a readability perspective: No comments, single-letter variable names, and overuse of the compact yet cryptic JScript ?: operator (used as a shortcut for the If...Else statement in JScript).

FIGURE 5.17

The FormatMoney function.

```
shopcart\PRODUCTS.ASP*

var WGdc="."; var WGgc=","; var WGnc="("; var WGcs="$";

function FormatMoney(A,W) {
    var N=Math.abs(Math.round(A*100));
    var S=((N<10)?"00":((N<100)?"0":""))+N;
    S=WGcs+((A<0)?WGnc:"")+
        WGgroup(S.substring(0,(S.length-2)))+
        WGdc+S.substring((S.length-2),S.length)+
        ((A<0&&WGnc=="(")?")":"");
    return (S.length>W)?"Over":S;
}

function WGgroup(S) {
    return (S.length<4)?S:
        (WGgroup(S.substring(0,S.length-3))+
        WGgc+S.substring(S.length-3,S.length));
}
```

Design   Source   Quick View

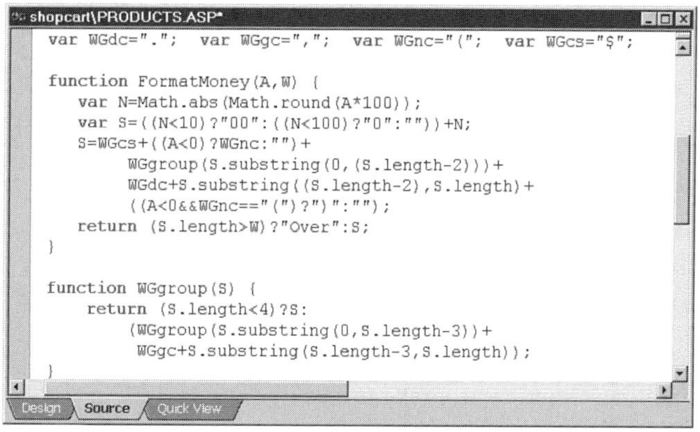

Stepping Through the Logic

First, you will examine the logic flow of the function by stepping through the code:

1. Use the Step Into (F11) function to move line by line through the function's logic flow. Notice that you even jump into the WGgroup function. When you reach the return for the FormatMoney function, select Continue from the Debug menu to allow the remaining script to resume execution. The breakpoint on FormatMoney will trigger again for the second row.

2. This time, use the Step Over (F10) function to move line by line through the function. This time, you will jump over the WGgroup function. Again, select Continue to allow the remaining script to execute.

TIP

When using JScript, you might want to consider using the If...Else statement instead of the ?: operator. Besides ?: being more difficult to read, it's also impossible to step through the conditions of the code using the ?: operator.

5

DEBUGGING WEB APPLICATIONS

> **NOTE**
>
> If you continue to Step Into the code past the return for FormatMoney, you will jump into the middle of the design-time control code that Microsoft wrote for the grid. This can be an interesting exercise, but is outside the scope of this case study.

Tracing the Call Stack

The Call Stack window is useful to help track your execution path, particularly when you have complex scripts to debug. This part of the case study gives you practice working with the Call Stack window.

1. With the execution still broken on the first var in the FormatMoney function, select the Call Stack window from the toolbar.

2. Use the Step Into function until you jump into the WGgroup function.

   Notice that when you step into the WGgroup function, a new row is added to the top of the Call Stack window, and FormatMoney is pushed down below it, shown in Figure 5.18.

FIGURE 5.18

The Call Stack window displaying WGgroup at the top.

3. Double-click the FormatMoney entry in the Call Stack window.

   The Source window is scrolled to reveal the exact line in FormatMoney that called the WGgroup function. Further, the line is highlighted in green.

4. Close the Call Stack window.

5. Continue the script execution, and the breakpoint at the beginning of the FormatMoney function will trigger again.

Viewing and Manipulating Local Variables

With the compact nature of the FormatMoney function, stepping through the code and viewing the call stack does not tell you much about what is going on. Therefore, the next step is to examine the code more closely by using the Locals and Watch debug windows to gain better insight into internal logic.

1. With the execution still broken on the first var in the FormatMoney function, select the Locals window from the toolbar.

   This will display the four variables: A, W, N, S. If your breakpoint is still on the first var statement, N and S will be undefined (see Figure 5.19).

FIGURE 5.19

The Locals window displaying variables in the FormatMoney.

2. Use the Step Over function to step through the code until you reach the return.

   Notice that N and S are assigned a value and data type. Also notice that some values are red and then turn black. Remember that a value in red means that it has changed since the last break. If you are stepping through the code and a value goes from black to red, it means that the statement just processed changed the variable's value.

3. Select Continue to return to the top of the function.

4. Double-click the value for A and change it to 25. Notice that the value for A has been updated.

5. Move the breakpoint from the var statement to the return statement and disable it using the shortcut menu. Select Continue so that Products.asp completes processing, and you can start the processing of the page over.

6. Enable the breakpoint and click Search again.

   The processing will break on the return, and with the Locals window open, you will now see the end values for the variables. Observe the four values, and see whether you can deduce the processing of this function. Keep selecting Continue and observing the variables until the Products.asp page is completely processed.

5

DEBUGGING WEB APPLICATIONS

Watching Expressions

The Locals window is a quick and easy way to view (and possibly modify) all the primitive variables currently in scope. However, sometimes the primitive values are not enough to understand complex script processing. Although you should now have some idea as to the purpose of the FormatMoney function, the specific details are still nebulous. You will now move to the Watch window for further insight. Its strength is that it is not limited to viewing only primitive variables in scope, but can evaluate more complex expressions.

1. Move the breakpoint to the first line following the two vars.

   The variable S is initialized based on two nested If...Elses (or more precisely, ?: operators). Because stepping does allow you to follow the flow within this statement, you will watch the two conditionals to help you follow the logic.

2. Select the expression N<10 in the var S line, and use the shortcut menu to add a Watch.

3. Open the Watch window.

4. Select the N<100 expression in the same var S line and drag and drop it into the Watch window. You've now practiced two different techniques to add Watches.

5. The next line in the function that makes an assignment to S is significantly more complex. Use the same techniques to create appropriate Watches. This enables you to decompose the assignment statement into manageable chunks.

6. Reposition the breakpoint to the var at the top of the function again.

7. Continue the script execution until you encounter the breakpoint.

8. Step through the code and examine the values in the Locals and Watch windows. You will be able to see the decomposed logic you specified in step 5.

9. Repeat stepping through the function until you feel comfortable with the logic flow.

At this point, you should have a good understanding of the purpose and function of the FormatMoney function. The FormatMoney function takes two numeric parameters: The first is an amount (A) parameter, and the second is the maximum width (W) parameter. It then converts the numeric amount to a string that is properly formatted to display money, that is, a dollar sign, commas in all the right places, and two decimal places for the cents. If the formatted string length is greater than the maximum width, the function simply returns over.

The Watch, Locals, and Call Stack windows, combined with the code-stepping functionality, constitute the core of InterDev's powerful debugging facility. The most obvious omission from the core is the Immediate window, which enters the equation next.

Testing Functions Immediately

Like the Watch and Locals windows, the Immediate window can also be used to view and modify variables and evaluate expressions. However, the Immediate window is unique in its capability to execute functions with user-specified parameters. In this case study, you have dissected the FormatMoney function to determine its logic, but so far you have used only valid data coming from the database. What about invalid or extreme test cases, such as negative, zero, or extremely large values for the amount parameter? What if you want to test the effects of specifying different maximum widths?

1. With the script execution broken, open the Immediate window.

2. Type the following into the Immediate window and press Enter:

   ```
   ? FormatMoney (-100,12)
   ```

   Notice that the format returned includes parentheses around the value to indicate that it is negative.

3. Try the following examples and observe their outcomes:

   ```
   ? FormatMoney (0,12)
   ? FormatMoney (.01,12)
   ? FormatMoney (123456,12)
   ? FormatMoney (1234567,12)
   ? FormatMoney (12.345,12)
   ```

   If you have properly deduced the logic of the FormatMoney function, the outcome of each function call should match your expectations. Now imagine more complex functions, and you can quickly see how easy it is to test them from the Immediate window.

Case Study Conclusion

This concludes the structured portion of the case study. As you can see, we only scratched this application's surface in terms of understanding its functionality. However, the objectives of this case study were to provide you with an opportunity to practice the most commonly used debugging features and to demonstrate how all the components in the new debugging environment work together.

Summary

This chapter gave you a detailed understanding of the new Visual InterDev 6 debugging environment and an appreciation for its power. The sample debugging case study stepped you through a sample debugging session to demonstrate how all the components in the new debugging environment work together. As you learned, the new environment brings InterDev into the same league as its companion products in Visual Studio.

This chapter is especially important because InterDev's debugging environment has radically changed from its previous version. With this chapter under your belt, you should be comfortable applying these new debugging techniques and tools to your own Web applications.

Team Development

by Steven Banick

Working with teams is a large part of Web application development. Rarely, however, are teams standardized on the same tools and development environment. In this chapter, you'll learn how to maximize your team development through careful version control and compatibility guidelines.

Local Mode Versus Master Mode Development

At the heart of most mid-scale to large-scale Web sites and applications is a team of developers. The development of complex Web applications is rarely a solitary effort and requires careful coordination and cooperation on the part of the developers and whoever acts as the project manager. In the past, multideveloper environments typically relied on a careful pattern of staging and merging of changes before publication. To simplify some of this process, Visual InterDev 6 provides a few facilities for team development, including the concepts of *local* versus *master* modes of development.

Understanding Development Modes

Traditionally speaking, developers worked on either a staging Web server or the production server and made their changes. The developer then (presumably) tested these changes before moving on to the next change. The dangers in this approach lay in the changes being made to the centralized "production" Web server that other developers use. A production Web server can, in essence, be a staging server in itself. Development teams might proceed through several "staging" servers (including their own local server) before proceeding to post their changes on the final staging server. This final staging server can be perceived as the production server for the Web team. When the material has passed muster, it can then again move on to a publication server external to the development team.

Regardless of what you classify as a development server, staging server, and production server, the dilemma remains the same. How do you enable multiple developers to work cooperatively on different aspects of the Web site without damaging the changes others make? Visual InterDev addresses this problem with two operational modes of development, master and local modes, respectively:

- *Master mode* is used to directly modify the contents of the production Web server used by the development team. Any and all changes are made directly to the files on the production server. In this approach, the production server is referred to as the "master Web."

Team Development
CHAPTER 6

153

6

TEAM
DEVELOPMENT

TEAM
DEVELOPMENT

- *Local mode* is used to create a duplicate, isolated copy of the Web application on a developer's personal Web server (on the same workstation). All changes are made to the local version of the Web site's files, leaving the original files on the production server untouched. When the changes to the local version have been completed, the changes can be merged into the production server.

To fully understand how the two modes differ, consider this example. Two developers are working at the same time to update a page. Developer A commits his changes on his workstation, firing the changes to the centralized production Web server. Meanwhile, developer B follows suit and does the same thing. He changes the same file and fires the changes to the centralized production Web server, mere moments after developer A. What happens? Visual InterDev recognizes that the timestamp on the file has changed and displays a dialog box, shown in Figure 6.1, to developer B.

FIGURE 6.1

Because of time-stamping, Visual InterDev can compare the date and time of the file before the changes and then after.

By clicking the Yes button to replace the master file with the local file, developer A's changes will be undone and saved over by developer B's new file. So much for version management.

> **NOTE**
>
> Of course, this alert dialog box is much better than it could have been. Without an environment that can compare timestamps (say, your standard HTML editor), developer B would overwrite developer A's changes without even knowing it.

Isolated Development with Local Mode

Rather than contend with these sorts of issues each time your developers must make changes, a better tactic is to use isolated development with local mode. Isolating developers with the local development mode provides tighter control over your Web site, preventing casual overwriting of other developers' work.

> **NOTE**
>
> Use of local mode in Visual InterDev requires that a local Web server be installed on the developer's workstation, along with the FrontPage Extensions. Typically, you will install Visual Studio with the NT Option Pack on each developer's station. For developers with Windows NT Workstation, NT Peer Web Services will be used, and Windows 95/98 users will use Microsoft Personal Web Services.

To enter local mode on a developer's workstation, follow these steps:

1. Right-click your project in the Project Explorer.

2. From the context menu, choose Working Mode, Local. The globe icon beside your project name changes (no lightening bolt appears) to indicate that you are working in local mode.

3. Open your files for development as you normally would. The most recent versions are automatically downloaded from the master Web.

Keep in mind that while you are working in local mode, you are not offline per se. You can still retrieve files from the master Web/production Web servers by double-clicking their icons in the Project Explorer. The difference lies in where the modified files are stored and tested—your local workstation.

> **TIP**
>
> You can download the entire contents of the master Web by right-clicking the project name in the Project Explorer and choosing Get Latest Version from the context menu. This will download the complete Web site once, rather than download select files as you need them.

Merging Working Files

When you are working as an isolated developer in local mode, all changes you make to your Web files are stored on the local workstation's hard disk drives. When you are ready to update the master Web with your new changes, you are merging the working files. This process is handled primarily by Visual InterDev, although you might be prompted in the event of a conflict (more on that in a moment). To merge your changes and update the master Web server, follow these steps:

6

1. Right-click your project in the Project Explorer.

2. From the context menu, choose Working Mode, Master. Visual InterDev recognizes that you are working in local mode and displays the prompt shown in Figure 6.2.

FIGURE 6.2

Visual InterDev warns you before you commit your changes to the master Web server, avoiding accidental file merging.

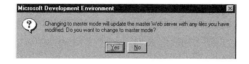

3. Click Yes to confirm the update and to dismiss the dialog box. The Refresh Project View window, shown in Figure 6.3, is displayed during the update.

FIGURE 6.3

When you update the master Web, Visual InterDev updates the Web site structure and compares time-stamps for all affected files.

During this update, Visual InterDev compares the timestamp from the local version of the file and the current timestamp on the master Web server. This comparison is used to determine whether the master Web file has changed since you entered local mode and retrieved a working copy of the file. In the event of a conflict, the Confirm Save to Master Web dialog box (refer to Figure 6.1) is displayed. However, how do you know what has changed?

Visual InterDev provides you with a means of comparing files so that you can visually identify what is different between two files. You can use this feature in the event of a conflict that results in the Confirm Save to Master Web dialog box. Follow these steps:

1. At the Confirm Save to Master Web dialog box, click No to dismiss the dialog box and leave the master Web file as is.

2. If the conflicting file is still open in the Source or Design editors, close the file.

3. Right-click the conflicting file's name in the Project Explorer and choose Compare to Master Web. This opens the Differences Between window shown in Figure 6.4.

FIGURE 6.4

The Differences Between window highlights differences between files, using color-coded lines.

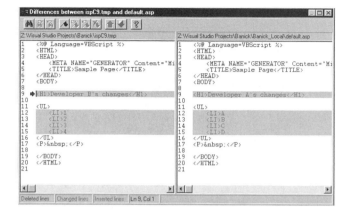

TIP

You can use the Compare to Master Web option at any time during your development. If you are working in master mode and try to compare a file, the result will always be the same: The local file and the remote file are identical. However, if you are working in local mode, you can use this feature to periodically compare your file against the master Web for changes.

4. Identify the lines that differ between the two files. The left pane displays the master Web version and the right pane, your local version.

TIP

Learn to identify the color of the changes in your files. All affected lines are grouped in a gray block to distinguish the changes from the rest of the document. Within those blocks, the changes are color coded according to the differences between the two files. Blue lines are lines that have been deleted, red lines are lines that have been modified in some way, and green lines are lines that have been added to the file.

5. Close the Differences Between window.
6. If you need to make additional changes to your local version before merging it with the master Web, double-click its icon in the Project Explorer. This displays the dialog box shown in Figure 6.5.

FIGURE 6.5

You have the option to either work with your newer, local copy or replace the local copy with the master Web version.

7. Click the Open Local button to open your locally edited version of the file.

8. Modify your file accordingly. This is when you usually will include the changes to the file you found in the differences comparison.

9. Save your changes. Because you have switched back to master mode, you will be prompted to confirm the replacement of the file on the master Web server.

10. If you are ready to replace the file, click the Yes button. Otherwise, click No and return to the editing stage.

Managing Development Teams

Developer isolation through local and master mode helps avoid common development conflicts. However, there are underlying issues with development teams that local and master mode cannot expressly address. The larger concerns when managing development teams are issues of process and security.

Working in Mixed Environments

Not every development team has the luxury of working with standardized environments. Often, different teams on a Web project will rely on different tools, because of either preference or technical requirements. When you are working in mixed environments with Visual InterDev projects, there are some points to keep in mind. I will discuss legacy versions of Visual InterDev and FrontPage interacting with Visual InterDev 6, but this information extends to any Web authoring or development tool your team might use.

Visual InterDev 1 and 6

The first version of Visual InterDev, version 1, was Microsoft's first attempt at a Web development tool from a developer's perspective (as opposed to a designer's). Using the Visual Studio IDE shell as an interface, Visual InterDev 1, shown in Figure 6.6, introduced powerful site management features and integration with the FrontPage editor. In comparison to Visual InterDev 6, the preceding version lacks many capabilities, potentially complicating mixed environment development. If you are not able (or willing) to upgrade all Visual InterDev 1 users to version 6, consider these points.

FIGURE 6.6

To take advantage of the new features in Visual InterDev 6, you should plan to upgrade Visual InterDev 1 users as soon as you can.

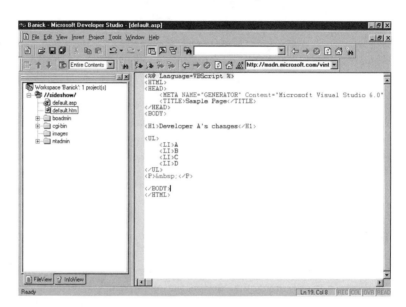

Debugging Capabilities

Visual InterDev 1 does not offer the debugging support found in 6. Your InterDev 1 users will not be able to take advantage of either server-side debugging or client-side debugging within Visual InterDev. For client-side debugging, your developers will have to rely on the Microsoft Script Debugger. In this case, InterDev 1 is better suited for a maintenance role than for an active development role.

Design-Time Controls

Visual InterDev 1 introduced design-time controls (DTCs) for simplifying Web application development. Many Visual InterDev 6 DTCs are not found in InterDev 1 and are not compatible with the preceding version. Additionally, make sure your Visual InterDev 1 DTCs are tested in Visual InterDev 6 for compatibility. Make sure that if you are relying on DTCs (especially custom developed ones), you test them carefully between the two versions before developing.

FrontPage Editor

The WYSIWYG editor provided in Visual InterDev 6 is built from the Microsoft DHTMLEdit control, whereas the editor found in Visual InterDev 1 is a customized version of the FrontPage 97 editor. This editor has been surpassed even by FrontPage 98's own editor, so keep in mind compatibility issues with this older editor. As I will soon explain, the FrontPage editor has difficulty understanding and interpreting some files, primarily ASP files, so exercise caution.

Newer Web Technologies

More recent additions to the Web, such as Cascading Style Sheets (CSS), scriptlets, and DHTML, are not supported in Visual InterDev 1. Using these technologies and InterDev 1, you must be cautious when developing.

FrontPage and Visual InterDev

Microsoft built Visual InterDev 6 and FrontPage 98 (and the upcoming FrontPage 2000) for slightly different, but overlapping, target markets. Although it tailored Visual InterDev for the creation of advanced Web-based applications, Microsoft designed FrontPage 98 for day-to-day Web site creation and maintenance. Figure 6.7 shows FrontPage 98.

FIGURE 6.7

FrontPage is the ideal tool for users who must update the content or appearance of pages—but not for application development.

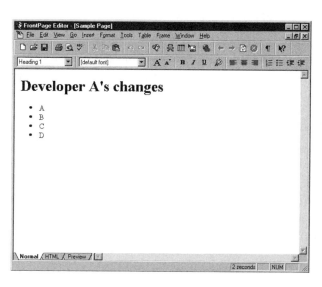

FrontPage is Microsoft's second-generation Web site creation and management tool, sporting a great interface. Many of the tools are available in Visual InterDev, but without the complication of Active Server Pages (ASP) authoring tools or multiproject workspaces. It has set the standard for Windows-based Web authoring and management, and many of the Web's best Webmasters create and maintain their sites completely within FrontPage.

Typical end users do not necessarily want or need the more advanced features and interface of Visual InterDev, but they still have to make occasional modifications and additions to the Web site. FrontPage's WYSIWYG-style HTML editor is one of the best in the field. In fact, the FrontPage WYSIWYG HTML page editor is so good that Visual InterDev includes a version of it. The FrontPage management tools also are well suited to a site maintainer's needs.

Given the limitations of FrontPage 98—compared to Visual InterDev's huge feature set—creating a site that can make the most of both management environments might seem a daunting task, but there are many compelling reasons to make the effort.

When you develop your Web sites with Visual InterDev, keeping FrontPage's capabilities in mind, you make maintaining them with FrontPage much easier. This way, you can deploy a Web application developed with the high-end tools of Visual InterDev and then turn over routine maintenance to a team, using the tools most appropriate to their needs. In many cases, this tool is FrontPage 98.

If you can keep the majority of your Web application editable with FrontPage, you are doing yourself (and your successors) a huge favor. How can you ensure that you do so? The following points provide you with some recommendations for surviving homogenous InterDev and FrontPage environments.

Use ASP Elements Only When Needed

As mentioned earlier, a few types of documents are "allergic" to the FrontPage Editor. This includes Active Server Pages. The FrontPage Editor tries to interpret tags in them, and it might reformat and rearrange the tags it cannot understand, causing them to stop working—not pretty and no fun to clean up. Make sure that the end users who will be maintaining your Web site are aware of these limitations. You should train them to leave ASP files alone, just as most home owners leave plumbing and electrical work to the professionals.

Modularize Your Web Application

Another strategy that can help is to borrow an old programmer's tactic: modularization. Keep the parts of your Web application that FrontPage users can edit in an "HTML-only" Web project and consider even segregating the ASP and other FrontPage-allergic pieces in their own child Webs.

Test Pages with the FrontPage Editor

Because the FrontPage Editor does not always damage ASP tags, you might want to test it on a specific page before assuming that it's not safe. Make a copy of the page you want to test, and then open it in the FrontPage Editor. Save it and then preview the page in the browser pane. Check carefully to see whether your tags survived the ride. If everything appears to be correct, then proceed, but be aware that changes to the page content can cause unexpected changes to its code. Remember the Cold War quotation, "Trust— but verify."

Generally, the best way to make your Visual InterDev–developed Web application FrontPage-friendly is to always keep in mind the target environment. For most Web development, that advice refers to the expected browsers. In the case of ASP, though, it means both the browser and editing environments.

FrontPage Security Issues

Because a Web server will present your documents to the world, you must test them constantly by using a Web server. That way, you can check any interpretation or other actions that you expect the server to perform. FrontPage 98 and Visual InterDev both include versions of the Personal Web Server/Personal Web Services. Also, both can connect to more robust and scalable servers, using the FrontPage Server Extensions.

Both FrontPage 98 and Visual InterDev use the same server extensions to enable you to work with documents on a live Web server. These extensions are available for all the Microsoft Web servers and most of the other popular Web server packages on the market. To configure the Server Extensions to enable either FrontPage or Visual InterDev to modify a server's documents, start by running the Server Administrator. The exact information listed varies, depending on what Web server software you are using.

For most Web servers, you can use the Security option to add authorized administrators to the server. Just enter the username and password that the administrator should supply from within FrontPage or Visual InterDev to gain access to the documents on your server. Before allowing FrontPage and Visual InterDev users access to your Web site for development, make sure you have your security model in place. Security is discussed in detail in Chapter 8, "Visual InterDev Security."

Introducing Visual SourceSafe

Managing Web sites and content can be a thankless and frustrating task. As Web projects grow in size and more people begin to work with projects in teams, the potential for errors increases dramatically. What is even more disconcerting is the possibility that a team member might inadvertently destroy or permanently damage content, without any immediate method of reversing the problem. Programmers who have experienced these headaches recognize the value in using a version control system (VCS) to manage their code and projects. The premise of a VCS is logically extensible to Web site management and ideally integrates with the Visual InterDev environment.

By using a VCS—in this case, Microsoft Visual SourceSafe (VSS)—you have the ability to safely archive your work on a regular basis, ensuring its protection. Visual SourceSafe, like most VCS software, behaves much like a librarian, who manages the integrity and safety of the library's contents. Think of your Web project as a library that is constantly growing and evolving. It's easy to imagine that as more people contribute to the library, you will need a reliable way of tracking the contributions. As more changes to the existing content occur, you will likely want a way of identifying who did what changes where. This is the role of the VCS, in short: to baby-sit the files that compose your project.

Understanding Revision Control

Visual SourceSafe operates on a simple premise: Two heads are better than one. When you enter a file into VSS's database, it is preserved there until you purge it. That's the first head. You never actually change that file; you sign out a working copy of it, the second head. You modify the working file and then sign it back into the VSS database; it replaces the original file you checked out. What about the original file? Is it now gone for good? Actually, it hasn't gone anywhere. Visual SourceSafe has a versioning control system that enables the history of a file to be recorded. You have the option of "rolling back" to whatever previous version of the file might exist in the database. If you find a mistake in your newly edited file just *after* you've checked it in, you can roll back the mistake a version, so your original file remains pristine.

You're thinking, "If I change a file 10 times, Visual SourceSafe stores 10 copies of that file? How grossly inefficient!" This isn't totally true. VSS stores the *original* file and then stores changes in a format *relative* to that original file. Therefore, if you add a *the* to your file and then check it into the VSS database, it doesn't create two copies of the file, producing overhead. Instead, VSS appends a note to the original file, saying *the* was added to this point on this date. This is known as creating a *delta*. Using the delta method of storing changes, you can have several files in the database for much less disk cost than you think. However, it's all well and good to store so many files, but how do you keep track of them?

Files are stored in Visual SourceSafe along the lines of a Project mentality. A Visual SourceSafe Project is in no way linked to your Visual InterDev project (although your

InterDev project may be stored within a SourceSafe Project). A Project is also not an exact mirror of your file's status on the hard drive. Visual SourceSafe operates on a database storage principle, and Projects are its internal means of keeping track of the files you have stored in it. Operations-wise, the Project structure mimics the organizational hierarchy found in an operating system's directory tree. The root project `$/` (which can be considered roughly analogous to `C:\`) can contain subprojects such as `$/Web/Client/Development`, much like directories and subdirectories found on your hard drive. Moreover, much like directories on your hard drive, you can divide and subdivide project folders in a nearly infinite array. It's important to note once more that although the organization of Projects mimics that of a hard drive, the actual files in VSS are not accessible that way. You can never write directly to the "hard drive" in a Visual SourceSafe Project. You can only move copies of it out, to be modified elsewhere before being written back into the database.

Visual SourceSafe Functions

If you look at Visual SourceSafe's implementation of Projects from another perspective, VSS can be considered a specialized disk operating system. Instead of pedestrian functions such as copy or delete, however, VSS can do things such as check in, check out, and get.

Checking out files is almost exactly like getting a book out of the library, except you don't have to be quiet all the time to do it. To safely work on a VSS project, you have to check out a file from the VSS database. Essentially, what *checking out* does is to tell Visual SourceSafe, "I'm going to be making some changes to this file, so be a dear and give it to me." Visual SourceSafe then uses a working directory to put a working copy of the file. The file remains in the working directory until you are finished with the file. The great advantage to a VCS and checking out a file is that (unless configured to do so) Visual SourceSafe will not allow multiple developers to check out the same file. This ensures that developer A will finish what she is doing before developer B gets his grubby fingers on the file.

> **NOTE**
>
> Visual InterDev manages your working directory for you, by default.

You have checked out your file, you have made all your changes and saved them, but your copy of your project in Visual SourceSafe is unchanged. What's wrong? Checking out the file is only the beginning. For your changes to be entered in the VSS database, they must be checked in.

Checking in files is almost exactly like returning a book to the library, except in VSS the librarian doesn't care if you've written all over the book and changed its text. (They still frown on you getting food on the pages, though.) *Checking in* a file takes the changes you've made to your working copy of a file and enters them into the VSS database. After a successful check in, your changes are applied to the VSS copy in the database.

Visual SourceSafe Version and Tracking Control

Nobody's perfect. Even technical reference authors make mistakes (sic). Luckily, Visual SourceSafe has several safeguards designed for clumsy and absent-minded people or even perfect people who make the occasional mistake.

The first of these safeguards is the Undo Check Out feature. It's a simple function. If you have something checked out, it unchecks it, and Visual SourceSafe never knows you had the file. Plausible deniability. The obvious utility of this is when you check out a file, edit it into incomprehensibility, and then want to restore the original file. You can't re–check out the file, and checking it back in would be counterproductive. You must undo the process of checking it out in the first place. However, Undo Check Out is only a first-line defense against casual mistakes and erroneous checkouts. For errors that are inadvertently checked back in, more serious measures are necessary.

The *History function* is one of these measures. It enables you to selectively pore over the cumulative changes made to the file ever since it was created and imported into the VSS database. If you've made a mistake and you know in which version it occurs, you can set the file to roll back to the preceding version. Rollback simply tells Visual SourceSafe to "remove modifications of the file back to this version." Rollback itself is a powerful command, but without the power of the History function to navigate among the various file versions, it would be an arcane tool to use.

NOTE

Unfortunately, to compare successive versions of a file and rollback changes, you must leave the Visual InterDev IDE and step into the Visual SourceSafe Explorer interface.

The *Differences function* is mostly a diagnostic tool, just like comparing a local file against the master Web server. You have a file in which you know something is wrong, but you don't know what. Differences displays a file you choose from the file History and a working version of the file, side by side. The discrepancies between the two are highlighted, so you can trace what changes exist from an older version to a newer. Differences can display whether a line has been deleted, changed, or added to the file in comparison to the other file—all in all, a powerful tool for tracking changes.

Setting Up VSS for Use with Visual InterDev

Before you can begin to use Visual SourceSafe on your workstation with Visual InterDev, you must correctly set up the Visual SourceSafe software. SourceSafe through Visual InterDev relies on a Visual SourceSafe Server being installed on the Web server. The Visual SourceSafe Server components are different from the Visual SourceSafe client components installed during a Visual Studio installation.

NOTE

Refer to the Microsoft documentation on instructions for installing the Visual SourceSafe client and server components.

Depending on your Visual InterDev and Web server configuration, you might be required to create a Visual SourceSafe user for your Web service account. If you are using Microsoft Internet Information Server 4.0, this user is typically called Iusr_MachineName; MachineName represents the Web server's name. For information on adding a Visual SourceSafe user, refer to "Adding Users to VSS" later in this chapter.

Using SourceSafe and Visual InterDev

Normally, within Microsoft Developer Studio, you utilize a set of options and features directly linked to Visual SourceSafe that removes the need to ever use the Visual SourceSafe Explorer client software. Because of the nature of the Web, all content is physically located on the Web server and is not necessarily located completely on your workstation at any given time. This makes the traditional form of interaction with VSS unusable. The main objective of VSS integration within Visual InterDev is to manage the updates to the files in your project. To remove the possibility of two or more people changing the same files simultaneously, Visual SourceSafe's library services monitor whenever a file is checked out. While the file is checked out for changes, no other person can open and edit the file, to prevent saving over the other person's changes. After the changes are complete, the file is checked back in and updated. The file is then returned to the pool of available files for editing, free for someone to check out again.

NOTE

The Visual SourceSafe server operates on the Web server itself, not on the workstation.

Before you can begin to derive the benefits of Visual SourceSafe within Visual InterDev, you must enable Source Control for your Web project. This tells Visual InterDev to start tracking requests to the Web server for files and to pass on the information to Visual SourceSafe on the Web server. Keep in mind that the VSS database is usually on the Web server and not the workstation for Visual InterDev integration. Enabling Source Control is a simple process:

1. Select your project from the Project Explorer.

2. Select Project, Source Control, Add to Source Control from the menu bar. This opens the Enable Source Control dialog box shown in Figure 6.8.

FIGURE 6.8

By choosing Add to Source Control from the Project, Source Control menu, you are telling Visual InterDev to start tracking Visual SourceSafe requests for all files.

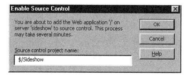

3. Enter the name for the SourceSafe project in the Source Control Project Name text box, with $/ being the root of the SourceSafe database—for example, $/MyWebProject.

> **TIP**
>
> You can specify an existing SourceSafe project to add your Web content to.

4. Click OK. Visual InterDev begins the process of adding all your Web files to Source Control. After all the existing files have been added, you are greeted with a prompt, telling you all is well, as shown in Figure 6.9.

FIGURE 6.9

The appearance of this dialog box reassures you that all is well with Source Control.

5. Click OK to close the dialog box, and get down to work.

> **TIP**
>
> When files or folders are added to source control and the SourceSafe database, local versions of the file are changed to read-only.

Working with Source Control

When Source Control is enabled for your project, working with your files is nearly identical to the way it was before, without SourceSafe. The main difference in behavior, with SourceSafe, is what happens when you begin to edit files. Previously, when you requested a working copy of a file to edit, Visual InterDev fetched it directly from the Web server and placed it in your working directory. When you were finished with your changes and released the working copy, Visual InterDev submitted your changes to the Web server and removed the local copy in your working directory. With Visual SourceSafe enabled, the process changes slightly.

When you request a working copy of a file, Visual InterDev first queries the Web server to see whether the file is available for editing. If the file is available, Visual InterDev retrieves a working copy for your changes and signs out the file from the server, using VSS's checkout facility. The file is then removed from the available pool of files for other users to edit, until you release your working copy. If a file is already checked out by someone else and you try to retrieve a working copy, you are issued a warning stating that the file is currently being edited by a different user. Visual SourceSafe can be configured to allow multiple checkouts, but does not by default let this happen.

Checking Out and Checking In Files

To work on files in your Web application, you must check out the file. This informs Visual SourceSafe that you are actively working on a file. In this regard, SourceSafe acts as a transaction controller, or a traffic cop, ensuring that no one else can modify the file while you are working on it. Checking out files retrieves the most recent version of the file from the SourceSafe database, not from the master Web server. This is an important concept to understand. Remember, the SourceSafe database is separate from the physical file system and the Web server. To avoid confusion, you should always update the Visual SourceSafe version of a file when you complete your changes and release your changes to the master Web server.

To check out a file for work, follow these steps:

1. Right-click the files or folders in the Project Explorer that you want to work on.

2. From the context menu, choose Check Out <filename>. This opens the dialog box shown in Figure 6.10.

FIGURE 6.10

The Check Out Item(s) dialog box is used to request a file from the SourceSafe database.

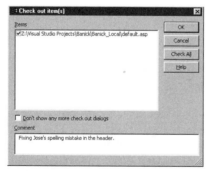

> **TIP**
>
> Double-clicking an item in the Project Explorer also checks out the file, if it isn't already checked out. The disadvantage to this method is that Visual InterDev does not prompt you to provide a comment, which can be used to record changes between versions.

3. Confirm that all the items listed in the Items list box are files you want to check out. Files selected with a check will be signed out of the SourceSafe database.

4. When checking out files, you should add a comment to the SourceSafe database to indicate why you are working on the file. Enter your comment into the Comment text box, such as `Updating date` and `email link`.

5. Click OK. This sends Visual InterDev to talk to the SourceSafe database. The files or folders are checked out, and the comment is added to the database.

NOTE

If a file is checked out by another developer, SourceSafe returns a message indicating such. You have the option to check out the file anyway (if the SourceSafe server has been configured to allow this), or you are asked to try again later.

TIP

When a file is checked out from the SourceSafe database, a red checkmark icon appears beside the file icon in the Project Explorer. This is a useful visual clue to spot checked-out files.

After you have completed your changes to the files you requested, you must save them and release the working copy. Releasing a working copy works in the same way that it did before you enabled Source Control, with one additional step. When you release the working copy to the server, you should instruct Visual InterDev to check in and update the file in the VSS database. To check in your local copy, follow these instructions:

1. Right-click the files or folders you want to release.

2. From the context menu, choose Check In <filename>. This opens the Check In Item(s) dialog box shown in Figure 6.11.

3. Confirm that the files listed in the Items list box are the files you want to check in to the SourceSafe database. If a file's check box is selected, the file is being checked back in.

4. If you want to update the SourceSafe database with your changes but still keep the file signed out, select the Keep Checked Out check box. If this box is not selected, the file is returned to the SourceSafe database for another developer.

5. Enter an update to the SourceSafe database on what you did in the Comments text box. This is ideal for making notes about what you did to a file.

6. To compare the differences between your local working copy and the latest version of the file in the SourceSafe database, click the Differences button. This opens the dialog box shown in Figure 6.12.

FIGURE 6.11

Checking items into the SourceSafe updates the database with your changes and makes the file available for another developer.

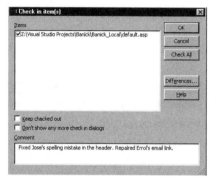

FIGURE 6.12

The Differences dialog box visually identifies the changes in your file.

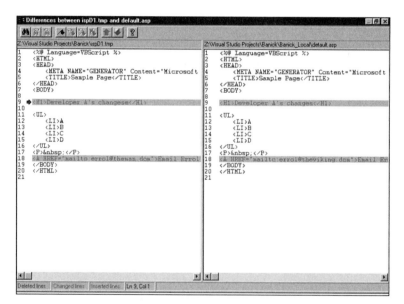

7. Close the Differences dialog box after you are finished comparing your differences.

8. Click OK to check in the file and update the database.

After you check a file in to the VSS database, where it is safely stored, the file is then unlocked for other users to check out the file for changes.

Administering Visual SourceSafe

The nature of Visual SourceSafe makes it a very simple matter to administrate a VSS database. Underlying its simple nature, Visual SourceSafe employs several sophisticated tools and features that might prove invaluable to you as a Web developer. From within the client software, the Visual SourceSafe Explorer, a developer may customize how he or she wants VSS to behave. These choices are unique to the developer and are not shared in a group environment. The VSS Administrator (that might be you) is able to set the standardized options and behaviors for the entire team in group environments, while still allowing individual developers the flexibility to add to that customization.

I will not explain the Visual SourceSafe Administration process in great detail. For more information on administering VSS, you should refer to the provided Microsoft documentation.

With the Visual SourceSafe Admin tool, shown in Figure 6.13, the VSS Administrator is also able to customize the operation of VSS. Of primary importance to VSS administrators is the implementation of security for the projects within the database.

FIGURE 6.13

The Visual SourceSafe Administrator is used to create databases, control user access, and modify the behavior of the SourceSafe database.

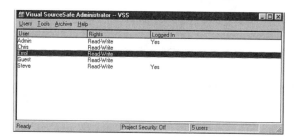

Adding Users to VSS

All aspects of VSS security work by keeping track of users and their access to the VSS database. Users are provided a name and password to enter, and Visual SourceSafe manages what they can and can't do. Usernames are usually the same name that the user has for the network, so they can automatically sign in to VSS. You may have a different name than the network username, but this will require the user to enter the username and password manually. Adding a user to Visual SourceSafe is a very simple process:

1. From the Users menu, choose Add User.
2. The Add User dialog box appears, as shown Figure 6.14. Within this dialog box, you must enter the user's name and password. You can also set this user to have read-only permissions.

FIGURE 6.14

When you are adding a new user to Visual SourceSafe, you may choose to use the same name that the user has on the network or an entirely differ-ent one with a password.

As you need more users, it's a simple matter to add them. If you want to remove users from accessing Visual SourceSafe, you may also delete users from the User menu.

Limiting Access to Projects

In some situations, you might want to control the more security-oriented issues of Visual SourceSafe. In a group environment, it might not be desirable to allow all developers equal access to every project and file under construction. The VSS Administrator has the power to determine who should have access to what and to prevent those developers from going where they shouldn't. By default, all VSS users have full access to all pro-jects (unless the user was created with read-only permissions).

Enabling Project Security

To limit access to specific projects, you must enable project security:

1. From the Tools menu, choose Options to open the SourceSafe Options dialog box. Click the second tab, Project Security, as shown in Figure 6.15.

FIGURE 6.15

The Project Security tab of the SourceSafe Options dialog box lets you enable project security.

2. Select Enable Project Security by clicking the check box.

3. Use the provided check boxes to specify the default user rights. You can specify what actions a user may do by default without further permissions.

After you have enabled the security features of VSS, you can begin setting up your permissions. You may control a user's access rights in two ways: Rights by Project or Rights Assignments for User.

Rights by Project

If you want to control security on a project-by-project basis, the Rights by Project view is the best choice for limiting access rights for users.

1. From the Tools menu, choose Rights by Project. The Project Rights dialog box appears, shown in Figure 6.16.

FIGURE 6.16

All projects are listed on the left side of the dialog; the users and their access rights are on the right.

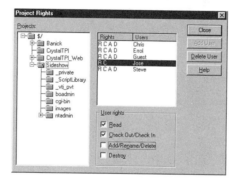

2. On the left side of the dialog box is the Project List. Select the project you want to limit access to.

3. On the right side of the dialog box are the users currently able to access the project. Below the list of users are the check boxes displaying the rights on the project.

4. By selecting a user from the list of users, you can alter the User Rights: Read, Check Out/Check In, Add/Rename/Delete, and Destroy.

5. To add a new user to the project, select the project from the list and click the Add User button.

6. To remove a user from the project, select the user from the list and click the Delete User button.

Rights Assignments for User

If you prefer to work on an assignment basis, you can specify the projects and the appropriate rights on a user-by-user basis.

1. Select the user you want to manage from the list in the Visual SourceSafe Administrator.

2. From the Tools menu, choose Rights Assignments for User. This opens the Assignments for User dialog box. The title of the dialog specifies which user you are currently managing. This is shown in Figure 6.17.

FIGURE 6.17

You can assign users specific tasks and limit their access rights with ease.

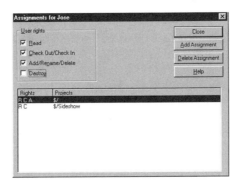

3. By default, the only assignment provided to the user will be permissions for the $/ root project. By selecting the project, you may specify the access rights for the user.

4. Using the check boxes for User Rights, select the access rights the user should have for the selected project.

5. To add a new project to the user's list of assignments, click the Add Assignment button. This enables you to select a project from the Visual SourceSafe database for the user to be assigned to.

6. To remove a project from the user's list of assignments, select the project and click the Delete Assignment button. This removes the selected project from the list of projects to which the user has access rights.

Locking the SourceSafe Database

At times, it might be appropriate to prevent users from checking out files and modifying them. To support this facility, VSS Administrator provides Lock the Visual SourceSafe Database. No user will be able to modify projects until it is unlocked. You may lock (and unlock) the database by choosing Tools, Lock SourceSafe Database. This calls up a dialog box that reports the connected users and enables you to lock (and unlock) the database with a check box, as shown in Figure 6.18.

FIGURE 6.18

By locking the SourceSafe database, you are preventing all users from checking out and modifying files.

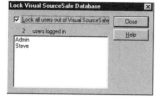

> **TIP**
>
> Locking the database is ideal when you must create backups of the SourceSafe database. This prevents a file from being in use when the backup is being made.

A Team Development Case Study

The Banick.com Web site is accessed by several developers at any given time. Used as a developer's resource and testing platform for many users, the Web site relies on the various team development aspects of Visual InterDev 6 to ensure that service from the site is not interrupted. First and foremost, developer isolation is used to ensure that developers don't step on one another's toes.

The core development for the Banick.com Web site is carried out locally from two different workstations connecting to the production Web server. Local Web servers are running on each of the workstations and act as "staging areas." The lead developer enters developer isolation through local mode during his changes and then propagates those changes to the first staging server. When he is satisfied that the changes are acceptable, the site is then deployed to the production Web server (the next chapter, "Deploying Web Applications," discusses site deployment in detail).

Several other developers contribute to Banick.com and take advantage of the available platform. These developers all connect via the Internet to work in their own development areas and the central site. Most of these developers use Visual InterDev 6, but a few users rely on Microsoft FrontPage 98 and other Web editors (including Allaire Homesite). The security for the site is restricted, based on a series of user groups: Site Authors, Site Administrators, and Site Contributors. These groups restrict the available areas of the site, depending on who the user is.

As the final line of defense for the site, Visual SourceSafe has been a mainstay of Banick.com for several years. All development is transacted through a central SourceSafe database. Several developers also maintain their own separate SourceSafe database on their workstation for individual version control.

Without the tactics adopted for Banick.com, the Web site would surely have fallen victim to accidental version conflicts and mistakes caused by single or multiple developers from the team.

Summary

Visual InterDev provides several facilities to simplify working in teams. Ultimately, however, team development requires careful cooperation and an attention to detail. Using the Visual InterDev collaborative features in combination with skilled and talented teams, you can feel confident that your team-oriented project will not suffer adverse disasters during development. Remember that careful revision control and isolated development are the keys to successful team development!

Deploying Web Applications

by Steven Banick

Deploying Web Applications to the Web

The time comes in any Web site's life to move into the spotlight and hit the big time. When you work with multistaged development and multiple developers, you typically work from a development Web server. This development server is the locale that all developers use to prepare a Web application for the adulation it surely deserves. When the development is complete, it's then a matter of how best to migrate the Web site from the development server to the production, or "live," Web server. Rather than rely on tedious, manual file copying and replication, Visual InterDev provides you with a facility for doing such a job: Web application deployment.

When you are working towards deploying your Web application, you must keep a mental (or physical, for that matter) deployment check list.

- *Do the links work?* Make sure that all your hyperlinks traverse the path you want. You can use Visual InterDev's tools for repairing and viewing links, including site maps.

- *Are all dependent files included in the Web project?* When deploying your Web site, you want to make sure that all the files used by that site are included in the project. You can include any kind of file inside a project, not just Web-specific files.

- *Are all the files updated on the master/development Web server?* Make sure to release *all* your working copies before deployment and check in any files that might be checked out in Visual SourceSafe. Synchronize your Web site with any files you might be working with in local mode.

- *Do you have data connections correctly configured?* If your Web application uses a data source, you will have to make sure that the database connection is properly configured for your production server.

- *Has the Web application been thoroughly tested and debugged?* Use Visual InterDev's debugging facilities to test all aspects of your Web application before deployment. It can be both troublesome and tiring to track down bugs that might have been introduced before deployment. You then have to debug not only the development server, but also the production server.

After you have deployed your Web application, be sure to verify the deployment target. You should test the Web application from several machines to ensure that it is running properly.

> **TIP**
>
> When you are testing Web applications, it's best to test from a machine that does not have any Web files stored locally.

The Deployment Methods

Visual InterDev provides you with two means of deploying Web applications. Their differences lie primarily in their scope. When you are deploying, the key questions you must ask yourself are "How complex of a site am I deploying?" and "Do I have to deploy to more than one server?" The two methods for deployment are

- Web application duplication
- Web application deployment

Copying Web Applications

The simplest method of deploying a Web application to another Web server is to use Visual InterDev's Copy Web Application feature. This method enables you to duplicate child Webs of your Web application, as well as copy and register server components used by the site. The Copy Web Application feature is suited to deploying sites to *one* target Web server. You may repeat the process for additional Web servers, as required.

> **TIP**
>
> You can use the Copy Web Application feature to duplicate an entire Web project or collection of Web projects between Web servers. You can use either the master Web server or the local project files as your source.

To copy a Web application from one server to another, follow these steps:

1. Open your Web application on your development server using Visual InterDev.

2. Locate the Copy Web Application button in the Project Explorer. Optionally, you may instead choose Project, Web Project, Copy Web Application from the menu bar.

3. The Copy Project dialog box appears, shown in Figure 7.1. Select the Source Web Server for your copying. This may be either the Master Web Server or the Local Web Server. Copying a Web application does not implicitly duplicate all dependencies the Web project might rely on, so exercise caution.

FIGURE 7.1

Copying a Web application is ideal for quickly duplicating sites for further development.

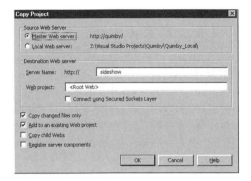

4. Enter the destination's Web server name into the Server Name text box. This should be the fully qualified domain name for your Web server, such as www.myserver.dom.

> **NOTE**
>
> The Copy Web Application feature requires that both the development and the target Web servers support the Microsoft FrontPage Server Extensions and the Visual InterDev Server Extensions.

5. Enter the Web project to be used for the duplication on the destination server. By default, the Web Project text box uses the <Root Web> project to copy your files to the root Web project.

6. If your destination Web server supports SSL (Secure Sockets Layer) and you want to copy your Web project securely, select the Connect Using Secure Sockets Layer check box.

7. By default, copying a Web application duplicates only files that have changed since you last copied the site. To copy all files, regardless of state, deselect the Copy Changed Files Only check box.

8. To create a new Web project, as opposed to adding to an existing project, deselect the Add to an Existing Web Project check box.

9. If you want to copy any child Webs that are part of your project, select the Copy Child Webs check box.

10. Finally, if specific server components (such as MTS components) are required by your Web project, select the Register Server Components check box to duplicate and register the components on the destination Web server.

11. Click OK to instigate the copying process. During the copy process, the Copy Web dialog box (see Figure 7.2) displays the status of the duplication.

FIGURE 7.2

The process of copying your Web application for the first time can take quite a while, depending on the size of your Web and the speed of your connection.

12. After the copying is complete, you are prompted by Visual InterDev with the dialog box shown in Figure 7.3. Click OK to continue.

FIGURE 7.3

In the event of a problem copying files, you would be advised. In this case, the copying was successful.

13. Open your Web browser and access the deployed Web site on the target Web server. Confirm that the Web application functions properly before returning to Visual InterDev.

TIP

If you are copying a Web project to another Web server, you might be prompted to provide a username and password. Always have this information ready.

Web Application Deployment

Visual InterDev 6 and Visual J++ 6 (both of which sport the same development environment) share a more extensive deployment facility, called the *Deployment Explorer*. The Deployment Explorer enables you to deploy complete solutions, including more than one project, to multiple deployment servers. The deployment features offered through the Deployment Explorer are more akin to developing on multiple Web servers than to developing and copying the changes. You can debug the deployed application remotely because the application responds to the same breakpoints you establish to the project locally.

> **NOTE**
>
> The deployment features of Visual InterDev require that both the development and the target Web servers support the Microsoft FrontPage Server Extensions and the Visual InterDev Server Extensions. To deploy server-side components, the target server also requires the Microsoft Posting Acceptor (version 2.0 or higher) to be installed.

Setting Up a Deployment Target

With a configured target Web server, you can specify deployment targets within Visual InterDev. Deployment targets consist of a URL for the target Web server, as well as the deployment services supported by the Web server. *Deployment services* refer to two kinds of services:

- Web content, controls, and applets—Typically referred to as *client-side content*, this content is executed within the client Web browser for the site visitors.

- Server-side components—Any and all content executed and controlled on the Web server is referred to as *server-side content*. This typically refers to components (for Microsoft Transaction Server) and ASP pages.

You can create multiple deployment targets for your Visual InterDev solution. Each deployment target can refer to different servers or perhaps different configurations on the same Web server. Each deployment target within the Deployment Explorer is associated with a URL that acts as the root for the Web application's deployment. To add a deployment target to your solution, follow these steps:

1. Open your Visual InterDev solution. Your solution may be composed of multiple projects.

2. Switch to the Deployment Explorer window and select it. To open the Deployment Explorer if it is not already open, choose View, Other Windows, Deployment Explorer from the menu bar. Figure 7.4 shows the Deployment Explorer.

FIGURE 7.4

When you first begin, the Deployment Explorer should contain only one entry referring to your computer.

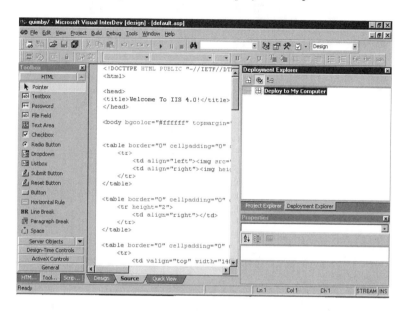

3. Click the New Deployment Target button in the Deployment Explorer or choose Project, New Deployment Target from the menu bar. This opens the New Deployment Target dialog box, shown in Figure 7.5.

FIGURE 7.5

The New Deployment Target dialog box enables you to select which projects you want to include.

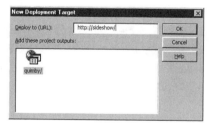

4. Enter the URL for your new deployment target in the Deploy to (URL) text box. For example, `http://sideshow/`. If you are specifying a specific Web for the target, specify it as part of the URL: `http://sideshow/myweb/`.

5. Each project in your solution appears in the Add These Project Outputs pane. If you want to include multiple projects in the deployment, select each project that should be included.

6. Click OK to add the target. The deployment target is added to the Deployment Explorer, as shown in Figure 7.6.

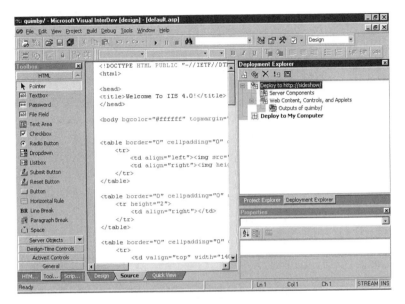

When you add a deployment target, Visual InterDev communicates with the deployment target to determine what services the server supports. If the deployment target has been configured correctly, both services (Web Content, Controls, and Applets and Server-Side Components) appear as nodes in the hierarchical tree in the Deployment Explorer. Otherwise, only the Web Content, Controls, and Applets service appears.

> **NOTE**
>
> Remember, your target Web server must support the FrontPage Server Extensions to use this method of deployment.

Adding Files to Deployment Services

Each deployment target contains references to the project files that are to be deployed. In the Deployment Explorer, you can see the projects that will be deployed using a specific target. All files contained within a project will be included in the deployment. At any time, you may choose to add additional files or projects to a deployment target. For example, your Web application may come to rely on a new project for additional content after its initial deployment. You can easily add a new project to the deployment target by following these steps:

1. Locate your deployment target in the Deployment Explorer window.

2. Select the deployment target service that will use your project's output. This may be either Web Content, Controls, and Applets or Server-Side Components.

3. Right-click the deployment target service and choose Add Project Outputs from the context menu. This opens the Add Project Outputs dialog box, shown in Figure 7.7.

FIGURE 7.7

Subsequent projects can be added to the deployment target.

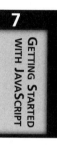

4. Select the projects to be included in the deployment target and click the OK button.

To remove an unneeded project from the deployment target, follow these steps:

1. Locate the project output name for the deployment target in the Deployment Explorer window.

2. Right-click the project name and choose Remove from the Context menu.

Just as you can add (or remove) projects to a deployment target, you can also include files that are not part of projects within your solution. The purpose could be to add additional files not directly referenced within your Web project, but which you might want to include with the site. (A good example of this is documentation for other developers.) To add files to the deployment target, follow these steps:

1. Locate your deployment target in the Deployment Explorer window.

2. Select the deployment target service that will use your project's output. This may be either Web Content, Controls, and Applets or Server-Side Components.

3. Right-click the deployment target service and choose Add Files from the context menu. This opens the Add Files dialog box, shown in Figure 7.8.

4. Using the Add Files dialog box, select the files you want to add to your deployment target. After you have finished selecting files, click the Open button. Your files appear under the service node in the Deployment Explorer, as seen in Figure 7.9.

FIGURE 7.8

Selecting individual files to add to your deployment target is much like adding files to your Web projects.

FIGURE 7.9

Each file you add to your deployment target service is listed underneath its node in the tree.

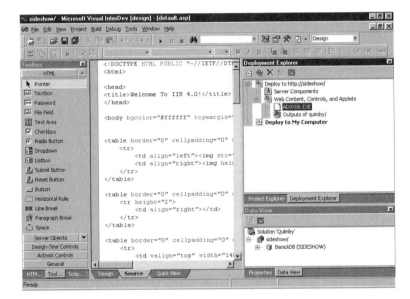

Removing files from the deployment target is identical to removing projects:

1. Locate the filename under the deployment target in the Deployment Explorer window.

2. Right-click the filename and choose Remove from the context menu.

> **NOTE**
>
> You cannot add more than 1,000 files at once to the Deployment Explorer. Try adding files in batches of fewer than 1,000 at a time.

Deploying to the Deployment Targets

With your deployment targets specified, you can quickly force the deployment of your Web application and files to the target server. For Visual InterDev, each project output that you deploy sends a complete copy of the entire Visual InterDev Web site and installs it on the deployment target's URL. To deploy your Web application, follow these steps:

1. Locate your deployment target in the Deployment Explorer.

2. Right-click your deployment target and choose Deploy from the context menu. You may instead choose Project, Deploy, and your deployment target from the menu bar.

Visual InterDev proceeds to deploy your Web application. The Task List is used to display any errors identified during the deployment, such as the one shown in Figure 7.10. The Output window is used to summarize the entire deployment process, as shown in Figure 7.11.

FIGURE 7.10

As with debugging, errors found during deployment are added to the Task List for correction.

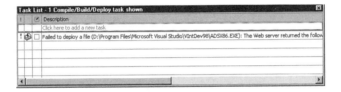

FIGURE 7.11

The Output window summarizes the entire deployment process.

TIP

One of the cleverest and most useful features of deployment through the Deployment Explorer is referential correction. Visual InterDev can modify deployed Web pages so that applet and object tag references refer to the proper items. This feature is controlled from the Deployment Target Settings dialog box. To open this dialog box, right-click a deployment target and choose Properties from the context menu.

Working with Non-Microsoft Web Servers

Deploying Web sites to servers that are not using Microsoft Internet Information Server introduces some complications. Essentially, you can deploy your Web application to any Web server that supports the Microsoft FrontPage Server Extensions. This includes UNIX and non-Microsoft Web servers.

> **NOTE**
>
> For up-to-date information on the Microsoft FrontPage Extensions and non-Microsoft Web servers, visit the Microsoft FrontPage Web Administrators resource at http://www.microsoft.com/frontpage/wpp/.

When FrontPage Extensions are not an option, the remaining method for deployment to non-Microsoft Web servers is traditional FTP. To deploy a Web site to a Web server using FTP, be sure that you have properly configured the remote Web server and have validated all hyperlinks within the site. You may choose to use an FTP client or the Microsoft Web Publishing Wizard, which acts as a friendly face in front of FTP.

> **NOTE**
>
> The Microsoft Web Publishing Wizard is included with Internet Explorer, Microsoft FrontPage, and Microsoft Office.

Deployment Issues

Regardless of the method used to deploy your Web applications, several underlying issues come to the surface. Keeping in mind the Deployment Checklist, as explored earlier in this chapter ("Deploying Web Applications to the Web"), consider the issues presented in this section.

Link Protection

Migrating links between servers can always be a tricky task, unless you are working with a completely closed and controlled environment. The safest method for linking resources within Web projects is relative links. Specify links between application pages and files using relative paths, as opposed to absolute paths. For example:

```
<A HREF="../mypage1.asp">
```

When you are linking to external sites and files (that is, resources that are not part of the Web project), use absolute paths. Specify the protocol and the complete URL to the resource. For example:

```
<A HREF="http://www.banick.com/personal/steve/index.html">
```

Ensuring Data and Data Connection Portability

For most Web applications that use databases, development is carried out using a development database that does not affect the production environment. When a Web application is deployed to its final resting place, the production server, you also want to be sure that any and all data connections point to the proper database. Make sure that all data connections contain the proper references to communicate with the production Web server. Also, ensure that the Web application has the proper access to connect to the production database.

Verifying Production Web Server Capabilities

When you are moving your application to the deployment target server, ensure that the production Web server has *all* the necessary software. The Web application may rely on several components or features that are not present on the production Web server. Make sure to verify that the security settings for the Web application and the Web server are appropriate. Make sure that you do not deploy your application to a Web server that does not support the features your application uses.

Including All Dependent Web Items

Remember to verify that all dependent files are part of your deployment target. When deploying Web sites, developers remember to deploy the pages that bring the core functionality of the Web application. However, many supplementary files are often forgotten. This includes downloadable documents and other items offered on the Web pages. If you have any files used by the Web application but not included in the deployed Web project(s), you have to add them to the deployment target.

Marking Components for Server Registration and MTS Packages

When you are deploying server components to your deployment target, make sure that they are marked as server components in the project. Additionally, ensure that any Microsoft Transaction Server components are included in an MTS package and have suitable permissions to operate.

A Web Application Deployment Case Study

The Banick.com Web site, as mentioned in Chapter 6, "Team Development," is a collaborative effort. Multiple developers use Banick.com as a staging area for their own development experiments and projects. Banick.com consists of several Web servers, including Microsoft Internet Information Server–based systems and non-Microsoft Web servers on a UNIX platform (specifically, Apache).

When a new Web project is begun, a development Web is created on one of the development Web servers. These servers, although accessible to the Internet, are not linked to the production Web server. Developers use the development servers to carry out their work. Using developer isolation (refer to Chapter 6 for information on developer isolation), developers work locally on their workstations and update the development servers. After development is complete, the developers are ready to deploy their applications to the staging server.

The staging server is used for the end-to-end testing for all Web applications. Developers have access to a single server that houses Internet Information Server, as well as Microsoft SQL Server. They may optionally choose to stage their applications on a UNIX server using a Sybase database, instead of the strictly Microsoft platform. The staging server is used simultaneously by several users to test their work.

After an application has passed through the staging process, developers may deploy their Web application to the production Web server. To simplify the entire development/staging/production deployment process, each developer uses several deployment targets within Visual InterDev. Each developer has suitable access to create his or her own Web folders on the Web server, as well as MTS packages. Using this access, the developers move through the deployment process, beginning with the development servers and ending with the production server.

Although most developers that use Banick.com utilize Visual InterDev and the Microsoft FrontPage Server Extensions, several developers rely on FTP to deploy their Web applications. These developers, who do not use Microsoft tools, do not share the advanced features and practicality of Visual InterDev's deployment functionality.

Summary

When you are working with multiple-stage development and different Web servers, the Visual InterDev deployment features will likely prove of immense value to you. Using the deployment features, you do not need to rely on manual file transfers and confirmation of each file version. Instead, using Visual InterDev you can feel confident that each Web application is deployed in its entirety from the most recent version.

Visual InterDev Security

by Michael Marsh

IN THIS CHAPTER

CHAPTER 8

Visual InterDev is all about allowing users controlled access to your data. The operative word for this chapter is *controlled*: I'll show you how to protect data that is part of your site but is not for public consumption.

Securing your Web site is something of an arms race between whatever measures you can put in place and whatever measures can be used to attack them. When trying to hack your site, intruders are nothing if not creative! You can also be creative in preventing these attacks, but you *can* go too far. Security is necessarily a trade-off between level of security and ease of use. These chapters provide you with measures that will ward off most attacks but not put undo burdens on your legitimate users or on you as the administrator of the site.

A Web Site Security Overview

The measures I'll discuss are a combination of host security and network security. The *host security* model depends on the host operating system to provide security, whereas the *network security* model works across operating systems. The first two sections cover topics generic to any security installation. The rest apply to sites using Visual InterDev. For the specific examples, I assume that you are running NT Server 4.0 and Internet Information Server 3.0 or above.

Hardware Security

A secure site must implement at least one hardware-based security component. More likely, your site will use components in some combination. Each component has an effect on level of security, ease of use, performance, and ease of administration.

Firewalls

A *firewall* is a system that separates two networks. Of specific interest here, firewalls separate your internal network from the Internet (see Figure 8.1). Firewalls control access to your network through a single point of entry and exit (a *choke point*). This enables the firewall to scrutinize the traffic and ensure that it is within the acceptable parameters defined by your security plan. That is, you configure the firewall to accept or reject traffic, based on criteria you select.

Firewalls are usually some combination of computers, routers, and software. They can be purchased as a system or built from scratch. These days, a commercial firewall usually comes in one box, making installation somewhat easier. Building a firewall from scratch is more difficult, but might be necessary in order to achieve custom configurations.

FIGURE 8.1

A firewall separates two networks: yours and the Internet.

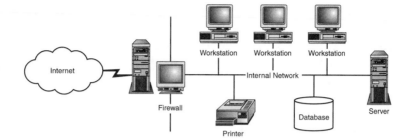

Firewalls are powerful tools, but they do have some drawbacks:

- They cannot protect data that does not pass through the firewall.
- They cannot protect against inside attacks.
- The data filtering through a firewall slows access, sometimes significantly.
- Some Internet services are not available to users through a firewall.
- Firewalls are expensive to implement and maintain.

That much said, today there is no better protection for your data against attacks from an outside network. If your site must be on the net and it needs the absolute best security, a firewall of some sort is your best choice for security. Check out the firewall FAQ at `http://www.v-one.com/newpages/FAQ.html`. That should get you started.

> **TIP**
>
> If your Web server happens to be on the other side of the firewall from your Visual InterDev workstation, you can still develop Web sites using Visual InterDev. You do this by communicating with the Web server via a *Web project proxy*. For more information, search the Visual InterDev help system, using the words *firewall* or *proxy*.

Packet-Filtering Routers

Networks function by sending information from machine to machine in small entities called *packets*. These vary in size and content, based on the network protocol being used. Here I'll assume an IP network because that's what the Internet is.

A *router* is a hardware device that connects networks by routing packets between them. Packets have information about their destination, but it's up to the router to choose the path by which they get there.

8

VISUAL INTERDEV SECURITY

Because routers read a packet's information, routers can filter them. Routers can either drop the packet or send it along its way, based on preprogrammed filtering rules. I'll show some examples of these rules later in the section. A packet can be filtered based on its address of origin or destination and on the protocol used.

Some advantages of packet-filtering routers, as they apply to Web site security, are the following:

- One router can protect an entire network if placed strategically (see Figure 8.2) and programmed properly.
- Filtering is transparent to users.
- Packet filtering is generally available. Many commercial routers are available with packet filtering. Additionally, software is available to use a computer to do routing with packet filtering.

FIGURE 8.2

Strategic router placement for protection of the entire network.

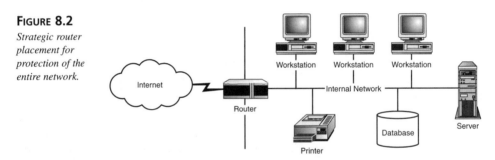

The following are some disadvantages:

- Not all protocols are routable, so filtering through a router is not possible for every protocol.
- Programming routers can be difficult, and testing programmed rules tends to be hard.
- The information available in packets limits the kinds of rules you can enforce. For example, you cannot limit the access of a certain user, because packets contain no information about users.

Configuring a packet-filtering router involves writing rules and sending them to the router. These rules tell the router which packets to allow or disallow. Your security plan might state something like this:

> Allow incoming SMTP mail from a particular machine and outgoing SMTP mail from any machine to a specific machine; allow incoming and outgoing HTTP from any machine to any machine; allow nothing else.

Table 8.1 shows the router rules for this statement. It's always a good idea to write a default rule. The router will look to apply each rule in turn on each packet; if no rule applies, the router will generally drop the packet. To be sure, write the last rule similarly to what I have here. This will ensure that the router will drop packets not covered by previous rules.

TABLE 8.1 RULES FOR PROGRAMMING A PACKET-FILTERING ROUTER

Rule	Direction	Source Address	Destination Address	Protocol	Destination Port	Action
A	In	External	Any	TCP	25	Accept
B	Out	Any	External	TCP	>1023	Accept
C	In	Any	External	TCP	25	Accept
D	Out	External	Any	TCP	>1023	Accept
E	In	Any	Any	TCP	80	Accept
F	Out	Any	Any	TCP	>1023	Accept
G	In	Any	Any	TCP	80	Accept
H	Out	Any	Any	TCP	>1023	Accept
I	Either	Any	Any	Any	Any	Accept

> **NOTE**
>
> Clients for both mail and Web services generally use a random port number above 1023, SMTP servers use port 25, and HTTP servers generally use port 80 (but not always!). The source and destination addresses should be translated to the specific IP addresses intended. *Internal* here implies a machine on your internal network, and *External* implies an address outside your network.
>
> I can't give the specifics for programming every type of router here, so I've shown the rules in a generic form. You should use a form like this to capture and save the filtering rules for your router. The advantage of a generic form will prove itself when you have to move to another manufacturer's router.

This is an example of filtering by service, which is generally more useful than filtering by address. Filtering by address alone can leave you open to attacks involving forged addresses.

8

VISUAL INTERDEV
SECURITY

Consider carefully which services you allow. Some services are known to be riskier than others. As a general rule, allow only those services that are required and no others. Be sure to set up rules so that you restrict the local port numbers as much as possible and so that you put only trustworthy servers on that port. That way, it doesn't matter if the client is using an untrustworthy application, because it will not be able to do anything against the trusted server. Consult your router's documentation for more tips on securing ports.

Proxies

A *Proxy Server* sits between users of the Internet and external hosts. It gives a user the illusion of being connected directly to the net, but doesn't allow data to pass directly from the net to the user's machine (and vice versa). Proxies are usually set up as *dual homed* machines; that is, they are machines with two Network Interface Cards (NICs). One NIC is attached to the external net, the other to the internal net. Data is passed back and forth through the proxy software, which can filter and log the transactions (see Figure 8.3).

FIGURE 8.3

The proxy commu-nicates between the two NICs.

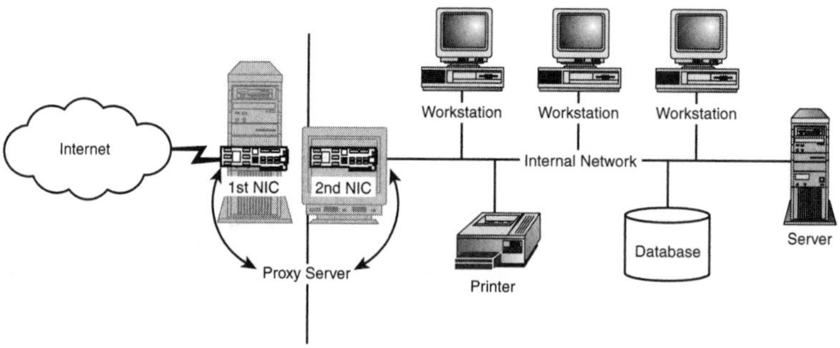

Proxies that are set up correctly can provide a good level of security for most sites. They are particularly effective for Web access because HTTP is designed to work with proxies. However, HTTP allows downloading of applets—for example, those written in Java or as ActiveX controls. A proxy will not know whether this code is malicious. Furthermore, surfing through a proxy can be significantly slower than surfing directly.

MICROSOFT PROXY SERVER

Microsoft offers Proxy Server as part of its Back Office suite. Proxy Server provides a high degree of safety, along with ease of use and maintenance. It also integrates extremely well with NT Server and the other Back Office components. Proxy Server features document caching for improved performance.

On dual-homed systems, Proxy Server provides exceptional security. Combined with a packet-filtering router, this security is equivalent to some firewalls. Microsoft claims that Proxy Server has been tested by an independent testing agency and has been shown to be "resistant" to spoofing, SATAN, and other common attacks.

Proxy Server comes with both Web Proxy (for HTTP, FTP, Gopher, and SSL) and WinSock Proxy (for a myriad of other protocols, including VDOLive and RealAudio, or any protocol written to the WinSock 1.1 API). See Figure 8.4 for a look at Proxy Server's interface. For more information about Proxy Server, try `http://www.microsoft.com/proxy/`.

FIGURE 8.4

Microsoft's Proxy Server interface.

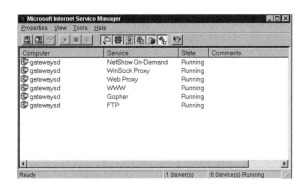

Software Security

This section talks about some generic security methods that are software based. These might be included in other components of your system (for example, NT manages passwords). I will discuss each as it applies to a general site security plan.

Passwords

When a user thinks about security, *passwords* is usually the first topic that comes to mind. Passwords can be a powerful tool in the security arsenal, but only if applied appropriately and managed continuously. A firm policy on passwords must be written into your security plan, must be enforced, and must be periodically reviewed. Here is a list of potential problems with passwords:

- An intruder might guess simple passwords. Readily available tools such as Crackerjack and Crack can be used to automate the guessing and are remarkably effective. The earliest versions of Crackerjack actually sent the cracked passwords back to an individual: He collected a huge database of compromised systems!

- Users might sometimes share their passwords.

- Passwords can be intercepted as they are sent across the net. An unencrypted password is easily compromised this way.

Here are some preventative guidelines to keep in mind when you are formulating your password policy:

- Passwords should be at least eight characters in length.

- Passwords should not be based on common information known about a user, such as birthdays, a pet dog's name, and so on.

- Passwords should have numbers and symbols, as well as letters. However, you should avoid passwords that are a word with a concatenated number.

- Passwords should have mixed case.

- Passwords should not be common words in any language.

- Passwords should not be related to popular themes such as Star Trek or Star Wars. *Wookie* is not a good password!

- Passwords should have a finite expiration date; the shorter the better. Users don't like this policy, so you might have to educate them on the issue.

- Users should be encouraged not to share their passwords.

- Do not send passwords out to the net in clear text. Always encrypt!

TIP

Here are a few strategies for good passwords you could suggest to your users:

Passwords can be words separated by symbols, such as *drum-vine*. The words should not be related.

You can use the first letters of a phrase, such as *tblpomam* ("the best laid plans of mice and men").

These rules should form the basis for a solid password scheme. Again, it's a good idea to review your password policy periodically and to monitor compliance. As new employees come on board and veterans become complacent, passwords can become a security risk again. An administrator never rests!

Encryption

The use of encryption on your system enables confidentiality, integrity, and nonrepudiability for your data. In a succeeding section, I discuss digital certificates and authentication; data integrity and nonrepudiability are covered then. Confidentiality is what we are concerned with here.

Encryption modifies a plain text message so that it becomes unreadable. *Decryption* unscrambles the coded message, rendering it into the original plain text. There are many types of encryption, but I will discuss only key-based systems because they are the most widely applicable here. The two types of key encryption systems are symmetric and non-symmetric or public key.

Symmetric systems, such as DES (Data Encryption Standard) and RSA's RC2, use a single key to encrypt and decrypt a coded message. These systems are fast and can actually be implemented in hardware. However, you must distribute the key to whomever you want to read your message. This is cumbersome and potentially dangerous: The more copies of a key are available, the higher the risk of theft or cracking.

Public key systems employ two keys: a *public key*, used by the author of a message for encoding, and a complementary *private key*, used by the recipient for decoding. A public key works to decode only those messages encoded by its private key pair, and vice versa. Private keys are guarded as secret.

Here's how it would work. I would use your public key to encode a message to you. You would receive the message and use your private key to decode it. If you had to respond, you would encode your response with my public key, and I would decode it with my private key. With this system, it doesn't matter how many copies of the public key are floating around, because it can't decode anything (except messages encoded with the sister private key, something that wouldn't ordinarily happen). PGP (Pretty Good Privacy) is a sample implementation of a public key system that is readily available on the net.

8

VISUAL INTERDEV
SECURITY

CAUTION

Key encryption systems depend for their level of security on the length in bits of the key. 40-bit systems are widely used, but have been recently hacked. They are no longer considered secure. 128-bit keys are less likely to be hacked, but cannot be exported from the United States.

Also, the algorithm is only as good as its implementation. In September 1995, two students from Berkeley reverse-engineered the process by which Netscape's Navigator generates random numbers. They were able to use this information to crack the 128-bit version in 25 seconds! Netscape has changed the way these numbers are generated and has been secure since.

S-HTTP

S-HTTP (Secure HTTP) is an extension of the HTTP protocol and provides secure trans-fers using encryption. Clients and servers negotiate security methodologies on connec-tion. These methodologies can be any combination of algorithms, key management, certificates, and policies. S-HTTP's flexibility makes it possible to implement public key certificates without requiring individual users to acquire public keys. This means that a user can be sure that he is sending information to a trusted system. However, the server cannot be sure the user is who the user claims to be, because client authentication is not required. S-HTTP can be set up to require client authentication, You will be seeing a lot of this in the future as commerce on the Net becomes more common.

SSL

About the same time that S-HTTP was introduced, Netscape introduced its Secure Sockets Layer (SSL). Unlike S-HTTP, which works with HTTP only, SSL can secure other TCP/IP protocols.

SSL consists of two parts: the *handshake protocol*, which establishes by negotiation the security services to be used, and the *record protocol*, which is used to transmit data. Server authentication is provided in all implementations of SSL, but client authentication is implemented only in some.

PCT

PCT (Private Communications Technology) is Microsoft's version of SSL. For the most part, PCT is similar to SSL, except that it has stronger client authentication. Currently, PCT is available only with Visual InterDev.

NT Security

Windows NT was designed and built to provide a high degree of security. Using NT, you can build a system in which the servers, workstations, and network are all secure. Furthermore, NT provides an unmatched ease of administration for security-related tasks. These tasks are centrally administered using GUI interfaces. Users can manage access to those resources they own. NT conforms to the government's C2-level guidelines, explained shortly.

I strongly recommend NTFS (NT File System) over FAT as the file system for your server. By using NTFS on the server, you can restrict access to folders and files, based on rules set out in your security plan. With FAT, you cannot. This discussion assumes that you are using NTFS.

NTFS file permissions and user and group profiles form the basis for security on NT Server. These are also the foundation for your Web site's security.

> **CAUTION**
>
> As secure as NTFS is, you should be aware of redirector utilities that allow DOS or Windows systems booted from a floppy to read files protected using NTFS security. The lesson here is that you should restrict physical access to machines with sensitive data. Physical security should be a part of your security plan.

What Is C2-Level Security?

The U.S. Government has described a standard for secure computer systems. One level of this standard is C2. Some important parts of C2-level security for an operating system are:

- User identification and authentication—Users must be identified uniquely. Furthermore, the system must guarantee user authenticity.

- Resource access control—The owner of a resource must be able to control its access.

- Protected memory—No resource stored in memory should be available to outside processes.

- Accountability—Security events must leave an audit trail for later perusal by an administrator.

Microsoft went to the National Computer Security Council (NCSC), a division of the National Security Agency, for verification that NT has met C2 security requirements. Windows NT (version 3.5) passed all requirements outlined in the NCSA's *Orange Book*. Certification of NT 4.0 is pending. See
`http://www.microsoft.com/security/issues/c2summary.asp` for more information on the C2 status of NT 4.0.

The following sections discuss two aspects of NT security in further detail: user identification and authentication and resource access control.

User Identification and Authentication

A user must log on to NT with a valid username and password before using any resources. A valid login generates an access token for the user, which is used in all subsequent attempts to use resources. Based on this token, a user is either allowed or denied access to a particular resource.

Users are added to an NT system, using the User Manager program (see Figure 8.5). You can use this program to administer the following for each user:

- User information, including username, password, and full name.
- User account restrictions, such as password expiration date, restricted login times, and restricted login workstations.
- User environment profile, including a home directory and a login script.
- User group membership.

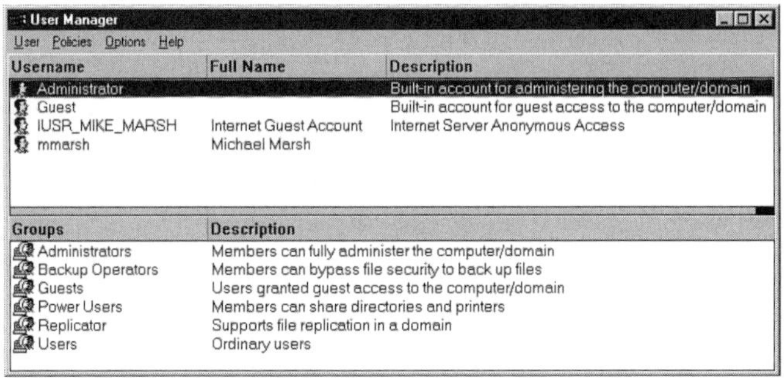

FIGURE 8.5

The User Manager program.

The user's group memberships determines what the user can do on the system. For example, an Administrator can create new users, but a Guest cannot.

If you have a sizable number of users on your system, it's a good idea to create groups. This will enable you to apply the various grants and restrictions to the group as whole, without having to set these for each user individually.

There are three types of groups:

- Local—Groups that apply to one machine only
- Global—Groups that apply on machines across the entire domain and into other trusted domains
- Special—A predefined set of groups that are used by NT internally

There are several built-in groups, just as for users. These groups are for users that need to perform similar tasks, such as backup and replication.

Resource Access Control

The NT resource security model protects resources by controlling their access. Associating a particular user with a particular resource controls access. If a user is not associated with a resource, the user is not allowed access.

The ACL (Access Control List) is the mechanism that NT uses to associate users and resources. The list not only permits or denies access, but also controls the level of permitted access. For example, if the resource is a file, the ACL will determine whether the user has permission to write to the file.

You use the Explorer to set folder and file permissions, and thus you can make an entry into the ACL, on NTFS partitions (see Figure 8.6). You must have Full Control access to the folder or file and have Change Permission; also, you must be the Owner. Again, it is often most expedient to assign permissions to groups, instead of individuals.

FIGURE 8.6

Using Explorer to set folder and file permissions.

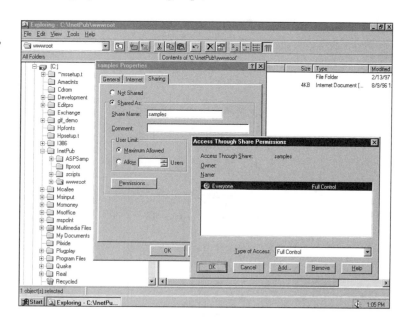

IIS Security

The Internet Information Server builds on the native NT security model by providing additional security features. This section describes NT security as it applies to IIS and native IIS security features.

Figure 8.7 shows the process that IIS uses to grant or deny an access request from a client.

FIGURE 8.7

How IIS determines whether to grant or deny an access request from a client.

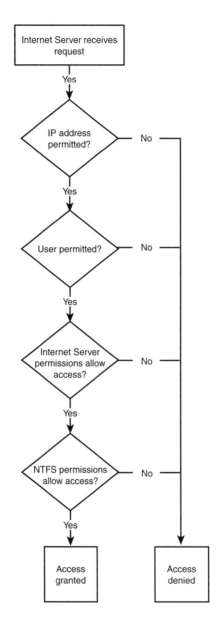

User Authentication

IIS uses authentication to grant or deny access to a client request. IIS can use NT groups and users to accomplish this, as well as its own mechanisms. IIS supports three types of user authentication:

- Windows NT Challenge/Response
- Basic authentication
- Anonymous login

You use the Internet Service Manager snap-in to the Microsoft Management Console (MMC) to set up your authentication scheme, as shown in Figure 8.8.

FIGURE 8.8

Setting up user authentication methods using the Internet Service Manager MMC snap-in.

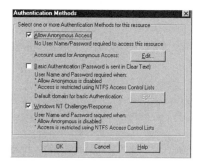

Windows NT Challenge/Response requires the client to pass user account information to the server. This information must match a valid NT user account; if it does not, the access is denied. An important part of this authentication scheme is that the account information is encrypted, making it very safe when put on the net. However, NT Challenge/Response is available in only a limited number of clients. Specifically, NT Challenge/Response works only with Internet Explorer. It is perhaps best used when you can control which browser your users will run.

Basic authentication passes unencrypted user account information between browser and server. The user must again have a valid NT account. This is the least safe method because plain-text user account information can be intercepted easily. Therefore, I strongly recommend avoiding this method, unless it is used with S-HTTP or SSL.

Anonymous login uses the IUSR_*computername* account generated automatically when you install IIS. This account is permitted to log on locally to the IIS server machine, and on that machine only. If you are careful about properly setting the permissions on your site's files, this anonymous account can be secure.

8

VISUAL INTERDEV SECURITY

If you have a mix of information on your site, some of which you don't want the entire public to see, you should set up a combination of anonymous login and authenticated login, preferably NT Challenge/Response, to control access. Create a group for users that may see the private material and give the desired permissions to the group for these folders and fields. This will deny access to these resources by an anonymous user, as long as the IUSR_*computername* account does not also have these privileges.

Access Control

You must carefully consider the permissions you grant to the folders and files that make up your Web site. As a general rule, grant read access to content folders, read and execute access to program files, and read and write access to database folders and files. Again, you would set these permissions using the Explorer application.

When you create a project with Visual InterDev, it automatically generates virtual directories for you on the server machine. You can see these directories in the Internet Service Manager MMC snap-in (see Figure 8.9). You can also use this application to change the two special IIS permissions: Read and Execute. These apply only to virtual directories. Clients will only be able to read from directories with the IIS read permission and will only be able to run programs from directories with the IIS execute permission.

FIGURE 8.9

Virtual directories in the Internet Service Manager MMC snap-in.

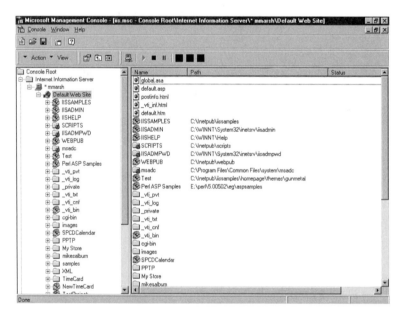

Logging

It is prudent to check for unauthorized access, or attempted access, to your site's folders from time to time. You can use the User Manager application to enable auditing for File and Object Access, as in Figure 8.10. You then use Explorer to specify particular resources to audit. The Event Viewer application shows you the audit entries (see Figure 8.11).

> **NOTE**
>
> To view the audited information, you use the Event Viewer's security log. This log is available only to system administrators.

FIGURE 8.10
User Manager is used to enable auditing for file and object access.

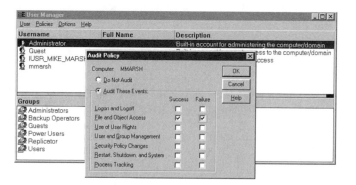

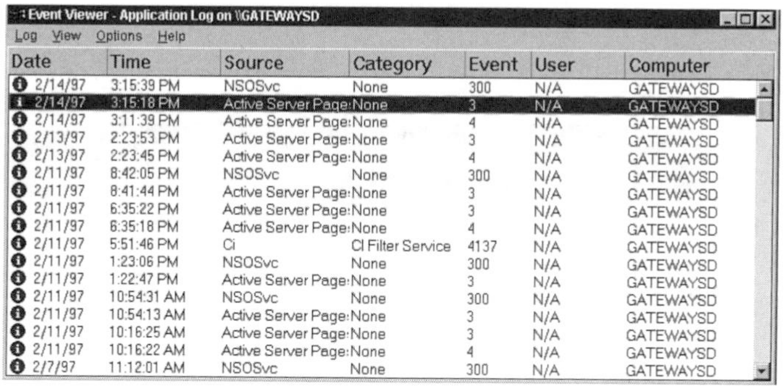

FIGURE 8.11
Using the Event Viewer to audit for unauthorized access.

Visual InterDev–Specific Security Issues

Visual InterDev allows programmers and authors write access to your site's content at design time. Administrators may also have protected access to your site. On the other hand, your end users may have only read access to the content. How is this accomplished?

FrontPage Server Extensions and Design-Time Security

Visual InterDev uses FrontPage Server Extensions to manage design-time security. FrontPage extensions use the native file-system security model to manage design-time access to your site's files. Specifically, the extensions provide gatekeeper DLLs through which design-time access is managed. These DLLs are ADMIN.DLL, AUTHOR.DLL, and DVWSSR.DLL, and they control administration, authoring, and browsing access, respectively. The ADMIN.DLL file is located at (SITE_DIRECTORY)/_VTI_BIN/_VTI_ADM, and AUTHOR.DLL and DVWSSR.DLL are found in (SITE_DIRECTORY)/_VTI_BIN/_VTI_AUT.

All design-time access is routed through one of these gatekeeper DLLs. The extensions have modified the ACLs on these files, allowing particular user accounts to have particular access rights. If a user with read permission makes an administration request via HTTP, that user will be allowed administration privileges on the site. If the user does not have read permission on ADMIN.DLL, he or she will be denied administration privileges.

> **NOTE**
>
> The FrontPage Server Extensions security model works best on NTFS. Because FrontPage uses the native security model of the file system, it makes sense to use NTFS for its tight security.

Permissions on the appropriate gatekeeper DLLs are managed via Visual InterDev's Permissions dialog box (see Figure 8.12). Changing Web permissions here causes FrontPage extensions to modify the ACLs on the appropriate gatekeeper DLL.

FIGURE 8.12

The Permissions dialog box from Visual InterDev.

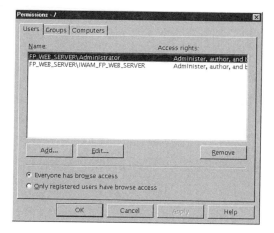

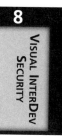

Runtime Security

By default, your Web is set up so that any user with a browser can access your site. To prevent users from gaining access to your site or parts of your site, you must apply runtime security. The FrontPage Server Extensions security model provides two ways for a user to access your site: unrestricted browsing and restricted browsing.

For *unrestricted browsing*, FrontPage extensions grant read access to the anonymous user account. This allows any user access to all Web content on your site.

To protect your site's content, FrontPage removes anonymous user account privileges from the protected content for *restricted browsing*. Then, only an identified and registered user may see these pages. This user must have explicit permissions set on the files. The next section shows you how to protect certain pages while allowing anonymous access to others.

Security Programming Issues

Imagine this scenario: Your company's Web site enables your customers to browse a catalog of products for purchase. You want all your customers to be able to access the product catalog and order form pages. You want customers to access their personal information pages, but not those of other customers. You want your employees to be able to update the catalog, process orders, and manage the customer information database. Employees will need full access to all pages.

Figure 8.13 illustrates a security architecture for this site. The architecture is based on two groups: Customer and Administrator. The Customer group allows a member to access the catalog and order form pages, and nothing else. The Administrator group allows a member to access all pages. Furthermore, customers can access their information pages, and theirs only, by login name and password. You can use a security architecture diagram like this to plan the security of your site.

FIGURE 8.13

A security architecture for a commercial Web site.

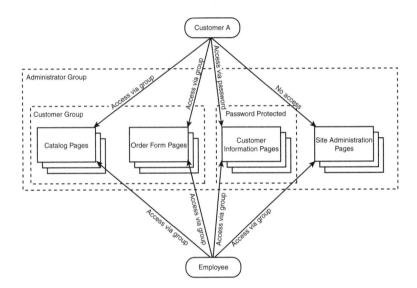

In this section, I'll show you how to use the features of Visual InterDev and its runtime environment to implement a security architecture for your site.

Access Level and Navigation

People have come to like the Web because it is easy to navigate. A click on a hot spot here, a click on the back arrow there, and that is all you really have to know to get around. This might be a slight exaggeration, but you get the idea: The Web is easy to navigate, and that is a big part of its charm.

When you need to limit a user's ability to access portions of your site, you must be careful not to interfere with ease of navigation. Users probably shouldn't even be aware that parts of your site are unreachable. The exception comes when a password is required. In this case, your users might even feel more comfortable, because you are protecting their interests, as well as your own.

Making your site secure, while still providing easy access when necessary, takes some planning. You must decide which pages are going to be available to which users. You then have to look at the resulting structure and discern any natural groupings. You can use these groupings to help administer controlled access to your site. It's much easier to create a group, set permissions for that group, and then add individuals as members than it is to set permissions for each individual.

After you have established your groups, you can get on with the nitty-gritty of managing navigation based on access privilege.

Defining Access Rights for Groups

Groups can be created at a number of levels: at the operating system level, the database level, and the application level. Each level has pros and cons, as you will see. It is often advantageous to coordinate groups from different levels, although even more careful planning is required in this case.

NT Groups

For our purposes, groups at the operating system level mean NT groups. NT uses groups for two purposes: to give rights to users to perform certain system tasks, such as backup, and to give users permission to access resources. We're interested in the latter.

NT has three types of groups:

- Local—Implemented on the local machine's account database, these groups apply only to that machine. One interesting aspect of local groups is that they can contain other groups. No other NT group type can do this. Use local groups to grant access to resources of the local server machine, for example, in a workgroup installation.

- Global—These are stored in the account database of the Primary Domain Controller (PDC) server machine of a domain. The permissions apply across the entire domain and into other trusting domains. Only user accounts from the domain, and not from other trusted domains, are allowed in the group. You would use global groups at sites with more than one server machine to allow access to other server machines in the domain. For example, your Web server may be on a different machine from your database server.

- Special—These are groups used internally by NT to accomplish automated system tasks. You cannot add users to these special groups, and it is generally best to leave them alone.

You use the programs User Manager and User Manager for Domains to create groups and add user members. Figure 8.14 shows the User Manager main screen.

FIGURE 8.14

The User Manager program.

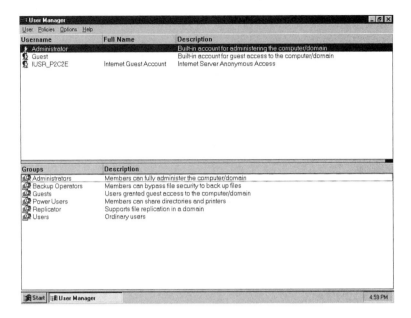

To create a group, Choose User from the main menu and then New Global Group, shown in Figure 8.15. Fill in the information for the new group and set the rights and permissions as appropriate.

FIGURE 8.15

Creating a new group, using the User Manager program.

To add a user to a group, double-click the username in User Manager. This opens the User Properties dialog (see Figure 8.16). Click the Groups button to open the Group Membership dialog, shown in Figure 8.17. Assign a user to any group that appears here.

FIGURE 8.16

The User Properties dialog from the User Manager program.

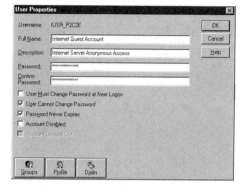

FIGURE 8.17

The Group Memberships dialog from the User Manager program.

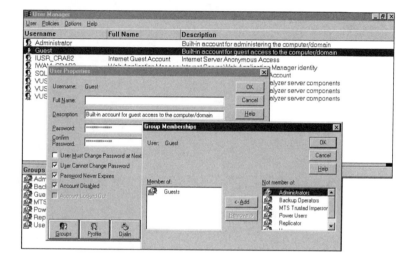

8

VISUAL INTERDEV SECURITY

If you add a user to more than one group, the user will have the lowest or least restrictive set of permissions that apply across the groups.

Database Groups

Some database products enable you to create groups similar in function to NT groups. I use Microsoft SQL Server 6.5 in my examples here.

Permissions in a database apply to access for database objects such as tables, stored procedures, and views. With SQL Server, you can actually apply permissions down to the column level in a table. It's important to plan your database schema with security and groups in mind. The decisions you make about how to apply permissions, and at what level, can affect performance.

To create a group in SQL Server 6.5, you use either the SQL Security Manager or the SQL Enterprise Manager applications. Figures 8.18 and 8.19 show each, respectively.

FIGURE 8.18

The SQL Security Manager program.

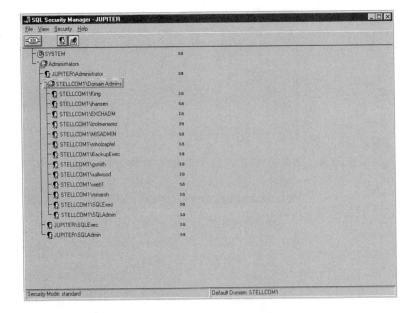

FIGURE 8.19

The SQL Enterprise Manager program.

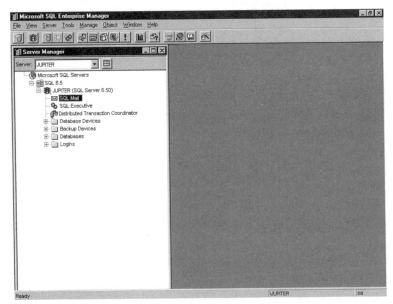

Using SQL Enterprise Manager, you choose Manage from the main menu and then Groups, after selecting a server and database from the Server Manager list view. This opens the Manage Groups dialog (see Figure 8.20). To add a group and users to that group, fill in the information in the dialog, shown in Figure 8.21.

FIGURE 8.20

The Manage Groups dialog from the SQL Enterprise Manager program.

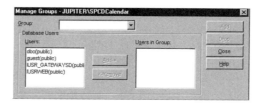

FIGURE 8.21

Using the Manage Groups dialog to add groups to your database.

Application-Defined Groups

You can keep track of users and groups at the application level. This might afford you finer control of how a user can access your site, but it obviously puts the burden on you to develop.

One method of tracking users and groups within your application is to use the database as the store for account information. Figure 8.22 shows a simple schema for doing this, and Listing 8.1 gives you a SQL Server script for implementing the schema.

FIGURE 8.22

A schema for implementing application-administered users and groups.

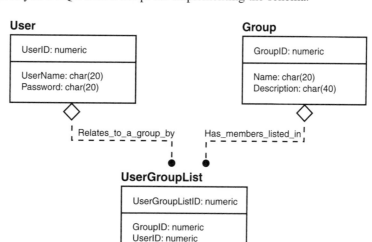

8

VISUAL INTERDEV SECURITY

LISTING 8.1 A SQL SERVER 6.5 SCRIPT FOR IMPLEMENTING THE SCHEMA IN FIGURE 8.22

```
CREATE TABLE Group (
       GroupID                numeric IDENTITY,
       Name                   char(20) NULL,
       Description            char(40) NULL
)
go
ALTER TABLE Group
       ADD PRIMARY KEY (GroupID)
go
exec sp_primarykey Group,
       GroupID
go
CREATE TABLE User (
       UserID                 numeric IDENTITY,
       UserName               char(20) NULL,
       Password               char(20 NULL
)
go
ALTER TABLE User
       ADD PRIMARY KEY (UserID)
go
exec sp_primarykey User,
       UserID
go
CREATE TABLE UserGroupList (
       UserGroupListID        numeric IDENTITY,
       GroupID                numeric NULL,
       UserID                 numeric NULL
)
go
ALTER TABLE UserGroupList
       ADD PRIMARY KEY (UserGroupListID)
go
exec sp_primarykey UserGroupList,
       UserGroupListID
go
ALTER TABLE UserGroupList
       ADD FOREIGN KEY (GroupID)
                                REFERENCES Group
go
ALTER TABLE UserGroupList
       ADD FOREIGN KEY (UserID)
                                REFERENCES User
go
exec sp_foreignkey UserGroupList, Group,
       GroupID
go
exec sp_foreignkey UserGroupList, User,
       UserID
go
```

The idea is to add users to the User table and groups to the Group table and then create group membership lists by associating a user with a group in the UserGroupList table. Listing 8.2 is a code fragment that shows you how to return the group for a particular user.

LISTING 8.2 QUERYING FOR GROUP MEMBERSHIP

```
<%
    strSQL = "SELECT UserGroupList.GroupID FROM `Group`,
    ➂UserGroupList, `User`"
    strSQL = strSQL & " WHERE `Group`.GroupID = '"
    strSQL = strSQL & "UserGroupList.GroupID AND "
    strSQL = strSQL & "UserGroupList.UserID = "
    strSQL = strSQL & "`User`.UserID AND "
    strSQL = strSQL & "`User`.UserName = '"
    strSQL = strSQL & "& Request.Form("UserName") & "'"
    ' execute the query
    Set rstUser = dbUser.Execute(strSQL)
    ' report the GroupID
    Response.Write(rstUser("GroupID"))
    ' close the connection
    dbUser.Close
%>
```

Planning Ahead

When planning an architecture for your site, think about security. This is the time to identify areas of your site that must be restricted and for recognizing the natural groupings of users, based on their access privileges. A diagram like the one in Figure 8.13 helps you visualize this architecture and identify all aspects of security as they relate to page access.

For added protection, you can combine the three types of groups in your site. NT privileges provide restricted access to your system's resources; you can allow Web users access only to those folders that you want and nothing else. Add to this groups within your database, and you will have the ability to restrict which database objects a user may see. Finally, at the application level, you can use groups of your own creation to further refine access to your site.

> **CAUTION**
>
> Remember that as you add levels of security, your administrative burden goes up as well. Some of the most frustrating problems to resolve involve access issues, so be forewarned!

Navigation Based on Group Membership

When you have the group membership information for a user, you can dynamically create a page with navigation to pages allowed for that group. Listings 8.3 and 8.4 show a simple example of this, using the application-level groups discussed previously.

LISTING 8.3   THE CODE FOR DEFAULT.ASP, REQUESTING A USERNAME AND PASSWORD

```
<%@ LANGUAGE="VBSCRIPT" %>

<HTML>

  <HEAD>
    <META NAME="GENERATOR" CONTENT="Microsoft Visual InterDev 6.0">
    <TITLE>Chapter 8 Sample Application</TITLE>
  </HEAD>

  <BODY>

    <H1>Visual InterDev 6 Unleashed</H1>
    <H2>Chapter 8 Sample Application</H2>
    <HR>

    <FORM ACTION="navigation.asp" METHOD="POST">
      <H3>User Name: <INPUT NAME="UserName" ></H3>
      <H3>Password:  
      <INPUT TYPE="PASSWORD" NAME="Password" ></H3>
      <INPUT NAME="Submit" TYPE="SUBMIT" value="Submit Query">
    </FORM>

  </BODY>

</HTML>
```

Listing 8.3 shows code for a simple .ASP page that requests a username and password (see Figure 8.23). When the user clicks the Submit button, the code opens the page in Listing 8.4.

FIGURE **8.23**

The login screen.

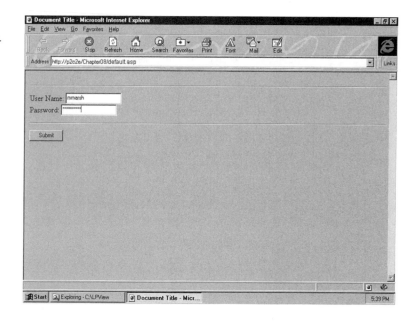

LISTING **8.4** BUILDING A PAGE BASED ON MEMBERSHIP IN A GROUP
(NAVIGATION.ASP)

```
<%@ LANGUAGE="VBSCRIPT" %>
<HTML>

  <HEAD>

    <META NAME="GENERATOR" Content="Microsoft Visual InterDev 6.0">
    <TITLE>Navigation Page</TITLE>

  </HEAD>

  <BODY>

    <%
    Response.Write "<H1>Visual InterDev 6 Unleashed</H1>"
    Response.Write "<H2>Chapter 8 Sample Application</H2>"

    ' Set the UserName and Password Session variables
    Session("UserName") = Request.Form("UserName")
    Session("Password") = Request.Form("Password")

    ' create and open the Connection object
    Set dbUser = Server.CreateObject("ADODB.Connection")
```

continues

LISTING 8.4   CONTINUED

```
dbUser.Open Session("Chapter28_ConnectionString"), _
            Session("Chapter28_RuntimeUserName"), _
            Session("Chapter28_RuntimePassword")

' build our SQL query
strSQL = "SELECT UserGroupList.GroupID FROM `Group`, "
strSQL = strSQL & "UserGroupList, `User`"
strSQL = strSQL & " WHERE `Group`.GroupID = "
strSQL = strSQL & "UserGroupList.GroupID AND "
strSQL = strSQL & "UserGroupList.UserID = "
strSQL = strSQL & "`User`.UserID AND "
strSQL = strSQL & "`User`.UserName = '"
strSQL = strSQL & Request.Form("UserName") & "'"

' execute the query
Set rstUser = dbUser.Execute(strSQL)

' build page based on Group membership
Select Case rstUser("GroupID")

  Case 1 ' customer

    Response.Write "Customer: "
    Response.Write(Request.Form("UserName"))

    Response.Write "<BR>"
    Response.Write "<HR>"
    Response.Write "<A HREF='Catalog.asp'>Catalog</A>"

  Case 2 ' administrator

    Response.Write "Administrator: " & Request.Form("UserName")
    Response.Write "<HR>"
    Response.Write "<A HREF='AdminGroups.asp'>Administer Groups</A>"
    Response.Write "<BR>"
    Response.Write "<A HREF='AdminUsers.asp'>Administer Users</A>"
    Response.Write "<BR>"

  Case Else ' invalid group type

    Response.Write "Not a valid User!"
    Response.Write "<BR>"

End Select

' close the connection
dbUser.Close
```

```
        %>

    </BODY>

</HTML>
```

This page queries the database for the GroupID of the member and then uses that ID to build itself, as in Figure 8.24. The page will display navigation links to pages that this user has access to, based on the user's group membership. For clarity, this example is extremely simple; in reality, you would want to do error trapping and decent formatting. Oh, and by the way, you might want to verify the user's password, too!

> **NOTE**
>
> The code for the entire project is on the CD-ROM that accompanies this book. This project includes all the code for the pages that support this sample application.

FIGURE 8.24

The navigation screen.

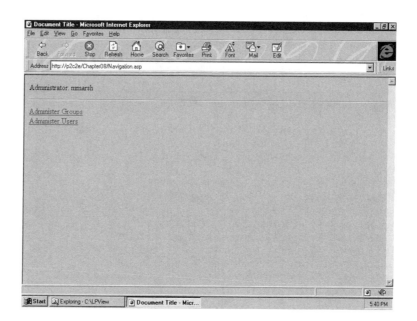

Preventing a Jump over the Login Screen

Users are smart. Even if you put your login screen as the first page of your site, they might find a way to jump over that screen and gain access to the other pages without logging in. Can you prevent this? Yes, in a couple of ways.

First, if you take a look at the code in Listing 8.4, you will see that the database query will fail if a user jumps directly here, because the `Request.Form("UserName")` variable is not set.

What if the user jumps to one of the other pages? There is no check in the code for these pages to verify that the user is logged in; if a user does jump here, access will be granted. You could add code to verify that the user has logged in, say, with an applicationwide Boolean variable, but you would have to add this code to every page in your site that needs protection. On a large site, this could be burdensome.

Fortunately, there is a better way: Use the Redirect method of the Response object in GLOBAL.ASA to send users to your login page, no matter where they land in your site. To be polite, you check to make sure that a user has not logged in before you do the redirect. Listing 8.5 shows the GLOBAL.ASA file for your project where the redirect is implemented. The code is in the OnStart subroutine called at the beginning of a session.

LISTING 8.5   THE GLOBAL.ASA FILE, SHOWING HOW TO REDIRECT A USER THAT HAS NOT LOGGED IN

```
<SCRIPT LANGUAGE=VBScript RUNAT=Server>
Sub Session_OnStart
  '==Visual InterDev Generated - DataConnection startspan==
  '--Project Data Connection
  Session("Chapter8_ConnectionString") =
  "DBQ=C:\INETPUB\WWWROOT\CHAPTER8\ch2.mdb;
  DefaultDir=C:\INETPUB\WWWROOT\CHAPTER8;
  Driver={Microsoft Access Driver (*.mdb)};
  DriverId=25;FIL=MS Access;
  ImplicitCommitSync=Yes;MaxBufferSize=512;
  MaxScanRows=8;PageTimeout=5;SafeTransactions=0;
  Threads=3;UID=admin;UserCommitSync=Yes;"
  Session("Chapter8_ConnectionTimeout") = 15
  Session("Chapter8_CommandTimeout") = 30
  Session("Chapter8_RuntimeUserName") = "admin"
  Session("Chapter8_RuntimePassword") = ""
  '==Visual InterDev Generated - DataConnection endspan==


  ' create a Session variable to track
  ' whether the user has logged in
  Session("LoggedIn") = False
```

```
' make sure that if users haven't logged in,
' they are redirected to the login screen
If Session("LoggedIn") = False then
  Response.Redirect("default.asp")
End If

End Sub
</SCRIPT>
```

You also have to add some code to set the Session variable `LoggedIn` to `True` when the user has successfully logged in. Listing 8.6 shows a code fragment from the NAVIGATION.ASP file, which is where a user is validated and logged in.

LISTING 8.6   THE MODIFIED NAVIGATION.ASP FILE, SHOWING THE MANAGEMENT OF THE `LoggedIn` SESSION VARIABLE

```
' build page based on Group membership
  Select Case rstUser("GroupID")

    Case 1 ' customer

      Session("LoggedIn") = True

      Response.Write "Customer: "
      Response.Write(Request.Form("UserName"))

      Response.Write "<BR>"
      Response.Write "<HR>"
      Response.Write "<A HREF='Catalog.asp'>Catalog</A>"

    Case 2 ' administrator

      Session("LoggedIn") = True

      Response.Write "Administrator: " & Request.Form("UserName")
      Response.Write "<HR>"
      Response.Write "<A HREF='AdminGroups.asp'>"
      Response.Write "Administer Groups</A>"
      Response.Write "<BR>"
      Response.Write "<A HREF='AdminUsers.asp'>Administer Users</A>"
      Response.Write "<BR>"

    Case Else ' invalid group type

      Response.Write "Not a valid User!"
      Response.Write "<BR>"

  End Select
```

8

VISUAL INTERDEV
SECURITY

This is quite an elegant solution, but it will work only if all your pages have the .ASP extension. That's because only Active Server Pages can use the objects in GLOBAL.ASA. There is a very small performance penalty for making all the protected pages in your site go through Active Server parsing, but the payoff in ease of implementation more than compensates. If you need to have pages that anybody can access alongside secure pages, make these public pages .HTM(L) files. They will not be redirected.

Keeping Track of a User

To keep track of users as they move from page to page, simply add Session variables to GLOBAL.ASA, as you did for the LoggedIn flag. You can access the variables anywhere in your code. The code fragment in Listing 8.7 shows the addition of the variables UserName and Password to GLOBAL.ASA. Listing 8.8 shows additions to NAVIGATION.ASP, where the variables are set. Finally, Listing 8.9 shows how to use the variables to display the username in the CATALOG.ASP page. Figure 8.25 shows the Catalog page with the username displayed.

LISTING 8.7   ADDING THE UserName AND Password VARIABLES TO OnStart IN GLOBAL.ASA

```
' create a Session variable to track whether the user has logged in
  Session("LoggedIn") = False

  ' create a Session variables to track username and password
  Session("UserName") = ""
  Session("Password") = ""

  ' make sure that if users haven't logged in,
  ' they are redirected to the login screen
  If Session("LoggedIn") = False then
    Response.Redirect("default.asp")
  End If
```

LISTING 8.8   SETTING THE UserName AND Password SESSION VARIABLES IN NAVIGATION.ASP

```
    ' Set the UserName and Password Session variables
    Session("UserName") = Request.Form("UserName")
    Session("Password") = Request.Form("Password")
```

LISTING 8.9 DISPLAYING THE USERNAME IN CATALOG.ASP

```
<%@ LANGUAGE="VBSCRIPT" %>

<HTML>

  <HEAD>
    <META NAME="GENERATOR" CONTENT="Microsoft Visual InterDev 6.0">
    <TITLE>Catalog</TITLE>
  </HEAD>

  <BODY>
    <H1>Visual InterDev 6 Unleashed</H1>
    <H2>Chapter 8 Sample Application</H2>
    <H3>Product Catalog.</H3>
    <HR>
    Customer: <%= (Session("UserName")) %>
  </BODY>

</HTML>
```

FIGURE 8.25

The Catalog page with the username displayed.

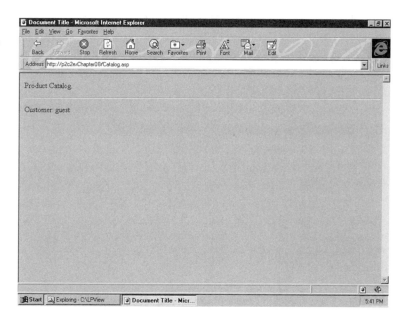

8

VISUAL INTERDEV
SECURITY

Security Versus Performance

Any time you add a layer to your code, you are going to slow things down. By how much depends on what kind of layer you apply. You've already seen that security is a trade-off with access, and performance is a part of this equation. The good news is that the techniques used here will not affect performance to any great degree. If your users complain that your site is unresponsive, it won't be because of these techniques. The peace of mind that you will gain makes the balance tip in security's favor this time!

Digital Certificates

One of the interesting properties of the Internet is that it enables us to communicate with one another even when we are not at the same location. I can have a long conversation with my friend in Germany or my editor in Indiana without hopping on plane, boat, or bus and without having to pay costly long distance phone bills! For casual conversations, these advantages outweigh the possible dangers.

Dangers? Yes, indeed. That you are not face to face with the person or entity you are communicating with poses serious problems of proof of identity. Consider these examples:

- You are shopping in an electronic mall on the Internet. You come across a store that is selling an item that you've wanted to buy for some time, but haven't been able to afford. The price is incredibly low, so you decide that now is the time. How can you be sure that this is not a bogus storefront set up to rip you off?

- Conversely, you have set up shop on the Internet. How can you be sure your customers are who they claim to be?

- You have to communicate sensitive information to a colleague at another facility. How can you reassure your colleague that the information in the message hasn't been tampered with and that it was in fact you who the sent the message?

- You have to send commercial transaction information over the net. How can you assure authorities that all parties properly authorized the transaction?

- You are surfing the Web. You come to a site that wants to download some executable software to your machine and run it from there. How can you be assured that the code is not malicious?

All these problems and more can be addressed by using authentication through digital certificates.

How Digital Certificates Work

Digital certificates work by associating a user's information with a public-key encryption key pair. The issuing certification authority *digitally signs* the digital certificate. If you have a digital certificate installed in your browser, it will serve as digital identification for sites that require it. A digital certificate has a finite expiration date and must be renewed periodically.

Public Key Encryption

Public key encryption is a method of encoding plain texts by using two keys: a public key and a private key. You use your *private key* to encode a message, and your message's recipient uses your *public key* to decode it. Private keys are kept secret, whereas public keys are made generally available.

Username and Other Identification

Depending on the level of authentication required for acquiring your public key, you might have to provide several forms of identification to the certification authority. Some require that you appear in person with a photo ID and a copy of your birth certificate. Others require fingerprints and a background check. For casual browsing on the Web, most certification authorities require only your email address and your name.

Digital Signatures

A *digital signature* is an encrypted message digest that is nonrepudiable. A *message digest* is the result of running the text of the message through a special hashing algorithm that produces a unique sequence of characters for the text. A particular text will produce only one digest, no other text will produce the same digest, and it's impossible to reproduce the text itself from the digest. After you create the digest for your message, you encrypt it using your private key. The encrypted digest is the digital signature for your message. Your digital certificate contains such a digital signature from the issuing certification authority.

Digital Certificate Expiration and Time-Stamping Agencies

A digital certificate has a finite valid life. You should not accept a digital certificate that has expired. You will periodically renew your digital certificate, just as you would a driver's license or credit card.

Some digitally signed documents must be kept for long periods of time, perhaps long past the expiration date of the certificate used. These documents can remain legal if they were registered with a time-stamping service at the time they were signed. It works this way: You create a message and its digest and then send the digest to the time-stamping agency. They time-stamp the digest by creating a new digital signature, consisting of the original digest, the date and time that the digest was received, and the digital signature of the time-stamping agency. You include both the message digest and the digital time stamp with your message (see Figure 8.26).

FIGURE 8.26

Digital time stamps.

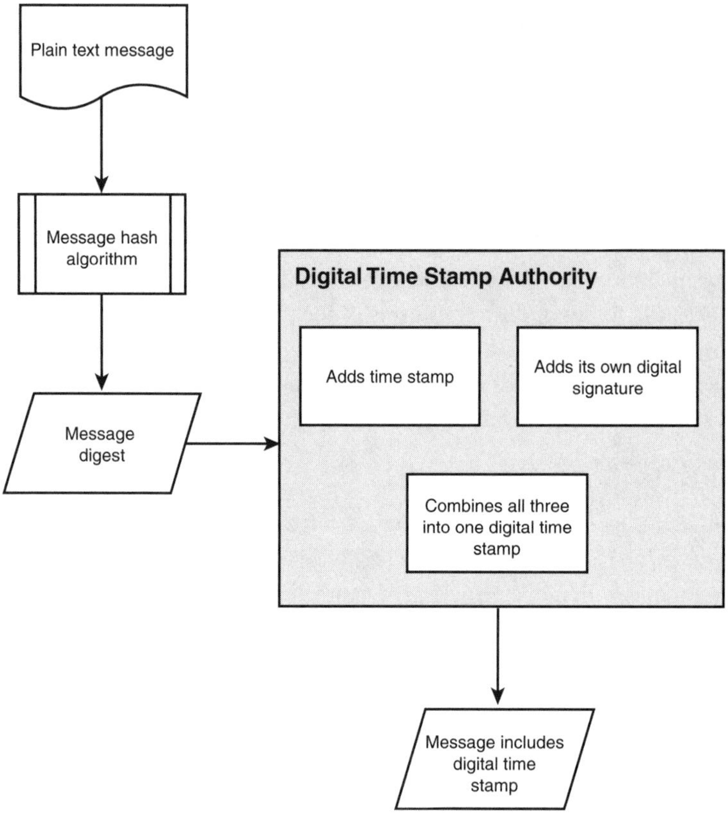

Obtaining Digital Certificates

There are several types of certificates: personal, code, and server. Each might have different levels of protection. For example, VeriSign offers a Class 1 Personal Digital ID that assures a unique email address and name; it also offers a Class 2 ID that verifies identity against an online consumer database. Class 2 IDs are more expensive. Both are for use in browsers. VeriSign also offers personal IDs for S/MIME applications, IDs for signing code, and server certificates. The requirements for each differ, as does the process for acquiring them. There are several other authorities. Here is a list of some of them:

- VeriSign Certification Authority (VeriSign, Inc.) `http://www.verisign.com/`.
- Entrust (Northern Telecommunications, Inc.) `http://www.entrust.com/`.
- Caviar (ISODE Consortium) `http://www.isode.com/ x509Certification Authority.htm`.
- BSafe/BCert (RSA Data Security, Inc.) `http://www.rsa.com/`.
- Intelligent Security Agent (Zoomit International, Inc.) `http://www.zoomit.com/`.

MICROSOFT CERTIFICATE SERVER

Microsoft includes Certificate Server with NT Option Pack 4.0. This software administers the issuing, renewing, and revoking of certificates for Web sites using SSL and PCT. It can also be used for S/MIME, secure payments (SET), and Authenticode.

Certificate Server works by accepting standard requests for certificates and issuing standard certificates. Because the product allows customizable policy, your organization can assume control of the certificate process, becoming a certification authority. This would be valuable for connecting remote users to your private intranet, for doing subscription-based business on the net, and for secure communications with vendors and suppliers.

Installing SSL and PTC with Your Digital Certificate

The first step in enabling SSL and PCT for your Web is to install a digital certificate on IIS. Here are the main steps:

1. Generate the Public Key Encryption key pairs for your server and a certificate request file. You use the Key Manager application to do this, shown in Figure 8.27.
2. Obtain a server Digital Certificate from a certification authority by sending them the Certificate Request file. The generated key pair will not be valid until a certification authority has issued a certificate for it.
3. Install the new certificate on your server, using Key Manager (see Figure 8.28).
4. Enable SSL and PCT on the virtual folders that require secure access. To do this, use the Internet Service Manager snap-in for the MMC, as shown in Figure 8.29.

FIGURE 8.27

Using the Key Manager to create a key pair for your server.

8

VISUAL INTERDEV SECURITY

FIGURE 8.28

Using Key Manager to install a Digital Certificate for your server.

FIGURE 8.29

Using the Internet Service Manager snap-in of the MMC to enable SSL and PCT on your site's folders.

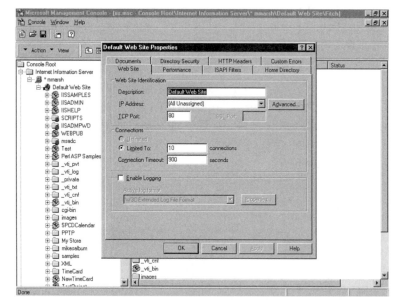

Here are a few more points to consider when enabling SSL and PCT on your Web:

- For best performance, enable SSL and PCT only on those directories that require security.

- Keep your secure content in separate directories from your public content.

- Use Key Manager to make a backup of your key pair. Don't forget your password! If you do, you will have to get a new certificate.

- To point to documents on an SSL-enabled and PCT-enabled folder, use `https://`. `http://` will not work on secured folders.

- After you are set up for SSL and PCT, remove the keys from the server machine onto a floppy disk. Use the floppy disk whenever you need the key. Obviously, guard this floppy disk jealously!

Enabling SSL and PCT Using Visual InterDev

After IIS has been set up to use SSL and PCT, enabling them for your Web is easy with Visual InterDev.

1. Use the Web Project Wizard to generate a new Web or connect to an existing Web.

2. In Step 1 of the wizard, be sure to check the Connect Using Secure Sockets Layer check box, shown in Figure 8.30.

3. Continue entering information with the wizard as usual.

4. Click the Finish button.

Your Web will now be enabled for SSL-secure and PCT-secure communications.

FIGURE 8.30

The Web Project Wizard of Visual InterDev can be used to enable SSL and PCT for your Web.

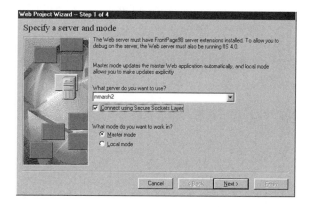

Programming with Digital Certificates

Most of the secure communication technology that you need to run your site is built in to IIS and Internet Explorer. For those times that you have to do something beyond what is provided, Visual InterDev provides the programming support.

The CryptoAPI

The CryptoAPI is the fundamental framework on which the Digital Certificate technology in IIS and Internet Explorer is built. It is part of the Win32 SDK and is, therefore, a set of C APIs in DLLs. It can be used with any language that can access C DLLs. The CryptoAPI includes support for symmetric-key and public-key encryption, key generation and management, encryption and decryption, message digests, and creating and verifying digital signatures. CryptoAPI 2.0, in beta as of this writing, further includes support for certificates. The CryptoAPI is approved for export.

CryptoAPI 2.0 provides COM interfaces for access; this means that you can use VBScript within your Web pages to add crypto functionality to your site. Check out http://www.microsoft.com/workshop/security/capi/cryptapi.asp for examples of how to do this.

Microsoft Authenticode Technology

Built in to Internet Explorer is the capability to authenticate a supplier of a software component: Authenticode. This technology is built on top of the CryptoAPI. It verifies to the user that the code about to be downloaded has not been tampered with and is in fact from a reputable supplier.

If you are creating ActiveX controls for distribution on the Web, you will want to sign your controls using Authenticode. Authenticode is available in the ActiveX SDK, which can be downloaded from http://www.microsoft.com/gallery/tools/activexsdk/axsdk.asp.

After you have created your control, you need to follow these steps to get it signed:

1. Make sure you have Internet Explorer version 3.0 or above and the latest version of the ActiveX SDK.
2. Get your credentials from a certification authority. You can apply as either an individual or a company. Each authority will have different procedures for certification. See the list of authorities in the previous section.
3. For a .cab file, add this entry in its corresponding .ddf file:

   `.Set ReservePerCabinetSize=6144.`

   For any other file type (.exe, .ocx, .dll, and so on), you don't have to do anything special.
4. Sign your files with the signcode program.
5. Check your signature with the chktrust program.

You have now signed your code. When a user downloads the file with Internet Explorer from a Web site, your certificate will be displayed. The user can accept or reject running your file, based on this certificate. If the code has been tampered with, the browser will inform the user.

The Request Object and the ClientCertificate Collection

Visual InterDev provides you with easy access to client certificates through the ClientCertificate collection of the Request object. The syntax is

```
Request.ClientCertificate(Key[subfield])
```

In this, the key can be

- Subject—A string made up of subfields (listed next). If a subfield is not included, a comma-delimited string of all subfields is returned in the form `C=US, O=Msft,` . . . .
- Issuer—Also a string of subfields. The same rules apply as with the Subject key.
- ValidFrom—A VBScript-formatted date that specifies when the certificate becomes valid.
- ValidUntil—A VBScript-formatted date that specifies when the certificate becomes invalid.
- SerialNumber—A string representing the serial number of the certificate as hexadecimal bytes separated by hyphens, as in `FF-FF-FF-FF`.
- Certificate—A string containing the entire certificate contents encoded as an ASN.1 format binary stream.
- Flags—These provide additional certificate information, `ceCertPresent` and `ceUnrecognizedIssuer`.

The subfields for Subject and Issuer are

- C—Country of origin
- O—Organization name
- OU—Organizational unit name
- CN—Common name of the user
- L—Locality
- S—State or province
- T—Title (of person or organization)
- GN—Given name
- I—Initials

8

VISUAL INTERDEV
SECURITY

Listing 8.10 illustrates how to report information about the client certificates currently in the collection. To test this code, make sure that you have set up a Web that expects client certificates and that you access that Web using a client certificate. Otherwise, you will just receive a message saying that no certificates are available. Also, the include file cervbs.inc is needed to use the Flags key.

LISTING 8.10 THE CERTIFICATE INFORMATION WEB PAGE

```
<%@ LANGUAGE="VBSCRIPT" %>

<HTML>
  <HEAD>
    <META NAME="GENERATOR" Content="Microsoft Visual InterDev 6.0">
    <META HTTP-EQUIV="Content-Type"
         content="text/html; charset=iso-8859-1">
    <TITLE>Certificate Info</TITLE>
  </HEAD>

  <BODY>
    <!--#include file="cervbs.inc"-->
<%
    Response.Write "<H1>Visual InterDev 6 Unleashed</H1>"
    Response.Write "<H2>Chapter 8 Sample Application</H2>"
    Response.Write "<HR>"

    You have the following Client Certificates
    in the Response object collection: <BR>

  <%
  If Len(Request.ClientCertificate("Subject")) = 0 Then
    Response.Write("None.<BR>")
  Else
    For Each key In Request.ClientCertificate
      Response.Write key & ": "
      Response.Write Request.ClientCertificate(key) & "<BR>"
    Next
  End If
  %>
  </BODY>

</HTML>
```

The Security Plan

A security plan for your site should be written, authorized, and implemented before you expose your site to the public. Without a coherent and shared vision for security, your site is more vulnerable to attack. For example, without the guidance of a formal policy, naive users might rely on passwords that can be cracked, exposing your site to infiltration.

In the ideal world, you could adhere to the preceding paragraph. Alas, the real world will probably have you scrambling to create pages for marketing's Latest Great Idea in a quarter of the time necessary. Security considerations might be pushed down a few levels in your stack. We've all been there, but you have to remember the security plan and come back to it as soon as possible. Convince management of the plan's importance, and you will have an ally the next time you're yanked.

Getting a security plan authorized is not an easy task. You probably have strong ideas about what should be protected and how. These might not entirely agree with management's ideas, so you should be prepared to defend your reasoning, but probably compromise. You should recognize that security policy decisions, because they affect access and ease of use, must be considered in the context of your company's entire business.

The Importance of a Companywide Security Plan

Your site is probably only a part of your company's overall network. Your security plan should therefore be a subset of a companywide security policy. If you have a strict security plan for your site, but your internal network is unsecured, your site is unsecured as well. Conversely, if your internal network has a strict security policy, but your site security is lax, you put the internal net at risk. Consider your site security plan carefully because it affects your general network.

Considerations When Designing a Plan

As with any plan, you should build using guiding principles. This helps resolve any conflicts and keeps things coherent. Here are some things to keep in mind as guiding principles:

- Cost—You will probably have a budget within which to operate. This will dictate what kinds and quantities of hardware and software you can use. It could also limit your development time.

- Ease of use—Security measures are necessarily a balance against ease of access. If users are continually stymied by your security, your business will suffer. Users might even rebel by ignoring security altogether, thus defeating the central purpose of the plan.

- Ease of administration—Make sure that you can easily accomplish the tasks associated with maintaining your site's security. If these tasks are too difficult, they will probably not be consistently performed.

- Legal issues—Consider your company's special legal issues, if any. These include items such as copyrights, electronic funds, special security laws, and so on.

- Enforcement—What will be the consequences of a violation of security policy? Will a user lose privileges? Will there be warnings? How will enforcement affect day-to-day business?

Elements of a Security Plan

What elements should you include in the plan? This varies from site to site, but you should minimally include the following:

- Specific security issues—Your site might have specific concerns such as dial-in access or the protection of a particular machine. List these specifically in the plan.

- Methods for dealing with identified issues—For all the specific issues just listed, provide a detailed method for dealing with each.

- Physical security—No site is safe if an intruder can walk up to a workstation that is already logged on and access information. Similarly, if your servers are not physically secure, they are vulnerable.

- Identification of responsibilities—Are you responsible for security of your site or of the entire network? How do you prove that you are living up to those responsibilities? What is your manager's responsibility? How are users responsible for security?

- Methods of enforcement—Write down the specific consequences for violations of security policy. Make sure all users are aware of these consequences. Get management approval for this section particularly. There will inevitably be violations, some mild, others gross. You will have to deal with these, so documentation is very helpful.

- Implementation details—In this section, describe exactly and technically how you will implement each part of the plan. This section is similar to a design document for a software project.

- Administration strategy—Here you identify the specific administrative tasks associated with the security plan and explain how these will be accomplished.

- User education—The security plan is necessarily a technical document. You should make it available to all users, but there must also be a version for nontechnical users. This smaller document should include sections on the reasons for the security policy, tips for using the system securely, user responsibilities, and a description of the consequences of violating the security policy. Other forms of user education should be considered: perhaps a Lunchtime Learning lecture on famous security breaches and their consequences or a demonstration of tips for using the system securely.

The written security plan is a crucial element in your site's overall security. It should be considered and written with the same care as any technical document. It's not an easy task and, depending on the size of your installation, can take weeks to accomplish. However, writing a security plan is considerably less onerous than dealing with the consequences of a security breach!

Summary

You've put your site on the Internet precisely to enable the public to access specific information about your company. However, being on the net also exposes your company to substantial risk. An attack on your site can compromise your data through theft or vandalism. Your reputation can be harmed, your business damaged, and revenue lost. Your site must be adequately protected.

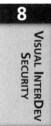

You can use hardware security measures such as firewalls, filtering routers, and proxies to physically separate your internal network from the Internet. NT Server and Internet Information Server provide a secure software infrastructure to control access to your resources. Visual InterDev provides some tools for implementing access control from within the IDE.

The time to consider security for your site is at the planning stage. Use a security architecture diagram to identify pages that require restricted visibility. You can then identify groups of users with varying degrees of access to these pages.

Groups are important because they facilitate security administration. Groups operate at three levels: the operating system, the database, and the application level. Each has particular strengths and weaknesses, and each can be implemented in combination with the others. You can use application groups for a finer level of control, but you have to do a little programming.

You can prevent a user from jumping over your login screen by using the Redirect method of the Response object. If you need to have unrestricted access to some pages alongside some secure pages, use a combination of .HTM(L) and .ASP files.

The Internet affords us great new opportunities for fast communication with people, regardless of their physical location. This also presents real problems of identification. How do you know that the person you are communicating with is who she says she is? How does she know who you really are?

Digital certificates provide a means for servers and clients to authenticate themselves. They use technologies such as symmetric-key and public-key encryption, message digests, and digital signing to accomplish this. Certification authorities issue certificates and administer them.

Microsoft provides technology to support secure and authenticated Internet communication. These are based fundamentally on the CryptoAPI. Authenticode technology enables developers to sign their executables, giving users some assurance that the code is not malicious. IIS can be set up to use secure communication with SSL and PCT. Visual InterDev provides facilities for accessing digital certificates through the Response object's ClientCertificate collection.

Finally, a security plan for your site should be written, authorized, and implemented before your site goes live. If this is not immediately possible, and in the real world it is often not, keep trying. A coherent security plan is vital to your site's health!

Creating a Secure Application

by Michael Marsh

CHAPTER 9

Introduction—The Electronic Time Card Application Overview

This chapter ties things together by describing an application that encompasses many of the security issues discussed in Chapter 8, "Visual InterDev Security." The application is an electronic time card for a small fictitious engineering consulting firm, Armadillo Engineering. I'll discuss the program in detail, point out interesting alternatives to what I've written, and suggest other features that could be added.

This chapter is presented as a narrative from the point of view of the CEO of Armadillo Engineering, the author of the software. With a focus on security issues, I show how the CEO built the system. I also point out some mistakes in his thinking regarding security and explain their possible consequences, along with some solutions.

Vision and Scope

Armadillo Engineering is a small consulting firm with two employees who are field engineers. These field engineers work at the client site and are rarely in the Armadillo office. Their time cards are due weekly. To avoid a trip to the office, the field engineers fax their time cards. On occasion, these faxes have been lost or garbled, preventing Accounting from billing in a timely manner. Furthermore, errors have occurred in transcribing the faxes into the accounting system's database.

The CEO, also an engineer, designed a system for inputting time card information by engineers from the field over the Web and for having these approved by the clients, again over the Web. The information goes directly into the database, thus avoiding transcription errors.

Armadillo Engineering's biggest client is a UNIX shop; the other two clients run Microsoft Windows. One of the Windows shops uses Windows for Workgroups 3.11; the other uses Windows 95 for client machines and NT 3.51 for servers. In designing the system, the CEO had to consider the variety of browsers and clients that would be accessing the Electronic Time Card application.

To make the system as easy as possible to use, the CEO wanted login information to route users to an appropriate page automatically, rather than force users themselves to do the navigation. Security was an issue here: The CEO had to make sure that clients could not view one another's data and that field engineers could not access the database directly, because this would allow them to change their time cards after authorization.

Accounting's complaints had become increasingly strident, so the CEO needed a quick, temporary solution to implement right away. The result of his effort is Armadillo Engineering's Electronic Time Card, a page of which is shown in Figure 9.1.

FIGURE 9.1

A page from Armadillo Engineering's Electronic Time Card application.

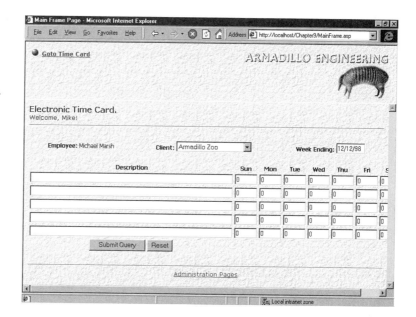

The Client Side

The Electronic Time Card application appears somewhat differently to each type of user, after the initial common login page (shown in Figure 9.2). There are three types of users, each with a particular set of privileges:

- *Administrators* are allowed full access to the system. Pages for maintaining the database are available only to members of this group. Furthermore, a link to the Database Maintenance menu appears on the time card page if the user is logged in as Administrator (see Figure 9.3).

- *Employees* can see the time card input page (see Figure 9.4) and the time card verification page (see Figure 9.5).

- *Clients* can search for pending time cards by employee (see Figure 9.6) and see the resulting pending time card authorization page (see Figure 9.7) and then the time card authorization verification page (see Figure 9.8). Only records for this particular client are displayed.

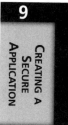

FIGURE 9.2

The login page.

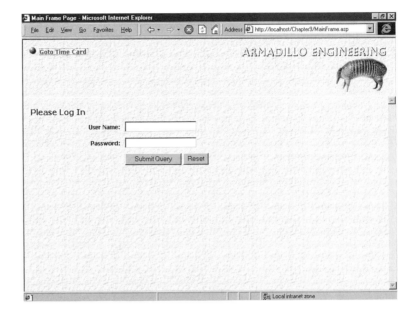

FIGURE 9.2

The login page.

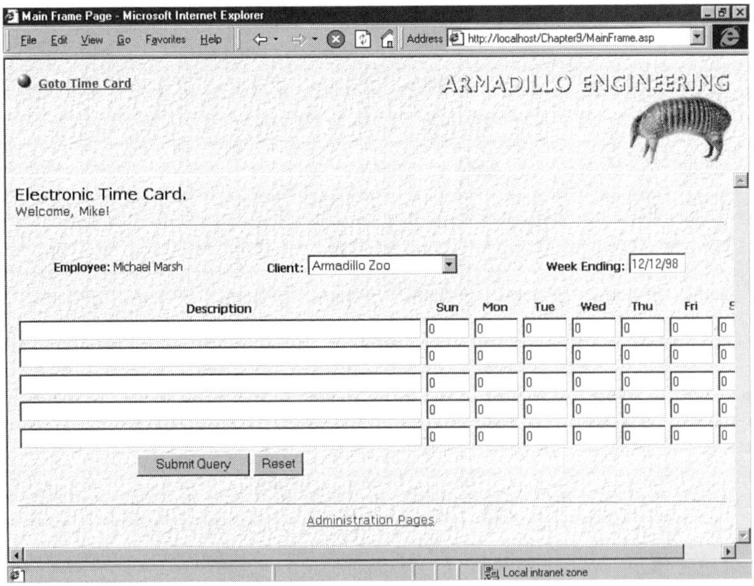

FIGURE 9.3

*The time card
input page with a
link to the admin-
istration menu.*

FIGURE 9.4

The time card input page, as seen by a member of the Employee group.

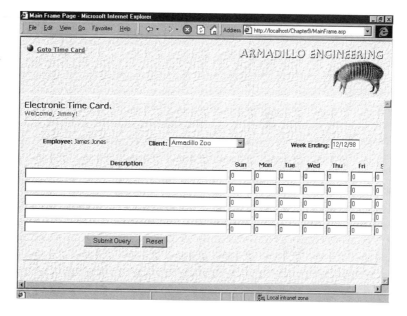

FIGURE 9.5

The time card verification page.

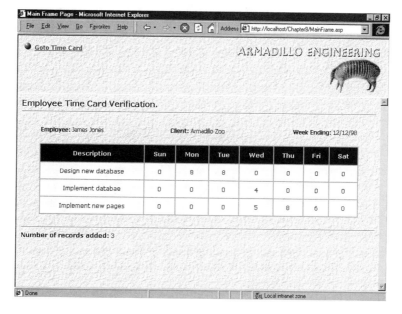

FIGURE **9.6**

The client time card page.

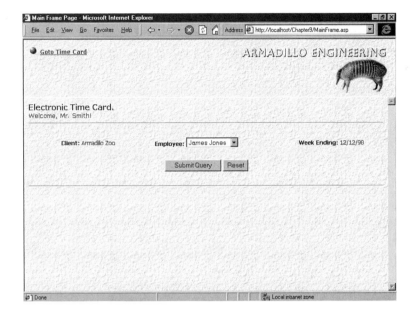

FIGURE **9.7**

The pending time card authorization page.

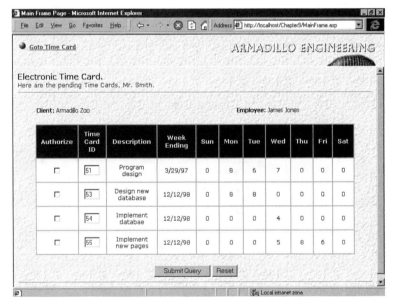

FIGURE 9.8

The pending time card authorization verification page.

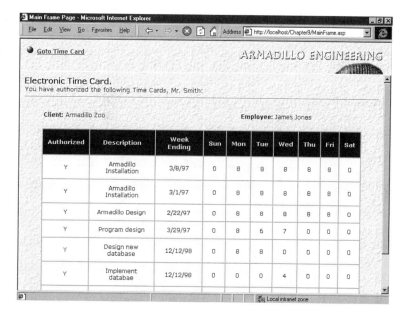

To ActiveX or Not to ActiveX

One of the CEO's main concerns when implementing this solution was to ensure that the client code would run on a variety of browsers. Initially, the CEO wanted to implement some of the features of the application using ActiveX. In particular, he wanted to use an ActiveX spreadsheet control for presenting the time card data. This would have offered a substantial number of features for much less coding and was therefore a very attractive solution. Unfortunately, one of his clients (the biggest one, in fact) did not have a browser that could use ActiveX. Reluctantly, the CEO abandoned ActiveX in favor of a pure HTML solution for the client side.

The Server Side

Armadillo Engineering is a Microsoft shop internally, with Windows 98 and Windows NT 4.0 Workstation on the clients and several server machines running Windows NT 4.0 Server. The dynamic nature of the client code made the choice of server software obvious: IIS with Active Server Pages. This in turn suggested the appropriate development tool, Visual InterDev.

After some thought, the CEO decided to use Access 97 as the database for the Electronic Time Card application. The accounting database runs under SQL Server 6.5 on its own machine. Using Access as a way station for the data—with an automated import procedure for inserting data into the appropriate accounting database tables—seemed the

safest method for a quick implementation. The CEO plans to revisit this issue if and when there are scalability problems with the implementation.

Figure 9.9 shows a general architectural diagram of the system.

FIGURE 9.9

The architecture of the Electronic Time Card application.

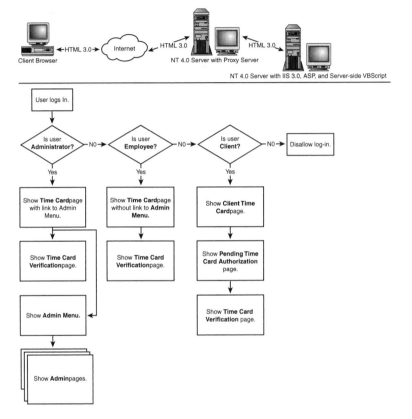

The Code

The three main components of the project are described here: the database, the client-side code, and the server-side code. First, though, I'll touch on how the CEO set up for the project.

Setting Up for the Project

The CEO set up his IIS server on a new machine running NT 4.0 Server. He put Proxy Server on another new machine with the same configuration. The Proxy Server machine has two NICs, one connected to his company's T1 line to the Internet and one connected to his internal network. He set up the Web Proxy to allow HTML and SSL in and out. He disallowed FTP and Telnet because at the moment he has no use for either. For the WinSock Proxy, he allowed RealAudio for himself because he likes to get his news from a radio station that broadcasts using this protocol over the net. He figured (correctly!) that he will have to revisit this setup and tune it as time goes on.

The CEO then installed the server-side extensions on the IIS machine necessary to support Visual InterDev. He tested his installation with one of the sample sites provided by IIS.

Finally, the CEO set up his workstation with NT 4.0 Workstation and the Visual InterDev development environment. He installed Access on this workstation as well. He was then ready to move forward with the first step in his project: the database.

The Database

Armadillo Engineering's accounting database is relatively straightforward. Simply supplying the name of the client, the field engineer's name, and the hours worked for that week would be sufficient time card information for Accounting's purposes. However, the CEO would like to give his clients a little more information: exactly what the engineer was working on for those hours reported. The CEO also has an idea that he would like to use this database to track basic client and employee information.

The Schema

Figure 9.10 shows the schema for the database that the CEO designed. Tables 9.1–9.5 detail the physical schema for the tables.

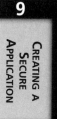

> **NOTE**
>
> The entire project, including the database with sample data, is on the CD-ROM that accompanies this book. The username and password for the administrator are mmarsh and hsramm, respectively. Another employee is jjones (password senojj), and a client is ssmith (password nutbrownale).

Table 9.1 shows how the user information is stored. The UserID is an AutoNumber field, which increments the value used as an ID automatically, guaranteeing uniqueness. The CompanyID field ties this user to a particular company.

FIGURE 9.10

The logical schema for the database.

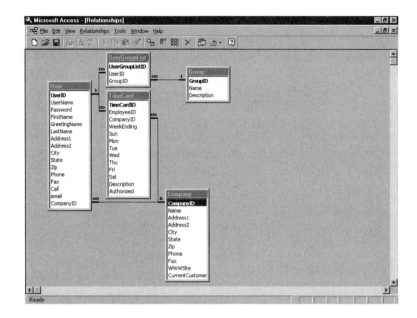

TABLE 9.1 THE PHYSICAL SCHEMA FOR THE USER TABLE

Column Name	Data Type
UserID	AutoNumber
UserName	Text(20)
Password	Text(20)
UserName	Text(20)
FirstName	Text(30)
GreetingName	Text(50)
LastName	Text(30)
Address1	Text(50)
Address2	Text(50)
City	Text(50)
State	Text(2)
Zip	Text(10)
Phone	Text(20)
Fax	Text(20)
email	Text(255)
CompanyID	LongInteger

For keeping track of groups, Table 9.2 shows the physical schema for the Group table.

TABLE 9.2 THE PHYSICAL SCHEMA FOR THE GROUP TABLE

Column Name	Data Type
GroupID	AutoNumber
Name	Text(20)
Description	Text(40)

To tie a particular user to a particular group, the join table UserGroupList is used. Table 9.3 describes this table. Note that by using a join table like this, a user may belong to more than one group. If you look at the logical schema shown in Figure 9.9, you can see how this table ties together elements of the Group and User tables.

TABLE 9.3 THE PHYSICAL SCHEMA FOR THE UserGroupList TABLE

Column Name	Data Type
UserGroupListID	AutoNumber
UserID	LongInteger
GroupID	LongInteger

The Company table stores information about companies, as shown in Table 9.4.

TABLE 9.4 THE PHYSICAL SCHEMA FOR THE COMPANY TABLE

Column Name	Data Type
CompanyID	AutoNumber
Name	Text(50)
Address1	Text(50)
Address2	Text(50)
City	Text(50)
State	Text(2)
Zip	Text(10)
Phone	Text(20)
Fax	Text(20)
WWWSite	Text(255)
CurrentCustomer	Text(1)

9

CREATING A
SECURE
APPLICATION

The TimeCard table, shown in Table 9.5, stores the hours worked by one employee for one company over a one-week period. Each separate job that the employee lists for a single customer for a particular week goes into the database as a separate record, but is recorded on one page. If an employee works for more than one company, the employee must submit a separate time card for each. The Authorized field is how the application keeps track of open time cards that need a client's authorization. The EmployeeID and CompanyID fields are foreign keys relating this table to the User table and Company table, respectively.

TABLE 9.5 THE PHYSICAL SCHEMA FOR THE TIMECARD TABLE

Column Name	Data Type
TimeCardID	AutoNumber
EmployeeID	LongInteger
CompanyID	LongInteger
WeekEnding	Date/Time
Sun	LongInteger
Mon	LongInteger
Tue	LongInteger
Wed	LongInteger
Thu	LongInteger
Fri	LongInteger
Sat	LongInteger
Description	Text(255)
Authorized	Text(1)

Relationships

Figure 9.10 shows the logical schema for the database, along with the relationships set up among tables. Table 9.6 shows these relationships in more detail.

TABLE 9.6 RELATIONSHIPS DEFINED FOR THE DATABASE

Parent Table	Related Table	Relationship Type	Join Type
User	UserGroupList	One-to-many	Inner
Group	UserGroupList	One-to-many	Inner
Company	User	One-to-many	Inner
Company	TimeCard	One-to-many	Inner
User	TimeCard	One-to-many	Inner

Access Versus SQL Server

As mentioned before, the CEO gave some consideration to the question of which database to use. He could have used the SQL Server machine that Accounting uses for its work, but he didn't want to rock that particular boat. He could have set up yet another machine as a database server, but for his small operation, that seemed like overkill. For now, he has decided to use Access 97, but will revisit the issue if necessary in the future.

The Client Side

The client for this application is obviously a browser, although which particular browser is an unknown. Because the code generated for client display and interaction will be pure HTML, the question of which browser will be used is moot anyway. For example, the code that the client sees for the login page is in Listing 9.1. This listing shows that the code is nothing more than HTML and can be run on almost any browser.

LISTING 9.1 THE HTML CODE THAT THE CLIENT BROWSER SEES FOR THE LOGIN PAGE

```
<HTML>
  <HEAD>
    <META NAME="GENERATOR" Content="Microsoft Visual InterDev 6.0">
    <META HTTP-EQUIV="Content-Type"
          content="text/html; charset=iso-8859-1">
    <TITLE>Main Frame Page</TITLE>
  </HEAD>

  <FRAMESET ROWS = "180, *">
    <FRAME NAME = "Header" SCROLLING = NO  SRC = "Header.asp">
    <FRAME NAME = "Login"  SCROLLING = YES SRC = "Login.asp">
  </FRAMESET>

</HTML>
```

Look and Feel

The CEO wanted the electronic time card to have the look and feel of a Web application. He also wanted to prominently display the company logo based on its mascot, the armadillo. Using frames would enable him to display this information everywhere without having to code it into every page.

9

CREATING A SECURE APPLICATION

> **TIP**
>
> If you use frames in your pages, be careful of one thing. Currently with ASP, if the first page that a user comes to contains frames, you get a Session object for each frame on that page. This can make keeping track of Session variables and the like, uh, somewhat difficult at best. Fortunately, there is a workaround: Have a default.htm page without frames that does nothing but redirect the browser to your main, framed page. The following code shows how the CEO did this for the Electronic Time Card example:
>
> ```html
> <HTML>
>   <HEAD>
>     <META NAME="GENERATOR"
>           Content="Microsoft Visual InterDev 6.0">
>     <META HTTP-EQUIV="Content-Type"
>           content="text/html; charset=iso-8859-1">
>     <META HTTP-EQUIV="Refresh"
>           CONTENT="1; URL=MainFrame.asp">
>      <TITLE>Default Page</TITLE>
>   </HEAD>
>   <BODY>
>
>     <!-- Don't do anything here -->
>
>   </BODY>
> </HTML>
> ```

User Interface

Because the CEO was limited to using HTML on the client, this dictated what kinds of controls he could use. Fortunately, the user interface is not complicated. All users will log in using the page shown in Figure 9.2. Employees will fill in their time cards using text boxes and input buttons, as shown in Figure 9.4. Clients will use check boxes to authorize time cards, as shown in Figure 9.7. Finally, the administrator will navigate via standard HTML page links to various administration pages and use text boxes and buttons to accomplish many tasks. Figure 9.11 shows a sample administration page.

Navigation

There is very little in the way of complex links on this site, so navigation is handled in a simple way. The main element is the Goto Time Card link on the logo frame. This allows the user to navigate back to the TimeCard page regardless of where the user is on the site. Otherwise, navigation is handled by the browser's Forward and Back buttons and by standard HTML links, such as those implemented in the administration menu (see Figure 9.12).

FIGURE 9.11

A sample administration page: Group Administration.

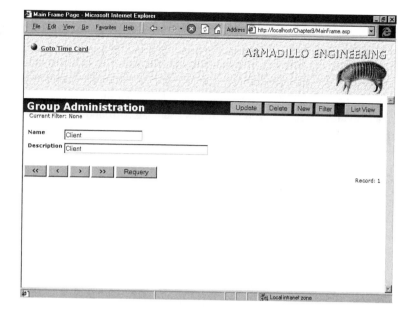

FIGURE 9.12

The Database Maintenance Menu page.

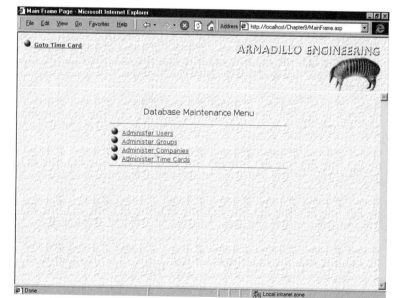

9

CREATING A
SECURE
APPLICATION

The Server Side

The server side is where most of the action is happening. The ASP source files all have server-side scripting in them that creates the client-side HTML dynamically. For example, Listing 9.2 shows an abbreviated ASP file for the time card input verification page, whereas Listing 9.3 shows the client-side HTML that the server-side code created, again in abbreviated form. The full text of this code can be found on the CD accompanying this book. Figure 9.13 shows how this page is displayed.

LISTING 9.2 THE ABBREVIATED ASP CODE FOR THE TIME CARD INPUT VERIFICATION PAGE

```
<%@ LANGUAGE="VBSCRIPT" %>

<HTML>
<HEAD>
<META NAME="GENERATOR" Content="Microsoft Visual InterDev 6.0">
<META HTTP-EQUIV="Content-Type"
      content="text/html; charset=iso-8859-1">
<TITLE>Employee Time Card Verification Page</TITLE>
</HEAD>
<BODY>

<BODY BACKGROUND = "images/Backgrnd.gif" BGCOLOR = "#FFFFFF"
      LEFTMARGIN = "10" TOPMARGIN = "10">

    <FONT SIZE="5" FACE="Trebuchet MS, Verdana, Arial, Helvetica">
        <B>Employee Time Card Verification.</B>
    </FONT>

    <HR>

<%
    ' keep track of records added
    nRecords = 0

    ' open database connection
    Set dbChapter9 = Server.CreateObject("ADODB.Connection")
    dbChapter9.Open Session("Chapter9_ConnectionString")

    nHours = CInt(Request("Sun1")) + CInt(Request("Mon1"))
    nHours = nHours + CInt(Request("Tue1")) + CInt(Request("Wed1"))
    nHours = nHours + CInt(Request("Thu1")) + CInt(Request("Fri1"))
    nHours = nHours + CInt(Request("Sat1"))

    If nHours > 0 Then

        ' create the SQL string
        strSQL = "INSERT INTO TimeCard(EmployeeID, CompanyID,
                    WeekEnding, Description, "
```

```
        strSQL = strSQL & "Sun, Mon, Tue, Wed, Thu, Fri,
                          Sat, Authorized) "
        strSQL = strSQL & "Values(" & Session("UserID") & ", " &
                   Request("CompanyID") & ", '"
        strSQL = strSQL & Request("WeekEnding") & "', '" &
                   Request("Description1") & "', "
        strSQL = strSQL & Request("Sun1") & ", " & Request("Mon1")
                          & ", "
        strSQL = strSQL & Request("Tue1") & ", " & Request("Wed1")
                          & ", "
        strSQL = strSQL & Request("Thu1") & ", " & Request("Fri1")
                          & ", "
        strSQL = strSQL & Request("Sat1") & ", 'N')"

        ' execute the SQL command
        Set rsResults = dbChapter9.Execute(strSQL)

        nRecords = nRecords + 1

    End If


...
and so on for each day
...

    <CENTER>

    <P>
    <TABLE ALIGN = CENTER WIDTH = 90%>
        <TR>
<%
            ' create the SQL string
            strSQL = "SELECT FirstName, LastName FROM User
                     WHERE UserID = " & Session("UserID")

            ' execute the SQL command
            Set rsResults = dbChapter9.Execute(strSQL)
%>
            <FONT SIZE = "4"
                  FACE="Trebuchet MS, Verdana, Arial, Helvetica">

            <TD ALIGN = LEFT>
                <B>Employee: </B><% = rsResults("FirstName") %> 
                                 <% = rsResults("LastName") %>>
            </TD>
<%
            ' create the SQL string
```

continues

9

CREATING A SECURE APPLICATION

LISTING 9.2 CONTINUED

```
                strSQL = "SELECT Name FROM Company WHERE CompanyID = "
                        & Request("CompanyID")

                ' execute the SQL command
                Set rsResults = dbChapter9.Execute(strSQL)
%>

                <TD ALIGN = CENTER>
                    <B>Client: </B> <% = rsResults("Name") %>
                </TD>

                <TD ALIGN = RIGHT>
<%                  strDate = DateAdd("w", -WeekDay(Now), Now)
                    strWeekEnding = Left(strDate, InStr(strDate, " "))
%>
                    <B>Week Ending: </B><% = strWeekEnding %>
                </TD>

                </FONT>
            </TR>

        </TABLE>
        </P>

        <P>
        <TABLE ALIGN = CENTER WIDTH = 90% CELLPADDING=10 CELLSPACING=2>
            <TR BGCOLOR="#000000">
                <TH>
                    <FONT SIZE = "4" FACE = "Trebuchet MS, Verdana,
                        Arial, Helvetica" COLOR="#FFFFFF">
                    Description
                    </FONT>
                </TH>
                <TH>
                    <FONT SIZE = "4" FACE = "Trebuchet MS, Verdana,
                        Arial, Helvetica" COLOR="#FFFFFF">
                    Sun
                    </FONT>
                </TH>
...
and so on for each day
...
<%      For x = 1 To nRecords %>
        <TR>
            <TD ALIGN = CENTER BGCOLOR="#FFFFB3">
                <FONT SIZE = "3" FACE = "Trebuchet MS, Verdana,
                    Arial, Helvetica" COLOR = "#000000">
<%
```

```
                    strTarget = "Description" & x
                    Response.Write(Request(strTarget))
    %>

                    </FONT>
              </TD>

              <TD ALIGN = CENTER BGCOLOR="#FFFFB3">
                    <FONT SIZE = "3" FACE = "Trebuchet MS, Verdana,
                        Arial, Helvetica" COLOR = "#000000">
    <%

                    strTarget = "Sun" & x
                    Response.Write(Request(strTarget))
    %>
              </TD>
    ...
    and so on for each day
    ...
    </TR>
    <%      Next %>

       </TABLE>
       </P>

       </CENTER>

       <HR>

       <FONT SIZE="4" FACE="Trebuchet MS, Verdana, Arial, Helvetica">
           <B>Number of records added: </B> <% = nRecords %>
       </font>

    <%
       ' close the connection
       dbChapter9.Close
    %>

    </BODY>
    </HTML>
```

LISTING 9.3   THE HTML CODE PRODUCED BY THE CODE IN LISTING 9.2 FOR THE TIME
CARD INPUT VERIFICATION PAGE

```
<HTML>
<HEAD>
<META NAME="GENERATOR" Content="Microsoft Visual InterDev 6.0">
<META HTTP-EQUIV="Content-Type"
      content="text/html; charset=iso-8859-1">
<TITLE>Employee Time Card Verification Page</TITLE>
```

continues

LISTING 9.3 CONTINUED

```
</HEAD>
<BODY>

<BODY BACKGROUND="images/Backgrnd.gif" BGCOLOR="#FFFFFF"
      LEFTMARGIN="10" TOPMARGIN = "10">

    <FONT SIZE="5" FACE="Trebuchet MS, Verdana, Arial, Helvetica">
        <B>
            Employee Time Card Verification.
        </B>
    </FONT>

    <HR>


    <CENTER>

    <P>
    <TABLE ALIGN = CENTER WIDTH = 90%>
        <TR>

            <FONT SIZE = "4" FACE="Trebuchet MS, Verdana, Arial,
                Helvetica">

            <TD ALIGN = LEFT>
                <B>Employee: </B>Michael Marsh
            </TD>


            <TD ALIGN = CENTER>
                <B>Client: </B> Armadillo Zoo
            </TD>

            <TD ALIGN = RIGHT>

                <B>Week Ending: </B>3/22/97
            </TD>

            </FONT>
        </TR>

    </TABLE>
    </P>

    <P>
    <TABLE ALIGN = CENTER WIDTH = 90% CELLPADDING=10 CELLSPACING=2>
        <TR BGCOLOR="#000000">
            <TH>
```

```
                <FONT SIZE = "4" FACE = "Trebuchet MS, Verdana,
                    Arial, Helvetica" COLOR="#FFFFFF">
                  Description
                </FONT>
            </TH>
            <TH>
                <FONT SIZE = "4" FACE = "Trebuchet MS, Verdana,
                    Arial, Helvetica" COLOR="#FFFFFF">
                  Sun
                </FONT>
            </TH>
...
and so on for each day
...

        <TR>
            <TD ALIGN = CENTER BGCOLOR="#FFFFB3">
                <FONT SIZE = "3" FACE = "Trebuchet MS, Verdana,
                    Arial, Helvetica" COLOR = "#000000">
                  Program maintenance
                </FONT>
            </TD>

            <TD ALIGN = CENTER BGCOLOR="#FFFFB3">
                <FONT SIZE = "3" FACE = "Trebuchet MS, Verdana,
                    Arial, Helvetica" COLOR = "#000000">
                  0
                </FONT>
            </TD>

...
and so on for each day
...

        </TR>

    </TABLE>
    </P>

    </CENTER>

    <HR>

    <FONT SIZE="4" FACE="Trebuchet MS, Verdana, Arial, Helvetica">
        <B>Number of records added: </B> 1
    </FONT>

</BODY>
</HTML>
```

FIGURE 9.13

*The time card
input verification
page displayed
from the code in
Listing 9.3.*

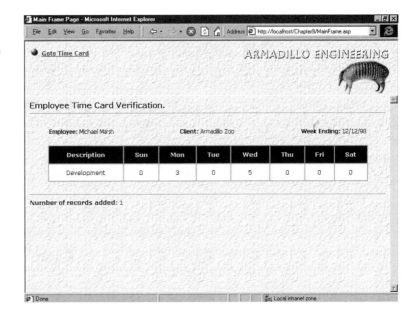

The Database Connection

The Electronic Time Card application uses a file DSN to communicate with the Access
database. Figure 9.14 shows the ODBC applet displaying this DSN.

FIGURE **9.14**

*The ODBC
Control Panel
applet displaying
the database's file
DSN.*

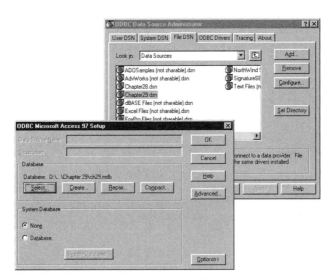

Listing 9.4 shows the GLOBAL.ASA that was modified by Visual InterDev when the CEO added the data connection.

LISTING 9.4   GLOBAL.ASA FOR THE ELECTRONIC TIME CARD APPLICATION

```
<SCRIPT LANGUAGE="VBScript" RUNAT="Server">

</SCRIPT>

<SCRIPT LANGUAGE=VBScript RUNAT=Server>

Sub Session_OnStart

'==Visual InterDev Generated - DataConnection startspan==

    '--Project Data Connection
    Session("Chapter9_ConnectionString") = "DBQ=C:\InetPub\WWWRoot\
    Chapter9\ch9.mdb;
    DefaultDir=C:\InetPub\WWWRoot\Chapter9;
    Driver={Microsoft Access Driver (*.mdb)};DriverId=25;
    FIL=MS Access;ImplicitCommitSync=Yes;MaxBufferSize=512;
    MaxScanRows=8;PageTimeout=5;SafeTransactions=0;Threads=3;
    UID=admin;UserCommitSync=Yes;"

    Session("Chapter9_ConnectionTimeout") = 15
    Session("Chapter9_CommandTimeout") = 30
    Session("Chapter9_RuntimeUserName") = "admin"
    Session("Chapter9_RuntimePassword") = ""

'==Visual InterDev Generated - DataConnection endspan==

    ' Session-wide variables to keep track of the user
    Session("UserName") = ""
    Session("UserGreetingName") = ""
    Session("UserID") = -1
    Session("Admin") = False

    ' Prevents a jump into the site w/o logging in
    if UserName = "" then
        Response.Redirect("MainFrame.asp")
    end if

End Sub

</SCRIPT>
```

Often it is much easier to hand-code certain pieces of a Visual InterDev application, particularly if the wizards provided don't create the things that you need. This was the case for the CEO in several places in the application. He needed to be able to access the database without the luxury of a wizard to write the code for him. Listing 9.5 shows an example of how he accomplishes database access by hand.

TIP

Notice that in Listing 9.5 all the script code happens before the <HTML> tag. This is so that the redirection to the appropriate pages will work. Remember that you can redirect only before you've written anything to the header of the page.

LISTING 9.5 LOGINVERIFICATION.ASP—AN EXAMPLE OF ACCESSING THE DATABASE BY HAND-CODING

```
<%@ LANGUAGE="VBSCRIPT" %>

<SCRIPT RUNAT=Server LANGUAGE="VBScript">

' this function cleans up spaces and NULLs in a string
Function ConvertNull(varTemp)
    If IsNull(varTemp) Then
        ConvertNull = ""
    Else
        ConvertNull = Trim(varTemp)
    End If
End Function

</SCRIPT>

<%
' open database connection
Set dbChapter9 = Server.CreateObject("ADODB.Connection")
dbChapter9.Open Session("Chapter9_ConnectionString")

' create the SQL string
strSQL = "SELECT UserID, UserName, GreetingName FROM User "
strSQL = strSQL & "WHERE UserName = '" &
                ConvertNull(Request.Form("UserName"))
strSQL = strSQL & "' AND Password = '" &
                ConvertNull(Request.Form("Password")) & "'"

' execute the SQL command
Set rsResults = dbChapter9.Execute(strSQL)

' see whether any records are returned
```

```
nCount = 0
While rsResults.EOF = False
    nCount = nCount + 1
    rsResults.MoveNext
Wend

If nCount = 0 Then
    Response.Redirect("Login.asp?Result=Failed")
Else
    rsResults.MoveFirst
    Session("UserName") = Request.Form("UserName")
    Session("UserGreetingName") = rsResults("GreetingName")
    Session("UserID") = rsResults("UserID")
    Response.Redirect("TimeCard.asp")
End If

dbChapter9.Close
%>

<HTML>
<HEAD>
<META NAME="GENERATOR" Content="Microsoft Visual InterDev 1.0">
<META HTTP-EQUIV="Content-Type"
      content="text/html; charset=iso-8859-1">
<TITLE>Login Verification Page</TITLE>
</HEAD>
<BODY>

</BODY>
</HTML>
```

Preventing Jumps Around the Login Page

A closer look at Listing 9.4, the GLOBAL.ASA file, shows that the CEO used a technique outlined in Chapter 8 to prevent a user from jumping past the login page. The little bit of code toward the end of the file checks whether the user has logged on and, if not, redirects the user to the login page. Again, this works because all the pages in this site are ASP, with the exception of the do-nothing DEFAULT.HTM page.

Keeping Track of the User

The GLOBAL.ASA file also declares Session variables to keep track of the user. In the file LOGINVERIFICATION.ASP in Listing 9.5, the user information Session variables are set on successful login. The variables are used in other places, for example, to greet the user with a friendly name in the time card input page.

Applying Security

Much of the application's security is handled within the application itself. The application prevents a user from accessing the system without logging in; after the user has logged in, it prevents that user from accessing anything other than what membership in the user's group allows. This, coupled with the physical setup of the system (just described) gave the CEO a sufficient comfort level with security while providing the necessary ease of access for the system's users.

> **CAUTION**
>
> The CEO's comfort level with this security might have had more to do with Accounting pressuring him for a solution than his thinking through the security implications. Although it is convenient to think that your application is limiting access to sensitive data, the fact is that you are distributing the code for your client on the Internet. It can be intercepted and used by an attacker to gain access. As you will see later on, however, an even more serious breach of security exists with this system.

Logging In

When users first enter the system, they are presented with the login page (refer to Figure 9.2). Users type in their username and password and then click the Submit button. The code, shown in Listing 9.6, uses the <FORM> tag to transfer control to the login verification page (refer to Listing 9.5). The login verification page code uses the Request object to retrieve the values from the UserName and Password variables and then uses these to query the database for a valid user.

LISTING 9.6   LOGIN.ASP

```
<%@ LANGUAGE="VBSCRIPT" %>

<HTML>
<HEAD>
<META NAME="GENERATOR" Content="Microsoft Visual InterDev 6.0">
<META HTTP-EQUIV="Content-Type"
     content="text/html; charset=iso-8859-1">
<TITLE>Login Page</TITLE>
</HEAD>
```

```
<BODY>

<BODY background="images/backgrnd.gif" bgcolor="#FFFFFF">

<% If Request.QueryString("Result") = "Failed" then %>
    <FONT SIZE="4" FACE="Trebuchet MS, Verdana, Arial,
                        Helvetica" color="#FF0000">
        <BR> 
        <B>Incorrect username or password. Please try again.</B>
    </FONT>
<% End If %>

<FORM ACTION="LoginVerification.asp" METHOD=POST>

<TABLE BORDER=0 CELLPADDING=5 CELLSPACING=0 WIDTH=500>

    <TR WIDTH = 500>

        <TD>
            <P ALIGN="LEFT">
                <FONT SIZE="5" FACE="Trebuchet MS, Verdana, Arial,
                                    Helvetica">
                    <B>Please Log In</B>
                </FONT>
            </P>
        </TD>

    </TR>

    <TR>
        <FONT SIZE = "4" FACE="Trebuchet MS, Verdana, Arial,
            Helvetica">
            <TD ALIGN = RIGHT>
                <B> User Name: </B>
            </TD>
            <TD ALIGN = LEFT>
                <INPUT NAME="UserName" SIZE=20>
            </TD>
        </FONT>
    </TR>

    <TR>
        <FONT SIZE = "4" FACE="Trebuchet MS, Verdana, Arial,
            Helvetica">
            <TD ALIGN = "RIGHT">
                <B> Password: </B>
            </TD>
            <TD ALIGN = "LEFT">
```

continues

LISTING 9.6   CONTINUED

```
                <INPUT NAME="Password" SIZE="20" TYPE="PASSWORD">
            </TD>
        </FONT>
    </TR>

    <TR>
        <FONT SIZE = "4" FACE="Trebuchet MS, Verdana, Arial,
            Helvetica">
            <TD ALIGN = "RIGHT">
            </TD>
            <TD ALIGN = "LEFT">
                <INPUT NAME="Submit" TYPE="SUBMIT">
                <INPUT NAME="Reset" TYPE="RESET">
            </TD>
        </FONT>
    </TR>

</TABLE>

</FORM>

</BODY>
</HTML>
```

If the login data is not in the database, the login is invalid, and the user is redirected back to the login page with the QueryString variable set to Result=Failed. The login page is redisplayed, this time with a message in red indicating that the login failed.

If the login data does exist in the database, the login is valid; the user information Session variables are updated, and the user is redirected to the TIMECARD.ASP page.

Listing 9.7 is a part of TIMECARD.ASP that shows how the CEO redirects a user to a page, based on the user's group membership.

LISTING 9.7   PORTIONS OF TIMECARD.ASP

```
<%
    ' open database connection
    Set dbChapter9 = Server.CreateObject("ADODB.Connection")
    dbChapter9.Open Session("Chapter9_ConnectionString")

    ' create the SQL string
    strSQL = "SELECT `Group`.Name FROM UserGroupList, `User`,
            `Group` "
    strSQL = strSQL & "WHERE UserGroupList.UserID =
                    `User`.UserID "
```

```
        strSQL = strSQL & "AND UserGroupList.GroupID =
                            `Group`.GroupID AND "
        strSQL = strSQL & "`User`.UserID = " & Session("UserID")

        ' execute the SQL command
        Set rsResults = dbChapter9.Execute(strSQL)

        ' store the result
        strUserType = rsResults("Name")

        ' close the connection
        dbChapter9.Close

        ' set up the rest of the page depending on group membership
        Select Case strUserType
            Case "Administrator"
                Session("Admin") = True
%>
        <!-- #INCLUDE FILE="EmployeeTimeCard.asp" -->
<%      Case "Client"
                Session("Admin") = False
%>
        <!-- #INCLUDE FILE="ClientTimeCard.asp" -->
<%      Case "Employee"
                Session("Admin") = False
%>
        <!-- #INCLUDE FILE="EmployeeTimeCard.asp" -->
<%      Case Else
                Session("Admin") = False
%>
                Error<BR>
<% End Select %>

<HR>

<%      if Session("Admin") = True Then %>
        <!-- #INCLUDE FILE="AdminNavigation.asp" -->
<%      End If %>
```

Why Not Let NT Do It?

The CEO initially toyed with the idea of using NT Challenge/Response, in addition to the application-level users and groups. The idea was to match the application users and groups with identical ones added using the User Manager for Domains program. That way, he could let NT itself handle the login chores, and he would simply query the system for the user information needed for his database queries. Because NT Challenge/Response uses a token to communicate with the client, the username and password never go out on the net. This would provide very good security indeed. The trouble is that only one of his three customers has browsers that would work with NT Challenge/Response, so he scrapped the idea.

This is an unhappy circumstance because the CEO knows that user login information, including passwords, is going out unencrypted over the net. He is concerned about this, but not overly so, because his system is small and nobody would be that interested in his data. Still, the CEO plans to obtain a Digital Server Certificate and implement SSL for his site. This would solve the encryption problem, but would entail rewriting some of the code. He would have to check whether the SSL handshake failed and, in that case, revert to the old system so that no users are locked out. He could easily parse the client certificate for the user information needed to verify the login. This is the next feature that the CEO is going to implement.

CAUTION

This is the most serious breach of security in this system. User information, including passwords, is going out on the net, which is an invitation to a site hack. The CEO recognizes this, but for expediency, ignores the issue for now. SSL will solve the CEO's major security problem, but his thinking about reverting to the old system is flawed: At a minimum, he should use some sort of encryption on the password. One solution would be to use the CryptoAPI for encryption algorithms. Alternatively, he could insist that any client trying to access his system must indeed use SSL. Most modern clients can do this, so it would not be a great burden on his users.

Thinking that his site is small, unadvertised, and therefore uninteresting is a curious net fallacy. Although it could be true (but not necessarily!) that professional spies and criminal hackers might bypass his site for something more interesting, it is certainly not true that his site might not be attractive to vandals. If it is easy to hack, they will hack it! There is no anonymity for sites on the Web: Remember, it is a public network!

Database Security

Access 97 implements users and groups, but the CEO thought this might be overkill for his first implementation. He could also have changed the RuntimeUserName in GLOBAL.ASA with an Access user having the appropriate restrictions, but then decided that this would complicate the code in the case of the Administrator. He decided to let all users have administration rights to the database and to protect his data within his application instead.

> **CAUTION**
>
> Again, in the name of expediency, the CEO has exposed himself to some risk. Access97's users and groups are, indeed, as powerful as he surmised. There would have been no complication in the code had he added users and groups to his database that matched those in his application. At a minimum, he should have used a different RuntimeUserName. Giving everyone administration access to the database gives everyone the power to do anything to the data. If an attacker gains access to his system, his data is left extremely vulnerable.

Summary

The Electronic Time Card application demonstrates some of the security features and techniques available using Visual InterDev. In particular, the system makes heavy use of application-level users and groups to control access to data. The physical setup of this site shows how a small-to-medium Web site might be configured using Microsoft Proxy Server or a similar product.

This sample application and accompanying scenario also point out some common mistakes made when installing a site on the (very public) Internet. I presented some solutions to these mistakes, such as using SSL when sending sensitive data across the net and using the built-in security provided by the database engine.

Finally, this chapter presents some realities of securing a site while still allowing access to your targeted group of users. Other pressures come to bear when you are making design decisions about security. You have seen, in practical terms, how much of a trade-off the relationship between access and security truly is!

9

CREATING A SECURE APPLICATION

Creating Data-Bound Web Applications

PART

II

IN THIS PART

CHAPTER 10

Working with Databases: Universal Data Access

by Paul Thurrott

IN THIS CHAPTER

In mid-1996, Microsoft's Blackbird project—then positioned as a multimedia creation tool for the Microsoft Network—was extensively revamped. Microsoft had caught the Internet bug, and the product, briefly named *Internet Studio* but soon changed to *Visual InterDev*, was repositioned as a way to combine back-end data from database servers such as SQL Server with Web sites. At the time, it was a radical idea, and most Web developers didn't quite get it.

Microsoft was pushing a new concept called the *Web application*. In Microsoft parlance, a Web application includes the collection of HTML and client scripting files most users would call a *Web site* and combines it with server-based scripting (ASP), site management logic, executable programs (ISAPI applications and IIS components), and a way to access information in a database.

Using these technologies, Web applications are *dynamic* (not static like a normal HTML-based Web site) because the content and business logic are separated from the HTML user interface. A Web application appears in the browser just like any other Web site, but offers the developer (and content creator) far more powerful options on the back-end. Perhaps most importantly, the need to hand-code and edit HTML pages is becoming a thing of the past. With a dynamic (that is, database-backed) Web application, content creators can use the tools they're most comfortable with and don't have to learn arcane languages such as HTML or JavaScript.

The move toward Web applications created a need for a tool, Visual InterDev, that could make these seemingly disparate technologies come together. However, the move to Web applications also created a major tremor in the then complacent data access industry. The client/server model of yore was suddenly thrust on its behind when the concept of n-tier or multitier applications appeared. With an *n-tier application* (typically three-tier, really), a third position is added to the classic client/server (two-tier) approach so that business logic is separated from the client *and* the server.

The very nature of the Web caused this change. Web clients (*Web browsers* to you) are connected to the server for very short periods of time and then disconnected immediately. More importantly, corporations don't want their business logic on the client (that is, exposed in client-side script that anyone can read). In the n-tier model (see Figure 10.1), the Web client is responsible only for displaying the user interface and making requests of the Web server. The middle tier, represented by the IIS Web server in the NT-based example, responds to requests from clients and acts as a middle man between the client and the database server. Business logic is typically stored in server-side script or executable server components that the user never sees. The client never directly accesses (or even knows about) the third (database server) tier. It's tidy, secure, and responsive.

FIGURE 10.1

An n-tier Web application separates the data source from the client.

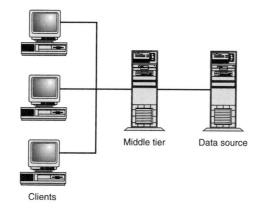

Middle tier   Data source

Clients

Around the time this transition to dynamic Web applications was taking place, Microsoft decided to shore up its data access strategy. Although it's taken a few revisions to get this right, Microsoft is finally delivering a comprehensive *universal* data access strategy that benefits both developers and users. Let's take a look at the current state of affairs and the rocky road we traveled to arrive there.

An Introduction to Microsoft's Universal Data Access Strategy

In the not too distant past, the methods you would use as a developer to access data in a database (or other data provider) depended heavily on the tools you used. Visual Basic developers in particular have been treated to a confusing and constantly changing list of data access methodologies that even the most diligent VB wizards have had trouble keeping up with.

The problem, of course, is the numerous kinds of data. I can quickly rattle off a long list of database applications and servers—including Microsoft SQL Server, Microsoft Access, Microsoft Visual FoxPro, Oracle 7.x, Oracle 8.x, Sybase SQL Server, Informix Dynamic Server/SE, Borland dBase, Borland Paradox, Powersoft PowerBuilder, Lotus Approach, and many others—and this doesn't even include other types of data providers, such as spreadsheets, email messages, and the like.

This can become ugly pretty quickly because all those databases have their own relatively proprietary methods for getting at the data programmatically. Every time you use a different database, you have to figure out the differences, and these can range from being a hassle to an all-out disaster.

Microsoft Open Database Connectivity (ODBC)

The first step to creating a manageable system for working with incompatible types of data was the creation of the Microsoft open database connectivity (ODBC) standard. ODBC defines the grammar rules for accessing data (using a language called SQL, which I discuss later in the chapter), as well as a C-based programming interface to SQL-based databases. The idea (and it's a good one) is to provide a common interface to data so that from the programmer's standpoint, it doesn't matter which database is on the back end. Database-specific drivers must be written, of course, to handle the conversion from ODBC-based interfaces to the database-specific routines that make it all come together (see Figure 10.2). It's comparable to a video driver. The driver abstracts the details of the hardware while providing standard interfaces to the operating system so that the card actually works. As long as the driver exists, you're good to go.

FIGURE 10.2

In the ODBC model, the ODBC library sits between the client and the database.

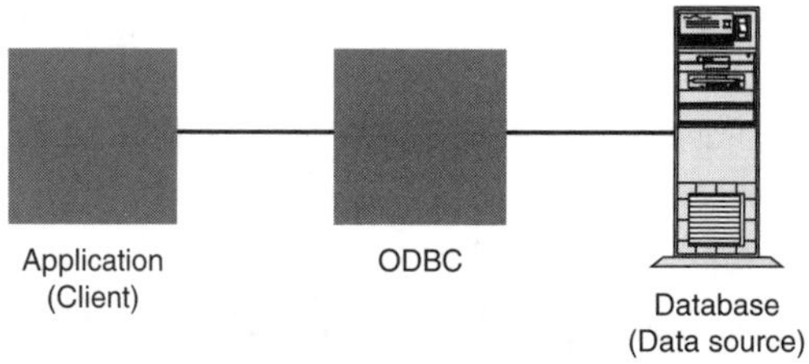

Application
(Client)

ODBC

Database
(Data source)

Developers have had only one big problem with ODBC: It doesn't allow applications to take advantage of the special features of individual databases. Arguments can be made both ways here, but the consensus is that compatibility among all these otherwise incompatible databases is far more important than the ability to take advantage of proprietary features. ODBC also frees developers to use the tools of their choice and not be locked into a particular vendor's solution. Oracle makes a powerful database, for example, but to create data-aware applications, most developers would rather use Visual Basic than Oracle's own tools. ODBC is the great equalizer.

ODBC has another weakness, however: It's hard to develop drivers for nondatabase data sources, because ODBC relies on the relational representation of data that most databases use. Something else was needed to take ODBC to the next level.

That something is OLE DB.

OLE DB

OLE DB is a Component Object Model–based (COM) alternative (and eventual replacement) to ODBC that provides the same sort of low-level interfaces to data that made ODBC famous. However, because it is built from reusable COM components, OLE

DB is expected to usher in an era of new componentized data sources, while providing backward compatibility with the monolithic databases we all know and love.

OLE DB wouldn't be a Microsoft technology if it didn't introduce its own special brand of terminology. In OLE DB, a data source (such as a database) is called a data *provider* or *component*. On the client side, the Visual Basic program, ASP page, and so on, that accesses the data is called a *consumer*.

OLE DB (see Figure 10.3) was developed to facilitate the creation of n-tier applications, while providing a more componentized interface for numerous types of data providers, including nonrelational data sources. Like ODBC, OLE DB is a low-level technology that exposes a rather ugly API for C and C++ programmers to access. Visual Basic users, and by extension, ASP developers such as you, access the benefits of OLE DB through ActiveX Data Objects (ADO), a simple object model that was written with Visual Basic in mind.

FIGURE 10.3

With OLE DB, data consumers access data providers directly or through an ODBC provider for OLE DB.

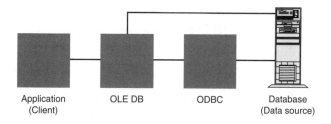

| Application (Client) | OLE DB | ODBC | Database (Data source) |

An interesting side note is that the very first OLE DB data providers were, in fact, ODBC data sources. Realizing that developers wouldn't embrace the new technology unless it was compatible with the widely accepted ODBC, Microsoft created the OLE DB provider for ODBC drivers so that ADO users could access familiar ODBC data sources. In fact, when ADO 1.0 shipped with Internet Information Server (IIS) 3.0, the only OLE DB providers were simple wrappers over the existing ODBC data sources. This was by design, of course. To get developers to move away from ODBC, the new technology had to be backward compatible.

Because there are already ODBC drivers for SQL Server, Microsoft Access, and every other major database product out there, OLE DB consumers have immediate access to the data sources already created. Frankly, ODBC will be around for some time to come. Even though OLE DB is a great concept, it lacks the universal (that is, non-Windows) support that greeted ODBC, because OLE DB is heavily tied to Windows-specific technologies such as COM and ActiveX.

10

WORKING WITH DATABASES

> **NOTE**
>
> Interestingly, Microsoft has created a native OLE DB provider for SQL Server 7.0. This means that you can create a data source for your SQL Server databases using either the existing ODBC driver or the new OLE DB driver. Microsoft did this to support the new Data Transformation Services in SQL Server 7.0. Because you can easily import data into SQL Server and work with it as if it were in its own native data format, SQL Server 7.0 is both an OLE DB provider and consumer.

All this is merely theory from the Web developer's point of view, however. OLE DB doesn't do anything tangible; it just provides the low-level interfaces that make connecting to data easy from ADO. Now take a look at ADO, which is something you will work with every day as you develop Web applications.

ActiveX Data Objects (ADO)

When it comes to data access from Active Server Pages, ActiveX Data Objects (ADO) is the object-based interface of choice. ADO is an object model in the sense that it provides a logical set of objects you can access from code. These objects, explained in Table 10.1 and in upcoming chapters, present an interface in the form of properties and methods that can be queried and manipulated. Microsoft has come up with a variety of Visual Basic–based data access object models over the years, but ADO is the future. If you're an ASP developer, it's really all you have. This is good news, frankly, because ADO was specifically developed to be small, lightweight, fast, and feature complete—everything you need when you're programming for the Internet.

TABLE 10.1 ADO OBJECTS

Object	What It Does
Connection	Manages the connection with the data source
Command	Defines the commands that will be executed against the data source
Recordset	Contains the data that is retrieved from the data source

ADO is a nonhierarchical object model in the sense that the objects in the object model are not dependent on one another (see Figure 10.4). This means that you can create instances of objects independently of one another (you can create a Recordset object without first explicitly creating a Connection object, for example). Older object models such as Data Access Objects (DAO) and Remote Data Objects (RDO) aren't this flexible, requiring a specific coding sequence and style. Because ADO de-emphasizes the hierarchy (and relationship) of the objects, ADO code is easier to write, read, and maintain.

FIGURE 10.4

ADO sits between OLE DB and your Web application.

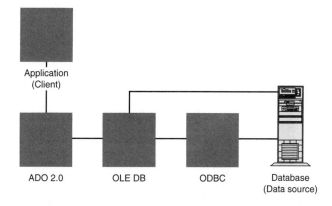

Application
(Client)

ADO 2.0   OLE DB   ODBC   Database
(Data source)

NOTE

By definition, ADO is not object oriented, but rather object based. ASP, like Visual Basic, doesn't support the more advanced features of an object-oriented programming language, such as inheritance. This isn't a huge shortcoming, however. ADO, like ASP and Visual Basic, was designed to do a job as easily and quickly as possible. Thus, the ADO object model is an excellent example of function over form.

ADO began its life with the release of IIS 3.0 in late 1996. It was updated to ADO 1.5 in late 1997, with minor updates (1.5a, 1.5b, and so on) appearing throughout the next year with various products such as the Windows NT 4.0 Option Pack. In September 1998, Visual Studio 6.0 introduced ADO 2.0 to an eager public. You can download the latest version of ADO for free from the Microsoft Web site if you're still using an older version of Visual Studio or want to update the data access components on a Web server that doesn't have Visual Studio installed. Check out `http://www.microsoft.com/data` for details (see Figure 10.5).

10

WORKING WITH DATABASES

FIGURE 10.5

Microsoft's Universal Data Access Web site contains all the latest information about ODBC, OLE DB, and ADO.

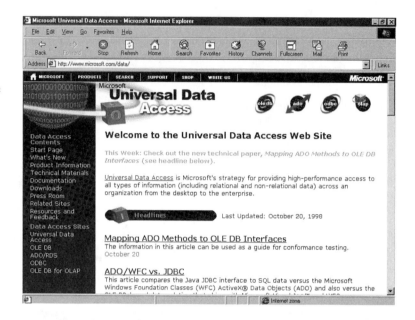

ADO 2.0 is an important release for Microsoft because it represents the first version of this object model that matches and finally surpasses previous Data Access Object (DAO) models. ADO even supports the ability to move data from the server to a Web client using Remote Data Services (RDS), although the only browser that currently supports this is Internet Explorer 4.0+. If anything, ADO is deceptively simple. Although it's not immediately obvious, the linear object model is surprisingly capable. Chapter 11, "Using the Visual Database Tools," contains a detailed look at ADO 2.0.

Connecting to Data

Before you can use the data in a database, you must be able to establish a connection. This can be accomplished with a variety of methods, including ODBC data source names (DSN), OLE DB data links, and the so-called DSN-less connection, where you provide enough information in your code to connect to a database.

Using ODBC Data Source Names

To connect to data using ODBC, you can use an ODBC data source name (DSN). A *data source* is a link or pointer to data that specifies the information required to access that data, including the username, password, and other data source–specific information. A *DSN*, which identifies a data source, abstracts the connection to the data source so that you can focus on working with the data that it refers to.

You access DSNs through the ODBC Data Source Administrator applet in the Windows NT Control Panel, shown in Figure 10.6.

FIGURE 10.6

The ODBC Data Source Administrator enables you to create and modify data source names.

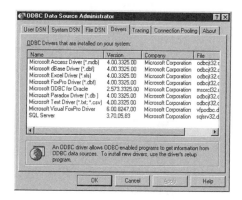

You can create the following three kinds of DSNs from this applet:

- User DSN—This type of DSN is available only to the current (interactive) user and is, as such, not compatible with ASP/ADO. In other words, you can't create a user DSN and expect it to work with your Web applications.

- System DSN (machine DSN)—A system DSN is available to all users on the current machine, including NT services, making it ideal for use with ASP/ADO. It's also the fastest type of DSN because the connection information is stored in the Windows Registry.

- File DSN—Like a system DSN, a file DSN is available to all users on the current system. However, a file DSN is written to a plain text file that must be opened and closed each time it is accessed. This is a slow operation and, therefore, it's not recommended that you use file DSNs. On the other hand, building a file DSN can be helpful if you have to create a DSN-less connection because it provides the information you need for that connection.

When Visual Studio 1.0 first appeared and Microsoft began preaching the benefits of ASP and ADO, the company claimed that file DSNs were faster than system DSNs. I was positive this wasn't true, and, sure enough, by the time that work began on Visual Studio 6.0, the tune had changed: Microsoft now acknowledges that system DSNs are at least three times faster than file DSNs! That's reason enough to never use a file DSN.

One small problem with a system DSN is that you must be able to physically access the machine to create the DSN, as in Figure 10.7. This probably won't be a serious issue for most users, however, and remote Web servers will probably be accessible via tools such as PC Anywhere. If you're really lucky, you won't have to create a data source yourself but can instead ask a database administrator to do it for you.

10

WORKING WITH DATABASES

FIGURE 10.7

The System DSN page of the ODBC Data Source Administrator enables to you add, remove, or configure system DSNs.

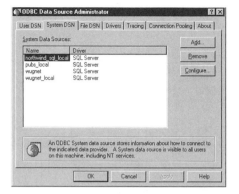

The other 99% of us, however, will have to create our own DSNs. To create a system DSN (see Figure 10.8), launch the Control Panel ODBC applet on the Web server (or development machine) and navigate to the System DSN page. Click the Add button and choose the correct driver for the database you will be using.

FIGURE 10.8

The first step of the Create New Data Source Wizard presents a list of application data providers.

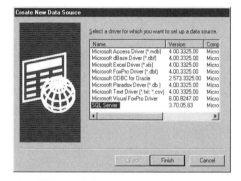

TIP

If you're working with Visual InterDev, you can also create a DSN by adding a data connection to your current project. This will prompt you to choose an existing DSN or create a new one as shown in Figure 10.7. Note that the Select Data Source dialog that appears includes only two tabs: one for System DSN and one for File DSN.

Generally speaking, SQL Server is the only viable Microsoft database engine for use with production Web sites (Oracle works well, too), but it's possible you will use Access during internal development. With the release of SQL Server 7.0, though, there's little reason to use Access anymore. All the user interface benefits of Access are equaled by the tools in Visual Studio 6.0, and SQL Server 7.0 now runs on Windows 95 and 98, making it an obvious choice for the client *and* the server (talk about scalability!). All the examples in this section of the book use SQL Server 6.5 or 7.0.

The second step for creating a system DSN to a SQL Server database requires that you identify the SQL Server, as in Figure 10.9. This server can be on the same machine as the Web server or, more appropriately, on any other machine on the network or the Internet. You can use the SQL Server's machine name if it's on the local network or use its IP address in either case. Using the IP address is the quickest method.

FIGURE 10.9

The second step of the wizard prompts you to identify the SQL Server.

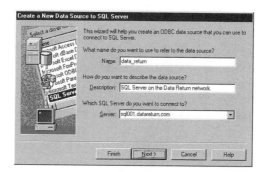

After you've established the name and location of the SQL Server database, the DSN Administrator will want to know how you plan to log in to the database. This login can be established through integrated Windows NT authentication if you're on the same network or by manually supplying a username and password to use SQL Server authentication. Enter the required information (SQL Server authentication is faster) and make sure that the client configuration is set up to use the TCP/IP network library. When you click the Next button, ODBC will try to establish a connection to SQL Server using the information you provided. If everything is okay, you will move on to the next step. Otherwise, you will see the nasty dialog shown in Figure 10.10, and it's back to the drawing board. The next section explains what to do when you can't establish a data source name.

FIGURE 10.10

The Connection Failed message in the Microsoft SQL Server Login dialog box.

The next step enables you to choose the default database and set some other options. The final step presents various advanced options, including the ability to log queries to a text file. Don't ever do this in a production setting unless you're experiencing some kind of problem. Writing to a text file is an expensive (in time and CPU usage) operation.

When you click the Finish button, you're given a chance to test the DSN. You should always do this before creating the DSN, because it's a quick and easy way to make sure you've supplied the right information. If the DSN is set up correctly (see Figure 10.11), the test will succeed, and you can start using the DSN with your Visual InterDev Web applications. Otherwise, you will be thrown into a hideous death spiral affectionately known as ODBC Hell (see Figure 10.12). But fear not, every problem has a solution. In the following section, you will take a look at what can go wrong and what you can do to make it right.

FIGURE 10.11

This is what you're looking for. Don't quit the wizard until the test works successfully.

FIGURE 10.12

Oh, the pain. Any number of things can go wrong to cause your DSN to malfunction.

Troubleshooting ODBC Connections

If you receive a `Test failed` message at the end of the New ODBC Data Source Wizard or another dialog box elsewhere in the wizard that indicates that something is wrong, the problem has to do with the connection options you entered or with the network library you're using. For Web applications, you should always use TCP/IP, not the default, Named Pipes. You can set the default network library in a couple places (see Figures 10.13 and 10.14). If you're in the middle of the wizard, the second step has a Client Configuration button that will let you set the network library. Otherwise, the SQL Server Client Network Utility that comes with SQL Server 7.0 can be used (called the SQL Client Configuration Utility in SQL Server 6.5, but it does the same thing). The SQL Server Client Network Utility should be run on the machine that contains the SQL Server, as well as any development workstations that might connect to the server.

FIGURE 10.13

While navigating through the wizard, you can set which default network library to use when connecting to the SQL Server.

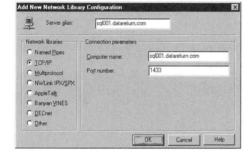

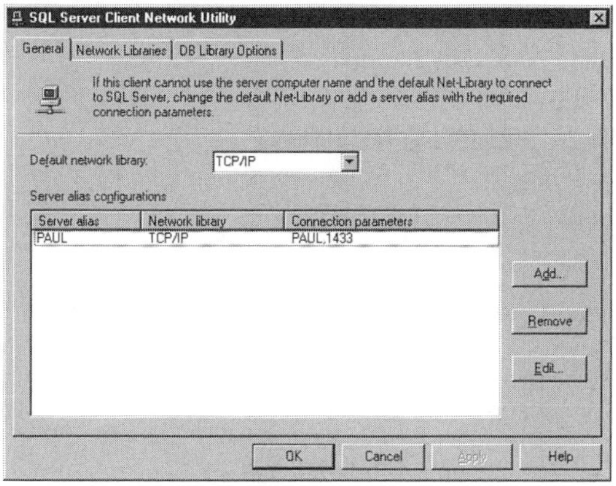

FIGURE 10.14

It's always a good idea to make sure TCP/IP is the default network library when using the SQL Server Client Network Utility.

One often overlooked problem: The SQL Server is unavailable because either it's offline currently or if things have really gone downhill, it's crashed. This will result in a SQL Server not found message. You can test the connection to SQL Server 7.0 by running the Enterprise Manager tool that comes with SQL Server and attempting to connect that way. If that doesn't work, check with the DBA. Those guys love to communicate with the outside world every now and then.

If you see the message Login failed for user "[username]", this probably means that you're trying to use Windows NT authentication with a user ID that isn't mapped to a SQL Server user ID. Try logging in with a specific SQL Server username and password instead. Another obvious problem: Your username and/or password were not correctly entered.

You will also run into problems with ODBC data sources and the ADO code you write. These problems are addressed in Chapter 11. In general, if you receive a TESTS COMPLETED SUCCESSFULLY message from within the wizard, you're good to go.

Using OLE DB Data Links

Windows NT 4.0 systems with Visual Studio 6.0 or SQL Server 7.0 installed and Windows NT 5.0 systems will have a Data Links applet in the Control Panel, in addition to the ODBC one. As shown in Figure 10.15, this applet creates OLE DB data links, which are conceptually identical to ODBC file DSNs. This applet presents a dialog box with four pages that enables you to create a data link to an OLE DB data provider such as SQL Server 7.0 or any ODBC data source. All this dialog box does is let you map a data link to an existing (or new) ODBC data source or more interestingly, build a connection string to a data source by hand.

FIGURE 10.15

An OLE DB data link is functionally similar to an ODBC file DSN.

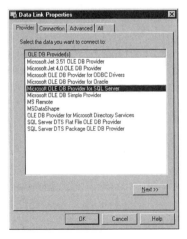

Currently, there's no compelling reason to use a data link instead of an ODBC data source name. It's possible that data links will eventually replace DSNs, but that's still a long way (and a lot of functionality) away from happening.

Working with SQL Server

SQL Server is Microsoft's industrial-strength relational database management system. Version 7.0, which became available in November 1998, adds an interesting wrinkle to this definition, however, because it can also function as a desktop database system comparable to (and compatible with) Microsoft Access. For the purposes of this book and the Web applications you will be working with, SQL Server represents the data source tier of the three-tier system discussed earlier. As a server application that integrates with Windows NT Server, SQL Server performs services for clients written in Visual Basic and other programming languages. When used in conjunction with your ASP-based Web applications, IIS is the client.

SQL Server began its life as a licensed version of the Sybase SQL Server that Microsoft created for OS/2. Microsoft ported the code for SQL Server to Windows NT when work began on that operating system in the early 1990s. The first version of SQL Server for Windows NT was version 4.2 (the first version of Windows NT was 3.1).

Today, Microsoft and Sybase both market a product, called SQL Server, for Windows NT. The Sybase product, however, has taken a back seat to the ever more popular Microsoft version. After its initial rollout, Microsoft released two major versions of SQL Server that were still built on the old Sybase code base, versions 6.0 and 6.5.

In 1998, Microsoft released SQL Server 7.0. This was completely rewritten to take advantage of new technology and upcoming features in Windows NT 5.0, which is due in late 1999 (as of this writing, anyway—Microsoft works loose-and-free with its shipping schedules).

SQL Server 6.5

SQL Server 6.5 for Windows NT shipped in April 1996, after only five months in beta. It proved to be an amazingly stable release and became very popular with NT-based Web sites that wanted to provide dynamic content. The product is designed to handle multiple connections efficiently, and it integrates nicely with the NT Server operating system.

The SQL Server engine is based on the powerful Transact SQL (TSQL) language, a superset of the industry standard Structured Query Language (SQL). Transact SQL extends standard SQL with powerful new extensions and capabilities designed to facilitate new features such as data warehousing and derived tables. The SQL Server 6.5 query

10

WORKING WITH DATABASES

optimizer uses a cost-based algorithm to automatically determine the fastest way to get at the data you're accessing. The SQL Server 6.5 Enterprise Manager is the central management location for this powerful DBMS (see Figure 10.16).

FIGURE 10.16

The SQL Server 6.5 Enterprise Manager.

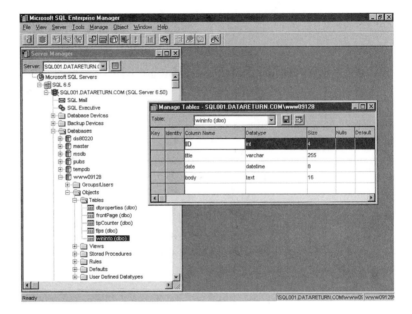

I'm not going to focus on SQL Server 6.5 that much because of the recent release of SQL Server 7.0. On the other hand, all the SQL Server–based code examples in this book will work fine with SQL Server 6.5 as well.

SQL Server 7.0

In development for more than two years, SQL Server 7.0 is one of the most exciting products to come out of Redmond in a long, long time. SQL Server 7.0 not only features backward compatibility with SQL Server 6.5, but also offers numerous enhancements to the architecture, functionality, and development tools in SQL Server. The following summarizes the new features in SQL Server 7.0:

- Dynamic locking with cost-based locking granularity
- Improved query processor
- New Transact SQL statements
- Trigger and cursor enhancements
- Distributed queries
- New data types, including Unicode data types
- Support for Windows 95/98
- Unicode support
- Data warehousing and OLAP services
- More tables and columns per query
- Improved support for very large databases (VLDB)
- Integration with NT security, using new user roles
- Native OLE DB, ADO, ODBC, and SQL-DMO programming interfaces
- Replication enhancements
- *And much more*, as they say

In addition to these features, SQL Server 7.0 sports a new Microsoft Management Console (MMC)-based Enterprise Manager that integrates nicely with the other MMC tools used in the NT 4.0 Option Pack and Windows NT 5.0. Anyone familiar with SQL Server will have no problem adjusting to the new interface, however, because it is very similar to the monolithic Enterprise Manager found in 6.x.

The new MMC-based version of Enterprise Manager exposes many of its administration tasks as easy-to-use wizards. I won't debate the merits of making these sorts of activities easy enough for any end user, but the HTML-based Enterprise Manager wizards are a joy to use (see Figure 10.17). You can always right-click the tree view in the left side of Enterprise Manager to get at functionality the old-fashioned way. SQL Server old-timers might need a few days to recover from the shock of using MMC, but it's a safe bet that most people will be won over by the new interface.

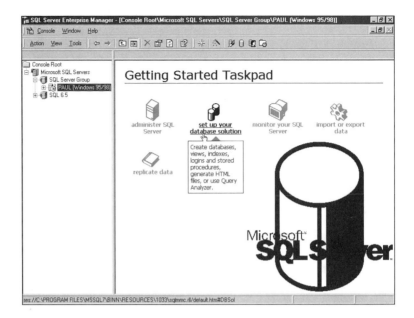

FIGURE **10.17**

*In SQL Server
7.0, Enterprise
Manager func-
tions are exposed
in an MMC-host-
ed snap-in.*

A Transact SQL Overview

As mentioned previously, Transact SQL (TSQL) is the heart of SQL Server. I don't have
the space to provide a full tutorial to TSQL, the native language of SQL Server, but a
short overview will be helpful if you've never come across it before.

> **TIP**
>
> Numerous excellent books about SQL and Transact SQL are available. *SQL Server
> 7.0 Unleashed* and *SQL Server 7.0 Programming Unleashed* by Sams Publishing
> are great places to start.

The original version of SQL was developed by scientists at IBM, and over the years the
language has been adapted to take advantage of modern programming language features.
TSQL, in particular, exposes numerous proprietary programming features, and the language itself is backward compatible with the latest ANSI standard for SQL, SQL-92.

Although TSQL is a simple language, some of the more advanced TSQL samples can
become as complicated as anything you will see in Visual Basic. If you're not a TSQL
guru and have no intention of ever becoming one, fear not: All the Visual Studio tools,

including Visual InterDev, include visual database tools that enable you to construct TSQL queries visually. This means, in theory, that you could get away without having to learn TSQL at all if you'd like. As with any advanced technical topic, however, it makes sense to understand the underlying language. Often times, you will want to tweak the TSQL code generated by the visual database tools so that it is more efficient, for example. Chapter 11, "Using the Visual Database Tools", covers these tools more in-depth.

Using TSQL

TSQL enables you to programmatically access information in SQL Server using far less code than most programming languages would require. Consider the following line of code:

```
SELECT * FROM MyTable
```

This code retrieves every single field of every single record in the table named MyTable. TSQL statements consist of at least one command, or *clause*, and a verb that indicates the action that is to occur. Table 10.2 shows the four main commands in TSQL.

TABLE 10.2   COMMON TSQL COMMANDS

Command	What It Does
SELECT	Retrieves data from SQL Server and sends it back in one or more result sets
UPDATE	Updates data in specific rows of a table
INSERT	Adds new data rows to a table
DELETE	Deletes data in specific rows of a table

The SELECT command is used most often because it is used to retrieve data. When you use SELECT to retrieve data, you're executing a *SELECT query* in TSQL terms. When you're dealing with Web applications, for example, you generally have to output data from a database, so you use a SELECT query almost exclusively.

When it comes to modifying data in a database (adding new data, removing data, or changing existing data), there are two ways to handle this: You can use the TSQL commands just mentioned or take advantage of features in ADO that accomplish the same thing. Because you're tackling SQL Server from a Web developer's perspective, you will use ADO to accomplish these tasks. Modifying data with ADO methods is covered in Chapter 17, "Modifying Web Application Data from the Web."

> **TIP**
>
> Like HTML, TSQL is not case sensitive. The coding style used here places all TSQL keywords in all caps, but that's just an arbitrary convention. You can capitalize your SQL code however you like.

Building SELECT Queries

To build SELECT queries, you can use the visual database tools in Visual InterDev or one of the tools that come with SQL Server 7.0, such as the SQL Server Query Analyzer. The SQL Server Query Analyzer makes its predecessor (ISQL/W) look sick by comparison, offering a host of advanced features such as color-highlighted code, an execution plan view, and the choice of text-based or grid-based output.

In this section, you will be using SQL Server Query Analyzer as you look at SELECT queries (see Figure 10.18). For the query examples, you will also be using the Pubs database that ships with SQL Server.

FIGURE 10.18

SQL Server Query Analyzer is one of the many new and improved tools in SQL Server 7.0.

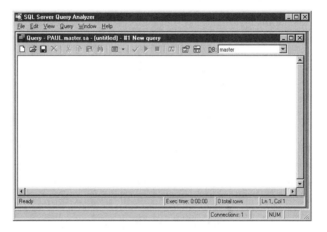

The simplest (and least efficient) query you can run will retrieve everything in a specific table. For example, the following returns the entire contents of the authors table in Pubs (assuming Pubs is set as the current database):

```
SELECT * FROM authors
```

The information retrieved by this query (23 rows, or records, with 9 fields each) is stored in a temporary area of memory called a *result set* or *recordset* (literally, *a set of records*).

The SELECT * portion of this code can be read as "Select all the records" (the * character is a wildcard that specifies *all*). The FROM clause specifies the location of the data. The entire line of code could be read as "Select all the records from the authors table," shown in Figure 10.19.

FIGURE 10.19

The result of your first query: Everything in the authors table is retrieved.

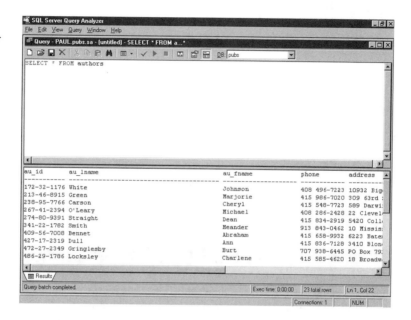

Using the * wildcard character in a SELECT statement is considered bad form on good days, and when it comes to Web applications, it's a major faux pas. Typically, you won't have to retrieve everything from a table like that. In the case of the authors table you're working with, you might want to retrieve only the first and last names (this can be done by specifying only the field names that you do want). The result might look like this statement, shown in Figure 10.20:

```
SELECT au_lname, au_fname FROM authors
```

As you can see, this query retrieves only the first and last names. As a result, the query will run faster and return control to your ASP page (and thus to the user) far more quickly.

FIGURE 10.20

By drilling down a bit, you can return only the data you need. This is much faster than retrieving all the data.

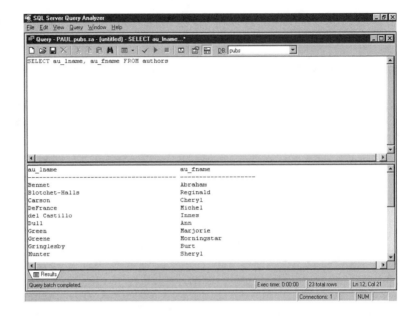

Limiting the Result Set with the WHERE Clause

In addition to specifying only the exact fields you want returned, you can also tell TSQL to return records that match certain criteria. This functionality is the responsibility of the WHERE clause. WHERE uses a condition or group of conditions to filter the result set of the query, using the following form:

```
SELECT field(s) FROM table(s) WHERE condition(s)
```

To extend the authors table example, you might want to display only the authors that live in a certain city, say Oakland. This can be accomplished with the following query and is shown in Figure 10.21:

```
SELECT au_lname, au_fname FROM authors WHERE city = "Oakland"
```

Figure 10.21

Although the city names are not displayed, you have filtered the result set down to authors from Oakland.

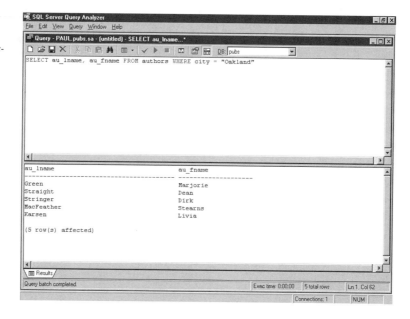

One interesting thing to note here is that the city field does not have to be specified in the SELECT clause unless you want it to be part of the result set. In other words, you can specify fields in the WHERE clause that are not being displayed by the SELECT cause.

The WHERE clause can use a variety of operators to accomplish its work. Here are some typical examples of WHERE syntax (these are not meant to correspond to the Pubs database):

```
SELECT * FROM tablename WHERE city = "Oakland" AND state = "CA"
SELECT * FROM tablename WHERE writer = "Stephen King"
        OR writer = "John Norman"
SELECT * FROM tablename WHERE writer IN
        ("Stephen King", "John Norman", "Isaac Asimov")
SELECT * FROM tablename WHERE ID <= 1280
SELECT * FROM tablename WHERE Num > 10 AND Num < 20
SELECT * FROM tablename WHERE ID != 6
```

The LIKE keyword is often used with WHERE to further filter the data that goes into the result set. LIKE works with its own set of wildcard characters so that you can do things such as find all the authors whose last names begin with the letter *w* or find all the authors from states beginning with *m* (see Figure 10.22).

```
SELECT au_lname, au_fname, state FROM authors WHERE state LIKE "m%"
```

10

WORKING WITH
DATABASES

FIGURE 10.22

The state name is outputted as well so that you can see how the query worked.

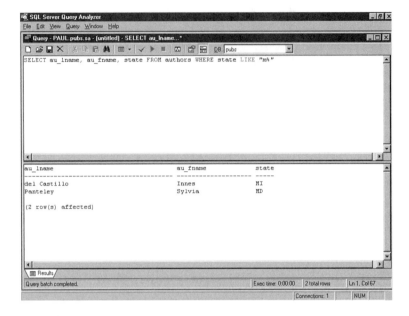

The % character works as * does in DOS batch files: It stands for any number of (or no) characters. Table 10.3 summarizes the wildcards you can use with LIKE.

TABLE 10.3 LIKE WILDCARD CHARACTERS

Wildcard	What It Filters
%	Any number of (or no) characters
- (Underscore)	Any single character
[a]	Any single character in a specified range (such as [a-m]) or set ([abcdefghijklm])
[^]	Any single character not within a specified range or set

These wildcard characters are treated like any other characters when not used with LIKE.

Sorting the Result Set with ORDER BY

Unless you sort the result set, SQL Server will return records in the order they were retrieved. This is almost never acceptable, so TSQL includes an ORDER BY clause that enables you to sort the result set before it is returned. The ORDER BY clause must appear after the WHERE clause, and it takes the following form:

```
SELECT field(s) FROM table(s) WHERE condition(s) ORDER BY field(s)
```

If you'd like to order the authors from Oakland by last name (a common enough operation), the code would look something like this query and Figure 10.23:

```
SELECT au_lname, au_fname FROM authors
  WHERE city = "Oakland" ORDER BY au_lname
```

FIGURE 10.23

Authors from Oakland sorted by last name.

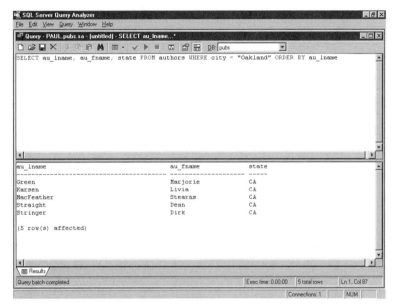

This query sorts the authors in ascending order by last name. To sort in descending (reverse) order (see Figure 10.24), you can use the DESC keyword:

```
SELECT au_lname, au_fname FROM authors
  WHERE city = "Oakland" ORDER BY au_lname DESC
```

Like other clauses, you can specify more than one field with ORDER BY. For example, to list all authors by city and then last name, you could use the following query:

```
SELECT au_lname, au_fname, city FROM authors ORDER BY city, au_lname
```

As you might imagine, you can get into some convoluted syntax very quickly, and I haven't even touched on some of the more advanced query topics such as inner and outer joins and subqueries. At heart, though, TSQL is a simple language as long as you learn to break it down into readable segments that are easy to understand.

10

WORKING WITH DATABASES

FIGURE **10.24**

Authors from Oakland sorted by last name in reverse order.

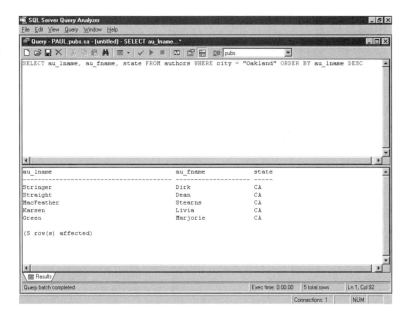

Stored Procedures

One other feature of SQL Server deserves a quick look. For most Web applications, it doesn't make sense to throw dynamic queries at SQL Server from ASP code, especially if your site gets many hits. Although repeated queries are cached so that subsequent hits of the same page should return more quickly, SQL Server also supports something known as *stored procedures*. These are designed specifically to make repeated queries execute faster.

A stored procedure is a group of TSQL statements that are compiled into a single executable unit (from within SQL Server, that is). As such, a stored procedure should always execute more quickly than the equivalent dynamic query. That way, you can code the query once, compile it within SQL Server, and just call the stored procedure with ADO code. You will take a closer look at stored procedures in Chapter 11.

Summary

The future of Web development hinges on database integration. In fact, it could be argued that the ability to create a dynamic, database-backed Web application is the dividing line between amateur personal Web sites and professional Web experiences that look and act just like native Windows applications. Microsoft has been working hard for the past few years to make Web/database integration a reality. Yes, there will always be a learning curve as we move into the brave new world of data access, but Microsoft technologies such as OLE DB, ADO, ASP, and Visual InterDev make it all come together in a way that any seasoned developer should be comfortable with.

This chapter discusses Microsoft's Universal Data Access strategy and the technologies you can use to realize this strategy. You were also introduced to SQL Server 7.0, perhaps the ultimate example of a universal database, and its native language of TSQL.

Using the Visual Database Tools

by Paul Thurrott

Chapter 10, "Working with Databases: Universal Data Access," presented an admittedly brief introduction to Transact SQL, the native language of Microsoft SQL Server. Most Web developers, however, are not experts in this somewhat obscure language, so Microsoft provides a variety of integrated Visual Database tools in Visual InterDev that make it easy to query databases so that you can locate the information you need. The functionality of the Visual Database tools doesn't stop here, though. Using only Visual InterDev, you can perform a variety of database functions, including the following:

- Connect to any ODBC-compliant or OLE DB-compliant data source.
- Navigate through the objects in such a database, examining its structure and contents.
- Create SQL Server databases visually, using database diagrams.
- Modify SQL Server databases.
- Design queries that generate Transact SQL script and run them in real time to see the results.
- Add, modify, and delete data in a database.
- Create SQL Server and Oracle database tables.
- Create SQL Server and Oracle triggers.
- Create SQL Server and Oracle stored procedures.

Naturally, these features work best with Microsoft's SQL Server (which is used in this chapter's examples), but you can also perform many of these functions on Oracle databases as well.

Another interesting, and often underused, visual database feature of InterDev is the capability to create a database project, which enables you to use InterDev as your sole database development tool. You can integrate database projects with Web application projects to create a solution that includes these two otherwise separate components. In this chapter, you will take a look at the Visual InterDev tools that make it easy to work with databases visually.

An Introduction to the Visual Database Tools

There are four primary components of the Visual Data tools: Data View, Database Designer, Query Designer, and the Source Code editor for triggers and stored procedures. The following sections take a quick look at these tools, and throughout the course of this chapter, you'll learn how they can be used to provide a single-stop interface to all your remote data.

Data View

The Visual InterDev Data View, typically available as its own tab in the Properties window (although it can be detached), provides a view of the live database connections in Web application and Database projects. With the Data View, you can access objects in the connected databases, including database diagrams, tables, views, and stored procedures.

> **NOTE**
>
> The various components in Visual Studio are not yet as integrated as they someday will be. However, the Data View is currently shared with Visual J++, Visual C++, and Visual Basic, although the implementation differs slightly in each environment. Regardless, when you become accustomed to the Data View in any of these components, you will be able to use it in any of the others.

The Data View window automatically appears whenever you add a data connection to your project. Figure 11.1 shows the Data View in a Database project that is connected to the SQL Server Pubs database.

FIGURE 11.1

The Data View window gives you easy access to all the objects in a live database connection.

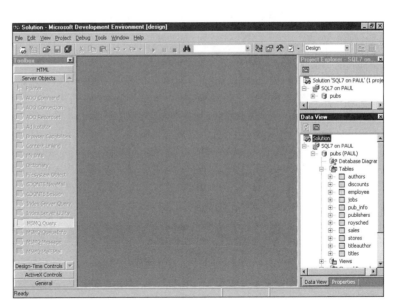

You should think of the Data View as the uppermost view of your database: From here, you can initiate almost anything that the Visual Database tools are capable of.

Database Designer

The Database Designer provides a visual way to create, edit, and delete database objects in remote and local databases. It enables you to not only view the tables and table relationships that store the data in the database, but also modify the actual structure of the database. The nice thing about the Database Designer is that it enables you to perform "what if" scenarios on your database: Changes you make to the database structure are not replicated to the live database until you save them. You can also have the Database Designer save the structural changes to a Transact SQL script, which enables you to apply the changes later.

The Database Designer, shown in Figure 11.2, enables you to work graphically with the table relationships in your database by displaying the tables in a diagram, which you can modify.

FIGURE 11.2

The Database Designer enables you to create visual database diagrams of the tables and table relationships in your databases.

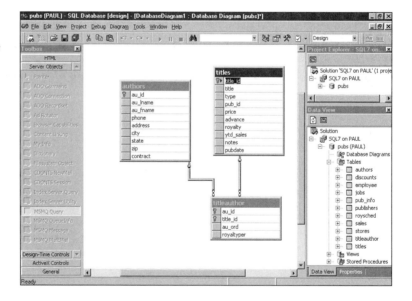

Query Designer

The Query Designer is a four-pane window (see Figure 11.3) that visually creates Transact SQL statements for you using an interface similar to the Query Designer in Access. The Query Designer consists of the Show Diagrams pane, the Show Grid pane, the Show SQL pane, and the Show Results pane. Any of these panes can be shown or hidden, and the Query Designer even checks the grammar of your SQL code if you try to write it by hand. The Query Designer is invoked any time you double-click a table in the Data View window. From the Query toolbar, you can modify the panes that are shown.

FIGURE 11.3

The Query Designer provides a graphical way to construct SQL queries.

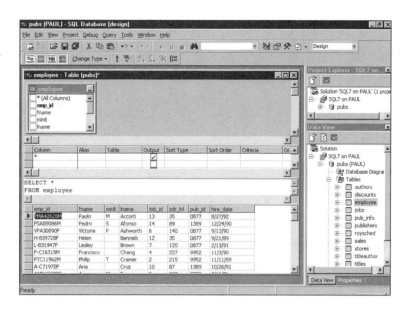

In addition to SQL queries, you can build views from the Query Designer. This is done by right-clicking the Views heading in the Data View window and selecting New View.

Source Code Editor

You can create triggers, stored procedures, and other SQL scripts using the Visual Studio editor that is built in to Visual InterDev. This color syntax-highlighting editor understands the SQL language and provides nice skeleton code for new stored procedures and triggers, as shown in Figure 11.4.

Right-clicking the Stored Procedure heading in the Data View window and choosing New Stored Procedure creates a new stored procedure. Likewise, right-clicking any table in the Data View window and choosing New Trigger creates a new trigger.

FIGURE 11.4

Although not as visual as the other database tools, the Source Code editor does provide color syntax highlighting.

Now that you've had a quick look at the tools involved, it's time to see how they're used. In the following sections, you will examine database projects and the various ways you can manage databases with InterDev's visual tools.

Using Database Projects

Although you will typically work with Web projects in Visual InterDev, the Visual Studio environment also supports database projects, as well as a small assortment of other, more special-purpose projects. A *database project* enables you to connect to a remote SQL Server database (in the same way that a Web project enables you to connect to a remote Web site) and manage that data, using the familiar Visual Studio environment. Best of all, you can also add a database project to an existing Visual InterDev solution, which typically includes a Web project as well. This gives you an integrated, one-stop environment in which to work with your data-backed Web sites.

> **TIP**
>
> You can also work with local Microsoft Access databases or any databases for which you can create an ODBC data source name (DSN) or OLE DB data link.

Another interesting, and often overlooked, aspect of Database projects is that you can connect to multiple databases. Simply add multiple data connections in the Project Explorer window. This has several implications: You could use a single database project to manage all your remote databases, creating, in effect, a developer's equivalent to the SQL Server Enterprise Manager, or you could create a Visual InterDev solution that includes a Web project and one or more database projects, so that the entire Web solution is managed as a single unit.

Creating a Database Project

To create a new database project, select New from the File menu and expand the Visual Studio option in the left side of the dialog box that appears. The first option, Database Projects, enables you to create a new database project (see Figure 11.5).

FIGURE 11.5
It's not as obvious as creating a Web project, but Visual InterDev lets you manage databases as well.

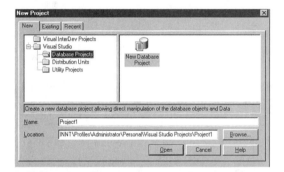

> **NOTE**
>
> A little advice on naming the project: If you're going to manage only a single database with your database project, by all means give it a logical name, such as Pubs database. Before you name it, though, think about how you will be using the database project. You might very well have to manage more than one database. If that's the case, consider a more generic name, such as SQL Server databases on SQL001.

After you've named the project and chosen a location to store it, you're prompted to choose a file or machine DSN. If you haven't already created a DSN for the database you want to connect to, you can create it now from this dialog (make sure you choose a machine DSN, not a file DSN, because machine DSNs are faster and more efficient). The DSN you choose will form the first data connection used by your database project. If you choose a SQL Server database, you are asked to log in, and then Visual InterDev presents you with a screen similar to Figure 11.6.

FIGURE **11.6**

Generally speaking, the default Design view isn't the best environment for managing a database.

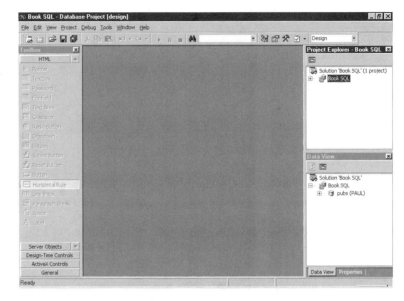

Depending on how you've configured Visual InterDev, you might find that the default view style (or *Window UI*, as Visual InterDev calls it), Design view, is inadequate for database management. That's because the Toolbox window, which is generally not used by database projects, takes up large chunks of the screen real estate. You could experiment with some of the other styles, but I recommend simply creating your own view style. To do this, change to Design view, close the Toolbox, and choose Define Window Layout from the View menu. Type Database as the name of the new view and click Add to create it. Then choose Database from the Load/Save Window UI drop-down list box when you work with database projects, as shown in Figure 11.7.

One of the first things you will notice about the database project is that the Project Explorer window consists solely of your project name and a single data connection, called Connection1. You should change this to something more descriptive right away, especially if you will be adding additional data connections to the project, as described in the next section.

In addition to the Project Explorer, you should see a Data View window displaying the database diagrams, tables, views, and stored procedures contained by the remote database. If you don't see the Data View window, you can enable it from the View, Other Windows, Data View menu item.

FIGURE 11.7

*Create your own
customized view
style when
working with
databases.*

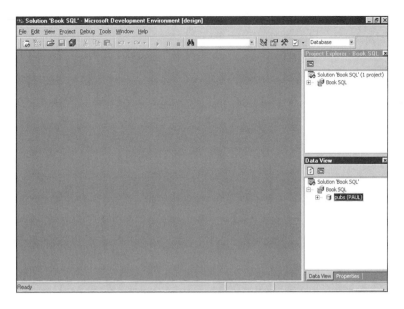

Adding Additional Data Connections to the Project

Adding more data connections to your database project is relatively simple. Right-click
the name of your database project in the Project Explorer and choose New Data
Connection. Once again, you can select (or alternatively, create) a DSN. If you select a
SQL Server database, you are asked to log in, and then the Project Explorer window displays a new data connection. If this is the second data connection, it will be named
Connection2. Again, you should name this something more logical. Figure 11.8 shows a
database project with two data connections.

Working this way, you can add as many databases as you'd like. They can be various
kinds of databases that exist at different physical locations, too. As long as you can create a DSN for the database, you can add it to your database project.

FIGURE **11.8**

In this example, the Northwind and Pubs data-bases from SQL Server 7 can be managed from the same database project.

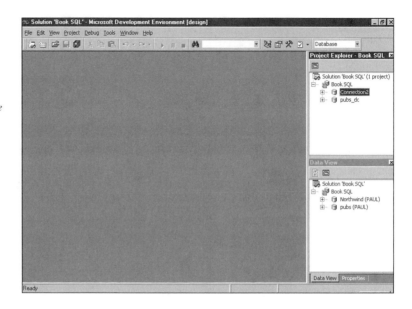

Using Database Projects in Web Project Solutions

If you're working on a database-based Web application in Visual InterDev, it makes sense to manage the Web site and the database from the same familiar environment. This type of integration is at the heart of Visual Studio, and Microsoft introduced a new concept called the *solution*, alluded to earlier. A Visual Studio solution is a group of one or more Visual Studio projects that can be considered a single container unit. In the past, the project was the uppermost container that you could work with: A *project* contains the files that make up a Web application, for example, or a Visual C++ application. Even today, most developers still work at the project level, although Visual InterDev (and the other Visual Studio tools) is transparently creating solutions for you as well. Every project you create—Web application, database, or whatever—is really part of a solution as well.

The maturity of Microsoft's visual tools has enabled a new type of application that embodies the best features from numerous tools. You might create a monster InterDev Web application that uses a Visual J++ Java applet in the browser and a Visual Basic component for database access on the back end. Even though three separate tools are used in this scenario, they work together to create a single entity, which you can think of as a *solution*.

Most Visual InterDev Web applications will require database functionality. This presents an obvious need for a solution that includes both the database and the Web application files. Thus, it makes sense to create a solution that includes a Web project and a database project.

To create this type of solution, you can add a new database project to an existing Web project, add a new Web project to an existing database project, or add an existing project of either type to an existing project of either type. In the following example, you will add an existing database project to an existing Web project. Then, you will take a quick look at how easy it is to add a new database project to an existing Web solution.

Adding an Existing Project to an Existing Solution

Open a Web project that uses (or will use) database connectivity. Notice that the top of the Project Explorer window displays the name of the solution along with the tag line 1 `project`. This indicates that your solution currently includes only a single project. Right-click the solution name in the Project Explorer and choose Add Project (alternatively, choose Add Project from the File menu) to open the familiar Add Project dialog. Navigate to the Existing tab and choose the database project (`*.dbp`, not `*.sln`) you'd like to add.

After you add the database project, your Visual InterDev environment will resemble Figure 11.9.

FIGURE 11.9

This Visual InterDev solution includes a Web project and a database project.

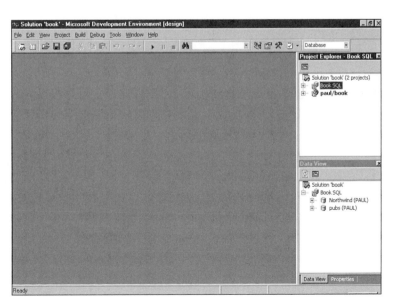

Notice that the tag line at the top of the Project Explorer window now indicates that two projects are included in the solution. When you save the solution, you will always have both these projects at your disposal.

Adding a New Database Project to an Existing Web Solution

Adding a new database project to an existing solution is just as easy, but while you're creating the database project, you must be careful that you don't create a new solution by mistake. As with the preceding example, you must open the Web solution you will be working with and select Add Project from the File menu. This time, however, you create a new database project from the Add Project dialog, ensuring that the choice marked Add to Current Solution (see Figure 11.10) is selected. As always, use or create a machine DSN and, voilà, you have a new multiproject solution.

FIGURE 11.10

Tread lightly here and make sure you're adding the project to the existing solution, not creating a new solution.

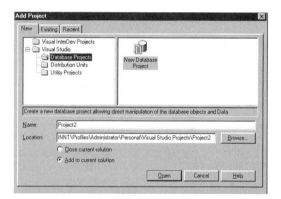

Managing Remote Databases with Visual InterDev

One primary benefit of a database project is that you can create and manage database objects from the familiar Visual Studio environment. These objects include tables and table relationships, views, indexes, constraints and triggers, stored procedures, and SQL scripts. These SQL scripts can perform simple SELECT queries or make changes to the structure of your database.

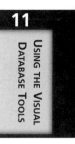

> **NOTE**
>
> The capability to make structural changes to a remote database is available only in the Enterprise Edition of Visual InterDev.

Depending on your view of database management, Visual InterDev might or might not be a better management tool than the built-in tool with SQL Server, the Enterprise Manager.

Visual InterDev Versus SQL Server Enterprise Manager

True database administrators are going to be excited about the Enterprise Manager MMC plug-in that comes with SQL Server 7.0. This amazing tool, shown in Figure 11.11, offers a greater variety of database management features than Visual InterDev.

FIGURE 11.11

The SQL Server Enterprise Manager is the apex of database management packages.

In addition to creating, modifying, and deleting database objects, Enterprise Manager enables you to import and export heterogeneous data, back up and restore databases, automate administrative tasks, manage database security, replicate data, monitor database performance, and much more. For the Web developer, however, Visual InterDev's tool set is more than adequate.

On the other hand, you might need some of these features, especially if you work at a small company and must assume many roles (we've all been there). If that's the case, you might consider installing the SQL Server client utilities on your development station so that you can access Enterprise Manager.

Visual InterDev Database Management

Using Visual InterDev as the management point for remote databases has its own benefits, however. The Visual Studio environment supports source control, so you can easily manage multiple-user access to the database and its SQL scripts. Database management in Visual InterDev involves the use of the Visual Database tools mentioned previously, including the Data View window, the Database Designer, and various other designers such as the Query Designer, the View Designer, and the Stored Procedure editor. For the rest of this chapter, you will examine the various management functions you can perform in Visual InterDev.

Creating Tables

In SQL Server and other relational databases, a *table* is a named entity that stores information in a row/column format in which each row references a single piece of data whose attributes are defined by the columns. Tables are, quite simply, the single most important data structure in a relational database.

> **NOTE**
>
> Many people are confused by the differences between tables and views. A *table* is the place where data is stored in a database. A *view* offers a look at that data; however, it can correspond to the data in one or more tables, like a recordset. For this reason, tables are sometimes referred to as *base tables* to separate them more clearly from views. This nomenclature is infrequently used, however.

In a simple database, tables can exist independently of one another, but it's more common for tables to refer to, or relate to, one another within a relational database (thus, the name). Figure 11.12 shows the relations between the tables in the Pubs database. Notice that a table's key fields are connected in this diagram: The job_id field in the jobs table relates to the emp_id field in the employee table, for example.

FIGURE **11.12**

Table relations are shown visually in this database diagram.

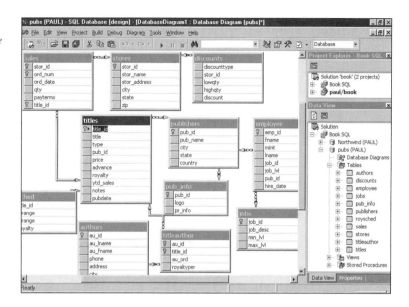

When you're creating your own database, you will want to develop a diagram of the database's structure beforehand. This diagram maps out the tables you will need, the fields in those tables, and the ways in which those fields relate to other fields in other tables. Proper database design, before physically creating the database, is crucial to the performance of your Web and database applications. When you're ready to implement your database, however, the first step (after creating the database) is to populate that database with tables. You can do this the old-fashioned way (with Transact SQL statements) or via the visual tools in Visual InterDev.

NOTE

How do you create a database? For SQL Server, you must use the tools that come with the database server. Most Web developers probably have access to an empty SQL Server database provided to them by their ISP or IT department. Normally, you will probably not have to create your own SQL Server databases. If you're using Access for the database (hopefully not in a production environment), create an empty document in Access, save it to disk, and create a machine DSN for that file.

Creating Tables with Transact SQL

If you're still living in the computing Stone Age, you will enjoy the Data Definition Language (DDL) method of creating SQL Server tables: The Transact SQL CREATE TABLE statement. You can create a SQL script by using SQL Server's Query Analyzer or Visual InterDev's SQL Script tool. Either way, you write the appropriate code and execute it against the server. The Visual InterDev method, incidentally, supplies a lot of error-checking skeleton code, so you will be taking a look at that method here.

To create a new table using a SQL script in Visual InterDev, open a database project or a solution that includes a database project. Locate the database in the Project Explorer, right-click, and choose Add SQL Script. The Add Item dialog appears, shown in Figure 11.13.

FIGURE 11.13

Using Visual InterDev, you can create scripts to create a table, query, stored procedure, trigger, or any other kind of SQL script.

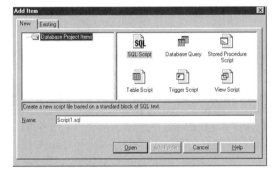

Select Table Script and give it a descriptive name (remember to retain the *.sql naming convention for Visual InterDev's purposes). When you're finished, you will be presented with the skeleton code shown in Figure 11.14.

This skeleton code is surprisingly powerful. It checks to make sure the table doesn't already exist. If it does exist and is a user-created table, that table is deleted and your table is created. You still must write your own code, however. In the InterDev-generated script, you must replace each reference to Table_Name with the name of your new table and then write the code in the CREATE TABLE block that actually creates the table. The CREATE TABLE block appears near the end of the skeleton code and resembles the following:

```
CREATE TABLE Table_Name
(

)
```

FIGURE 11.14

Visual InterDev's base SQL scripts provide skeleton scripting to get you started.

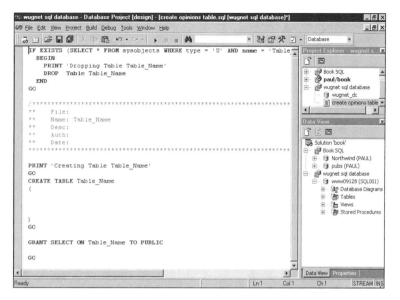

FIGURE 11.14

Visual InterDev's base SQL scripts provide skeleton scripting to get you started.

If you'd like to create a simple table for storing opinion articles, for example, you could use code such as the following to create the table:

```
CREATE TABLE Opinions
(
    title    varchar(255) NOT NULL,
    date     datetime NOT NULL,
    body     text NOT NULL
)
```

To execute this code, save it and then right-click the script name, which now appears in the Project Explorer; then choose Execute. The Output window will appear, showing the results of the table creation, as shown in Figure 11.15.

To verify that the table was created, you can refresh the Data View window and expand the correct database.

Getting Data into the New Table

There are a variety of ways to input data into a table. In fact, Chapter 17, Modifying Web Application Data from the Web, covers some of the programmatic ways to do so using the Web and technologies such as Active Server Pages and ActiveX Data Objects. You can also copy data from other tables and/or views into your new table, manually enter it using a front-end application written in Visual Basic or Visual C++, or even write a SQL script that uses Transact SQL statements to add data.

FIGURE **11.15**

*When you execute
a SQL script from
Visual InterDev,
the Output win-
dow displays the
results.*

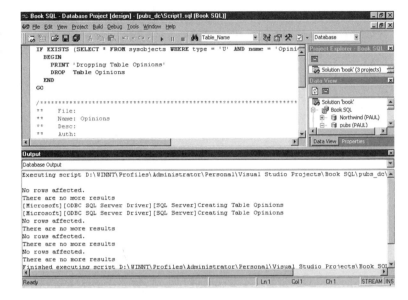

Creating Tables Visually

Creating a table with a SQL script is all well and good, but it assumes an in-depth
knowledge of Transact SQL. Creating anything more than a simple table such as the one
in the preceding example would require some pretty serious code. For most Web developers, this is a bit much to ask and is better left to experienced database administrators.
For the mere humans out there, Microsoft has added visual table creation to Visual
InterDev.

When you're creating a table in Visual InterDev, you still must decide ahead of time
what fields you will need, the data type of each field, and any other table design issues
(such as which fields will accept NULL values). The Visual InterDev table creation tools
make it much easier to create complex tables as well, especially when you consider that
you won't have to verify any complex SQL syntax before committing the creation.

You can launch the visual table designer in a couple of ways, including right-clicking the
Tables entry under the correct database in the Data View window and choosing New
Table. However, many more options are available to you when you have a database diagram open. A *database diagram* is a visual representation, or schema, of a subset of your
database layout. That is, you can create database diagrams that display all or just some of
the data in your databases. Database diagrams work specifically with tables, the relationships between tables, and table objects such as fields and keys.

Using a Database Diagram to Create a New Table

To create a new table, then, you will want to work with a new or existing database diagram. If you decide to create a new database diagram, you don't have to save it when you're finished if you won't use it later. It's just a good idea to create tables within a diagram because of the extra options you have. On the other hand, when you're working with a blank database (especially) and you're adding tables to that database, it's a good idea to save a diagram that includes all the tables in the new database. A database diagram enables you to tell, at a glance, what the table relationships are in your database.

The first step is to create a new diagram. Locate the database you will be working with and expand it in the Data View window so that the database objects (database diagrams, tables, views, and stored procedures) are visible. Right-click Database Diagrams and choose New Diagram. This opens a blank diagram window and displays the Database Diagram toolbar, shown in Figure 11.16. (If the Database Diagram toolbar doesn't appear, be sure to display it by choosing that option when you right-click any toolbar in Visual InterDev.)

FIGURE 11.16

A new database diagram enables you to work with the tables in your database and add new tables.

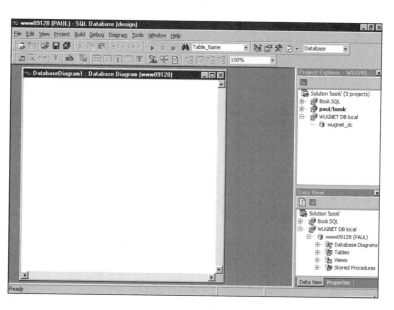

To create a new table, click the New Table button on the Database Diagram toolbar or choose New Table from the context menu that appears when you right-click a blank area of the Database Diagram window. Choose a name when prompted, and a blank table design window will appear inside the diagram window. Notice, too, that a variety of table option buttons on the Database Diagram toolbar become available.

At this point, you can add a new field (Column) name. As you can see in Figure 11.17, after a field name is entered and you've moved to the Datatype property, you're provided with a drop-down list of possible data types. This list is dependent on which version of which database you're using (the server shown is SQL Server 7.0). Then, depending on which data type you choose, you might have the option to change the Length, Precision, and Scale properties. If you want to allow NULL values for that field, check the Allow Nulls property.

FIGURE 11.17

The Database Designer window enables you to select properties rather than type them into a complex SQL script.

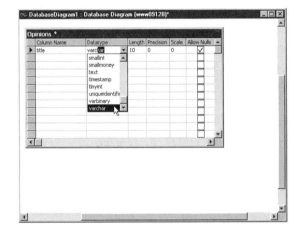

The Database Designer also makes it easy to create primary keys and identity fields. As shown in Figure 11.18, I've added to the Opinions table an ID field that will automatically increment each time a row is added to this table. Also, because ID is a primary key, that field will uniquely identify each row. This is possible, of course, using straight Transact SQL (in fact, everything you can do with SQL Server is possible from Transact SQL), but it would require much more complex code, which you'd have to write by hand. Using Visual InterDev, it's easy to create more complex tables.

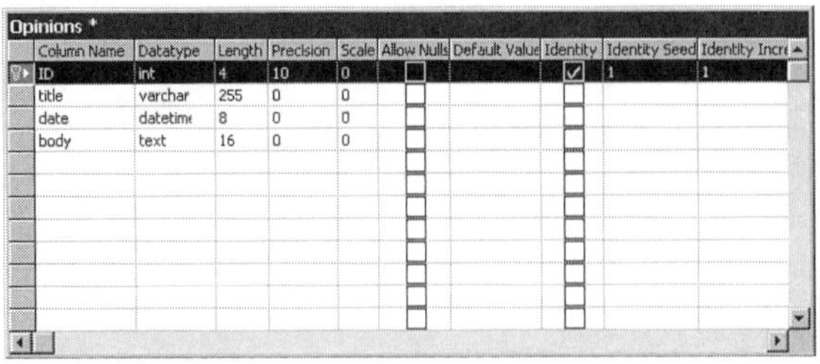

FIGURE 11.18

Creating identity fields and primary keys is a snap with the Database Designer.

After you've finished designing the table, you can display it in the Database Designer, using the more common column names view; the mode it's in currently is called *column properties*. To do this, right-click the table and choose Column Names or click the Column Names toolbar button. You can also drag other tables into the diagram and, if you'd like, create and display table relationships. Let's take a look at how to create table relationships.

Creating Table Relationships

Any time two or more tables share data, you can create a relationship between them. This enables you to store data in one table but refer to it from another. Consider the case of a field such as authorID in the Opinions table. You could create a key called ID in another table (perhaps called *authors*) that refers to authorID in the Opinions table. That way, the Opinions table would store the title, date, and body of the opinion article, but the authors table could store other information related to that article, in this case, information about the article's author.

To create table relationships with Visual InterDev, you must drag two or more tables from the Data View window into the Database Designer. Locate the field in one table that you want to relate to a field in another table, click the gray box (called a *row selector*) to the left of the field name, and drag the mouse to the field in the other table. As shown in Figure 11.19, this opens the Create Relationship dialog, which presents options for defining this new relationship. Check that everything is in order and click OK. Instant relationship!

FIGURE 11.19

Creating table relationships in Visual InterDev is as simple as drag and drop.

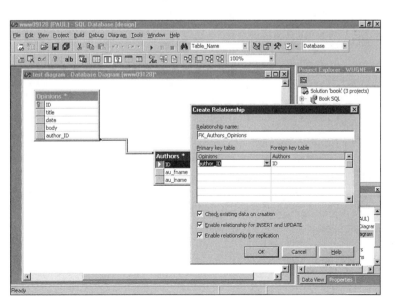

> **NOTE**
>
> When you close your database diagram, you will be prompted to save your diagram and then, separately, any tables you've created. Even if you don't intend to keep the diagram, save it anyway and then save the tables. Go back later and delete the diagram, if you want. It will appear under the Database Diagrams heading for your database in the Data View window.

Editing Database Objects

Each database object you work with—tables, views, and so on—can be edited within InterDev as well. Also, as you might expect, database diagrams play a central role when you must modify tables. The nice thing about a database diagram, incidentally, is that you can modify the database objects without affecting the live database. When you save the changes, however, they will be replicated to the live database. This enables you to experiment with changes without worrying about destroying critical data. You can even have Visual InterDev generate a SQL script that will perform the changes you've made so that they occur later when you decide to execute the script.

Editing a Table

Toedit a table in Visual InterDev, load a database diagram or create a new database diagram and make sure the table you'd like to change is visible. Then, make your changes. Some changes, obviously, will destroy data. For example, you can't easily change data stored in a text field to datetime. On the other hand, other changes are nondestructive and might actually improve the performance of queries. Say you'd like to make a field the primary key for the table. This field is already an identity field, so you know that the value of this field in each row, or record, is unique and therefore uniquely identifies the record. Therefore, it makes sense to make this field the primary key.

In this example, all you must do is select the field name you want and then select the Set Primary Key toolbar button (this option is also available from a pop-up menu). Just how complex is this little change? Well, on a simple table named wininfo, which has just four fields (ID, title, date, and body), here's the SQL script generated by this change:

```
BEGIN TRANSACTION
SET QUOTED_IDENTIFIER ON
GO
SET TRANSACTION ISOLATION LEVEL SERIALIZABLE
GO
COMMIT
```

```
BEGIN TRANSACTION
CREATE TABLE dbo.Tmp_wininfo
    (
     ID int NOT NULL IDENTITY (1, 1),
     title varchar(255) NOT NULL,
     date datetime NOT NULL,
     body text NOT NULL
     ) ON [PRIMARY]
      TEXTIMAGE_ON [PRIMARY]
GO
SET IDENTITY_INSERT dbo.Tmp_wininfo ON
GO
IF EXISTS(SELECT * FROM dbo.wininfo)
    EXEC('INSERT INTO dbo.Tmp_wininfo(ID, title, date, body)
        SELECT ID, title, date, body FROM dbo.wininfo TABLOCKX')
GO
SET IDENTITY_INSERT dbo.Tmp_wininfo OFF
GO
DROP TABLE dbo.wininfo
GO
EXECUTE sp_rename 'dbo.Tmp_wininfo', 'wininfo'
GO
ALTER TABLE dbo.wininfo ADD CONSTRAINT
    PK_wininfo PRIMARY KEY NONCLUSTERED
    (
    ID
    ) ON [PRIMARY]
GO
COMMIT
```

You can view this script by clicking the Save Change Script on the Database Diagram toolbar. If at a later time you'd like to execute this *change script*, as it's called, save it and execute it against the database later. On the other hand, if you're sure you want to execute the change right away, you can close and save the database diagram when prompted. Any changes you've made to database objects, such as the addition of a primary key to the table, will be executed against the database automatically.

To ensure that your changes occurred, you can open a database diagram that uses that table or right-click the table name in Data View and choose Design. In the case of the wininfo table, the addition of a primary key graphic next to ID indicates that the changes were made (see Figure 11.20).

Clearly, editing tables after you've added data to them is a disaster waiting to happen. It's more likely that you will be editing noncritical objects such as views.

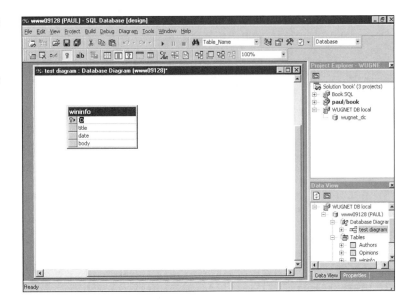

Editing Other Database Objects

To edit a view in Visual InterDev, locate the view in the Views section of the database in the Data View window. Right-click the view you want to edit, and choose Design. The Query Designer window will appear (see Figure 11.21), loaded with the Show Diagram, Show Grid, Show SQL, and Show Results panes by default. If it doesn't appear, be sure to display the Query toolbar as well because all its options apply to views, also.

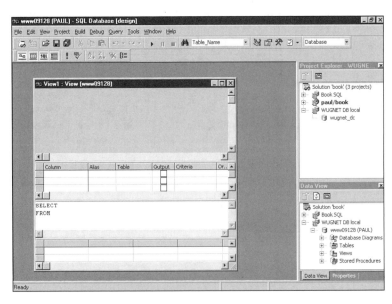

Likewise, stored procedures, triggers, and other objects can be edited after they're created. Each will open in a designer that is appropriate to the object, and the types of changes you will be able to make depend on the object. In the next section, you will take a look at some of the other common database objects you would have to create and work with.

Working with Other Database Objects

Although tables are, by far, the most common type of database object, it's likely that most Web developers will have to work with other database objects as well, such as stored procedures and triggers. You can also use Visual InterDev to create any other type of SQL script you'd like. For example, if you're more comfortable writing Transact SQL code, you can use the SQL code editor to write code that adds or deletes records. All these functions are possible in Visual InterDev.

Using Stored Procedures

A *stored procedure* is a special feature of SQL Server that enables you to execute a batch of Transact SQL code as a single unit precompiled by the server for improved performance. Perhaps more importantly, stored procedures enable you to use some of the more programmatic features of Transact SQL, such as control flow statements and parameters, and use them with a group of code that will run much faster than any dynamic query you might generate with ADO code.

Consider the table of news articles you used before. This table includes ID, title, date, and body fields. You could write a stored procedure that grabs a single article from this table, using a parameter to pass the article ID you want. The code for this might resemble the following:

```
Create Procedure GetArticle @articleID int
As
SELECT * FROM wininfo WHERE ID=@articleID
Return
```

This stored procedure can then be executed from any of the SQL Server client tools (see Figure 11.22) or from an Active Server Page (which I discuss in Chapter 15, "Displaying Data in a Web Application"). However, Visual InterDev (naturally) provides a slightly better way to code a stored procedure. Granted, it's not as visual as some of the other database tools, but we *are* dealing with straight Transact SQL code here.

FIGURE 11.22

*The results of
your stored proce-
dure, as shown in
the SQL Server
Query Analyzer.*

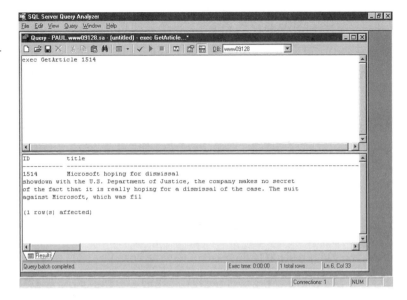

Creating Stored Procedures in Visual InterDev

To create a stored procedure by using Visual InterDev, locate the Stored Procedures heading under the database you're using in the Data View window. Right-click the heading and choose New Stored Procedure. This launches the Visual InterDev SQL code editor and presents the following skeleton code:

```
Create Procedure StoredProcedure1
/*
    (
        @parameter1 datatype = default value,
        @parameter2 datatype OUTPUT
    )
*/
As
    /* set nocount on */
    return
```

When you remove the comments and clean this up a bit, it becomes a little easier to read:

```
Create Procedure StoredProcedure1 As <SQL code here> return
```

An option list of parameters can follow the name of the stored procedure. You can specify output parameters as well. An explanation of the intricacies of stored procedures is beyond the scope of this book, but SQL Server 7.O Books Online and MSDN Library have great references that should get you started.

With this skeleton as a starting point, you can easily code your own stored procedures, using the nice color syntax-highlighting editor. Best of all, you can execute and debug them from within, using Visual InterDev. To execute a stored procedure, right-click the name of the stored procedure in the Data View window; then choose Execute. The Execute dialog (see Figure 11.23) appears, prompting you to choose values for any parameters the procedure might require.

FIGURE 11.23

The Execute dialog box enables you to provide test parameter values or accept the default.

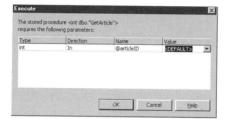

After you've supplied these values, the Output window shown in Figure 11.24 appears, displaying the results of the stored procedure.

FIGURE 11.24

The Output window displays the results of the stored procedure execution.

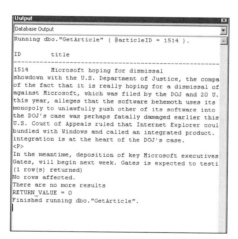

After you create a stored procedure, you can modify it by double-clicking its name in the Data View window. This displays the code you created previously, with one difference: The reference to Create Procedure changes to Alter Procedure because any changes you make to the code will alter the design of the stored procedure:

```
Alter Procedure GetArticle @articleID int
As
SELECT * FROM wininfo WHERE ID=@articleID
Return
```

One note of interest about the SQL code editor: If you're uncomfortable writing Transact SQL code, you can right-click anywhere in the code window and choose Insert SQL to use Visual InterDev's Query Designer to visually create the code you need. Alternatively, if you have a block of SQL code you'd like to edit, you can right-click it in the editor and choose Edit SQL to edit that code visually (see Figure 11.25).

FIGURE 11.25

The Query Designer loads pre-existing code and lets you edit it visually.

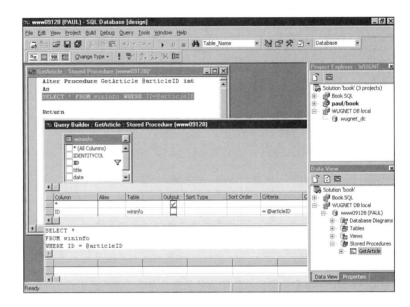

To debug a stored procedure, right-click the procedure name in the Data View window and choose Debug. The Execute dialog will appear, as it does when you execute the procedure, to let you enter values for any parameters the procedure might take.

Using Triggers

A *trigger* is a special type of stored procedure that is automatically executed in response to a specific event. In other words, a trigger isn't manually executed like a regular stored procedure. Typically, a trigger is executed when an INSERT, DELETE, or UPDATE statement causes data to change in the database. Each SQL Server 7.0 table can have multiple triggers associated with it (SQL Server 6.5 was limited to three triggers per table).

Because a trigger is essentially the same as a stored procedure, the syntax for creating one is very similar, also. The following pseudocode shows the basic syntax for a trigger:

```
CREATE TRIGGER <trigger name>
ON <table name>
```

```
FOR <INSERT, DELETE or UPDATE>
AS
<SQL code>
```

Note that the SQL code section can be any valid block of Transact SQL, including the execution of one or more stored procedures (which are executed with the EXEC statement). As with a stored procedure, you can create a trigger by using any SQL Server–compatible query tool, but Visual InterDev makes it easy to create triggers right from the comfortable Visual Studio environment.

Creating Triggers in Visual InterDev

To create a trigger, locate the table you'd like the trigger associated with, in the Data View window. Unlike stored procedures, triggers are always associated with a particular table. Then, right-click the table name and choose New Trigger. The SQL code window appears with the following block of skeleton code (where the Pubs authors table was chosen):

```
Create Trigger authors_Trigger1
On dbo.authors
For /* Insert, Update, Delete */
As
    /* If Update (column_name) ...*/
```

Replace authors_Trigger1 with the name you want to give the trigger; choose Insert, Update, or Delete in the For line and remove the other choices (and the comment characters, /* and */). Finally, add the code you'd like in the As section. Like a stored procedure, this can consist of any number of lines of valid Transact SQL code. Remember, too, that you can use the visual Query Designer to build a SQL query by right-clicking the editor window and choosing Insert SQL.

Any triggers you create will appear as an object below the fields for its associated table in the Data View window.

Using Other SQL Scripts

Although stored procedures and triggers are the most common types of SQL scripts you will create, you can write batch scripts of any type and save them in a database project as a generic SQL script that can be executed against the database at any time. You might create a generic SQL script that executes several stored procedures, for example, so you would have to run only the one script rather than manually launch the stored procedures separately. Also, SQL scripts are stored locally on your workstation, not on the server, as stored procedures are. This makes them faster to debug and work with while in development.

To create a SQL script, right-click a data connection in the Project Explorer window and choose Add SQL Script. The Add Item window appears (refer to Figure 11.13), enabling you to choose from a variety of SQL script types. Choose SQL Script, give your script a name, and then click the Open button.

The resulting SQL code window is as plain as they come. Because Visual InterDev has no idea about the type of script you plan to run, you're pretty much on your own here. This script can contain any number of valid Transact SQL statements, including the execution of stored procedures. When you save the script, it is placed under its associated data connection in the Project Explorer window, along with any other scripts or queries you might have created. You can execute this script as you would a table create script: Right-click the script name and choose Execute.

A Case Study: Managing the WUGNET Databases with Visual InterDev

In my work with WUGNET (the Windows User Group Network) during its move to a SQL Server database-backed Web site, Visual InterDev has proved invaluable as a development environment and one-stop database administration tool. WUGNET's Web site is stored locally on my workstation and then replicated up to the Data Return Web servers when any updates are considered complete. Perhaps more importantly, WUGNET's SQL Server database, also located at Data Return, can be managed almost completely from Visual InterDev.

Using Visual InterDev's visual database tools, I can make quick-and-dirty changes to the data, although WUGNET's own users have Web-based and Win32 applications that provide a much nicer way to access their data (the Web-based management tools are examined in Chapter 17). Some tables in the WUGNET database are quite large. The WinInfo table, for example, contains every article ever written for that online newsletter, dating back to December 1996. Two years later, that has amounted to more than 2,000 articles. Other WUGNET tables handle the content for various parts of its site, such as the front-page news items, shareware picks of the week, and tips of the day. As of this writing, the WUGNET database is stored on a SQL Server 6.5 database, although it's expected to be updated to SQL Server 7.0 by the time this book is published.

Summary

This chapter discusses the visual database tools provided by Visual InterDev, including the Data View window, the Database Designer, the Query Designer, and the Visual Studio source code editor. Although most InterDev users are familiar with Web application projects, the concept of a Database project might be unfamiliar ground. Visual InterDev provides excellent tools to manage databases that, for developers, rival those that come with SQL Server 7.0.

Database projects can be combined with Web application projects and even other database projects to form complex solutions that work as a single unit within InterDev. The creation and management of database objects such as tables, triggers, stored procedures, queries, and more has never been easier, thanks to the tools included in InterDev. For the Web/database developer, Visual InterDev is truly a one-stop solution.

ActiveX Data Objects 2.0

by Paul Thurrott

IN THIS CHAPTER

Visual InterDev is at an interesting point in its development: The latest version, 6.0, is far more visual than the preceding edition, but it's still a far cry from the wizard-like niceties of Visual Basic. Although it's probably true that the future of Web development will be more visual, the reality now is that we have a lot of code to write. When it comes to database integration, there's almost no way to get around the necessity of writing code. The good news, of course, is that Microsoft is doing everything it can to make this sort of activity easier than ever. With the move to ActiveX Data Objects 2.0, Web developers finally have a data access library that's as powerful as it is simple.

Accessing Databases Programmatically

The move to simplified programming languages such as Visual Basic caused Microsoft to begin developing simple data access schemes soon after the release of Windows 3.1. The first object-based, instead of truly object-oriented, data access libraries appeared with Visual Basic 3.0 and were dubbed Data Access Objects (DAO), based on the Microsoft Access Jet database engine. Before DAO, developers wanting to access information in databases had to program directly to the ODBC API, a nasty collection of C-based function calls that largely ignores the Visual Basic world. DAO offers developers a simplified object model for working with local databases, and it was an instant success with VB programmers.

With the release of a 32-bit Visual Basic 4.0 in 1995, Microsoft developed a new data access library, Remote Data Objects (RDO), that provides for access to remote databases and introduces a concept Visual Basic programmers now take for granted: bound controls. Using RDO, programmers can "attach" database fields to standard text boxes and other controls so that navigating through a recordset automatically updates the display in the bound controls. RDO was designed as a wrapper around ODBC, and it uses an object model based on that API. Although RDO was a big success, it remained largely unchanged through the releases of Visual Basic 5.0 and 6.0 because Microsoft had moved on to yet another data access model and a universal data access strategy that would change the face of database programming forever.

Introduced with Visual Basic 5.0, ActiveX Data Objects (ADO) is the end result of Microsoft's universal data access strategy (described in Chapter 11, "Using the Visual Database Tools"). Based on COM-based OLE DB technology instead of straight ODBC, ADO has been upgraded over the course of several product releases, including Internet Information Server 3.0, the Windows NT 4.0 Option Pack, and Visual Basic 6.0. As of this writing, the current version is ADO 2.1, which ships with Office 2000.

ADO 1.x

The various 1.x releases of ADO are limited, offering most of the functionality that pro-grammers need, but only a subset of the features developers were accustomed to with DAO and RDO. Designed primarily as a fast, lightweight data transport technology that would work effectively on TCP/IP networks such as the Internet, most ADO 1.5 develop-ers used ADO 1.x exclusively with server-side scripting languages such as JScript and VBScript. It wasn't until the more full-featured ADO 2.0 arrived in late 1998 that Microsoft made it obvious that the future was all ADO and that there was no turning back.

> **NOTE**
>
> Because we're dealing with Visual InterDev and VBScript specifically here, I am taking a very Visual Basic–centric view of things. The ADO object model does work with other languages as well, however, including Visual C++ and Visual J++ (Java).

An Introduction to ADO 2.x

ActiveX Data Objects 2.0 provides a simple, Visual Basic–centric way to access remote and local data using COM-based OLE DB technology. Although OLE DB itself is avail-able to Visual Basic developers (but not to Visual Basic Script or JScript developers) who must offer generic ways to access heterogeneous data, ADO is designed specifically to access data in relational databases such as SQL Server. In this sense, ADO is a bridge technology between the relatively complex world of OLE DB and simplified program-ming environments such as Visual Basic, Visual Basic for Applications, and VBScript/JScript.

ADO is implemented as a set, or library, of discrete objects. That is, unlike other data access libraries, such as DAO and RDO, the objects in ADO are not dependent on one another, and they can be created separately from one another. This works nicely with the non–object-oriented Visual Basic (and with VBScript and JScript for Visual InterDev developers) because these languages do not support the full range of OOP features but do support simplified object-based programming models. Other, more hierarchical object models require that base objects be instantiated before objects lower in the hierarchy are created. ADO removes this complexity.

Any object in an object model such as ADO supports a variety of characteristics called *properties*. An object also performs actions called *methods*, which are basically functions that are attached to the object and cannot be run separately from the object. An object also responds to *events*, which notify the object when they occur, or *fire*.

Web Development Features in ADO 2.x

As mentioned previously, ActiveX Data Objects 2.0 enables you to create independent objects. This means that your ADO code is smaller and faster than similar code written in DAO or RDO (not that it matters, frankly, because as a VBScript or JScript writer, you're pretty much limited to ADO 2.0 when it comes to data access anyway). Like RDO, ADO includes features for batch updating of data to a database, enabling you to compile a list of updates locally and then execute the entire batch as a single unit. The batch-updating features in ADO, however, are far more powerful than those in RDO.

For SQL Server users, ADO 2.0 supports stored procedures with both input and output parameters (ADO 1.5 supports only input parameters), return values, and multiple result sets. Although you will be working through the full range of ADO data access features in this chapter, it is no exaggeration that truly scalable production systems will always use stored procedures, rather than initiate repetitive dynamic queries using ADO called from an ASP page. Before ADO 2.0, this was impossible because the object model didn't support the variety of ways information can pass to and from a stored procedure. That limitation no longer exists, however, so now there is little excuse. Oftentimes, you can't be sure that a stored procedure executed properly, without examining its return code. With ADO 2.0, you can now do this and write conditional code based on this value. In Chapter 15, "Displaying Data in a Web Application," you will take a long look at calling stored procedures from ASP pages using ADO.

ADO 2.0 also supports a new client-side cursor that currently isn't applicable to Web development. If you'd like to implement client-side cursors for Web clients, however, ADO 2.0 and Internet Explorer 4.0+ (but not Netscape Navigator) support Remote Data Services (RDS). This lessens the load on the server, passing control and management of recordsets to the browser.

Another key feature for Web developers is the capability to limit the number of rows returned when a recordset is generated. When you're working over the Web, you don't want a dynamic query to generate 1,500 records. With the proper cursors and/or the appropriate code, you can limit the number of recordsets retrieved, improving performance and speed for your clients.

In ADO 2.0, Microsoft has provided native OLE DB data providers for SQL Server, Jet, and Oracle so that you don't have to work through the ODBC drivers for these databases. Native OLE DB providers tend to be faster than their ODBC equivalents and will only improve over time. By moving to native data providers now, you ensure that future driver updates provide automatic performance improvements without you having to update any code.

In addition to these features, ADO 2.0 adds dozens of new capabilities that are more easily realized from application programming languages such as Visual Basic or Visual C++. I am limiting this discussion of ADO to those features that directly affect Web developers. In upcoming sections, you will look at the ADO object model and the ways these objects can be used in your ASP pages.

Using the ADO Objects

The ADO object model (shown in Figure 12.1) defines the base objects you work with to perform specific actions in your ultimate quest to access data. The base objects, such as Connection, Recordset, and Command, can be created independently of one another and are related in a hierarchical sense. On the other hand, you will typically relate a Recordset object to a Connection object, for example. In fact, many ADO objects do work together, even though they aren't dependent on one another.

FIGURE 12.1
The ADO 2.0 object model.

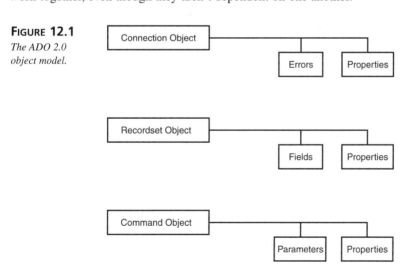

12

ACTIVEX DATA OBJECTS 2.0

Now for a look at each object in the ADO object model.

Using the Connection Object

The *Connection object* lies at the top of the ADO object model and represents the actual data connection, or data source. That is, the properties of the Connection object *identify* the data source and determine its characteristics. Connection object properties and methods can be used to configure the connection before it is opened, determine whether batch updates are supported, set the default database, specify the OLE DB data provider, physically establish (and then later break) the connection to the data source, execute a command (that can be encapsulated by a Command object), and much more. Table 12.1 summarizes the properties and methods of the Connection object.

TABLE 12.1 THE CONNECTION OBJECT PROPERTIES AND METHODS

Name	Type	What It Does
Attributes	Property	Determines whether the Connection object can automatically start new transactions.
BeginTrans	Method	Begins a new transaction.
Cancel	Method	Cancels a pending Execute or Open method call.
Close	Method	Closes an open Connection object.
CommandTimeout	Property	Determines the amount of time a command will attempt to execute before timing out and causing an error.
CommitTrans	Method	Saves changes and ends the current transaction.
ConnectionString	Property	Contains a detailed string of text that provides the information necessary to connect to a data source.
ConnectionTimeout	Property	Determines the amount of time a connection will be attempted before a time out occurs and an error is generated.
CursorLocation	Property	Determines whether a client or server cursor is used (the server is the default; only RDS can use client cursors).
DefaultDatabase	Property	Determines which database is accessed by default when a connection is made to the data source.

Name	Type	What It Does
Execute	Method	Executes a SQL query or script, or stored procedure without using a separate Command object.
IsolationLevel	Property	Determines the level of isolation for the Connection object and is used only within transactions.
Mode	Property	Determines the access permissions used when connecting to a data source.
Open (connection)	Method	Opens a connection to a data source.
OpenSchema	Method	Retrieves information about the database schema of the associated data source. The schema info is returned in a read-only recordset.
Provider	Property	Determines the name of the data provider for the connection.
RollbackTrans	Method	Cancels changes and ends the current transaction.
State	Property	Indicates whether the Connection object is currently open or closed.
Version	Property	Retrieves the version number of the ADO engine currently in use.

12

ACTIVEX DATA OBJECTS 2.0

Looking over this massive list of properties and methods, you might think that the Connection object is unwieldy and hard to use. Actually, most of these properties and methods are used rarely, if ever, and you can create simple Connection objects with a minimum of code. Consider the following code snippet:

```
<%
Set cn = Server.CreateObject("ADODB.Connection")
cn.ConnectionString = "driver={SQL Server};server=NTS;uid=sa;pwd=;"
cn.Open
cn.DefaultDatabase = "pubs"

cn.Close
%>
```

Here you see a simple Connection object created, with a connection string that identifies the data provider (SQL Server), the server name (NTS—in this case, an IP address is also valid), and the username and password required for authentication. When the data connection is opened, the default database for the connection is set to the Pubs database, and then the connection is closed.

You could achieve this same effect in a variety of ways. For example, the following code snippet does basically the same thing but explicitly uses a machine DSN (pubs_local) in the connection string. Because the Pubs database is set as the default database by the DSN, there's no need to explicitly set that property here.

```
<%
Set cn = Server.CreateObject("ADODB.Connection")
cn.ConnectionString = "DSN=pubs_local;uid=sa;pwd=;"
cn.Open

cn.Close
%>
```

In fact, this code could be further compressed by simply passing the connection string to the Open method, rather than explicitly using the ConnectionString property:

```
<%
Set cn = Server.CreateObject("ADODB.Connection")
cn.Open "DSN=pubs_local;uid=sa;pwd=;"

cn.Close
%>
```

In fact, this is the way that most people use the Connection object (if they use it at all) in Active Server Pages. Simply set up a DSN with all the connection information and use the Open method to connect to that data source, while providing the login name (UID) and password (pwd).

Connection Object Collections

In addition to the properties and methods you will commonly work with, the Connection object also supplies a set of two collections that handle errors and properties. The *Errors collection* contains any errors that are generated by any objects associated with the current connection. In other words, if you've associated a Recordset or Command object with the current connection, errors generated by these objects will be stored in that Command object's Errors collection.

The Errors collection supports a read-only Count property that provides the number of errors stored in the collection and an Item property that lets you access each error in the collection by number. For example, if no errors are generated during the lifetime of the current connection, the Count property will contain a value of 0. Each time an error is generated, the property is incremented by one. To view a list of the errors generated during the lifetime of the current Connection object, you could use code such as the following:

```
<%
For x = 1 to cn.Errors.Count
    Response.write x & "<BR>"
Next
%>
```

The problem with this feature is that it's almost impossible to use from Active Server Pages: Visual Basic Script supports only part of Visual Basic's error-handling routines, On Error Resume Next, but not On Error Goto <error handler>. Because of this limitation, there is no way to easily integrate VBScript error handling with the Errors collection. Ideally, you would want to place your database access code into subroutines, mark them with On Error blocks, and then trigger the error handler block if the Error Count property exceeds 0. In the real world, unfortunately, this is impossible. Because of this, in only a few instances is this collection useful in the real world.

The other Connection object collection, *Properties*, stores all the properties for the current connection in a collection. Like the Errors collection, Properties supplies a Count property that stores the number of items in the collection and an Item property that lets you access each collection object individually.

Using the Recordset Object

Perhaps the most used object in the ADO object library is the *Recordset object*, which is used to temporarily store the set of records (also called a *result set* or more simply, *recordset*) that is returned by a SQL query. Technically, a recordset contains zero or more records, as well as other (sometimes optional) information about the data, such as the number of records contained by the recordset and the fields that make up the recordset columns. Additionally, recordsets have a *cursor* that indicates the current pointer position within the recordset (that is, the current row). As such, only one record is available at a time when working with a recordset, and the cursor can point to no row (when the recordset contains no data), before the first row, at any row, or at the position after the last row. To handle those instances when the cursor is pointing before the first row or after the last row, Microsoft has resurrected a blast from Basic's past, the BOF (Beginning Of File) and EOF (End Of File) markers. Don't be confused by the nomenclature, however; a recordset is not a file.

NOTE

This section deals with the server-side, or ADODB Recordset, not the client-side, or ADOR Recordset object. The ADOR Recordset is covered later in this chapter.

12

ACTIVEX DATA OBJECTS 2.0

Perhaps the most exciting thing about the ADO Recordset is that you can create one without having to explicitly create Connection or Command objects. On the other hand, there's no good reason not to create these objects, except for the desire to create more compact code. The highly flexible nature of ADO and its nonhierarchical object model makes for an overly generous number of ways to get data out of a database. Naturally, I describe some of the better ways here in this section. Table 12.2 summarizes the properties and methods of the Connection object.

TABLE 12.2 THE RECORDSET OBJECT PROPERTIES AND METHODS

Name	Type	What It Does
AbsolutePage	Property	When you divide a recordset into logical pages with PageSize, this property specifies the page that the current record (the cursor) resides in.
AbsolutePosition	Property	Retrieves the number of the current record, where the first record is record 1.
ActiveConnection	Property	Determines the Connection object that the recordset is associated with.
AddNew	Method	Creates a new record in the recordset (assuming the recordset is updatable).
BOF	Property	Indicates that the current record position is before the first record in the recordset.
Bookmark	Property	Saves the current record position so that you can easily return to that position later.
CacheSize	Property	Determines how many records may be stored in RAM; must be greater than 0. A value of 5 would store five recordsets in RAM.
Cancel	Method	Cancels the execution of an Execute or Open method.
CancelBatch	Method	Cancels a batch update.
CancelUpdate	Method	Cancels any changes to the current record or a new record before the execution of the Update method.
Clone	Method	Creates a duplicate copy of the recordset that may optionally be read-only.
CursorLocation	Property	Determines whether the cursor is server based (default) or client based (IE only).

Name	Type	What It Does
CursorType	Property	Determines the type of cursor used by the recordset; forward-only, keyset, dynamic, or static cursors are possible.
Delete	Method	Deletes the current record.
EditMode	Property	Determines whether the current record is being edited, is not being edited, is a new record, or was recently deleted.
EOF	Property	Indicates that the current record position is after the last record in the recordset.
Filter	Property	Enables you to filter the result set stored by the recordset, based on any type of valid criteria.
LockType	Property	Determines the type of lock placed on the recordset during editing: read-only, pessimistic locking, optimistic locking, or optimistic batch locking.
MaxRecords	Property	Limits the number of rows returned by a recordset.
Move	Method	Moves the current record position to a new position.
MoveFirst	Method	Moves the current record position to the first record.
MoveLast	Method	Moves the current record position to the last record.
MoveNext	Method	Moves the current record position to the next record.
MovePrevious	Method	Moves the current record position to the preceding record.
NextRecordset	Method	Returns the next recordset when the results of a query require multiple recordsets.
Open	Method	Opens a recordset that represents the entire contents of a table, the results of a SQL query, or the contents of a previously saved recordset.

continues

TABLE 12.2 CONTINUED

Name	Type	What It Does
PageCount	Property	Indicates how many logical pages a recordset is divided into when the PageSize property is set.
PageSize	Property	Divides a recordset into logical pages of records, effectively dividing the recordset into manageable units.
RecordCount	Property	Retrieves the number of records in the recordset, if possible.
Requery	Method	Re-executes the SQL query that populated the recordset and repopulates the recordset.
Resync	Method	Manually synchronizes the data in a recordset with the underlying database data it represents when the actual data has been modified (useful for recordsets with a forward-only or static cursor).
Save	Method	Saves the recordset to a file (persists the recordset).
Sort	Property	Specifies which field(s) the recordset is sorted on.
Source	Property	Indicates the type of source for the recordset: Command object, SQL query/statement, table name, or stored procedure.
State	Property	Determines whether the recordset is open or closed.
Status	Property	Determines the status of the recordset, based on a long list of possible values (new record, modified, deleted, and so on).
Supports	Method	Determines whether the recordset supports specific types of functionality, for example, whether the recordset supports AddNew, bookmarks, or the ability to move the cursor backward through the result set.
Update	Method	Saves any changes you've made to the current record, assuming the recordset supports updates. This affects the underlying database, not just the recordset.
UpdateBatch	Method	Saves all pending batch changes to the underlying database.

Displaying Data with a Recordset

As with the Connection object, this list of possible properties and methods can be somewhat daunting, but in real-world use, the recordset is surprisingly useful. If anything, there are too many ways to do the same things. Consider a simple example that uses an explicit Connection object:

```
<%
Set cn = Server.CreateObject("ADODB.Connection")
Set rs = Server.CreateObject("ADODB.Recordset")

cn.Open "DSN=pubs_local;UID=sa;Password=;"
rs.ActiveConnection = cn
rs.Open "SELECT au_fname, au_lname FROM authors"

Do While NOT rs.EOF
    Response.write rs("au_fname") & " "
    Response.write rs("au_lname") & "<BR>"
    rs.MoveNext
Loop

rs.Close
cn.Close
%>
```

In this code, two server-based ADO objects are created: a Connection object (cn) and a Recordset object (rs). The Recordset uses cn for its data connection and then executes the Open method, passing a plain text SQL query as the only parameter. Then, the results of this query are displayed using a simple loop that iterates through the recordset, using the MoveNext method. Figure 12.2 shows the resulting Web page.

The nice thing about a Recordset object, however, is that you can create one independently of a Connection object. This type of recordset is sometimes referred to as a *firehose* recordset because of its speed, and it's an ideal recordset to use on public Web sites because you typically have to display read-only data in the fastest possible way.

To create a firehose recordset, you have to work with some of the optional parameters to the Recordset's Open method. This effectively duplicates the functionality of a Connection object by transparently creating a non-named data connection for you. The Open method takes a number of comma-separated parameters with the following form:

```
<recordset name>.Open
  <Source,> <Active Connection,> <Cursor Type,> <Lock Type,>
```

FIGURE 12.2

The results of your simple query displayed in a Web page.

Specifically, you have to work with the following parameters:

- Source—A valid SQL query, Command object, table name, stored procedure call, or saved (persisted) recordset.

- Active Connection—A valid Connection object or connection string.

- Cursor Type—The type of cursor that should be used (you will use a forward-only cursor in this example; see the next section for details).

- Lock Type—The type of locking used (you will use read-only locking here; see the next section for more information).

Therefore, a firehose recordset takes the following form:

```
<%
Set rs = Server.CreateObject("ADODB.Recordset")
rs.Open "SELECT au_fname, au_lname FROM authors", _
  "DSN=pubs_local;UID=sa;Password=;", 0, 1

Do While NOT rs.EOF
    Response.write rs("au_fname") & " "
    Response.write rs("au_lname") & "<BR>"
    rs.MoveNext
Loop

rs.Close
%>
```

When you compare this code to the previous example, you can see that the Recordset's Open method optionally can take on the functionality of the Connection object's Open method.

The methods you choose in order to display data via an ASP page (typically, through a mixture of HTML and ASP/ADO code) depend on the type of site you're creating and the data you're accessing. These issues are thoroughly explored in Chapter 15.

Working with Cursors and Locks

In the previous examples, we've created read-only recordsets with forward-only cursors. If you don't specify the type of cursor or lock type to use with a recordset, ADO gives you these values by default. What if you want to do something more powerful, though, than display read-only data quickly? The Recordset object supports different kinds of cursors and locks that enable you to do all kinds of things, such as update or add new data, delete data, and obtain the number of records in a recordset. These features are inaccessible to read-only, forward-only recordsets. Table 12.3 lists the various cursor types (accessible through the Recordset object's Open method CursorType parameter), and Table 12.4 lists the various lock types (accessible via the LockType parameter to the same method).

TABLE 12.3   THE CURSORTYPE PARAMETERS FOR THE RECORDSET OPEN METHOD

Cursor Type	Numeric Equivalent	What It Does
adOpenForwardOnly	0	Forward-only cursor optimized for scrolling quickly through records. Changes made by other users are invisible to this cursor (default).
adOpenKeyset	1	A keyset cursor that isn't aware of records added by other users. Records deleted by other users are inaccessible, however. The cursor can move in any direction.
adOpenDynamic	2	A dynamic cursor that is aware of additions, changes, and deletions by other users. The cursor can move in any direction.
adOpenStatic	3	A static cursor that is similar to a forward-only cursor (in that changes made by other users are not visible) except that the cursor can move in any direction.

TABLE 12.4   THE LOCKTYPE PARAMETERS FOR THE RECORDSET OPEN METHOD

Numeric LockType	Equivalent	What It Does
adLockReadOnly	1	Read-only recordset (default).
adLockPessimistic	2	Locking occurs when a record is edited; handled by the OLE DB provider.
adLockOptimistic	3	Records are locked only when the Update method is called.
adLockBatchOptimistic	4	Used when updating records in batch mode, instead of single-record immediate mode.

To access the CursorType and LockType constants, you must add a reference to ADOVBS.INC, an include file that provides numerous ADO constant names for VBScript. By default, this file can be found in C:\Program Files\Common\System, but it's a good idea to simply copy the file to your Web application project's root directory and use code such as the following to "include" this file's constants:

```
<!--#include file="ADOVBS.INC"-->
```

Conversely, you could simply use the numeric equivalents and forego the include file altogether. It's up to you.

Depending on the type of cursor and lock you use, various other recordset features become available. To obtain the number of records in a recordset, for example, you can use the Recordset object's RecordCount property, but this property contains a value of -1 if the recordset is forward-only, read-only. To obtain an accurate count, you must set the CursorType parameter to adOpenKeyset or adOpenStatic (the second choice is a little faster).

The following code block resembles the preceding example, but provides a printout of the number of records, as shown in Figure 12.3.

```
<%
Set rs = Server.CreateObject("ADODB.Recordset")
rs.Open "SELECT au_fname, au_lname FROM authors", _
        "DSN=pubs_local;UID=sa;Password=;", _
        adOpenStatic, adLockReadOnly

Do While NOT rs.EOF
    Response.write rs("au_fname") & " "
    Response.write rs("au_lname") & "<BR>"
```

```
    rs.MoveNext
Loop

Response.write "<P>This recordset contains " & rs.RecordCount & _
    " records."

rs.Close
%>
```

FIGURE 12.3

By using the right kind of cursor, you're able to easily retrieve the number of records in the recordset.

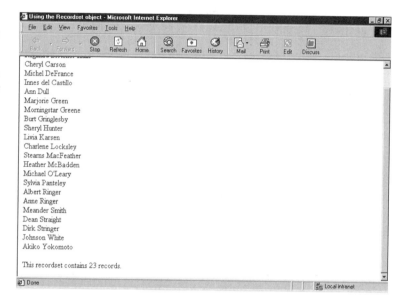

Note that adOpenStatic and adLockReadOnly could have been replaced by 3 and 1 in the code, respectively, so that the line of code that populates the recordset would read as follows:

```
rs.Open "SELECT au_fname, au_lname FROM authors", _
    "DSN=pubs_local;UID=sa;Password=;", 3, 1
```

This would have exactly the same effect as the previous example.

Adding a New Record to a Recordset

Often, you will want to add a new record to the recordset, thus affecting the underlying database when the information is updated. To do this, you have to use the *AddNew* and *Update methods* in tandem with a pessimistic or optimistic lock. Consider the following code, which adds a new record to the authors table in Pubs:

```
<%
Set rs = Server.CreateObject("ADODB.Recordset")
rs.Open "authors", "DSN=pubs_local;UID=sa;Password=;", _
        adForwardOnly, adLockPessimistic

rs.AddNew
rs("au_id") = CStr("123-45-6789")
rs("au_lname") = CStr("Thurrott")
rs("au_fname") = CStr("Paul")
rs("phone") = CStr("123 456-7890")
rs("address") = CStr("123 Visual InterDev Way")
rs("city") = CStr("Phoenix")
rs("state") = CStr("AZ")
rs("zip") = CStr("85018")
rs("contract") = CInt(1)
rs.Update

rs.Close
%>
```

This code opens the authors table with a pessimistic lock and adds a new record. First, the AddNew method creates a new blank record in the recordset. Then, the fields in the new record are filled in with appropriate data. Finally, the changes are saved to the recordset and the underlying table in the database with the Update method. You can prove that the table was updated by loading it into Visual InterDev (see Figure 12.4) or using a Web page to view the records in the table.

FIGURE 12.4

When the Update method is called, the new record is added to the table.

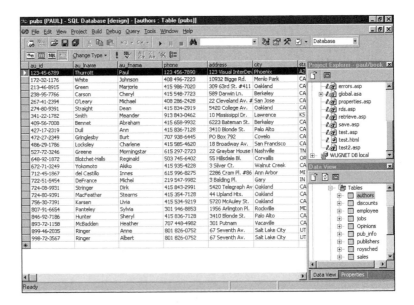

Incidentally, the Update method can be used apart from the AddNew method to update any data that's changed in the current recordset. Chapter 17, "Modifying Web Application Data from the Web," discusses in more detail adding and changing data in a database (and the various issues that surround these operations).

Deleting Records

You can also delete records from a recordset, and therefore from the underlying database, when you're using the right kind of cursor. The Recordset object's *Delete method* marks the current record for deletion: If the record can be deleted (the lock isn't read-only), it will be deleted. Otherwise, an error will occur. Also, when you've deleted a record, you have to move the cursor position to another record.

The following code lists the authors in the Pubs database, deletes the record added earlier, and then redisplays the list of authors. Figure 12.5 shows the results.

```
<%@ Language=VBScript %>

<!--#include file="ADOVBS.INC"-->

<HTML>
<HEAD>
<META NAME="GENERATOR" Content="Microsoft Visual Studio 6.0">
<TITLE>Deleting a record</TITLE>
</HEAD>

<BODY BGCOLOR="#FFFFFF">

<TABLE WIDTH=600 BORDER=1 CELLPADDING=5 CELLSPACING=0>
    <TR>
        <TD WIDTH=50% ALIGN=LEFT VALIGN=TOP>
<%
Set rs = Server.CreateObject("ADODB.Recordset")
rs.Open "authors", "DSN=pubs_local;UID=sa;Password=;", _
        adOpenDynamic, adLockOptimistic

Response.write "<H2>Authors before deletion:</H2>"
Do While NOT rs.EOF
    Response.write rs("au_fname") & " " & rs("au_lname") & "<BR>"
    rs.MoveNext
Loop
%>
        </TD>
<%
rs.MoveFirst
rs.Delete
rs.MoveFirst
%>
        <TD WIDTH=50% ALIGN=LEFT VALIGN=TOP>
```

```
<%
Response.write "<H2>Authors after deletion:</H2>"
Do While NOT rs.EOF
    Response.write rs("au_fname") & " " & rs("au_lname") & "<BR>"
    rs.MoveNext
Loop

rs.Close
%>
        </TD>
    </TR>
</TABLE>

</BODY>

</HTML>
```

FIGURE 12.5

Now you see him, now you don't. First, the authors are displayed. Then one is deleted. Finally, the authors are displayed again.

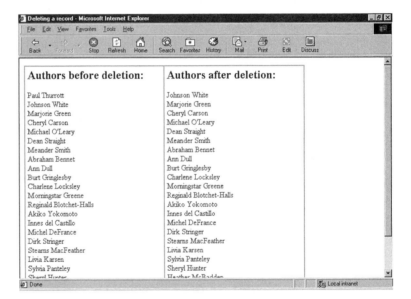

This bears some examination. As an example, it's not a good representation of the type of code you will use in the real world, but rather a demonstration of the Delete method (again, check out Chapter 17 for real-world recordset manipulation). This code assumes that the preceding AddNew example has been executed. As such, a new author (*Paul Thurrott*) has been added to the table; it displays as the first record in the recordset, which simply grabs the whole table. In the far left column of the HTML table, the list of authors (including the recent addition) is displayed. Then, the cursor is moved back to the first record, and that record is deleted with the Delete method. Finally, the list of authors is displayed again in the far right column of the HTML table, this time minus

Paul Thurrott. Notice that a call to MoveFirst occurs after the deletion as well: The delete operation is performed as soon as the cursor is moved away from the record being deleted.

Using the Command Object

The third major base object in the ActiveX Data Objects object model is the *Command object*, which is used to store information about the SQL query you plan to run against the database. Both the Connection object and the Recordset object enable you to bypass the Command object by coding command parameters directly into their Open and Execute methods, but the Command object offers its options in a more accessible and flexible format. It should be noted that a Command object implicitly is created automatically by a Connection or Recordset object if you don't create one explicitly.

Like the Connection and Recordset objects, the Command object offers a number of properties and methods for you to use. Table 12.5 summarizes these.

TABLE 12.5   THE COMMAND OBJECT PROPERTIES AND METHODS

Name	Type	What It Does
ActiveConnection	Property	Determines which Connection object the Command object is associated with.
Cancel	Method	Cancels a pending Execute or Open method call.
CommandText	Property	Contains the text of the command you are executing against the database; typically a SQL statement, a table name, or a stored procedure call.
CommandTimeout	Property	Determines the amount of time, in seconds, that the system will wait before terminating a command execution that hasn't completed.
CommandType	Property	Determines the type of command: text, table name, and so on.
CreateParameter	Method	Creates a new Parameter object.
Execute	Method	Executes the SQL query, table name, or stored procedure represented by the current Command object.

continues

TABLE 12.5 CONTINUED

Name	Type	What It Does
Prepared	Property	Determines whether a prepared (that is, *compiled*) version of the command should be saved the first time the command is executed. This is slower the first time, but much faster on subsequent executions.
State	Property	Describes whether the Command object is open or closed.

For the most part, you use a Command object to improve readability and explicitly set command options. In the following example, you explicitly create a Command object that is associated with a database table, the Pubs authors table, in this case. Rather than use the Recordset Open method to execute a SQL string, you can simply pass it the Command object.

```
<%
Set cn = Server.CreateObject("ADODB.Connection")
Set rs = Server.CreateObject("ADODB.Recordset")
Set cm = Server.CreateObject("ADODB.Command")

cn.Open "DSN=pubs_local;UID=sa;Password=;"

cm.CommandType = adCmdTable
cm.CommandText = "authors"
cm.ActiveConnection = cn

rs.ActiveConnection = cn
rs.Open cm

Do While NOT rs.EOF
    Response.write rs("au_fname") & " "
    Response.write rs("au_lname") & "<BR>"
    rs.MoveNext
Loop

rs.Close
cn.Close
%>
```

The results are similar to past examples: The contents of the authors table are displayed. An admittedly more elegant version of this code could pass a SQL string through the Command object instead:

```
<%
Set cn = Server.CreateObject("ADODB.Connection")
Set rs = Server.CreateObject("ADODB.Recordset")
Set cm = Server.CreateObject("ADODB.Command")

cn.Open "DSN=pubs_local;UID=sa;Password=;"

cm.CommandType = adCmdText
cm.CommandText = "SELECT au_fname, au_lname FROM authors"
cm.ActiveConnection = cn

rs.ActiveConnection = cn
rs.Open cm

Do While NOT rs.EOF
    Response.write rs("au_fname") & " "
    Response.write rs("au_lname") & "<BR>"
    rs.MoveNext
Loop

rs.Close
cn.Close
%>
```

You might have noticed the use of CommandType constants (adCmdTable and adCmdText) in the preceding two examples. Table 12.6 summarizes the available constants.

TABLE 12.6   THE COMMANDTYPE CONSTANTS

CommandType	Numeric Equivalent	What It Does
adCmdText	&H0001	The Command object contains a SQL query.
adCmdTable	&H0002	The Command object contains a table name.
adCmdTableDirect	&H0200	The Command object contains a table name (this is slightly faster than adCmdTable).
adCmdStoredProc	&H0004	The Command object contains the name of a stored procedure.
adCmdUnknown	&H0008	The type of command is unknown. This is slower than the other methods and should not normally be used (default).

continues

TABLE 12.6 CONTINUED

CommandType	Equivalent	What It Does
adCmdFile	&H0100	The Command object contains the name of a saved (persisted) recordset.
adExecuteNoRecords	4	The Command object contains a SQL query or stored procedure that doesn't return any rows.

Working with Command Parameters

Command objects are particularly useful when you're working with stored procedures. Many stored procedures make extensive use of *parameters*, which are used to pass data to and from the procedure. For this reason, the Command object contains a *Parameters collection*, which enables you to store a group of parameter objects that you can pass to a stored procedure. You can also use the Command object's *CreateParameter method* to create individual parameters. These parameters can be added to the Parameters collection by using its *Append method*. Here is an example. The Pubs database includes a stored procedure, *byroyalty*, that returns the IDs of the authors that match the royalty rate passed into the procedure. To see an example of this, locate the byroyalty stored procedure in the Data View window, right-click, and choose Execute. Enter 100, and a set of author IDs displays, shown in Figure 12.6.

FIGURE 12.6

Stored procedures with input parameters can be executed from the Visual InterDev IDE.

Here's the code for the stored procedure:

```
Alter PROCEDURE byroyalty @percentage int
AS
select au_id from titleauthor
where titleauthor.royaltyper = @percentage
```

Pretty simple isn't it? The byroyalty stored procedure accepts a single integer input parameter, percentage, and matches the entered value against the royalty types in the titleauthor table.

Let's get this on the Web. What you have to do is create explicit Command and Parameter objects. The Command object will have a CommandType of stored procedure, and the CommandText will be set to the name of the stored procedure (`"byroyalty"`). Then, you can create a Parameter object that will be named *percentage* to match the name of the parameter that's passed to the stored procedure. This parameter will be of type integer (like the stored proc parameter) and will be an input parameter. After this object is created, you can append it to the Command object's Parameters collection and assign it a value of 100.

Finally, you will return the results of the stored procedure to a recordset. Because the results contain a list of author IDs, this is the only data that will populate the recordset, and you will display this on the Web page. Here's the code:

```
<%
Set cn = Server.CreateObject("ADODB.Connection")
Set rs = Server.CreateObject("ADODB.Recordset")
Set cm = Server.CreateObject("ADODB.Command")
Set pr = Server.CreateObject("ADODB.Parameter")

cn.Open "DSN=pubs_local;UID=sa;Password=;"

cm.CommandType = adCmdStoredProc
cm.CommandText = "byroyalty"
cm.ActiveConnection = cn

Set pr = cm.CreateParameter("percentage", adInteger, adParamInput)
cm.Parameters.Append pr
pr.Value = CInt(100)

rs.ActiveConnection = cn
rs.Open cm

Do While NOT rs.EOF
    Response.write rs("au_id") & "<BR>"
    rs.MoveNext
Loop
```

12

ACTIVEX DATA OBJECTS 2.0

```
rs.Close
cn.Close
%>
```

Sure enough, the results are the same: A set of 10 author IDs is displayed, this time on a Web page (see Figure 12.7).

FIGURE 12.7

It might not look like much, but this required the explicit creation of Connection, Command, Parameter, and Recordset objects.

Creating Persistent Recordsets

One subject that's come up here and there over the course of this chapter is the idea of a *persistent recordset*, which is simply a recordset that's been saved to a text file on the Web server. This file can be saved, and later accessed, to re-create the recordset. In general, saving anything to a text file on the server is a major no-no, but some repeatedly used recordsets are so complex that it's actually faster to do it this way. One could argue that this type of recordset is a prime candidate for a stored procedure, but poorly written stored procedures can create their own problems. If you're comfortable creating dynamic recordsets in ADO code, you might find some use for creating persistent recordsets as well.

Saving a Persistent Recordset

Saving a recordset as a text file is as simple as opening a recordset and callings its *Save method*. The Save method takes two parameters, FileName and PersistFormat. The FileName, obviously, will contain the filename and, optionally, the path of the file you're saving. PersistFormat currently has only one valid possible value, adPersistADTG (make sure to include that ADOVBS.INC file).

What happens when you execute the following ASP file?

```
<%@ Language=VBScript %>

<!--#include file="ADOVBS.INC"-->
```

```
<HTML>
<HEAD>
<META NAME="GENERATOR" Content="Microsoft Visual Studio 6.0">
<TITLE>Saving a persistent recordset</TITLE>
</HEAD>

<BODY BGCOLOR="#FFFFFF">

<%
Set rs = Server.CreateObject("ADODB.Recordset")
rs.Open "SELECT au_fname, au_lname FROM authors", _
        "DSN=pubs_local;UID=sa;Password=;", _
        adOpenStatic, adLockReadOnly

rs.Save "myrs.txt", adPersistADTG

rs.Close
%>

</BODY>

</HTML>
```

You might think that myrs.txt would be saved to the same directory that the ASP file was stored in. However, if you don't specify a path, it's actually stored in C:\WINNT\ SYSTEM32 by default on an NT Server system(!). Clearly, this isn't what you're after, and, indeed, most ISPs would never allow you to write to that directory. If you know the Windows-style path you'd like to save the file to, you could specify that as follows:

```
rs.Save "C:\myrs.txt", adPersistADTG
```

I suspect, however, that this isn't going to be a solution for many people. Therefore, it might make more sense to figure out the current path (that is, the path your ASP/HTML files are stored to) and save the file there. The path can be obtained with the *MapPath method* of the *Server object*. To get the path to the root of your Web site, for example, execute an ASP page that contains the following script:

```
Server.MapPath("/")
```

On my own system, this returns the following:

```
C:\Inetpub\wwwroot
```

Armed with this knowledge, you could rewrite the preceding example so that the record-set is saved to the root of your Web site (or, obviously, you could add more path information if you are working in a subdirectory off the root):

```
<%
Set rs = Server.CreateObject("ADODB.Recordset")
```

```
rs.Open "SELECT au_fname, au_lname FROM authors", _
        "DSN=pubs_local;UID=sa;Password=;", _
        adOpenStatic, adLockReadOnly

thePath = Server.MapPath("/") & "\myrs.txt"
rs.Save thePath, adPersistADTG

rs.Close
%>
```

Now that you've persisted the recordset, you need to be aware of what happens when you try to save it again. If you reload this page, you will see a message indicating that the file already exists. To get around this, you can save the recordset again without specifying any parameters.

Retrieving the Persisted Recordset Later

To retrieve the information from the saved recordset, you must use ADO code to create a new recordset. As with everything you've examined here, there are a multitude of ways to do this with any combination of Connection, Command, and Recordset objects. However, because you're dealing with just recordsets here, it makes sense to go down the path of least resistance. The following code creates a Recordset object and uses the Open method to open the persisted recordset file. For completeness, the recordset is displayed to prove that it can be done, as shown in Figure 12.8.

```
<%@ Language=VBScript %>

<!--#include file="ADOVBS.INC"-->

<HTML>
<HEAD>
<META NAME="GENERATOR" Content="Microsoft Visual Studio 6.0">
<TITLE>Retrieving a persisted recordset</TITLE>
</HEAD>

<BODY BGCOLOR="#FFFFFF">

<%
Set rs = Server.CreateObject("ADODB.Recordset")
rs.Open Server.MapPath("/") & "\myrs.txt"

Do While NOT rs.EOF
    Response.write rs("au_fname") & " "
    Response.write rs("au_lname") & "<BR>"
    rs.MoveNext
Loop
```

```
rs.Close
%>
```

```
</BODY>
</HTML>
```

FIGURE 12.8
*This recordset
was retrieved
from a text file,
not a database.*

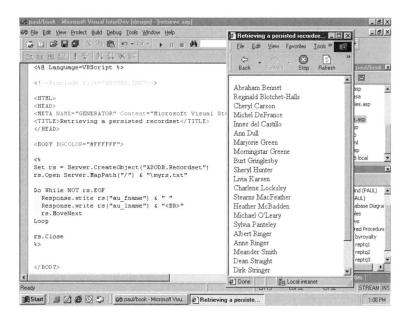

Using Remote Data Service

Until now, you have dealt solely with server-side database components that are implemented using ADO technology. One of the more recent additions to ADO, however, enables developers to take much of the load off the server and store data results on the client, which at this writing is only Internet Explorer 4.0 or higher. This client-side technology, known as Remote Data Service (RDS), is an extension to ADO that enables users to modify and view data directly in their browser without the need for frequent round-trips to the server. The benefit of RDS is that all Internet Explorer 4.0+ users can automatically take advantage of the technology: The feature is built right in. The problem, of course, is that it *requires* Internet Explorer; Navigator users need not apply.

For the foreseeable future, it's likely that RDS will be an option only for corporate intranets, where you can be sure what client your users are running. Over the Web, it doesn't currently make sense to spend much time working with RDS right now. For this reason, I only mention this emerging technology for completeness and will spend most of the time on the browser-independent, server-side ADO.

Summary

ActiveX Data Objects 2.0 is a full-featured object model offering amazing power, flexibility, and speed. In fact, it might be argued that ADO is *too* flexible because it offers a staggering number of ways to accomplish your work. An understanding of ADO is the key to mastering Web application with Visual InterDev, even if you plan on using some of the more visual tools that appear in the most recent release.

The Connection, Command, and Recordset objects form the heart and soul of ADO 2.0, the version of ADO that ships with Visual InterDev 6.0. Using these objects, you can display, edit, add, and delete data in remote databases quickly and easily.

A Case Study: The WinInfo Newsletter on the WUGNET Web Site

I've published a daily Windows news and information newsletter called *WinInfo* since 1994. WinInfo is provided free of charge via email to anyone who's interested, and its readers—including numerous people at Microsoft, Sun, Netscape, and other high-tech firms—tend to be in the forefront of computing technology. If you're interested in more information, please visit the WinInfo Web site (`http://www.wugnet.com/wininfo`), shown in Figure 12.9.

FIGURE 12.9

The WinInfo Web site provides a searchable database of more than 2,000 news articles.

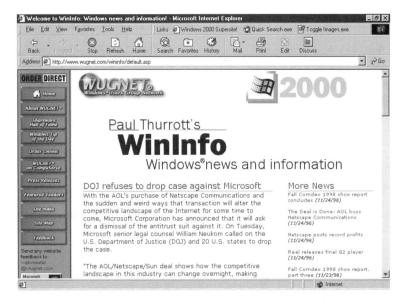

Since December 1996, every article written for WinInfo has been saved to a SQL Server database. The WinInfo Web site provides a dynamic view of this data, with up-to-date news articles, a list of the week's headlines, and a search function that enables users to probe the entire WinInfo database for articles of interest.

From day one, WinInfo has been at the forefront of the Web/database phenomena. As a member of Microsoft's SiteBuilder 3 group, I attended the very first Visual Studio ("Boston") seminar at the Microsoft campus in early 1997, a few months after receiving the first beta of Visual InterDev 1.0 (then known as *Internet Studio*) and discovering this emerging technology. As I worked away at InterDev in the days leading up to the seminar, it became clear that this was the future of Web development, and I immediately went to work on getting WinInfo into a database that could be published on the Web. As such, WinInfo was the first InterDev-based Web application to deliver daily news and information over the Internet.

After working with WUGNET for more than a year as the Webmaster at Big Tent Media Labs, I eventually moved WinInfo to the WUGNET Web site so that I could take advantage of its enormous user base, as well as the Microsoft and Windows community. WinInfo on WUGNET is a powerful SQL Server-based Web application that is easily managed and updated by using Web-based tools created in Visual InterDev, a Visual InterDev solution that includes Web and Database projects (see Figure 12.10), and a Visual Basic–based management tool that uses ADO to retrieve only the most recent articles so that I can easily modify them as needed. In the fast and furious world of Internet news, these tools are all I need to keep my Web site, and its SQL Server database, running in top form.

FIGURE 12.10

The WinInfo Visual InterDev solution is a one-stop management point for my Web and Database projects.

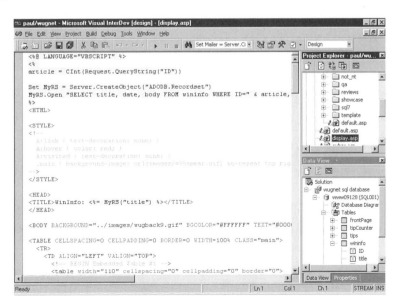

CHAPTER 13

Programming the Visual InterDev Data Environment

by Paul Thurrott

Using straight ActiveX Data Objects (ADO) and ASP scripting, it's possible to connect to a database, retrieve data, and display that data in ASP pages, using the Connection, Command, and Recordset objects described in Chapter 12, "ActiveX Data Objects 2.0." However, ADO itself doesn't offer any sort of code reuse capabilities. For example, an ADO Recordset you create on one ASP page can't be reused in another without first persisting it to disk.

With these limitations in mind, Microsoft created the Data Environment (DE), a new Web application feature that stores reusable data components to be used on any of the ASP pages in your Web site. The Data Environment works in two basic ways: through a simplified version of the ADO object model that you can access in script or via visual design-time ActiveX controls (DTCs), which provide a stepping stone between the all-text world of Web scripting and environments such as Visual Basic. In this chapter, you will examine the scripting capabilities in the Data Environment and its object model. Check out Chapter 14, "Using Data-Bound Controls," for details on using the visual Data Environment DTC controls.

An Introduction to the Data Environment (DE)

In Chapter 12, you had a look at the ADO object model and its core objects. The ADO object model is a decentralized, or nonhierarchical, object model that provides ways to access each of its objects independently of one another. This is contrary to previous data access object models such as DAO and RDO, but consistent with the simplified programming model we've come to expect with Visual Basic and Visual Basic Scripting Edition (VBScript). The Data Environment is, in many ways, a somewhat visual wrapper over ADO: It provides simple access to core ADO functionality without forcing you to get down-and-dirty with any real programming...that is, unless you want to.

There are some good reasons to learn the bare metal approach to the Data Environment and its object model. Although the move to visual environments such as Visual Basic is a good thing market-wise, it creates a market of people who don't understand what's going on behind the scenes. This trend also affects Windows NT system administration because the administration tools resemble the simple Windows applications we all know and love. With Visual InterDev 6.0 and FrontPage 2000, it's becoming a problem for Web development as well. The reality here is that Web development has matured from simple "Look at my cat" HTML-based Web sites to data-backed Web applications that incorporate Web scripting and server-side components. It's a brave new world out there.

Although I will be discussing the visual aspects of the Data Environment in the next chapter, it cannot be overstated that a basic understanding of what's happening is crucial to mastering this technology and the tools you use to create Web applications, such as Visual InterDev 6.0.

Okay, enough pontificating. The first step in using the Data Environment is to connect to some data.

Connecting to a Database with the Data Environment

To enable the Data Environment in your Web application, you have to add a *data connection*, which provides your project with a global database connection object. This is done by right-clicking the global.asa file in Project Explorer and choosing Add Data Connection. Grab a machine DSN and then give your data connection a descriptive name such as dcPubs (you will be using the SQL Server Pubs database for the examples in this chapter).

You might have noticed that a Data Environment heading was added right under your global.asa file in the Project Explorer. As soon as you add a data connection to your project, the Data Environment is automatically added. The Data Environment gives you a visual front end to any data connections and data commands that you add to your project. The thing to note here, of course, is that these objects are now available to any file in your Web application; you won't have to write code to create a Connection object or Command object on every single page that needs one.

NOTE

A quick caveat about the Data Environment: The data connections and commands you create in the DE are available only to server-side, not client-side, scripts.

Let's add a simple data command as well. A *data command* represents the database object or SQL code that you will execute against a data source, as defined by a data connection. Right-click the global.asa file or the Data Environment heading and choose Add Data Command. The dialog shown in Figure 13.1 appears.

FIGURE **13.1**

When creating a data command, you can choose a stored procedure, table, or view, or you can write your own SQL statement.

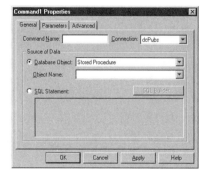

This dialog offers you the following options for your data command:

- Stored Procedure—Choose a stored procedure from the list of available procedures. If you want to write a new stored procedure for the data command, you must create it ahead of time.

- Table—Grab the entire contents of a base table, including every row (record) and column (field). You cannot create a new table from this dialog.

- View—Grab the entire contents of a view, which can consist of information from any number of base tables. You cannot create a new view from this dialog.

- Synonym—For use only with Oracle databases, this enables you to use an Oracle synonym as the basis for your data command.

- SQL Statement—The most advanced option, this enables you to hand-code any SQL statement or visually construct one using the SQL Builder button, which launches the Query Builder. The SQL statement can be any valid SQL code, including SELECT, INSERT, UPDATE, and DELETE queries. You could even code a CREATE TABLE SQL statement if you were feeling adventurous.

For this example, you will write a simple SQL statement. Add the following code under the SQL statement heading, give the command a descriptive name (such as cmAuthors), and click OK:

```
SELECT * FROM authors
```

As shown in Figure 13.2, the new data command offers a quick look at the fields that will be accessed when this command is executed.

FIGURE 13.2

This global data command grabs all the information stored in the authors table.

au_id	au_lname	au_fname	phone
172-32-1176	White	Johnson	408 496-7223
213-46-8915	Green	Marjorie	415 986-7020
238-95-7766	Carson	Cheryl	415 548-7723
267-41-2394	O'Leary	Michael	408 286-2428
274-80-9391	Straight	Dean	415 834-2919
341-22-1782	Smith	Meander	913 843-0462
409-56-7008	Bennet	Abraham	415 658-9932
427-17-2319	Dull	Ann	415 836-7128
472-27-2349	Gringlesby	Burt	707 938-6445
486-29-1786	Locksley	Charlene	415 585-4620
527-72-3246	Greene	Morningstar	615 297-2723
648-92-1872	Blotchet-Halls	Reginald	503 745-6402
672-71-3249	Yokomoto	Akiko	415 935-4228
712-45-1867	del Castillo	Innes	615 996-8275
722-51-5454	DeFrance	Michel	219 547-9982
724-08-9931	Stringer	Dirk	415 843-2991
724-80-9391	MacFeather	Stearns	415 354-7128
756-30-7391	Karsen	Livia	415 534-9219
807-91-6654	Panteley	Sylvia	301 946-8853
846-92-7186	Hunter	Sheryl	415 836-7128
893-72-1158	McBadden	Heather	707 448-4982
899-46-2035	Ringer	Anne	801 826-0752
998-72-3567	Ringer	Albert	801 826-0752

The information you see under the data command is dependent on the type of database object you've associated the command with. If you connect the command to a database table, it will show a list of the fields in that table; a structured query data command, however, will display only a list of the fields returned by the procedure.

Another key concept here is that each data command is associated with a data connection, not the entire Data Environment. This is because you might have numerous data connections that could, conceivably, point to different data sources. The data command you've created is associated with the Pubs database through the dcPubs data connection, but you could also connect to the Northwind database and create separate data connections and data commands associated with that database as well.

On that note, you can have only a single Data Environment for each Visual InterDev solution.

Code Reuse and the Data Environment

Before moving on, let's consider the code reuse features that you've already implemented, despite the fact that the Web application doesn't yet use the data connection or data command. In pre–Data Environment days, you would have hand-coded an ADO Connection object (or at the very least, hand-coded the information necessary to create an implicit data connection in a recordset) that duplicates the functionality of the data connection you just created. Also, you would have duplicated this code on any ASP page that had to connect to the same data source, effectively using the oldest (and weakest) form of code reuse known to man. We call it *cut and paste*. Ditto for the data command. Regardless of how you get at your data from ADO (through a Connection, Command, or

Recordset object), at some point you will have duplicated the same SQL string over a potentially enormous number of pages. Using a data command, however, enables you to write it once and use it on any page that needs that data access.

Perhaps more importantly, you can later update your data connections and data commands without having to recode every single one of your pages. Using the data environment, you do it once, and your whole site is updated automatically. Before the Data Environment made this possible, ASP developers were left creating skeleton templates for their data access pages so that they wouldn't have to rewrite the same code again and again. Those days are over.

Programming the DE Object Model

As mentioned previously, there are two ways to access Data Environment objects: visually, using the new Visual InterDev 6.0 DTCs, or through scripting code that directly accesses the Data Environment object model. The straight scripting method might seem more difficult, but it enables you to create much cleaner-looking ASP files because the DTCs create a mess of code that's hard to decipher. Also, as previously noted, you can't be expected to effectively debug your ASP scripts if you don't understand what's going on.

If you're familiar with ActiveX Data Objects, you know that the following code presents a typical way to access information from a database and display it, using a standard VBScript Do loop (if this doesn't sound familiar, check out Chapter 12 for details):

```
<%
Set cn = Server.CreateObject("ADODB.Connection")
Set rs = Server.CreateObject("ADODB.Recordset")

cn.Open "DSN=pubs;UID=sa;Password=;"
rs.ActiveConnection = cn
rs.Open "SELECT au_fname, au_lname FROM authors"

Do While NOT rs.EOF
    Response.write rs("au_fname") & " "
    Response.write rs("au_lname") & "<BR>"
    rs.MoveNext
Loop

rs.Close
cn.Close
%>
```

Data Environment code is similar, but even simpler. In ADO, you create instances of core ADO objects such as the Connection and Recordset objects used here (cn and rs, respectively). The Data Environment abstracts the ADO object model so that the Data Environment itself is the base object and ADO objects, such as the Command object, are exposed as methods of the Data Environment.

Confused? An example will clear up things. The first step to using the Data Environment is to create at least one data connection and data command, which you've done. Open a new ASP file and add the following small block of code:

```
<%
Set de = Server.CreateObject("DERuntime.DERuntime")
de.Init(Application("DE"))
%>
```

The first line should look familiar, at least in passing; it creates an instance of the Data Environment object, using the same basic syntax you use in ADO to create Connection, Recordset, and Command objects. The second line executes the Data Environment's Init method to initialize the environment for scripting. Now that you have this under your belt, you're ready to actually do something, such as retrieve some data. Here's what it looks like:

```
<%
de.cmAuthors
Set rs = de.rscmAuthors

Do While NOT rs.EOF
    Response.write rs("au_fname") & " "
    Response.write rs("au_lname") & "<BR>"
    rs.MoveNext
Loop
%>
```

Most of this will probably look familiar, but the first two lines will likely cause a bit of head scratching. The first line of code

```
de.cmAuthors
```

causes the Data Environment to open, or execute, the command. In this particular case, you're dealing with a SQL string that retrieves a set of records. You can access this "recordset" using the Data Environment's built-in *result set object*. Functionally equivalent to an ADO Recordset object, the DE result set can be dynamically created and assigned the set of records from an open data command. This is, indeed, what the second line of code does:

```
Set rs = de.rscmAuthors
```

13

THE VISUAL INTERDEV DATA ENVIRONMENT

But what's with the syntax? You never created an object called rscmAuthors! It turns out that this is a function of the Data Environment. To assign a set of records to a dynamically created DE result set object, use the following syntax:

```
Set rs = <Data Environment object name>.rs<Command object name>
```

Incidentally, the variable name rs is at your discretion as well: Like any variable, you can name this as you see fit. I use rs here only because it's easy to remember.

As you might expect, the Data Environment result set can use the full complement of ADO Recordset record navigation functions, such as MoveFirst, MoveLast, MoveNext, and the rest.

Working with Data Environment Collections

As you work with Data Environment objects in script, you will notice that the Visual InterDev auto-complete feature will pop up with three collection names as you type. These collections include Commands, Connections, and Recordsets, and they provide a way to programmatically access the features of the Data Environment object. The Commands collection contains information about the command objects you've created, and the Connections collection contains information about the connection objects. The Recordsets collection is a little more complicated, but I'll explain that later in the chapter. Each Data Environment collection features the same property and method, shown in Table 13.1.

TABLE 13.1   DATA ENVIRONMENT COLLECTION PROPERTIES AND METHODS

Method	*Type*	*What It Does*
Count	Property	Retrieves the number of members in the collection
Item	Method	Retrieves a member of the collection by its position in the collection

Take a look at these collections and see how they might be used in scripting.

Using the Collections

The Data Environment Connections collection contains information about the Connection objects you've created. Specifically, it contains the number of Connection objects you've created and a way to access each Connection object programmatically.

The number of Connection objects is stored with the Count property, which can be accessed like so:

```
x = de.Connections.Count
```

The Item property, meanwhile, enables you to access information about the connections by their index, or position, in the Connections collection. To retrieve information about the first Connection object in your project, you can use code such as the following:

```
<%
strConnInfo = de.Connections.Item(1)
Response.Write strConnInfo
%>
```

For your SQL Server data connection, the output from this code will resemble Figure 13.3.

FIGURE 13.3

The Item property enables you to get at information about the data connection.

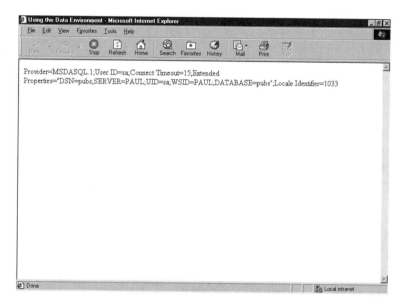

That's about it. The Commands and Recordsets collections work in the same basic way, and generally speaking, you won't have to programmatically access this information.

Stored Procedures and the Data Environment

In keeping with the theory that stored procedures are the single best way to access result sets that will be returned to a Web page, it's only fair that I dedicate some coverage to this advanced feature here. Using the Data Environment data command, it's easy to create global access to a stored procedure in your Web site. For the examples in this section, you will be working with the byroyalty stored procedure that comes with Pubs, because it requires an input parameter and returns a result set.

Creating a Stored Procedure Data Command

To add a data command to your project that references a stored procedure, right-click your dcPubs data connection and choose Add Data Command. In the resulting Command Properties dialog box, ensure that Stored Procedure is the database object and choose byroyalty from the Object Name drop-down list.

If you look at the Parameters tab of this dialog box (see Figure 13.4), you will see that the byroyalty stored procedure has two parameters: a return value that tells the client whether the procedure executed properly and an input parameter named *percentage*. This parameter is an integer, and it is required for the stored procedure to run properly. If no input value is provided, the stored procedure will exit with a return value of 1, indicating that a problem occurred. This dialog enables you to hard-code a value that will be passed as the percentage. Generally, though, you will want to pass this value dynamically, so you should leave that blank. On that note, if you know that the value of an input parameter is never going to change, why make an input parameter?

FIGURE 13.4

The Parameters tab of the Command Properties dialog box provides a wide range of information about the parameters for a stored procedure.

For simplicity's sake, call this data command cmSP. If you expand the data command in the Project Explorer, you will see that it retrieves a single-field result set consisting of the au_id field from the titleauthor table.

Passing Parameters to the Data Environment Object

The setup for a stored procedure–based data command is identical to that of a table or SQL string–based data command. Create an instance of the Data Environment object and initialize it. Then, execute the command as before to generate a result set. The difference here is that this stored procedure requires a parameter. To pass parameters to a command, use the following syntax:

```
<DE variable>.<data command name> (parameter, <parameter>, <...>)
```

The parameters should be enclosed in parentheses following the name of the data command and should be separated by commas. In the case of the single-parameter stored procedure, the following line of code will do:

```
de.cmSP(100)
```

This passes the integer value 100 to the stored procedure, which executes on the SQL Server and returns a result set. The result set can, of course, be applied to the built-in Data Environment result set and displayed as before:

```
Set rs = de.rscmSP

Do While NOT rs.EOF
    Response.write rs("au_id") & "<BR>"
    rs.MoveNext
Loop
```

This displays a list of 10 author IDs, demonstrated in Chapter 12. The difference here, of course, is that you've used the simplified Data Environment object model to get at your data.

Retrieving Single Values from a Stored Procedure

The preceding code works fine if the stored procedure returns a result set, but what if the data command returns a single value instead of (or in addition to) a result set? Unsurprisingly, it's easy to access the return value of a stored procedure or any other single value that's returned by a data command. The following code will retrieve the return value of data command:

```
intReturnValue = de.cmSP(100)
```

13

THE VISUAL INTERDEV DATA ENVIRONMENT

In this example, you're retrieving the return value of the byroyalty stored procedure, but the same general code will work fine for any kind of data command. The variable intReturnValue can be any name you happen to like.

Summary

Although it's true that the Data Environment really comes alive when you start working with the visual design-time controls described in the next chapter, the DE also provides a vastly simplified way to get at data when compared to the ActiveX Data Objects (ADO) object model. Like most things, coding the Data Environment by hand is a trade-off. ADO is a feature-rich object model with an almost overwhelming number of ways to do the same things. The Data Environment, in contrast, is far simpler to work with, offering only a couple of objects and collections that work in conjunction with global data connections and data commands to provide much, though not all, of the functionality of ADO.

The Visual InterDev Data Environment was designed around the concept that drag-and-drop server objects are the wave of the future. You will be able to decide whether that's true in the next chapter, when you explore the more visual side of the Data Environment and discover whether it will eventually replace ADO as the Web development tool of choice.

Using Data-Bound Controls

by Paul Thurrott

IN THIS CHAPTER

In Chapter 13, "Programming the Visual InterDev Data Environment," you took a look at the Data Environment, a new feature of Visual InterDev 6 that provides global, projectwide access to data connections and data commands, eliminating the need to manually re-create common database functionality from page to page. However, the Data Environment exposes far more functionality than its simplified object model, which can be coded by hand if desired. Using its drag-and-drop visual tools, the Data Environment works hand in hand with new design-time ActiveX controls (DTC) to provide developers with an incredibly powerful visual environment for adding database functionality to Web applications.

Microsoft's original design-time control specification dates back to the ActiveX Control Pad, a client-side scripting tool the company released in 1996 to facilitate the easy use of ActiveX controls, JScript, and VBScript in HTML documents. *Design-time controls* are ActiveX controls that provide a graphical user interface to the developer during design time (as opposed to runtime) so that control settings can be changed in a visual manner. During runtime, DTCs expose their functionality through scripting code to their ActiveX container, typically a Web browser for client-side controls or the ActiveX runtime in IIS for server-based controls. In other words, a DTC is basically a friendly front end to some prebuilt functionality that was implemented in VBScript or JavaScript (JScript). If programmed correctly, it can even act like a wizard, stepping the developer through various configuration options.

Although there are some client-side design-time controls floating around, the use of ActiveX controls in Web browsers never really caught on. When Microsoft introduced Dynamic HTML with Internet Explorer 4.0 in late 1997, the final nail was effectively struck in the coffin of client-side DTCs (and browser-hosted ActiveX controls, in general). Regardless, Visual InterDev users generally work with server-side controls. This eliminates any browser compatibility concerns, because the scripting code runs on the server, returning only simple HTML text to the browser.

In Visual InterDev 1.0, Microsoft introduced its first server-side DTCs and a rather weak way of using them in Web applications. VI 1.0 included only three design-time controls: the Data Command control, Data Range Header control, and Data Range Footer control. These somewhat limited controls were the basis of InterDev's buggy Data Form Wizard, which was subsequently dropped from the VI 6 project (although, interestingly, a similar wizard was added to Visual Basic 6). In Visual InterDev 6, server-side design-time controls were significantly updated with an array of new controls, and integration with the Scripting Object Model and the Data Environment. With the release of Visual InterDev 6, many Web developers will likely make the change from hand-coded ADO for database access to this more visual approach.

> **NOTE**
>
> To access every element in an HTML document, the Scripting Object Model provides an object-based method that will be familiar to Visual Basic and VBScript developers. The Scripting Object Model is covered in Chapter 3, "Programming the Scripting Object Model."

On that note, the design-time controls in Visual InterDev 6 are geared primarily toward data access, although a few interesting nondata controls are thrown in for good measure as well. InterDev 6 DTCs use a concept called *data binding* that is central to Web/database integration in your Web applications. With data-binding, specific fields in a recordset or other result set are bound, or connected, to specific controls. This concept will be familiar to anyone who has programmed database access in Visual Basic. By bringing this concept forward to Web developers, Microsoft has provided an obvious and familiar way to visually code database access in a Web application.

> **NOTE**
>
> Using methods specific to Internet Explorer, it is possible to work with client-side, data-bound controls. Because this would severely limit the potential audience, I will be covering only browser-independent, server-side methods here.

Design-Time Controls and the New Data Environment

Seasoned Visual InterDev developers will typically hand-code database access in their Web applications by writing to the ADO object model. Consider the following sample code:

```
<%@ Language=VBScript %>
<HTML>
<HEAD>
<META NAME="GENERATOR" Content="Microsoft Visual Studio 6.0">
```

14

USING DATA-
BOUND CONTROLS

```
</HEAD>
<BODY>

<%
Set cn = Server.CreateObject("ADODB.Connection")
Set rs = Server.CreateObject("ADODB.Recordset")

cn.Open "DSN=pubs;UID=sa;Password=;"
rs.ActiveConnection = cn
rs.Open "SELECT au_fname, au_lname FROM authors"

Do While NOT rs.EOF
    Response.write rs("au_fname") & " "
    Response.write rs("au_lname") & "<BR>"
    rs.MoveNext
Loop

rs.Close
cn.Close
%>

</BODY>

</HTML>
```

This code creates ADO Connection and Recordset objects, connects to the Pubs database, and retrieves the first and last name of each author in the authors table. Then, using a simple Do While loop, it outputs this information to plain HTML. There's nothing inherently wrong with this approach, but this sort of hand-coding adds significant overhead to your Web applications. What if, for example, the SQL Server username and/or password change? You would have to recode the page for the connection to complete, of course, and then recode every single other page that includes the old username and/or password. For large applications, this can be cumbersome. Furthermore, it's likely that you will eventually create some data-access skeleton code that you will want to reuse again and again on each page that requires this functionality.

In Chapter 13, I introduced the Data Environment, which provides a way to create data connections and data commands that are accessible throughout an entire Web application. This means that you can create a data connection to the Pubs database (as in the preceding example) just once and reference that connection on any ASP page you like. To create a recordset, all you have to do is literally drag a data command—which can contain the same SQL code you'd use in your hand-coded ADO code—onto an ASP page. Voilà! Instant code generation. Now you will see how this works.

Creating a DE Data Connection

The first step is to create a data connection. To do so, open a Web application project, right-click the global.asa file in the Project Explorer window, and choose Add Data Connection. If this is the first data connection you've added to the project, a new Data Environment heading will appear beneath global.asa, and the Select Data Source dialog box will appear. Select the appropriate machine data source (you will be using Pubs for these examples), and you will be prompted to log in to the database. Then, the Properties dialog box for your new data connection will appear. Here, you can give your data connection a logical name (such as dcPubs) and set other, authentication-related options. When you're finished, you will see a new data connection heading under the Data Environment heading in the Project Explorer.

Creating a DE Data Command

When you have established a data connection, you can add data commands to that connection. To do so, right-click the appropriate data connection (note that you can have more than one data connection in a single project) and choose Add Data Command. The Properties dialog appears for the connection, enabling you to set a wealth of properties for the command. As described in Chapter 13, a Data Command object can use a variety of data sources, including a stored procedure, an entire table, an entire view, a synonym (if you're using an Oracle database), or any valid block of SQL code. In keeping with the ADO example, you will use a simple SELECT statement here (SELECT au_fname, au_lname FROM authors), but the visual Query Builder (listed here as SQL Builder, for some reason) is also available for the SQL-phobic. You should also name the command something logical, such as cmAuthorNames.

The Advanced tab of this dialog box is particularly important. For some reason, Microsoft chose to use a client-side cursor as the default for DE Command objects. You can use the Cursor Location section of the Advanced tab to change this to a server-side cursor and set up the cursor type and lock type appropriately. For purposes of this introductory example, you will use a simple (and fast) forward-only cursor with a read-only lock type. The Advanced tab also enables you to limit the number of records returned, and frankly, this is an important feature for most Web applications. You won't be using it here because you know that the authors table contains a limited number of records anyway. However, it's interesting to note that you *can*, in fact, limit the number of records on a read-only, forward-only Data Environment recordset. This won't work with a similar ADO recordset.

When you're finished configuring the Command object, you will see, in the Project Explorer window, a new command heading below the data connection it's associated with. Depending on the type of database object you associated the command with, you will also see a list of the records the command will return (if it does, indeed, return records). If the command does return records (as the example does), that means you can use it to visually create a recordset DTC.

Creating a DE Recordset

Open a blank ASP page and make sure you're in Source mode. Hover over the data command you just created and literally drag it over to an empty portion of the BODY section. When you release the mouse button (*drop* the Command object), Visual InterDev will prompt you about adding support for the Scripting Object Model. Because this support is required, choose Yes, and a new recordset DTC will appear directly in the code, shown in Figure 14.1.

FIGURE 14.1

Even though you're in Source code mode, DTC controls appear as visual elements in Visual InterDev.

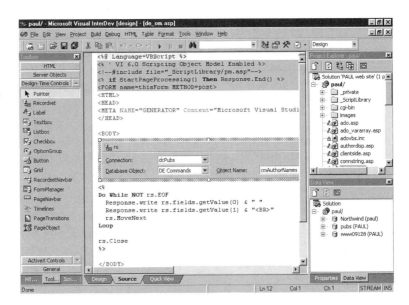

To access the recordset's properties, right-click it and choose Properties. The Recordset Properties dialog box enables you to name the recordset (rs in the example) and determine other attributes, such as the database object it's associated with. Because you dragged a global data command to the ASP file, however, you either can't or don't want to set most of these options. Primarily, they are provided for those instances when you create a new recordset not already associated with a Command object. You can do this by dragging a DTC Recordset from the Visual InterDev Toolbox window onto any ASP or HTML document, but this circumvents the best reason to use DTCs: code reuse through the Data Environment.

Now that you have a working DE recordset, you want to display the records it retrieves. This can be done in a variety of ways: You could write directly to the Data Environment Object Model, use data-bound controls such as the Label in conjunction with a recordset navigational bar, or use a recordset grid to display any number of records in a spreadsheet-like format. Additionally, you could use the Form Manager control to create pages that resemble the pages generated by the old Data Form Wizard in Visual InterDev 1.0. The choices, as they say, are unlimited. I will describe the more visual choices throughout this chapter, so for this section I present a code-based approach that most closely resembles the ADO code used in the original example.

Recall from earlier in the chapter that you used a Do While loop to cycle through the records contained in the ADO recordset and display the fields you retrieved. The code looks like this:

```
Do While NOT rs.EOF
    Response.write rs("au_fname") & " "
    Response.write rs("au_lname") & "<BR>"
    rs.MoveNext
Loop
```

Remember that the `<Recordset name>.("<Field name>")` syntax used here is just one of many ways to get at a field name. There are actually numerous ways to get at the same data. For example, all the following will retrieve the same data:

```
rs(0)
rs("au_fname")
rs.Fields(0)
rs.Fields("au_fname")
rs.Fields.Item(0)
rs.Fields.Item("au_fname")
```

And there are probably others. The reason these all work is that Visual Basic Script, like Visual Basic, supports default properties. Most developers, however, tend to find a way they prefer of writing this code and then go with that. Incidentally, the versions that use field indexes instead of names are faster, as are the versions that use the most extended syntax, because VBScript won't have to manually search for the default property of each object. Thus, the code that reads `rs.Fields.Item(0)` is actually the single fastest way to get at the au_fname field in that recordset.

You can write similar code to cycle through the information stored by a Data Environment recordset, but remember that the Data Environment uses a different,

14

USING DATA-BOUND CONTROLS

although similar, object model than ADO (described in the Chapter 13) that doesn't offer the same shortcuts. Although I do expect this feature to be added in a future release, you currently have to use a syntax similar to some of the more extended code (such as the code shown previously) when accessing specific fields in a DE recordset:

```
<%
Do While NOT rs.EOF
    Response.write rs.fields.getValue("au_fname") & " "
    Response.write rs.fields.getValue("au_lname") & "<BR>"
    rs.MoveNext
Loop
%>
```

Incidentally, the following code will work as well, and although it's a little harder to read, it's a little faster. Trying to remove anything to the left of getValue will not work, however. The DE object model just isn't that elegant yet.

```
<%
Do While NOT rs.EOF
    Response.write rs.fields.getValue(0) & " "
    Response.write rs.fields.getValue(1) & "<BR>"
    rs.MoveNext
Loop
%>
```

Used in conjunction with the DE recordset you just created, this code will display the first and last names of each author in the Pubs authors table, as the ADO example did. The only real difference is that the functionality previously provided by ADO Connection and Recordset objects is now exposed via global objects that you can use with any ASP document in your Web application, without the need for cut and paste. Also, you will have to change that username and password only *once* (in the Command object) if they ever change.

Other than that, the two examples are similar. However, Visual InterDev 6 offers a host of data-bound controls that make working with data access a visual, instead of code-based, task. For the rest of this chapter, you will explore these design-time controls.

Using the Recordset Control

Just as experienced ADO developers will tell you that the ADO Recordset object is the most frequently used object in the ADO Object Model, the Recordset design-time control (or *Recordset Script object*, as it's sometimes called) is the DTC you will use the most often for database access. In fact, the Recordset DTC is the springboard for any data-bound DTCs you might use, including the Label, Textbox, Listbox, or any other controls in the Design-Time Controls portion of the Visual InterDev Toolbox window.

A Recordset DTC can exist on its own, for single page or specialty use, but it is more commonly associated with a Data Command object, as demonstrated in the preceding section. When you use an unattached Recordset DTC (that is, a recordset not associated with a Data Command object), it functions in a way similar to an ADO Recordset, although offering a few visual simplicities. To use a Recordset DTC this way, simply place the mouse cursor where you'd like the DTC inserted and double-click the Recordset choice in the Design-Time Controls portion of the Visual InterDev Toolbox window. If prompted, enable the Visual InterDev Scripting Object Model for that page and then apply the appropriate properties. The only advantage of using a DTC such as this over straight ADO code is that you can choose the recordset properties visually, as shown in Figure 14.2.

FIGURE 14.2

You can create standalone recordsets that are not associated with a Data Command object in the Data Environment.

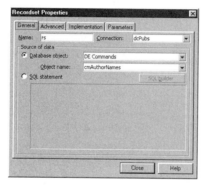

Note that you will still need at least a single Data Connection object, and thus a Data Environment associated with the project, to create a Recordset DTC. The caveat about client-side versus server-side cursors applies as well: For some reason, Microsoft made a client-side cursor the default. Make sure you change this to server-side.

You will be using Recordset DTCs for all the examples in the rest of this chapter. Although these recordsets will be associated with a Data Command object in the Data Environment, their use is functionally identical to standalone Recordset DTCs.

Working with Recordset DTC Properties and Methods

Like the ActiveX Data Objects (ADO) Recordset object, the Recordset DTC, or Recordset Script object, has numerous attributes that you can access programmatically. Table 14.1 lists properties and methods of the Recordset Script object.

TABLE 14.1 THE RECORDSET SCRIPT OBJECT'S PROPERTIES AND METHODS (FOR SERVER-SIDE RECORDSETS ONLY)

Name	Type	What It Does
absolutePosition	Property	Specifies the absolute position of the current record in the Recordset Script object.
addRecord	Method	Creates a new record and adds it to the current Recordset Script object.
advise	Method	Hooks an event so that a function or Sub you specify executes whenever that specific event occurs.
BOF	Property	Indicates whether the cursor is positioned before the first record in the Recordset Script object.
cancelUpdate	Method	Cancels any pending changes to the current Recordset Script object.
close	Method	Closes the Recordset Script object.
deleteRecord	Method	Deletes the current record in the Recordset Script object.
EOF	Property	Indicates whether the cursor is positioned after the last record in the Recordset Script object.
fields	Property	Represents the fields script object associated with this Recordset Script object.
getBookmark	Method	Obtains a bookmark for the current record that was set with setBookmark.
getConnectString	Method	Retrieves the connection string that makes up the connection object associated with the Recordset Script object.
getCount	Method	Retrieves the number of records in the recordset (or –1 if the recordset is empty).
getParameter	Method	Retrieves a parameter used by the stored procedure or parameterized query that built the recordset contained by the Recordset Script object.
getRecordSource	Method	Retrieves the underlying ADO recordset that created the Recordset Script object, so that you can access ADO recordset properties and methods that might not be available to the DTC Recordset.
getSQLText	Method	Retrieves the SQL query that built the recordset contained by the Recordset Script object.
isOpen	Method	Returns a Boolean value that indicates whether the recordset is currently open.

Name	Type	What It Does
maintainState	Property	Determines whether the Recordset Script object's state is maintained. The default is `True`.
move	Method	Moves the cursor the specified number of records, relative to the current cursor position. Negative values move backward through the recordset.
moveFirst	Method	Moves the cursor to the first record in the recordset.
moveLast	Method	Moves the cursor to the last record in the recordset.
moveNext	Method	Moves the cursor to the next record in the recordset.
movePrevious	Method	Moves the cursor to the preceding record in the recordset.
name	Property	The read-only value that identifies the Recordset Script object at runtime.
open	Method	Opens the Recordset Script object.
requery	Method	Requeries the database to repopulate the recordset. Useful if the data has been changed elsewhere.
setBookmark	Method	Sets a bookmark to point to the current record.
setParameter	Method	Adds parameter information for the stored procedure or parameterized query referenced by the Recordset Script object.
setRecordSource	Method	Sets the data connection properties that will be used to open the recordset. You can use an ADO Recordset object as the basis for the Recordset Script object or specify a valid data connection string and SQL statement to open the recordset.
setSQLText	Method	Sets the SQL statement that will be used to query the database and retrieve records to populate the Recordset Script object.
unadvise	Method	Cancels an event hooking that was established with the advise method.
updateRecord	Method	Updates the current record with any changes that were made.

14

**USING DATA-
BOUND CONTROLS**

Although much of the Recordset Script objects' functionality is best exploited by other data-bound DTCs, take a look at several the common things you might do with a recordset, using straight code.

Navigating the Recordset

Perhaps the most common recordset operation is *navigation*, the capability to move around within the recordset. Your ability to move forward and backward through the records in the recordset depends on the type of cursor you use. A forward-only cursor cannot use the MovePrevious method, for example, although it can move back to the beginning of the result set with the MoveFirst method.

For this example, you will create a new data command that points to the titles table in Pubs. The data command will feature a dynamic cursor with an optimistic lock type. As always, ensure that the cursor location is server-side, not client-side.

When you have an appropriate data command, it's a simple matter to drag it into an empty ASP file and create a Recordset Script object called rs (you can name it whatever you'd like, of course). Choose yes when InterDev prompts you to add the Scripting Object Model to this page.

The following example implements a simple hand-coded record navigator that enables you to move forward and backward through the list of book titles in the titles table. Here's the code, with the Scripting Object Model and Recordset DTC code removed for readability:

```
<%@ Language=VBScript %>
<%
intCurrent = CInt(Request.QueryString("ID"))
%>
<HTML>
<HEAD>
<META NAME="GENERATOR" Content="Microsoft Visual Studio 6.0">
</HEAD>

<BODY alink=#6633ff link=#6633ff vlink=#6633ff>

<!--METADATA TYPE="DesignerControl" startspan

<<<<< Recordset Script object inserted here >>>>>

    METADATA TYPE="DesignerControl" endspan-->

<%
' Establish the last record number
intEnd = Int(rs.fields.getCount())
```

```
' Establish the current record number
If intCurrent = "" Then
    intCurrent = 0
Else
    If intCurrent > intEnd Then
        intCurrent = intEnd
    End If
End If

' Establish the next record number
If intCurrent < intEnd Then
    intNext = intCurrent + 1
Else
    intNext = intEnd
End If

' Establish the preceding record number
If intCurrent > 0 Then
    intPrevious = intCurrent - 1
Else
    intPrevious = 0
End If

' Navigate to the appropriate record and display
rs.moveFirst
rs.move(intCurrent)
Response.write intCurrent & ": " & rs.fields.getValue("title")
%>
<BR>
<A HREF="navigate_rsdtc.asp">Start</A> ¦
<A HREF="navigate_rsdtc.asp?ID=<%= intPrevious %>">Go Back</A> ¦
<A HREF="navigate_rsdtc.asp?ID=<%= intNext %>">Go Forward</A> ¦
<A HREF="navigate_rsdtc.asp?ID=<%= intEnd %>">End</A>

<% rs.Close %>
</BODY>
</HTML>
```

What's happening here might not be immediately obvious. First, the URL is parsed for an attribute called ID. If there is an ID attribute in the URL, its value is assigned to the local variable intCurrent. This will represent the current cursor position within the recordset that you are going to retrieve, after some short processing.

Then the recordset is instantiated, and you retrieve the number of records in this record-set with the field object getCount method. This value is assigned to the local variable intEnd, which represents the end of your set of records.

Now that you have the recordset's size, you parse the intCurrent value a bit. If no ID attribute was used in the URL, your intCurrent variable will contain no value. If this is so, you assign 0 to intCurrent. Otherwise, you must make sure that the value of intCurrent doesn't exceed intEnd or represent a negative value.

When this is completed, you establish the record number of the next record. This is assigned to intNext. The preceding record's number is assigned to intPrevious. In both cases, you ensure that the page won't attempt to load a value that exists outside the range of possible record numbers for your recordset.

When you have these values, you can navigate to the current record by moving to the first record (just in case) and then moving forward the proper number of records, using Move. Then, you display the record number and the value of the title field (a book title).

Finally, a simple navigation menu is created, using a mixture of ASP code and HTML. Notice that the Go Back, Go Forward, and End choices use an ID attribute to the URL so that the correct record number is loaded when the page is refreshed. This page actually calls itself and denotes the record to load in the URL, as shown in Figure 14.3.

FIGURE 14.3

It's possible to hand-code your own recordset navigation, using Recordset Script object methods.

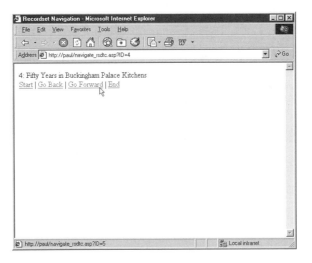

There are some good reasons to provide your own recordset navigation in this way. If you're code adverse, however, Visual InterDev 6 does include various recordset navigation controls, which you will be looking at later in this chapter.

Updating a Database

Using Recordset Script object methods, it's also possible to update specific records in the current recordset, thereby updating the underlying data as well. There are various ways to update a database. The most common actions include deleting a record, adding a new record, or modifying the information in a specific record. It is possible to perform any of these operations with a Recordset Script object, as long as the underlying recordset was created with the proper cursor and lock types.

Using the preceding example as a starting point, we can create a page that not only navigates among the records in a recordset but also enables you to change the underlying data. The key here is to provide separate ASP documents that are passed record information from the main page. For example, to the navigational choices in the preceding example, you might add two new choices that allow the user to modify or delete the selected record:

```
<A HREF="update.asp?ID=<%= intCurrent %>">Modify</A> ¦
<A HREF="delete.asp?ID=<%= intCurrent %>">Delete</A>
```

These pages are passed the ID number of the record to work with, so it's a simple manner to then supply data forms to modify or delete the record. In fact, later in the chapter, you will learn a variety of ways to do this.

Troubleshooting Recordset DTCs

If you see an exclamation point (!) in a red circle on a Recordset DTC in your code, there is a data problem. This could be caused by something as simple as changing the recordset's associated object type without choosing an object name that matches that type. It could also be as serious as a problem with the associated Data Connection object.

If the exclamation point appears in the Object Name drop-down list box on the Recordset DTC, you simply select a name that matches the selection in the Database Object drop-down list. For example, say you have a Recordset DTC connected to the Pubs database, and you set the Database Object setting to Tables and then choose Authors from the Object Name drop-down list box. If you then choose Views from the Database Object list, you're going to see an exclamation point in a red circle in the Object Name list because Authors is not a valid choice anymore (see Figure 14.4). To fix this, choose a valid view from the Object Name drop-down list box.

14

**USING DATA-
BOUND CONTROLS**

FIGURE 14.4

You will see a red exclamation if you change the database object without choosing a new object name.

An exclamation point next to the recordset name in the upper-right corner of the Recordset DTC indicates a more serious problem: There is something wrong with the data connection. This could be caused by the SQL Server being offline or an incorrect Data Connection object in the Data Environment. First, ensure that your SQL Server is online. Then, to resolve the problem, check the recordset's properties, followed by the Data Connection properties in the Project Explorer window. Generally speaking, Visual InterDev will not allow you to create an invalid Data Connection object, so it's possible that something is wrong with the physical connection between your Web application and the database server. If that's the case, there's little you can do anyway.

Using the Grid Control

The Grid control is one of those rare gifts from the heavens, a fully functional wizard that creates a data-bound HTML table with navigational and paging capabilities. It really is a work of art.

If you're familiar with the old Data Form Wizard from Visual InterDev 1.0 and were upset to see it removed from VI 6, the Grid DTC might make you happy if you'd like a bare-bones, read-only data display. Basically, the control presents a five-pane dialog box that enables you to set all kinds of properties for the HTML table that it generates, including the fields to display, how to display them, the page and row navigation features you want, the look and feel of the table (including more than a dozen prebuilt themes that are quite nice), text formats for headers and data cells, and more. It's easily the most extensive control included with Visual InterDev, and it's a real time saver if you want a structured, spreadsheet-style layout. The easiest way to explain it, however, is to take a look at the options it presents.

The first step, of course, is to create a Recordset Script object by dragging a data command from the Data Environment onto a blank ASP page.

Then, select the area where you'd like to create an HTML table for laying out the data represented by the recordset and double-click the Grid choice in the Design-Time Controls section of the Toolbox window. The screen will resemble Figure 14.5.

FIGURE 14.5

It's not much to look at (yet), but the Grid control offers a tremendous array of features.

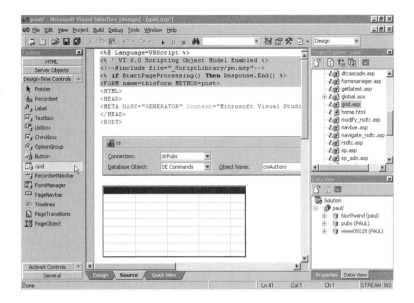

To access the Grid control's properties, right-click it and choose Properties. You're presented with the Grid Properties dialog box, which enables you to set numerous options, using the following pages:

- General—Choose from predefined table styles, set the Grid control's name, and determine the width of the HTML table that will be created. You can also choose whether to display the header row, which will display the fields' names by default.

- Data—Determine which recordset the grid is associated with, the fields to display, as well as the order to display them (this is determined by the order in which you choose the fields, although you can change the order later, using this page), and the text to use for each field's header.

- Navigation—Determine how many recordsets to display per page, which navigational buttons to use, and whether to enable row navigating as well.

- Borders—Modify the style of the table borders, gridlines (internal borders), colors, and border size. You can choose a table style in the General page and then modify it here, one item at a time.

- Format—Determine the fonts, colors, and alignment of the cells in the header and data rows. You can even change formatting for individual cells, if desired.

- Advanced—Assign additional HTML attributes to the TABLE, TR, TH, and TD tags used to generate the table.

14

**USING DATA-
BOUND CONTROLS**

Although the sheer number of options here is impressive, it's all quite straightforward. What's amazing is how configurable this control is. Figure 14.6 shows a pretty nice table generated by the Grid control.

FIGURE 14.6

The Grid control makes it easy to generate spreadsheet-like data displays.

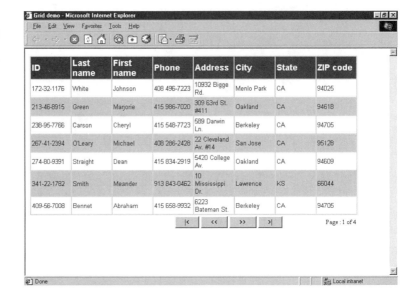

Advanced Grid Use

Although the Grid control seems straightforward after you get over the number of options it presents, some advanced features are not immediately obvious. For example, say you want to provide more functionality than a simple read-only display. The page with the Grid control could be used as the front end to other database management pages that perform more complex operations, such as data modification, creation, and deletion. Take a look at one way to accomplish this.

For this example, you will be using a Recordset Script object that is based on a data command representing the authors table in Pubs. A Grid control will be used to display the ID and each author's first and last name, displaying five authors per page.

To give the user the ability to view all the information for each author, and optionally modify this data, you can place both the first and last name in a single field and make that name a hyperlink. The hyperlink will load a second Web page that displays the information for only that author.

First, you must create the data grid page. Drag over a recordset that's based on the authors table and create a new grid. Right-click on the grid and choose Properties. Choose an appropriate theme and then navigate to the Data page. Associate the grid with the recordset you just created and then select au_id from the Available Fields list box. This will add the field to the Grid Columns section. In the Edit Columns section, change this field's header to Author ID.

Now, click the Add Unbound Column button to add a new column to the grid that isn't explicitly bound to an individual field in the table. In the Field/Expression text box in the Edit Columns section, change the line of text to read like so:

```
= "<A HREF=authordisp.asp?ID=" + [au_id] + ">" + _
  [au_fname] + " " + [au_lname] + "</A>"
```

This expression creates a hyperlink, consisting of the current author's first and last name, that loads a second ASP page when clicked, passing the author's au_id along with it. The Grid control enables you to create expressions for individual cells that use the following rules:

- An equal sign (=) denotes the beginning of an expression.
- Field names must be surrounded by brackets, as in [field name]. Otherwise, the syntax is identical to JavaScript, not VBScript, and thus the use of a plus sign (+), instead of an ampersand (&), for string concatenation.
- If you'd like to use brackets in the text displayed in the grid, be sure to enclose them in double quotes (as in "[This text will be displayed]").
- HTML code (such as the ANCHOR tag created here) must be enclosed within double quotes like any other text.
- The expression must evaluate to a string.

Incidentally, you can see the strings created by this expression by mousing over the hyperlinks while the ASP document is loaded in the browser. The status bar at the bottom of the window will display the string that was created.

Now, change the header to Name and then navigate to the Navigation page. Change the Records/Page choice to 10 and then click OK to close the Properties dialog box. When you save this document and load it into your Web browser, your screen will resemble Figure 14.7.

14

USING DATA-BOUND CONTROLS

FIGURE 14.7

You can enter complex expressions into grid cells to create more complex documents.

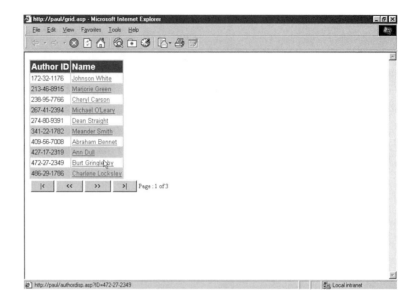

As you can see, each author name is now a hyperlink that loads a second page. This page should retrieve the ID value passed to it and then, as you like, display more information about the author. This page can use any database access method you want. Here's a simple example that uses straight ADO to display all the information stored about the author that is passed to the document:

```
<%@ Language=VBScript %>
<%
ID = CStr(Request.QueryString("ID"))
%>
<HTML>
<HEAD>
<META NAME="GENERATOR" Content="Microsoft Visual Studio 6.0">
</HEAD>
<BODY>

<FONT FACE="Verdana, Arial" SIZE=2>

<%
Set cn = Server.CreateObject("ADODB.Connection")
Set rs = Server.CreateObject("ADODB.Recordset")

cn.Open "DSN=pubs;UID=sa;Password=;"
rs.ActiveConnection = cn
rs.Open "SELECT * FROM authors WHERE au_id='" & ID & "'"

Response.write "<B>ID: </B>" & rs("au_id") & "<BR>"
Response.write "<B>First name: </B>" & rs("au_fname") & "<BR>"
```

```
Response.write "<B>Last name: </B>" & rs("au_lname") & "<BR>"
Response.write "<B>Phone: </B>" & rs("phone") & "<BR>"
Response.write "<B>Address: </B>" & rs("address") & "<BR>"
Response.write "<B>City: </B>" & rs("city") & "<BR>"
Response.write "<B>State: </B>" & rs("state") & "<BR>"
Response.write "<B>ZIP: </B>" & rs("zip") & "<BR>"
Response.write "<B>Contract: </B>" & rs("contract") & "<BR>"


rs.Close
cn.Close
%>

</FONT>

</BODY>
</HTML>
```

Figure 14.8 shows some sample output from this page, but remember that you can use nearly any sort of code here: ADO, Data Environment Object Model, design-time controls, whatever. Also, the capabilities you build into this type of page are limitless. You can provide ways to modify the author's information or delete that author's record, for example.

FIGURE 14.8

By passing an author's ID to this page, you can display information about that author.

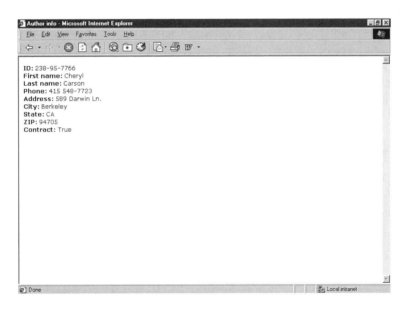

14

USING DATA-BOUND CONTROLS

Using the RecordsetNavBar Control with Other Controls

If you're interested in creating a more customized display, you might consider working with data-bound controls in conjunction with the RecordsetNavBar control, which supplies a VCR-like control panel for navigating through the records in your recordset. The controls you will typically use with the RecordsetNavBar include the following:

- Label—Creates a data-bound string of read-only text
- Textbox—Creates a data-bound HTML <TEXTAREA> tag or <INPUT> tag where the TYPE attribute is set to "TEXT"
- Listbox—Creates a data-bound HTML <SELECT> tag
- Checkbox—Creates a data-bound HTML <INPUT> tag where the TYPE attribute is set to "CHECKBOX"
- OptionGroup—Creates a group of data-bound HTML <INPUT> tags where the TYPE attribute is set to "RADIO" for each
- Button—Creates a data-bound HTML <INPUT> tag where the TYPE attribute is set to "BUTTON"

Combining the RecordsetNavBar with any combination of these other design-time controls gives you virtually unlimited control over the look and feel of your database-backed ASP documents. If the recordset is write-capable, you can optionally set the RecordsetNavBar to automatically update each record as you move forward or backward through the recordset. This way, the user can make changes to the data by using an editable control (such as a text box) and have the changes take place seamlessly.

Navigating with the RecordsetNavBar

To see how this all comes together, you can create a simple ASP document consisting of a couple Label controls and a RecordsetNavBar. As always, create a Recordset object by dragging a Data Environment data command to a blank ASP page (you will be using the tried and true authors table again, which uses a forward-only, read-only cursor).

Now you can start adding labels. For this example, you will take the time to create a table to contain the labels and navigational bar you're using, but you are obviously free to use any sort of formatting you like. Here's the skeleton code for the page you will be creating (less the Recordset control and the code generated by adding the Scripting Object Model to this document):

```
<%@ Language=VBScript %>
<HTML>
<HEAD>
<META NAME="GENERATOR" Content="Microsoft Visual Studio 6.0">
</HEAD>
<BODY>

<TABLE WIDTH=600 CELLPADDING=0 CELLSPACING=0 BORDER=0>
    <TR>
        <TD WIDTH=100 ALIGN=LEFT VALIGN=TOP>
        </TD>
        <TD WIDTH=500 ALIGN=LEFT VALIGN=TOP>
        </TD>
    </TR>
    <TR>
        <TD WIDTH=100% COLSPAN=2 ALIGN=LEFT VALIGN=MIDDLE>
        </TD>
    </TR>
</TABLE>

</BODY>
```

Now you can add three labels: one in the first table cell (TD) of the first row (TR) and the other two in the second table cell of the first row, separated by a space. When this is done, the screen will resemble Figure 14.9.

FIGURE 14.9

Label controls aren't laid out well in Design view.

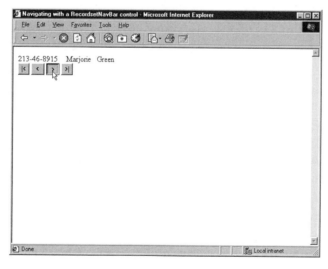

For each label, you must open the Properties dialog, associate them with the recordset you created, and then choose a field or expression from that recordset that the label will be bound to. The first label should be associated with the au_id field in the recordset, and the remaining two should be associated with the fields representing the author's first and last names.

Now, position the cursor in the table cell in the second row and double-click the RecordsetNavBar control in the Toolbox window. Associate this control with the record-set as well (right-click, Properties), save the document, and load it into a browser. The result, a fully functional table navigator, should resemble Figure 14.9.

Incidentally, if you'd rather not use design-time controls to display data from the record-set, you can always use the Data Environment Object Model to hand-code this output. For example, to display the au_id field in the first table cell, you could insert the following line of code instead of a DTC label:

```
<%= rs.fields.getValue("au_id") %>
```

As always, the choices are virtually endless; the method you employ is up to you.

Other Data-Bound Design-Time ActiveX Controls

For a simple database update page, you might create a Data Environment data command that enables the objects it contains to be updated and then place a recordset based on this control into an ASP page. You can then use Textbox controls to display the fields from the database, with a RecordsetNavBar control that will allow navigation. The user will be able to edit the value of each field as desired, right in the text boxes, and then update the database automatically by navigating to another field. To do this, you must check the Update on Move check box on the General page of the RecordsetNavBar's Properties dialog box.

Creating this page is deceptively simple, especially because you won't have to write a line of code. The first step is to create a Data Command object in the Data Environment, which enables you to update the data source. This can be done by using a static cursor with optimistic row locking. Then, drag this data command onto a blank ASP document to create a Recordset Script object.

From here, you have to add a Textbox design-time control for each field in the recordset that will be displayed and, as a result, be available for updating over the Web. Finally, add a RecordsetNavBar control to allow record navigation. In the Properties dialog for the RecordsetNavBar control, ensure that the Update on Move check box on the General page is checked (see Figure 14.10).

FIGURE **14.10**

By selecting Update on Move, you ensure that any changes you make to the current record are propagated to the live database when you navigate away from that record.

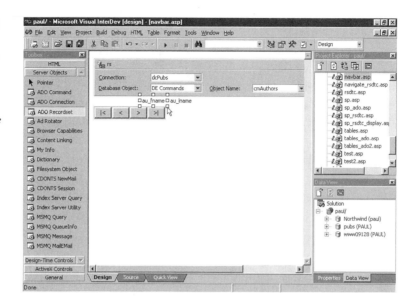

When you're finished, you will have a single ASP document that allows you to edit live data from a database, using the Web. Any edits you make in the text box controls will be applied to the live database when you navigate away from that record.

Other Design-Time Controls Included with Visual InterDev 6

In addition to the controls already described, Visual InterDev 6 includes a variety of other design-time controls.

FormManager

The FormManager control enables a single ASP document with several data-bound controls to behave in a variety of modes. For example, you might supply Button controls that enable you to switch between insert, delete, and modify modes. The FormManager, when used in conjunction with a Recordset Script Object and a variety of other data-bound controls, can duplicate the functionality of the Data Form Wizard from Visual InterDev 1.0. Of course, you can also duplicate this functionality by using a variety of code-based and visual methods.

PageNavBar

This control automatically generates a navigational toolbar or set of navigational links for your Web site, using a variety of display styles. The PageNavBar control supplies a three-page Properties dialog that enables you to set the style of a navigational bar (HTML buttons, plain text, or custom HTML), the orientation of the navigational bar (horizontal or vertical), and the sets of pages that should be included.

Timelines

The Timelines design-time control enables you to add any number of timeline objects to an ASP document. These timeline objects can respond to events that fire at specific intervals, giving your documents the capability to automatically trigger scripted actions at these intervals or in response to user actions (clicked hyperlink, clicked form button, and the like).

In general, use of this control should be limited to nonobtrusive actions. It's not wise to affect the user's visit with obnoxious interruptions.

PageTransitions

The PageTransitions control is another debatable addition to the Visual InterDev Toolbox. By this point, you've probably seen Web pages that fade in, possibly using a circular or rectangular slide effect. These page transitions are generally slow moving and annoying. If this hasn't turned you off yet, the PageTransitions control makes it all possible, supplying a number of prebuilt transitions. These include box in/out, circle in/out, wipe up/down/right/left, vertical/horizontal blinds, checkerboard across/down, random dissolve, split horizontal/vertical in/out, strips left down/left up/right down/right up, random bars horizontal/vertical, random, and blend. That's an awful lot of ways to annoy someone. Tread cautiously.

Summary

The design-time controls supplied with Visual InterDev 6 provide a rich palette for creating data-bound ASP documents that require virtually no code. As with any other visual programming solution, these controls are best used by those who thoroughly understand the system's underpinnings, which, in this case, are based on the Data Environment Object Model, a simplified way to access ActiveX Data Objects.

To use these controls, you will also have to master the Recordset Script object, which is generally created by dragging a Data Environment data command onto an ASP document. This recordset is the basis for all the work you will perform with the data-bound design-time controls, and its object model is very similar to that of the ADO Recordset, with which you're probably familiar.

Displaying Data in a Web Application

by Paul Thurrott

IN THIS CHAPTER

In previous chapters in this section, you've looked at the various methods available to Visual InterDev developers for integrating information in live databases with the Web. Only a few years ago, this very concept was an industry bugaboo. It was clearly the way things were headed, but the methods for getting there were rudimentary at best. Today, with Visual InterDev and Microsoft's array of Web/database technologies, the biggest problem isn't *putting* data on the Web; it's deciding *how* to. Ironically, there are now almost too many ways to make this happen.

Navigating through the rat's nest of acronyms and bizarre technology terms, you must face many issues: ODBC versus OLE DB, ActiveX Data Objects versus the Data Environment, hand-coded database access versus ActiveX controls, server-side versus client-side…the list goes on.

How you decide which methods to use depends largely on the project at hand, but you should also take a hard look at the future of your sites and where you see them heading technologically. Settling on a Windows server-based Internet Information Services (IIS) solution is the easiest decision you will ever make. Clearly, Windows is the future of the Web. But which Windows technologies will most clearly benefit the developer, offering automation without sacrificing power and speed?

Choosing a Data Access Provider

With the release of Visual Studio 6 and Microsoft Data Access Components (MDAC) 2, Web and database developers now have some very basic choices to make about the low-level way their applications will access data. In the past, there wasn't much of a choice. You could choose open database connectivity (ODBC) and, well, that was it. This wasn't a huge problem necessarily; ODBC was and is a fast interface to the underlying relational databases with which it is designed to work.

Microsoft realized, though, that the future of data access would require an interface to more heterogeneous types of data, including email stores, spreadsheets, word processing documents, and any other type of file you can think of that uses its own format to store any kind of data. Because ODBC is so closely tied to the structure of relational databases, it wouldn't have been efficient to modify that standard to fit these other kinds of data. Instead, Microsoft developed OLE DB, the COM-based, object-oriented successor to ODBC. OLE DB provides the low-level infrastructure necessary to access nearly any type of data using consistent COM interfaces.

For the database developer, Microsoft developed ActiveX Data Objects (ADO) and, later, the Data Environment Object Model (DEOM). Both ADO and DEOM are designed to abstract OLE DB into simple object models that offer the types of interfaces Visual Basic developers have come to expect (objects, collections, and the like). Although previous chapters explore both these technologies, the next section takes a close look at the differences between the two.

ODBC Versus OLE DB

Before Visual InterDev/Visual Studio 6, connecting to a database almost always involved creating an ODBC data source name (DSN) as the first step and then connecting to that data source through ADO methods. Because ADO actually works with OLE DB in the background, one of the less obvious issues here was the way that OLE DB got at your data. OLE DB 1.0 essentially offered a pass-through interface to any ODBC data source. Stated more accurately, the first OLE DB data provider was, in fact, an ODBC data provider that essentially enabled ADO developers to work directly with ODBC data sources. The reason for doing this should be obvious: ODBC, for the most part, provided the only real interface to data back then. The first version of OLE DB wasn't exactly brimming with native providers.

With MDAC 2 (which includes ADO 2), this has changed. Microsoft now provides native OLE DB data providers for a variety of data sources, including the following:

- Any ODBC data source
- Microsoft Index Server
- Microsoft Active Directory Services
- Microsoft Jet databases (MS Access)
- Microsoft SQL Server
- Oracle databases

This means that you now have a choice. You can keep working with the ODBC data sources that we all know and love, or you can jump forward and start working with the new native OLE DB data providers.

Frankly, working directly with the OLE DB providers can be more efficient. If you can use a native OLE DB provider, the underlying mechanism can skip the middle man (ODBC) and work directly with the data source, as long as that data source exposes a COM-based OLE DB interface. The reality, of course, is that not all data sources work this way yet. You are working with SQL Server almost exclusively here (and I would argue that most Web developers should do the same), and SQL Server does, in fact, expose an OLE DB interface for developers. On the other hand, working through the ODBC data provider for OLE DB, you can access *any* ODBC data source in a consistent matter, regardless of whether it exposes an OLE DB interface. It's the old chicken-and-the-egg syndrome, and your choice boils down to which data source(s) you have to work with.

15

DISPLAYING DATA
IN A WEB
APPLICATION

Specifying an OLE DB Provider

If you want to work with a specific OLE DB provider, you can specify this in the connection string you use to connect to the data source. If you are already connecting to an ODBC data source', the connection string takes the following syntax:

```
"Provider=<provider identifier>; { DSN=<DSN name> } ; " & _
  "DATABASE=<database name>; UID=<user name>; PWD=<password>"
```

It's also possible to construct a connection string that will connect to a data source without requiring an underlying DSN. This takes the following form:

```
"Provider=<provider identifier>; DRIVER=<driver name>; " & _
  "SERVER=<server>; DATABASE=<database name>; UID=<user name>;
  ➥PWD=<password>"
```

Table 15.1 lists the various provider identifiers you can use in a connection string.

TABLE 15.1   PROVIDER IDENTIFIERS FOR SPECIFIC OLE DB DATA PROVIDERS

Data Provider	Provider Identifier
ODBC	MSDASQL
Index Server	MSIDXS
Active Directory	ADSDSOObject
Microsoft Jet	Microsoft.Jet.OLEDB.3.51
SQL Server	SQLOLEDB
Oracle	MSDAORA

> **NOTE**
>
> In the DSN-less connection string just mentioned, the server can be a server name (if the servers are on the same local network), a fully qualified DNS name (such as sql002.datareturn.com), or an IP address (for example, 192.168.0.2).

Now you will see how you would use this connection string information in actual ASP code. There are a number of ways to associate a connection string with an ADO Connection or Recordset object. You will be using the Open method of a Connection object. The following code sample uses an existing DSN to establish a connection to the Pubs database, using the OLE DB provider for ODBC:

```
<%@ Language=VBScript %>
<HTML>
<HEAD>
<META NAME="GENERATOR" Content="Microsoft Visual Studio 6.0">
<TITLE>Using Connection Strings</TITLE>
</HEAD>
<BODY Link=Blue vLink=Blue aLink=Blue>

<H2>Using a connection strings -- with a DSN</H2>

<%
Set cn = Server.CreateObject("ADODB.Connection")
Set rs = Server.CreateObject("ADODB.Recordset")

cn.Open "Provider=MSDASQL;DSN=pubs;UID=sa;password=;"
rs.ActiveConnection = cn
rs.Open "SELECT * FROM authors"

Do While NOT rs.EOF
    Response.write rs("au_fname") & " "
    Response.write rs("au_lname") & "<BR>"
    rs.MoveNext
Loop

rs.Close
cn.Close
%>
</BODY>
</HTML>
```

The following version uses a DSN-less connection that directly accesses the native OLE DB provider for SQL Server:

```
<%@ Language=VBScript %>
<HTML>
<HEAD>
<META NAME="GENERATOR" Content="Microsoft Visual Studio 6.0">
<TITLE>Using Connection Strings</TITLE>
</HEAD>
<BODY Link=Blue vLink=Blue aLink=Blue>

<H2>Using a connection strings -- without a DSN</H2>
```

15

DISPLAYING DATA
IN A WEB
APPLICATION

```
<%
Set cn = Server.CreateObject("ADODB.Connection")
Set rs = Server.CreateObject("ADODB.Recordset")

cn.Open "Provider=SQLOLEDB;DRIVER=SQLServer;" & _
  "SERVER=PAUL;DATABASE=pubs;UID=sa;PWD=;"
rs.ActiveConnection = cn
rs.Open "SELECT * FROM authors"

Do While NOT rs.EOF
    Response.write rs("au_fname") & " "
    Response.write rs("au_lname") & "<BR>"
    rs.MoveNext
Loop

rs.Close
cn.Close
%>
</BODY>
</HTML>
```

The second method makes sense when you cannot (or may not) establish a DSN on the Web server. In general, however, you should take a minute to create an ODBC data source, even if you intend to bypass it to use a native OLE DB data provider. The ODBC DSN can still provide valuable connection information to the OLE DB provider you will be using.

Recommendations

If you can, always create ODBC data source names for your data sources. This will benefit you in a number of ways, especially if you have to use the DSN to store login information or use a data source with the more visual data access methods in InterDev, such as the Data Environment and design-time controls.

When you have a DSN, you can still use the appropriate native OLE DB provider for that data source. Simply specify the provider to use in a connection string in your code. This will effectively bypass the slower ODBC interface.

In the end, the issue of ODBC versus OLE DB is almost moot because the technologies can work together to give you the best of both worlds.

Choosing a Data Retrieval Method—ActiveX Data Objects Versus the Data Environment Object Model

If you decide that the manual coding of database connectivity is the way to go, you still have two choices: ADO or the DEOM. ADO 2.x is a full-featured, Visual Basic–style object model that basically gives you everything necessary to connect to and manipulate databases from your Web applications. Based on ADO (indeed, it uses ADO behind the scenes), the DEOM is a stripped-down object model that offers a simpler interface with most of ADO's functionality.

The choice here isn't as easy as it might seem. Hard-core Web developers who wouldn't even consider using the visual tools in InterDev will lean toward straight ADO coding. However, this approach brings some inefficiencies. For example, there's no easy way to reuse data connections and commands across different pages. One (bad) approach to this problem is to store the ADO Connection object in the ASP Application object, effectively making the connection global to all users. This wreaks havoc with the connection-pooling feature of ODBC, which maintains the state of connections to increase perfor-mance and reduce reuse of open connections when possible. Another related approach is to store Commands objects in the Application object. Although this is less costly than storing connections there, it still creates automatic overhead for your Web application.

Thus, ADO developers are left with few choices when it comes to creating dynamic queries in an ASP page. There really aren't any efficient ways to reuse connections and commands across multiple pages. Incidentally, this is where the DEOM comes in. You can create applicationwide Connection and Command objects, using the techniques described in Chapter 13, "Programming the Visual InterDev Data Environment," and Chapter 14, "Using Data-Bound Controls," and then use a combination of the visual tools and hand-coding as a method of code reuse. Although it's possible to hand-code the DEOM from the ground up, this approach is problematic. The Data Environment Object Model was designed for the new design-time controls that come with Visual InterDev 6 and aren't an efficient way to hand-code database access. Because of integration with the Visual InterDev environment, however, the Data Environment is a very efficient way to

15

DISPLAYING DATA
IN A WEB
APPLICATION

reuse data connections and data commands: Simply create these objects visually in the Data Environment and then use the DEOM to hand-code manipulation of the data you retrieve. For example, you could create a recordset, named rs, that is associated with a SQL query, table name, stored procedure, or other database object and then simply navigate through the result set, using a simple Do While loop.

```
<%
Do While NOT rs.EOF
    Response.write rs.fields.getValue(0) & " "
    Response.write rs.fields.getValue(1) & "<BR>"
    rs.MoveNext
Loop

rs.Close
%>
```

The DE recordset uses methods and properties similar to the ADO recordset, so it's not a huge leap moving from one to the other. However, the DE recordset does away with some of the nicer (and most commonly used) shortcuts that ADO developers are accustomed to (this is discussed in Chapter 14).

This effectively gives hand-coders the best of both worlds, while requiring only a minimal learning curve: You can hand-code your recordset navigation while using the visual tools to establish global data connections and commands that won't bog down the server. Best of all, a Command object is effectively precompiled, or cached, so that it will run a bit faster than a dynamic query that passes a SQL string to an Open or Execute method.

Recommendations

Although it might appear that the DEOM has a leg up on ADO, creating dynamic queries directly from an ASP page is inefficient, regardless of which method you use. There are two solutions to this problem: Use stored procedures or create server components in a high-level language such as Visual Basic or Visual C++. Stored procedures are compiled in the database server and therefore don't incur any overhead on the Web server (assuming the Web server and the database server are two different machines, which, of course, they should be). A stored procedure is the single best method you can employ to speed up your response time on the server, although this requires you to learn how to create one. On the other hand, you won't incur any cost to this approach, because you're (I hope) already using SQL Server. If you have Visual Basic 6, it's not a big stretch to create for your Web applications ActiveX server components that access a database and return result sets. On the other hand, there are some problems with this approach. The pro's and cons of creating your own server components are explored in Chapter 19, "Building Web Application Components with Visual Basic."

In general, any type of database access is an *expensive* operation in the sense that opening data connections, executing data commands, retrieving recordsets, and then keeping these recordsets open so that you can display the data they contain or work with them in some other way, are all operations that can tax a server, especially if the server is hit by a large number of users.

One way to minimize this issue is to use variant arrays to store a result set, rather than keep a data connection open. Yes, the arrays will incur a bit of temporary storage overhead, but that's far more efficient than keeping a number of objects open on the server, especially if you're simply outputting the data. For example, you might consider the following approach:

1. Establish a data connection.
2. Send a command to the SQL Server server.
3. Retrieve a recordset.
4. Copy the contents of the recordset into variant arrays.
5. Close immediately all the database objects you've opened (Connection, Command, Recordset).
6. Work with the data in the variant arrays, displaying it in HTML as needed.

If you're creating your own ActiveX server components, this is the *only* way to go. Your server components will effectively handle the first five steps, returning only variant arrays to the ASP page, *not* ADO recordsets. Think of the overhead you'd incur by taking the time to develop your own components, only to have them return ADO recordsets. You'd have to instantiate an ADO recordset in the ASP page (just as you would if you had never created your own components), making the creation of the component pointless. Again, I cover this in more detail in Chapter 19, but now you will learn how variant arrays can work, using a dynamic query. Consider the following code, which opens a simple dynamic query and then copies into variant arrays the contents of the two fields it returns.

```
<%@ Language=VBScript %>
<HTML>
<HEAD>
<META NAME="GENERATOR" Content="Microsoft Visual Studio 6.0">
</HEAD>
<BODY>

<%
Set cn = Server.CreateObject("ADODB.Connection")
Set rs = Server.CreateObject("ADODB.Recordset")
```

```
cn.Open "DSN=pubs;UID=sa;Password=;"
rs.Open "SELECT au_fname, au_lname FROM authors",cn,3,1

Dim Count

Count = rs.RecordCount

Dim fnames()
ReDim fnames(Count)
Dim lnames()
ReDim lnames(Count)

rs.MoveFirst

For x = 1 to Count
  fnames(x) = CStr(rs("au_fname"))
  lnames(x) = CStr(rs("au_lname"))
  rs.MoveNext
Next

rs.Close
cn.Close

For x = 1 to Count
    Response.Write fnames(x) & " " & lnames(x) & "<BR>"
Next
%>

</BODY>
</HTML>
```

Admittedly, this is a simple example, and there is no real HTML/ASP combination code, but the point is to show you how this code would work. Rather than parse through the recordset to display its contents, the fields of the recordset are copied into variant arrays, which are then used in the display routine (the second For Next loop), after the recordset and connection are closed. For this particular example, there is no real benefit to this approach, but the benefits of using variant arrays become more obvious when you have complicated HTML formatting (such as embedded tables) that will be applied to the recordset as it is outputted in a loop.

Straight Code Versus DTCs and ActiveX Controls

Whereas the combination of straight code and visual creation of data connections and data commands described in the preceding section might make a few converts from the hard-core hand-coding crowd, a large number of Web developers might be turned off by the necessity to hand-code database access at all. It depends on the developer. There will always be those people who feel the need to get their hands dirty and learn the ins and outs of the ADO (or Data Environment) Object Model so that they can massage their application into a living, breathing testament to efficiency.

Then there are the rest of us mere mortals.

Some people just want to get the job done. Using the Data Environment and the visual tools described in Chapter 14, it's possible to create a full-featured Web application without having to write any database access code at all. You can create data connections, data commands, and recordsets visually, even using the visual Query Designer to handle the back-end work. Then, with the design-time controls, you can display the data you'd like (or create navigational database edit applications) without writing any code at all.

As with most decisions you will make, either approach involves trade-offs. The all-code approach requires an almost intimate knowledge of the object model you decide to use, and that means a serious time commitment. On the other hand, you will always know what's going on, so if you decide to later use a combination of DTCs and code or, God forbid, finally make the move to a fully visual development style, you will be able to easily debug your Web applications when something goes wrong.

Using the straight visual approach has some trade-offs as well. The design-time controls used by Visual InterDev 6 provide a nice visual interface, but they're just creating scripting code to get the job done behind the scenes. Consider the lowly recordset DTC. Say you create a Data Environment data command that is associated with the authors table in the Pubs database. When you drag this command to an ASP page, a nice visual control appears, enabling you to work with its properties in a straightforward way. However, you can also view the actual code generated by this DTC by right-clicking it and choosing Always View as Text. Here it is, including the skeleton HTML and the Scripting Object Model code that's required by these controls:

```
<%@ Language=VBScript %>
<% ' VI 6.0 Scripting Object Model Enabled %>
<!--#include file="_ScriptLibrary/pm.asp"-->
<% if StartPageProcessing() Then Response.End() %>
<FORM name=thisForm METHOD=post>
<HTML>
<HEAD>
<META NAME="GENERATOR" Content="Microsoft Visual Studio 6.0">
</HEAD>
<BODY>

<!--METADATA TYPE="DesignerControl" startspan
<OBJECT classid="clsid:9CF5D7C2-EC10-11D0-9862-0000F8027CA0"
```

```
    id=rs style="LEFT: 0px; TOP: 0px" VIEWASTEXT>
      <PARAM NAME="ExtentX" VALUE="12197">
      <PARAM NAME="ExtentY" VALUE="2090">
      <PARAM NAME="State" VALUE="(TCConn=\qdcPubs\q,TCDBObject=
\qDE\sCommands\q,TCDBObjectName=\qcmAuthors\q,TCControlID_
Unmatched=\qrs\q,TCPPConn=\qdcPubs\q,RCDBObject=\qRCDBObject\
q,TCPPDBObject=\qDE\sCommands\q,
TCPPDBObjectName=\qcmAuthors\q,TCCursorType=\q0\s-\sForward\sOnly\
q,TCCursorLocation=\q2\s-\sUse\sserver-side\scursors\q,TCLockType=\
q1\s-\sRead\sOnly\q,TCCacheSize_Unmatched= \q100\
q,TCCommTimeout_Unmatched=\q30\q,CCPrepared=0,CCAllRecords=1,
TCNRecords_Unmatched=\q10\q,TCODBCSyntax_Unmatched=\q\
q,TCHTargetPlatform=\q\q,TCHTargetBrowser_Unmatched=\qServer\s(ASP)\
q,TCTargetPlatform=\qInherit\sfrom\spage\q,RCCache=\qRCBookPage\
q,CCOpen=1,GCParameters=(Rows=0))"></OBJECT>
-->
<!--#INCLUDE FILE="_ScriptLibrary/Recordset.ASP"-->
<SCRIPT LANGUAGE="JavaScript" RUNAT="server">
function _initrs()
{
    thisPage.createDE();
    var rsTmp = DE.Recordsets('cmAuthors');
    rs.setRecordSource(rsTmp);
    rs.open();
    if (thisPage.getState('pb_rs') != null)
        rs.setBookmark(thisPage.getState('pb_rs'));
}
function _rs_ctor()
{
    CreateRecordset('rs', _initrs, null);
}
function _rs_dtor()
{
    rs._preserveState();
    thisPage.setState('pb_rs', rs.getBookmark());
}
</SCRIPT>

<!--METADATA TYPE="DesignerControl" endspan-->


</BODY>
<% ' VI 6.0 Scripting Object Model Enabled %>
<% EndPageProcessing() %>
</FORM>
</HTML>
```

Pretty ugly, isn't it? There are some other problems, too. For one thing, the controls are scripted in JavaScript, not VBScript, so editing them might be a problem if you're not familiar with that language. Of course, editing this code is a dicey proposition anyway because of the iffy connection between the scripting code and the visual control that you see at design time. It's likely that the edits you make will render the control inoperable. For the most part then, what you see is what you get. Some developers will be okay with this, but others won't want anything to do with these controls.

What's really amazing about this code is how much of it there is. Hand-coding this would require only a few lines of VBScript. Of course, you'd have to know how to construct that code.

Recommendations

As mentioned in the preceding section, there's no good reason to choose one approach over the other. In most instances, it's best to use a combination of code and design-time controls so that your data connections and data commands are hosted in the Data Environment. Then you can decide how you want to proceed from there. If the other DTCs provide the functionality and simplicity you want, use them. Otherwise, you can hand-code your database routines from there, after dragging and dropping a recordset on your page from a data command in the Data Environment. The point here is that the tools are available. It's up to you to use them efficiently.

For the dedicated hand-coders, the recommendation is to at least take a look at the Data Environment. The benefits of using global data connections and commands outweigh any religious issues about visual tools. If you're in the total visual tool camp, I cannot stress enough how important it is to understand the underlying code. Even with many of the visual tools, it's important to understand what's going on code-wise to be able to use them properly. At least, a basic understanding of ADO and/or the DEOM is a must. Any time you spend looking into these important technologies is time well spent.

Server-Side Versus Client-Side Data Binding

It's hard not to be cavalier about this topic. There are almost no good reasons to use client-side data binding, not in this day of crossbrowser incompatibilities. Currently, the only browser that supports this feature is Internet Explorer 4.0 and higher, and with Netscape matching or beating IE's market share, there's no way to justify using this technology right now. Besides, it totally defeats the purpose of using server-side ASP technology: the capability to deliver plain HTML text to any client, regardless of who makes it.

The only place where it makes sense to use client-side data binding is in an intranet situation when the corporation has standardized on Internet Explorer. Even then, you're typically dealing with a small enough group that the performance benefits of client-side data binding are rendered moot.

In short, stick with server-side data binding until Internet Explorer controls a commanding lead in the browser wars or until Microsoft creates Java-based client-side data binding that works in all browsers.

Presentation Issues: Embedding Data Within HTML

There are different kinds of ASP documents. Some ASP pages consist entirely of code, such as form handlers that grab information the user entered in a form, process it in some way, and then return control to another Web page with a redirect. Although these types of pages are useful, most ASP documents consist of a mixture of HTML and ASP code. The way you code these documents has a huge effect on the speed with which they can be downloaded, especially if you're doing any kind of database access.

At its simplest level, an *ASP document* is a text file that can be loaded into a browser just like an HTML document. Because an ASP document can contain a mixture of ASP (server-side) code and HTML tags, though, it is processed differently by IIS and incurs an instant performance penalty because of this. Simply renaming an HTML file with a .asp extension will cause that page to load somewhat slower, despite recent improvements in the way that IIS handles "scriptless" ASP documents. From that point, things can only slow down. This is because ASP files must be parsed by the ASP engine in IIS before any output is sent to the client. IIS 5.0 will include a feature to speed up the parsing of scriptless ASP files, however.

Mixing HTML and ASP

One of the most common tasks you perform in a Web application is displaying read-only data from a database. Web news sites such as news.com and WinInfo use this technique to bring the latest computer industry news to readers on a daily basis. These sites have to combine the data in the database (article fields such as title, date, body, and others) with HTML formatting to present a consistent and attractive interface to users. Consider the following code sample, which displays the title, date, and body text from the WinInfo news table, using embedded HTML formatting and a Data Environment Recordset object named `rs`:

```
<% Do While NOT rs.EOF %>
<FONT FACE="Verdana, Arial" COLOR="NAVY">
<H2><%= rs.fields.getValue(0)%></H2></FONT>
<FONT FACE="Verdana, Times" SIZE=2 COLOR="BLACK"><I>
<%= rs.fields.getValue(1) %>
</I><P>
<%= rs.fields.getValue(2) %>
<BR><BR><BR>
<%
rs.MoveNext
Loop
%>
</FONT>
```

Aside from being hard to read, this code is a disaster of ASP and HTML and will cause some nasty context switches up on the server. When you have a block of code like this, it's better to rewrite the whole thing as a clean block of ASP, using Response.write methods to output the HTML tags. Consider the following replacement:

```
<%
Do While NOT rs.EOF
    Response.Write "<FONT FACE='Verdana, Arial' COLOR=NAVY>"
    Response.Write "<H2>" & rs.fields.getValue(0) & "</H2></FONT>"
    Response.Write "<FONT FACE='Verdana, Times' SIZE=2 COLOR=BLACK><I>"
    Response.Write rs.fields.getValue(1) & "</I><P>"
    Response.Write rs.fields.getValue(2) & "<BR><BR><BR>"
    rs.MoveNext
Loop
Response.write "</FONT>"
%>
```

This achieves the same goal—nice HTML formatting of database data—but will display more quickly because the server does not have to constantly switch back and forth between HTML and ASP. If you're really retentive, you might consider formatting your ASP pages entirely this way, placing each HTML tag into a Response.write line. This would become unwieldy very quickly, however, and be hard to read. The goal is to create an efficient middle ground between readability and execution speed.

Working with Tables

The table issue is a little more complicated. Because Cascading Style Sheets haven't been implemented consistently in Netscape Navigator and Internet Explorer, Web developers have been forced to turn to HTML tricks such as single-pixel GIFs and embedded tables to achieve the formatting and spacing that desktop publishers take for granted. For example, many Web sites are still hard-coded for specific widths, either because they've decided their target market consists largely of users with certain resolutions or because text becomes difficult to read past specific widths.

Design issues aside, you're going to run into the necessity of using HTML tables to create specific formatting. Consider the output shown in Figure 15.1. The text wraps only at the edge of the browser window, which can be quite wide when used full-screen on a high resolution display.

FIGURE 15.1

Letting the browser wrap text for you can be a mistake. It's hard to read wide areas of text.

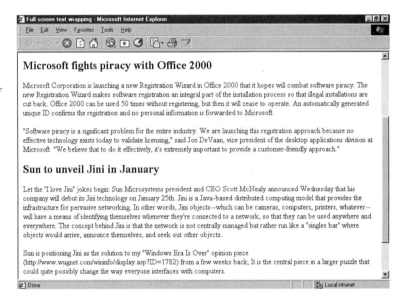

The answer to this problem is to use an HTML table to limit the width of the text. This can be set to a hard-coded pixel value or a percentage of the browser width. Figure 15.2 shows the same text, but contained within a table that is 600 pixels wide. The border has been kept to show the individual rows and general shape of the table.

Of course, we've all seen the complicated table tricks in which embedded tables are used to further offset text and create specific looks. This can be a very effective technique, given the current limitations of crossbrowser design. Just don't do it in conjunction with ASP code that accesses a database. Rendering tables, especially complex tables, slows down the processing of an ASP document dramatically. If you absolutely must use tables (and frankly, that's understandable), use a minimalist approach. Following are a couple of examples.

FIGURE 15.2

HTML tables can be used to limit the placement of text.

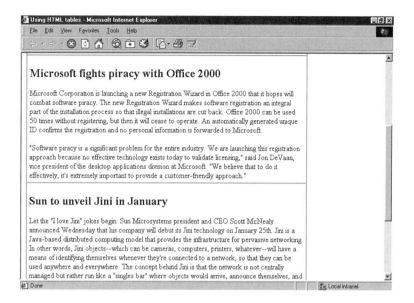

Here's some pretty inefficient code that dynamically generates table rows as it parses the fields in a recordset, displaying information as it goes:

```
<TABLE WIDTH=600 CELLPADDING=0 CELLSPACING=0 BORDER=1>
<TR>
<TD ALIGN=LEFT VALIGN=TOP WIDTH=100%>
    <FONT FACE="Verdana"><H1>Windows news</H1></FONT>
</TD>
</TR>
<%
Do While NOT rs.EOF
%>
<TR>
<TD ALIGN=LEFT VALIGN=TOP WIDTH=100%>
<%
        Response.write "<FONT FACE=Verdana SIZE=5><B>" & _
        rs("title") & "</B></FONT><BR>"
%>
</TD>
</TR>
<TR>
<TD ALIGN=LEFT VALIGN=TOP WIDTH=100%>
<%
```

15

DISPLAYING DATA IN A WEB APPLICATION

```
    Response.Write "<FONT FACE=Verdana SIZE=2>"
    Response.write "<I>" & rs("date") & "</I><BR>"
    Response.Write "</FONT>"
%>
</TD>
</TR>
<TR>
<TD ALIGN=LEFT VALIGN=TOP WIDTH=100%>
<%
    Response.Write "<FONT FACE=Verdana SIZE=2>"
    Response.write rs("body") & "<BR><BR><BR>"
    Response.Write "</FONT>"
%>
</TD>
</TR>
<%
    rs.MoveNext
Loop
%>
</TABLE>
```

The table border was kept so that you can see what's going on, as shown in Figure 15.3. Why is this so inefficient? Each time you display a field from the recordset, a new table row is generated. This means that three new table rows (in this example) must be generated for every single recordset. Because the generation of a table row is overkill for this example (it adds nothing to the page's layout or design), you can rewrite this page far more efficiently, using a single table row to display the entire set of records.

FIGURE 15.3

Mixing table code with ASP/ADO database output is very inefficient.

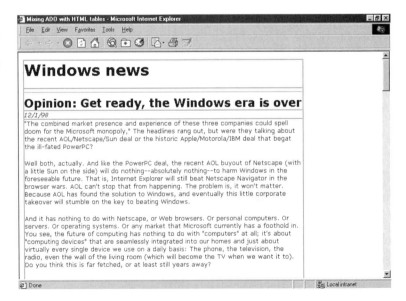

Here's a far more elegant code sample that achieves the same effect.

```
<TABLE WIDTH=600 CELLPADDING=0 CELLSPACING=0 BORDER=1>
<TR>
<TD ALIGN=LEFT VALIGN=TOP WIDTH=100%>
    <FONT FACE=Verdana SIZE=2>
    <H1>Windows news</H1>
<%
Do While NOT rs.EOF AND Count <= 5
    Count = Count + 1
    Response.write "<FONT FACE=Verdana SIZE=5><B>" & _
       rs("title") & "</B></FONT><BR>"
    Response.Write "<FONT FACE=Verdana SIZE=2>"
    Response.write "<I>" & rs("date") & "</I><BR>"
    Response.Write "</FONT>"
    Response.Write "<FONT FACE=Verdana SIZE=2>"
    Response.write rs("body") & "<BR><BR><BR>"
    Response.Write "</FONT>"
    rs.MoveNext
Loop

rs.Close
cn.Close
%>
</TD>
</TR>
</TABLE>
```

Also, as mentioned previously, you might consider displaying the table tags in Response.write method calls. Figure 15.4 shows the output from this version of the code. Note that separate rows and cells are not generated for each field; rather, the entire output is displayed in a single cell in a single row.

Recommendations

Because blocks of ASP script in the ASP document must be parsed by the server before the document can be displayed in the browser, you must keep in mind a couple of basic issues when working with ASP documents:

- Never convert a document from .htm or .html to .asp unless you plan on using specific ASP features in that document.

- Limit the number of ASP script blocks you use in each document. The fewer you have, the faster it will load.

- Limit the number of times you dynamically query a data source from an ASP document. Ideally, this querying will occur somewhere else, perhaps in a SQL Server stored procedure or an ActiveX server component written in a language such as Visual Basic or Visual C++.

- When mixing HTML and ASP code in an ASP loop, rewrite the HTML as ASP Response.write statements to improve performance.
- Limit the use of tables to display data from a database in an ASP document. Parsing a recordset and then displaying the data in discrete table cells is one of the slowest operations you can perform in ASP.

FIGURE 15.4

A more efficient approach: Minimize the mixing and matching of HTML tables and ASP/ADO database code.

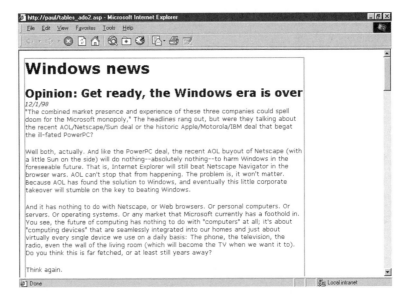

Accessing Databases Directly

Earlier in this chapter, you looked at connection strings and the ways that you can use OLE DB providers and ODBC data sources to connect to remote or local databases. The so-called "DSN-less" connection mentioned in that section is a way to directly connect to a database without having first created an ODBC DSN or OLE DB data link.

Why might this be valuable? Well, for the most part, it's not a good idea. Using a DSN-less connection requires you to hand-code a connection string in each ASP document. Any change to the location, username, password, or other attribute of the database requires that you change each document by hand or hope that some automated grep-type method will work properly. Aside from these reuse issues, DSN-less connections are also far slower than DSNs and data links because they aren't cached or managed by a service on the server.

Still, there are going to be times when this might come in handy. For example, perhaps you'd like to work with an Access database on your NT-based ISP, but the ISP won't create a DSN on the server for you. Go figure.

No problem. Upload the Access database to your account, find out the path to the directory it's located in (using Server.MapPath, as described in Chapter 12, "ActiveX Data Objects 2.0") and then access the database by using a DSN-less connection that points to that location. Sure, it's an ugly approach, but when you don't have much choice, any port in a storm will do.

Recommendations

For production environments (and for your own local workstation), using a DSN-less connection isn't a good idea. If you have to use a DSN-less connection in the ISP scenario just described, please consider local development instead. It will be faster and more portable when you do decide to move your code to a production server.

Using SQL Server Stored Procedures

SQL Server stored procedures appear over and over again in the chapters in this section because they represent an efficient way to improve the performance of your Web/database applications without having to create ActiveX server components in a high-level language such as Visual C++ or Visual Basic. They also provide a way to pass information back and forth from these procedures, using input and output parameters. Best of all, from the Web developer's standpoint, stored procedures function in a similar way to the functions and procedures you might write inline in your ASP code: Stored procedures act as a single, named unit that can be called in code. They offer control flow and conditional execution statements for more powerful SQL processing, local variables, and other features that make their use compelling. Also, because stored procedures are compiled on the database server, not on the Web server, they offer serious performance benefits over straight dynamic queries called from ASP documents.

Stored Procedures in the Real World

Past excursions into stored procedures have dealt mostly with the ways to create and use them, but you have worked largely with the stored procedures built into the sample databases that come with SQL Server. Next, you will see how SQL Server stored procedures are used in the real world.

15

DISPLAYING DATA
IN A WEB
APPLICATION

In my work with WUGNET, the Windows User Group Network, I publish the WinInfo newsletter to the Web, using SQL Server. The WinInfo article table has a very simple structure, but it consists of thousands of articles. The main WinInfo news page on WUGNET.COM displays, as clickable hyperlinks, the full articles for the most recent day and the article titles for the most recent couple of days. Beyond that, we offer search functionality, which is described in detail in Chapter 17, "Modifying Web Application Data from the Web." With thousands of articles in the table, we have to limit the number of records we retrieve on the news display page; a SELECT * (select all) query won't do.

You can get this information in a variety of ways, and, as you might imagine, some are quite inefficient. If you're using the Data Environment, you can create a Data Command object that limits the number of records returned. We haven't fully switched to this visual approach, at least not on the main WinInfo pages, so this isn't an option yet. The straight ASP approach would be to use the ADO Recordset's RecordCount method. For example, the following code displays the number of records in the WinInfo table:

```
<%
Set rsCount = Server.CreateObject("ADODB.Recordset")
rsCount.Open "SELECT ID FROM wininfo", _
  "DSN=wugnet;UID=sa;Password=;", 3, 1
Response.Write rsCount.RecordCount
rsCount.Close
%>
```

You could also use a Transact SQL–based method; there are two basic ways to do this. You could use the COUNT(*) method, but this is pretty slow. It simply runs a query that returns all the rows and then counts them. A better approach is to query the rows column in the SQL Server sysindexes table. This column stores a row count for each table in the database. Thus, you could use the following code to retrieve the number of records in the WinInfo table as well:

```
<%
Set rsCount = Server.CreateObject("ADODB.Recordset")
rsCount.Open "SELECT rows FROM sysindexes WHERE " &_
  "(id = OBJECT_ID('wininfo')) AND (indid < 2)", _
    "DSN=wugnet;UID=sa;Password=;", 0, 1Response.Write rsCount("rows")
rsCount.Close
%>
```

That's an awful lot of code, though. Because this is probably the fastest method (you have no way of knowing how the RecordCount method works internally, but you do know that it can't possibly be faster than the Transact SQL equivalent), it makes sense to put this code in a stored procedure and call it from your ASP code. However, it's not enough to return the number of rows in the recordset. For an online newsletter such as WinInfo, you have to return only a certain number of rows, say the 15 most recent articles. Thus, you can incorporate the preceding basic SQL code into a more complicated SELECT query that will, in fact, return the 15 most recent articles in the table.

The first step, of course, is to create the stored procedure.

Writing a Stored Procedure That Returns a Single Value

Creating a stored procedure is fairly simple: Use Visual InterDev to expand the database in the Data View window, right-click the Stored Procedures heading, and select New Stored Procedure. This gives you the skeleton code necessary to start a stored procedure:

```
Create Procedure StoredProcedure1
/*
    (
        @parameter1 datatype = default value,
        @parameter2 datatype OUTPUT
    )
*/
As
    /* set nocount on */
    return
```

Remove the comment blocks and enter the appropriate SQL code. When completed, this particular stored procedure resembles the following code:

```
Create Procedure GetLatest15
As
SELECT title,date,body
FROM wininfo
WHERE ID >= (SELECT rows FROM sysindexes WHERE
  (id = OBJECT_ID('wininfo')) AND (indid < 2)) - 14
ORDER BY ID DESC
return
```

Here's what's happening: The SELECT statement has an embedded SELECT statement within it that returns the number of rows. By subtracting 14 from this value, you can use this query to return only the 15 most recent articles (the ID field is an identity column that increments by one each time a new record is added).

You could use this stored procedure to grab a recordset that consists of only the 15 newest articles in the database, but maybe it would make sense to create a more versatile stored procedure, one that can return any number of records. For example, if you want the 10 most recent articles, it could handle that request. For this to work, you must add an input parameter. Consider the following, improved version of your stored procedure:

```
Create Procedure GetLatest @numRecords int=15
As
SELECT title,date,body
FROM wininfo
WHERE ID >= (SELECT rows FROM sysindexes WHERE
  (id = OBJECT_ID('wininfo'))
  AND (indid < 2)) - (@numRecords - 1)
ORDER BY ID DESC
return
```

This version is passed an input parameter named @numRecords, which is an integer value that defaults to 15 (that is, if no value is passed to the procedure, the value 15 will be used). Then, you simply insert this value into the SELECT statement so that the appropriate number of records is returned.

Incorporating a Stored Procedure in Your ASP Document

Now it's a simple matter to call this stored procedure from an ASP document. Because the stored procedure returns a set of records, it makes sense to execute the procedure from the Open method of a Recordset object. If you want to accept the default value of 15 records, this can be accomplished with the following code:

```
<%
Set rs = Server.CreateObject("ADODB.Recordset")

rs.Open "EXECUTE GetLatest", "DSN=wugnet_local;UID=sa;Password=;", 0, 1

Do While NOT rs.EOF
    Response.write rs("title") & "<BR>"
    ' Display other fields as desired
    rs.MoveNext
Loop

rs.Close
%>
```

If, however, you want to tell the stored procedure how many records to return, you must deal with the input parameter. There are two ways to deal with this. The simplest is to supply the value inline when the stored procedure is executed, which takes the following form:

```
<%
Set rs = Server.CreateObject("ADODB.Recordset")

Count = 3
rs.Open "EXECUTE GetLatest " & Count, _
  "DSN=wugnet_local;UID=sa;Password=;", 0, 1

Do While NOT rs.EOF
    Response.write rs("title") & "<BR>"
    ' Display other fields as desired
    rs.MoveNext
Loop

rs.Close
%>
```

In this case, the stored procedure will retrieve the three most recent articles.

The second possibility for dealing with stored procedure parameters is to work with ADO Command and Parameter objects. This requires much more code and, in this case, offers no real benefits. However, for more complex stored procedures with more input (and output) parameters, it might make sense to use these more powerful ADO objects.

Recommendations

SQL Server stored procedures are powerful tools that you should use as often as possible in your own Web applications. This might seem severe, but there are rarely instances when dynamically querying a database from an ASP document is a good idea. Rather, it makes far more sense to implement your Transact SQL code inside SQL Server stored procedures so that they execute as quickly as possible. Although stored procedures require a bit of knowledge about Transact SQL, this falls under the same category as ADO: The more you know, the better.

Summary

There are numerous issues to consider when you create data-backed Web applications, everything from the low-level data access provider you will use to more personal preference issues, such as the never-ending visual tools versus straight ADO coding debate. For many of these issues, it all boils down to the developer, but it pays to have an educated opinion. Many of these decisions will create numerous side effects on your projects.

To summarize the recommendations presented in this chapter, it's best to use a native OLE DB data access provider when available and bypass the slower ODBC data sources. Avoid file DSNs and DSN-less connections whenever possible. Perhaps the most surprising recommendation here is choosing the Data Environment over hand-coded ADO. As a developer who has worked with ActiveX Data Objects since it was in beta three years ago, I can admit that it's easy to become comfortable with ADO and not want to switch gears into the more visual Data Environment. However, the code reuse features of the Data Environment, combined with its capability to work with whatever combination of visual controls and hand-coding you prefer makes the choice easy. The Data Environment is the way to go.

Unless you're developing an intranet site that's running exclusively on Internet Explorer, I strongly recommend avoiding client-side data binding altogether. Server-side data binding will work with all browsers, now and in the future. However, this forces you to deal with ASP/HTML presentation issues. Be sure to reduce the number of server-side code blocks in your ASP documents to a minimum and limit your use of HTML tables, especially embedded tables. Also, if possible, use stored procedures whenever you can: They are much faster and far more efficient than the dynamic queries used in most ASP documents today.

Creating Personalized Web Applications

by Paul Thurrott

One of the biggest problems with Web-based development is the transient nature of the Web itself. Information on the Web is designed to be transmitted quickly, and any connection between the client and server is closed as soon as possible. This makes it difficult to maintain state in your Web applications. For example, you might want to require users to log in to a secure portion of your site and then navigate freely among any documents in that part of the site. Without the ability to maintain state, you'd be forced to have users log in again and again, each time they navigated to a new document.

This is unacceptable, of course. Fortunately, Microsoft has built in to its Web server software various technologies that you can access programmatically so that this need not happen. However, it's also advisable to allow users to personalize their experience on your Web site so that their settings are automatically reinstated when they return to the site. In this scenario, a user can be disconnected from the site for long periods of time before he or she returns, but the site still "remembers" the user's personal settings.

You can implement these features in a variety of ways, which you will explore in this chapter. It all begins with that much maligned and little understood Web technology called a *cookie*.

Maintaining State with Cookies

A *cookie* is a small file that is saved on the user's computer. It is used to store information about the user that will be used on the site that wrote the cookie. This information can, therefore, be passed back to the Web site, using the Web browser the next time the user visits the site.

That's the problem for many people. Cookies have a somewhat bad reputation among those who suspect that this information is being used to collect and use information about them. However, cookies have built-in security guards that prevent other Web sites from viewing the information these other sites didn't create. In fact, each cookie contains information about a single user (or more technically, a single machine) and the set of URLs for which the cookie can be used.

> **TIP**
>
> For more information on cookies, look at `htt://home.netscape.com/newsref/std/cookie_spec.html` or `http://developer.netscape.com/docs/manuals/communicator/jsguide4/cookies.htm`. To understand why some people hate cookies, look at `http://www.cookiecentral.com/`.

Cookies are very small and can never grow beyond a fixed size, so they're not going to overrun your hard drive. The most paranoid among us can simply turn off cookie use in their browser altogether. Also, a cookie file is encrypted in such a way that it's impossible to understand the information it contains, using a text editor.

Cookies offer a powerful, yet simple, solution to the problem of state management. Say you want a user to log in to your site (or a secure part of your site). You could store this information in a cookie. Perhaps you'd like to offer personalization options on your Web site. This, too, is a logical choice for a cookie. Far from being a tool for evil, the cookie is a logical choice when you want to provide state management for users who disconnect and reconnect again and again, that is, for almost all the people who visit your site. Because cookies are automatically sent in the HTTP header for each HTTP request made against the Web server, you don't have to do any low-level work to make this happen.

> **NOTE**
>
> One often overlooked point about cookies is that they're related to the browser that is used, not the actual user. If you're using Internet Explorer and Netscape Navigator, you can't use your cookies from one browser in the other. This means that the same Web site will write different cookies to your computer for each browser if you happen to use both to view the site. IE cookies are typically stored in C:\Windows\Cookies (Windows 9x) or C:\Winnt\Profiles\<User name>\Cookies. Netscape typically stores its cookies in C:\Program Files\Netscape\Users\<Profile name>\cookies\, although this could change as new versions are released.

Cookies can be accessed from your ASP documents by using server-side scripting or from any HTML or ASP document by using client-side scripting.

Programming Cookies with Client-Side Scripting

It's possible to read and write cookies using client-side scripting languages such as JavaScript and VBScript, but it's frustrating and difficult. It's likely that most UNIX-based Web developers rely on a combination of JavaScript and server-side Perl scripting to accomplish any useful cookie work at all. Web developers with a foothold in Windows NT don't ever have to deal with the complications and limitations of scripting client-side cookies, however, because of Active Server Pages. For the Visual InterDev developer, there are just too many powerful features in ASP to make client-side scripting worthwhile at all. It offers absolutely no benefits over server-side cookie access and creates such a long list of problems that's it's not even worth mentioning further. You have a great Web server and a wonderful set of tools at your disposal, so use them.

Programming Cookies with ASP

Scripting cookies with Active Server Pages is far easier and more powerful than using them from a client-side scripting language. Because server-side cookies open up more possibilities, you will concentrate on these in this chapter.

With ASP, you work with two Cookies collections, one each for the Response and Request objects. Both Cookies collections represent a list of the cookies associated with the Web site. When you're writing a value to a cookie, you can use the following syntax:

```
Response.Cookies(<cookie name>)<(key name or attribute)> = value
```

Therefore, you might write the value of a simple cookie named userName like so:

```
<%
Response.Cookies("userName") = "Paul Thurrott"
%>
```

If you look at this syntax example, however, you will see an optional key name as well. This enables you to construct complex cookies that require multiple values. For example, you might write the values of a complex cookie (sometimes called a *dictionary cookie* because of the name/value pairing) this way:

```
<%
Response.Cookies("userName")("firstName") = "Paul"
Response.Cookies("userName")("middleInitial") = "B"
Response.Cookies("userName")("lastName") = "Thurrott"
%>
```

One important concept to note here: ASP cookies must be written *before* any HTML text is sent to the browser. If you attempt to write the preceding values inside any HTML, the server will respond with an error. For this reason, cookies must be written within an ASP page that returns no HTML or directly below the line that reads <%@ Language=VBScript %>, above any HTML code.

Consider the following ASP document:

```
<%@ Language=VBScript %>
<%
' Response.cookies("name") = ""
```

```
name = CStr(Request.QueryString("name"))
If name <> "" Then
    Response.cookies("name") = name
End If
%>
<HTML>
<HEAD>
<META NAME="GENERATOR" Content="Microsoft Visual Studio 6.0">
</HEAD>
<BODY>
<%
If name= "" and Request.cookies("name") = "" Then
%>
<FORM ACTION="setcookie.asp" METHOD="GET">
    Please enter your name to write cookie:
    <BR><INPUT TYPE="TEXT" SIZE=20 NAME="name">
    <INPUT TYPE="SUBMIT">
</FORM>
<%
Else
    Response.Write "The value for 'name' is " & Request.cookies("name")
End If
%>
</BODY>
</HTML>
```

This document contains a form that posts to itself, allowing a user to enter his name. If the name has been posted to the page, it is written to a cookie. Otherwise, you check whether the cookie is set. If it is, the value held by the cookie is returned. Otherwise, the form is presented so that the user can enter a value. Because this is a single-page solution, things can become convoluted: The commented-out line near the top allows you to write a blank value into the cookie to get the form back. A more elegant solution would contain at least two pages, one to write the cookie and a second to display its value. For example, you could construct a multipage site that does this. The front end to this site could be a simple HTML file (index.html) that provides options to write and display the cookie:

```
<HTML>

<HEAD>
<META NAME="GENERATOR" Content="Microsoft Visual Studio 6.0">
<TITLE>Cookie front-end</TITLE>
</HEAD>

<BODY>

<FORM ACTION="write.asp" METHOD="GET">
Please enter your name to write cookie:
```

```
<BR><INPUT TYPE="TEXT" SIZE=20 NAME="name">
<INPUT TYPE="SUBMIT">
</FORM>

<A HREF="display.asp">Display the cookie</A>
</BODY>

</HTML>
```

Then, you could create the ASP-only write.asp page that would write the value of the cookie and return the user to the front end:

```
<%@ Language=VBScript %>
<%
name = CStr(Request.QueryString("name"))
If name <> "" Then
    Response.cookies("name") = name
    Response.Redirect "display.asp"
Else
Response.Redirect "index.html"
End If
%>
```

This page retrieves the value sent by the form on the front-end page and writes the cookie if the value is valid. The user is then sent to the display page. If the value sent from the form is invalid, however, the user is sent back to the front end.

Finally, a third ASP document, display.asp, displays the value of the cookie or an error message if the cookie is not present or contains a null value:

```
<%@ Language=VBScript %>
<%
name = Request.cookies("name")
%>
<HTML>
<HEAD>
<META NAME="GENERATOR" Content="Microsoft Visual Studio 6.0">
<TITLE>Cookie display</TITLE>
</HEAD>

<BODY>

<%
If name = "" Then
    Response.Write "_
        The cookie hasn't been written or contains an empty value."
Else
```

```
      Response.Write "The cookie contains the value " & name & "."
End If
%>

<P>Return <A HREF="index.html">home</A>

</BODY>
</HTML>
```

Figure 16.1 shows some sample output from the display page.

FIGURE 16.1

The display page determines whether the cookie is present and acts accordingly.

Using Session-Level and Application-Level Variables for Personalization

When you've developed the ability to read and write cookies like this, the possibilities are endless. However, it might not make sense to perform these operations on each page. It probably makes more sense to check the value of a user's cookies once, when he or she first enters the site, and then apply the information to the appropriate session-level or application-level variables. This gives you the ability to create personalization features for your site and then provide a way for the user to set his or her options. After the options are set, the values can be written to a cookie. When the user returns, the values are read back and applied to session-level variables, and then these variables are appropriately applied throughout the site. If the user hasn't configured personalization settings, default values are used. Now you will see how to make this work.

Using Session Variables to Apply Personalization Settings

Here's a typical Web page (see Figure 16.2):

```
<%@ Language=VBScript %>
<HTML>
<HEAD>
<META NAME="GENERATOR" Content="Microsoft Visual Studio 6.0">
<TITLE>Welcome to my home page</TITLE>
</HEAD>

<BODY>

<H1>Welcome to my home page</H1>

<UL>
<LI><A HREF="">Find out more about UFOs</A>
<LI><A HREF="">My favorite musical bands</A>
<LI><A HREF="">I like cats!</A>
<LI><A HREF="">Why my child is cuter than yours</A>
<LI><A HREF="">View my Web cam!</A>
<P>
<LI><A HREF="config.asp">Personalize your experience!</A>
</UL>

</BODY>

</HTML>
```

To implement personalization features, you must create a way to read cookie information whenever users enter the site, regardless of which page they hit (you can't assume that users will begin at the home page; they can bookmark any page in the site). Fortunately, ASP supplies a Session object that makes this possible. If you'd like to cause ASP code to execute whenever the site is entered (that is, whenever a new user session begins), you can add to your global.asa file a block of code that resembles the following:

```
<SCRIPT LANGUAGE=VBScript RUNAT=Server>
Sub Session_OnStart
'  --- Add code here --
End Sub
</SCRIPT>
```

Creating Personalized Web Applications

CHAPTER 16

439

16

CREATING PERSON-
ALIZED WEB
APPLICATIONS

FIGURE 16.2

Someday there won't be Web sites like this.

The Session object has an OnStart event that occurs, logically enough, whenever a new user session begins. You could write the code directly into this file, but it's usually a better idea to forward the user to a script-only ASP page, execute the appropriate code, and then redirect the user seamlessly to the page he or she intended to visit. For example, you might add the following Session_OnStart code to the global.asa file:

```
<SCRIPT LANGUAGE=VBScript RUNAT=Server>
Sub Session_OnStart
  Session("StartURL") = Request.ServerVariables("SCRIPT_NAME")
  Response.Redirect "http://www.wugnet.com/wininfo/ personalize.asp"
End Sub
</SCRIPT>
```

The first line of code in this event handler grabs the URL to which the user was trying to navigate. The second line redirects the user to your personalization code. (Please note that this URL doesn't exist; it's provided for demonstration purposes only.) If you are following along, be sure to provide the full path to the personalize.asp (which can, of course, be named whatever you want) and not just the filename.

To personalize.asp, for now, you can add code that simply redirects users back to the page they were attempting to access in the first place. Here's the complete code for that file (for now):

```
<%@ Language=VBScript %>
<%
Response.Redirect Session("StartURL")
%>
```

What you have now is a place (personalize.asp) to read personalization information from cookies stored on the users' machine without the need for users to manually log in every time they enter your site. Best of all, it won't matter which page they navigate to first when they enter your site: The personalize.asp file will always execute first. Of course, before you can read any cookies, you have to write them. This can be done from a personalization configuration page.

Providing a Way to Configure Personalization

The final hyperlink on this home page points to a file called config.asp, which you will use to provide configuration choices. For now, you will stick to some simple configuration options (background and text color) because, as you will see, the amount of coding you have to implement for each choice can quickly become daunting.

The code for config.asp is a simple form that provides these choices for users:

```
<%@ Language=VBScript %>
<HTML>

<HEAD>
<META NAME="GENERATOR" Content="Microsoft Visual Studio 6.0">
<TITLE>Configure personalization</TITLE>
</HEAD>

<BODY>

<H2>Configure Personalization</H2>

<FORM METHOD="POST" ACTION="config2.asp">
    Select background color: 
    <SELECT NAME="bgColor">
        <OPTION VALUE="white"> White
        <OPTION VALUE ="yellow"> Yellow
        <OPTION VALUE ="aqua"> Aqua
    </SELECT>
    <P>
    Select text color: 
    <SELECT NAME="txtColor">
        <OPTION VALUE="black"> Black
        <OPTION VALUE="#333333"> Dark gray
        <OPTION VALUE="navy"> Navy blue
    </SELECT>
    <P><INPUT TYPE="SUBMIT" VALUE="Submit">
</FORM>

</BODY>
</HTML>
```

Creating Personalized Web Applications

CHAPTER 16

441

16

CREATING PERSON-
ALIZED WEB
APPLICATIONS

This form is submitted to config2.asp, which shows users the effects of choices they've made. If users are happy with their choices, they can move on. Otherwise, they're prompted to press BACK to return to the configuration page. Here's the code for config2.asp:

```
<%@ Language=VBScript %>
<%
bgColor = CStr(Request.Form("bgColor"))
txtColor = CStr(Request.Form("txtColor"))
%>
<HTML>
<HEAD>
<META NAME="GENERATOR" Content="Microsoft Visual Studio 6.0">
</HEAD>

<BODY BGCOLOR="<%= bgColor %>" TEXT="<%= txtColor %>">

This page demonstrates the choices you made. If this
is what you want, please click the button below to
save your settings and return to the homepage. Otherwise,
click page to adjust your settings.

<FORM ACTION="saveconfig.asp" METHOD=POST>
    <INPUT TYPE=HIDDEN VALUE="<%= bgColor %>" NAME="bgColor">
    <INPUT TYPE=HIDDEN VALUE="<%= txtColor %>" NAME="txtColor">
    <INPUT TYPE=SUBMIT VALUE="Save settings">
</FORM>

</BODY>
</HTML>
```

Note that you don't have to provide any sort of validation here, because the original personalization configuration form contains only two HTML list boxes: There is no way for the user to enter an invalid choice. This is not the case for more complex configuration pages, on which you will likely provide text boxes and other HTML form entities that might require validation. You should always validate form submissions when necessary.

The config2.asp page supplies a form that is submitted to a script-only ASP document, saveconfig.asp, which writes the user-defined values to cookies and then redirects users to the home page. The code for this page is brief:

```
<%@ Language=VBScript %>
<%
Response.cookies("bgColor") = CStr(Request.Form("bgColor"))
Response.cookies("txtColor") = CStr(Request.Form("txtColor"))
Response.Redirect "default.asp"
%>
```

With that, users are returned to the home page. Of course, none of the configuration choices are displayed on the site yet because you haven't provided a way to access these cookie values and then use them in HTML/ASP blocks. In the following section, you will add this capability to the site.

Putting It All Together

Now that you have a functional way to configure some simple personalization features, you must provide a way to access this information when users enter the site. Then, you will apply the text and background colors they've chosen so that they will see a totally customized version of the site.

The first step is to edit the personalize.asp document, which is executed every time a user enters the site. In this page, you can attempt to retrieve the cookies values. If they exist, you apply them to session-level variables; otherwise, you apply default values (white background with black text) to those variables. Either way, users are then redirected to the page they requested, none the wiser about all the work you've done to make them happy. Here's the new version of personalize.asp (the changes are noted in bold):

```
<%@ Language=VBScript %>
<%
Session("bgColor") = Request.Cookies("bgColor")
If Session("bgColor") = "" Then
    Session("bgColor") = "white"
End If
Session("txtColor") = Request.Cookies("txtColor")
If Session("txtColor") = "" Then
    Session("txtColor") = "black"
End If
Response.Redirect Session("StartURL")
%>
```

To take advantage of these variables, you must appropriately code the home page (and any other pages in the site). Here is the updated version of the home page (default.asp), which integrates the new session variables. Again, changes are noted in bold.

```
<%@ Language=VBScript %>
<HTML>
<HEAD>
<META NAME="GENERATOR" Content="Microsoft Visual Studio 6.0">
<TITLE>Welcome to my home page</TITLE>
</HEAD>

<BODY TEXT="<%= Session("txtColor") %>"
 BGCOLOR="<%= Session("bgColor") %>">

<H1>Welcome to my home page</H1>
```

```
<UL>
<LI><A HREF="">Find out more about UFOs</A>
<LI><A HREF="">My favorite musical bands</A>
<LI><A HREF="">I like cats!</A>
<LI><A HREF="">Why my child is cuter than yours</A>
<LI><A HREF="">View my Web cam!</A>
<P>
<LI><A HREF="config.asp">Personalize your experience!</A>
</UL>

<%= "Start URL= " & Session("StartURL") %>
</BODY>
</HTML>
```

The nice thing about this feature is that users who choose not to use cookies or take advantage of the personalization can still view the site normally. People who are interested in customizing their experience, though, can do so easily.

There's one more change to be made: The customization page (config.asp) must be edited so that the form list boxes display the proper value if users return there and decide to change their settings. Here's the modified version of this document:

```
<%@ Language=VBScript %>
<HTML>

<HEAD>
<META NAME="GENERATOR" Content="Microsoft Visual Studio 6.0">
<TITLE>Configure personalization</TITLE>
</HEAD>

<BODY>

<H2>Configure Personalization</H2>

<FORM METHOD="POST" ACTION="config2.asp">
    Select background color: 
    <SELECT NAME="bgColor">
        <OPTION VALUE="white" <% If Session("bgColor") = "white" Then _
        Response.write "SELECTED" End If %>> White
        <OPTION VALUE="yellow" <% If Session("bgColor") = "yellow" Then _
        Response.write "SELECTED" End If %>> Yellow
        <OPTION VALUE="aqua" <% If Session("bgColor") = "aqua" Then _
        Response.write "SELECTED" End If %>> Aqua
    </SELECT>
    <P>
    Select text color: 
    <SELECT NAME="txtColor">
        <OPTION VALUE="black"
```

```
        <% If Session("txtColor") = "black" Then _
            Response.write "SELECTED" End If %>> Black
    <OPTION VALUE="#333333"
     <% If Session("txtColor") = "#333333" Then _
        Response.write "SELECTED" End If %>> Dark gray
    <OPTION VALUE="navy"
     <% If Session("txtColor") = "navy" Then _
        Response.write "SELECTED" End If %>> Navy blue
</SELECT>
<P><INPUT TYPE="SUBMIT" VALUE="Submit">
</FORM>

</BODY>
</HTML>
```

That's it. From here, it's only up to you to decide which options will be configurable. For advanced personalization, however, you will want to integrate these settings into a database so that users can persist their settings on the server. In the following section, you will see how this works and explore the reasons you might consider supplying this functionality.

Using a Database to Store Personalization Options

After you get past a few simple personalization features, it becomes laborious to store and access all that information with cookies. A more elegant approach would be to create a table in SQL Server to store personalization information, along with usernames for the people who access your site. That way, you could store only the username (and, optionally, an encrypted password) for each user in a cookie that would reside on the user's machine.

When the user accesses your site, you can check the username against the information in the database and apply the customization features you've saved for that user. It's the same basic approach as the preceding example, except that most of the personalization information is stored in a database rather than in a cookie.

The big advantage here is that users can access your site from anywhere, with any browser, because you provide a page that allows them to log in if they're using a browser that doesn't yet store their cookie. Granted, you would not use this approach for a secure site. Rather, it's designed solely as a way to facilitate personalization features that might affect the user interface or other visual niceties.

Now take a look at how you would change the example to work with a database.

Creating the Database Table for Personalization

First, you need a table to store the personalization information for each user. In keeping with the simple nature of the example, it will contain the fields shown in Table 16.1.

TABLE 16.1 FIELDS AND DATA TYPES FOR THE PERSONALIZATION TABLE

Field Name	Data Type
userName	varchar(255)
bgColor	varchar(50)
txtColor	varchar(50)
lastAccess	datetime(8)

Note that you're not providing a field for a password. This is by design because of the simplicity of the site, but implementing a password is an obvious, and simple, addition. You're adding the lastAccess field so that you can record the date that the user last accessed the site. This way, you can periodically run a stored procedure or trigger that will search for old accounts and delete them automatically.

After you create the table, you should seed it with a few test records so that you can see how the personalization works before the site goes live. This is done easily enough in Visual InterDev's Data View window: Right-click the table name and choose Open. Then, supply a few records' worth of test data (see Figure 16.3).

FIGURE 16.3

Seeding the new table with test data.

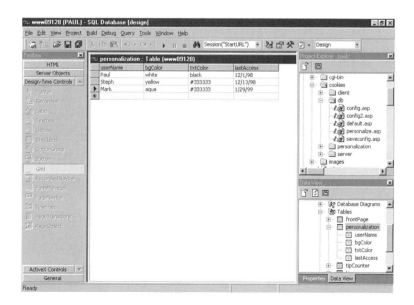

Using the preceding personalization example as a starting point, you want to add the ability to work with a new cookie that will represent the user's name. In the file config.asp, you can add a single line to the HTML form that presents a text box for this username. Here's the updated code for this document:

```
<%@ Language=VBScript %>
<HTML>

<HEAD>
<META NAME="GENERATOR" Content="Microsoft Visual Studio 6.0">
<TITLE>Configure personalization</TITLE>
</HEAD>

<BODY>

<H2>Configure Personalization</H2>

<FORM METHOD="POST" ACTION="config2.asp">
    User name: <INPUT TYPE="TEXT" NAME="userName"
      VALUE="<%= Request.Cookies("userName") %>"><P>
    Select background color: 
    <SELECT NAME="bgColor">
        <OPTION VALUE="white"
         <% If Session("bgColor") = "white" Then _
            Response.write "SELECTED" End If %>> White
        <OPTION VALUE="yellow"
         <% If Session("bgColor") = "yellow" Then _
            Response.write "SELECTED" End If %>> Yellow
        <OPTION VALUE="aqua"
         <% If Session("bgColor") = "aqua" Then _
            Response.write "SELECTED" End If %>> Aqua
    </SELECT>
    <P>
    Select text color: 
    <SELECT NAME="txtColor">
        <OPTION VALUE="black"
         <% If Session("txtColor") = "black" Then _
            Response.write "SELECTED" End If %>> Black
        <OPTION VALUE="#333333"
         <% If Session("txtColor") = "#333333" Then _
            Response.write "SELECTED" End If %>> Dark gray
        <OPTION VALUE="navy"
         <% If Session("txtColor") = "navy" Then _
            Response.write "SELECTED" End If %>> Navy blue
    </SELECT>
    <P><INPUT TYPE="SUBMIT" VALUE="Submit">
</FORM>

</BODY>
</HTML>
```

If the user hasn't entered a username, the text box will be left blank. In the config2.asp document, to which config.asp posts, some code will have to be added to grab the username and ensure that it is valid. Here you could do a variety of things. For simplicity, you will redirect the user back to config.asp if the username text box is left blank.

```
<%@ Language=VBScript %>
<%
userName = CStr(Request.Form("userName"))
bgColor = CStr(Request.Form("bgColor"))
txtColor = CStr(Request.Form("txtColor"))

If userName = "" Then
    Response.Redirect "http://<full path>/config.asp"
End If
%>
<HTML>
<HEAD>
<META NAME="GENERATOR" Content="Microsoft Visual Studio 6.0">
</HEAD>

<BODY BGCOLOR="<%= bgColor %>" TEXT="<%= txtColor %>">

User name = <%= userName %><P>

This page demonstrates the choices you made. If this
is what you want, please click the button below to
save your settings and return to the homepage. Otherwise,
click page to adjust your settings.

<FORM ACTION="saveconfig.asp" METHOD=POST>
    <INPUT TYPE=HIDDEN VALUE="<%= bgColor %>" NAME="bgColor">
    <INPUT TYPE=HIDDEN VALUE="<%= txtColor %>" NAME="txtColor">
    <INPUT TYPE=HIDDEN VALUE="<%= userName %>" NAME="userName">
    <INPUT TYPE=SUBMIT VALUE="Save settings">
</FORM>

</BODY>

</HTML>
```

Now that you have a valid username, text color, and background color, you can submit the form to a significantly changed saveconfig.asp:

```
<%@ Language=VBScript %>
<%
userName = CStr(Request.Form("userName"))
```

```
bgColor = CStr(Request.Form("bgColor"))
txtColor = CStr(Request.Form("txtColor"))

' First, find out if the username already exists
Set rs = Server.CreateObject("ADODB.Recordset")

rs.Open "SELECT * FROM personalization WHERE userName='" & _
userName & "'", "DSN=<DSN name>;UID=;Password=;",1,3

If rs.RecordCount > 0 Then
    ' Update the record
    rs("bgColor") = bgColor
    rs("txtColor") = txtColor
    rs("lastAccess") = Date()
Else
    ' Create a new record
    rs.AddNew
    rs("userName") = userName
    rs("bgColor") = bgColor
    rs("txtColor") = txtColor
    rs("lastAccess") = Date()
End If
rs.Update
rs.Close

Response.Cookies("userName") = userName

Response.Redirect "default.asp"
%>
```

This document now determines whether the username that was entered matches an existing username in the database. If it does, that record is updated with the new information. Otherwise, a new record is created and populated with the personalization information. Finally, the userName cookie is written, and the user is redirected back to the homepage.

There's only one more step: The personalize.asp file, which is automatically executed every time a user enters the site, will have to be updated so that it checks for the userName cookie only. If the cookie exists, the database will be accessed for the personalization information, and that information will be used to provide values for the session-level variables used in the preceding example. Otherwise, default values will be applied to these variables. Here's the new version:

```
<%@ Language=VBScript %>
<%
If Request.Cookies("userName") = "" Then
    Session("userName") = ""
    Session("txtColor") = "black"
    Session("bgColor") = "white"
Else
```

```
    Set rs = Server.CreateObject("ADODB.Recordset")
    rs.Open "SELECT txtColor,bgColor FROM personalization " & _
      "WHERE userName='" & _       Request.Cookies("userName") & "'", _
      "DSN=<DSN name>;UID=;Password=;",0,1
    Session("userName") = Request.Cookies("userName")
    Session("txtColor") = rs("txtColor")
    Session("bgColor") = rs("bgColor")
End If
Response.Redirect Session("StartURL")
%>
```

That's that. Now the personalization will be triggered whenever users re-enter the site, but users who want to bypass the personalization features can view the site normally. Best of all, with database integration, you have to store only one or two cookie values.

No Cookies! How to Handle the Overcautious User

There will probably always be a subculture of individuals who do not trust cookies. Despite increased awareness and the obvious benefits of these intriguing little packets of information, cookies will probably always have a certain aura of untrustworthiness. Unfortunately, as Visual InterDev developers, you're going to be stuck with cookies, because the InterDev Web interface uses FrontPage server extensions, which give off cookies to each and every visitor of your site, whether you want them to or not. It's unfortunate that Microsoft couldn't have implemented a more unobtrusive format for its server extensions, but you do have a few options, each of which presents its own challenges:

- You cannot use the FrontPage server extensions, but rather must develop your InterDev sites locally and upload them manually with FTP or the Microsoft Web Publishing Wizard to a non-FrontPage Web site. Probably thousands of InterDev developers are doing this. Obviously, this isn't an elegant solution, because you can't take advantage of some of InterDev's advanced features, such as the Data Environment.

- You can provide separate sites, one with the FrontPage extensions and one without. This requires a lot of back-end maintenance, however, because you will be duplicating content. Also, there's no way to apply the extensions to only certain directories on your site (wouldn't that be nice?).

- Many developers provide a cookie information page that explains how and why cookies are used on the site. Users can always turn off cookies in their browsers (and many do; indeed, many turn off Java and JavaScript functionality as well, another reason to stick with server-side development). Remember to provide defaults for users who don't use cookies.

Although it's easy to act enlightened about cookies, it's important to understand why some people feel the way they do about them. Rather than ostracize these potential customers, it's best to simply let them have their way and not flood them with unnecessary error dialogs.

Summary

Cookies provide an elegant and useful way to store personalization information or, at the least, username and/or password information that can be used with a database to provide personalization functionality. Cookies are best used in conjunction with server-side, rather than client-side, technologies—especially ASP, which provides two logical collection objects with which to work.

Although cookies have a bad reputation in certain circles, it's hard to deny their advantages, especially when you consider the myriad ways they can be used to make your sites more personable and helpful to users. In the end, that's what all Web technologies should be about: Making life better for the people who use the Web for business and pleasure.

CHAPTER 17

Modifying Web Application Data from the Web

by Paul Thurrott

IN THIS CHAPTER

A large portion of this book deals with the display of dynamic data, drawn from a database, in a Web page. Although this is an important functionality—indeed, Microsoft has created two data access object models and a variety of other related technology to the task—it's only half the puzzle. When you create a dynamic Web application for a customer, you have to supply a solution that allows the customer to update the information in the database, thus transparently updating the site as well.

In some (rare) cases, existing tools are enough. The customer might use Microsoft Access as a front end for SQL Server, for example, and, certainly, a case can be made for an Access form-based solution. You might also write simple Visual Basic applications that connect remotely to the database and allow the user to update, delete, and add new records. This, too, is a worthy approach. Probably dozens of such solutions exist.

In this chapter, however, you're going to focus on Web-based solutions that offer some tremendous benefits over the methods just mentioned. Most importantly, a Web-based solution enables customers to use virtually any Web browser (Internet Explorer, Netscape, Opera, and so on) running on any computing platform (Windows, Mac, UNIX, whatever) to update the data behind their site. Like any other hand-made solution, you can custom-tailor it to the technical level of the customer and shield him or her from the intricacies of the underlying data.

Providing Customers with a Web Front End to Their Data

The goal behind any Web front end to data should be to provide the customer with a central management system for his or her site. By integrating a database with the Web site, you give a customer the ability to deal directly with the content of the site and not worry about the technical HTML presentation details. Also, data-backed sites tend to be far smaller than static sites. Consider the case of the WinInfo Web site on WUGNET.com (`http://www.wugnet.com/wininfo`). As of this writing, WinInfo contains more than 2,000 news and information articles about Microsoft Windows and the entire computing industry. If this information were stored on a static Web site, we'd need more than 2,000 HTML documents, each of which would contain a single article. Instead, WinInfo is stored in a SQL Server database, and a single ASP document is used to display any of those articles.

This isn't a convoluted example: The very types of sites that are obvious candidates for Web/database integration will all benefit from the change. News and informational sites, product sites, and the like, are all better served by databases. Best of all, the reduction in page count makes it far easier to update the look and feel of the site. With fewer than a dozen individual ASP documents in the WinInfo site, for example, it's a short job to update the entire site now and then. If the site had more than 2,000 documents, it would be a nightmare.

From the customers' standpoint, the Web/database integration is also a benefit because you can supply a Web-based database front end to their data and not require them to understand HTML to update the site. Rather, you can supply simple Web pages with HTML forms for updating purposes, which enables any user (regardless of his or her technical level) to update the site. In the early days of the Web, a confusing blurring occurred in the roles each person played. For example, graphic artists and writers were forced to learn HTML so that they could update Web sites, or, perhaps more infuriatingly, they had to rely on a Web developer to make these changes for them.

Now, with Web/database integration, you can supply a nice management site that anyone can use. Let's take a look.

Managing a Database from the Web

A Web front end can resemble WUGNET's solution, shown in Figure 17.1. This private Web site, which requires a secure login (read a little further for details on implementing this feature), superficially resembles WUGNET's public Web site but allows WUGNET employees to update the various parts of the site.

FIGURE 17.1

WUGNET's Web site management site provides the user with a simple front end to the SQL Server data that drives the site.

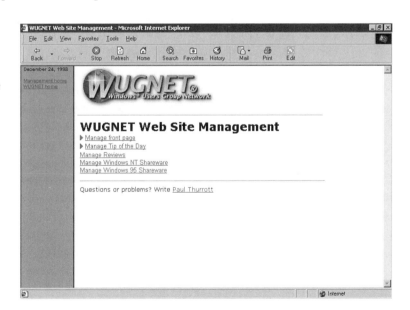

17

MODIFYING WEB
APPLICATION
DATA

For example, WUGNET's front page management, shown in Figure 17.2, specifically resembles the WUGNET front page so that users can immediately see how their changes will look. While working within the front page management portion of the site, WUGNET employees can move What's New items up and down or to the top or bottom. They can also delete items and add new items. This management page works with a temporary copy of a table on the SQL Server; when the user is ready to update the front page, it's only a mouse-click away. Later in this chapter, I discuss how this type of page can be created. Compare WUGNET's front page management (see Figure 17.2) with the actual front page on the WUGNET public Web site (see Figure 17.3).

FIGURE 17.2

WUGNET's front page management site is designed to resemble the WUGNET front page so that users can see how their changes will affect the live site.

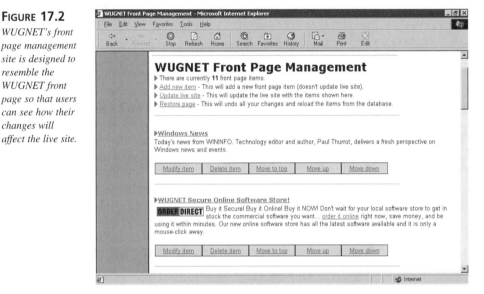

Each Web application has specific requirements when it comes to Web-based management. Regardless, there are some basic issues you usually have to deal with: The user will want to add information, delete information, and modify existing information. The makeup of the Web application determines how this all comes together, but I'll present a few approaches here, some of which are loosely based on the Database Forms Wizard from Visual InterDev 1.0. This buggy tool had its heart in the right place: Although the sites it created were nothing special to look at, it did give users a place to perform all the necessary database management functions just mentioned.

FIGURE 17.3

*The WUGNET
front page.*

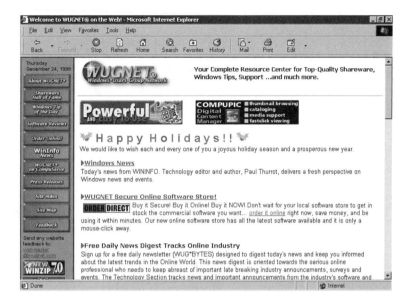

…when it worked, that is. The problem with the Database Forms Wizard is that the documents it generated rarely ever worked correctly. When Microsoft revamped the design-time controls for Visual InterDev 6.0, the Database Forms Wizard disappeared, although you can create similar DTC-based solutions now that are slightly less automated. This is covered in Chapter 14, "Using Data-Bound Controls"; I will cover hand-coded solutions here because they provide the greatest flexibility.

Security Issues

It should be fairly obvious that the biggest problem with providing Web-based access to your live data is security. There are various ways to minimize the risk, but the most obvious thing you can do is to require a login for those directories that will contain the forms used to update the database. This is simple enough, and depending on your situation, you can ask the system administrator or perhaps the Webmaster to perform this task for you. If, however, you're not working in a Fortune 100 company with an IS department the size of Rhode Island, you might have to do this yourself.

Setting NT User Security for Web Site Folders

On the NT-based (or Windows 2000-based) Web server, navigate to the folder you've created to contain the secure Web management documents. Right-click the folder and select Properties, which will open the Properties sheet for the folder. Navigate to the Security tab, and you will be presented with a list of the users that currently have access to the folder. This could include the Administrator account, the IUSR account for this machine, your user account, and perhaps the SYSTEM account. Use the Remove button to remove all these accounts from the security rules for the folder.

Now you have to add the user(s) or user group(s) who will have access privileges to the folder. Simply click the Add button, and then locate those users in the list of users and user groups that appears. Make sure that you give each user you add the following permissions: Read, Write, and Read & Execute. When you're done, close the Properties sheet.

The best thing you can do when you have security applied is to load a document into that directory and attempt to access it from the Web. If you do everything correctly, you should see a login dialog similar to Figure 17.4.

FIGURE 17.4

Internet Explorer allows your users to store their password in cache, so they don't have to re-enter it every time they use the management site. You might recommend that they not do this.

 Voilá! Now, it's time to get cracking on that front end. For the examples in this chapter, you will work with the WinInfo database, which is supplied on the CD-ROM that accompanies this book.

Creating the Front End

For this example, you will create a front end for the WinInfo database that contains a single table called wininfo. This table represents a small subset of the articles I've written for WinInfo (`http://www.wugnet.com/wininfo`), an email-based newsletter delivered to thousands of industry insiders every day. The front end won't be designed in any particular way per se, because you will be focusing on the content.

The first step is to create a new Web or a folder in an existing Web to hold the Web management files. The main entry page (default.htm) consists of a simple menu with three choices:

- Add a New Article walks the user through a wizard-like interface for adding new articles to WinInfo.

- Manage Recent Articles loads a list of the 10 most recent articles posted to WinInfo, allowing the user to modify or delete an existing article.

- Search for Article provides a variety of ways to find a particular article, such as search by ID, title, date, or phrase in the body text. After an article is found, it can be modified or deleted.

The code for this document will resemble the following:

```
<HTML>

<HEAD>
<META NAME="GENERATOR" Content="Microsoft Visual Studio 6.0">
<TITLE>Manage WinInfo</TITLE>
</HEAD>

<STYLE>
<!--
    A:link { text-decoration: none; }
    A:hover { color: RED; }
    A:visited { text-decoration: none; }
-->
</STYLE>


<BODY BGCOLOR="#FFFFFF" TEXT="BLACK"
 LINK="BLUE" ALINK="BLUE" VLINK="BLUE">

<FONT FACE="Verdana" SIZE=2>
<H2>Manage WinInfo</H2>
<HR SIZE=1 NOSHADE>
<LI><A HREF="addnew.asp">Add a new article</A>
<LI><A HREF="recent.asp">Manage recent articles</A>
<LI><A HREF="search.asp">Search for article</A>
<HR SIZE=1 NOSHADE>
<LI><A HREF="http://www.wugnet.com/wininfo">Goto live site</A>

</BODY>
</HTML>
```

Figure 17.5 shows the WinInfo Management page in a Web browser.

FIGURE 17.5

*The WinInfo Web
Management site
allows users to
manage an online
news and infor-
mation data
source.*

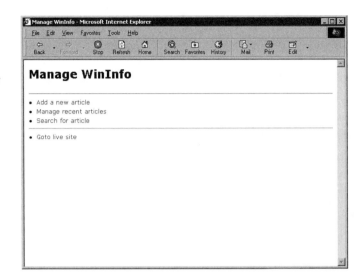

From here, you can tackle the menu options in order. Each option requires a handful of
ASP documents.

Adding New Data

First up is the Add a New Article option, which enables you to create a new WinInfo
news article. Each article consists of the fields `title`, `date`, and `body`, as well as an ID
field that is automatically assigned a value by the database. This option requires three
pages:

- addnew.asp—This presents an HTML form to the user so that the title, date, and
  body text can be submitted.

- addnew2.asp—The data entered into the form in addnew.asp is submitted here.
  This page does two things: It shows the user how the article will look on a Web
  page and then provides a form so that the user can make modifications. If the user
  decides to post the article as is, that's an option. Otherwise, he or she can make
  changes to the article over and over again, posting it to the same page each time a
  change is made. (This will be made clearer presently.)

- addnew3.asp—This accepts the submission from addnew2.asp and posts the new
  article to the database as long as no fields were left empty. In this case, an error
  message is shown, and the user is prompted to press Back to return to
  addnew2.asp.

The first file, addnew.asp, is the simplest:

```
<%@ Language=VBScript %>
<HTML>

<HEAD>
<META NAME="GENERATOR" Content="Microsoft Visual Studio 6.0">
<TITLE>Manage WinInfo: Add a new article</TITLE>
</HEAD>

<STYLE>
<!--
    A:link { text-decoration: none; }
    A:hover { color: RED; }
    A:visited { text-decoration: none; }
-->
</STYLE>

<BODY BGCOLOR="#FFFFFF" TEXT="BLACK"
 LINK="BLUE" ALINK="BLUE" VLINK="BLUE">

<FONT FACE="Verdana" SIZE=2>
<H2>Manage WinInfo: Add a new article</H2>
<HR SIZE=1 NOSHADE>
<TABLE WIDTH=400 CELLPADDING=5 CELLSPACING=5 BORDER=0 COLS=2>
  <TR>
        <TD WIDTH=50 ALIGN=RIGHT VALIGN=TOP>
          <FONT FACE="Verdana" SIZE=2 COLOR=BLACK>
            Title
        </TD>
        <TD WIDTH=350 ALIGN=LEFT VALIGN=MIDDLE>
          <FONT FACE="Verdana" SIZE=2 COLOR=BLACK>
                <FORM METHOD=POST NAME="post" ACTION="addnew2.asp">
                <INPUT TYPE="TEXT" SIZE=80 NAME="title">
        </TD>
    </TR>
  <TR>
        <TD ALIGN=RIGHT VALIGN=TOP>
          <FONT FACE="Verdana" SIZE=2 COLOR=BLACK>
            Date
        </TD>
        <TD ALIGN=LEFT VALIGN=MIDDLE>
          <FONT FACE="Verdana" SIZE=2 COLOR=BLACK>
                <INPUT TYPE="TEXT" SIZE=40 NAME="theDate"
                VALUE="<%= Date() %>">
        </TD>
    </TR>
    <TR>
        <TD ALIGN=RIGHT VALIGN=TOP>
          <FONT FACE="Verdana" SIZE=2 COLOR=BLACK>
```

```
        Body
    </TD>
    <TD ALIGN=LEFT VALIGN=MIDDLE>
      <FONT FACE="Verdana" SIZE=2 COLOR=BLACK>
            <TEXTAREA COLS=80 ROWS=15 NAME="body"></TEXTAREA>
    </TD>
</TR>
<TR>
    <TD ALIGN=RIGHT VALIGN=TOP>
      <FONT FACE="Verdana " SIZE=2 COLOR=BLACK>
         
    </TD>
    <TD ALIGN=LEFT VALIGN=MIDDLE>
      <FONT FACE="Verdana " SIZE=2 COLOR=BLACK>
            <INPUT TYPE="Submit" VALUE="Submit">
    </TD>
</TR>
</TABLE>
</FORM>
<HR SIZE=1 NOSHADE>
<A HREF="default.htm"><< Cancel</A>

</BODY>
</HTML>
```

As shown in Figure 17.6, this document presents an HTML form to the user so that a new article can be submitted.

FIGURE 17.6

The first step for adding a new article involves filling out a simple HTML form.

After the user fills out the form, he or she can submit it to addnew2.asp:

```asp
<%@ Language=VBScript %>
<%
'-- Get the title text ----------
title = CStr(Request.Form("title"))

'-- Get the date ----------
theDate = CStr(Request.Form("theDate"))
If IsDate(theDate) = True Then
    theDate = CDate(theDate)
Else
    theDate = date()
End If

'-- Get the body text ----------
str = CStr(Request.Form("body"))
body = ""
For x = 1 to Len(str)
    body = body & Right(Left(str, x), 1)
    If Right(body, 4) = Chr(13) & Chr(10) & Chr(13) & Chr(10) Then
        body = Left(body, Len(body) - 4)
        body = body & Chr(13) & Chr(10) & "<P>" & Chr(13) & Chr(10)
    End If
Next
%>
<HTML>

<HEAD>
<META NAME="GENERATOR" Content="Microsoft Visual Studio 6.0">
<TITLE>Manage WinInfo: Add a new article (Step 2)</TITLE>
</HEAD>

<STYLE>
<!--
    A:link { text-decoration: none; }
    A:hover { color: RED; }
    A:visited { text-decoration: none; }
-->
</STYLE>

<BODY BGCOLOR="#FFFFFF" TEXT="BLACK"
 LINK="BLUE" ALINK="BLUE" VLINK="BLUE">

<FONT FACE="Verdana" SIZE=2>
<H2>Manage WinInfo: Add a new article (Step 2)</H2>
<HR SIZE=1 NOSHADE>

<H3><FONT FACE="Verdana">Here's how the article currently looks:
</FONT></H3>
```

```
<TABLE WIDTH=600 CELLPADDING=5 CELLSPACING=5 BORDER=0>
   <TR>
      <TD WIDTH=100% ALIGN=LEFT VALIGN=TOP>
            <FONT FACE="Verdana" SIZE=2>
            <%
            Response.Write "<B>" & title & "</B>"
            Response.Write "<BR><I>(" & theDate & ")</I>"
            Response.Write "<BR>" & body
            %>
            </FONT>
         </TD>
      </TR>
</TABLE>

<BR><BR><H2>Now you have two choices:</H2>

<P><FONT FACE="Verdana" SIZE=4><B>1. It's ready! Post it to the
      database</B></FONT>
<TABLE WIDTH=600 CELLPADDING=5 CELLSPACING=5 BORDER=0>
   <FORM METHOD=POST ACTION="addnew3.asp">
   <TR>
      <TD WIDTH=100% ALIGN=LEFT VALIGN=TOP>
            <INPUT TYPE=HIDDEN NAME="title" VALUE="<%= title %>">
            <INPUT TYPE=HIDDEN NAME="theDate" VALUE="<%= theDate %>">
            <TEXTAREA COLS=1 ROWS=1 NAME="body"><%= body %></TEXTAREA>
              <INPUT TYPE=SUBMIT VALUE="Post it to the database!">
         </TD>
      </TR>
      </FORM>
</TABLE>

<P><FONT FACE="Verdana" SIZE=4><B>2. Edit the HTML and repost
</B></FONT>
<TABLE WIDTH=600 CELLPADDING=5 CELLSPACING=5 BORDER=0>
   <FORM METHOD=POST ACTION="addnew2.asp">
   <TR>
      <TD WIDTH=100% ALIGN=LEFT VALIGN=TOP>
            <INPUT TYPE=TEXT SIZE=80 NAME="title" VALUE="<%= title %>">
            <BR>
            <INPUT TYPE=TEXT SIZE=40 NAME="theDate"
             VALUE="<%= theDate %>"><BR>
              <TEXTAREA COLS=80 ROWS=15 NAME="body"><%= body %>
              </TEXTAREA>
              <P><INPUT TYPE=SUBMIT VALUE="Submit and review changes">
         </TD>
```

```
    </TR>
    </FORM>
</TABLE>

<HR SIZE=1 NOSHADE>
<A HREF="default.htm"><< Cancel</A>

</BODY>
</HTML>
```

This document probably requires some explanation, so let's walk through it. When the form is submitted to addnew2.asp, the document first retrieves the title, date, and body values, which are initially stored locally as `title`, `theDate`, and `str`. As demonstrated by this document, you should always explicitly convert values posted from a form if you will later copy them into a database. This ensures that the data is stored in the correct format before you try to update the database. The VBScript conversion functions (CStr, CDate, CInt, and the like) should be applied as soon as the values are passed from the form. Also, note that this must happen before the any HTML code is parsed.

You do some simple error checking on the date value because it would be easy for the user to enter a date incorrectly, even though a default value (today's date) is supplied. If the date entered is a valid date, that date is accepted. Otherwise, today's date is substituted.

The block of code dealing with the body text might also look a bit odd. Here it is:

```
'-- Get the body text ----------
str = CStr(Request.Form("body"))
body = ""
For x = 1 to Len(str)
    body = body & Right(Left(str, x), 1)
    If Right(body, 4) = Chr(13) & Chr(10) & Chr(13) & Chr(10) Then
        body = Left(body, Len(body) - 4)
        body = body & Chr(13) & Chr(10) & "<P>" & Chr(13) & Chr(10)
    End If
Next
```

This code grabs the text entered as the body text and parses through it, one character at a time. If it finds a double carriage return (each carriage return is represented in VBScript as `Chr(13)` & `Chr(10)`, it replaces these characters with a single carriage return, the text `"<P>"`, and then another carriage return.

Well, you know that these articles are going to be displayed in HTML. Let's say the user submits an article with the following body text:

```
Intel Corporation will ring in the new year with the first of a series
of new microprocessor introductions designed to attack both the
low-end and high-end computing markets. In addition to the expected
Celeron additions, Intel will introduce a new line of Pentium II CPUs,
which it will call "Pentium II Enhanced." Essentially a Pentium II
with 256KB of L2 cache integrated into the processor, the Pentium II
Enhanced will blow past the performance of the current generation of
Pentium IIs, which feature 512KB of external cache (that is, the
cache is not integrated into the processor, so it runs at only half
the speed of the processor). 333 and 366 MHz Pentium II Enhanced
processors will debut in January.

Also expected in January are the new 366 and (earlier than previously
expected) 400 MHz Celerons, which will include a 100 MHz bus. In
mid-1999, Intel will add a 433 MHz version as well.

For mobile users, Intel will introduce a 300 MHz Pentium MMX and 266
and 300 MHz Celeron processors. These chips are expected to launch an
era of full-featured $1000-1500 laptops.

At the extreme high end, Intel will release a 450 MHz Pentium II Xeon
with a choice of 512KB, 1MB, or 2MB of L2 cache. This chip will be
officially announced in January and be available in early 1999.
```

A double carriage return indicates a new paragraph. In HTML, a new paragraph is created with the <P>tag. This parsing code simply replaces each double carriage return with a <P> tag, so the preceding example would be converted to the following:

```
Intel Corporation will ring in the new year with the first of a series
of new microprocessor introductions designed to attack both the
low-end and high-end computing markets. In addition to the expected
Celeron additions, Intel will introduce a new line of Pentium II CPUs,
which it will call "Pentium II Enhanced." Essentially a Pentium II
with 256KB of L2 cache integrated into the processor, the Pentium II
Enhanced will blow past the performance of the current generation of
Pentium IIs, which feature 512KB of external cache (that is, the
cache is not integrated into the processor, so it runs at only half
the speed of the processor). 333 and 366 MHz Pentium II Enhanced
processors will debut in January.
<P>
Also expected in January are the new 366 and (earlier than previously
expected) 400 MHz Celerons, which will include a 100 MHz bus. In
mid-1999, Intel will add a 433 MHz version as well.
<P>
For mobile users, Intel will introduce a 300 MHz Pentium MMX and 266
and 300 MHz Celeron processors. These chips are expected to launch an
era of full-featured $1000-1500 laptops.
<P>
```

```
At the extreme high end, Intel will release a 450 MHz Pentium II Xeon
with a choice of 512KB, 1MB, or 2MB of L2 cache. This chip will be
officially announced in January and be available in early 1999.
```

This is done as a timesaver for users and as a way to circumvent the need for them to know any HTML. The common HTML <P> tag is automatically inserted for them. When the code is done parsing the text, it's copied into the local variable body.

From here, the HTML portion of the document is rendered. There are two main sections to this document, a top half displaying the article as it now looks, rendered in HTML (see Figure 17.7) and a bottom half presenting a form (see Figure 17.8) much like the form in addnew.asp. If the user likes the article as is, he or she can submit it by using the Submit button in the top half of the page. This will submit the data to addnew3.asp. Otherwise, the user can work with the form in the bottom half of the page, which is pre-filled with the proper submitted data. If the Submit button at the bottom is pressed, the page submits the changes *to itself* and refreshes the page. This is incredibly powerful, if you think about it: Users can work with the page for as long as they like, changing things and reposting it until it's just the way they want it. When it's complete, they can use the Submit button in the top half of the page to write the new record to the database.

17

MODIFYING WEB
APPLICATION
DATA

FIGURE 17.7

In the top half of the document, the submitted information is previewed in HTML.

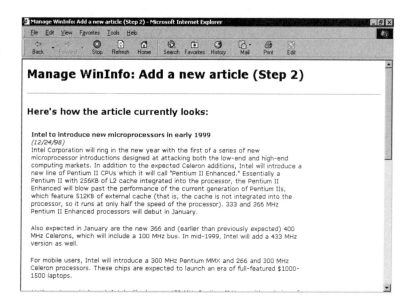

FIGURE 17.8

See a mistake?
Use the form in
the bottom half of
the document to
make changes.

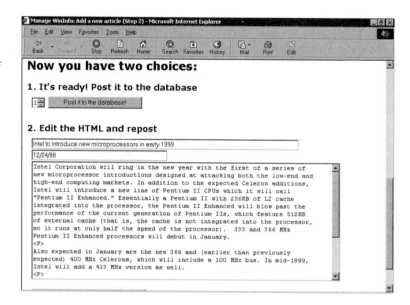

When addnew2.asp is submitted, addnew3.asp is called, and the new article information is passed along. Addnew3.asp retrieves the values, does some simple error checking, and writes the new record to the database if all is well. Otherwise, an error message is generated, depending on the error. Here's the code:

```
<%@ Language=VBScript %>
<%
title = CStr(Request.Form("title"))
theDate = CDate(theDate)
body = CStr(Request.Form("body"))

Errors = 0

If title = "" Then
  Errors = 1
End If

If theDate = "" Then
    Errors = 2
End If

If body = "" Then
  Errors = 3
End If

If Errors = 0 Then
  Set rs = Server.CreateObject("ADODB.Recordset")
```

```
    rs.Open "EXECUTE GetLatest 1", _
      "DSN=wugnet;UID=<login>;Password=<pass>",3,2

      rs.AddNew
      rs("title") = title
      rs("date") = theDate
      rs("body") = body
      ' rs.Update
%>
<HTML>

<HEAD>
<META NAME="GENERATOR" Content="Microsoft Visual Studio 6.0">
<TITLE>Manage WinInfo: New article added!</TITLE>
</HEAD>

<STYLE>
<!--
    A:link { text-decoration: none; }
    A:hover { color: RED; }
    A:visited { text-decoration: none; }
-->
</STYLE>

<BODY BGCOLOR="#FFFFFF" TEXT="BLACK"
 LINK="BLUE" ALINK="BLUE" VLINK="BLUE">

<FONT FACE="Verdana" SIZE=2>
<H2>Manage WinInfo: New article added!</H2>
<HR SIZE=1 NOSHADE>

<LI><A HREF="addnew.asp">Add another article</A>
<LI><A HREF="default.htm">Return to WinInfo management</A>
<HR SIZE=1 NOSHADE>

<LI><A HREF="http://www.wugnet.com/wininfo">Goto live site</A>

</BODY>

</HTML>
<%
Else
%>
<HTML>

<HEAD>
<META NAME="GENERATOR" Content="Microsoft Visual Studio 6.0">
<TITLE>Whoops!</TITLE>
</HEAD>

<STYLE>
<!--
```

```
    A:link { text-decoration: none; }
    A:hover { color: RED; }
    A:visited { text-decoration: none; }
-->
</STYLE>

<BODY BGCOLOR="#FFFFFF" TEXT="BLACK"
 LINK="BLUE" ALINK="BLUE" VLINK="BLUE">

<FONT FACE="Verdana" SIZE=2>
<H2>Whoops!</H2>
<HR SIZE=1 NOSHADE>

<%
If Errors = 1 Then
    Response.write "The title field cannot be blank."
Else
    If Errors = 2 Then
        Response.write "The date field cannot be blank."
    Else
        If Errors = 3 Then
            Response.write "The body field cannot be blank."
        End If
    End If
End If
Response.write "<BR>Please press <B>BACK</B>" & _
  and fill in the title field."
%>

<HR SIZE=1 NOSHADE>

</BODY>

</HTML>
<%
End If
%>
```

The one confusing thing here might be the recordset Open line, which executes a stored procedure called GetLatest, passing along a value of 1. The GetLatest stored procedure looks like this:

```
Create Procedure GetLatest @numRecords int=15
As
SELECT ID,title,date,body
FROM wininfo
WHERE ID >= (SELECT rows FROM sysindexes
    WHERE (id = OBJECT_ID('wininfo'))
    AND (indid < 2)) - (@numRecords - 1)
ORDER BY date DESC, ID DESC
Return
```

The creation of this stored procedure is detailed in Chapter 15, "Displaying Data in a Web Application." In short, it takes a single optional parameter called numRecords that determines the number of records to return. You pass a value of 1 so that the smallest possible recordset is generated.

If all goes well, the new record will be added, and you will see a screen similar to Figure 17.9. Otherwise, an error will be generated, and you will be prompted to return to the preceding page and make some changes.

FIGURE 17.9

Success! Even a user with no HTML skills can easily enter articles with this wizard-like article entry site.

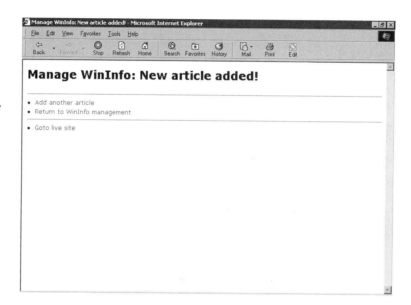

Modifying Existing Data

The Manage Recent Articles option on the front end loads recent.asp, which contains a list of the titles of the 10 most recent articles in the WinInfo database. Each title includes Modify and Delete choices so that the user can manage those articles accordingly. Here's the code:

```
<%@ Language=VBScript %>
<%
Set rs = Server.CreateObject("ADODB.Recordset")
rs.Open "EXECUTE GetLatest 10",_
  "DSN=wugnet;UID=<login>;Password=<pass>",0,1
%>
<HTML>

<HEAD>
<META NAME="GENERATOR" Content="Microsoft Visual Studio 6.0">
```

```
<TITLE>Manage WinInfo: Manage recent articles</TITLE>
</HEAD>

<STYLE>
<!--
    A:link { text-decoration: none; }
    A:hover { color: RED; }
    A:visited { text-decoration: none; }
-->
</STYLE>


<BODY BGCOLOR="#FFFFFF" TEXT="BLACK"
 LINK="BLUE" ALINK="BLUE" VLINK="BLUE">

<FONT FACE="Verdana" SIZE=2>
<H2>Manage WinInfo: Manage recent articles</H2>
<HR SIZE=1 NOSHADE>

<TABLE WIDTH=600 CELLPADDING=5 CELLSPACING=0 BORDER=1
 BGCOLOR="#FFFFFF" BORDERCOLOR="NAVY">
<% Do While NOT rs.EOF %>
  <TR>
        <TD WIDTH=500 ALIGN=LEFT VALIGN=TOP BGCOLOR="#FFFFEE">
            <FONT FACE="Verdana" SIZE=2>
            <%= rs("title") %>
            </FONT>
        </TD>
        <TD WIDTH=50 ALIGN=CENTER VALIGN=TOP>
            <FONT FACE="Verdana" SIZE=2>
            <A HREF="modify.asp?ID=<%= rs("ID") %>">Modify</A>
            </FONT>
        </TD>
        <TD WIDTH=50 ALIGN=CENTER VALIGN=TOP>
            <FONT FACE="Verdana" SIZE=2>
            <A HREF="delete.asp?ID=<%= rs("ID") %>">Delete</A>
            </FONT>
        </TD>
    </TR>
<% rs.MoveNext: Loop %>
</TABLE>

<HR SIZE=1 NOSHADE>
<A HREF="default.htm"><< Cancel</A>

</BODY>
</HTML>
```

Once again, you use the GetLatest stored procedure, although you pass a value of 10 this time. The article titles are arranged in a dynamically generated HTML table; each row represents the title and options for an article. The resulting page resembles Figure 17.10.

FIGURE 17.10

The Manage Recent Articles page lists the 10 most recent articles and provides links to modify and delete individual articles.

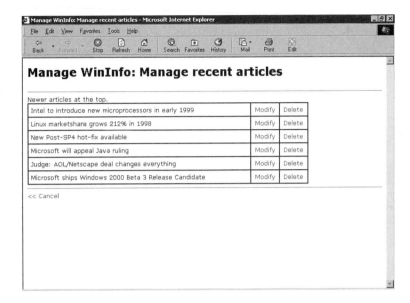

If the user clicks the Modify link, he or she will be presented with a document very similar to addnew2.asp. This document, modify.asp, also presents a two-tiered view of an article, although this time it's an existing article. The top half of modify.asp displays the article as it will appear in HTML. The user can then update the database from here or edit the article in an HTML form at the bottom of the page. Like addnew2.asp, the lower half of this document contains code to post the information to itself, so the user can edit the article over and over again until it's right. Here's the code for modify.asp:

```
<%@ Language=VBScript %>
<%
ID = CInt(Request.QueryString("ID"))

If CStr(Request.Form("title")) = "" _
  and CStr(Request.Form("theDate")) = "" _
  and CStr(Request.Form("body")) = "" Then
    Set rs = Server.CreateObject("ADODB.Recordset")
    rs.Open "EXECUTE GetArticle " & _
      ID,"DSN=wugnet;UID=<login>;" & _
      "Password=<pass>",0,1
    title = rs("title")
    theDate = rs("date")
    body = rs("body")
Else
    title = CStr(Request.Form("title"))
    theDate = CStr(Request.Form("theDate"))
    body = CStr(Request.Form("body"))
```

```
End If
%>
<HTML>
<HEAD>
<META NAME="GENERATOR" Content="Microsoft Visual Studio 6.0">
<TITLE>Manage WinInfo: Modify article "<%= title %>"</TITLE>
</HEAD>

<STYLE>
<!--
    A:link { text-decoration: none; }
    A:hover { color: RED; }
    A:visited { text-decoration: none; }
-->
</STYLE>


<BODY BGCOLOR="#FFFFFF" TEXT="BLACK"
 LINK="BLUE" ALINK="BLUE" VLINK="BLUE">

<FONT FACE="Verdana" SIZE=2>
<H2>Manage WinInfo: Modify article</H2>
<HR SIZE=1 NOSHADE>

<H3><FONT FACE="Verdana">Here's how the article currently looks:
  </FONT></H3>
<TABLE WIDTH=600 CELLPADDING=5 CELLSPACING=5 BORDER=0>
  <TR>
      <TD WIDTH=100% ALIGN=LEFT VALIGN=TOP>
            <FONT FACE="Verdana" SIZE=2>
            <%
            Response.Write "<B>" & title & "</B>"
            Response.Write "<BR><I>(" & theDate & ")</I>"
            Response.Write "<BR>" & body
            %>
            </FONT>
        </TD>
    </TR>
</TABLE>

<BR><BR><H2>Now you have two choices:</H2>

<P><FONT FACE="Verdana" SIZE=4><B>1. It's ready! Post it to
  the database</B></FONT>
<TABLE WIDTH=600 CELLPADDING=5 CELLSPACING=5 BORDER=0>
  <FORM METHOD=POST ACTION="modify2.asp?ID=<%= ID %>" >
  <TR>
      <TD WIDTH=100% ALIGN=LEFT VALIGN=TOP>
            <INPUT TYPE=HIDDEN NAME="title" VALUE="<%= title %>">
```

```
              <INPUT TYPE=HIDDEN NAME="theDate" VALUE="<%= theDate %>">
              <TEXTAREA COLS=1 ROWS=1 NAME="body"><%= body %></TEXTAREA>
                <INPUT TYPE=SUBMIT VALUE="Update the record!" >
          </TD>
      </TR>
      </FORM>
</TABLE>

<P><FONT FACE="Verdana" SIZE=4><B>2. Edit the HTML and repost
  </B></FONT>
<TABLE WIDTH=600 CELLPADDING=5 CELLSPACING=5 BORDER=0>
  <FORM METHOD=POST ACTION="modify.asp?ID=<%= ID %>">
  <TR>
      <TD WIDTH=100% ALIGN=LEFT VALIGN=TOP>
          <INPUT TYPE=TEXT SIZE=80
          NAME="title" VALUE="<%= title %>"><BR>
          <INPUT TYPE=TEXT SIZE=40 NAME="theDate"
          VALUE="<%= theDate %>"><BR>
          <TEXTAREA COLS=80 ROWS=15 NAME="body"><%= body %>
          </TEXTAREA>
          <P><INPUT TYPE=SUBMIT VALUE="Submit changes">
      </TD>
  </TR>
  </FORM>
</TABLE>

<HR SIZE=1 NOSHADE>
<A HREF="recent.asp"><< Return to Manage recent articles</A>

</BODY>
</HTML>
```

The big difference between this document and addnew2.asp comes at the top: In addition to passing the ID value of the article along in the URL, you must check whether the article information was posted from this page. Remember that there are two ways this page could have loaded: The user could have clicked the Modify link on recent.asp, or the page could have posted to itself. If the page posted to itself, form information will be passed along as well. Right away, you check for this form information: If it exists, you simply grab that information and store it in the local variables title, theDate, and body. If the page hasn't posted itself, this information will not have been passed, so you simply grab the ID value from the URL and open a recordset that consists of only the record with that ID. Then, you populate the local variables as before and continue.

From here on, the code should be familiar because it is based largely on addnew2.asp. When the user is ready to update the record, the form information is posted to modify2.asp, which performs an operation similar to addnew3.asp:

```
<%@ Language=VBScript %>
<%
ID = CInt(Request.QueryString("ID"))
title = CStr(Request.Form("title"))
theDate = CDate(Request.Form("theDate"))
body = CStr(Request.Form("body"))

Errors = 0

If title = "" Then
  Errors = 1
End If

If theDate = "" Then
    Errors = 2
End If

If body = "" Then
  Errors = 3
End If

If Errors = 0 Then
  Set rs = Server.CreateObject("ADODB.Recordset")
  rs.Open "SELECT * FROM wininfo WHERE ID = " & ID, _
    "DSN=wugnet;UID=<login>;Password=<pass>",3,2

    rs("title") = title
    rs("date") = theDate
    rs("body") = body
    rs.Update
%>
<HTML>

<HEAD>
<META NAME="GENERATOR" Content="Microsoft Visual Studio 6.0">
<TITLE>Manage WinInfo: Article updated!</TITLE>
</HEAD>

<STYLE>
<!--
    A:link { text-decoration: none; }
    A:hover { color: RED; }
    A:visited { text-decoration: none; }
-->
</STYLE>
```

```
<BODY BGCOLOR="#FFFFFF" TEXT="BLACK"
 LINK="BLUE" ALINK="BLUE" VLINK="BLUE">

<FONT FACE="Verdana" SIZE=2>
<H2>Manage WinInfo: Article updated!</H2>
<HR SIZE=1 NOSHADE>

<LI><A HREF="recent.asp">Return to Manage recent articles</A>
<LI><A HREF="default.htm">Return to WinInfo management</A>
<HR SIZE=1 NOSHADE>

<LI><A HREF="http://www.wugnet.com/wininfo">Goto live site</A>

</BODY>

</HTML>
<%
Else
%>
<HTML>

<HEAD>
<META NAME="GENERATOR" Content="Microsoft Visual Studio 6.0">
<TITLE>Whoops!</TITLE>
</HEAD>

<STYLE>
<!--
    A:link { text-decoration: none; }
    A:hover { color: RED; }
    A:visited { text-decoration: none; }
-->
</STYLE>

<BODY BGCOLOR="#FFFFFF" TEXT="BLACK"
 LINK="BLUE" ALINK="BLUE" VLINK="BLUE">

<FONT FACE="Verdana" SIZE=2>
<H2>Whoops!</H2>
<HR SIZE=1 NOSHADE>

<%
If Errors = 1 Then
    Response.write "The title field cannot be blank."
Else
    If Errors = 2 Then
        Response.write "The date field cannot be blank."
    Else
        If Errors = 3 Then
            Response.write "The body field cannot be blank."
```

```
        End If
    End If
End If
Response.write "<BR>Please press <B>BACK</B> and " & _
  "fill in the title field."
%>

<HR SIZE=1 NOSHADE>

</BODY>

</HTML>
<%
End If
%>
```

The difference, of course, is that the ID of the current record is passed so that you modify the correct article. A recordset object is instantiated that contains only the article you have to change. Then, the form values are passed into the fields of the recordset (note that you don't try to change or affect the ID field), and the record is updated.

As with addnew3.asp, a simple set of error situations can occur if one of the fields was left blank. In this case, the user is prompted to return to the form at modify.asp and make corrections.

Deleting Data

The second option for each record displayed on recent.asp allows the user to Delete a Record. Depending on the type of data used, this option may or may not be as frequented as the modify option; regardless, you should always build in some sort of safeguard when it comes to deleting data: After data is deleted, it's essentially gone for good, especially from the customer's perspective. Although it is, of course, possible to get SQL Server to roll back deletions if it's configured for that or to restore a backup that is (you hope) made on a regular basis (I recommend at least once a night for production sites that rely on a database), I don't want to give the impression that these operations are easy, fast, or inexpensive. You can do your part to save users from themselves by making it fairly difficult to delete information or, at the least, by giving the user an obvious prompt indicating how serious this action is.

For the WinInfo management site, the delete page presents an HTML table resembling a Windows dialog box, asking users whether they're sure they'd like to delete the article (see Figure 17.11).

FIGURE 17.11

Make the user think about the deletion before carrying out the action.

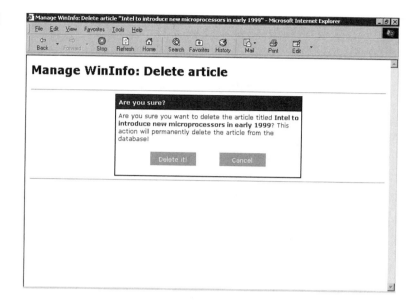

Here's the code for this document:

```
<%@ Language=VBScript %>
<%
ID = CInt(Request.QueryString("ID"))
Set rs = Server.CreateObject("ADODB.Recordset")
rs.Open "EXECUTE GetArticle " & ID,"DSN=wugnet;" & _
  "UID=<login>;Password=<pass>",0,1
title = rs("title")
%>
<HTML>
<HEAD>
<META NAME="GENERATOR" Content="Microsoft Visual Studio 6.0">
<TITLE>Manage WinInfo: Delete article "<%= title %>"</TITLE>
</HEAD>

<STYLE>
<!--
    A:link { text-decoration: none; }
    A:hover { color: BLUE; }
    A:visited { text-decoration: none; }
-->
</STYLE>


<BODY BGCOLOR="#FFFFFF" TEXT="BLACK"
 LINK="WHITE" ALINK="WHITE" VLINK="WHITE">
```

```
<FONT FACE="Verdana" SIZE=2>
<H2>Manage WinInfo: Delete article</H2>
<HR SIZE=1 NOSHADE>

<CENTER>
<TABLE WIDTH=400 CELLPADDING=5 CELLSPACING=0 BORDER=1
 BORDERCOLOR="BLACK">
    <TR BGCOLOR="NAVY">
        <TD ALIGN=LEFT VALIGN=MIDDLE>
            <FONT FACE="Verdana" SIZE=2 COLOR="WHITE">
            <B>Are you sure?</B></FONT>
        </TD>
    </TR>
    <TR BGCOLOR="WHITE">
        <TD ALIGN=LEFT VALIGN=MIDDLE>
            <FONT FACE="Verdana" SIZE=2 COLOR="BLACK">
            Are you sure you want to delete the article titled
            <B><%= title %></B>? This action will permanently
            delete the article from the database!
            <P>
            <TABLE WIDTH=100% CELLPADDING=5 CELLSPACING=0 BORDER=0>
                <TR>
                    <TD WIDTH=75 ALIGN=CENTER VALIGN=MIDDLE
                     BGCOLOR="#FFFFFF">
                    </TD>
                    <TD WIDTH=100 ALIGN=CENTER VALIGN=MIDDLE
                     BGCOLOR="#999999">
                        <FONT FACE="Verdana" SIZE=2>
                        <A HREF="delete2.asp?ID=<%= ID %>">Delete
                        it!</A></FONT>
                    </TD>
                    <TD WIDTH=50 ALIGN=CENTER VALIGN=MIDDLE
                     BGCOLOR="#FFFFFF">
                    </TD>
                    <TD WIDTH=100 ALIGN=CENTER VALIGN=MIDDLE
                     BGCOLOR="#999999">
                        <FONT FACE="Verdana" SIZE=2>
                        <A HREF="recent.asp">Cancel</A>
                        </FONT>
                    </TD>
                    <TD WIDTH=75 ALIGN=CENTER VALIGN=MIDDLE
                     BGCOLOR="#FFFFFF">
                    </TD>
                </TR>
            </TABLE>
            <BR>
            </FONT>
        </TD>
    </TR>
```

```
</TABLE>
</CENTER>

<HR SIZE=1 NOSHADE>

</BODY>
</HTML>
```

If the user cancels, the browser returns to recent.asp. Otherwise, delete2.asp is loaded, and from here, there's no looking back. The record is deleted, using the ADO Recordset object's Delete method.

```
<%@ Language=VBScript %>
<%
ID = CInt(Request.QueryString("ID"))

Set rs = Server.CreateObject("ADODB.Recordset")
rs.Open "SELECT * FROM wininfo WHERE ID = " & ID, & _
  "DSN=wugnet;UID=<login>;Password=<pass>",3,2
title = rs("title")
rs.Delete
%>
<HTML>

<HEAD>
<META NAME="GENERATOR" Content="Microsoft Visual Studio 6.0">
<TITLE>Manage WinInfo: Article deleted!</TITLE>
</HEAD>

<STYLE>
<!--
    A:link { text-decoration: none; }
    A:hover { color: RED; }
    A:visited { text-decoration: none; }
-->
</STYLE>

<BODY BGCOLOR="#FFFFFF" TEXT="BLACK"
 LINK="BLUE" ALINK="BLUE" VLINK="BLUE">

<FONT FACE="Verdana" SIZE=2>
<H2>Manage WinInfo: Article deleted!</H2>
<HR SIZE=1 NOSHADE>

The article titled <B><%= title %></B> has been deleted.
<P>
```

```
<LI><A HREF="recent.asp">Return to Manage recent articles</A>
<LI><A HREF="default.htm">Return to WinInfo management</A>
<HR SIZE=1 NOSHADE>

<LI><A HREF="http://www.wugnet.com/wininfo">Goto live site</A>

</BODY>
</HTML>
```

The deletion code is pretty straightforward: Load a recordset that contains only the record you want to delete, and then execute the Delete method.

Adding Search Capabilities

A final bit of functionality you might consider for Web-based management of a database is a way to search for data. The options you present here depend on the type of data used in the site. In the case of WinInfo, you have a table full of articles, each of which has certain attributes (ID number, title, date posted, and body text). It makes sense, then, to provide a way to search for articles, based on the following criteria:

- Search by specific ID—The user can enter in an ID value and locate the corresponding article.

- Search by ID range—The user can specify a range of IDs to search.

- Search by title—The user can enter text that will be compared against all article titles. An exact title match is not required (or desired, usually): The user could enter Microsoft, for example, and see a list of all articles that contain the word *Microsoft* in the title.

- Search by specific date—The user can enter a date and see a list of all articles published on that date.

- Search by date range—The user can enter a range of dates and see a list of all articles published within that time frame.

- Search by body text—The user can enter a text string that will be compared against text in the bodies of all articles.

The main search page (search.asp), shown in Figure 17.12, shows these options:

```
<%@ Language=VBScript %>
<HTML>

<HEAD>
<META NAME="GENERATOR" Content="Microsoft Visual Studio 6.0">
```

```
<TITLE>Search WinInfo</TITLE>
</HEAD>

<STYLE>
<!--
    A:link { text-decoration: none; }
    A:hover { color: RED; }
    A:visited { text-decoration: none; }
-->
</STYLE>


<BODY BGCOLOR="#FFFFFF" TEXT="BLACK"
 LINK="BLUE" ALINK="BLUE" VLINK="BLUE">

<FONT FACE="Verdana" SIZE=2>
<H2>Search WinInfo</H2>
<HR SIZE=1 NOSHADE>
<LI><B>Search by ID</B>
<TABLE WIDTH=600 BORDER=0 CELLPADDING=0 CELLSPACING=0>
    <TR>
        <TD WIDTH=20> </TD>
        <TD ALIGN=LEFT VALIGN=TOP>
            <FONT FACE="Verdana" SIZE=2>
            <FORM METHOD=POST ACTION="search2.asp">Enter an ID:<BR>
            <INPUT TYPE=TEXT SIZE=5 NAME="ID">
            <INPUT TYPE=SUBMIT VALUE="Search">
            <INPUT TYPE=HIDDEN NAME="type" VALUE="ID"></FORM>
        </TD>
        <TD ALIGN=LEFT VALIGN=TOP>
            <FONT FACE="Verdana" SIZE=2>
            <FORM METHOD=POST ACTION="search2.asp">Enter an ID range:
            <BR><INPUT TYPE=TEXT SIZE=5 NAME="ID1"> to
            <INPUT TYPE=TEXT SIZE=5 NAME="ID2">
            <INPUT TYPE=SUBMIT VALUE="Search">
            <INPUT TYPE=HIDDEN NAME="type" VALUE="ID2"></FORM>
        </TD>
    </TR>
</TABLE>

<LI><B>Search by title</B>
<TABLE WIDTH=600 BORDER=0 CELLPADDING=0 CELLSPACING=0>
    <TR>
        <TD WIDTH=20> </TD>
        <TD ALIGN=LEFT VALIGN=TOP>
            <FONT FACE="Verdana" SIZE=2>
            <FORM METHOD=POST ACTION="search2.asp">Search article
            titles for the following text:<BR>
```

```
                    <INPUT TYPE=TEXT SIZE=40 NAME="title">
                    <INPUT TYPE=SUBMIT VALUE="Search">
                    <INPUT TYPE=HIDDEN NAME="type" VALUE="title"></FORM>
            </TD>
        </TR>
</TABLE>

<LI><B>Search by date</B>
<TABLE WIDTH=600 BORDER=0 CELLPADDING=0 CELLSPACING=0>
        <TR>
            <TD WIDTH=20> </TD>
            <TD ALIGN=LEFT VALIGN=TOP>
                <FONT FACE="Verdana" SIZE=2><FORM METHOD=POST
                 ACTION="search2.asp">Enter a date:<BR>
                <INPUT TYPE=TEXT SIZE=15 NAME="date" VALUE="<%= date %>">
                <INPUT TYPE=SUBMIT VALUE="Search">
                <INPUT TYPE=HIDDEN NAME="type" VALUE="date"></FORM>
            </TD>
            <TD ALIGN=LEFT VALIGN=TOP>
                <FONT FACE="Verdana" SIZE=2><FORM METHOD=POST
                 ACTION="search2.asp" id=form3 name=form3>Enter a
                 date range:
                <BR><INPUT TYPE=TEXT SIZE=15 NAME="date1"
                VALUE="<%= date - 10 %>"> to <INPUT TYPE=TEXT SIZE=15
                NAME="date2" VALUE="<%= date %>">
                <INPUT TYPE=SUBMIT VALUE="Search">
                <INPUT TYPE=HIDDEN NAME="type" VALUE="date2"></FORM>
            </TD>
        </TR>
</TABLE>

<LI><B>Search for text in body</B>
<TABLE WIDTH=600 BORDER=0 CELLPADDING=0 CELLSPACING=0>
        <TR>
            <TD WIDTH=20> </TD>
            <TD ALIGN=LEFT VALIGN=TOP>
                <FONT FACE="Verdana" SIZE=2><FORM METHOD=POST
                 ACTION="search2.asp">Search article bodies for
                 the following text:<BR>
                <INPUT TYPE=TEXT SIZE=40 NAME="body">
                <INPUT TYPE=SUBMIT VALUE="Search">
                <INPUT TYPE=HIDDEN NAME="type" VALUE="body"></FORM>
            </TD>
        </TR>
</TABLE>

<HR SIZE=1 NOSHADE>
<A HREF="default.htm"><< Cancel</A>

</BODY>
</HTML>
```

FIGURE **17.12**

The search options you supply will be based on the type of data you're using. Some of these options can carry over nicely to the public site as well.

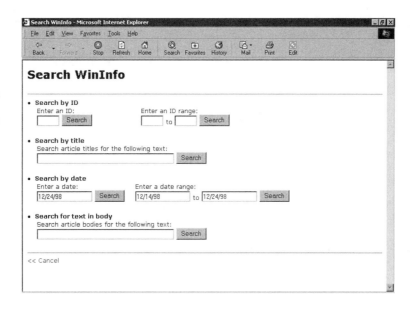

Each option on this page represents its own HTML form, and each form posts to the same document, search2.asp. This ASP document parses the searchType form item, which is passed by each form. Depending on the type of search type specified (ID, ID2, title, and so on), a recordset will be created using the passed criteria. This is done in a massive Select Case statement right at the top of search2.asp:

```
<%@ Language=VBScript %>
<%
searchType = CStr(Request.Form("type"))
Select Case searchType
    Case "ID"
        ID = CStr(Request.Form("ID"))
        If ID = "" Then
            Response.Redirect ("search.asp")
        Else
            Set rs = Server.CreateObject("ADODB.Recordset")
            rs.Open "SELECT * FROM wininfo WHERE ID = " & ID, _
             "DSN=wugnet;UID=<login>;Password=<pass>",1,3
        End If
    Case "ID2"
        ID1 = CStr(Request.Form("ID1"))
        ID2 = CStr(Request.Form("ID2"))
        If ID1 = "" or ID2 = "" Then
            Response.Redirect ("search.asp")
```

```
        Else
            Set rs = Server.CreateObject("ADODB.Recordset")
            rs.Open "SELECT * FROM wininfo WHERE ID >= " & ID1 & _
                " AND ID <= " & ID2 & " ORDER BY ID DESC", _
                "DSN=wugnet;UID=<login>;Password=<pass>",1,3
        End If
    Case "title"
        title = CStr(Request.Form("title"))
        If title = "" Then
            Response.Redirect ("search.asp")
        Else
            Set rs = Server.CreateObject("ADODB.Recordset")
            rs.Open "SELECT * FROM wininfo " & _
                "WHERE title LIKE '%" & title & "%' ORDER BY ID DESC", _
                "DSN=wugnet;UID=<login>;Password=<pass>",1,3
        End If
    Case "date"
        theDate = CDate(Request.Form("date"))
        If theDate = "" Then
            Response.Redirect ("search.asp")
        Else
            Set rs = Server.CreateObject("ADODB.Recordset")
            rs.Open "SELECT * FROM wininfo WHERE date= '" & _
                theDate & "' ORDER BY ID DESC",_
                "DSN=wugnet;UID=<login>;Password=<pass>",1,3
        End If
    Case "date2"
        date1 = CDate(Request.Form("date1"))
        date2 = CDate(Request.Form("date2"))
        If date1 = "" or date2 = "" Then
            Response.Redirect ("search.asp")
        Else
            Set rs = Server.CreateObject("ADODB.Recordset")
            rs.Open "SELECT * FROM wininfo WHERE date >='" & _
                date1 & "' AND date <='" & date2 & _
                "' ORDER BY ID DESC", _
                "DSN=wugnet;UID=<login>;Password=<pass>",1,3
        End If
    Case "body"
        body = CStr(Request.Form("body"))
        If body = "" Then
            Response.Redirect ("search.asp")
        Else
            Set rs = Server.CreateObject("ADODB.Recordset")
            rs.Open "SELECT * FROM wininfo WHERE " & _
                "body LIKE '%" & body & "%' ORDER BY ID DESC", _
                "DSN=wugnet;UID=<login>;Password=<pass>",1,3
        End If
```

```
End Select
%>
<HTML>

<HEAD>
<META NAME="GENERATOR" Content="Microsoft Visual Studio 6.0">
<TITLE>WinInfo Search results</TITLE>
</HEAD>

<STYLE>
<!--
    A:link { text-decoration: none; }
    A:hover { color: RED; }
    A:visited { text-decoration: none; }
-->
</STYLE>


<BODY BGCOLOR="#FFFFFF" TEXT="BLACK"
 LINK="BLUE" ALINK="BLUE" VLINK="BLUE">

<FONT FACE="Verdana" SIZE=2>
<H2>WinInfo Search results</H2>
<HR SIZE=1 NOSHADE>

Newer articles at the top
<BR>
<TABLE WIDTH=600 CELLPADDING=5 CELLSPACING=0
 BORDER=1 BGCOLOR="#FFFFFF" BORDERCOLOR="NAVY">
<%
Count = 0
Do While NOT rs.EOF
    Count = Count + 1
%>
  <TR>
        <TD WIDTH=450 ALIGN=LEFT VALIGN=TOP BGCOLOR="#FFFFEE">
            <FONT FACE="Verdana" SIZE=2>
            <%= rs("title") %>
            </FONT>
        </TD>
        <TD WIDTH=50 ALIGN=CENTER VALIGN=TOP>
            <FONT FACE="Verdana" SIZE=2>
            <A HREF="view.asp?ID=<%= rs("ID") %>">View</A>
            </FONT>
        </TD>
        <TD WIDTH=50 ALIGN=CENTER VALIGN=TOP>
            <FONT FACE="Verdana" SIZE=2>
            <A HREF="modify.asp?ID=<%= rs("ID") %>">Modify</A>
            </FONT>
```

```
        </TD>
        <TD WIDTH=50 ALIGN=CENTER VALIGN=TOP>
            <FONT FACE="Verdana" SIZE=2>
            <A HREF="delete.asp?ID=<%= rs("ID") %>">Delete</A>
            </FONT>
        </TD>
    </TR>
<%
rs.MoveNext: Loop
If Count = 0 Then
    Response.Write "<TR><TD WIDTH=100% ALIGN=LEFT VALIGN=TOP>"
    Response.Write "<FONT FACE=Verdana SIZE=2>"
    Response.Write "There were no records returned a match of" & _
      "that search criteria. Please press BACK and try again."
    Response.Write "</TD></TR>"
End If
%>
</TABLE>

<HR SIZE=1 NOSHADE>
<A HREF="search.asp"><< Search page</A>

</BODY>
</HTML>
```

When this page loads, a recordset is created, and the results are displayed in an HTML table (see Figure 17.13) very similar to the one used by recent.asp.

FIGURE 17.13

Here is a sample search result that occurs when the body is searched for the phrase Paul Thurrott.

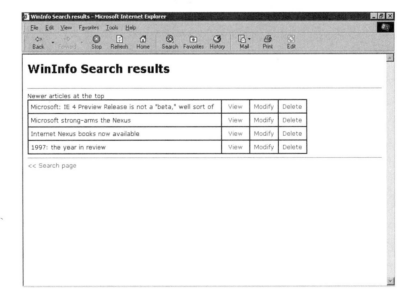

The major difference is that you supply a View option that shows a read-only version of each record returned. This is in addition to the Modify and Delete options that actually load the previously created modify.asp and delete.asp documents you created for the View Recent Articles section of the management site.

Here is the view.asp page, which also provides links to modify and delete the article it displays:

```
<%@ Language=VBScript %>
<%
ID = CInt(Request.QueryString("ID"))

Set rs = Server.CreateObject("ADODB.Recordset")
rs.Open "EXECUTE GetArticle " & ID, _
   "DSN=wugnet;UID=<login>;Password=<pass>",0,1
title = rs("title")
theDate = rs("date")
body = rs("body")
rs.Close
%>
<HTML>
<HEAD>
<META NAME="GENERATOR" Content="Microsoft Visual Studio 6.0">
<TITLE>Manage WinInfo: View article "<%= title %>"</TITLE>
</HEAD>

<STYLE>
<!--
    A:link { text-decoration: none; }
    A:hover { color: RED; }
    A:visited { text-decoration: none; }
-->
</STYLE>


<BODY BGCOLOR="#FFFFFF" TEXT="BLACK"
 LINK="BLUE" ALINK="BLUE" VLINK="BLUE">

<FONT FACE="Verdana" SIZE=2>
<H2>Manage WinInfo: View article</H2>
<HR SIZE=1 NOSHADE>

<TABLE WIDTH=600 CELLPADDING=5 CELLSPACING=5 BORDER=0>
  <TR>
      <TD WIDTH=100% ALIGN=LEFT VALIGN=TOP>
          <FONT FACE="Verdana" SIZE=2>
          <%
          Response.Write "<B>" & title & "</B>"
```

```
            Response.Write "<BR><I>(" & theDate & ")</I>"
            Response.Write "<BR>" & body
            %>
            </FONT>
        </TD>
    </TR>
</TABLE>

<HR SIZE=1 NOSHADE>
<A HREF="modify.asp?ID=<%= ID %>">Modify this article</A>
<BR><A HREF="delete.asp?ID=<%= ID %>">Delete this article</A>
<BR><A HREF="search.asp"><< Return to Search page</A>

</BODY>
</HTML>
```

Summary

Web-based management of live data can take many forms (no pun intended), and the resulting site will largely depend on the database you're working with. The key thing to remember is that the people using the management site will likely possess minimal technical skills, so make it as simple and obvious as possible.

Beyond the options discussed in this chapter are other issues to consider. Error checking is of primary importance in this type of site because of the type of users and the nature of the work they're doing. Beyond the simple error checking presented here, you should consider more extensive data verification each time information is passed from page to page. I've presented a basic turnkey solution here, and it shouldn't be hard to massage this into something you could use on your own sites. Also, you didn't worry too much about the look and feel of the site here because you were focusing on the technical details. It's likely that you will want to create something a little easier on the eyes when you present such a site to your own customers.

Visual InterDev Integration

PART

III

Building Web
Application
Components with
Visual Basic

by Paul Thurrott

Although many Web applications out there probably use nothing but dynamic queries running directly in ASP documents, this solution doesn't provide the type of performance that heavily trafficked sites demand. A *dynamic query*—that is, a block of ASP code that uses scripted ADO objects to retrieve data from a live data source—is quick only from the developer's point of view: It's not the most efficient solution for real-world use, however.

In previous chapters, I discussed some of the alternatives, including stored procedures, that compile and execute on the database server, and components that you write in a high-level programming language such as Visual Basic or Visual C++. A *component* in this sense is simply a dynamic link library (DLL) containing functions and procedures that can be called from any application, including Internet Information Server (IIS). In this chapter, you will focus on developing components in Visual Basic, the most popular programming language ever created.

Reasons to Build Your Own Components

There are plenty of good reasons to build your own components. Here's a Top 10 list:

1. Performance—Components written in any high-level language (Visual Basic, Visual C++, Visual J++, and so on) execute more quickly than script-based ASP documents. Because database access is an expensive operation, it makes sense to speed up this sort of thing as much as possible.

2. Microsoft Transaction Server—Visual Basic components can leverage the programming interface to Microsoft Transaction Server (MTS), so operations can be executed within a transaction, thus ensuring that the entire operation either succeeds or fails and returns a logical message explaining what happens. Previously, developers had to hand-code this functionality, but with Visual Basic and MTS, it's built in.

3. Isolate Business Logic—As a developer conceivably delivering an entire solution to a client, do you really want to reveal the business logic (think of this as your trade secret) to the client? By wrapping this into a component, the client will be more likely to come to you again rather than try to decode what you've done in-house. This protects you from changes that clients might attempt to make to your files as well and future frantic phone calls for help when they mess them up beyond recognition. This happens all too often.

4. Separate Data Access from the User Interface—As in the preceding step, it's generally not a good idea to reveal your methods for accessing data. More importantly, data access executes more quickly when done from a component. Then, you can use variant arrays (not ADO recordsets) in the ASP documents to deal with any result sets returned. This simplifies your ASP code dramatically and gives clients something that's easier to work with, should they decide to modify it later.

5. Avoid Scripted ADO Object Creation—Except for the smallest Web applications and learning exercises, you should never, ever process dynamic queries from an ASP document. Never. It makes more sense to access a stored procedure from an ASP document, but it makes even more sense to use variant arrays in ASP to store result sets returned from components that access the data.

6. Scalability—Your components will scale automatically with the Web server as it is enhanced with new hardware.

7. Isolate Username and Password References—This is another bugaboo with ASP-based data access: You have to specify the username and password in a plain text file. Although previous attacks on IIS that revealed the contents of these files over the Web have been fixed, there is always the chance that some enterprising hacker will figure out a way to reveal the source code in ASP documents again. Likewise, within a corporation might be employees who have access to certain ASP documents but who shouldn't have access to certain SQL Server usernames and passwords. For situations in which it's acceptable to store usernames and passwords in an ASP document, you can pass this information to a component and not hard-code it into the component, where it will be hard to alter when the logins change.

8. It's Easy: Leverage the Language You Already Know—If you know Visual Basic Script, you know Visual Basic. Ironically, VBScript developers will arguably have an easier time coding VB-based components than typical Visual Basic developers because they're already used to the "all-code" programming model used in component design. Any properly coded ASP document that uses data access can be easily converted to a combination of ASPs and Visual Basic components.

9. Learning More SQL Is Not Required—Stored procedures offer a huge performance gain over dynamic ASP queries, but you have to know a lot about Transact SQL to code them properly. With components, you can use the same SQL code from the dynamic queries you're already using and not worry about knowing advanced SQL syntax (on the other hand, you can't go wrong knowing as much about SQL as possible). The point is that components leverage the knowledge about Visual Basic that you probably already have, whereas coding stored procedures might require a

new skill. If time is money, components are the way to go. It's worth noting, of course, that the ultimate performance gain would be to call components that themselves use stored procedures to access data. You will look at that approach in this chapter.

10. Components Run In-Process with IIS—Technically, ASP documents can too, but they run more slowly and tend to be far more transient because of the sheer number of such documents. Code that doesn't have to cross process boundaries is more efficient and executes more quickly. On the other hand, in-process components can also crash IIS: Make sure that they're fully debugged before implementing them on a production server. If you use the Microsoft Transaction Server, you can choose to let your components run out-of-process (they will run within the process space of MTS instead), saving IIS from any problems.

Working with Components

Although you might have never thought of it this way, every time you create an instance of an ADO object in an ASP document, you are working with a prebuilt component that is stored in a DLL somewhere on your system (or if you're working on a live site, the DLL is somewhere on the Web server). For example, the following code snippet creates an instance of the ADO Connection object:

```
<%
Set cn = Server.CreateObject("ADODB.Connection")
%>
```

The string `"ADODB.Connection"` identifies the component, which is part of the ADODB library. The first half of this identifier, `ADODB`, is the component's name (not to be confused with the component's filename, which can be different). The second half of the identifier, `Connection`, refers to a specific object within the component. The ADODB component, as you know, contains the definitions of several objects: Connection, Recordset, Command, and Parameter.

In Visual Basic, these entities are defined by projects and classes, where a Visual Basic ActiveX DLL project will encapsulate a component and each class within that component will define a specific object. For example, if you create a component in Visual Basic that encapsulates information about various kinds of fruit, you might end up with the following entities (note that all these names are arbitrary):

- Visual Basic project: prjFruit.vbp

- Visual Basic project name: fruit

- Object definitions (VB classes): apple (apple.cls), orange (orange.cls), and strawberry (strawberry.cls)

After this component is created and registered on the system (this process will be described presently), you could create an instance of the apple object, using the following code in an ASP document:

```
<%
Set myApple = Server.CreateObject("fruit.apple")
%>
```

As you can see, there's no difference in the way that you access system-supplied components (such as ADO) and ones you might create yourself in Visual Basic (or any other language). In the following section, you will explore the process of component creation.

Using Visual Basic to Develop ASP Controls

When you first start Visual Basic, you're confronted with a dialog box that presents a wide variety of project types, including Standard EXE (for regular Windows applications), ActiveX EXE, and others. To create a software component that runs in-process with IIS, you have to create an ActiveX DLL project. An *ActiveX DLL* is simply a library of class definitions. These classes are used to describe the objects that you will be making available via the DLL created by the project. This type of application doesn't supply a user interface because it is designed to work within the context of a host application (such as the IIS Web server in our case) that will provide these features.

In fact, a component is simply the server half of the so-called client/server programming model, in which the host application (IIS) becomes the client. Don't confuse the terms *client* and *server* when used this way: A component is the server here because it supplies services to the host application, which can request these services through ASP documents in this example.

In-Process Versus Out-of-Process

You might see the terms *in-process* and *out-of-process* thrown about during any discussion of components. Generally speaking, a component that is compiled into a DLL (such as the ActiveX DLLs you will work with in this chapter) is an in-process component that will run within the process space of the host application (IIS in this case). Actually, it's also possible to create an out-of-process ActiveX DLL component, but this is rare unless you're using Transaction Server.

Out-of-process components are usually compiled into EXE files, and Visual Basic supplies an ActiveX EXE project type for this. In-process components run more quickly than otherwise identical out-of-process components because the system doesn't have to context-shift across process boundaries each time a property, method, or event handler for the component is accessed by the host application.

Because you will be working with ActiveX DLL projects, you will be creating in-process components. In-process components run more quickly but can cause the host application to crash if not debugged thoroughly. Out-of-process components are slower but won't bring down the host application should they crash. You are going to use in-process components here, but MTS components (covered later in this chapter) run out-of-process with regards to IIS.

> **NOTE**
>
> Before the release of IIS 4.0, it was almost impossible to use out-of-process components with Microsoft's Web servers (actually, you could make it work by hacking the Registry). Now, even particular Web applications can be run within their own address spaces, further segregating processes and minimizing the risk that any errant application will bring down the whole system.

Setting Component Options in Visual Basic

After you create a new ActiveX DLL project in Visual Basic, you will be confronted with a blank class module code window, shown in Figure 18.1. Coding an ActiveX DLL in Visual Basic will be a bit of a throw-back for grizzled Visual Basic veterans, but those ASP scripters in the crowd will be happy in the familiar code-only environment. Unlike most Visual Basic programs, where drag-and-drop visual development is the norm, creating an ActiveX DLL requires a lot of typing with absolutely no graphical niceties.

The first thing you should do is logically name the classes you will need and the project itself. For purposes of this example, you will create a simple component that accesses information in the SQL Server Pubs database, so prjPubs.vbp might be a good filename for your project, and cPubs would make a good name for the component. Each class in the component can access different types of information in the database, so you might have classes such as authors (authors.cls), employees (employee.cls), and titles (titles.cls), although you might also think of other logical schemes.

FIGURE **18.1**

*When coding
ActiveX DLLs in
Visual Basic,
you'll be working
with straight code,
not visual compo-
nents.*

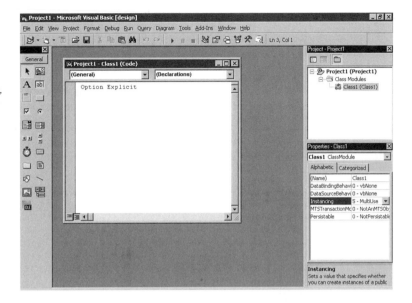

The first (and least obvious) step is to name the project: This is done from the Project
Properties dialog, which is accessed from the Project 1 — Properties menu. As shown in
Figure 18.2, this dialog box offers a number of options, including the following, which
are important for the type of work you will be performing:

- Project Type—This should be set to ActiveX DLL.

- Startup Object—Components can be configured to optionally execute a block of
  code stored in the Main procedure when they are instantiated. If you have a need
  for certain code to execute whenever a component is first called, this is the place.
  You won't be using the Main procedure in this example, however.

- Project Name—Not to be confused with the name of the project file (which is
  determined when you save the project to disk), the project name used here will
  identify your component to the system and provide a way to access it via code. For
  this reason, you're going to want to choose something short but descriptive. You
  will use cPubs for this example.

- Threading Model—For components that are going to run on IIS, you must set this
  to Apartment Threaded, which guarantees that each thread of execution within the
  component is thread safe and will not overwrite or interfere with other threads.

Apartment-threaded components are said to be *re-entrant*, which means that multiple clients can access its code simultaneously, automatically switching as needed between code in the component and code in the host without causing any problems. Apartment-threaded components also run more quickly and efficiently than single-threaded components, which is the other choice for a threading model. Visual Basic 6.0 automatically chooses Apartment-threading for ActiveX DLLs, but the original release version of Visual Basic 5.0 contained only Single Threaded as an option, making VB 5.0 essentially useless for IIS component development. This problem was fixed with the first Service Pack for Visual Studio 97, however. If you're using VB 5.0, make sure that you upgrade to the latest Service Pack before attempting to develop components for your Web applications.

FIGURE 18.2

Don't start coding your component until you've set up the project options correctly.

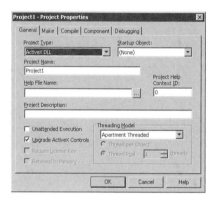

After you have properly set the project options, you should save the project, thus naming the first code module and the project. For this example, you will name the code module `authors.cls` (internal name authors) and the project, `prjPubs.vbp`. After you do this, the screen will resemble Figure 18.3.

Component 101: A Quick Guide to the Development Process

Now that you have a blank class to work with, it's time to write a simple function so that you can see how the Visual Basic code you write ends up being called from a Web application. For this quick guide to the component development process, the first step is to add the infamous Hello, world! function to the beginning of the authors class:

```
Public Function helloWorld()
    helloWorld = "Hello, world!"
End Function
```

FIGURE **18.3**

After you've established the project options, you're ready to begin coding.

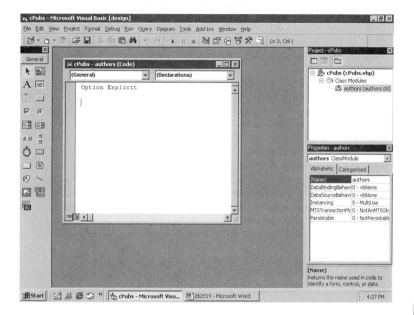

After you add this code to the module, you can create the first version of the target DLL file. Visual Basic will prompt you for a directory to save this file in (you are naming your example `cpubs.dll`). While you're developing the DLL (on a developmental workstation, I hope, which, incidentally, requires a Microsoft Web server such as Personal Web Services for Windows NT Workstation or Personal Web Server for Windows 98), you might consider creating a separate directory for any components you create. I generally save DLL works in progress in C:\Inetpub\comp where comp is a directory I created for just this purpose.

The next step is to register this component with the system. This involves running the command line program regvr32.exe, which will announce the availability of your DLL to Windows. To unregister the DLL, which you have to do before you can save a new version from Visual Basic, you can run regsvr32.exe with the /u switch. I will cover this in detail in the next section because there are some issues to be aware of when you're changing DLLs over and over again.

Now, navigate to the directory where you've saved the DLL, and type the following at the command line:

```
regsvr32 cpubs.dll
```

The system will then display the dialog box shown in Figure 18.4, indicating that your DLL is now available to any program that chooses to use it.

FIGURE 18.4

When you've successfully registered a component with the system, you will see this dialog box.

Now it's time to build an ASP document in Visual InterDev that will open an instance of the authors object and execute its helloWorld function. The following code demonstrates how this might be done:

```
<%
Set myPubs = Server.CreateObject("cpubs.authors")
Response.Write myPubs.helloWorld
%>
```

Note that InterDev's AutoComplete feature actually works here: When you type myPubs followed by a period, a list of available subroutines appears (right now, you have only the one), as shown in Figure 18.5.

FIGURE 18.5

Come on, admit it. It's cool seeing your own function show up in Auto-Complete.

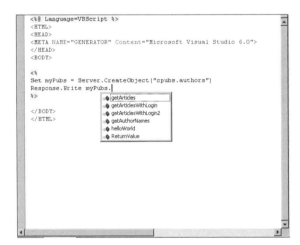

When you execute this document on the Web server, you do indeed see the expected hello message (see Figure 18.6).

FIGURE 18.6

*Hello, world!,
courtesy of your
first component.*

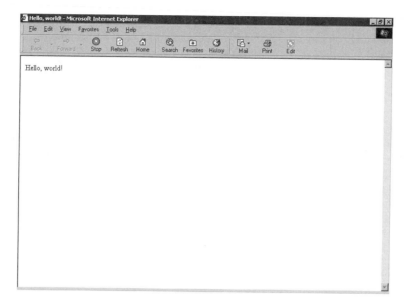

Riding the Component
Development Merry-Go-Round

Okay, so far so good: You have created a simple component with one class (an object definition) that contains one function, and you've executed that function from an ASP document, displaying its return value in a Web page.

But it's not usually this simple: ASP component development requires a sometimes frustrating series of repetitive steps that differ slightly from system to system, depending on which version of Windows you're running. Here are the basic steps:

1. Create an ActiveX DLL project (a component) with at least one class in Visual Basic, and populate that class with at least one subroutine.

2. Save the project and generate a DLL.

3. Register the DLL on the system, using regsvr32.exe.

4. Execute the ASP document that uses the component (test the component).

From here, you might think that the next step would be to return to Visual Basic, make changes, and repeat. This is where things become sticky, however: A DLL isn't like a standalone program. When you exit the program that uses the DLL (IIS in this case or one of its derivatives for Windows NT Workstation or Windows 9x), the DLL will still exist in memory. Furthermore, the DLL is still registered with the system. You won't be able to overwrite the DLL with a newer version until you've unregistered it (using regsvr32 /u) and made sure that the current version is no longer in memory. To make sure of this, you have to remove the host application (again, IIS in this case) from memory as well.

This isn't as easy as it looks.

On Windows NT Server and Workstation, a Services Control Panel applet can start and stop services. Windows 98, however, offers no such applet. There is, however, a Personal Web Manager (see Figure 18.7) front end that lets you start and stop the IIS service (Windows NT Workstation includes this rather sorry program as well)...sort of.

FIGURE 18.7

Microsoft has created Personal Web Manager with an almost overly simple interface for Workstation and Windows 9x users.

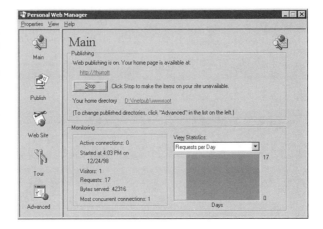

The problem is this: If you unregister your component, stop the Web server by using the Personal Web Manager, and then try to compile and save a new version of the DLL file from Visual Basic. You are in for a nasty surprise, shown in Figure 18.8:

FIGURE 18.8

Stopping the IIS service will not remove its hold on your DLL: This dialog indicates that more work needs to be done before you can recompile your DLL.

Something still has its tendrils in your component, and there's no way to save a new version to disk until you break that lock. I'll spare you the agony of guessing and tell you that it's the Microsoft Web server (inetinfo.exe) that still has a lock on the component. It turns out that the Personal Web Manager doesn't perform the action you need: It does, technically, stop the Web server service, but it doesn't remove inetinfo.exe (the Web server executable) from memory. As long as this program is still in memory, there's no way to create a new version of the component.

I know of developers who literally reboot their Windows 98 or NT Workstation system every time they have to compile a new version of a component because Microsoft doesn't include a tool with their operating systems that makes it possible to kill processes. If you have the Windows 98, Windows NT Workstation, or Windows NT Server Resource Kit (the freebie version on the Windows 98 CD-ROM doesn't count), you're good to go. Otherwise, you will have to download the tools from the Web (available free if you sign up for a 15-day evaluation membership to MSPress ResourceLink, at least as of this writing). Microsoft Press maintains separate Resource Kit Web sites for Windows 98 (`http://mspress.microsoft.com/reslink/win98/Book/`) and Windows NT 4.0 (`http://mspress.microsoft.com/reslink/nt40/kits/`). These sites make available the entire suite of tools that you receive when you purchase any of these book/CD packages in a bookstore.

What you are interested in is the programs Task List Viewer (tlist.exe) and Task Killing Utility (kill.exe). Task List Viewer is a command-line program that displays a list of the processes (also called *tasks*) currently running on your system. This is where you can see that inetinfo.exe is, indeed, still running even after you stop the service. Figure 18.9 shows the display from this utility on a typical Windows 98 workstation.

The Task Killing Utility can be used to end, or *kill*, one or more tasks (processes). It takes an optional argument (`/f`) that forces the kill (this is equivalent to the UNIX kill -9 command). These two tools can be used together to figure out which tasks are running and then kill the appropriate tasks. For example, you use the Task Killing Utility to kill inetinfo.exe so that you can recompile the component as desired. You can find these utilities on the Web at the following locations (at least at the time of this writing—locations on the Web seem to change rapidly, so head to the main Microsoft Press Web site if these don't pan out):

- Windows NT

  kill.exe—`http://mspress.microsoft.com/reslink/nt40/toolbox/default.asp?filechosen=tools/kill.htm`

  tlist.exe—`http://mspress.microsoft.com/reslink/nt40/toolbox/default.asp?filechosen=tools/tlist.htm`

18

BUILDING WEB
APPLICATION
COMPONENTS

- Windows 98

    kill.exe—http://mspress.microsoft.com/reslink/win98/Toolbox/
    default.asp?filechosen=htm/kill.htm

    tlist.exe—http://mspress.microsoft.com/reslink/win98/Toolbox/
    default.asp?filechosen=htm/tlist.htm

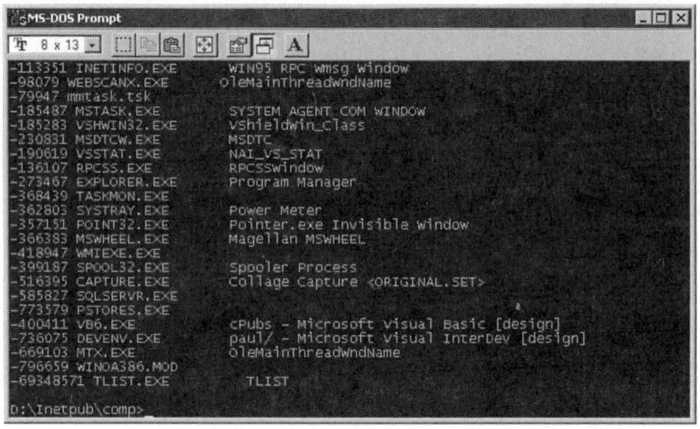

FIGURE 18.9

TLIST.EXE supplies a list of the currently running tasks.

Using Task List Viewer with the Task Killing Utility

The first step, then, is to use TLIST to get a list of the tasks that are currently running. TLIST doesn't take any arguments, but if the list of tasks scrolls off the top of the command prompt window, you might pipe its output to a text file that you can view later. This can be accomplished with the following commands:

```
C:\tlist > tlist.txt
C:\type tlist.txt ¦ more
```

There are two ways to kill a task using KILL: You can specify the process ID (which will include the "-" sign) or the name of the process (such as inetinfo.exe). It's easier to just use the process name because that won't change each time the process starts, although the process ID will. You can also kill a number of processes by using wildcard pattern matching. The KILL command also takes a single option, /f, which tells the system to force the kill. You specify this option each time you kill the inetinfo process, and this can be accomplished with the following command:

```
C:\kill /f inetinfo.exe
```

The Component Development Cycle Revisited

Okay, now that you have all the tools you need and know how to use them, it's time to refine the steps required to create an IIS component:

1. Create an ActiveX DLL project (a component) with at least one class in Visual Basic, and populate that class with at least one subroutine.

2. Save the project and generate a DLL.

3. Register the DLL on the system, using regsvr32.exe.

4. Execute the ASP document that uses the component (test the component).

5. Stop the Web server with Personal Web Manager (Windows 98 or Windows NT Workstation), the IIS snap-in for MMC (Windows NT Server), or the Services Control Panel applet (Windows NT Workstation or Server). Close the PWM window when done.

6. Unregister the DLL using regsvr32 /u.

7. Kill the inetinfo.exe process by typing the following at the command line: `kill /f inetinfo.exe`.

8. Implement any changes in the Visual Basic project and regenerate the DLL.

9. Restart the Web server (using PWM or similar).

10. Repeat steps 3–9 as needed.

There's another, more elegant way to develop components, however: You could create a Standard EXE project and add a code module that will essentially duplicate the functionality of the component you will later build. Add the functions and procedures to the code module as you would for the component, and then call these subroutines from code in the form module. This way, you can take advantage of the tools in Visual Basic, such as the debugger, to hone your creation. Then, after you have a working set of functions that you'd like to test from an ASP document, you could paste the contents of the code module into a code module in an ActiveX DLL project.

Accessing Databases in a Component

As previously stated, one of the best reasons to use components with your Web applications is to segregate your business logic (such as database access) from the HTML presentation. Because you're now using the full Visual Basic IDE to code data access, you will find some niceties that aren't available in Visual InterDev. You also have your pick from a variety of data access methods, but you will be sticking with the tried and true (and familiar) ActiveX Data Objects (ADO).

Consider a simple example for your cPubs component: The following code can be added to the authors class (code module), creating a component-based method of returning the name of each author in the Pubs authors table:

```
Public Function getAuthorNames(ByRef names As Variant)
    Dim Count, x As Integer
    Dim rs As ADODB.Recordset
    Set rs = New ADODB.Recordset

    rs.Open _
      "SELECT au_fname,au_lname FROM authors ORDER BY au_lname", _
"DSN=pubs;UID=sa;Password=;", adOpenStatic, adLockReadOnly
    Count = rs.RecordCount

    ReDim names(Count)

    For x = 1 To Count
      names(x) = CStr(rs("au_fname")) & " " & CStr(rs("au_lname"))
      rs.MoveNext
    Next

    rs.Close
End Function
```

Before you can compile this and save it as a DLL, you have to add a reference to the ADO library. To do this, select References from the Project menu, and select the choice labeled Microsoft ActiveX Data Objects 2.0 Library (or similar).

Now, register the component and restart the Web server. Start InterDev if it isn't already running, and create an ASP document that will access this new function. The following will do:

```
<%
Dim nameList()
myPubs.getAuthorNames(nameList)

For x = 1 to  UBound(nameList)
    Response.Write nameList(x) & "<BR>"
Next
%>
```

As Figure 18.10 shows, the resulting output from this ASP document is very similar to previous work you've done with the authors table. But the way you went about getting at and displaying this data is decidedly different. Let's go over it line by line, starting with the ASP file.

FIGURE **18.10**

The Pubs authors list, courtesy of your first component.

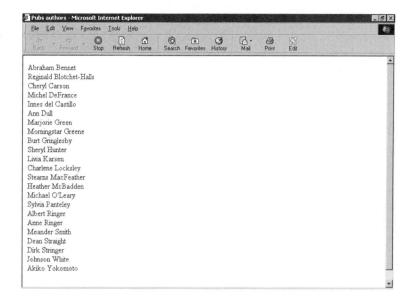

Dissecting Component/ASP Interaction

First, the ASP document declares a dynamic variant array named nameList. A *dynamic array* is an array that can change size after it's created: This is a crucial capability because you won't know the final size of the array until you access the authors table (which occurs in the component). A *variant array* is an array that can contain any kind of data, in any of its elements. Because all the database access is now occurring in a component, you need some way to store the result set that is retrieved when you query the database. A variant array is perfect for this, and you can pass it back and forth to the component.

In the second line of code in the ASP document, you call the object's getAuthorNames function, passing the variant array along as an argument. This passes control into the component, where a reference to the nameList array from the ASP document is created, ensuring that the original array is affected, should any changes to the reference be made. The other alternative is to create a copy of the array, which would be separate from the original array. (In Visual Basic, this is known as *passing an array by value only*. You can use the ByVal keyword to accomplish this). Then, a read-only, static ADO recordset is created. This recordset is populated with the first and last names of every author in the Pubs authors table.

The reference to nameList (known locally as *names*) is then redimensioned so that it is big enough to contain all the records in the recordset. A For Next loop is used to populate the array with data from the recordset. Then, the recordset is closed and the function ends, returning control to the ASP document.

Because a reference to the nameList array was passed to the component, all the changes made to the local copy of the array were also made to nameList. Thus, nameList has been resized and populated with data from the recordset that was created in the component. You use a For Next loop in the ASP document to display the information contained by the array. Note that the UBound function contains the subscript of the last element in an array; in other words, it contains the number of elements in the array (think of it as a Count property for an array).

The most important concept to come away with is that the database access in this example is performed in the component and no ADO objects are instantiated in the ASP document. This gives you the best of both worlds: fast execution speed and a separation of data and design. It sounds ludicrous, but I've seen inexperienced Web developers take the time to create components but then return an ADO Recordset to the ASP page instead of a variant array! This completely bypasses all the benefits of component design while effectively slowing down the site because ADO objects are being created twice on the server. This would be kind of hilarious if it wasn't so stupid. Please don't make this mistake.

Using Error-Checking Features

Another great feature you can use in the component is Visual Basic's rich error-checking capabilities, which are largely absent in VBScript. For example, your function can return certain values, enabling you to check the returned value from the ASP page so that you can make decisions about what to do next. For example, you might indicate whether the database access was successful and return an appropriate value. If the returned value indicates a problem, you can have execute different code in the ASP document that won't rely on the returned result set.

Here's a new version of the getAuthorNames function that returns a value of 0 if all is well and a value of 1 if there is a problem:

```
Public Function getAuthorNames(ByRef names As Variant) As Integer
    On Error GoTo ErrorHandler

    Dim Count, x As Integer
    Dim rs As ADODB.Recordset
```

```
Set rs = New ADODB.Recordset

rs.Open _
  "SELECT au_fname,au_lname FROM authors ORDER BY au_lname", _
  "DSN=pubs;UID=sa;Password=;", adOpenStatic, adLockReadOnly
Count = rs.RecordCount

ReDim names(Count)

For x = 1 To Count
  names(x) = CStr(rs("au_fname")) & " " & CStr(rs("au_lname"))
  rs.MoveNext
Next

rs.Close
getAuthorNames = 0
Exit Function
ErrorHandler:
getAuthorNames = 1
End Function
```

Now, you can wrap the ASP code that calls this function into a loop that checks for the return code. For example, the following ASP code can be used to check whether the function exited on a good note:

```
<%
Set myPubs = Server.CreateObject("cpubs.authors")

Dim nameList()

If myPubs.getAuthorNames(nameList) = 0 Then
    For x = 1 to  UBound(nameList)
        Response.Write nameList(x) & "<BR>"
    Next
Else
    Response.Write "Houston, we have a problem."
End If
%>
```

Granted, you're probably going to want something a little nicer than this error message, but the basics are there. If you test this page, you will get the same list of author names as before, or turn off the SQL Server and test it. You will see the error message you supplied, not the nasty SQL Server error message you'd receive if you attempted to access the SQL Server directly from the ASP document. The possibilities, as they say, are endless.

> **NOTE**
>
> If you're creating a dynamic Web site that relies on a database, it's always a good idea to supply some sort of nondynamic version of the site, should the database not be available. Like any other kind of computer, the SQL Server might not be available from time to time.

A More Complex Example

Now that you have some working component examples, it's probably a good idea to sit back and consider the ramifications of what you're doing. Components aren't an efficiency cure-all when not used correctly. One thing to consider, for example, is the issue of logins and passwords. It's generally not a great idea to hard-code these values into a component, as you did for simplicity in the previous examples. Logins and passwords are the types of things that change regularly, and it's not feasible to stop the Web server and recompile all your database components every time there's a change. Rather, it makes more sense to pass login and password values as arguments to the component functions that require this information.

There are two ways to handle this, and, frankly, how you handle it is up to you. First, you could dynamically assign these values in every ASP document that accesses the database component. Alternatively, you could assign these values to Application-level variables. For all but the smallest sites, the second approach is probably best. Otherwise, you'd have a management nightmare each time a login or password changed, and that's what we're trying to avoid here. For this reason, you will use Application-level variables to store the login and password for the SQL Server database.

The first step is to create the Application-level variables. These should be placed in the Application object's OnStart event handler in global.asa. If you don't already have this event handler there, the skeleton code looks like this:

```
<SCRIPT LANGUAGE=VBScript RUNAT=Server>
Sub Application_OnStart
    ' Add code here
End Sub
</SCRIPT>
```

Adding two Application-scope variables might take this form:

```
<SCRIPT LANGUAGE=VBScript RUNAT=Server>
Sub Application_OnStart
    Application("sqlLogin") = "<username>"
```

```
        Application("sqlPassword") = "<password>"
    End Sub
</SCRIPT>
```

Here, <username> and <password> are replaced with the correct SQL Server login and password. For the component, you want to create a function that accepts username and password arguments, in addition to a variant array for storing the result set. For this particular example, you will be working with the WinInfo table, which is supplied on the CD-ROM that accompanies this book. The WinInfo table contains a number of Windows news and information articles, and the purpose of this particular function will be to return a certain number of articles. For this reason, you will also pass a fourth argument, num, that will contain the number of articles to return. Here's the code:

```
Public Function getArticlesWithLogin(ByRef articles As Variant, _
    ByVal num As Integer, _
    ByVal theLogin As String, _
    ByVal thePassword As String) As Integer
    On Error GoTo ErrorHandler

    Dim x As Integer
    Dim rs As ADODB.Recordset
    Set rs = New ADODB.Recordset

    rs.Open "EXECUTE getLatest " & num, _
        "DSN=wininfo;UID=" & theLogin & ";Password=" & _
        thePassword & ";", adOpenStatic, adLockReadOnly

    ReDim articles(num)

    For x = 1 To num
      articles(x) = CStr(rs("title"))
      rs.MoveNext
    Next

    rs.Close
    getArticlesWithLogin = 0
Exit Function
ErrorHandler:
    getArticlesWithLogin = 1
End Function
```

A few notes here: The WinInfo table is contained in a database also called wininfo, so you've created a wininfo DSN as well. The WinInfo table has four fields: ID, title, date, and body. For this example, you are just returning an array of article titles, but you could have just as easily returned other information as well. The recordset is constructed by executing the getArticles stored procedure, which you built in a previous chapter. If there aren't any errors, this function will return a value of 0; a returned value of 1 indicates that some sort of problem occurred.

The final piece of this puzzle is the code needed to access this function from an ASP document. Because you can save this component as wininfo.dll and can name the code module that contains this function as wininfo.cls, the code to access the getArticlesWithLogin function might take the following form:

```
<%
Set w = Server.CreateObject("wininfo.wininfo")

Dim articleList()

If w.getArticlesWithLogin(articleList,5, _
  CStr(Application("sqlLogin")),_
  CStr(Application("sqlPassword"))) = 0 Then
    For x = 1 to  UBound(articleList)
        Response.Write articleList(x) & "<BR>"
    Next
Else
    Response.Write "Houston, we have a problem."
End If
%>
```

In this example, you are requesting five article titles and sending along the Application-level sqlLogin and sqlPassword variables. If all is well, you should see a list of five article titles displayed, as shown in Figure 18.11.

FIGURE 18.11

Yes, Virginia, you can use ASP, ActiveX components, and stored procedures together in a logical, efficient way.

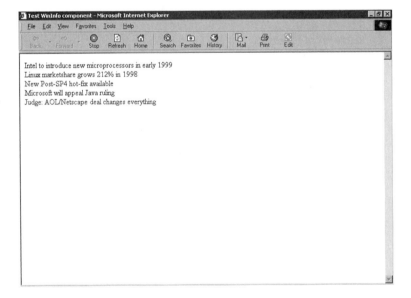

> **NOTE**
>
> Before loading the ASP document, you have to stop and start the Web server so that the Application-level variables are created.

As always, the code for these examples is on the CD-ROM that accompanies the book.

Registering Components on a Remote Web Server

When you have a component that's ready for prime time, you have to register it on the Web server so that you can use it with your production sites. There are various ways to accomplish this:

- If you have physical or telnet access to the Web server, you can copy the DLL file to the Web server and register it there, using regsvr32.exe as you did on the development workstation.

- Third-party products such as PC Anywhere (highly recommended, especially when working with a Web server that is off-site) enable you to work with a virtual desktop on the server. You can FTP the DLL up to the Web server and then register it from a command line with regvr32.exe.

- You can use the Visual Basic Package and Deployment Wizard to create a Setup program for the component that you, or someone else physically at the Web server, can install.

- If you're using Microsoft Transaction Server (which is recommended), deploying components is even easier. Transaction Server is covered in the next section.

Using Microsoft Transaction Server

Microsoft Transaction Server (MTS) is, perhaps, one of the most confusing yet useful technologies Microsoft has recently developed. The confusion comes partly from the name, Transaction Server, which only partially describes its capabilities. In fact, Microsoft realizes this: With the release of Windows 2000 (formerly Windows NT 5.0), currently expected in mid to late 1999, Microsoft has renamed MTS as *Component Services*. This seemingly more generic name is actually a more accurate description of the technology, which is, in fact, geared toward providing automated services for components. Transactions, as it turns out, are only part of it.

MTS is a technology that enables the building, deploying, managing, and automating of ActiveX components. One of its more powerful features, and the cause of its current naming confusion, is its capability to provide *transactional processing* for components. MTS literally provides this feature without requiring the programmer to hand-code it at all. You might be familiar with the concept of transactions from your work with databases: A *transaction* is essentially a unit of work that consists of one or more jobs, each of which must be completed successfully before the transaction is considered successful. If any one job does not complete successfully, all the other jobs are undone, or *rolled back*, and the transaction ends.

The classic example of a transaction in the real world, of course, is a money transfer at the bank. When you transfer $1,000 from a savings account to a checking account, both jobs (the savings withdrawal and the checking deposit, respectfully) must complete successfully for the transaction to process successfully. If only one of the two occurs, the other is rolled back (undone), and it's as if the transaction never took place (which, in many ways, it didn't). SQL Server users are familiar with this concept, and now, with Transaction Server, it's possible to seamlessly apply this capability to component development.

MTS is an important addition to component development because most components act as the business logic "middle man" that exists between the user interface (an ASP document in your case, although it could also be a Visual Basic form or other entity) and the data source (typically SQL Server). In this scenario, you often have to perform a series of operations in a component that can be considered a single transaction. By using the built-in functionality of MTS, you can take advantage of its transactional capabilities without you yourself having to hand-code them.

But again, MTS isn't just about transactions. MTS also provides a framework to manage and install components easily on a local or remote machine. There's another important benefit to MTS: MTS components can run out-of-process with regards to IIS (that is, MTS components run within the process space of MTS itself), so they cannot bring down the host application (IIS, in your case) by mistake. This is probably a wise move for the components you are developing in Visual Basic for IIS.

We All Live in a Transactional World

To facilitate transactional processing and other component services, MTS provides the MTS runtime environment, which runs by default on the Web server (and any other

machine that includes a Microsoft Web server, including your developmental workstation). The MTS runtime environment provides the transaction capability described in the
preceding section, as well as automatic process, thread, and instance management and a
graphical user interface for managing and administering MTS components. This is
known as the *Transaction Server Explorer*, which is a nice MMC plug-in for Windows
NT users (and Windows 2000 users) or a slightly less capable standalone program for
Windows 98 users. Figure 18.12 shows the Windows 98 version of Transaction Server
Explorer; the Windows NT version is similar but provides an Explorer-style pane to the
left, which makes navigating the MTS hierarchy simpler.

FIGURE 18.12

*The Transaction
Server Explorer in
Windows 9x is not
nearly as nice as
the NT version.*

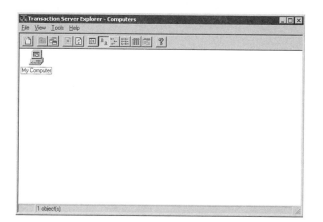

Regardless of which version of the MTS Explorer you're using, the goal is the same: To
manage existing components and install any components you yourself create. Best of all,
you can manage remote computers through this interface, in addition to your local
machine, enabling you to easily install components on remote computers as well. This
is, for many people, the real benefit: As long as you have access rights on the Web server, you can install your components there easily with MTS. In the following section, you
will explore how it's possible to install existing components within the MTS framework.

Porting an Existing Component into MTS

If you've already created an IIS component such as the cPubs component you've been
working on in this chapter, it's a relatively simple matter to move this component into
the MTS environment. Generally speaking, you move a component (or group of related
components) into MTS only when development is complete or nearly complete. Think of
MTS as the last step before deployment; you have to delete any components you install
in MTS each time a change is made, which can be maddening. It's better to develop

components as described earlier in the chapter and then deploy them with MTS when you're done.

To migrate a component to MTS, start the Transaction Server Explorer and navigate into the My Computer folder to display the list of choices shown in Figure 18.13. The first choice, Packages Installed, contains a list of the MTS packages installed on the local system.

FIGURE 18.13

Transaction Server Explorer enables you to browse and manage the components installed on local and remote computers.

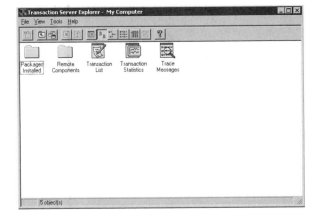

An *MTS package* is simply a logical name and grouping for a set of related components. When you group components together in an MTS package, they will run within the same process, sharing security settings. You have to create a new package for the cPubs component if you want to move it into the MTS runtime environment. After you double-click on Packages Installed, you will see a list of the packages installed on the local system. Packages are represented in MTS Explorer by black ActiveX balls (components) sitting in an open box, as shown in Figure 18.14.

FIGURE 18.14

Packages Installed contains a list of the MTS packages installed on your local system.

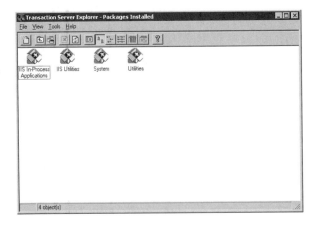

To create a new package, choose New from the File menu. This launches the Package Wizard (see Figure 18.15).

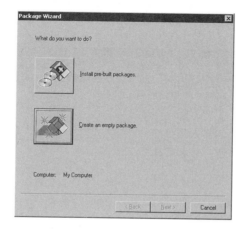

You are going to have to create a new package, so select the Create an Empty Package Choice. Then, you will be prompted for the name of the package. This can be anything logical, such as `Pubs` or `pkgPubs`. After you create the package, it will show up in the Packages Installed section of MTS Explorer. You can then open the package and navigate to its Components folder, which will be empty, naturally. From this window, however, you can add your own components to the package by selecting New from the File menu. This launches the MTS Component Wizard (see Figure 18.16). If you're adding a component that's never been registered on the machine, go with the first choice. In this case, however, you have already registered the component, so you select Import Component(s) That Are Already Registered.

18

BUILDING WEB APPLICATION COMPONENTS

At this point, you're provided with a list (admittedly long) of the components registered on the local system. Select the component you'd like to add to MTS (yours is listed as cPubs.authors) to continue. When you're done, the component will appear within the Components section of MTS as a little ActiveX ball (see Figure 18.17).

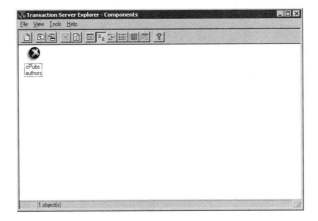

Alternatively, if you unregistered the component before launching the MTS Explorer, you could choose Install New Components from the Component Wizard's opening window. This enables you to navigate to the DLL file stored somewhere in the file system. Either way, when you're done, you will have registered your component on the system, using MTS.

When you double-click on your component in MTS, you're presented with an Interfaces folder. This folder contains the public interfaces supplied by your component. Open this, and you will see a predefined interface grouping for your component (called _authors in this case). When you open the interface, you will be presented with one or more folders. Because you created functions and procedures for your component, you will see a Methods folder. It can also have a Role Membership folder, which contains an MTS class of users who are allowed to access the component. This is the integrated package security mentioned earlier.

When you open the Methods folder, you will see a list of the method interfaces (functions and procedures) that you provided, as well as a set of standard method interfaces supplied automatically by any COM component (see Figure 18.18).

FIGURE 18.18

Public interfaces, such as functions and methods, are considered methods of the component.

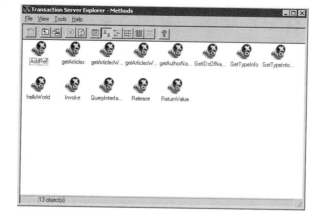

For a nontransactional component, there isn't much more to do, except one very geeky (yet somehow compelling) test. Navigate in the MTS Explorer to the component (cPubs.authors), and make sure that it's set to large icon view. Now, open a browser window and size it so that you can see the entire contents of both the Web browser and the MTS Explorer window. Navigate to an ASP document that accesses the cPubs.authors component, and watch the ActiveX ball as the Web page loads (see Figure 18.19).

18

BUILDING WEB
APPLICATION
COMPONENTS

FIGURE 18.19

It's alive! The ActiveX ball spins the first time it is loaded into memory.

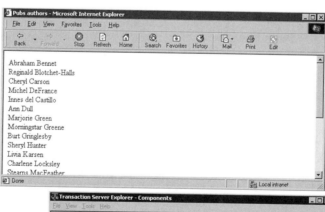

Looking at Visual C++ and Visual J++ for Control Creation

In addition to Visual Basic, you can use Visual C++ and Visual J++ to create components that will run on the Web server and interact with your Active Server Pages. Each of these languages has specific benefits and detriments when compared to Visual Basic.

Visual C++

Visual C++ supplies the ActiveX Template Library (ATL), a lightweight collection of C++ templates that encapsulates the creation of components and other COM objects. ATL components are smaller and faster than equivalent components written with Visual C++'s bloated Microsoft Foundation Classes (MFC), a massive collection of C++ classes. They are also much, much faster than components created in Visual Basic (four to eight times faster, depending on the functionality). Of course, programming components in ATL is also an order of magnitude more difficult than in Visual Basic.

If you're a C++ wizard, the ATL is exactly what you're looking for. Otherwise, leave ATL (and Visual C++) to the experts. Unlike Visual Basic, it's not something you can easily pick up.

Visual J++

Microsoft added the capability to create COM objects such as components using Java with its Visual J++ product. I attended Microsoft's first public demonstration of Visual Studio about three years ago and sat, in amazement, as a Visual J++ product manager created a COM component with Java. My amazement had less to do with the fact that it was possible than the fact that anyone would want to do this. Even with recent advances in the execution speed of Java programs, Visual J++ today (as it did then) creates the absolutely slowest possible COM components. Visual J++ components execute more slowly, in general, than components created in Visual Basic.

But if you're not turned off by this news, it's still possible to do it. Visual J+ enables Java developers to create COM objects, using Java classes that are exposed as COM classes. It's likely that the COM-on-Java approach is valid in certain situations, such as when a Java developer needs to access existing COM components (say, from Microsoft Office or Windows itself) in his or her own programs. Creating COM objects in Visual J++ that will run on a Web server in a production environment is not advised, however.

Summary

The ability to create powerful, full-featured components in Visual Basic is a major victory for Active Server developers. Visual Basic is a language most ASP developers all know and use on a daily basis, and the switch from dynamic queries in Active Server Pages to component-based database access is relatively painless. Yet the performance benefits are enormous: When handled correctly (with variant arrays used in an ASP document to contain a returned result set), Visual Basic components outperform dynamic ASP queries dramatically.

Visual Basic opens up the world of automated component management and transactions through Microsoft Transaction Server (MTS, soon to be renamed *Component Services* in Windows 2000). MTS enables developers to easily register and maintain components locally and remotely, a feature any component developer will appreciate after trying to accomplish these tasks by hand.

Although other approaches to component development are available in Visual Studio, using tools such as Visual C++ or Visual J++, Microsoft Visual Basic offers the ultimate combination of speed and power, while leveraging your existing knowledge of the underlying language. Visual Basic's prowess at component creation could occupy an entire book, but I hope that this introduction will excite you enough to explore Visual Basic further.

18

BUILDING WEB
APPLICATION
COMPONENTS

Programming Microsoft Transaction Server

by Doug Mitchell

IN THIS CHAPTER

Microsoft has integrated Microsoft Transaction Server (MTS) into Internet Information Server (IIS) 4.0 so successfully that you might easily be using it without knowing. In fact, all Web applications automatically use MTS when they run on IIS 4. What exactly is it? Good question, but not an easy one to answer simply.

The goal of this chapter is to discuss how to develop your Web applications using MTS. However, to set the stage for this discussion, MTS and related topics must first be introduced.

Depending on your level of experience and knowledge, the discussion of MTS and its related concepts in this chapter might be an insufficient introduction. For this reason, at the end of the chapter I have assembled a list of additional MTS resources for further research.

The Microsoft Transaction Server and Related Concepts

In a sentence, the *Microsoft Transaction Server (MTS)* is Microsoft's distributed runtime environment for COM components. MTS combines the scalability and reliability of a transaction-processing (TP) monitor and the convenience and flexibility of an Object Request Broker (ORB). An ORB is the middleware that handles the communication details between distributed objects. In doing so, it provides the underlying infrastructure or "plumbing" that a scalable application needs: transactional support using stateless objects, database connection pooling, object instance management, simplified component administration, and more.

Conceptually, this description might make sense. However, it might leave you unsatisfied if you are relatively new to the world of large-scale distributed systems. It assumes you have a complete grasp of transactions, TP monitors, stateless objects, and the like. Furthermore, if you are new to large-scale distributed systems, you might not immediately grasp why MTS is even necessary in the first place.

To help you understand MTS, this section discusses some critical and related concepts, such as transactions, TP monitors, and stateless objects. It also introduces you to the N-tier architecture, which emphasizes why MTS is so important in the first place.

Transactions

Understanding transactions and why they are so important to application development is the key to understanding MTS. If you have been developing Web applications exclusively, it is entirely possible that you are not familiar with transactions, because many Web applications only disseminate information (read-only).

For example, many companies provide information about their products on the Internet. In the infancy of the Web, this was typically accomplished by using static Web pages written in HTML and using a tool such as Microsoft FrontPage.

As the popularity of the Web grew, so did the amount and volatility of information. In response to this shift, companies began to provide extensive, ever changing, product information via Web pages dynamically generated from information stored in replicated databases outside corporate firewalls. These Web applications were relatively inexpensive and quick to develop, using products such as InterDev, and proved to be very popular with the customers because they can contain detailed and current information.

Sometimes these read-only Web applications proved to be too popular. This popularity resulted in slow response times and sometimes timeouts, which soured the customer's perception of the company. In response, companies were forced to upgrade and tune their servers, increase their network bandwidth, and take advantage of techniques such as server load balancing and database connection pooling.

Competition was fierce, and profit margins were tight, so companies increasingly looked to the Web for additional ways to differentiate themselves from one another. The next evolutionary step typically taken was a big one: e-commerce. Rather than advertise and educate on the Web, they began to sell products directly to their customers via virtual Web storefronts. With these transactional Web applications, the amount of additional complexity with regard to application development, security, process, and infrastructure became staggering.

To help minimize the application complexity, many software vendors, such as Microsoft with its Site Server (Commerce edition) product, provided off-the-shelf Web storefronts that could be tailored to a company's needs. However, many challenges were still ahead for transactional Web application developers. MTS does help address two of the more important issues: transactional support and, to some degree, scalability.

Transactional support is the new requirement with e-commerce Web applications, compared to the read-only Web applications. The essence of transactional support is the requirement that a series of steps be treated as a single unit of work. If any step in the unit of work fails, the entire unit of work is considered a failure, and any previous steps are undone, as if nothing happened in the first place. (See "The ACID Test for Transaction Validity.")

The textbook example of the transactional support requirement is the account transfer method. An account transfer requires debiting one account and crediting another. A bank

19

PROGRAMMING
MICROSOFT
TRANSACTION SERVER

would rather not have your savings account credited if the money is not available in your checking account. Therefore, it is a requirement that unless the credit and debit both are successfully completed, nothing occurs.

THE ACID TEST FOR TRANSACTION VALIDITY

To be considered valid or reliable, a transaction must satisfy the following ACID criteria, as first introduced in the 80s:

- Atomic—All or none of the transaction must be executed.

- Consistent—Any discrete step within the transaction must not be left in an inconsistent state when the transaction is completed, regardless of its success or failure. For example, in the case of a RDBMS, referential integrity of data cannot be violated.

- Isolated—The intermediate states must not be visible to other transactions.

- Durable—The results of a successful transaction must be stored in a permanent or durable medium.

Transactional support simplifies programming because it provides protection against anomalies caused by incomplete transactions. That is, you can be assured that your application will not leave your data in an inconsistent state. Furthermore, by supporting the isolation transaction property, MTS allows for the processing of multiple-customer transactions in serial or parallel without affecting one another's outcome.

If your environment does not provide transactional support, error recovery has to be manually coded into your application to restore the state of your system to the state it was in before the transaction started. This can be simple if you are using a single database to store your information, because all the popular database vendors provide their own transactional support. However, what do you do if your transaction has to span multiple databases from various vendors? Traditionally, the answer would mean a lot of extra code to manually coordinate the transaction.

Scalability is not a new concept for companies that already have popular Web sites. However, transactional Web applications add a whole new dimension to this scalability issue. A transactional Web application involves data capture, which requires additional server resources as it attempts to manage the user's state. Scalability is a recurring theme throughout the remainder of this chapter.

Transaction-Processing (TP) Monitors

The challenge of building large-scale systems that must handle thousands of transactions a second is not new. For example, IBM's CICS (Customer Information Control System) is a TP monitor and has been in use for a long time. The concept is simple enough. All applications have a finite amount of system resources, such as CPU, memory, threads, handles, and database connections. A TP monitor has two objectives: First, it attempts to maximize the use of these limited resources across thousands of concurrent users. Second, by monitoring the transactions being executed by the application, it can improve an application's reliability by ensuring that each transaction conforms to the ACID test. Database connections and thread pooling are two examples of MTS's TP monitor-like features.

N-Tier Application Development

As applications increase in their size and complexity, steps must be taken to support scalability. These steps take the form of adapting the traditional two-tier (client/server) architecture to a more versatile N-tier architecture. At a minimum, the N-tier application is logically partitioned into presentation (or user), business, and data services. This architecture is also known as *servercentric* because often the bulk of the application logic is contained in the business tier that often resides on an intervening application server. The *N* signifies that the number of tiers is not fixed, but is at least more than two. It is easy to get hung up on what a tier is and what it is not, but what is important is that the application is partitioned.

This partitioning is the key step that results in improved scalability, reusability, reliability, and manageability. For example, if the business methods are partitioned from the interface (presentation), they are more likely to be reused across similar applications. By keeping the client (that is, a Web browser client) thin or zero and moving as much of the application logic as possible to the business tier, it becomes relatively simple to provide multiple client front ends to suit various user communities. From a management perspective, by keeping the business logic separated and centralized, routine updates to the business logic can be deployed with relative ease.

Using Microsoft's N-tier architecture, the partitioning units are likely to be COM components. You build components to encapsulate your presentation, business, and data access logic. Components can be developed and used by a variety of popular languages, such as Visual Basic, J++, and C++. Of course, nothing comes for free, and the cost of N-tier architecture is a relative increase in application complexity.

MTS's purpose is to minimize this complexity by providing you the necessary infrastructure to build N-tier applications without all the typical concerns. MTS has many features that help make a component-based N-tier scalable. These features include database connection pooling, automatic thread pooling, transaction management, and object instance management. By maximizing the limited system resources, such as memory, threads, and database connections, an application can be built to scale. Remember that scalable applications require upfront planning; retrofitting an existing architecture to be scalable, after the fact, can be difficult at best.

Stateless Versus Stateful Objects

Part of the upfront planning involves designing your objects so that they can take maximum advantage of MTS. Transaction management is a very important feature of MTS. However, a requirement of transactional objects is that the objects be stateless.

An object that is *stateless* does not persist any information (or has none to begin with) from one method call to the next. This is a bit unsettling at first because an *object* is classically defined as the encapsulation of data (or state) and behavior. Moreover, stateless objects have a downside: Initialization information required by the method must be passed as parameters. This parameter passing not only results in some tedious coding, but also has a potential effect on scalability because the extra parameters increase network traffic.

Why Use Stateless Objects?

Stateful objects have some problems when it comes to building transactional Web applications. First, users of Web applications are notorious for getting half way through a transaction (such as ordering a CD) and taking a break (such as checking the competitor's prices) before completing it. If the Web application is using stateful objects, the system resources (threads, memory, and database connections) allocated to the user are sitting idle, but still dedicated, during the breaks.

Second, Web applications sometimes must take advantage of load balancing with multiple servers in order to support a large number of users. A traditional stateful object does not have the luxury of being relocated to another, less busy server over the course of its life. This limits the usefulness of server load balancing.

> **CAUTION**
>
> The problem of maintaining state across servers is significant and affects more than just objects. For example, the use of ASP's Session or Application objects and even MTS's Shared Property Manager cannot span servers. Therefore, consider your options carefully if you foresee that your Web application will need to take advantage of server load balancing for scalability reasons.

Do I Always Have to Use Stateless Objects?

There is a common misconception that in order to use MTS, you must use only stateless objects. This misconception is due to an oversimplification of how MTS works. To set the record straight, this statement is simply not true. Both stateless and stateful objects can be used together in MTS. Nontransactional objects can retain state as normal within MTS. Even transactional objects can retain their state, but the state must be stored programmatically outside the object.

Techniques to programmatically store state external to the object include the use of cookies, the ASP's Session object, or MTS's Shared Property Manager. The Shared Property Manager is introduced in the next section. During the life of a transaction, it is also possible to use MTS to store interim state in a "stateless" object. This topic is addressed more thoroughly in the section "The MTS Development Environment."

The MTS Runtime Environment

The MTS runtime environment consists of many parts working together to support your component-based applications. It is important to understand the internal mechanics of MTS if you are to understand how to use it to program. Some elements used by MTS's runtime environment are leveraged from other Microsoft products and integrated into the MTS architecture. Figure 19.1 illustrates how the various parts are integrated.

MTS Packages

Rather then host discrete COM components, MTS works with groups of components referred to as *packages*. A package is a collection of one or more components that can be managed and deployed as a logical unit. These packages also define the security and process boundaries for the components running in MTS. Components in the same package run in the same process and therefore have better performance. NT inflicts a performance penalty when components interact across process boundaries. This interaction among processes is achieved through a process known as *marshalling*. However, by placing components in different packages, you can have a better chance of isolating the problematic component and limiting its effect to the Web server. This feature is known as *fault isolation*. Therefore, you must balance security, performance, and fault-isolation requirements when you create your packages.

FIGURE 19.1

The MTS runtime environment.

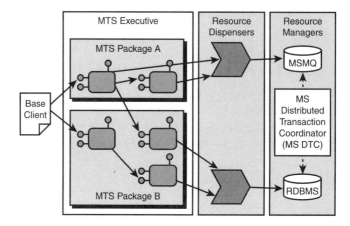

The Base Client

Any application, outside the MTS environment, that invokes an MTS component is considered a *base client*. This can be anything from a VB desktop application to an ASP script running on IIS.

The MTS Executive

The MTS Executive is a DLL that provides runtime services, such as thread and context management, for your MTS components running in their packages.

Resource Dispensers

A *resource dispenser* manages nondurable, shared state on behalf of components within a process. Typically, a resource dispenser manages the connections to a resource manager. MTS provides two resource dispensers:

- ODBC Resource Dispenser—For the MTS components, it manages a pool of connections to ODBC data sources. In the cases when the connection information is the same, this dispenser can allocate connections quickly and efficiently.

- Shared Property Manager—This provides access to application-defined variables (anything that can be stored as a variant) within a process. It is one mechanism that can be used to store state external to the component.

> **CAUTION**
>
> Because the sharing of data by the Shared Property Manager is limited to a single process, be careful that objects implemented in different DLLs do not reference common shared properties. This works only if both the DLLs are contained in the same package, because each package runs in its own process. If the DLLs are ever moved to different packages, they will no longer share the same process and therefore will not be able to share the property.

The Microsoft Distributed Transaction Coordinator (MS DTC)

MS DTC is a system service used by MTS to coordinate transactions. Originally, it was designed for SQL Server 6.5, but was later leveraged by MTS for transactional support. It uses a two-phase commit protocol to ensure transactional consistency across resource dispensers. It is through the MS DTC that MTS provides support for distributed transactions that can even span across databases (or other resource managers), if necessary.

The Resource Manager

As a system service, a resource manager manages *durable* (that is, persistent) data, such as an ODBC data source. Its job is to ensure that data is not lost or corrupted in the event of a system failure. The MS DTC manages the transaction through these resource managers. MTS supports resource managers, such as Microsoft's SQL Server and MSMQ, as long as they implement the OLE or XA transaction protocol. OLE and XA transaction protocols are two industry-standard APIs for communicating between resource managers and the MS DTC. Resource managers permit XA-compliant databases, such as Oracle, DB2, and Informix, to be involved in a transaction coordinated by MS DTC.

Object Context

A component contained in a package is referred to as an *MTS component*. An instance of an MTS component is known as an *MTS object*. For each MTS object created, MTS maintains information about each object's execution environment. This information is known as the object's *context* and includes information such as the identity of the object's creator, security, and its transactional nature. The object context persists across deactivations (discussed next), but is destroyed when the base client releases the object's reference. In Visual Basic or VBScript, this occurs when the object goes out of context or if you explicitly set the object instance to nothing. Because the object context is maintained by MTS, it simplifies your development tasks because it masks the complexity in tracking the object's state information.

Component Deactivation and Reactivation

When a user first requires an MTS object, it is created, performs the desired operation, and then is deactivated. This process is sometimes referred to as *as-soon-as-possible (ASAP) deactivation*. What do I mean by *deactivated*? Technically, the object is destroyed. However, from a base client's prospective, a valid object reference still exists, thanks to the creation of an object context wrapper by MTS. The object context wrapper is created by the MTS Executive whenever an MTS object is created; it serves as a persistent object reference. Because the object is destroyed, some of the system resources (such as database connections and threads) that are dedicated to the object can be released and made available for others to use. When that object instance is referenced again (for example, the base client invokes another method), the object is reactivated and performs the desired action. This process is sometimes referred to as *just-in-time (JIT) activation*. Of course, if the object maintains state between method calls, it is impossible to recycle the system resources, which is why stateless objects are preferred by MTS.

Technically, these "reactivated" objects are not coming from a pool of waiting objects, but instead are being re-created each time they are reactivated. The object-pooling feature is not presently available in MTS 2.0.

> **NOTE**
>
> In Don Box's ActiveX Q&A column for *Microsoft System Journal* (MSJ), March 1998, he provides a comprehensive discussion of MTS and the issues involved with state. This excellent article provides many more technical details and clears up several common misconceptions. For example, he makes a convincing argument that object pooling is no silver bullet for MTS. First, the pool hit rate will

be low because an object can be reactivated only on the same execution thread. Second, the object pooling concept is based on using memory to save CPU cycles.

At the time this chapter was written, the article was available online from MSJ's Web site: `http://www.microsoft.com/MSJ/default.htm`.

The MTS Explorer

The MTS Explorer is a Microsoft Management Console (MMC) snap-in that permits the configuration, administration, and deployment of MTS components (see Figure 19.2). Although, strictly speaking, the MTS Explorer is not part of the MTS runtime environment, it is the mechanism used to install and configure the components used at runtime.

FIGURE 19.2

Microsoft Management Console (MMC).

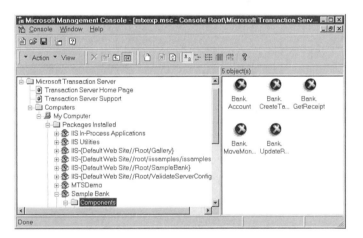

Programming with MTS

Now that you understand how MTS works, the next step is to learn how to program, using it. This section introduces and discusses the following topics:

- The MTS development environment and related concepts
- The rules that govern transactions in MTS
- The use of MTS from within a Web application
- A few quick tips for creating COM components for use in MTS

The MTS Development Environment

As previously discussed, MTS automatically provides some of the infrastructure features necessary to build scalable applications based on components. These features include database connection pooling, automatic thread management, process isolation, and improved manageability. However, to take full advantage of MTS requires that you have some in-depth knowledge of MTS and a willingness to add some MTS-specific code. This section introduces and discusses relevant MTS development concepts that serve as a foundation for the remaining topics discussed in this chapter.

A Transaction's Root Object

When you consider transactions according to MTS, the concept of a root object becomes important. Remember that one or many components can be enlisted in a transaction and if any one of these components fail, the entire transaction fails, and all actions are undone. Because all transactions must have a beginning, the object that initiates a new transaction is called the *root object*. This root object can also create and use other MTS components, although their involvement in the root object's transaction is dependent on the new object's transactional support setting.

Transaction Support Settings

All components placed into an MTS package have a transaction support setting. If you are using Visual Basic 5 to build your COM components, this setting must be set manually when adding the component to the MTS package (see Figure 19.3). If you are using Visual Basic 6, the setting will be mapped, by default, to the component class's corresponding MTSTransactionMode setting. As you can surmise, the transaction support setting indicates to MTS how the object will involve itself in transactions.

The following are the four possible settings:

- Requires a Transaction—This setting is the most common for transactional objects. Obviously, by name, this setting indicates that the component requires a transaction. This means that if the object is created outside a transaction, it becomes the root object of a new transaction. If the object is created within the context of a transaction, it will participate (or enlist) in the invoking object's transaction. For example, consider an object whose job is to authorize a customer's credit card purchase. It takes the credit card number, amount, and expiration date and performs the following highly simplified steps:

    1. Verify that the number is a valid, active account.

    2. Verify that the expiration date matches the card's number and that the card has not expired.

3. Check whether the amount is allowed, based on the credit limit.

4. Request a unique authorization number.

5. Update the account to reflect the authorized amount.

FIGURE 19.3

The MTS compo-nent's properties.

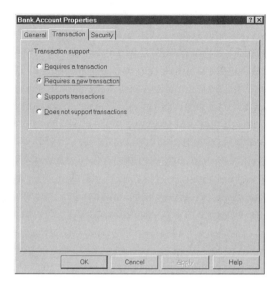

Clearly, this object would require a transaction. For example, if the account num-ber verification failed, you would not want the account updated to reflect the pur-chase amount. Furthermore, this process can stand alone as an independent transaction or belong to another larger transaction.

- Requires a New Transaction—Sometimes an object requires its own transaction, regardless of the transactional nature of its invoking object. This occurs when a base object's transaction invokes a transactional object whose success or failure should not determine the root object's success or failure.

For example, the object that determines a unique authorization number might be set to require a new transaction. In the example, perhaps the authorization number is based on the current time, the store vendor's ID, and the card number. If, for some reason, the authorization transaction fails, you do not care that the unique number generated is wasted. Moreover, you do not want to prevent the customer from buying the merchandise just because the server generating the unique num-bers is down. Instead, you can still record the transaction and flag the record to indicate that it requires further attention. By not involving this object's transaction in the authorization transaction, you conserve your server's resources because you can free up the resources as soon as a new authorization number returns. This

19

PROGRAMMING
MICROSOFT
TRANSACTION SERVER

improves the application's scalability by minimizing the amount of resources held by any given transaction at any point in time.

- Supports Transactions—This transaction support setting plays both sides of the transactional fence. If the root object has a transaction, it will participate in the invoking root object's transaction. That is, if this supporting object fails, it will result in the root object's transaction failing. However, if the root object is not transactional, this object will not create a new transaction for itself.

  Use this setting if the object does not require transactional support for itself, but its failure or success can have meaning to a transactional base object. For example, the verification of the card's information could be set to support transactions because the process itself does not require a transaction, but its failure or success affects the entire authorization transaction.

- Does Not Support Transactions—This setting indicates that the object is not transactional; it neither participates in nor creates a new transaction. Use this setting whenever an object does not require transactional support for itself and its actions have no effect on the outcome of a transactional root object's transaction.

Automatic Transactions

Traditional transaction systems require you to be explicit about the transactional boundaries. For example, if you are using the transactional support of an RDBMS, you explicitly specify the boundaries of your transaction, using key words such as these:

```
BEGIN TRANSACTION
VerifyAccount
...
COMMIT TRANSACTION
```

The transaction support option, such as Requires a Transaction, permits a component to act alone or as part of another transaction. Microsoft refers to this feature as *automatic transactions* and offers a good deal of flexibility when designing components.

As you have already seen, setting the transaction support option for a component is a simple, nonprogrammatic first step. However, with a tiny bit of code, you can make MTS more aggressive at reclaiming system resources effectively by indicating to MTS when you are done with an object.

Object Context Revisited

As previously discussed, MTS manages the object's execution environment by creating and managing an object context. MTS exposes this information to you via an ObjectContext object. This object has four methods that help you control the transaction's outcome and the persistence of an object's state over the course of a transaction. In addition, the ObjectContext object exposes a method that helps create new instances of objects that can be enlisted in the current transaction. These five methods are summarized in Table 19.1 and discussed in greater detail in the following section.

TABLE 19.1 OBJECTCONTEXT'S METHODS

Method	*Description*
SetComplete	Call this method to indicate that the object involved in a transaction has completed and is satisfied (that is, no errors occurred) with the current state of events. If called from a root object, the transaction is considered complete, but not necessarily successful (more on this later). If called from an enlisted object, the transaction continues, but the object is free to be deactivated and its resources reclaimed.
SetAbort	Call this method to indicate that the method involved in a transaction has completed all its actions and you are not satisfied (that is, unrecoverable errors occurred) with the results. If called from a root object, the transaction is considered complete and a failure. If called from an enlisted object, the transaction continues but is doomed to fail. Like SetComplete, the object is free to be deactivated and its resources reclaimed.
DisableCommit	Related to a SetAbort, but the object cannot be deactivated. Use this when the state must be maintained in the interim, but as far as the object is concerned, the transaction is a failure unless the object later calls EnableCommit or SetComplete before the transaction is completed.
EnableCommit	Related to SetComplete, but the object cannot be deactivated. Use when state must be maintained in the interim, but as far as the object is concerned, the transaction is valid.
CreateInstance	Use this method to create objects that you want to participate in the root object's transaction.

Transactions According to MTS

Although you already know what a transaction is from an abstract perspective, it is important to learn specific rules by which MTS governs its transactions. To maximize your application's scalability, you must understand the mechanics of transactions according to MTS. The preceding section introduces you to the four ObjectContexts' methods that affect an object's state and a transaction's success. Table 19.2 summarizes the effect of these methods on the overall transaction and each object's state:

TABLE 19.2 THE OBJECTCONTEXT METHODS' EFFECT ON THE TRANSACTION AND OBJECT STATE

ObjectContext Method	Vote to Commit Transaction?	Preserve Object's State?
SetComplete	Yes	No
SetAbort	No	No
EnableCommit	Yes	Yes
DisableCommit	No	Yes

The following list and associated commentary summarizes the major MTS rules that govern transactions and object state:

- A transaction's outcome is either a complete success or a failure—Following the ACID test, all or none of the transaction is committed. MTS relies on MS DTC to ensure that this is accomplished.

- Each transaction has a root object that initiates the transaction—An object that is specified to either Require a New Transaction or Require a Transaction and is called from a nontransactional object or script will initiate a new transaction. The object that initiates the transaction is known as the root object.

- A transaction can involve one or more objects—Often, a root transaction will enlist other objects to participate in its transaction. Other objects can be enlisted in the root object's transaction if they themselves are transactional objects and either require or support a transaction.

  A participating component can also enlist other transactional components to participate in its transaction, but these nested objects must be created using the ObjectContext.CreateInstance method instead of the New operator or Server.CreateObject method. When you create an object, using CreateInstance, the new object's context is derived from the current object's ObjectContext. This ensures that the new object always executes within the same execution thread as the object that created it. If the current object has a transaction, the transaction attribute of the new object determines its involvement.

- Each object participating in the transaction has equal input in determining the transaction's outcome—Each object participating in the transaction has an equally weighed vote in determining the transaction's outcome. More specifically, if even one object indicates its desire to abort the transaction, the entire transaction will abort, and the system's state will revert to its original condition.

- Each object involved in the transaction can optionally maintain state during the life of the transaction—Throughout the life of a transaction, it might be necessary for an object to maintain state across method calls. Calling EnableCommit and, if necessary, DisableCommit prevents the object from being released until after the transaction is complete. A key point is that the state is maintained only while the transaction is in progress. Therefore, this mechanism can be used only to store interim state. If object state must be maintained across transactions, you store the state externally, using an approach such as MTS's Shared Property Manager.

- By default, each participating object is optimistic about the transaction's success— Objects start out assuming that the transaction will be successful. For the transaction to fail requires an object to explicitly specify its desire to abort. An object can abort a transaction by calling SetAbort or DisableCommit without calling EnableCommit or SetComplete before the transaction completes.

- By default, each participating object maintains state throughout the life of the transaction—Objects will not deactivate until the transaction is complete, unless an explicit SetAbort or SetComplete is called. Therefore, state during the life of the transaction will be preserved by default. However, it is a better practice to call EnableCommit or DisableCommit if interim state is needed.

- If a participating transactional object does not call any of the object context's transaction-related methods, neither the object's state nor the transaction's status will be affected—If SetAbort, SetComplete, EnableCommit, or DisableCommit are not called in an enlisted object's method, the object's vote to commit and preserve state flags is not changed. Do not assume that one of the transaction-related methods is implicitly called if you do not call on it explicitly.

- Transactions can be nested—A *nested transaction* is a new transaction that is spawned in the middle of another transaction. This can occur if an object enlisted requires a new transaction or if you fail to use the CreateInstance method appropriately.

- The outcome of a nested transaction has no input in determining the outcome of the parent's transaction—Remember that nested transactions are independent of the current transaction and that their success or failure has no effect on the current transaction's success or failure.

- The object's commit status is not considered until the transaction is completed— An enlisted object's input (or vote) as to whether to commit or abort the transaction is not considered until the transaction is complete. This means that an object can, in effect, change its mind during the life of the transaction. An important exception is when SetAbort is called. Subsequent calls to the object that called SetAbort will fail, and the transaction itself is ultimately doomed to failure.

- The transaction is completed when the method of the root object that initiated the transaction is completed—The objects are polled when a transaction is completed. Because of MTS's use of automatic transactions, the transactional boundaries are not always obvious. Typically, a transaction is complete when the method call of the transactional root object calls SetAbort or SetComplete and returns from the method. Given the optimistic assumption regarding transactions, calling SetComplete is strictly unnecessary, but should be called anyway to be explicit. Note that if the transaction timeouts, the transaction is considered aborted.

MTS Meets the Web

As stated in the introduction, MTS has been fully integrated into IIS 4. When you are building Web applications, this integration directly affects you in several ways.

Transactional Active Server Pages (ASP) Scripts

Using the transactional directive, ASP scripts can become transactional and serve as the root object. For example:

```
<%@ Transaction=required Language=VBScript %>
```

Visual InterDev 6 makes this even easier by setting the directive for you, if you set the transaction property by using the document's Properties window (see Figure 19.4).

FIGURE 19.4

The ASP page's transaction property.

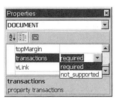

Technically, the transaction directive has the allowable values shown in Table 19.3.

TABLE 19.3   TRANSACTION DIRECTIVE SETTINGS

Value	*Result*
Required	Initiates a transaction
Requires_New	Initiates a transaction
Supported	Does not initiate a transaction
Not_Supported	Does not initiate a transaction
<NO TRANSACTION DIRECTIVE>	Does not initiate a transaction

I say *technically* because with the current version of ASP, an ASP script can serve only as a "root object", and the transaction cannot span multiple ASP files. Therefore, the only significant setting at this time is @transaction=required. If the ASP script does not requires transactional support, leave out the transaction directive.

After the transaction directive has been specified, any objects created, using Server.CreateObject, that either require or support a transaction will be enlisted in the ASP's transaction. You might be wondering why the ObjectContext's CreateInstance method is not used. To clarify, CreateInstance is required only when components want to enlist other components in the current transaction.

> **TIP**
>
> When you create your objects within your ASP scripts, make sure you use the CreateObject method of the Server built-in ASP object. The HTML <OBJECT> tag creates the object outside the MTS environment.

ObjectContext Built In

The ObjectContext object is automatically exposed, permitting access to the object's context. This enables the ASP script to call SetComplete or SetAbort as appropriate. For example:

```
ObjectContext.SetComplete ' all is well
```

or

```
ObjectContext.SetAbort ' problem encountered
```

> **TIP**
>
> Strictly speaking, calling the SetComplete is not necessary, because an ASP page will commit when it ends if no enlisted object explicitly aborts. However, it is a good practice to explicitly call SetComplete.

Transactional Events

When a transactional ASP script has completed its transaction, an event will be raised, depending on the outcome:

- OnTransactionCommit if the transaction was successful
- OnTransactionAbort if the transaction was aborted

This provides you with an opportunity to respond accordingly, based on the transaction's outcome. You will see how these events can be used in the case study at the end of this chapter.

> **CAUTION**
>
> A commit or rollback of a transaction affects only objects managed by MS DTC. For example, the Application and Session collections must be manually handled because these built-in objects do not have a resource manager. Any variables set or changed during the course of the transaction will *not* be undone if the transaction aborts. Therefore, you might want to defer the setting of application and session variables until the transactional events are triggered, if possible. If it is not possible to defer, it will be necessary to manually reset the variables. The transactional events are a perfect place to add the required logic.

Improved Crash Protection for Your Web Server

By default, Web applications run together in the Web server's own process. However, with IIS 4, individual Web applications can be marked to run in their own memory space (isolated process), shown in Figure 19.5. By having a Web application run in its own memory space, IIS automatically creates an MTS package for the application to run in. Because Web applications can now run within their own MTS package, your Web server's stability will be improved. With each Web application isolated in its own process, the chances of a problematic application bringing down your whole Web server is minimized. Keep in mind that there is a performance-versus-stability trade-off in having your packages run in different processes, because of the interprocess marshalling overhead.

Tips for Designing COM Components for Use with MTS

Designing COM components for use with MTS has already been covered in the discussion on stateless objects. However, it is worth a quick detour to highlight some important design considerations on how to build COM components for use with MTS.

- Minimize the use of object state as much as possible. This is the first step to maximizing the use of your system resources with MTS.
- Call SetComplete (or as necessary, SetAbort) explicitly at the conclusion of each method when state is not needed. This will deactivate the object and free up system resources on returning from the object's method.

- Avoid the use of properties and, instead, pass the necessary information as parameters. This minimizes network round trips and is particularly important when using DCOM.

- Acquire database connections as late as possible and release them as soon as you are done with them, to take advantage of connection pooling.

FIGURE 19.5

The Web application's properties.

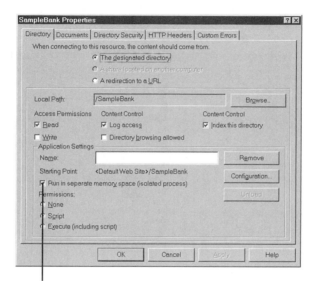

Run in separate memory space

An MTS Case Study

This case study demonstrates how to take advantage of MTS, using ASP. To focus on the relevant points in the most expedient manner, the case study builds on the Microsoft Bank Sample that comes with MTS.

This section walks you through the more important sections of the ASP code. If you want to try this for yourself, the InterDev project that accesses the Bank components in MTS is included on the CD-ROM that accompanies this book. Of course, you will have to install the Bank package included with MTS and set up the MTS Bank Application.

19

TRANSACTION SERVER
PROGRAMMING MICROSOFT

TIP

To install the samples included with MTS (such as the MTS Sample Bank), you must install MTS by using the Custom Install option. See the topic "Setting Up the MTS Sample Bank Application" in Microsoft Transaction Server Reference Help for complete details.

The purpose of this case study is to reproduce the sample Visual Basic banking application as a Web application. This sample banking application makes use of an MTS package that contains a Bank component.

The bank application makes use of these components to perform some basic banking services: Credit, Debit, and Account Transfer. The bank accounts are persistent, using a SQL Server database. If you have installed the Bank application already, you might want to quickly familiarize yourself with its operation, shown in Figure 19.6.

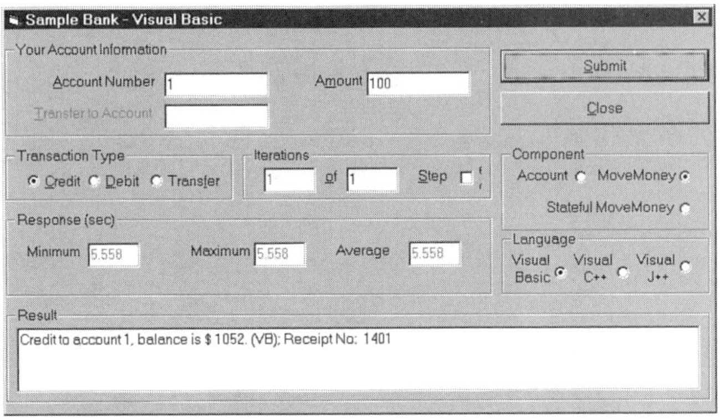

FIGURE 19.6

The sample bank VB application.

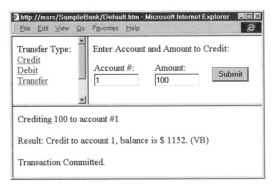

The Web application equivalent of the VB Bank application client provides similar access to the credit, debit, and account methods, shown in Figure 19.7.

FIGURE 19.7

The sample bank Web application.

The bulk of the Bank Web application pages supports the typical flow and data capture you have seen before with your Web application. The only page relevant to this chapter is ATM.asp. ATM.asp processes the user's request by extracting the type of request and any necessary information from the QueryString collection. Based on the type of request, the appropriate transactional object is

```
<%@ Transaction=required Language=VBScript %>
```

ATM.asp is a transactional script, as indicated by the @ `Transaction=required` directive.

```
On Error Resume Next
```

If an error is encountered, the script continues with the next line. This is desirable because you want to handle errors more gracefully when they occur.

```
PrimeAcct = Request.QueryString("txtAccount")
Amount = Request.QueryString("txtAmount")
...
```

The preceding code extracts from the QueryString collection and stores the parameters in local variables.

```
Set objAcct = Server.CreateObject ("Bank.Account")
```

This creates an instance of the desired class. In this case, it is an instance of the Account class from the Bank component.

```
Res = objAcct.Post(PrimeAcct, Amount)
```

This invokes the desired method. In this case, you are posting the amount to a specified account.

```
If Err.Number <> 0 Then bAbort = True
```

After all method calls to your objects, it is necessary to test for an error because of the On Error Resume Next statement. If an error occurs, your only indication will be that Err.Number is not equal to 0. In this case, you set a flag to signify that the application was aborted. This flag can be used to "drop through" any remaining logic that should not be executed if an error occurs and get to the ASP script's SetAbort.

```
If bAbort Then
ObjectContext.SetAbort
Else
    ObjectContext.SetComplete
End If
```

You might think that this If...Else statement is unnecessary. Each enlisted object will call SetAbort after it encounters a critical problem. After all, when the script completes, the outcome of the transaction will be determined, based on the enlisted components' votes anyway, right? This If...Else statement is useful when an error occurs before the enlisted object's method is executed. For example, imagine a user who makes a typo and enters

$$100 for the amount. Because the amount parameter for the post method expects a valid number, the method call fails outright with a Type Mismatch error. Unfortunately, the method never had a chance to call SetAbort, so the transaction is not considered a failure. If the SetAbort is not explicitly called, the OnTransactionCommit event is triggered because, as far as the transaction is concerned, it is a success.

```
Sub OnTransactionCommit ()
    Response.Write "Result: " & Res & "<P>Transaction Committed."
End Sub
Sub OnTransactionAbort ()
    Response.Write "An error has occurred: " & Err.description
    Response.Write "<P>Transaction Aborted."
End Sub
```

The two transactional events are trapped, depending on the outcome of the transaction. If the transaction is successful, the results returned by the method are displayed. If aborted, the user is notified that an error has occurred, and a description is displayed.

The MTS Sample Bank example provides a great test bed to get first-hand experience with MTS and transactions. Using the Web version provided, you can become comfortable with MTS and its transactional support for ASP scripts.

The Future of MTS

MTS has a bright future ahead in distributed application development. Although things can change, it appears that the first version of COM+, the next generation of COM, is going to take the form of a more generalized and universal MTS. COM+ will take Microsoft's products, such as MTS, COM, and MSMQ, and integrate them together into a single package. The next version of MTS (3.0) is expected to ship as an option pack for Windows NT Server 5.0. The two obvious enhancements expected to be included in the next version are object pooling and dynamic load balancing.

Additional MTS-Related Resources

MTS is a large topic that has received much coverage by industry periodicals and publishers. It's likely that with the release of COM+, this coverage will only intensify as MTS takes on a more significant role in Microsoft's architecture.

The best place to look for additional MTS-related resources is Microsoft itself. Unlike the static list of recommended resources I provide here, Microsoft maintains a dynamic list of MTS-related sites on its Web site: http://www.microsoft.com/com/mts.asp.

In addition to the articles that I have referenced directly in the chapter, I have included a list of my favorite MTS-related articles. At the time of this writing, all these articles are available on the Web (see the URLs listed next):

"How Microsoft Transaction Server Changes the Programming Model" by David Chappell, *Microsoft Systems Journal*, January, 1998

`http://www.microsoft.com/msj/0198/mtscom/mtscom.htm`

David Chappell's landmark article does an outstanding job explaining the nitty-gritty details of how COM components work within MTS. His secret is in his generous use of figures to help illustrate some of the more important concepts.

"Building Scalable Apps" by John Lam, *PC Magazine*, April 21, 1998

`http://www.zdnet.com/pcmag/pctech/content/17/08/tf1708.001.html`

John Lam does an excellent job covering a large amount of material in a concise manner. Many topics covered in this chapter (MTS services, session management, transactions, context wrappers, context objects, and more) are also addressed in his article. Moreover, he introduces MTS security.

- "Writing a Microsoft Transaction Server App" by John Lam, *PC Magazine*, April 21, 1998,
  `http://www.zdnet.com/pcmag/pctech/content/17/08/pp1708.001.html`

  This follow-on article by John Lam is a case study that demonstrates how to build an MTS page-counter component for IIS, using Visual Basic 5.0. Along the way, he addresses important topics, such as how durable and nondurable storage of data affects the scalability and safety of your Web application.

- "Build Reliable and Scalable N-Tier Applications That Run on Both Windows NT and UNIX" by Mai-lan Tomsen, *Microsoft Systems Journal*, December 1998,
  `http://www.microsoft.com/msj/1298/ntUnix/ntUnixtop.htm`

  The focus of this article is how to replace front-end legacy logic on UNIX with COM components running on Windows NT, but it also contains a good discussion on N-tier application architecture.

- "MTS: Fast Train Coming?" by Max Dolgicer, *Application Development Trends Magazine*, August 1998, `http://www.adtmag.com/pub/Aug98/fe801-f.htm`

  This article provides a good overview of MTS and related concepts.

- "Building Distributed Applications with DCOM and MTS" by Vlad Kroutik, *Application Development Trends Magazine*, November 1998,
  `http://www.adtmag.com/pub/Aug98/fe801-f.htm`

19

PROGRAMMING MICROSOFT TRANSACTION SERVER

In addition to some of the usual MTS topics, this article discusses several interesting approaches to server-side state management, with a focus on scalability.

Summary

MTS is a critical technology for large-scale Web applications. This chapter provides you not only with an understanding of MTS itself, but also with an introduction to related key concepts. It is difficult to do justice to MTS and its related topics in a single chapter, considering entire books have been written on the subject. However, this chapter gives you the necessary foundation to get you jump started and enough additional MTS references to keep you going in the right direction.

Sending Email with Collaboration Data Objects

by Ken Cox

IN THIS CHAPTER

Using the IIS SMTP Component

The Simple Mail Transfer Protocol (SMTP) is a standard for the exchange of mail between two computers using TCP/IP. SMTP has related standards that set out the format of the mail messages, the inclusion of nontext attachments, and how mail is routed via the domain name system. SMTP is an end-to-end delivery system. That is, an SMTP client that has mail for delivery contacts the destination host's SMTP server directly. The SMTP client holds on to the mail until it successfully completes the transfer of the mail to the destination computer. Note that SMTP is not the same as Post Office Protocol version 3 (POP3). POP3 is the protocol used to retrieve email messages from an individual's mailbox. For the most part, the standards and inner workings of SMTP are transparent to you when run an SMTP site on Windows NT.

Installing the SMTP Service on IIS

The SMTP Service runs on Windows NT 4.0 Server, not NT Workstation. The service is an option during the setup of Internet Information Server (IIS). One way to check whether you have installed SMTP is to open the Internet Service Manager and under Internet Information Server, look for Default SMTP Site. If SMTP was not installed, you can do so by running the Windows NT 4.0 Option Pack Setup (see Figure 20.1). As shown in Figure 20.2, the SMTP Service is a subcomponent of IIS. To see the SMTP option, select Internet Information Server and then click Show Subcomponents.

FIGURE 20.1

To install the SMTP Service, you run the NT 4.0 Option Pack Setup.

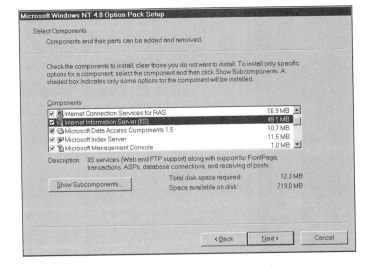

FIGURE 20.2

The Microsoft SMTP Service is an optional component of IIS.

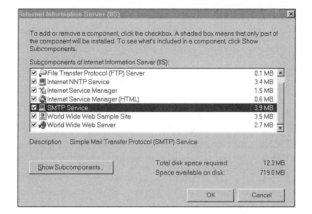

To confirm that the SMTP Service is listening for email on the usual port (port 25), you can run the Telnet utility from any computer on the network, as shown in Figure 20.3. From the Windows Start button, click Run. Substituting your IIS server name for *<servername>*, type the following:

```
telnet <servername> 25
```

From the SMTP Service, you should receive a response confirming that it is ready to go:

```
220-p133.winnt Microsoft SMTP MAIL ready at
Mon, 9 Nov 1998 21:18:59 -0500 Version: 5.5.1877.977.9
220 ESMTP spoken here
```

FIGURE 20.3

Use the Telnet utility to confirm that the SMTP Service is listening on port 25.

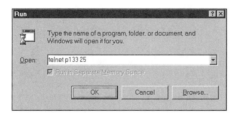

Configuring the SMTP Service

To send and receive email, you might have to configure your SMTP site. Open the Internet Service Manager and expand the Internet Information Server node to reveal the SMTP site. Right-click Default SMTP Site (assuming you haven't renamed the site), open the Properties pages, and click the Delivery tab, which appears in Figure 20.4. By default, the setup program inserts the name of your IIS server in the Fully Qualified Domain Name box. You don't have to change it unless your server name has changed.

20

SENDING EMAIL WITH CDO

If your company uses a centralized server such as Microsoft Exchange Server to handle the messaging on your network, you might be able to direct email through what is called *a smart host*. If so, type that server's name in the Smart Host box. Click Apply and OK to exit the Properties pages.

A *smart host* is a TCP/IP host that routes mail for the TCP/IP network, usually through the domain name service (DNS). Organizations that have several SMTP hosts can designate one smart host to route all messages between the Internet and the other SMTP hosts. The remaining SMTP hosts are configured to forward all messages to the smart host. A smart host is sometimes called the mail routing host or SMTP router.

FIGURE 20.4

You can configure a smart host to redirect SMTP Service email.

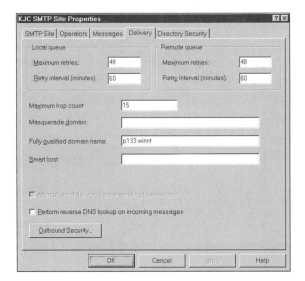

About DNS Configuration

Depending on your server and network setup, you might require changes to your domain name server configuration for message handling via SMTP. For instance, the mail exchanger record (or MX record) in the zone file of the DNS might require updating. This file associates the domain name of the mail handler with your company's usual domain name. Also, the mail address record (or A record) might have to be changed. DNS configuration is beyond the scope of this book, so check with your ISP or network administrator on where and how to define mail exchanger and mail address records for your system.

SMTP Default Directories

The SMTP Service uses several directories on the server to store and manipulate text messages. By default, these are subdirectories of c:\InetPub\Mailroot\. Table 20.1 shows the names of the subdirectories and their purposes. Later in this chapter, you will see how scripts can use these subdirectories to send and receive email.

TABLE 20.1 SUBDIRECTORIES USED BY THE SMTP SERVER

Subdirectory	Purpose
Badmail	Holds messages that can't be delivered and can't be returned to the sender.
Drop	Holds all incoming messages, including messages that have been generated by scripts. You can change this folder as long as it isn't the same as the Pickup subdirectory.
Pickup	The drop directory for outgoing messages. As soon as the SMTP Service detects a text file in the Pickup directory, the service picks up the message and attempts to deliver it.
SortTemp	Stores messages temporarily during processing. Outgoing messages are sorted by domain and sent as a group, for efficiency.
Queue	Holds messages for delivery. When the service determines that a message cannot be delivered within the number of retries that you've set, the message goes from Queue to Badmail.

Introducing Collaboration Data Objects for NT Server (CDONTS)

The Collaboration Data Objects for Windows NT Server (CDONTS) Library that comes with the Windows NT Option Pack exposes messaging objects that you can use to read, write, and send SMTP messages. CDONTS is a subset of the CDO 1.2 Library that ships with Microsoft Exchange Server. Whereas CDO 1.2 uses MAPI to access and store data, CDONTS works directly with messages. You don't need an Exchange Server installation to use CDONTS, but you do need IIS.

CDONTS Library is far less complex than CDO 1.2. For instance, CDONTS isn't designed for advanced uses such as scheduling, workflow, and calendars. However, CDONTS appeals to Web developers because it's lightweight, simple, and fast. With very few commands (as few as three lines of code), you can add mailing applications to Web sites.

20

SENDING EMAIL
WITH CDO

The CDONTS Object Model

The CDONTS Object Model defines a collection of programmable objects that support the Component Object Model and OLE Automation. As a result, its objects, methods, and properties are available to programs and, especially for your purposes, Active Server Pages (ASP) script.

Before you begin using CDONTS in script, take a look at the seven objects and three collections that make up the CDONTS Object Model. These objects are shown in Figure 20.5 and briefly described in Table 20.2.

FIGURE 20.5

The CDONTS Object Model.

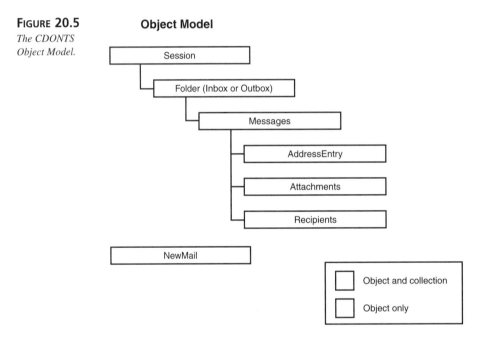

TABLE 20.2 THE CDONTS OBJECT MODEL'S SEVEN OBJECTS AND THREE COLLECTIONS

Object	Description
NewMail	A special shortcut object for sending messages
AddressEntry	Defines addressing information such as a person or process
Attachment	Represents a file or message that is an attachment of a message
Attachments collection	Contains the Attachment objects
Folder(Inbox or Outbox)	Represents a folder or container in a message store

Object	Description
Message	Represents a single message, item, document, or form in a folder
Messages collection	Contains the Message objects
Recipient	Represents a recipient of a message
Recipients collection	Contains the Recipient objects and specifies the recipients of a message
Session	A top-level object that contains sessionwide settings and options

> **TIP**
>
> Thanks to Visual InterDev's IntelliSense feature, you don't have to look up or remember the parameters that you can pass to component objects. Just start typing the object's name. At each point where there's a choice to be made (usually at the dot or a bracket), VI presents a list of options. As you select an option from the list, watch for a ToolTip that describes the type of value that the property or method expects.

The NewMail Object

The NewMail object is a special object that, with a few lines of code, you can use to create and send email messages. Although NewMail doesn't fit with the normal hierarchical style of objects, it makes up for its lack of sophistication with speed and ease of use. As you will see later in this chapter, NewMail is handy for automating a quick courtesy response to a customer's inquiry. With NewMail, you don't have to create a logon or manage the folders or Messages collections. Using an automated process, you create the Message object, address the mail, and send it through the SMTP Service.

The NewMail object contains the properties and methods described in Table 20.3 and Table 20.4, respectively.

TABLE 20.3   PROPERTIES OF THE NEWMAIL OBJECT

Name	Description
Bcc	Adds an address to the list of blind copy recipients
Body	Sets the text content of the message
BodyFormat	Sets the text format of the message body: 0=HTML and 1=text

continues

TABLE 20.3 CONTINUED

Name	Description
Cc	Adds an address to the list of copy recipients
ContentBase	Sets the base path for resource names included in the message
ContentLocation	Sets the relative path to resource names included in the message
From	Sets the address of the message sender
Importance	Sets the importance of the message, 0–3
MailFormat	Sets the encoding format of the message: 0=MIME and 1=text
Subject	Sets the subject of the email message
To	Adds to the list of primary (To) recipients
Value	Adds additional headers to the message
Version	Returns the version information of the CDO for the NTS Library

TABLE 20.4 METHODS OF THE NEWMAIL OBJECT

Name	Description
AttachFile	Adds an attachment to the message
AttachURL	Adds an attachment to the message and associates a URL to the attachment
Send	Sends the message
SetLocaleIDs	Sets a code page identifier

The AddressEntry Object

An AddressEntry object represents addressing information about the sender of a message. In CDONTS, the key properties are Name, which represents a friendly name such as *John Oliver*, and Address, such as olivej@anywhere.com. The AddressEntry object is available through the Sender property of a Message object. The Type property is always SMTP in CDONTS. The AddressEntry object contains the properties described in Table 20.5.

TABLE 20.5 PROPERTIES OF THE ADDRESSENTRY OBJECT

Name	Description
Address	Returns the email address of an address entry
Application	Returns the name of the active application; CDO for NTS Library

Name	Description
Class	Returns the object class of the CDO for NTS Library objects
Name	Returns the display or friendly name of an address entry
Parent	Returns the immediate parent of this object
Session	Returns the top-level Session object associated with this object
Type	Returns SMTP as the message type

The Attachment Object

An Attachment object represents a file or message that is embedded in or adjacent to the main body of a message. Depending on the attachment's content, the mail reader software might display the attachment as an icon until opened.

The Name property is the display name of the attachment, such as New Statistics. The Source property is the path and filename of the attachment, such as c:\outbound\new-stats.zip. The Type property takes a value of 1 for a file or 4 for an embedded message. The most common attachment is a file, such as a graphic or zipped document. However, you can embed a message within an email message.

You can delete all attachments from a message by using the Delete method.

The Attachment object contains the properties and methods described in Table 20.6 and Table 20.7, respectively.

TABLE 20.6 PROPERTIES OF THE ATTACHMENT OBJECT

Name	Description
Application	Returns the name of the active application, CDO for NTS Library
Class	Returns the object class of the CDO for NTS Library objects
ContentBase	Returns the Content-Base header of a MIME (multipurpose Internet mail extensions) message attachment
ContentID	Returns the Content-ID header for the appropriate MIME body part and is used for MIME HTML
ContentLocation	Returns the Content-Location header for the appropriate MIME body part and is used for MIME HTML
Name	Returns or sets the display name of the Attachment object as a string
Parent	Returns the immediate parent of this object

continues

20

SENDING EMAIL WITH CDO

TABLE 20.6 CONTINUED

Name	Description
Session	Returns the top-level Session object associated with this object
Source	Returns or sets the location of the data for the attachment
Type	Determines the valid values for the Source property (1=Attachment is the contents of a file; 4=Attachment is an embedded message.)

TABLE 20.7 METHODS OF THE ATTACHMENT OBJECT

Name	Description
Delete	Removes the Attachment object from the Attachments collection
ReadFromFile	Loads the contents of an attachment from a file, requires the full path and filename
WriteToFile	Saves the attachment as a file in the file system; requires the full path and filename

The Attachments Collection Object

The Attachments collection contains the Attachment objects in a message. You can return the number of attachments through the Count property and a specific attachment through the Item property. The properties of the Attachments collection object are described in Table 20.8.

TABLE 20.8 PROPERTIES OF THE ATTACHMENTS COLLECTION OBJECT

Name	Description
Application	Returns the name of the active application; CDO for NTS Library
Class	Returns the object class of the CDO for NTS Library objects
Count	Returns the number of Attachment objects in the collection
Item	Returns a single Attachment object from this collection
Parent	Returns the immediate parent of this object
Session	Returns the top-level Session object associated with this object

The Folder Object

The Folder object represents a folder (an Inbox or Outbox) for messages. See the Session object and its GetDefaultFolder method to return the name of a folder. The Folder object's Messages property returns a collection of messages within the folder. The Folder object does not contain any methods. Table 20.9 describes its properties.

TABLE 20.9   PROPERTIES OF THE FOLDERS OBJECT

Name	Description
Application	Returns the name of the active application; CDO for NTS Library
Class	Returns the object class of the CDO for NTS Library objects
Messages	Returns a Messages collection object within the folder
Name	Returns the name of the Folder object
Parent	Returns the immediate parent of this object
Session	Returns the top-level Session object associated with this object

The Message Object

The Message object represents a single message in a folder. The extensive properties enable you to set or retrieve key elements of a message, including the sender, the subject, and the body of the message text. Because message contents cannot be changed when put in the Inbox, received message properties are read-only. The Send method saves all changes to the message and puts the message into the current user's Outbox folder. The Message object contains the properties and methods described in Table 20.10 and Table 20.11, respectively.

TABLE 20.10   PROPERTIES OF THE MESSAGE OBJECT

Name	Description
Application	Returns the name of the active application; CDO for NTS Library
Attachments	Returns a single Attachment object or an Attachments collection object
Class	Returns the object class of the CDO for NTS Library objects.
ContentBase	Returns or sets the Content-Base header of a MIME message body
ContentID	Returns or sets the Content-ID header of a MIME message body
ContentLocation	Returns or sets the Content-Location header of a MIME message body
HTMLText	Returns or sets the HTML content of the message
Importance	Returns or sets the importance of the message, 0–3
MessageFormat	Sets the encoding format of the message: 0=MIME and 1=text

continues

20

SENDING EMAIL WITH CDO

TABLE 20.10   CONTINUED

Name	Description
Parent	Returns the immediate parent of this object
Recipients	Returns a collection of Recipient objects
Sender	Returns or sets the sender of a message as an AddressEntry object
Session	Returns the top-level Session object associated with this object
Size	Returns the message length in bytes
Subject	Returns or sets the subject of the message
Text	Returns or sets the text content of the message
TimeReceived	Returns the date and time that the message was received
TimeSent	Returns the date and time the message was or is being sent

TABLE 20.11   METHODS OF THE MESSAGE OBJECT

Name	Description
Delete	Removes the Message object from the Messages collection
Send	Sends the message to the recipients

The Messages Collection Object

The Messages collection contains the Message objects. You can return the number of messages through the Count property and return an individual message through the Item property. To navigate through the collection of messages, you can use the GetFirst, GetNext, GetPrevious, and GetLast methods. The Messages collection object contains the properties and methods described in Table 20.12 and Table 20.13, respectively.

TABLE 20.12   PROPERTIES OF THE MESSAGES COLLECTION OBJECT

Name	Description
Application	Returns the name of the active application; CDO for NTS Library
Class	Returns the object class of the CDO for NTS Library objects
Count	Returns the number of Message objects in the collection
Item	Returns a singke Message object from the Messages collection
Parent	Returns the immediate parent of this object
Session	Returns the top-level Session object associated with this object

TABLE 20.13   METHODS OF THE MESSAGES COLLECTION OBJECT

Name	Description
Add	Creates and returns a new Message object in the Messages collection.
Delete	Removes *all* the Message objects from the Messages collection.
GetFirst	Returns the first Message object in the Messages collection.
GetLast	Returns the last Message object in the Messages collection. If there is no last object, it returns `Nothing`.
GetNext	Returns the next Message object in the Messages collection. If there are no more messages, it returns `Nothing`.
GetPrevious	Returns the preceding object in the Messages collection. If there is no preceding object (already at the first), it returns `Nothing`.

The Recipient Object

The Recipient object represents a recipient of a message. The Address property is commonly an email address such as `olivej@kjc.com`, whereas the Name property is a friendly name such as John Oliver. Use the Type property to indicate whether the recipient is in the To, Cc, or Bcc category. Note that messages and recipients in the Inbox are read-only. The Recipient object contains the properties and the method described in Table 20.14 and Table 20.15, respectively.

TABLE 20.14   PROPERTIES OF THE RECIPIENT OBJECT

Name	Description
Address	Returns or sets the email address of the recipient
Application	Returns the name of the active application; CDO for NTS Library
Class	Returns the object class of the CDO for NTS Library objects
Name	Returns or sets the name of the Recipient
Parent	Returns the immediate parent of this object
Session	Returns the top-level Session object associated with this object
Type	Returns or sets the recipient type: 1=To, 2=Cc, and 3=Bcc

TABLE 20.15   THE RECIPIENT OBJECT'S METHOD

Name	Description
Delete	Removes the Recipient object from the Recipients collection

The Recipients Collection Object

The Recipients collection object represents all recipients of a given message. You can determine the number of recipients by using the Count property and can access individual recipients by using the Item object. The Recipients collection object contains the properties and the methods described in Table 20.16 and Table 20.17, respectively.

TABLE 20.16   PROPERTIES OF THE RECIPIENTS COLLECTION OBJECT

Name	Description
Application	Returns the name of the active application; CDO for NTS Library Class Returns the object class of the CDO for NTS Library objects
Count	Returns the number of Recipient objects in the collection
Item	Returns a single Recipient object from the Recipients collection
Parent	Returns the immediate parent of this object
Session	Returns the top-level Session object associated with this object

TABLE 20.17   METHODS OF THE RECIPIENTS COLLECTION OBJECT

Name	Description
Add	Adds and returns a new Recipient object in the Recipients collection
Delete	Removes all the Recipient objects from the Recipients collection

The Session Object

The Session object is a top-level object that contains sessionwide settings and options that exist during a user's messaging activity. To initialize the Session object, call the LogonSMTP method. The Session object contains the properties and methods described in Table 20.18 and Table 20.19, respectively.

TABLE 20.18   PROPERTIES OF THE SESSION OBJECT

Name	Description
Application	Returns the name of the active application; CDO for NTS Library.
Class	Returns the object class of the CDO for NTS Library objects.
Inbox	Returns or sets a Folder object representing the user's Inbox folder. In IIS, the Inbox is a common folder shared by all recipients and applications and containing all undeleted messages.

Name	Description
MessageFormat	Sets the encoding format of the message: 0=MIME and 1=text.
Name	Returns or sets the display name used to log on to this session.
Outbox	Returns or sets a Folder object representing the user's Outbox folder.
Parent	Returns the immediate parent of this object.
Session	Returns the top-level Session object associated with this object.
Version	Returns the version of the CDO for NTS Library.

TABLE 20.19 METHODS OF THE SESSION OBJECT

Name	Description
GetDefaultFolder	Returns the default Folder name or Nothing if the name does not exist: 1=Inbox and 2=Outbox
Logoff	Logs off the messaging system
LogonSMTP	Logs on to CDONTS and initializes the Session object
SetLocaleIDs	Sets a code page identifier

CDO CONSTANTS AND ASP

Some CDO documentation refers to numeric constants for values such as the object class of a CDO component. These constants are not available when you are programming in ASP unless you yourself include them in your code. Table 20.20 shows some common numeric constants and the values you must supply.

TABLE 20.20 CDONTS NUMERIC CONSTANTS

Name	Value
CdoAttachments	18
CdoBodyFormatHTML	0
CdoBodyFormatText	1
CdoDefaultFolderInbox	1
CdoDefaultFolderOutbox	2
CdoEmbeddedMessage	4

continues

TABLE 20.20 CONTINUED

Name	Value
CdoEncodingBase64	1
CdoEncodingUUencode	0
CdoFileData	1
CdoFolder	2
CdoHigh	2
CdoLow	0
CdoMailFormatMime	0
CdoMailFormatText	1
CdoMessages	16
CdoMime	0
CdoMsg	3
CdoNormal	1
CdoRecipient	4
CdoRecipients	17
CdoSession	0
CdoText	1

Creating Web Forms for Email

One common requirement in a Web application is a customer response form. Using the Web browser, the user fills in comments and other information inside the form. In this sample, you create a comments form and a small ASP script. The script forwards the form's contents as an email message to the Customer Relations Department's email alias. The sender needs only a Web browser to send email. He or she doesn't need an email account or email software.

> **NOTE**
>
> This example and all others in this chapter assume that you have already config-ured Internet Information Server's SMTP Service as explained at the beginning of this chapter.

Creating the HTML Form

In your Visual InterDev environment, add an HTML page to your project and name it Comments.htm. Shown in Figure 20.6, this will be the form that collects the information from the user. Listing 20.1 shows the code that creates the form. Notice that you submit the form's contents to a file called process.asp.

LISTING 20.1 A SIMPLE HTML FORM TO SUBMIT COMMENTS TO AN ASP SCRIPT

```
<FORM action="process.asp" method="post"><P>
<INPUT id=comments name=comments style="HEIGHT: 142px; WIDTH: 293px"
    maxLength=1000 value="Your comments here."></P><P><FONT face=Arial>
    <NOBR>Your e-mail address here</FONT>:
<INPUT id=email name=email></NOBR></P>
<INPUT id=submit1 name=submit1 type=submit value=Send>
</FORM>
```

FIGURE 20.6

A sample form for collecting customer comments.

Creating the Active Server Pages Script

Next, you create the ASP page that sends the email and gives the user some feedback. The complete code in process.asp appears in Listing 20.2. Process.asp starts by checking the contents of the form variables that are called *comments* and *email*. If either variable is empty, it means that the person has not completed the form. In that case, the script

20

SENDING EMAIL
WITH CDO

redirects to the form page called *comment.htm*. The next portion of the script uses the Set statement to instantiate the CDONTS.NewMail object, making its properties and methods available for use.

> **TIP**
>
> If you receive an error message
>
> `Server object error 'ASP 0177 : 800401f3' Server.CreateObject Failed,`
>
> check to ensure that Collaboration Data Objects is installed on the Web server.

The remaining code in process.asp demonstrates the efficiency of the NewMail object. Notice that no logon or validation is required. You set the Body property to the value of the form's Comments field, the From property to the value that the person entered as his or her email address, and the To property to the email address of the Customer Relations Department. To help the department identify the source of the email, you can include a brief heading in the Subject property.

When you call the Send method (theMail.Send), the message goes to the SMTP server for delivery, and the page provides confirmation to the sender, shown in Figure 20.7.

LISTING 20.2   THE ASP PAGE PROCESS.ASP USES CDONTS.NEWMAIL TO SEND MAIL

```
<%@ Language=VBScript %>
<%
if Request.Form("comments")="" _
  OR Request.Form("email")="" then
  Response.Redirect "comments.htm"
end if
%>
<HTML>
<HEAD>
<TITLE>We appreciate your comments</TITLE>
</HEAD>
<BODY>
<CENTER>
<P><IMG alt="" border=0
src="comments.gif" align=middle></P>
<P><FONT face=Arial><STRONG>Thank you for your comments.<P>
<%
Set theMail=server.CreateObject("CDONTS.NewMail")
theMail.Body=Request.Form("comments")
theMail.From=Request.Form("email")
```

```
theMail.To="crelations@kjc.com"
theMail.Subject="Web form comment"
theMail.BodyFormat=1
theMail.Send
Set theMail  = Nothing
%>
<P>Your message has been sent to Customer Relations.</P>
</STRONG></FONT></P>
<INPUT type=button value="Home" onclick="location.href='default.htm'">
</BODY>
</HTML>
```

FIGURE 20.7

The HTML page provides feedback after sending the form's contents to the SMTP Server.

Viewing Email from an ASP Page

In the default SMTP site setup, all incoming mail ends up in one drop box. Therefore, you can sort and view all email by using an ASP page. For instance, in the preceding example, the mail for the Customer Relations Department can be stored on the mail server. Employees in the department use their Web browsers to check for new mail and read whatever is there. By formatting the email address as a hyperlink, you let workers click the sender's name and launch their email utility to reply to the message. For this example, you will use the CDONTS Session object. Although it requires more code than the NewMail object, Session is far more flexible.

20

SENDING EMAIL WITH CDO

Here's a description of the major features found in Viewcom.asp. The code itself is in Listing 20.3.

1. Instantiate the CDONTS Library's Session object by using `server.CreateObject`.

2. Log on to the SMTP session as `crelations@kjc.com`, using `myobjSession.LogonSMTP`.

3. Set the Folder object as the Inbox.

4. Set the Messages collection as the messages in the Folder object.

5. Display the number of messages for the logged-on user, using `myobjMessages.count`.

6. Loop through each message in the Messages collection, using `for i = 1 to myobjMessages.count`.

7. Display the sender's name, using `myobjMessages.item(i).sender`, and format it as a hyperlink.

8. Display the subject of the message by using `myobjMessages.item(i).subject`.

9. Get the AddressEntry collection for this message object by using `myobjAddrEntry = myobjMessages.item(i).Sender`.

10. Display the address of the sender by using `myobjAddrEntry.Address`.

11. Display the body of the message by using `myobjMessages.item(i).text`.

12. Display other details about the message, such as the time received, time sent, importance, and size.

13. Get the Recipients collection for the message by using `set rcpient = myobjMessages.item(i).recipients`.

14. Loop through and display each recipient in the collection, using `for each person in rcpient`.

15. After all loops are complete, log out and release the objects.

The code in Listing 20.3 produces a page such as the one in Figure 20.8.

LISTING 20.3   THE FILE VIEWCOM.ASP ENABLES THE BROWSER TO VIEW EMAIL MESSAGES

```
<%@ Language=VBScript %>
<HTML>
<HEAD>
<META NAME="GENERATOR" Content="Microsoft Visual Studio 6.0">
</HEAD>
<BODY bgcolor=white>
<center>
<p><img border="0" src="comments.gif" align="middle"
  WIDTH="306" HEIGHT="50"></p>
```

```
<p>
<%
Set myobjSession = server.CreateObject("CDONTS.Session")
myobjSession.LogonSMTP "Customer Relations",
➥"crelations@kjc.com"
set myobjFolder= myobjSession.inbox
set myobjMessages = myobjFolder.messages
response.write "There are " & myobjMessages.count & " messages.<br>"
%>
<table border="1" cellpadding=2  cellspacing=0
bordercolor=#cccccc bgcolor=white border=1  rules=ALL>
<tr><td BGCOLOR=000099 HEIGHT=6 COLSPAN=9>
<IMG border=0 SRC="1pixel.gif" WIDTH=1 HEIGHT=2></td></tr>
  <tr>
    <th bgcolor="#c3c299">Sender</th>
    <th bgcolor="#c3c299">Subj.</th>
    <th bgcolor="#c3c299">Addr.</th>
    <th bgcolor="#c3c299">Text</th>
    <th bgcolor="#c3c299">Recvd</th>
    <th bgcolor="#c3c299">Sent</th>
    <th bgcolor="#c3c299">Imp.</th>
    <th bgcolor="#c3c299">Size</th>
    <th bgcolor="#c3c299">Recipnts</th>
  </tr>
<%
for i = 1 to myobjMessages.count
response.write "<tr>"
response.write "<td><a href=mailto:" &
➥ myobjMessages.item(i).sender & ">" &
➥ myobjMessages.item(i).sender & "</td>"
response.write "<td>" & myobjMessages.item(i).subject & "</td>"
Set myobjAddrEntry = myobjMessages.item(i).Sender
response.write "<td>" & myobjAddrEntry.Address & "</td>"
response.write "<td>" & myobjMessages.item(i).text & "</td>"
response.write "<td>" & myobjMessages.item(i).timereceived & "</td>"
response.write "<td>" & myobjMessages.item(i).timesent & "</td>"
response.write "<td>" & myobjMessages.item(i).importance & "</td>"
response.write "<td>" & myobjMessages.item(i).size & "</td>"
set rcpient = myobjMessages.item(i).recipients
response.write "<td>"
for each person in rcpient
response.write person & "<br>"
next
response.write "</td></tr>"
next
myobjSession.Logoff
set myobjSession=Nothing
%>
</table><P>
```

20

SENDING EMAIL
WITH CDO

continues

LISTING 20.3   CONTINUED

```
</center>
</BODY>
</HTML>
```

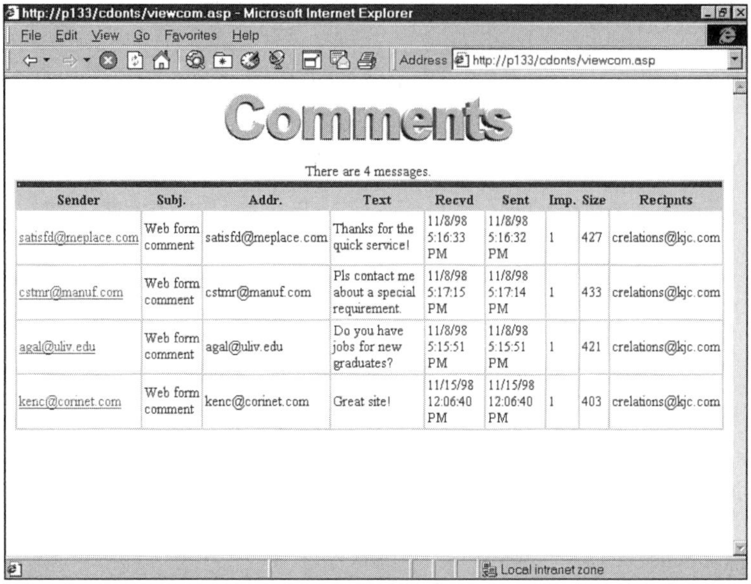

FIGURE 20.8

A browser view of the messages to crelations@kjc.com.

TIP

Before writing a lot of code to send email across the Internet via ASP, check with your Internet service provider (ISP) as to what email handler he or she uses and whether you actually have access to CDONTS. Some ISPs use third-party email utilities. Just because an ISP supports ASP, you can't assume that the ISP makes CDONTS available to customers. However, check whether you can use the FrontPage Extensions to send email.

Sending Mail from a Web Application with CDONTS and ASP

Another use for CDONTS is the creation of email, based on records in a database. Although spam has given this abuse of bulk email a bad name, targeted email has many legitimate uses. For instance, consider the case of a computer club that wants to send meeting reminders to members via email. Because the membership list changes constantly, it is more efficient to use a database-driven mailer. In addition, the club can attach the meeting's agenda as a Word document.

Listing 20.4 demonstrates how a very small ASP script hooked to a database can send thousands of messages in short order.

CAUTION

If you are using a compiled program that sends a large number of messages with CDONTS and uses multiple threads, you might get a sharing violation in Windows NT. Some messages might be lost and never sent, because one thread incorrectly uses the same message file identifier used by another thread. The workaround is to make sure that only one message file is created at a time. For more information or updates, check Microsoft's Knowledge Base, article Q181697.

The script starts by connecting to an Access database and retrieving a recordset that contains the records of all members who are listed as Active=true. Then, it starts a loop that will take it from the first record in the recordset to the last. As it moves on to the CDONTS activity, the script sets the various properties that you expect in an email message, such as the sender, message body, and the email address of the recipient. Notice that the script retrieves the recipient's address (the To property) from the `rsmail("emailaddr")` field. To attach the agenda, the script passes the path and filename as a parameter with the AttachFile method. It calls the Send method to hand the message over to the SMTP Service. Before looping back for the next address, the script provides some onscreen feedback to reassure the operator that it is working. Figure 20.9 shows the Web page after bulkmail.asp has completed its task.

LISTING 20.4   BULKMAIL.ASP USES ADDRESSES FROM A DATABASE TO SEND REMINDERS

```
<html>
<head>
<title>Bulk Mail</title>
</head>
<body bgColor=white text=black>
<p align="center"><img SRC="compuclub.gif"
WIDTH="397" HEIGHT="141"></p>
<h2 align="left">Processing mail list at
<%=time%>
 ....</h2>
```

20

SENDING EMAIL
WITH CDO

continues

LISTING 20.4   CONTINUED

```
<%
Session("DataConn_ConnectionString") =
➥"DBQ=c:\Inetpub\wwwroot\cdonts\ccmemlst.mdb;
➥DefaultDir=c:\Inetpub\wwwroot\cdonts;Driver=
➥{Microsoft Access Driver (*.mdb)};DriverId=25;FIL=
➥MS Access;ImplicitCommitSync=Yes;MaxBufferSize=512;
➥MaxScanRows=8;PageTimeout=5;SafeTransactions=0;
➥Threads=3;UID=admin;UserCommitSync=Yes;"
Session("DataConn_ConnectionTimeout") = 15
Session("DataConn_CommandTimeout") = 30
Session("DataConn_RuntimeUserName") = "admin"
Session("DataConn_RuntimePassword") = ""

Set DataConn = Server.CreateObject("ADODB.Connection")
DataConn.ConnectionTimeout = Session("DataConn_ConnectionTimeout")
DataConn.CommandTimeout = Session("DataConn_CommandTimeout")
DataConn.Open Session("DataConn_ConnectionString"),
➥Session("DataConn_RuntimeUserName"),
➥Session("DataConn_RuntimePassword")
Set cmdTemp = Server.CreateObject("ADODB.Command")
Set rsmail = Server.CreateObject("ADODB.Recordset")
theSQL = "SELECT members.FirstName, members.LastName,
➥members.Emailaddr "
theSQL= theSQL & "FROM Members "
theSQL= theSQL & "WHERE [Active]=True ORDER BY 'Emailaddr' "
cmdTemp.CommandText=theSQL
cmdTemp.CommandType = 1
Set cmdTemp.ActiveConnection = DataConn
rsmail.Open cmdTemp, , 1, 3
If rsmail.BOF and rsmail.EOF Then
   Response.Write "<BR><h2 align='left'>Sorry,
   ➥there has been a database error.</h2>"
Else
   rsmail.MoveLast
   rsmail.MoveFirst
End If
Do While Not rsmail.EOF
   Set theMail = CreateObject("CDONTS.NewMail")
   theMail.From = "remind@compuclub.ca"
   theMail.To = rsmail("emailaddr")
   theMail.Subject = "CompuClub Meeting Tues. 7 pm"
   theMail.Body = "Don't forget Tuesday's meeting.
   ➥Agenda attached."
   theMail.AttachFile
   ➥"c:\inetpub\wwwroot\cdonts\agenda.doc","Agenda.doc"
   theMail.Send
   Response.Write rsmail("emailaddr") & "<BR>"
   rsmail.MoveNext
   Set theMail = Nothing
```

```
Loop
rsmail.Close
dataconn.Close
Set rsmail = Nothing
Set dataconn = Nothing
Response.Write "<h2>Done at " & time & "</h2>"
%>
</body>
</html>
```

FIGURE 20.9

The bulk mailer script provides feedback as it sends messages.

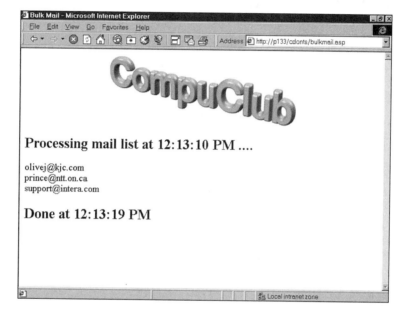

Integrating the SMTP Component with Exchange Server

As mentioned at the beginning of this chapter, CDONTS is designed for simple and rapid email solutions. It is not intended for complicated messaging applications that harness Outlook and Exchange for scheduling, task management, and personal calendars. However, because CDONTS is a subset of the CDO 1.2 Library that ships with Exchange Server, you are well on your way to developing more sophisticated applications. Except for the NewMail object, your CDONTS applications should continue to work after upgrading to Exchange Server 5.5, with a little tweaking. For instance, the CDONTS Session object uses LogonSMTP, whereas CDO for Exchange uses the Logon method.

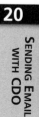

Microsoft Exchange version 5.5 includes the Internet Mail Service (IMS) Setup Wizard that configures CDO for NTS to use the SMTP Service that Exchange provides. If you don't run the IMS Wizard, you will continue using the SMTP Service that was installed by IIS.

A Case Study: The WinInfo Subscription Form

The WinInfo case study creates a small database, ASP, and CDONTS application for a fictional company named *WinInfo*. The company offers a daily summary of news via email. The news is attached as a Word document. In this Web application, subscribers sign up for the email package, receive feedback about the information they have just provided, and get their first copy of the news summary right away. You will find the complete source code and database for WinInfo in this chapter's subdirectory on the accompanying CD-ROM.

Collecting User Information

The script and HTML in WinInfo.asp carry out several functions:

- Collect and validate data from subscribers
- Write the data to the database, wininfo.mdb
- Pass subscriber information to the feedback page, thanks.asp

Data Collection and Validation

The ASP page's first task is to collect subscribers' names and email addresses. This function is handled by a Web form that was created using the design-time controls (DTC) in Visual InterDev 6. To avoid cluttering the database with null entries (such as when users click OK on a blank form), the server-side script checks that the user has entered values into all the fields. This is one of those occasions when it is necessary to convert the design-time control information to text so that you can add code to it. In this case, you add some rudimentary validation and move to a feedback page called thanks.asp. Figure 20.10 shows the form.

In Listing 20.5 (a snippet from wininfo.asp), notice the second If statement. It checks whether the form fields are not empty. If there's no data, the page simply refreshes.

FIGURE 20.10

The WinInfo project gathers information from subscribers.

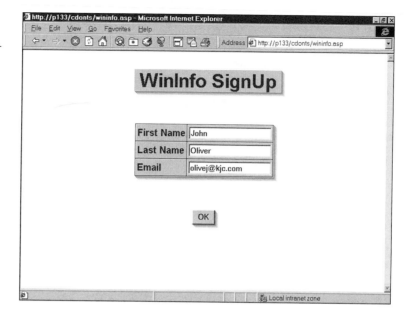

LISTING 20.5 WININFO.ASP INCLUDES FUNCTIONS TO VALIDATE AND FORWARD FORM DATA

```
function _UserModeManager_Save_onclick()
{

    if (thisPage.getState("UserModeManager_formmode") ==
    ➥"Opened")
    if ((textbox_Email.value!="") &&
    ➥(textbox_FirstName.value!="") && (textbox_LastName.value!=""))
     {

    {
       RS_RZ1.updateRecord();
       thisPage.navigateURL('thanks.asp?'+ 'Email=' +
       ➥textbox_Email.value + '&FirstName=' +
       ➥textbox_FirstName.value + '&LastName=' +
       ➥textbox_LastName.value);
       _UserModeManager_SetMode("Browse");

    }
     }
    else _UserModeManager_SetMode(thisPage.getState
    ➥("UserModeManager_formmode"))

}
```

Storing the User Data in Wininfo.mdb

If there is data in the form fields, the code writes the form's information to the WinInfo.mdb database. Listing 20.6 shows a snippet, from wininfo.asp, that prepares the database. By the way, the code in Listing 20.6 was generated by RuleZero, a handy design-time control from Vertigo Software.

Listing 20.6 Data Handler Code from Wininfo.asp

```
<!--#INCLUDE FILE="_ScriptLibrary/Recordset.ASP"-->
<SCRIPT LANGUAGE="JavaScript" RUNAT="server">
function _initRS_RZ1()
{
    var DBConn = Server.CreateObject('ADODB.Connection');
    DBConn.ConnectionTimeout =
    ➥Application('Connection2_ConnectionTimeout');
    DBConn.CommandTimeout =
    ➥Application('Connection2_CommandTimeout');
    DBConn.CursorLocation =
    ➥Application('Connection2_CursorLocation');
    DBConn.Open(Application('Connection2_ConnectionString'),
    ➥Application('Connection2_RuntimeUserName'),
    ➥Application('Connection2_RuntimePassword'));
    var cmdTmp = Server.CreateObject('ADODB.Command');
    var rsTmp = Server.CreateObject('ADODB.Recordset');
    cmdTmp.ActiveConnection = DBConn;
    rsTmp.Source = cmdTmp;
    cmdTmp.CommandType = 2;
    cmdTmp.CommandTimeout = 30;
    cmdTmp.CommandText = '"subscribers"';
    rsTmp.CacheSize = 100;
    rsTmp.CursorType = 3;
    rsTmp.CursorLocation = 3;
    rsTmp.LockType = 3;
    RS_RZ1.setRecordSource(rsTmp);
    RS_RZ1.open();
    if (thisPage.getState('pb_RS_RZ1') != null)
        RS_RZ1.setBookmark(thisPage.getState('pb_RS_RZ1'));
}
function _RS_RZ1_ctor()
{
    CreateRecordset('RS_RZ1', _initRS_RZ1, null);
}
function _RS_RZ1_dtor()
{
    RS_RZ1._preserveState();
    thisPage.setState('pb_RS_RZ1', RS_RZ1.getBookmark());
}
</SCRIPT>
```

Passing Subscriber Information to the Feedback Page

After the database update, the function uses the PageObject's navigateURL method (this-page.navigateURL) to navigate to thanks.asp for feedback. The script concatenates a string onto the end of thanks.asp's URL. The concatenation technique effectively posts the subscriber's first name, last name, and email address to thanks.asp. That completes the work of the first ASP page in your WinInfo application.

Sending Feedback

Figure 20.11 shows the feedback page, thanks.asp. This page accomplishes the following tasks:

- Assures the subscriber that the information has been received
- Double-checks that the email address is in the database
- Emails the first issue of WinInfo to the customer, using CDONTS

Onscreen Feedback

By passing the user's first name, last name, and email address from the form page (win-info.asp) to thanks.asp, you can personalize the feedback. The page uses the Request object to fetch the subscriber's details.

A Double Check of the Database

As a way of confirming the subscriber's record in the database, the script uses the email address that the form passes. The snippet of thanks.asp in Listing 20.7 shows how to incorporate the subscriber's email address into a SQL command. If the address wasn't added correctly by the preceding ASP page, the script lets the customer know. If the email address is found in the database, the script sends the first issue of WinInfo, using CDONTS's NewMail object.

LISTING 20.7 THE SCRIPT CONFIRMS THE EMAIL ADDRESS IN THE DATABASE

```
theSQL = "SELECT subscribers.Email "
theSQL= theSQL & "FROM subscribers "
theSQL= theSQL & "WHERE " & "Email='" & Request("Email") & "'"
cmdTmp.CommandText=theSQL
```

FIGURE 20.11

WinInfo's feed-back page sends the first news summary issue.

Using CDONTS to Mail the First Issue

Listing 20.8 shows the portion of the script that sends the email and attachment. As you see, it retrieves the email address from the database rather than from the preceding form. To include the date as part of the title and body text, you use the VBScript date function.

LISTING 20.8   WININFO USES CDONTS TO SEND THE DOCUMENT AS AN ATTACHMENT

```
Set theMail = CreateObject("CDONTS.NewMail")
theMail.From = "wininfo@wininfo.ca"
theMail.To = rsmail("Email")
theMail.Subject = "Attached is your WinInfo for " & date
theMail.Body = "Here's your WinInfo for " & date & "."
theMail.AttachFile
➥c:\inetpub\wwwroot\cdonts\wininfo.doc","WinInfo.doc"
theMail.Send
Set theMail = Nothing
```

The WinInfo project is far from being a complete solution. You would want another form on which users could remove themselves from the subscription list. A useful feature would be to send an email message to which the subscriber replies and confirms that he or she did, in fact, ask for the daily WinInfo messages. For a robust Web application on a busy site, you should look at SQL Server instead of the Access database shown here.

Summary

In this chapter, you've seen how to install and configure the Simple Mail Transfer Protocol (SMTP) service on Windows NT and integrate SMTP with Collaboration Data Objects for NT Server (CDONTS) and Internet Information Server (IIS). As part of a Web application on IIS, you can create Web pages and HTML forms that send customer comments to you by email. The user does not need an email account or even email software to send email directly from an HTML form; a browser is sufficient.

With Active Server Pages (ASP) code, you can display email messages in a Web page. You can create a database-driven application that automatically sends bulk email or subscription service messages through the SMTP Service. Because CDONTS is a subset of the messaging object offered by Microsoft Exchange Server, the code and the descriptions you've seen here will be useful if you need to go on to creating richer messaging applications for Microsoft Exchange and Outlook clients with MAPI.

Programming
Index Server

by Steven Banick

IN THIS CHAPTER

Searching Static Content on a Web Site

Locating information in a mammoth Web site can be a fate worse than death. Too many bloated Web sites exist on the Internet (and in many intranets) that provide visitors with no successful means of locating information. You know that the piece of information you want is buried deep in the Web site, but how do you find it? The traditional solution for searching sites with a wide array of *static* (that is, unchanging) content is to implement a search engine.

Search engines are common enough. Undoubtedly, everyone who uses a Web browser on the Internet has, at least at one time, used a search engine. Although the Internet search engines provide a facility for locating sites that hold content, a local search engine is a tool for locating that very content within a single site (typically). Regardless of how efficient or effective your Web site's navigational system is, some users will want to search for information and immediately jump to it. Enter Microsoft Index Server.

Introducing Microsoft Index Server

A variety of search engine options are available to Web developers and site administrators. Microsoft Index Server is but one in a teeming horde of products competing for organizations' knowledge management dollar. The key advantage to Index Server is its cost: It is (essentially) free. As part of the Windows NT Option Pack, Index Server has become an integral part of the Internet Information Server (IIS) suite. In fact, Index Server and the technology behind it form the foundation for the more comprehensive Microsoft Site Server suite (more on that later in this chapter), in addition to the search facilities integrated into Windows 2000.

Index Server 2.0, included with the NT Option Pack, has several significant advantages over other search options on the market:

- Tight integration with IIS
- Active Scripting (for ASP) support
- Comprehensive content filters for many document types (including Microsoft Office)
- Simplified administration through the Microsoft Management Console (MMC) and HTML Administrator
- Speed (Index Server performs very well with large content)

> **NOTE**
>
> This chapter assumes that you have previously installed the Index Server components as part of the Windows NT Option Pack installation process. If you haven't, please do so before proceeding any further in this chapter.

Starting Out with Index Server and Administration

Index Server is an intangible addition to your server. You won't see much of it or interact directly with its components all that often. Instead, you will rely on the administrative tools Microsoft has provided. The two key means of administering an Index Server installation are the Microsoft Management Console (MMC), shown in Figure 21.1, and the Index Server Manager (HTML version), shown in Figure 21.2.

FIGURE 21.1

You can add the Index Server snap-in to an existing MMC console to centralize your server management.

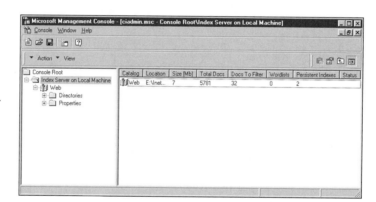

When you are working with either administration tool, the key concepts to understand are *catalogs* and *directories*. Catalogs can be analogized as a collection of information. This collection of information represents a unified "lump" of data that can be searched and indexed. Catalogs are composed of directories, also known as *virtual roots*, that contain the actual content for indexing. Both the MMC and HTML administration tools enable you to work with catalogs and directories, but only the MMC enables you to create new catalogs and add new directories. Figure 21.3 illustrates the concepts of catalogs and directories within Index Server.

FIGURE 21.2

If you prefer to manage your Index Server from a remote workstation that does not use the MMC, you can use the HTML administration tool.

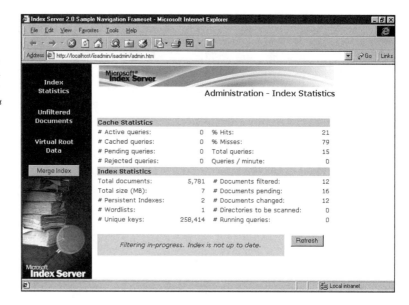

FIGURE 21.3

Your Web site may contain many catalogs, which in turn, may contain many directories of information for indexing.

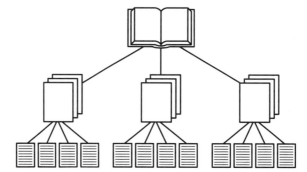

Creating an Index Catalog

The basic requirement for use of Index Server is to have a populated catalog. Catalogs in themselves are similar to a shell container; they act as the referential object used throughout Index Server to access the documents within the catalog. Typically, you will create a catalog related to the content you are indexing. For example, a Knowledge Base catalog may contain information that composes a help desk's knowledge or solution base articles. Another example would be an ACD-Statistics catalog, which would be used to index and search statistical information relevant to the same help desk's automatic call distribution system.

Index Server's flexibility in creating multiple catalogs gives you a considerable advantage over traditional top-down searching. You can create catalogs that not only contain the kind of information you want to search, but also establish relevance between pieces of information. You might very well have the same content indexed in several catalogs, because of its relationship with other content within your site. Your Web site can define a particular catalog to search, giving you impressive flexibility in controlling how your content is organized and accessed. Figure 21.4 illustrates this concept.

FIGURE 21.4

Your content may be included in more than one catalog, enabling you to establish the relationship among pieces of information.

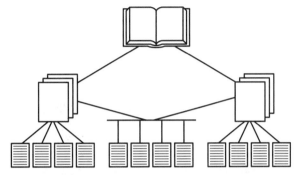

To begin with Index Server, you must create a catalog. Index Server does include a default catalog when it is installed, but you will ignore that one and create your own by following these steps:

1. Begin by opening the MMC version of the Index Server Manager from the Start menu. By default, this is located in Start, Program Files, Windows NT Option Pack, Microsoft Index Server, and Index Server Manager.

2. The Index Server Manager, shown in Figure 21.5, lists each catalog hierarchically below the Index Server folder. Right-click the Index Server folder and choose New, Catalog from the context menu.

FIGURE 21.5

You can use the MMC version of the Index Server Manager to connect to other servers running Index Server.

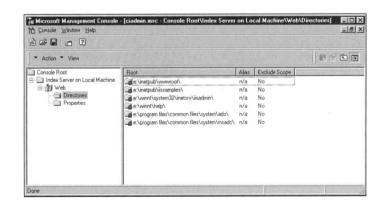

3. The Add Catalog dialog box, shown in Figure 21.6, appears. Enter a name for the new catalog into the Name text box. For this example, enter `Documents`.

FIGURE 21.6

Your catalog is referenced by its name and must be stored in a unique location.

4. In the Location text box, enter the physical directory path to store your index files. The index file must be in its own unique subdirectory. You can use the Browse button to locate a directory. In this example, you will create a new subdirectory off the default location. Enter `C:\InetPub\Index`.

5. Click the OK button to commit your changes and add the catalog to the Index Server. Your new catalog appears in the hierarchical list in the Index Server Manager, shown in Figure 21.7.

FIGURE 21.7

Each catalog appears below the Index Server folder, distinctly identifying it as a unique and separate item in the hierarchy.

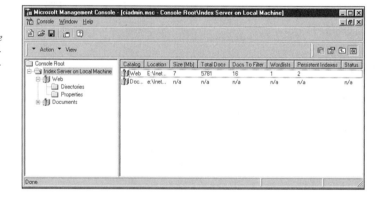

When you examine the hierarchical tree below your new catalog, you will notice two subfolders: Directories and Properties. In the next step, you will create a searchable directory and view the changes made to the Properties folder.

Populating Catalogs with Directories

With the catalog added to Index Server, the next step is to populate that catalog through directories. Directories within Index Server refer to the physical directory locations, on your server or your network, that store content files. In using directories, you are creating sets of searchable data within Index Server. The contents of your searchable directory then contribute to the catalog's master index. One significant advantage to Index

Server's directory approach is how it removes you from physical directory topology restrictions. You can index directories of information on disparate file systems and servers without moving all content files to a centralized location. To the catalog, the content appears to be contained within one contiguous file location, but the files themselves can remain in the separate locations.

> **TIP**
>
> An important lesson to learn is that Index Server does not modify your content files. Index Server acts as a spider and crawls through your catalogs and catalog directories to scan each file, creating a master index. The contents of your files are untouched. Be that as it may, you should ensure that the Index Server has sufficient security access to scan your files.

To begin populating your catalog, you must add one or more directories. For this example, you will be adding two: one directory that contains Web content (HTML pages) and another that contains Microsoft Office files. Follow these steps to create the directories.

> **NOTE**
>
> For this example, you will require two separate directories on your server (or network). One directory should contain only Web-related content, such as HTML pages, and the other directory should contain Microsoft Office files. Your Microsoft Office files may be Microsoft Word documents or Microsoft Excel spreadsheets. The content of these files is largely irrelevant, but try to choose content that will be useful for your Web site.

1. Locate your new catalog folder in the Index Server Manager's hierarchical list. Right-click the folder and choose New, Directory from the context menu.

2. The Add Directory dialog box, shown in Figure 21.8, appears. In the Path text box, enter the physical directory path to your Web-related files. You may choose to use the Browse button to locate the directory.

3. Often you will want to hide the physical path for a file and replace it with an alias. The Alias (UNC) text box is used to return a UNC (*\\servername\directory*) alias to clients executing a query on this directory. If you want an alias, enter it into this text box. The alias is not required for this example.

FIGURE 21.8

The Add Directory dialog box is used to include or exclude directories from the index.

4. If your directory is referencing a mapped drive or UNC share name, enter the account information required for Index Server to access the directory. You must provide a username and a password.

5. Make sure that the Include radio button on the Type panel is selected.

TIP

You can use the Exclude directory Type to define a directory that is not indexed. For example, if you had a directory named C:\Finance that you wanted indexed, but the C:\Finance\Payroll directory contained information not meant for public eyes, you would use the Exclude type to remove the subdirectory from indexing.

---

6. Click the OK button to commit your changes and dismiss the dialog box.

7. Again, right-click your catalog's name in the hierarchical tree and choose New, Directory from the context menu.

8. In the Add Directory dialog box, enter the path to the directory that contains your Microsoft Office files. Again, you may choose to use the Browse button to locate the directory.

9. Optionally, provide the alias (UNC) for the directory and the account information, if it is required.

10. Ensure that the Include radio button is selected within the Type panel.

11. Click the OK button to add your second directory and dismiss the dialog box.

12. Click the Directories folder below your catalog. Your two directories have been added to the catalog, as shown in Figure 21.9.

FIGURE 21.9

The Index Server Manager identifies the physical path to your catalog directory, as well as its alias, and whether it has been excluded from the search.

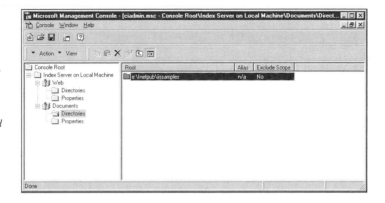

> **NOTE**
>
> Index Server refers to directories as *nonvirtual*. Virtual directories from your Web site can also be indexed and included for searching. All directories (virtual or otherwise) included in a catalog for searching are referred to as within the *scope* of the search.

Examining Catalog Properties

As Index Server progressively works through your catalogs, it gleans a pool of properties from the documents it interacts with. These properties are based on the type of files that Index Server makes contact with, such as Web pages, Word documents, and even Adobe Acrobat files. These properties can be used within your index to create more comprehensive searches and meaningful results. You should understand that you do not manually add properties, but rather you work from the properties that are defined based on your files. You can view the properties for your catalog by selecting the Properties folder below your catalog in the Index Server Manager's hierarchical tree, shown in Figure 21.10.

Index Server enables you to cache these properties (colloquially known as *caching properties*) to speed up the retrieval of frequently retrieved values, such as a file's path or an abstract summarizing its contents. This caching reduces the overall time taken for Index Server to retrieve values for key properties.

FIGURE 21.10

The catalog properties are defined through Index Server's contact with your files.

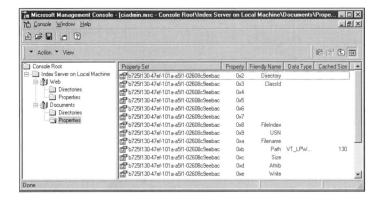

> **NOTE**
>
> Remember, caching properties speeds up access to property *values*, not necessarily searching the index itself. Caching also has no direct effect on the time Index Server takes to index the catalog.

To cache a property, follow these steps:

1. Click the Properties folder for your catalog, if you have not already done so.

2. Locate the property set you want to cache from the list. For example, choose DocCreatedTm to cache the value for the document creation date and time.

3. Right-click the property set (in this case, DocCreatedTm) and choose Properties from the context menu. This opens the Properties dialog box, shown in Figure 21.11.

FIGURE 21.11

Each Property dialog box refers to a property set that can be cached to speed value retrieval.

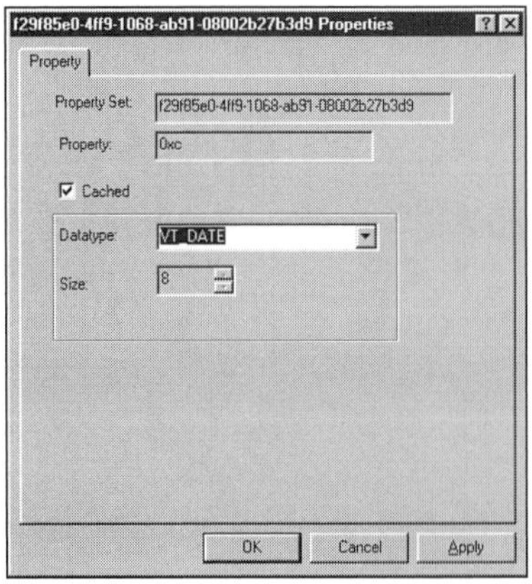

4. Click the Cached check box to cache this property. The Datatype drop-down list becomes selectable.

5. Choose the data type for your property set. The default is VT_LPWSTR. For this example, choose VT_DATE because you are caching a time and date value.

6. Click the OK button to dismiss the dialog box. The Pending Change dialog box appears to inform you that your change to the property cache will not take place until the Commit command has taken place. Figure 21.12 shows this dialog.

FIGURE 21.12

Before your change is made, you are informed of a pending change.

7. Click the OK button to dismiss the dialog box and return to the Index Server Manager window.

8. Right-click the Properties folder for your catalog and choose Commit Changes from the context menu. This forces the Commit Changes to Property Cache? dialog box to appear, shown in Figure 21.13.

FIGURE 21.13

Committing changes forces the index properties to be modified.

9. Click the Yes button to commit your changes. After a few moments, the dialog box will disappear, and Index Server will begin to cache your property set.

Alternatively, you may choose to remove a property from caching. For example, you might find that the VT_DATE property is infrequently used by your Web site. To remove the property from cache, follow these steps:

1. Right-click your property set in the property list. For example, right-click the DocCreatedTm item.

2. Choose Properties from the context menu to open the Properties dialog box.

3. Deselect the Cached check box. This grays out the Datatype drop-down list.

4. Click the OK button. The Pending Change dialog box (refer to Figure 21.13) appears and informs you that the change will not take place until it has been committed.

5. Click the OK button to dismiss the dialog box and return to the Index Server Manager window.

6. Right-click the Properties folder for your catalog and choose Commit changes. The Commit Changes to Property Cache? dialog box appears again.

7. Click the Yes button to commit your changes and remove the property from cache.

CAUTION

Just like indexes for databases, adding too many properties to cache might, in fact, cause more performance delays than you would expect. Cache only the most frequently used properties to improve access time. The more properties cached, the less effective the cache.

Building and Monitoring Indexes

After your catalog has been created with content to index (in the form of directories within the search scope), you must instruct Index Server to begin indexing (or *scanning*) the catalog. Before Index Server can scan a catalog, it must be restarted to recognize the new addition. To stop and restart the Index Server, follow these steps:

1. Right-click the Index Server folder in the Index Server Manager. From the context menu, choose Stop.

2. After a moment, the Index Server services come to a halt. Now you must restart Index Server to recognize your new catalog. Right-click the Index Server folder once again.

3. From the context menu, choose Start. This instructs Index Server to begin indexing all catalogs.

When Index Server begins to index its catalog, you can view its progress, using the Index Server Manager. Click the Index Server folder in the Index Server Manager. The left pane of the window identifies each catalog and its status. This is shown in Figure 21.14.

Index Server periodically reindexes catalogs to update them. You can also force Index Server to reindex a catalog's directory by right-clicking the directory and choosing Rescan from the context menu. Index Server Manager prompts you to confirm that you want to manually force a full rescan of the directory.

FIGURE 21.14

You can use this display to view the total number of documents being indexed, as well as the size of the index itself.

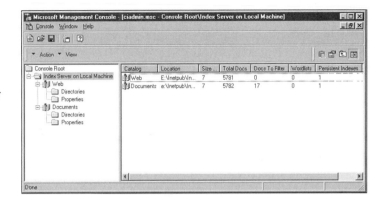

21

PROGRAMMING
INDEX SERVER

CAUTION

Exercise caution when rescanning directories. If your directory contains many files, the rescan could take considerable time and cause undo duress to your server.

Maximizing Performance by Merging Indexes

From time to time, the response time to queries made on your catalogs might begin to slow down. Behind the scenes, Index Server creates multiple indexes for catalogs for searching. By combining these smaller indexes into larger ones, Index Server frees space in both memory and disk space to improve performance. To merge indexes for a catalog, follow these steps:

1. Click the Index Server folder in the Index Server Manager.

2. Right-click your catalog's name in the right pane. In the example, the catalog is named *Documents*.

3. From the context menu, choose Merge. The Merge Catalog? dialog box appears, shown in Figure 21.15.

FIGURE 21.15

This tiny dialog box acts as your last step before merging indexes.

4. Click the Yes button to proceed with the merge. After a few moments, the indexes will be merged, and performance should improve.

Building HTML Search Forms for Index Server

With your back-end indexes and catalogs in place, you are ready to proceed with creating your end user interface to Index Server. Most users are familiar with search forms because they are used today by the large Internet search engines, as shown in Figure 21.16. The premise behind a search form is simple: User enters search criteria into form, server analyzes form contents, server searches site contents, and server delivers search results to user.

FIGURE 21.16

Most users are familiar with search forms from the large search engines, such as this page from Excite.

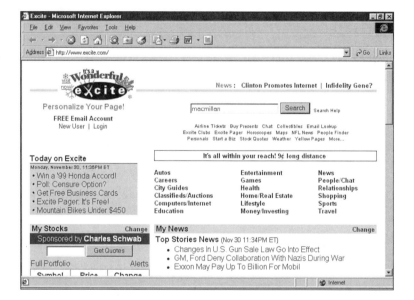

The goal behind your search form is threefold:

- Provide a means for users to enter search criteria
- Enforce reasonable rules or restrictions on the search
- Set the expectations of users for the results of their search

A search form should be regarded as more than a simple Fill In the Blanks and Click Search screen. You should design your search forms to inform your users and encourage quality criteria for searches. For example, all too often search forms make references to *Enter keywords for search.* A more reasonable and effective tactic might be to rephrase the form to read *Provide the name or names of the products you would like information on.* Although the two sentences can be argued on semantics alone, the discernable difference between them comes down to the form asking the user for exactly what is needed.

Conceptual arguments aside, the methods used for putting an Index Server search form in place are very easy to grasp. Your interface to Index Server is broken down into two components:

- The search form itself, used by visitors to provide search criteria
- The results page, displaying the results of the visitor's query to the Index Server

Behind the scenes, these two components are represented by three files:

- The HTM search form
- The IDQ file used to control the search
- The HTX file used to display the results of the search

> **NOTE**
>
> Later in this chapter, I will discuss using Active Server Pages (ASP) and Index Server.

Creating a Basic HTM Search Form

At its most basic, the search form is a Web page (HTM or ASP) that is used as the interface for visitors making a search query. The page itself is composed of a form that establishes the search criteria from user input and hands the information to the intermediary IDQ control file. For this chapter, you will create a very simple search form to access the catalog created earlier. You may choose to customize the appearance of the search form however you want and to implement it within your sites. To begin, follow these steps:

1. Open Visual InterDev, if you have not already done so. Connect to your Web server and an existing Web project. You may choose to create a new project, if it better suits your needs.

2. With a Web project open, begin by adding a new page to your project. From the menu bar, choose Project, Add Web Item, HTML Page. This opens the Add Item dialog box shown in Figure 21.17.

FIGURE 21.17

The Add Item dialog box should be familiar to most Visual InterDev users.

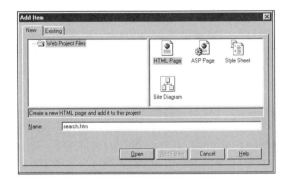

3. From the document types, choose HTML Page.

4. In the Name text box, enter a name for your search page. In this example, you will use the very generic name of search.htm.

5. Click the Open button to add the new page to your project. Your new page should open in the Visual InterDev editor.

6. Switch to Source view in the editor and select the page's contents.

7. Replace the contents of the page with the code in Listing 21.1.

8. Save the changes to your page by choosing File, Save search.htm.

LISTING 21.1   THE SEARCH.HTM BASIC SEARCH FORM

```
<HTML>
<HEAD>
<META NAME="GENERATOR" Content="Microsoft Visual Studio 6.0">
<TITLE>Index Server Search</TITLE>
</HEAD>
<BODY BGCOLOR="White">
<FONT FACE="Arial" SIZE="+3">Index Server Search</FONT>
<HR WIDTH="80%" SIZE="1" ALIGN="LEFT" NOSHADE>
<P ALIGN="LEFT">
    <FONT FACE="Arial">
        This page will search the <I>Documents</I> catalog based
on what information you enter in this form. Please enter search
criteria specific to what information you need.
    </FONT>
</P>
<CENTER>
    <FORM ACTION="search.idq" METHOD="GET" id=form1 name=form1>
    <TABLE BORDER="0">
    <TR>
        <TD ALIGN="CENTER" COLSPAN="2">
            <FONT FACE="Arial" SIZE="+1">
```

```
                    <B>Search Criteria</B>
            </FONT>
        </TD>
    </TR>
    <TR>
        <TD ALIGN="CENTER" COLSPAN="2">
            <INPUT TYPE="TEXT" NAME="CiRestriction" SIZE="30"
            ➥MAXLENGTH="100" VALUE="">
        </TD>
    </TR>
    <TR>
        <TD ALIGN="CENTER">
            <INPUT TYPE="SUBMIT" VALUE="Execute Query" id=SUBMIT1
            ➥name=SUBMIT1>
        </TD>
        <TD ALIGN="CENTER">
        <INPUT TYPE="RESET" VALUE="Clear Query" id=RESET1
        ➥ name=RESET1>
        </TD>
    </TR>
    </TABLE>
    </FORM>
</CENTER>
<HR WIDTH="80%" SIZE="1" ALIGN="LEFT" NOSHADE>
<FONT FACE="Arial" SIZE="-1">.HTM/.IDQ/.HTX Query Example</FONT>
</BODY>
</HTML>
```

When you preview your page, it should resemble the one in Figure 21.18.

FIGURE 21.18

*This very basic
search form can
be expanded to
create a more
complete interface
to Index Server.*

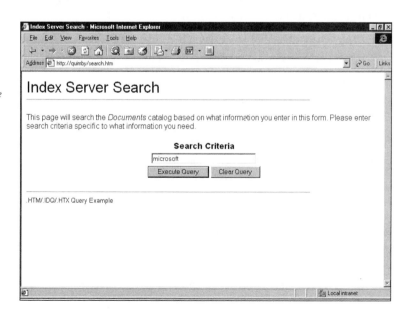

There are two key lines in this listing. The following provides the instructions for the form:

```
<FORM ACTION="search.idq" METHOD="GET" id=form1 name=form1>
```

This form will submit its information using a standard HTTP GET to the middle-tier search.idq file (which you will create in just a moment).

The following describes the text box in which users will input their search criteria:

```
<INPUT TYPE="TEXT" NAME="CiRestriction" SIZE="30"
➡ MAXLENGTH="100" VALUE="">
```

Of note is the NAME assigned to the text box, CiRestriction. This variable is passed to the Index Server as the search criteria. When the user clicks the Execute Query button, the search criteria are passed to the IDQ file and on to the Index Server.

Controlling the Search with an IDQ File

The IDQ (*Internet Data Query*) file is used to define the parameters for your search. Your parameters may include the scope of your search, restrictions on the results, the number of results to return, and the template (HTX file) to use for displaying the results. IDQ files are very straightforward and easy to read because they do not require any markup or code to write. The IDQ file is a plain text file located on your Web server, typically in the same directory as your search form.

For this example, you will create a very simple IDQ file, named search.idq, to control the search. You can create search.idq by following these steps:

1. With Visual InterDev still open, choose Project, Add Web Item, HTML Page from the menu bar. This opens the Add Item dialog box.

2. From the available file types, choose HTML Page.

3. In the Name text box, enter the name for the IDQ file. In this case, enter search.idq (note the lack of the .htm suffix).

4. Click the Open button to create the file and add it to your Web project.

5. When the search.idq file is opened in the Visual InterDev editor, replace the contents of the file with the code in Listing 21.2.

6. Save your changes by choosing File, Save search.idq.

LISTING 21.2 THE SEARCH.IDQ FILE USED TO CONTROL THE SEARCH

```
[Query]
CiCatalog=e:\InetPub\Index\Documents
CiColumns=filename,size,rank,characterization,vpath,DocTitle,write
```

```
CiRestriction=%CiRestriction%
CiMaxRecordsInResultSet=300
CiMaxRecordsPerPage=10
CiScope=/
CiFlags=DEEP
CiTemplate=/search.htx
CiSort=rank[d]
CiForceUseCi=true
```

There are two lines that you should change to suit your own server. Line 2 points to the physical path of your catalog's indexes. When you first created your catalog, you specified a directory for your index to reside in. Replace the CiCatalog value in line 2 with the path to the Documents catalog index on your system. On the line containing CiTemplate, replace the CiTemplate value with the relative path to your HTX template, which you will create in the next step.

Creating a Basic HTX Results Page

The last step of your search interface is the results page. When Index Server completes its query, it returns its results through the HTX template page. This template page formats the query results for your users to view. Your results page can contain as little or as much information as you need. To create your HTX file, named search.htx, follow these steps:

1. With Visual InterDev still open, choose Project, Add Web Item, HTML Page from the menu bar. This opens the Add Item dialog box.

2. From the available file types, choose HTML Page.

3. In the Name text box, enter the name for the HTX file. In this case, enter search.htx (note the lack of the .htm suffix).

4. Click the Open button to create the file and add it to your Web project.

5. When the search.htx file is opened in the Visual InterDev editor, replace the contents of the file with the code in Listing 21.3.

6. Save your changes by choosing File, Save search.htx.

LISTING 21.3 THE SEARCH.HTX FILE USED TO FORMAT THE SEARCH RESULTS

```html
<HTML>
<HEAD>
    <META NAME="GENERATOR" CONTENT="Microsoft Visual Studio 6.0">
    <TITLE>Index Server Search Results</TITLE>
</HEAD>
<BODY BGCOLOR="White">
```

continues

LISTING 21.3 CONTINUED

```html
<FONT FACE="Arial" SIZE="+3">Index Server Search Results</FONT>
<HR WIDTH="80%" SIZE="1" ALIGN="LEFT" NOSHADE>
<P ALIGN="LEFT">
<FONT FACE="Arial">
    <%if CiMatchedRecordCount eq 0%>
    No documents matched the query &quot;
    ➥<%EscapeHTMLCiRestriction%>&quot;.
    <%else%>
    Documents <%CiFirstRecordNumber%> to <%CiLastRecordNumber%> of
    <%if CiMatchedRecordCount eq CiMaxRecordsInResultSet%> the
    ➥first
    <%CiMatchedRecordCount%> matching the query
    &quot;<%CiRestriction%>&quot;.
    <%endif%>
    <%endif%>
</FONT>
</P>
<CENTER>
    <TABLE BORDER="0">
    <TR>
    <TD>
    <TABLE WIDTH="80%">
    <%if CiContainsFirstRecord eq 0%>
    <TD ALIGN="LEFT">
    <FORM ACTION="query.idq" METHOD="GET">
    <INPUT TYPE="HIDDEN" NAME="CiBookMark" VALUE="<%CiBookMark%>">
    <INPUT TYPE="HIDDEN" NAME="CiBookmarkSkipCount" VALUE="-
    ➥<%EscapeRAW CiMaxRecordsPerPage%>">
    <INPUT TYPE="HIDDEN" NAME="CiMaxRecordsInResultSet" VALUE="
    ➥<%EscapeRAW CiMaxRecordsInResultSet%>">
    <INPUT TYPE="HIDDEN" NAME="CiRestriction" VALUE="
    ➥<%CiRestriction%>">
    <INPUT TYPE="HIDDEN" NAME="CiMaxRecordsPerPage" VALUE="
    ➥<%EscapeRAW CiMaxRecordsPerPage%>">
    <INPUT TYPE="HIDDEN" NAME="CiScope" VALUE="<%CiScope%>">
    <INPUT TYPE="HIDDEN" NAME="TemplateName" VALUE="
    ➥<%TemplateName%>">
    <INPUT TYPE="HIDDEN" NAME="CiSort" VALUE="<%CiSort%>">
    <INPUT TYPE="HIDDEN" NAME="HTMLQueryForm" VALUE="
    ➥<%HTMLQueryForm%>">
    <INPUT TYPE="SUBMIT" VALUE="Previous <%CiMaxRecordsPerPage%>
    ➥documents">
    </FORM>
</TD>
<%endif%>
<%if CiContainsLastRecord eq 0%>
<TD ALIGN="RIGHT">
<FORM ACTION="query.idq" METHOD="GET">
<INPUT TYPE="HIDDEN" NAME="CiBookMark" VALUE="<%CiBookMark%>">
```

```
<INPUT TYPE="HIDDEN" NAME="CiBookmarkSkipCount" VALUE="
➥<%EscapeRAWCiMaxRecordsPerPage%>">
<INPUT TYPE="HIDDEN" NAME="CiMaxRecordsInResultSet" VALUE="
➥<%EscapeRAWCiMaxRecordsInResultSet%>">
<INPUT TYPE="HIDDEN" NAME="CiRestriction" VALUE="
➥<%CiRestriction%>">
<INPUT TYPE="HIDDEN" NAME="CiMaxRecordsPerPage" VALUE="
➥<%EscapeRAWCiMaxRecordsPerPage%>">
<INPUT TYPE="HIDDEN" NAME="CiScope" VALUE="<%CiScope%>">
<INPUT TYPE="HIDDEN" NAME="TemplateName" VALUE="<%TemplateName%>">
<INPUT TYPE="HIDDEN" NAME="CiSort" VALUE="<%CiSort%>">
<INPUT TYPE="HIDDEN" NAME="HTMLQueryForm" VALUE="
➥<%HTMLQueryForm%>">
<INPUT TYPE="SUBMIT" VALUE="Next <%CiRecordsNextPage%> documents">
</FORM>
</TD>
<%endif%>
</TABLE>
<HR WIDTH="80%" SIZE="1" ALIGN="LEFT" NOSHADE>
<%begindetail%>
<TABLE BORDER="0">
<TR CLASS="RecordTitle">
<TD ALIGN="right" VALIGN="top" CLASS="RecordTitle" STYLE="
➥background-color:white;">
<%CiCurrentRecordNumber%>.
</TD>
<TD><B CLASS="RecordTitle">
<%if DocTitle isempty%>
<A HREF="<%EscapeURL vpath%>" class="RecordTitle"><%filename%></A>
<%else%>
<A HREF="<%EscapeURL vpath%>" class="RecordTitle"><%DocTitle%></A>
<%endif%>
</B></TD>
</TR>
<TR>
<TD></TD>
<TD>
<B><I>Abstract:  </I></B><%characterization%>
</TD>
</TR>
<TR>
<TD></TD>
<TD>
<I CLASS="RecordStats"><A HREF="<%EscapeURL vpath%>" class="
➥RecordStats" style="color:blue;">http://<%server_name%>
➥<%vpath%></A>
<BR><%if size eq ""%>(size and time unknown)<%else%>size <%size%>
➥ bytes - <%write%> GMT<%endif%>
</I>
```

continues

LISTING 21.3   CONTINUED

```
</TD>
</TR>
</TABLE>
<BR>
<%enddetail%>
</DL>
<P>
<%if CiMatchedRecordCount ne 0%>
<%endif%>
</TD>
</TABLE>
</CENTER>
<HR WIDTH="80%" SIZE="1" ALIGN="LEFT" NOSHADE>
<FONT FACE="Arial" SIZE="-1"><A HREF="<%HTMLQueryForm%>">New
➥query</A></FONT>
</BODY>
</HTML>
```

Listing 21.3, a hefty one indeed, establishes a formatted template used to display the search results. The document properties are inserted into the formatting to create a page of information and hyperlinks for users to interact with. The appearance of the results is entirely at your mercy. The core of this page lies in between the line starting with <%begindetail%> and the line <%enddetail%>. These lines specify the formatting used for each individual result, or *record*, in the search. For each result returned on the page, this code is repeated.

> **TIP**
>
> You can specify the number of results returned per page in the IDQ file.

Based on the number of results, the template inserts navigational buttons. If more results are available after the current page, a Next button is added. If results are available before the current page, a Previous button is added. This simple navigational scheme enables users to move through their search results. A sample result using the search.htx template is shown in Figure 21.19.

FIGURE 21.19

This basic results page displays the title of a document, a brief abstract, and a hyperlink to the file, as well as the file information.

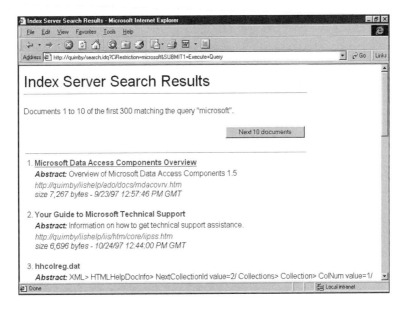

Programming Index Server with ASP

Working with Index Server and HTM/IDQ/HTX files is simple enough, but it isn't ideal. The original method for implementing Index Server relied exclusively on the combination of HTM/IDQ/HTX files. With the advent of Active Server Pages (ASP), the traditional method doesn't seem so appealing. Active Server Pages are likely used throughout your Web application, so it stands to reason that ASP would be the best method for you to implement Index Server. Implementing Index Server through ASP enables you to take advantage of the flexibility and power of ActiveX scripting. You can use ASP to leverage various scripting languages, such as VBScript or Jscript/ECMAScript, rather than rely on a different set of code.

At the heart of ASP access to Index Server are two objects:

- The Query object
- The Utility object

The Query Object

The Query object is at the heart of Index Server, acting as your window to catalogs and indexes. The Query object, just like other ASP usable objects, provides you with different methods and properties. These methods and properties are your means of interacting with the Index Server components. Each property and method for the Query object is detailed in Table 21.1 and Table 21.2, respectively.

TABLE 21.1 THE QUERY OBJECT PROPERTIES

Property	Syntax	Description
AllowEnumeration	TRUE | FALSE	When set to TRUE, enables queries to use enumeration to resolve the result set. Otherwise, queries are forced to use indexes only for resolution. The default is FALSE.
Catalog	*indexname*	Specifies the catalog name on a local server. If no name is supplied, the default catalog is used.
Columns	*Fname1 [,Fname2]...*	Gives friendly column names separated by commas. This list of columns appears as columns in the result. The column names are not case sensitive and can be enclosed in quotation marks if they contain nonalphanumeric characters.
LocaleID	*number*	Specifies the language code and optional country code used for the query.
MaxRecords	*number*	Limits the number of records a provider returns from a data source. The default setting of zero means that the provider returns all requested records. MaxRecords is a read/write property when the recordset is closed and read-only when it is open.
OptimizeFor	performance | recall	Replaces the IDQ `CiDeferNonIndexedTrimming` parameter. Choosing the performance option forces scope and security trimming to be deferred until after the maximum number of hits are collected. If set to recall, this trimming occurs during the query. The default is recall.

Property	Syntax	Description
Query	*query string*	Determines the documents to be returned in a search. This is referred to as the *query restriction*.
SortBy	*Fname [a	d]...*	Sorts results in ascending order, by default. The [a] and [d] options specify ascending or descending sorting.

TABLE 21.2   THE QUERY OBJECT METHODS

Method	Syntax	Description
CreateRecordSet	*recordset*=CreateRecordSet (*CursorType*)	Executes a query and creates or returns an ADO recordset for navigating through the query results. The *CursorType* is either sequential or nonsequential.
DefineColumn	DefineColumn *strColumnDef*	Defines a friendly name for a column.
QueryToUrl	*strQueryString* = QueryToUrl()	Produces a URL string reflecting the state of the query object.
Reset	Reset	Resets the state of the query object.
SetQueryFromUrl	SetQueryFromUrl (*strQueryString*)	Sets query parameters from a Web a Web client request. The QUERY_STRING variables are listed in Table 21.3.

TABLE 21.3   THE QUERY_STRING VARIABLES USED BY THE QUERY OBJECT

Variable	Description
qu	Full text of the query, associated with the Query property.
so	Sort, associated with the SortBy property.
sd	Sort down (in descending order), associated with the SortBy property.
ct	Catalog, associated with the Catalog property.
mh	Maximum hits, associated with the MaxRecords property.
ae	Allow enumeration, associated with the AllowEnumeration property. If this is set to any value other than zero, enumeration is allowed.
op	Optimize for, associated with the OptimizeFor property. The value can be x for *performance* or r for *recall*.

Before a query can be executed using the Query object (the CreateRecordset method), the properties for the query must be defined. This requires your ASP script to define the search criteria for the query (the Query property) and, optionally, your sorting and catalog specifications.

The Utility Object

The Utility object is used by ASP developers to work with the Query object. As an Automation object, the Utility object simplifies your interaction with Index Server and obscures the more intricate inner workings from your view. The Utility object defines five methods, outlined in Table 21.4.

TABLE 21.4   THE UTILITY OBJECT METHODS

Method	*Syntax*	*Description*
AddScopeToQuery	AddScopeToQuery *QueryObj, Path[, Depth]*	Used to add virtual or physical directories to a search's scope. The *Depth* scope can be *shallow* (only the named directory) or *deep* (the named directory and all its subdirectories).
GetArrayElement	*varResult*=GetArrayElement (*varArray, iElem*)	Accesses a variant array element and returns the *iElem* element of the array.
ISOToLocaleID	*LocaleID*=ISOToLocaleID (*strLanguage*)	Converts an ISO 639 language code into a Win32 locale identifier.
LocaleIDToISO	*strLanguage*=LocaleIDToISO	Converts a Win32 locale identifier to an ISO 639 language code.
TruncateToWhitespace	*Newstring*=TruncateTo WhiteSpace(*String, Length*)	Ends a string at a whitespace character for displaying short forms of long strings.

Creating an ASP Index Server Interface

Much like the previous example for creating an Index Server interface, the ASP interface requires different components. To create an interface for Index Server with ASP scripting, you need two parts:

- The Query using the Query object
- The formatted results

Again, you will create a search form, followed by a results page. For this example, the search form you use will be a slightly modified version of the search.htm file created earlier in this chapter. The search.htm file will then pass on the search criteria to the second page, results.asp, for display. To create the interface, follow these steps:

1. Open your search.htm file in Visual InterDev. If you want to keep your existing form, make a backup copy of it. Your current file will be modified in these steps to work with the ASP Index Server example.

2. You must change two lines in the search.htm file. Locate the line that reads

   ```
   <FORM ACTION="search.idq" METHOD="GET" id=form1 name=form1>
   ```

   Replace the line with the following:

   ```
   <FORM ACTION="results.asp" METHOD="GET" id=form1 name=form1>
   ```

3. Locate the second line, which reads

   ```
   <INPUT TYPE="TEXT" NAME="CiRestriction" SIZE="30" MAXLENGTH="100"
   ➥ VALUE="">
   ```

   Replace the line with the following:

   ```
   <INPUT TYPE="TEXT" NAME="qu" SIZE="30" MAXLENGTH="100" VALUE="">
   ```

4. Save the changes to your form by choosing File, Save search.htm.

5. To create your new results page, choose Project, Add Web Item, Active Server Page from the menu bar. This opens the Add Item dialog box.

6. Make sure that ASP Page is selected from the available file types.

7. In the Name text box, enter the name for your results page. In this example, you will enter `results.asp`.

8. Click the Open button to add your new file and open it in the Visual InterDev editor.

9. Switch to the Source editor, if you are not already there, and replace the contents of the results.asp page with the code in Listing 21.4.

10. Replace the directory reference with the physical directory path to the Documents catalog you created earlier in this chapter.

11. Save your changes by choosing File, Save results.asp from the menu bar.

LISTING 21.4 THE RESULTS.ASP RESULTS PAGE

```
<%@ Language=VBScript %>
<HTML>
<HEAD>
<META NAME="GENERATOR" Content="Microsoft Visual Studio 6.0">
```

continues

LISTING 21.4   CONTINUED

```
<TITLE>Index Server Search Results</TITLE>
</HEAD>
<BODY BGCOLOR="White">
<FONT FACE="Arial" SIZE="+3">Index Server Search Results</FONT>
<HR WIDTH="80%" SIZE="1" ALIGN="LEFT" NOSHADE>
<%
'   Create the query and record set objects.
set objQuery = Server.CreateObject("IXSSO.Query")
if IsObject(objQuery) = FALSE then
    Response.Write("The IXS SSO has not been installed correctly.
    ➥Please reinstall the Index Server components.")
    else
    objQuery.SetQueryFromURL(Request.QueryString)
    objQuery.SortBy = "rank[d]"
    objQuery.Catalog = "e:\InetPub\Index\Documents"
    objQuery.Columns = "DocTitle, vpath, filename, size, write,
    ➥characterization, rank"
    objQuery.MaxRecords = 300
    set objQueryRS=objQuery.CreateRecordSet("sequential")
end if
%>
<TABLE CELLPADDING=5 BORDER=0>
<TR>
  <TD ALIGN=CENTER>
    <FONT STYLE="ARIAL" SIZE=1>Record</FONT>
  </TD>
  <TD ALIGN=CENTER >
   <FONT STYLE="ARIAL" SIZE=1>File name</FONT>
  </TD>
  <TD ALIGN=CENTER WIDTH=160 >
   <FONT STYLE="ARIAL"  SIZE=1>Path</FONT>
  </TD>
  <TD ALIGN=CENTER >
   <FONT STYLE="ARIAL" SIZE=1>Size</FONT>
  </TD>
  <TD ALIGN=CENTER >
   <FONT STYLE="ARIAL" SIZE=1>Write</FONT>
  </TD>
</TR>
<%NextRecordNumber = 1%>
<% Do While Not objQueryRS.EOF%>
 <TR>
  <TD ALIGN=CENTER>
   <FONT STYLE="ARIAL" SIZE=1><%=NextRecordNumber %>.</FONT></TD>
  <TD ALIGN=CENTER>
    <FONT STYLE="ARIAL" SIZE=1><%=objQueryRS("FileName")%></FONT>
```

```
➥</TD>
<TD ALIGN=CENTER>
 <FONT STYLE="ARIAL" SIZE=1><A HREF="http::<%=objQueryRS("vpath"
➥)%>"> <%=objQueryRS("vpath")%></A></FONT></TD>
<TD ALIGN=CENTER>
 <FONT STYLE="ARIAL" SIZE=1><%=objQueryRS("Size")%></FONT></TD>
<TD ALIGN=CENTER>
 <FONT STYLE="ARIAL" SIZE=1><%=objQueryRS("Write")%></FONT></TD>
</TR>
<%
 objQueryRS.MoveNext
 NextRecordNumber = NextRecordNumber+1
Loop
%>
</BODY>
</HTML>
```

This page sports the familiar ASP conventions for navigating through ADO data sources. That, perhaps, is one of the most appealing reasons to use Index Server with ASP scripting—your experience with databases and OLEDB/ODBC sources is directly applicable to working with Index Server results. You might notice that in the following lines an action is taken if there is a problem creating the Index Server objects. This enables your scripts to gracefully exit without dying on the spot.

```
if IsObject(objQuery) = FALSE then
    Response.Write("The IXS SSO has not been installed correctly.
    ➥Please reinstall the Index Server components.")
    else
```

Open your modified search.htm page in your Web browser and enter a search criterion into the text box. After submitting your query to the results.asp page, you should see a result similar to Figure 21.20.

The key to the linkage between the search.htm form and the results.asp page is the text box in the search form. As instructed, you renamed the text box to qu. This name is used as an Index Server query variable. When a user clicks the Execute Query button, the URL for the results.asp page resembles this:

```
http://sideshow/search.asp?qu=Microsoft&SUBMIT1=Execute+Query
```

The qu value is read into Index Server, using the SetQueryFromURL method for the Query object. By giving this method the actual query string from the browser (using the Request object), the search criterion is passed to Index Server. The remaining portion of the URL is ignored by Index Server because it is not understood. Simplicity itself!

FIGURE 21.20

This results page is acted on by ASP as if it were stepping through a database recordset.

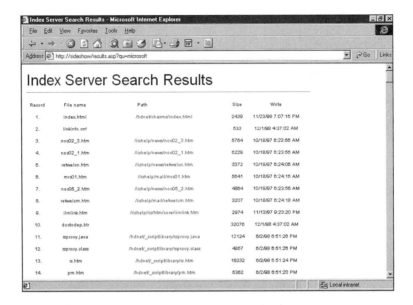

Record	File name	Path	Size	Write
1.	index.html	/hdnet/chasms/index.html	2439	11/23/98 7:07:16 PM
2.	linkinfo.cnf		533	12/1/98 4:37:02 AM
3.	noc02_3.htm	/iishelp/news/noc02_3.htm	5764	10/18/97 6:23:56 AM
4.	noc02_1.htm	/iishelp/news/noc02_1.htm	6229	10/18/97 6:23:56 AM
5.	refwelcn.htm	/iishelp/news/refwelcn.htm	3372	10/18/97 6:24:06 AM
6.	mrc01.htm	/iishelp/mail/mrc01.htm	5641	10/18/97 6:24:16 AM
7.	noc05_2.htm	/iishelp/news/noc05_2.htm	4864	10/18/97 6:23:56 AM
8.	refwelcm.htm	/iishelp/mail/refwelcm.htm	3207	10/18/97 6:24:18 AM
9.	iimlink.htm	/iishelp/iis/htm/core/iimlink.htm	2974	11/13/97 9:23:20 PM
10.	doctodep.btr		32076	12/1/98 4:37:02 AM
11.	rsproxy.java	/hdnet/_scriptlibrary/rsproxy.java	12124	6/2/98 6:51:26 PM
12.	rsproxy.class	/hdnet/_scriptlibrary/rsproxy.class	4857	6/2/98 6:51:26 PM
13.	rs.htm	/hdnet/_scriptlibrary/rs.htm	16332	6/2/98 6:51:24 PM
14.	pm.htm	/hdnet/_scriptlibrary/pm.htm	5362	6/2/98 6:51:20 PM

TIP

You can see the SetQueryFromURL method at work when you visit the Microsoft Support Online Web site at `http://support.microsoft.com`. The Microsoft Knowledge Base takes advantage of Index Server to create a searchable pool of information for visitors. When you establish your search criteria (using a combination of a drop-down list, a text box, and radio buttons), the URL for the Index Server query embeds all the information Index Server requires. Next time you drop by the site, make a search and examine the URL.

Searching Dynamic Web Applications

Index Server is ideally suited to working with static, unchanging content. Conveniently, Web sites are moving away from static, unchanging content. What is a dynamic Web developer to do? Through intelligent design and careful planning, dynamic Web applications can coexist with Index Server. When you are working with dynamic Web applications, there are two kinds of content:

- Content stored in the file system
- Content stored in a database

When you are working with content files that are altered dynamically, you should plan your Index Server implementation carefully. One method of ensuring your content is searchable is to establish a rigid and predictable directory structure. When you are indexing file content that is altered on a regular basis, one of the biggest pains is the dreaded dead link. By establishing a predictable directory structure and combining that with regular rescans of your catalog directories, you can reduce the number of dead links that your search results return.

Here are a few tips for designing searchable content:

- Regularly rescan your directories to ensure your indexes are up to date.

- If you have particular directories that have a high *churn* (deletion) for files, consider creating a separate catalog for the content. This catalog could be updated more regularly than your conventional catalog indexes.

- Keep a predictable directory structure. You can use URL query strings to load dynamic content from its respective directory. The more complicated your directory structure, the more difficult it will be to search.

- Determine what content should be searchable and what content shouldn't. There isn't always a requirement to maintain a searchable index of your entire site. Choose the content that users will *want* to search.

Microsoft's Site Server 3.0 is ideally suited to searching dynamic Web applications. Built on the foundation of Index Server, Site Server sports powerful extensions that can empower searches within your site. Site Server enables you to search SQL data sources, Exchange Servers, and even multiple Web sites. You can then tag content and establish a common dictionary or dialect for your content, making searches more effective. If you plan on working with demanding dynamic Web applications, you should investigate Site Server or a like-minded project.

> **NOTE**
>
> For more information on Site Server, visit `http://www.microsoft.com/siteserver`.

An Index Server Case Study

As a customer support call center, the TELUS PLAnet Help Desk services Internet-related problems via telephone, the World Wide Web, and electronic mail. Most problems that help desks experience are common and have predictable solutions. To improve the call-handling time and the staff's effectiveness, the TELUS PLAnet Help Desk maintains a solutions base. Commonly referred to as a *knowledge base*, this pool of information establishes a consistent and common approach for solving customer problems. The solutions base is composed of many separate text files that are inserted into a Web page, using Server Side Includes. These files are cataloged and indexed by Index Server to create a searchable resource.

As shown in Figure 21.21, the knowledge base provides the Help Desk staff with a means of querying the available information pool with specific criteria. Rather than you relying exclusively on full-text searching, a keyword system was established, using check boxes and drop-down lists. These interface elements create a consistent means of retrieving information and identifying its relationship within the solutions base. Staff can contribute new knowledge entries based on their experiences. Hourly, each knowledge article is added to the index, creating a living and breathing pool of information.

Figure 21.21

Each knowledge article contains only the raw text of the article, as opposed to HTML interface code. The HTML interface is created using a template.

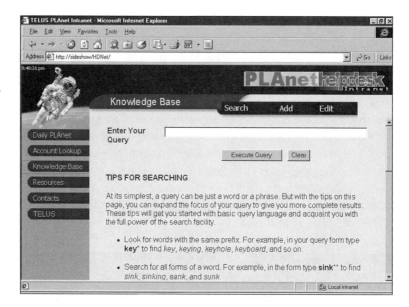

Through the combination of a trouble/customer tracking system and the solutions base, the Help Desk is in a better position to resolve customer problems quickly. Through more effective problem management, costs are lowered and help contribute to a more efficient organization.

Applying Visual InterDev in the Real World

PART

IV

IN THIS PART

CHAPTER 22

Building a User Registration Web Site

by Steven Banick

IN THIS CHAPTER

Introducing the User Registration Web Site

At the heart of most Web applications is some form of user management. Typically, you will want to exercise some kind of restrictions and control over your application, as well as some means of tracking how users interact with it. The user registration Web site in this chapter highlights several techniques that you can adapt for your own site to suit your needs. Most of the techniques shown in this chapter may be used for Internet or intranet applications.

Leveraging the flexibility and features of Visual InterDev, you can easily create a user registration scheme that fulfills your needs. Most user registration systems follow a common thread, obtaining a set of information from potential users before permitting them access to your site contents. Often you might provide a basic guest access to users before registration, but the full features of your site remain unavailable until they consent to registration. Many user registration sites obtain similar information, such as the following:

- A login or username for the site
- The user's first and last name
- A (surface) mailing address
- An electronic mail address
- The user's profession

The information you request from users ultimately depends on your requirements. Most sites use this information as a method for establishing demographics: What kinds of people are visiting your site? What is their background? What are their habits? Many sites use this information to tailor content or advertising to make the user's experience more customized.

TIP

Exercise good judgement when you are deciding what information you want from your users. Many people are reluctant to share information that they do not feel is appropriate (for example, a computer games site asking users how much money they make). Balance the need for information with the comfort and privacy of your users.

Determining a Registration Strategy

Before you proceed with building a user registration system, you should first establish your strategy behind the scenes. Your user registration strategy outlines your requirements, what information you want, how you plan to use the information, and how you will approach users for this information. Your strategy should fit within the scope and direction of your Web site/application and not alienate users before they even get into your site. For example, ask yourself these questions:

- Why am I asking users to register?
- What value will the users get for registering?
- How will I encourage users to register?
- Will there be restrictions or penalties for users who do not register?
- What information do I want from the user?

To address these basic questions, you will work through two sample scenarios.

Scenario 1: The Internet Storefront

ElectroShack is an online reseller of industrial electrical supplies. Its clientele is mainly composed of independent contractors and electrical professionals who demand high-quality electrical supplies at wholesale prices. ElectroShack has elected to adapt its business model to include Internet sales, in addition to its traditional catalog and telephone-based ordering. ElectroShack is working within the confines of its existing distribution model, so the storefront requires from the user considerable information relating to shipping and billing.

ElectroShack services only professionals who have credentials proving their status. The ElectroShack e-commerce Web team chose to restrict all access to its electronic storefront to registered users only. A user who has not registered is only able to view a welcome screen and access the registration process. When registered and validated, the user may proceed to browse the online catalog and make orders.

In the case of ElectroShack's registration process, validation is somewhat unique. Users must provide several pieces of information, including the following:

- The company name
- The billing address
- The shipping address
- The billing method: a purchase order or corporate card
- The user's position
- Contact information

> **Tip**
>
> In determining what data must be tracked, remember that you are defining your database structure. Try to be as thorough as possible when creating the system, but leave yourself room to change and evolve.

This information is provided electronically, but ElectroShack requires that the applicant also fax documentation to prove his or her professional status to the ElectroShack office. The ElectroShack registration system processes the application and provides a reference number to the user, which he or she includes in the fax. On receipt of the fax, the ElectroShack staff validates the applicant's professional status and processes the application. Only after the user's status is confirmed is an account created and open for use.

Scenario 2: The Information Exchange

The Internet Toothpick Collectors Society (ITCS) maintains a comprehensive Web site for members and nonmembers alike. The Web site is dedicated to their common passion, the collection of toothpicks from around the world. As a nonprofit organization, ITCS mainly focuses on information sharing, not money. Members pay a yearly membership fee, which covers the cost of maintaining the Web site and their yearly convention in Danbury, Connecticut. The goal behind the ITCS user registration system is to recruit potential members, as well as to customize content for users, based on their locale.

The ITCS Web site is open for all visitors, inviting them to preview the gallery of the world's toothpicks (including the award-winning 1998 champion: the serrated Royal Whites from Australia) and collector's information. Users who do not register are free to explore, but certain site areas are unavailable to them. Registration is free of charge and is primarily a means of identifying potential new members and increasing membership revenues.

Users who register for the site are provided with access to collectors' conference rooms and auction sites. One important feature for registered users is the customized event listings, based on their geographic location. For this reason, the ITCS registration system requires information specific to their collection interests and their location:

- The user's first and last name
- The user's mailing address
- The user's ITCS membership number, if applicable
- The category the user collects: domestic, rare, or foreign

Based on this information, the ITCS Web site tailors its appearance and approach to the user's information.

> **NOTE**
>
> These sample scenarios and questions do not imply that all user registration strategies are this simple (or complicated, for that matter). Make sure you keep your user registration strategy in line with your overall site strategy.

Mapping Out the Registration Process

With a strategy in place, the next step is to define the user registration process. The process itself outlines the steps for registration application, validation, and postregistration. A common term for the logic behind these steps is *workflow*. With the workflow for your registration process mapped out, you can create the requisite pages and code to form your registration system. Creating a map of the workflow also makes it less likely that you will forget something or leave a noticeable hole in the process.

Continuing with the two examples (the ElectroShack site and the Internet Toothpick Collectors Society), you can explore sample workflow.

Scenario 1: The Internet Storefront

As you read earlier, ElectroShack is looking to maintain a closed site that will allow only registered users into the online catalog and purchasing system. Their needs can be mapped to a workflow model much like the one in Figure 22.1.

FIGURE 22.1

The workflow behind the ElectroShack site prevents unregistered visitors from accessing most features.

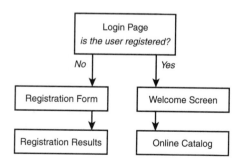

> **TIP**
>
> It is important to realize that there are typically several ways to model work-flow behind a process, whether it is for a registration system or for another aspect of your Web application. A good practice is to create several workflow models and determine which is most in sync with your business or site requirements. Remember that your Web application should not mold your business or your customers, but rather you and your customers should mold the application.

Scenario 2: The Information Exchange

Unlike ElectroShack, the Internet Toothpick Collectors Society maintains an open site that promotes registration but does not enforce it. Its workflow looks considerably different from ElectroShack's, but the intent is the same: to encourage registration in order to use additional services. Figure 22.2 shows the ITCS workflow.

FIGURE 22.2

Registered users benefit from enhanced service in the ITCS Web site, but registration is not a requirement.

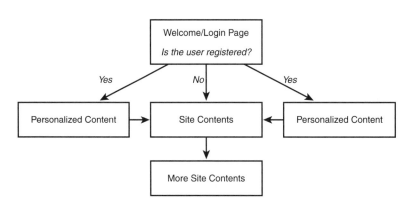

Building the User Database

After you have outlined your workflow and data requirements, you are ready to begin creating your user registration site. For the rest of this chapter, you will be using the ElectroShack example outlined earlier. Behind your registration system, you need a system for storing and retrieving user data. Almost always, this is housed in some sort of database (even a flat text file can be thought of as a database). In this section, you will work from a simple Microsoft Access database, but the instructions here could just as easily be translated to a Microsoft SQL Server or Oracle database.

> **NOTE**
>
> For these instructions, you will require a copy of Microsoft Access to create the tables used in this example. If you have only SQL Server, use the SQL Server Enterprise Manager (or your database's counterpart) to create the required tables.

Your objective in this very simplistic database is to store the user's registration information. This includes the following:

- First name
- Last name
- Company name
- Mailing address
- City
- State/province
- Postal/Zip code
- Telephone number
- Fax number
- Site login
- Site password

To begin, open your copy of Microsoft Access (the instructions here relate to Access 97 but can easily be translated to Access 95) and create a new (blank) database with the name of `RegistrationDB`. For the sake of simplicity, you will be creating one table (tblCustomerInfo) to store the customer information. Your RegistrationDB database will take on the form of Table 22.1.

TABLE 22.1   THE REGISTRATIONDB tblCUSTOMERINFO TABLE

Column Name	Data Type
CustomerID	AutoNumber
FirstName	Text
LastName	Text
CompanyName	Text
Telephone	Text

continues

TABLE 22.1 CONTINUED

Column Name	Data Type
FAX	Text
StreetAddress	Text
City	Text
StateProvince	Text
ZipPostalCode	Text
Username	Text
Password	Text

> **TIP**
>
> For simplicity, you can leave the options for each column as the default. If you are ambitious, however, you might want to restrict the column sizes to realistic values.

For the tblCustomerInfo table, set the CustomerID column as the primary key. Save the changes to your database so that you can use it in the next step.

Creating the Login Page

Open Visual InterDev and create a new project for your registration system. In this example, you are using a clean project with no other contents, but you may choose to work with an existing project. To begin, you're going to create the first screen the user sees: the login page. Your site visitor will enter a username and password into a form in the login page. If the username and password are not recognized, the visitor will automatically be forwarded to the registration page, which you will build in the next step. To create the login page, follow these steps:

1. Right-click your project in the Project Explorer and choose Add, Active Server Page from the context menu. This opens the Add Item dialog box shown in Figure 22.3.

FIGURE 22.3

*The all too famil-
iar Add Item dia-
log box.*

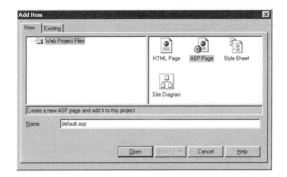

2. In the Name text box, enter the name for your login page. For this example, enter
   `default.asp`.

3. Click the Open button to add the page to your project. In the Visual InterDev editor, the default.asp page opens for you to work with.

4. Replace the contents of the default.asp page with the code in Listing 22.1.

LISTING 22.1 THE DEFAULT.ASP PAGE FOR USER LOGINS

```
<%@ Language=VBScript %>
 <HTML>
<HEAD>
<META NAME="GENERATOR" Content="Microsoft Visual Studio 6.0">
<TITLE>ElectroShack Login</TITLE>
</HEAD>
<BODY>
<H1>Welcome to ElectroShack</H1>
<HR ALIGN="LEFT" WIDTH="80%" SIZE="1" NOSHADE>
<P ALIGN="LEFT">
 Please enter your ElectroShack username and password to continue.
</P>
<CENTER>
<FORM action="login.asp" method=POST id=Register name=Register>
<TABLE>
<TR>
 <TD>     Username</TD><TD><INPUT type="text" id=Username name=
➥Username></TD>
</TR>
<TR>
<TD>      Password</TD><TD><INPUT type="password" id=Password name=
➥Password></TD>
 </TR>
<TR>
<TD COLSPAN="2" ALIGN="CENTER">
<INPUT type="submit" value="Login" id=Submit name=Submit>
</TD>
```

continues

LISTING 22.1   CONTINUED

```
</TR>
</TABLE>
</FORM>
</CENTER>
<P> </P>
<HR ALIGN="LEFT" WIDTH="80%" SIZE="1" NOSHADE>
Registration Site Example
</BODY>
</HTML>
```

5. Save your changes by choosing File, Save default.asp from the menu bar. If you preview your page, you should see a page similar to the one in Figure 22.4.

FIGURE 22.4

The default.asp page is the first screen used for logging in.

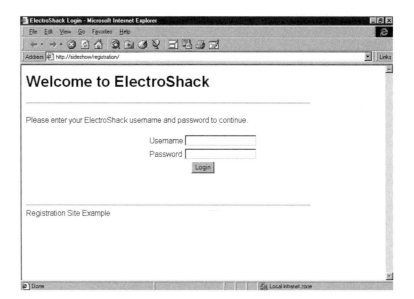

This page is straightforward. It provides two text boxes for the visitor to enter his or her login information and a submission button. In the code, the form action is defined as the login.asp page you will create later in this chapter. Don't try to use this page yet, because next you will jump into creating the registration form and subsequent results page.

Creating the Registration Form

The registration form for the example is split into two pages: The first page, named register.asp, is the form itself. This is the page users will see, asking them to enter their

registration information. The second page, named finish.asp, is the results page inform-
ing the user that the registration has been completed. In actuality, the registration itself
will take place within the finish.asp page after receiving the form information from the
register.asp page. First, you create the register.asp page by following these instructions:

1. Right-click your project in the Project Explorer and choose Add, Active Server
   Page from the context menu. This opens the Add Item dialog box.

2. In the Name text box, enter the name for your registration form. For this example,
   enter register.asp.

3. Click the Open button to add the page to your project. In the Visual InterDev editor, the register.asp page opens for you to work with.

4. Replace the contents of the register.asp page with the code in Listing 22.2.

LISTING 22.2   THE REGISTER.ASP REGISTRATION FORM PAGE

```
<%@ Language=VBScript %>
<HTML>
<HEAD>
<META NAME="GENERATOR" Content="Microsoft Visual Studio 6.0">
<TITLE>ElectroShack Registration Page</TITLE>
</HEAD>
<BODY>
<H1>Welcome to ElectroShack</H1>
<HR ALIGN="LEFT" WIDTH="80%" SIZE="1" NOSHADE>
<P ALIGN="LEFT">
 Please complete the following form to submit your application for
ElectroShack's online catalog. When you are finished, click the
<B>Submit Registration</B> button to proceed.
</P>
<CENTER>
<FORM action="finish.asp" method=POST id=Register name=Register>
<TABLE>
<TR>
<TD>First Name</TD><TD><INPUT type="text" id=FirstName name=
➥FirstName></TD>
</TR>
<TR>
<TD>Last Name</TD><TD><INPUT type="text" id=LastName name=
➥LastName></TD>
</TR>
<TR>
<TD>Company Name</TD><TD><INPUT type="text" id=CompanyName name=
➥CompanyName></TD>
</TR>
<TR>
<TD>Telephone Number</TD><TD><INPUT type="text" id=Telephone name=
➥Telephone></TD>
```

continues

LISTING 22.2   CONTINUED

```
</TR>
<TR>
<TD>FAX Number</TD><TD><INPUT type="text" id=FAX name=FAX></TD>
</TR>
<TR>
<TD>Street Address</TD><TD><INPUT type="text" id=StreetAddress
➥name=StreetAddress></TD>
</TR>
<TR>
<TD>City</TD><TD><INPUT type="text" id=City name=City></TD>
</TR>
<TR>
<TD>State or Province</TD><TD><INPUT type="text" id=StateProvince
➥name=StateProvince></TD>
</TR>
<TR>
<TD>Zip or Postal Code</TD><TD><INPUT type="text" id=ZipPostalCode
➥name=ZipPostalCode></TD>
</TR>
<TR>
<TD>Desired Username</TD><TD><INPUT type="text" id=Username name=
➥Username></TD>
</TR>
<TR>
<TD>Desired Password</TD><TD><INPUT type="password" id=Password
➥name=Password></TD>
</TR>
<TR>
<TD COLSPAN="2" ALIGN="CENTER"><INPUT type="submit" value="Submit
➥Registration" id=Submit name=Submit></TD>
</TR>
</TABLE>
</FORM>
</CENTER>
<P> </P>
<HR ALIGN="LEFT" WIDTH="80%" SIZE="1" NOSHADE>
Registration Site Example
</BODY>
</HTML>
```

5. Save your changes by choosing File, Save register.asp from the menu bar. If you
   preview your page, you should see a page similar to Figure 22.5.

FIGURE 22.5

The register.asp page is a simple form used to enter registration information for processing.

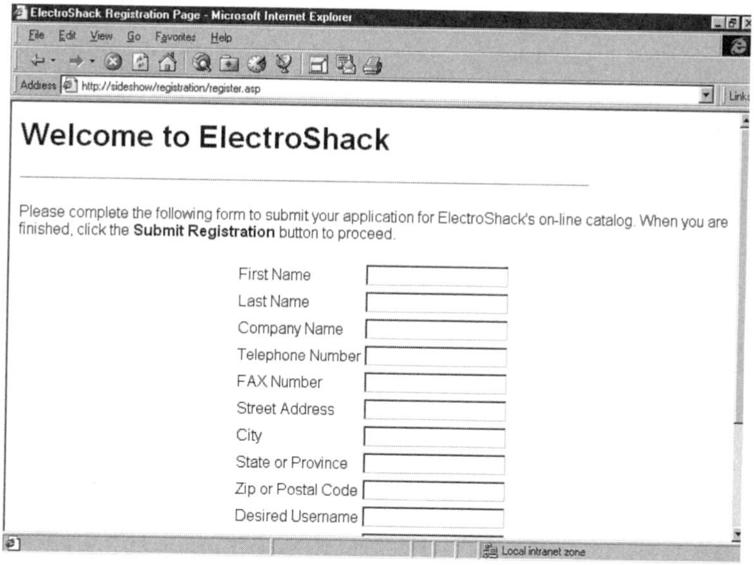

Much like the default.asp form, the form in the register.asp page is straightforward. The user is asked to provide several pieces of information, including a desired username and password. This information is then sent to the finish.asp page. You might notice that I chose to use a password text box, masking the user's requested password with asterisks (*). The password itself is stored correctly in the database, but for security it is not displayed on the screen.

> **CAUTION**
>
> This form does not carry out any input validation. Each field is required for the next page, but the page itself does not ensure that the values are there. Here's a good improvement opportunity: Add input checking and validation to the registration process after you've finished this example.

The next component of the registration form, the finish.asp page, is where the actual registration process takes place. To create this page, follow these steps:

1. Right-click your project in the Project Explorer and choose Add, Active Server Page from the context menu. This opens the Add Item dialog box.

2. In the Name text box, enter the name for your results page. For this example, enter `finish.asp`.

3. Click the Open button to add the page to your project. In the Visual InterDev editor, the finish.asp page opens for you to work with.

4. Replace the contents of the finish.asp page with the code in Listing 22.3.

LISTING 22.3   THE FINISH.ASP RESULTS PAGE

```
<%@ Language=VBScript %>
<HTML>
<HEAD>
<META NAME="GENERATOR" Content="Microsoft Visual Studio 6.0">
<TITLE>ElectroShack Registration Page</TITLE>
</HEAD>
<BODY>
<H1>Thank You for Registering!</H1>
<HR ALIGN="LEFT" WIDTH="80%" SIZE="1" NOSHADE>
<P ALIGN="LEFT">
Your registration information has been received and will be
processed shortly. You will be contacted once your registration has
 been accepted.</P>
<%
strFirstName = Request.Form("FirstName")
strLastName = Request.Form("LastName")
strCompanyName = Request.Form("CompanyName")
strTelephone = Request.Form("Telephone")
strFAX = Request.Form("FAX")
strStreetAddress = Request.Form("StreetAddress")
strCity = Request.Form("City")
strStateProvince = Request.Form("StateProvince")
strZipPostalCode = Request.Form("ZipPostalCode")
strUsername = Request.Form("Username")
strPassword = Request.Form("Password")
curDir = Server.MapPath("\registration\registrationdb.mdb")
Set oConn = Server.CreateObject("ADODB.Connection")
oConn.Open "DBQ="& curDir &";Driver={Microsoft Access Driver
➥(*.mdb)};DriverId=25;FIL=MS Access;"
Set oRs = Server.CreateObject("ADODB.Recordset")
Set oRs.ActiveConnection = oConn
 oRs.Source = "INSERT INTO tblCustomerInfo (FirstName, LastName,
➥CompanyName, Telephone, FAX, StreetAddress, City, StateProvince,
➥ZipPostalCode, Username, Password) VALUES ('" & strFirstName &
➥"', '"& strLastName & "', '" & strCompanyName & "', '" &
➥strTelephone & "', '" & strFAX & "', '" & strStreetAddress &
➥"', '" & strCity & "', '" & strStateProvince & "', '" &
➥strZipPostalCode & "', '" & strUsername & "', '" & strPassword
➥& "')"
oRs.Open
%>
<P> </P>
<HR ALIGN="LEFT" WIDTH="80%" SIZE="1" NOSHADE>
```

```
Registration Site Example
</BODY>
</HTML>
```

5. Save your changes by choosing File, Save finish.asp from the menu bar. If you preview your page, you will see a page similar to the one in Figure 22.6.

FIGURE 22.6

The finish.asp page informs users that their information has been received.

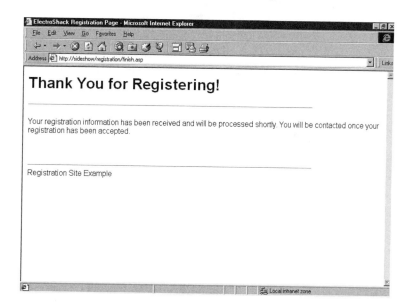

In Listing 22.3, the str lines retrieve the user's registration information from the form submitted from the register.asp page. Each form field is stored in a variable, which, in turn, is stored in the database. The Access database connection is managed quite simply. You use the Server.MapPath function to determine the physical path to the Web root, and then append the path to the registration database. In the example, you have the database stored in the registration directory under WWWRoot. You might have to change this path for your own system.

Notice the lines that create the ADO database connection to the Microsoft Access database and enable you to get down to work. The line starting with oRs.Source, a hefty one indeed, is where the actual database command is specified. You're using a simple INSERT query to pop each of the user's variables into a database record. This is a very simple way to manipulate the database, and it enables you to execute the database command on the next line.

Creating the Welcome Page

The final leg of the registration example is to create the welcome screen that registered users see after they have logged in. This page, in fact, plays double duty. When a user submits his or her login information (username and password) in the default.asp page, the information is submitted to the login.asp page, which you are about to create. The login.asp page (which I will refer to as the *welcome page*) verifies the username and password to determine whether the user should be granted access to the ElectroShack Web site. If the username that the visitor entered is invalid, he or she is redirected to the register.asp page to register for an account. If, on the other hand, the user provides a valid username but an invalid password, he or she is redirected back to the login page.

After a user has correctly provided a valid username and password, the login.asp page displays greeting information to the user and summarizes his or her account information. In reality, you would use this opportunity to present the user with his or her available options and hyperlinks.

To create the login.asp page, follow these instructions:

1. Right-click your project in the Project Explorer and choose Add, Active Server Page from the context menu. This opens the Add Item dialog box.

2. In the Name text box, enter the name for your results page. For this example, enter login.asp.

3. Click the Open button to add the page to your project. In the Visual InterDev editor, the login.asp page opens for you to work with.

4. Replace the contents of the login.asp page with the code in Listing 22.4.

LISTING 22.4   THE LOGIN.ASP WELCOME PAGE

```
<<%@ Language=VBScript %>
<%
 strUsername = Request.Form("Username")
 strPassword = Request.Form("Password")
 curDir = Server.MapPath("\registration\registrationdb.mdb")
Set oConn = Server.CreateObject("ADODB.Connection")
oConn.Open "DBQ="& curDir &";Driver={Microsoft Access Driver(*.mdb)
➥};DriverId=25;FIL=MS Access;"
Set oRs = Server.CreateObject("ADODB.Recordset")
Set oRs.ActiveConnection = oConn
oRs.Source = "SELECT * FROM tblCustomerInfo WHERE tblCustomerInfo.
➥Username = '" & strUsername & "'"
oRs.Open
If oRs.EOF = TRUE Then
Response.Redirect("register.asp")
```

```
End If
If strPassword <> oRS("Password").Value Then
Response.Redirect("default.asp")
End If
 strFirstName = oRS("FirstName").Value
strLastName = oRS("LastName").Value
strCompanyName = oRS("CompanyName").Value
strTelephone = oRS("Telephone").Value
strFAX = oRS("FAX").Value
strStreetAddress = oRS("StreetAddress").Value
strCity = oRS("City").Value
strStateProvince = oRS("StateProvince").Value
strZipPostalCode = oRS("ZipPostalCode").Value
 %>
<HTML>
<HEAD>
<META NAME="GENERATOR" Content="Microsoft Visual Studio 6.0">
<TITLE>ElectroShack Login</TITLE>
</HEAD>
<BODY>
<H1>Welcome to ElectroShack</H1>
<HR ALIGN="LEFT" WIDTH="80%" SIZE="1" NOSHADE>
<P ALIGN="LEFT">
Welcome back <%= strFirstName  %> <%= strLastName %>.
Your account information is:
</P>
<UL>
<LI>Company Name: <%= strCompanyName %>
<LI>Telephone Number: <%= strTelephone %>
<LI>FAX Number: <%= strFAX %>
<LI>Street Address: <%= strStreetAddress %>
<LI>City: <%= strCity %>
<LI>State or Province: <%= strStateProvince %>
<LI>Zip or Postal Code: <%= strZipPostalCode %>
</UL>
<P ALIGN="LEFT">
Thank you for choosing ElectroShack.
51 </P>
<P> </P>
<HR ALIGN="LEFT" WIDTH="80%" SIZE="1" NOSHADE>
Registration Site Example
</BODY>
</HTML>
```

5. Save your changes by choosing File, Save login.asp from the menu bar.

The login.asp page receives the login information from the form on the default.asp page. Before anything else is done, the page retrieves the username and password. The page queries the RegistrationDB database for all information for the username provided in the form in the following line:

```
oRs.Source = "SELECT * FROM tblCustomerInfo WHERE tblCustomerInfo.
➥Username = '" & strUsername & "'"
```

The script checks whether the recordset is at End of File (EOF), meaning no result was found. In the case that no result was found, the user is redirected to the registration form (register.asp) to fill out a registration application.

Next, the script determines whether the password provided by the visitor is valid for the given username. If it does not match, the user is redirected to the login page to try again (without an error message, for simplicity). If the password matches, the script continues and stores all the user's information from the database to variables.

This information is displayed to the user with a simple greeting and a list of values. You might notice that in the code, you use the shorthand <%= %> form to directly display the variable value, rather than use the Response.Write method.

If you run through the full process of registration and then connect as a registered user, you will see a page similar to the one in Figure 22.7.

FIGURE 22.7

The login.asp page acts as your site's welcome page for registered users.

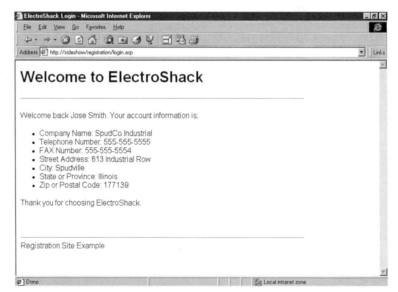

Future Paths

This registration system is incredibly simplistic. It contains no error checking, no real security, and no input validation. It does, however, provide you with a functional framework from which to evolve. Here are some suggestions on improving the registration system outlined in this chapter:

- Add input validation for each form field in the register.asp page. For example, ensure that a telephone or fax number is actually a phone number.

- Enforce constraints on your usernames and passwords. Usernames and passwords should be at least six characters, and passwords should include alphanumeric characters.

- Check for duplicate usernames. Currently, no checking for duplicate usernames exists. The first instance of the username works, but others won't. Add code to ensure that a user is not requesting a username already in use.

- Add record keeping for the last time the user logs in. You can do this by adding a column in the database of the DateTime type and updating its value in the login.asp page whenever a user connects.

- Expire usernames and accounts that have not been used in some time.

- Using CDO, email the user his or her account information after the user completes the registration in the finish.asp page.

These are just a few ideas that you can use to create a flexible and functional registration system for your Web applications.

Summary

The user registration process is typically a cornerstone to your Web application. If your application relies at all on some form of security or integrity control, your user registration process should be well thought out and executed. When developing your registration system, be sure to plan for the future. Leave yourself development room in your architecture to allow for future needs and changes. After all, the last thing you want to do is start recording everyone's favorite compact discs when they all move on to DVDs, right?

Creating an Online Catalog

*by Michael Starkenburg and
Brian Fino*

IN THIS CHAPTER

Introduction—The Monster Modem Company

Although many corporate Web sites are nothing more than simple brochures about the company, more and more people are using the Web as another method of presenting their product information. An online catalog of products is an inexpensive and effective way to make extensive information on an entire product line available to a wide variety of people. A potential customer can get the most up-to-date information on your products any time of the day or night.

Using Visual InterDev, a Web developer can add catalog functionality to an existing site easily and quickly. As you will learn in this chapter, an online catalog is easy to implement and can be easily maintained through a Web interface. The online catalog is also the basis for a later expansion into electronic commerce, as you will see later in this book.

In this chapter, you will create an online catalog for a fictional company called Monster Modem. Monster is in the business of selling modems of all shapes and sizes through a network of stores and catalogs across America.

Monster has had a Web site for several months, but it provides very limited functionality, such as contact information and a company mission statement. Now Monster wants to list its product information and show pictures of its products to potential end users and resellers.

Features of the Monster Catalog

Monster asked for the following functionality in its online catalog:

- A catalog home page—Allowing access to the category navigation feature and the product search feature.
- Navigation by category—Giving the user the ability to look for products, based on two types of categories. Each modem belongs to a form factor category (for example, internal modems versus external modems) and a modem speed category (56.6KB versus ISDN). A user should be able to get a listing of modems that belong to any category combination.
- Product search—Giving the user the ability to find products through a keyword search. The search results should look similar to the category listing pages and let the user choose a modem for display.

- Product detail—Displaying specific information about a modem after the user has selected it from a category list.

- Catalog management—Giving Monster's product managers the ability to update the catalog in real-time, using a simple Web tool. They must add products, delete products, and edit product information.

Setting Up the Environment

Before you can start developing the catalog project, you must make sure that you've properly set up the server environment. You have to define the Web server configuration, the database configuration, and the development environment.

Monster expects several thousand visitors to the catalog every day. Because Monster sells products all over the world, these visitors might come from any country. In addition, Monster is a fast-growing company, so it expects that traffic will triple over the next several months. Its Web server and database have to be available 24 hours a day, but must handle only a moderate load.

Our Web server consists of a Microsoft IIS 4.0 server running on a P2-300 machine with 128MB of RAM. We've installed the server, using all the default settings for simplicity, and added the FrontPage server extensions so that the Visual InterDev development environment can be fully integrated.

One nice feature of Visual InterDev is that it is extremely flexible in database handling. You can work with any ODBC-compliant database, using the same simple toolset. We chose to use Microsoft SQL Server for this project, running on the same machine as the Web server.

Depending on the database you choose, you have to do some prep work before you start building the catalog application. For example, you must do the following to get SQL Server ready:

- Install SQL Server 6.5.
- Create a database device.
- Create a database.
- Set up database users.

> **NOTE**
>
> Be aware that your choice of database will affect your ability to fully use the Visual InterDev tools. For example, if you choose to use an MSAccess database, the Database Diagram tools will not be available to you, and you might have trouble with parameterized queries.

After your Web server and database are configured and tested, you're ready to begin developing the catalog. Going forward, almost every single step can be completed within the impressive toolset of Visual InterDev 6. At this point, we're assuming that you have read most of this book before attempting your first project and are familiar with the basics.

Creating Your Visual InterDev Project

There are a few important points about the way you will build this project. You will see that the examples are pretty plain vanilla in appearance—not because we don't know how to build good-looking Web pages, but rather to keep the focus on using Visual InterDev and the DTCs to create functionality. After going through this exercise, you should be familiar enough with the tools to add the look and feel without confusing the issues.

We also want to say, right up front, that at times just opening the Source window and writing functions yourself in ASP is an easier way to get this functionality. We've gone out of our way here to show that nearly everything can be done through a DTC. This isn't necessarily the way you'd do it in real life. All the same, doing it in these examples is a great learning experience. In the next chapter, on e-commerce, you will see a lot more "real" coding and less use of DTCs.

To get started with the Monster catalog, you have to create the Visual InterDev Project. You will call your project *Monster*, and you will choose not to use any themes or layouts at this time. Start with the following steps:

1. Open Visual InterDev 6.
2. At the New Project dialog, enter the name Monster and choose the New Web Project icon. Select Open. The New Web Project Wizard will launch.

3. Enter the name of the server you've set up for this project. Choose whether to work in Master or Local mode. (for information on Master and Local modes, see Chapter 6, "Team Development." Select Next.

> **NOTE**
>
> If you can, avoid using the name *localhost* for your server, even if you will be working with Visual InterDev on the same machine as the Web server itself. Microsoft's ODBC driver has some known problems with the use of the name *localhost*. In addition, try not to use an IP address to specify the server. If later you have to move the server and the IP address changes, you will have much work to do making sure that all references to the IP change as well.

4. Enter `Monster` as the Web application name. Select Next.

5. Select None for the layout. You can add a layout later if you like. Select Next.

6. Select None for the theme (you can add a theme later). Select Finish.

At this point, Visual InterDev creates your project file and copies the script library into your project directory. If you choose a layout or theme, it will copy the necessary files into your directory as well. Your Project Explorer window will contain the new project, as seen in Figure 23.1.

FIGURE 23.1

The Visual InterDev Project Explorer for the project Monster.

Designing the Database

The most important part of creating a database-driven project is the design of the data schema itself. If you do this right the first time, the rest of the project will be easy.

Mistakes made now will be a lot tougher to fix later. You will have to check every piece of the project to make sure that your changes are reflected in all the right places.

In Visual InterDev, you have to take two main steps to create your data environment. First, you define what database you will be using and set up the connection. Then, you design the database schema and tables you will need. Visual InterDev provides a tool called the Database Designer for this purpose. Before you start, you might want to review Chapter 10, "Working with Databases: Universal Data Access," and Chapter 11, "Using the Visual Database Tools."

> **NOTE**
>
> If you are using Microsoft Access, you won't be able to use the Database Designer tool. Instead of performing the following steps, create the tables using Access. Then you can create an ODBC connection to the Access MDB file on disk. Visual InterDev will be able to see the database and use it as any other data source, but will not be able to modify tables or build relationships.

Setting Up Your Database Connection

Before you can start working with your database, you have to add a data connection to your project. The *data connection* defines the particulars of the database you will be connecting to. Although you can have several data connections in a project, you will be using only one for the catalog. Here are the steps for adding a data connection:

1. Select Project, Add Data Connection from the menu in Visual InterDev.

2. You are asked to choose a data source from your operating system's existing ODBC definitions. If you have already defined the correct database in the ODBC control panel, select it and move on to step 3. If you haven't set up an ODBC definition, do this now. Refer to Chapter 10 for specific instructions.

3. Depending on your database, you might be prompted to log in. After you log in, you can name your connection and click OK. We named our connection dbconn1.

Your new data connection appears in the Project Explorer. Below the Project Explorer, you should now see your database reflected in the Data View window, shown in Figure 23.2. You will be spending a lot of time in this window as you build the data schema.

FIGURE 23.2

The Visual InterDev Data View window for the project Monster.

Creating Your Database Diagram and Tables

Now that you're connected to the database, you're ready to start building the database tables that will be the core of the catalog. Visual InterDev's Database Designer tools make this painless.

You will create one data diagram for your catalog. The diagram will contain three simple, related tables. The main table will be the mm_product table, which contains all the product information you want to make available to the users.

TIP

The categorization scheme you're working with here is almost painfully simple. A category is determined by the contents of two fields within each product. It works great when you have only a few products and even fewer categories, but the real world isn't that simple. For example, almost every catalog application we've seen works better when a single product can belong to more than one category, which you can't do with this categorization scheme.

If you have many products or many categories, you will want to use a different categorization scheme. You still need only three tables, but they work differently. One table contains all the products. A second table contains a category list. The third table is simply two fields (product id and category id), which are related to the other two tables by many-to-many relationships. To put a product *into* a category, you create a row in this table with the product id and the category id. To look up all the products in a category, you search the third table. You can then have a much longer list of categories and can put products in more than one category.

The other two tables, mm_category1 and mm_category2, are simple lookup tables. They define the product categories you will use for navigation and are related to the mm_product table by one-to-many keys. To get started, follow these steps:

1. Select your database name in the Data View. Select Project, Add Database Item, Diagram from the menu bar. This opens the Database Designer with a blank diagram.

2. You will start by creating the mm_product table. To create a table, right-click in the Database Designer window, and select New Table.

3. Enter the table name, in this case, mm_product, and click OK.

> **NOTE**
>
> As you create the mm_product table, you will see a couple fields that have no obvious purpose: the ec_weight and ec_export fields, which are not used in this chapter. They are used in the next chapter as part of the e-commerce solution. If you are not planning on working with the e-commerce project in Chapter 24, "Implementing E-Commerce," these fields can be safely omitted.

4. Enter the field names and properties for the mm_product table. You can find the suggested fields in Figure 23.3.

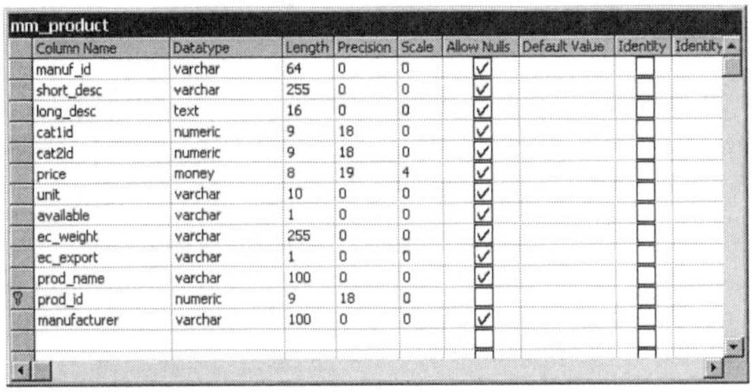

FIGURE 23.3

The Table view for mm_product.

Column Name	Datatype	Length	Precision	Scale	Allow Nulls	Default Value	Identity	Identity
manuf_id	varchar	64	0	0	✓			
short_desc	varchar	255	0	0	✓			
long_desc	text	16	0	0	✓			
cat1id	numeric	9	18	0	✓			
cat2id	numeric	9	18	0	✓			
price	money	8	19	4	✓			
unit	varchar	10	0	0	✓			
available	varchar	1	0	0	✓			
ec_weight	varchar	255	0	0	✓			
ec_export	varchar	1	0	0	✓			
prod_name	varchar	100	0	0	✓			
prod_id	numeric	9	18	0				
manufacturer	varchar	100	0	0	✓			

5. When you complete entering the field information for the mm_product table, you can save the data diagram by clicking the Save button on the toolbar. Name this data diagram catalog. This automatically creates the table in your database.

6. Create the mm_category1 table by repeating steps 3–5, using the information in Figure 23.4.

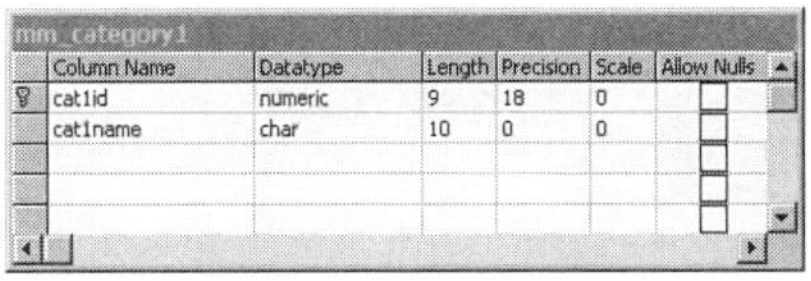

FIGURE 23.4

The Table view for mm_ category2.

7. Create the mm_category2 table by repeating steps 3–5, using the information in Figure 23.5.

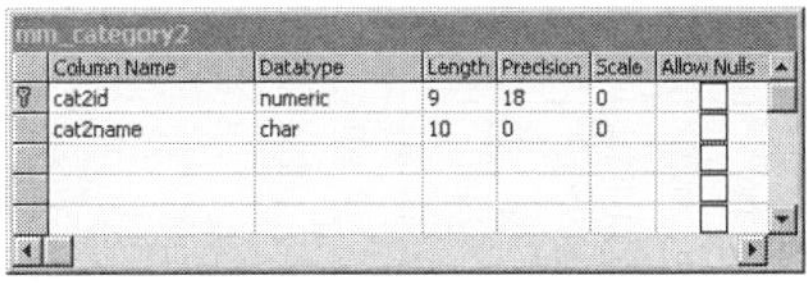

FIGURE 23.5

The Table view for mm_ category2.

Your data diagram should now contain the necessary three tables. All that remains is to create the relationships between the tables, and your database will be ready to go. The Database Designer also enables you to create relationships, as follows:

1. Highlight the cat1id field in the mm_product table. Drag this field over the title bar of the mm_category1 table. This creates a relationship line and allows you to define the relationship.

2. Verify that the relationship is properly represented in the window. Because you named the fields and kept the fields' sizes identical in the two tables, the designer assumed the proper relationship. You don't have to change anything, so click OK.

3. Repeat steps 1 and 2 for the cat2id field and the mm_category2 table.

If you look closely at Figure 23.6, you will see that the relationships are now indicated by gray lines. At the end of the relationship lines are small icons that show the nature of the relationship (that is, one-to-many).

All the work you've just done is easy to review through the Data View window in Figure 23.7. You can access your database diagrams and tables and look at the fields' specifications within this tool. Take a moment now to go through your data environment to check for any errors you might have made thus far. Remember, it is far easier to fix them now than after you've built the whole application!

After you've checked your work, that's it. You have created your data structure and are ready to begin building your site.

23

CREATING AN
ONLINE CATALOG

FIGURE 23.6

The Visual InterDev Database Designer for the project Monster.

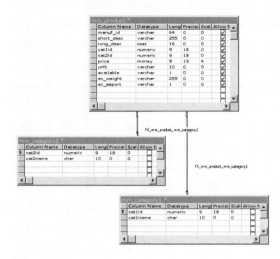

FIGURE 23.7

The completed Data View for the project Monster.

Creating the Site Diagram

Before you begin work on the individual pages of the application, it's helpful to create a site diagram of all the pages and their relationship. Because you've just worked with the Database Designer, you should be ready to use the Site Designer. These are very similar in function and usability.

Because your catalog is completely data driven, you can get away with only a few pages in your site diagram. Your site is so dynamic, in fact, that the site diagram isn't all that useful. You will create one anyway, though, because as the site grows, it will be helpful to have a structure to build around. Also, if you want to add a theme or layout later, the site diagram will enable you to quickly apply it across the entire site.

1. Highlight the project name *Monster* in the Project Explorer. From the menu, select Project, Add Item.

2. At the Add Item dialog, choose Site Diagram, and enter the name `monster` in the Name box. Click Open. This opens the Site Designer.

3. A new site diagram contains a single page called *home*. Change the name of this file to *default* by highlighting the word *home* and typing over it.

4. To add the product_navigation ASP, right-click on the site diagram, and choose Add New ASP. Change the name of this file to `product_navigation`. Drag this box next to the default page to create a link between the two.

5. Add the product_detail ASP. Create a link between this page and the product_navigation page.

6. Add the search_results ASP. Create a link between this page and the default page.

7. Add the product_management ASP. Because this page should not be accessed by users, it can be set off to the side and not linked to any other page.

Your site diagram is now an accurate logical map of the pages you are about to create and should now look like Figure 23.8. When you save the site diagram, it adds these pages to your project. You're now ready to begin working with the actual application pages themselves.

FIGURE 23.8

The Visual InterDev site diagram for the project Monster.

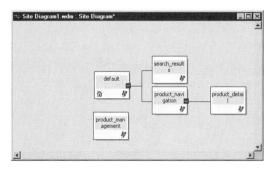

Implementing the Catalog Tools

When you think about an online catalog, you probably think of searching and product display. However, ask someone who's built an e-commerce site or a production product catalog, and he or she will tell you that the most important part of an online catalog is entirely behind the scenes. The product management tools allow a user to quickly add, edit, and delete products in the catalog and can require as much development to make right as the rest of the site combined.

For this project, you're going to combine the functionality of all three tasks into a single ASP. Visual InterDev makes this easy for you. The RecordSet DTC does all the heavy lifting.

The steps to building this ASP include setting up the recordsets for data access and then creating a good entry form for displaying and editing product information. To start work on the product_navigaton ASP, highlight it in the Project Explorer and double-click the file. This opens the editor with that file.

Creating Your RecordSet Design-Time Controls

Your product_management page needs to access the mm_product, mm_category1, and mm_category2 tables. The RecordSet DTC acts as the data source for data-bound controls elsewhere in the page. You have to set up three separate RecordSet DTCs, one for each table.

You will also use a tool called the RecordsetNavBar design-time control. This very useful DTC creates a set of HTML buttons that enable you to step back and forth through rows in a recordset.

To set up a recordset for mm_category1, follow these steps:

1. Put the editor into Design mode by selecting the Design tab at the bottom of the editor window.

2. Find the RecordSet design-time control in the toolbox. If your toolbox is not present, you can activate it by choosing View, Toolbox from the menus. Drag a RecordSet DTC to the top of the editor design window (you might be prompted to log in to your database).

3. Answer Yes when asked to enable the Visual InterDev Scripting Object Model (for more information on the Scripting Object Model, refer to Chapter 3, "Programming the Scripting Object Model").

4. Right-click on the recordset object, and select Properties.

5. On the General tab, the settings should be as follows (see Figure 23.9):
   - Name: Categories
   - Connection: dbconn1
   - Database Object: Tables
   - Object Name: mm_category1

FIGURE 23.9

The Recordset Properties window.

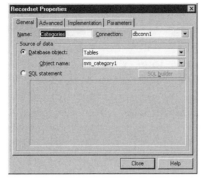

6. On the Advanced tab, change the lock type to 1 — Read Only. Click Close.

To set up a recordset for mm_category2, perform the following steps:

1. Drag a RecordSet DTC to the top of the editor design window.

2. Right-click on the recordset object, and select Properties.

3. On the General tab, the settings should be as follows:

   - Name: Categories2
   - Connection: dbconn1
   - Database Object: Tables
   - Object Name: mm_category2

4. On the Advanced tab, change the lock type to 1 — Read Only. Click Close.

To set up a recordset for mm_product, follow these steps:

1. Drag a RecordSet DTC to the top of the editor design window.

2. Right-click on the recordset object, and select Properties.

3. On the General tab, the settings should be as follows:

   - Name: Products
   - Connection: dbconn1
   - Database Object: Sql Statement
   - Select SQL Statement

4. In the SQL window, enter the following statement:

```
Select * from mm_product order by prod_name;
```

> **NOTE**
>
> You might notice that we used a table object on the category tables and a SQL statement on the product table. We found that when using a table object in the recordset, we couldn't update product information. The SQL statement in the product table's recordset was the workaround we found. We've heard a number of stories like this regarding trouble with the data-bound DTCs. Whenever we run into trouble, we find that it helps to try experimenting with various SQL statements and with converting the DTCs to program text code in the Visual InterDev Source window.

5. On the Advanced tab, *make sure* that the lock type is set to Optimistic. Click Close.

To set up the RecordsetNavBar, here are the steps:

1. Drag the RecordsetNavBar DTC from the toolbox onto the page, below the recordset DTCs themselves.

2. Right-click on the RecordsetNavBar, and set the following properties:
   - Recordset: Products
   - Update on Move: Unchecked
   - Name: RecordsetNavbar1

3. Optionally, you can change the way the RecordsetNavBar appears, with the Format tab. Click OK.

At this point, your page has access to all the data it will need. The next step is to display that data through an entry form.

Setting Up the Data Entry Form

To create the user interface for updating and viewing products, you will use a few useful design-time controls.

The TextBox DTC creates an HTML <INPUT> or <TEXTAREA> tag and allows these tags to be bound to a data source. You will use this to display and edit field data out of the mm_product table. The ListBox DTC can create an HTML list box or drop-down that can be bound to a data source. In your page, you will bind the Listbox Entry to the products table to view and edit the categories; you will populate the list choices by binding to the category table. Finally, the FormManager DTC creates a set of event-driven forms that are bound to a recordset. You will use this to create your browse, edit, and delete functionality.

First, you create a table to hold the entry form, using the Visual InterDev table tool. Choose Table, Insert Table from the menu. Build a table, using the following parameters:

- Width: 600 Pixels
- Border: 1
- Columns: 2
- Rows: 13

Now you have to populate the table. In the left column, type the name of each field in the mm_product table. There's an easy way to see the fields: In the Data View, expand the mm_product object under the Tables section. When a table is expanded, the Data View lists the field names, which you can use as a guide.

> **TIP**
>
> A common mistake of new Visual InterDev users is to use HTML list boxes, drop-downs, and text areas instead of the DTC versions and then do lots of work to handle the data interface. The DTCs will create the necessary HTML for you at runtime and make the data access painless. You'll see!

In the right column of each row, you place the data-bound design-time controls for each field. You start with the category drop-downs, which will use the ListBox DTC. To set up the category fields, perform these steps:

1. Drag a ListBox DTC into the right column of the row labeled Category 1. Right-click the ListBox DTC, and choose Properties.

2. On the General tab, set the following:
   - Name: Cat1
   - Style: DropDown
   - Recordset: Products
   - Field: Cat1id

3. On the Lookup tab, set the following:
   - Row Source: Categories
   - Bound Column: cat1id
   - ListField: cat1name

4. Click Close.

5. Drag a ListBox DTC into the right column of the row labeled Category 2. Right-click the ListBox DTC, and choose Properties.

6. On the General tab, set the following:

   - Name: Cat2
   - Style: DropDown
   - Recordset: Products
   - Field: Cat2id

7. On the Lookup tab, set the following:

   - Row Source: Categories2
   - Bound Column: cat2id
   - ListField: cat2name

8. Click Close.

In the rest of the fields, you have to place and configure textbox DTCs. To do this, follow the next steps once for each field, replacing the appropriate field information where needed:

1. Drag a TextBox DTC into the right column of each remaining row.

2. On each DTC, right-click and choose Properties. The first one is shown in Figure 23.10. Change the following, and then click apply:

   - Name: (Field name)
   - Style: Text Area (for short_desc and long_desc), Textbox (for all others)
   - Recordset: Products
   - Field: (Field name)

FIGURE 23.10

The Textbox Properties window.

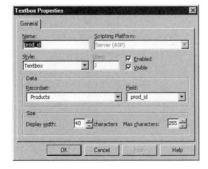

3. Click OK.

TIP

When working on many objects of the same kind, as you are doing with the TextBox DTC, you don't have to click to reopen the Properties window every time you change the object you are working on. You can complete your editing of one textbox, click Apply, and then click on another textbox. The Properties box will be automatically updated. You don't have to click OK to close the window until you are through editing all the objects.

Configuring Data Entry Form Actions

You're almost finished with this page: You have made the data connection with the recordset DTC and created the entry form using the TextBox and ListBox DTCs. Now, you only have to add the form actions. You will implement NEW, DELETE, EDIT, CANCEL, and SAVE form buttons using the FormManager DTC.

The FormManager DTC is the most complicated DTC in the Visual InterDev toolkit, but it is also the coolest. To use the FormManager, you set up any number of date entry modes. In each mode, you can define specific behavior for objects on the page. The FormManager can be confusing because the word *action* is used in about 10 places without the DTC. We'll try to take you through it in a logical manner, but be prepared to play with it a bit before you really understand it.

In the example, you will create a Default browse mode and an edit mode. In each mode, you will specify which buttons are enabled: In the Default mode, you can use the NEW, DELETE, and EDIT buttons and the RecordsetNavBar. In the Edit mode, you will hide the RecordsetNavBar and enable the Save and Cancel buttons. Finally, you have to set up *transitions*, which means defining what actions the page will take when switching between modes.

1. Use the Button DTC to create the NEW, DELETE, EDIT, CANCEL, and SAVE buttons. Drag the DTC onto the page, and change the following properties for each button (we will do the NEW button; you can figure out the other four):
   - Name: action_new
   - Scripting Platform: Inherit from page
   - Caption: New
   - Visible: Checked
2. Drag the FormManager DTC onto the page. Right-click to open Properties.

3. Create the Default mode by typing `Default` in the New Mode box and clicking the button to add it to the Modes List.

4. To get the desired behavior in the Default mode, you have to enter the rows in Table 23.1 in the Actions Performed for Mode.

TABLE 23.1   DEFAULT MODE ACTIONS

Object	Member	Value
action_edit	Disabled	false
action_new	Disabled	false
action_delete	Disabled	false
action_cancel	Disabled	true
action_save	Disabled	true
RecordSetNavBar1	Show	()

5. Create the Edit mode by typing `Edit` in the New Mode box and clicking the button to add it to the Modes List.

6. To get the desired behavior in the Edit mode, you have to enter the rows in Table 23.2 in the Actions Performed for Mode.

TABLE 23.2   EDIT MODE ACTIONS

Object	Member	Value
action_edit	Disabled	true
action_new	disabled	true
action_delete	Disabled	false
action_cancel	Disabled	false
action_save	Disabled	false
RecordSetNavBar1	Hide	()

7. Now that both modes are created, you have to define what actions cause a switch between modes and what happens during the transition. Ask this question: In each mode, what does this button do? If it causes a mode switch, it needs a row in this table. Notice that each button in this example has one transition defined, except DELETE. This is because DELETE is the only button enabled in both modes. Switch to the Action tab, and populate the Form Mode Transitions Table with the rows shown in Table 23.3.

TABLE 23.3   FORM MODE TRANSITIONS TABLE

Current Mode	Object	Event	Next Mode
Default	action_new	onclick	Edit
Default	action_edit	onclick	Edit
Default	action_delete	onclick	Default
Edit	action_delete	onclick	Default
Edit	action_save	onclick	Default
Edit	action_cancel	onclick	Default

8. For each transition, the DTC gives you the opportunity to specify some actions that should occur before the mode changes. For example, when a user clicks NEW, you switch to the Edit mode. However, you have to tell the system to create the blank record and place the cursor in it. To set these values, highlight the row in the Form Mode Transitions Table, and in the table below the row, enter the values from Tables 23.4–23.7. Note that the values for action_delete have to be entered twice, once for each mode. Also, there are no entries for action_edit.

TABLE 23.4   ACTIONS TO BE PERFORMED BEFORE ACTION_NEW

Object	Member	Value
Products	Addrecord	()
Products	Movelast	()

TABLE 23.5   ACTIONS TO BE PERFORMED BEFORE ACTION_CANCEL

Object	Member	Value
Products	CancelUpdate	()

TABLE 23.6   ACTIONS TO BE PERFORMED BEFORE ACTION_SAVE

Object	Member	Value
Products	UpdateRecord	()

23

CREATING AN
ONLINE CATALOG

TABLE 23.7 ACTIONS TO BE PERFORMED BEFORE ACTION_DELETE

Object	Member	Value
Products	Addrecord	()
Products	Movelast	()

9. Click Close and save your ASP.

That's it for the product management ASP. You should now be able to add, edit, and delete products in the mm_product table, using the mm_category tables as lookups for category values. Now, you will move on to the user interface pages. Although there are more of them, they are much simpler (now that you've come this far, the rest should be a breeze).

> **NOTE**
>
> At this point, you should populate your category and product tables with some information. Later, as you implement your user interface, you'll be using RecordSet DTCs that behave strangely when a query returns zero rows.

Implementing the User Interface

The user interface for the catalog breaks down into four dynamic pages: a User home page, the Product Navigation page, the Product Detail page, and the Search Results page. Each by itself is easy to put together, but combined, they make a very usable catalog.

Each page in the user interface will contain a PageObject DTC. The PageObject defines the ASP as an object, with properties and methods that can be referenced from other pages in the application. You use this functionality to help the user navigate and to pass value from one page to the next.

The Product Navigation ASP

The product navigation ASP takes two parameters off the URL, cat1 and cat2, which represent the categories that the user has requested. In the example, the parameters are built into the URL on the preceding page (the User home page) by drop-downs. You could also hardcode the URLs into static HTML and achieve the same effect.

Like the product_management ASP, this page is built on a recordset. Whereas your previous recordsets were bound to tables, however, this recordset will be bound to a query. The query gets the list of products from the product table that match the passed-in category parameters.

After the data is gathered, you use the Grid DTC to display the query results. The Grid DTC makes it easy to control the contents and formatting of the results table. You will create an unbound column in the Grid tool, which will allow users to link from a result to the specific product detail they want to see.

To get started, you will have to create the page and set up the recordset and page object.

1. Open the product_navigation ASP.
2. Drag a recordset DTC from the toolbar into the page.
3. Right-click on the RecordSet, and open Properties. Name the RecordSet `NavigationRS`.
4. In the Source of Data box, choose SQL Statement, and enter the following statement (shown in Figure 23.11):

```
Select * from mm_product where cat1id=? And cat2id=?;
```

23

CREATING AN
ONLINE CATALOG

FIGURE 23.11

The SQL statement entry in the Recordset Properties window.

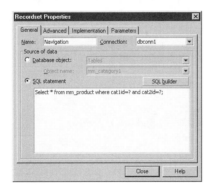

5. Select the Parameters tab. You will see that two parameters exist in the table, one for each question mark in the SQL statement you entered. You have to pass the cat1 and cat2 parameters into these rows. You do that by entering the following into the value fields on the table. In the first row, Param1, enter

```
thisPage.getCat1()
```

In the second row, for Param2, enter

```
thisPage.getCat2()
```

6. Drag a PageObject DTC to the page. Name the PageObject `product_navigation`.

7. Enter a row in the Properties table containing the settings shown in Table 23.8.

Table 23.8   PRODUCT_NAVIGATION PageObject Settings

Name	Lifetime	Client	Server
Cat1	Session	None	R/W
Cat2	Session	None	R/W

Now that you have your data source all set up, you have to display the results set, using the Grid DTC.

All you really want to show about each product is the product name, the manufacturer, and the price. But you want the product name to be a link to the product detail, so you can't just display the field. You will see, as you go through the process, that you do a little extra work to make this happen.

> **CAUTION**
>
> For some reason, you have to click Apply on *each* tab in the Grid DTC, or you will lose your changes. Whatever.

1. Drag the Grid DTC onto the page, below the RecordSet. Right-click the Grid, and open the Properties page.

2. On the General tab, set the following and click Apply:
   - Name: NavigationGrid
   - Style: Basic Navy
   - Width: 600 Pixels
   - Display Header Row: Checked

3. On the Data tab, set the following and click Apply:
   - RecordSet: Navigation
   - Available Fields: Check Manufacturer and Price

4. Click Add Unbound Column. You will see a new column created in the Grid Columns window.

5. In the Edit Columns box, enter the following in the Field/Expression area:
```
="<a href=\'product_detail.asp?prod_id=
"+[prod_id]+"\'title=\'"+[prod_name]+"\'>"+[prod_name]+"</a>"
```

We know, by the way, that this is totally unwieldy. Sorry, but we really wanted to show you how cool the grid can be.

6. In the Heading box, enter Name. Your list of fields should look like Figure 23.12. Click Apply.

FIGURE 23.12

The Grid DTC property window.

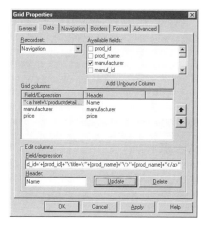

7. Optionally, change the font size in the Format tab. We found the default to be too large, so we chose Arial -3. Click Apply.

You're finished. You should now have a very clean listing of all the products in a given category.

The Product Detail ASP

The product_detail ASP is probably the simplest page in the whole catalog. All the page has to do is grab a single product out of the database and display the attributes. To some extent, the Product Detail page is just a simple display-only version of the product_management page. You will see a lot of similarities in the steps to create the pages.

You will use the Label DTC instead of the TextBox DTC to handle the individual fields. There is no need to set up the forms buttons or FormManager actions, but you will have to write a SQL statement to get the category names out of the related tables. You will also have to handle the prod_id parameter to tell the page which product to show.

1. Select Project, Add Item from the menu, and create an ASP called
   `product_detail`.

2. Drag a RecordSet DTC from the toolbar into the page.

3. Right-click on the RecordSet, and open Properties. Name the RecordSet `product`.

4. Choose SQL Statement, and enter the following in the window. This query will get the product information and the related long category names:

   ```
   SELECT * from mm_product, mm_category1, mm_category2
   WHERE mm_product.cat1id = mm_category1.cat1id
   AND mm_product.cat2id = mm_category2.cat2id
   AND mm_product.prod_id = ?
   ```

5. On the Advanced tab, make sure that the lock type is set to Read Only. Click Close.

6. On the Parameters tab, enter the following for Param1:

   ```
   Request.Querystring("prod_id")
   ```

7. Choose Table, Insert Table from the menu. Build a table, using the following parameters:
   - Width: 600 Pixels
   - Border: 1
   - Columns: 2
   - Rows: 13

8. Drag a PageObject DTC to the page. Name the PageObject `product_detail`. You don't have to set up any other properties for this object because it is only being referenced by the static links in product_navigation and search_results, not by any other objects.

9. In the left column, type the name of each field in the mm_product table.

10. Drag a Label DTC into the right column of each row. Right-click the Label, and choose Properties. For each label, set the Recordset to product and the Field/Expression to the appropriate field.

> **NOTE**
>
> Note that there are two additional fields in the recordset that don't exist in the mm_product table itself. Cat1name and cat2name were created by the SQL statement in the recordset and contain the category description for the product. When you set up the Label DTCs for the two categories, use these fields instead of the cat1id and cat2id fields. This way, the product description will show Internal (instead of 1) for the category, which is much nicer for the user.

The Search Results ASP

The search results ASP takes the name parameters off the URL. This page should seem really familiar because it's almost exactly like the product_navigation page.

Like the product management page, this recordset will be bound to a query. The query gets the list of products from the products table that match the passed-in category parameters. Again, you use the Grid DTC to display the query results. The end result is a page that looks and acts exactly like category navigation, but returns only those products whose name matches the search term.

> **NOTE**
>
> In this example, we've done a simple search, using a SQL statement containing a LIKE clause. This is a very database-intensive operation and shouldn't be used in a production environment. We're using it here to show the relationship between your search and navigation pages. In real life, you can get the same effect from a search by using Index Server functionality. Index Server is much more efficient at this kind of search. See Chapter 21, "Programming Index Server," for more information about using Index Server.

23

CREATING AN
ONLINE CATALOG

To get started, you must create the project and set up the page object and recordset.

1. Open the search_results ASP.
2. Drag a RecordSet DTC from the toolbar into the page.
3. Right-click on the RecordSet, and open Properties. Name the RecordSet Search.
4. Select the Implementation tab and Uncheck Automatically Open the Recordset.
5. Drag a PageObject DTC to the page. Name the PageObject search_result.
6. Enter a row in the Properties table containing the settings in Table 23.9.

TABLE 23.9 SEARCH_RESULTS PAGEOBJECT SETTINGS

Name	Lifetime	Client	Server
search_text	Session	None	R/W

Now you have to set up the SQL query that will be run against the database. Because of the nature of the parameter, you can't do this easily in the recordset. The best way to do this is to insert some simple functions.

1. In the editor, switch to the Source window.

2. Insert the following code immediately after the HTML <BODY> Tag. This defines the close_rs and set_rs functions, which control the querystring within the recordset:

```
<%
'*************************************************************
' Subroutine: close_rs
' Parameters: None
' Purpose: close the existing recordset
'*************************************************************
        sub close_rs()
                Search.close()
        end sub


'*************************************************************
' Subroutine: set_rs
' Parameters: None
' Purpose: set the sqltext of the search recordset
'*************************************************************
        sub set_rs()
                sqlText = "select * from mm_product " &_
                          "where prod_name like '%" &_
                          search_results.getsearch_text() &_
                          "%' order by prod_name"

                Search.setSQLText (SqlText)
                Search.open()
        end sub
'*************************************************************

call set_rs()

%>
```

3. Insert this line at the end of the page, immediately before the HTML </BODY> page. This calls the close_rs function.

```
<% call close_rs() %>
```

Now that you have set up your data source, you have to display the results set, using the Grid DTC. You will be setting this up exactly as you did for product_navigation.

1. Drag the Grid DTC onto the page, below the RecordSet, but above the call to close_rs(). Right-click the Grid, and open the Properties page.

2. On the General tab, set the following and click Apply:
   - Name: NavigationGrid
   - Style: Basic Navy
   - Width: 600 Pixels
   - Display Header Row: Checked

3. On the Data tab, set the following and click Apply:
   - RecordSet: Search
   - Available Fields: Check Manufacturer and Price

4. Click Add Unbound Column. You will see a new column created in the Grid Columns window.

5. In the Edit Columns box, enter the following in the Field/Expression area:
   ```
   ="<a href=\'product_detail.asp?prod_id="+[prod_id]+"\'
   title=\'"+[prod_name]+"\'>"+[prod_name]+"</a>"
   ```

6. In the Heading box, enter Name. Click Update.

7. Optionally, change the font size in the Format tab.

The User Home Page

It might seem strange that you're building the User home page last, but in fact, it's necessary. You need the PageObject DTCs to be configured in the search_results and category_navigation ASPs so that you can link to them from this page. Your sample home page will allow the user to search your product catalog in two ways: Search by Category and Search by Name.

You implement the Search by Category by offering two data-bound drop-downs to users, one for each set of categories. They can choose one value for each category; when they click Submit, they'll be passed to the Category Navigation page. Search by Name is almost exactly the same functionality, implemented on this page with a text box to gather the parameter.

To set up recordsets for mm_category1 and mm_category2, follow these steps:

1. Put the editor into Design mode by selecting the Design tab at the bottom of the editor window.

2. Drag a RecordSet DTC to the top of the editor design window (you might be prompted to log in to your database).

3. Right-click on the RecordSet object, and select Properties.

4. On the General tab, name the RecordSet `Category1`, and choose the object name mm_category1.

5. On the Advanced tab, change the lock type to 1 — Read Only. Click Close.

6. Drag another RecordSet DTC into the window.

7. On the General tab, name the RecordSet `Category2` and choose the object name mm_category2.

8. On the Advanced tab, change the lock type to 1 — Read Only. Click Close.

9. Drag a PageObject DTC to the page. Name the PageObject home. We found that you can't name it `default`, even though the page name is *default*. This page object doesn't require any properties because the page isn't referenced in any other objects.

10. Add two rows in the References table containing the settings shown in Table 23.10.

TABLE 23.10 DEFAULT PAGEOBJECT SETTINGS

Name	Client	Server
search_results	uncheck	check
product_navigation	uncheck	check

Okay, you've set up the data sources. You now have to create the input fields and button for the Search by Category functionality.

1. Drop a ListBox DTC on the page.

2. Open the Properties window, on the General tab:

   - Name: Cat1
   - Style: Dropdown
   - Recordset: Category1
   - Field: Cat1id

The name is very important because it ends up being the parameter name passed to the next page.

3. Switch to the Lookup tab.

   - Rowsource: Category1

   - Bound Column: cat1id

   - List Field: cat1name

4. Drop another ListBox DTC on the page.

5. Open the Properties window, on the General tab:

   - Name: Cat2

   - Style: Dropdown

   - Recordset: Category2

   - Field: Cat2id

6. Switch to the Lookup tab:

   - Rowsource: Category2

   - Bound Column: cat2id

   - List Field: cat2name

7. Drop a button DTC on the page. Name the button `btn_search_cat` and change the caption to Find.

If you view the page in the browser now, you will be able to see the functionality of the drop-downs, although clicking on the button won't yet work.

The last steps are to add the Search by Name functionality and the FormManager to handle the form actions.

1. Drop a TextBox DTC on the page, and name it `search_text`.

2. Drop a second Button DTC on the page, and name it `btn_search_text` modifying the caption to Search.

3. Drag the FormManager DTC onto the page. Right-click to open Properties.

4. You have some experience with FormManager from your work on the product_management ASP. This FormManager needs three modes: Default, Navigate, and Search. Create each mode by typing the name in the New Mode box and clicking the button to add it to the Modes List.

5. To get the desired behavior in each mode, you have to enter the rows in the Actions Performed for Mode table for each mode. There are no actions for the Default mode, but the actions for the Navigate and Search modes can be found in Tables 23.11 and 23.12.

TABLE 23.11   NAVIGATE MODE ACTIONS

Object	Member	Value
thisPage	navigateURL	(product_navigation.asp)

TABLE 23.12   SEARCH MODE ACTIONS

Object	Member	Value
thisPage	navigateURL	(search_results.asp)

6. Switch to the Action tab, and populate the Form Mode Transitions Table with the rows shown in Table 23.13.

TABLE 23.13   FORM MODE TRANSITIONS TABLE

Current Mode	Object	Event	Next Mode
Default	btn_search_cat	onclick	Navigate
Default	btn_search_text	onclick	Search

7. Highlight each row in the Form Mode Transitions Table, and in the table below each row, enter the values shown in Tables 23.14 and 23.15.

TABLE 23.14   ACTIONS TO BE PERFORMED BEFORE TRANSITION TO NAVIGATE

Object	Member	Value
Product_navigation	setCat1	(Cat1.getValue())
Product_navigation	setCat2	(Cat2.getValue())

TABLE 23.15   ACTIONS TO BE PERFORMED BEFORE TRANSITION TO SEARCH

Object	Member	Value
search_results	setsearch_text	(search_text.value)

Summary

In this chapter, you learned how to build all the key pieces of an online catalog. This includes a dynamic home page that allows users to search by category or name, and product management tools that allow product managers to update the product list. You've also built a category navigation page listing the products that belong to a given set of categories, a search results page listing the products that match a specific search term, and finally, a product display page displaying all the attributes of a specific product.

You managed to do this almost exclusively using the Visual InterDev toolkit, including the Database Designer, the Site Designer, and the DTCs.

An online catalog such as this one is also the core of any e-commerce application. In the next chapter, we'll take the functions you've built here and add a shopping cart and checkout procedure to create a fully functional retail site.

CHAPTER 24

Implementing
E-Commerce

*by Michael Starkenburg, Brian Fino,
and James Kindred*

IN THIS CHAPTER

Introduction—Selling Monster Modems Online

The explosion of Internet commerce in 1998, especially during the holiday shopping season, proved that selling goods over the Internet is a viable business plan. Microsoft's Active Server infrastructure is employed by a number of successful e-commerce companies, and as more companies commerce-enable their Web sites, ASP will become even more widespread.

In the quickly changing world of e-commerce, fast time-to-market is essential. An e-commerce company must be able to quickly respond to its customers' demands and its competitors' innovations. Visual InterDev gives you the tools to build a basic e-commerce site quickly, and you can easily add powerful features to the site.

In this chapter, you will build on the catalog work you did in Chapter 23, "Creating an Online Catalog," by extending the story of the fictional Monster Modem Company. After building a successful product catalog, the Monster Modem Company decided it could increase revenues and reach its customers effectively by selling its products online. Its existing site allows customers to peruse product information, but they must use traditional means to purchase the product. Now, rather than force the customers to call or go to a store, Monster wants to let them order the product from the Web site and have it shipped to their home.

Features of the Monster E-Commerce Site

The core features of any e-commerce site are the catalog features. Customers must be able to browse the product catalog or search for the products they want to purchase. From the catalog work in Chapter 23, the Monster site has the following features:

- A catalog home page—Customers can access the category navigation feature and the product search feature.
- Navigation by category—Customers can look for products, based on two types of categories.
- Product search—Customers can find products through a keyword search.
- Product detail—Customers can see specific information about any single product.
- Catalog management—Monster's product managers can add products, delete products, and edit product information.

In this chapter, you will add the following functionality to allow purchasing:

- Shopping cart—Customers must be able to add and remove items from a temporary shopping cart, which will hold the products for them until they are ready to place an order. The shopping cart should be able to hold any quantity of a given item and should show the total costs of all items in the cart.

- Checkout—Customers must provide payment, billing, and shipping information. They need to confirm the contents of their order and see the final totals. Finally, the order must be recorded in a database for later fulfillment.

Setting Up the Environment

The work in this chapter assumes that the developer has already created a working server environment and catalog application. If you followed the instructions in Chapter 23, you are ready to begin. If not, you must complete the following steps:

- Set up a database—In the example, we use SQL server, but you can use Access, Oracle, or any ODBC-compliant database.

- Set up a Web server—You must use IIS to use the full feature set of Visual InterDev and ASP.

- Develop catalog functionality—You must build a product database with the appropriate tools and with features that allow browsing and selection of products.

For the rest of the chapter, we'll assume that your environment and catalog application are identical to that of the Chapter 23 application.

Extending the Catalog Database

After completing the database work for the catalog application, you had the three tables, shown in Figure 24.1:

- mm_product contains the product information for each modem in the Monster catalog.

- mm_category1 contains the category definitions for the form factor categories. Each product has one form factor setting, for example, Internal or External.

- mm_category2 contains the category definitions for the modem speed categories. Each product has a modem speed, for example, 28.8KB.

FIGURE 24.1

*The Monster
Catalog schema.*

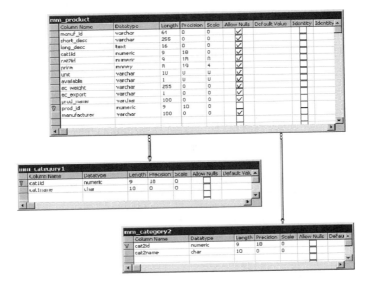

mm_product									
Column Name	Datatype	Length	Precision	Scale	Allow Nulls	Default Value	Identity	Identity
manuf_id	varchar	64	0	0	✓			
short_desc	varchar	255	0	0	✓			
long_desc	text	16	0	0	✓			
cat1id	numeric	9	18	0	✓			
cat2id	numeric	9	18	0	✓			
price	money	8	19	4	✓			
unit	varchar	10	0	0	✓			
available	varchar	1	0	0	✓			
ec_weight	varchar	255	0	0	✓			
ec_export	varchar	1	0	0	✓			
prod_name	varchar	100	0	0				
prod_id	numeric	9	10	0				
manufacturer	varchar	100	0	0	✓			

mm_category1						
Column Name	Datatype	Length	Precision	Scale	Allow Nulls	Default Val
cat1id	numeric	9	18	0		
cat1name	char	10	0	0		

mm_category2						
Column Name	Datatype	Length	Precision	Scale	Allow Nulls	Defau
cat2id	numeric	9	18	0		
cat2name	char	10	0	0		

As you can see in Figure 24.1, these three tables are related. For the e-commerce application, you have to add a number of additional tables. You will do this in two parts: by creating a Customer schema and then by creating an Order schema.

The Customer schema contains two related tables. You will create a new database diagram for this schema, create the two tables, and create a relationship based on the customer ID.

1. Open the Monster project from Chapter 23.

2. Create a new database diagram by selecting Database Diagrams in the Data View window. Right-click and select New Database Diagram. The Database Diagram tool should open.

3. Create a table called mm_shopcart. This table temporarily holds the customer's product selections until checkout. Create this table using the field specs in Figure 24.2.

4. Create a table called mm_customer. This table holds the customer's personal information. Create this table using the field specs in Figure 24.2.

Check your Customer schema against Figure 24.2, and click the Saveall button. The diagram will be saved, and the tables will be created.

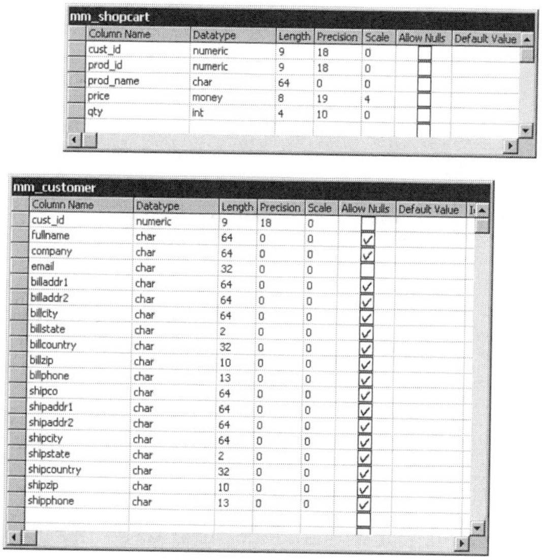

FIGURE 24.2

The Monster Customer schema.

mm_shopcart

Column Name	Datatype	Length	Precision	Scale	Allow Nulls	Default Value
cust_id	numeric	9	18	0		
prod_id	numeric	9	18	0		
prod_name	char	64	0	0		
price	money	8	19	4		
qty	int	4	10	0		

mm_customer

Column Name	Datatype	Length	Precision	Scale	Allow Nulls	Default Value
cust_id	numeric	9	18	0		
fullname	char	64	0	0		
company	char	64	0	0	✓	
email	char	32	0	0	✓	
billaddr1	char	64	0	0	✓	
billaddr2	char	64	0	0	✓	
billcity	char	64	0	0	✓	
billstate	char	2	0	0	✓	
billcountry	char	32	0	0	✓	
billzip	char	10	0	0	✓	
billphone	char	13	0	0	✓	
shipco	char	64	0	0	✓	
shipaddr1	char	64	0	0	✓	
shipaddr2	char	64	0	0	✓	
shipcity	char	64	0	0	✓	
shipstate	char	2	0	0	✓	
shipcountry	char	32	0	0	✓	
shipzip	char	10	0	0	✓	
shipphone	char	13	0	0	✓	

Next, you create an Orders schema. Because an order can contain any number of items, you will create two tables. The main table will contain one record for *each order* (the order header), and a related table will contain a record for *each item* on an order (the order detail).

1. Create a new database diagram by selecting Database Diagrams in the Data View window. Right-click and select New Database Diagram. The Database Diagram tool should open.

2. Create a table called `mm_orderheader`. This table holds the order-specific information. Create this table using the field specs in Figure 24.3.

3. Create a table called `mm_orderdetail`. This table holds the item-specific information. Create this table using the field specs in Figure 24.3.

4. Create a relationship between the tables on order_id by dragging the order_id field from mm_orderheader and dropping it on mm_orderdetail. Click OK when the dialog box appears.

Check your Order schema against Figure 24.3, and click the Saveall button. The diagram will be saved, and the tables will be created.

24

IMPLEMENTING
E-COMMERCE

FIGURE 24.3

*The Monster
Order schema.*

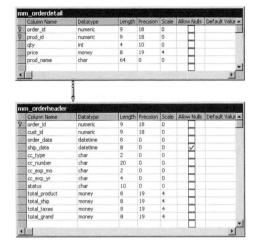

Finally, you must create a table that will hold the "next seed," our unique identifier for orders and customers. This table doesn't relate to any of the others, so you won't bother to create a data diagram for it. You should, however, initialize the next_seed table by entering default values for the order_id and cust_id fields. We chose starting values of 2000. In Data View, you can select Tables and right-click to create a new table. Use the structure in Figure 24.4.

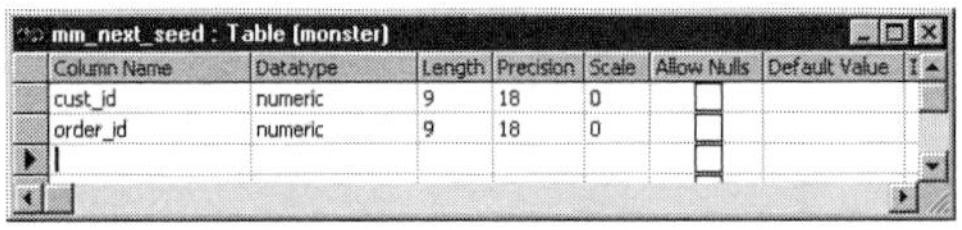

FIGURE 24.4

*The
mm_next_seed
table.*

At this point, you should have all the database structure necessary to complete the e-commerce project.

Modifying the Catalog Functionality

Before you begin working on the shopping cart, you have to go back and place the proper "hooks" in the catalog application. You will want to make changes to the product_detail, search_results, and product_navigation pages. In each page, you will insert code to create Click to Buy links. Customers will use these links to enter the shopping cart and to add items to the cart when appropriate.

Do the following in the product_detail.asp:

- Insert a Label DTC using the products Recordset.

- Set its Field/Expression to

```
="<a href=\'sc_additem.asp?prod_id="+[prod_id]
➥+"&qty=1\'>Click to Buy</a>"
```

- Under the Format tab, check Data Contains HTML.

In the search_results.asp:

- Add the following unbound column to the grid:

```
="<a href=sc_additem.asp?prod_id="+[prod_id]+
➥"&qty=1>Click to Buy</a>"
```

In the product_navigation.asp:

- Add the following unbound column to the grid:

```
="<a href=sc_additem.asp?prod_id="+[prod_id]+
➥"&qty=1>Click to Buy</a>"
```

Implementing the Shopping Cart

In Chapter 23, you tried to implement as much functionality as possible using design-time controls. In this chapter, you will use DTCs occasionally, but in many cases you will write functions as a part of the ASP page. In the shopping cart, you will use these functions to handle the passing of variables from one page to the next. By using Querystring variables instead of PageObject session variables, you can distribute Click to Buy URLS anywhere on your site, including within Grid DTCs, and on other sites as well. This is extremely useful in an e-commerce application: You might want to allow other sites to link directly into your shopping cart, bypassing the product catalog entirely.

Rather than try to implement all actions on the shopping cart page, we've created separate "action pages." These action pages will perform all the necessary functions to the shopper's items: adding items, removing items, and clearing the basket. The shopping cart functionality consists of a main page, which displays the contents of the cart, and three action pages:

- sc_additem.asp adds an item to the shopping cart
- sc_delitem.asp deletes an item from the shopping cart
- sc_clearall.asp clears all the items from the shopping cart

Action pages do not do anything that is noticeable to the user: They simply perform their functions and redirect the user back to the main shopcart page. On the action pages, you won't use DTCs at all, but instead will insert a series of VBScript functions.

24

IMPLEMENTING E-COMMERCE

Creating shopcart.asp

The first page you will build is the page that displays the cart's contents. This page is called by each of the action pages after they complete their work. In this page, you will use DTCs to access and display the shopping cart itself, but you will write some simple functions to format the summary information.

1. Create a new ASP page shopcart.asp.

2. Add the following function in the Head portion of the ASP page:

```
<SCRIPT LANGUAGE=VBScript RUNAT = Server>
        dim subtotal, tax, shipping, total
                subtotal = 0
        function format_price(price)
                format_price = formatcurrency(price)
        end function
        function calc_price(price, qty)
                subtotal = formatcurrency(subtotal + (price * qty))
                calc_price = formatcurrency((price * qty))
        end function
</SCRIPT>
```

3. Add a Recordset DTC with the following properties:

   - Name: rs_shopcart

   - Connection: dbconn1

   - Lock Type: Read Only

   - SQL Text:

     ```
     Select * from mm_shopcart where cust_id = ?;
     ```

   - Parameters: Value: session.sessionid

4. Add a Grid DTC with the following properties:

   - Size: 600 pixels

   - Style: Basic Navy

5. On the Data tab, map it to your rs_shopcart recordset and add the following fields:

   - prod_id

   - prod_name

   - qty

6. Add the following unbound columns:

   - Name: Remove

     ```
     ="<a href=\'sc_delitem.asp?prod_id="+[prod_id]+"\'>Remove</a>"
     ```

- Name: Price

  ```
  =format_price([price])
  ```

- Name: Cost

  ```
  =calc_price([price],[qty])
  ```

7. On the Navigation tab, disable Enable Paging.

8. On the Format tab, set the font to Arial and size to -2.

Now you have a page that will display the contents of the cart. You must add some additional functionality at the bottom of the page to present totals and allow some navigation.

1. Below the Grid DTC, add an HTML table as follows:
   - One column
   - One row
   - Width=600 pixels
   - border=0

2. Switch to Source view, and add the following within the table you just created:
   ```
   <b>SubTotal: </b><%=ccur(subtotal)%>
   ```

3. Below that table, add a second HTML table for navigation:
   - Three columns
   - One row
   - Width=600 pixels

4. Populate the table by inserting the following navigation links in each cell:
   - First cell: Continue Shopping
     ```
     <DIV align=right><A href="http://monster/default.asp">

     Continue Shopping</A>   </DIV>
     ```
   - Second cell: Clear Basket
     ```
     <DIV align=center><A href="http://monster/sc_clearall.asp">

     Clear Basket</A></DIV>
     ```
   - Third cell: Proceed to Checkout
     ```
     <DIV align=left><A href="http://monster/checkout_start.asp">

     Proceed To Checkout</A></DIV>
     ```

This completes the shopcart page. Now you build the three action pages that will modify the shopcart contents.

24

IMPLEMENTING
E-COMMERCE

Creating sc_additem.asp

The sc_additem ASP is an action page, and therefore no data will be physically displayed. The ASP simply adds the items to the shopper's basket and redirects him or her to the shopcart page. You implement this by writing functions in VBScript, rather than using DTCs.

1. Set up the scripting environment by inserting the following immediately after the first line of the page, `<%@language=VBScript%>`:

```
<% Response.buffer = true
on error resume next %>
```

2. Immediately following the HTML `<BODY>` tag, insert the following code to create the prod_exists function. The prod_exists function checks whether a row exists in the mm_shopcart table for this user and item. If so, you then increment that row's quantity in the update_count function, rather than create another row.

```
<%
'*************************************************************
'    Function:    prod_exists
'    Parameters:    prod_id, oconn
'    Purpose:
'        Checks for another identical prod_id in basket
'        and returns true if found using an existing
'        database connection
'*************************************************************
function prod_exists(byVal prod_id, byRef oconn)
    sqlText = "Select prod_id, qty from mm_shopcart " &_
                "WHERE cust_id = " & session.SessionID & " " &_
                "AND prod_id = '" & prod_id & "'"
    set rs = oConn.Execute(sqlText,affect)
    if( rs.EOF or rs.BOF )then
Err.Clear
        prod_exists = false
        exit function
    else
        qty = rs("qty") + qty
        Err.Clear
         prod_exists = true
        exit function
    end if
end function
%>
```

3. Create the Add_item function by inserting the following code after the prod_exists function. The add_item function handles the insertion of a new row in the mm_shopcart database for the requested item.

```
<%
'*************************************************************
```

```
'     Function:     add_item
'     Parameters:    cust_id, prod_id, prod_name, price, qty, oconn
'     Purpose:
'         Add the passed item to the shopping cart
'*************************************************************
Function add_item(byVal cust_id, byVal prod_id,
➥byVal qty, byRef oconn)
    SqlText = "Select prod_name, price from mm_product" &_
"where prod_id = '" & prod_id & "'"
        set rs = oConn.Execute(sqlText)
        prod_name = rs("prod_name")
        price = rs("price")

    sqlText = "INSERT INTO mm_shopcart" &_
"(cust_id, prod_id, prod_name, price, qty)" &_
            "VALUES (" &_
                cust_id & "," &_
            prod_id & "," &_
            "'" & prod_name & "'," &_
            price & "," &_
                qty & ");"

    oConn.Execute sqlText
    if Err.number <> 0 then
        '** Handle Error **'
        Err.Clear
    end if
end function
%>
```

4. Create the Update_Count function by inserting the following code in the body of the HTML page:

```
<%
'*************************************************************
'     Function: update_count
'     Parameters: prod_id, qty, oconn
'     Purpose:
'         Updates the count of an item if it already exists
'         in the shopping cart
'*************************************************************
function update_count(byVal prod_id, byVal qty, byRef oconn)
    sqlText = "UPDATE mm_shopcart SET qty = " & qty & " " &_
            "WHERE( cust_id = " & session.SessionID & " " &_
            "AND prod_id = '" & prod_id & "');"

    oConn.Execute sqlText

    if Err.number <> 0 then
        '** Handle Error **'
        Err.Clear
```

```
        end if

    end function
    %>
```

5. Insert the following code as the main script, which sets up the database connection and calls the other functions as needed:

```
<%
'****************************************************************
dim qty, prod_id, cust_id, oConn
    qty = Request.QueryString("qty")
    prod_id = Request.QueryString("prod_id")
    cust_id = session.SessionID

set oConn = Server.CreateObject("ADODB.Connection")
    oConn.Open Application("dbconn1_ConnectionString"), _
    Application("dbconn1_RunTimeUserName"), _
    Application("dbconn1_RunTimeUserPassword")

if (prod_exists(prod_id, oconn)) then
    update_count prod_id, qty, oconn
else
    add_item cust_id, prod_id, qty, oconn
end if

oConn.Close
set oConn = nothing

if Err.number <> 0 then
    '** Handle Error **'
    Err.Clear
else
    Response.Redirect ("shopcart.asp")
end if
%>
```

Save the current page as sc_additem.asp.

Creating sc_delitem.asp

The sc_delitem ASP is an action page and also displays no data. This ASP simply removes the specified items from the shopcart and redirects the user to the shopcart page. This page is implemented with some simple VBScript functions.

1. Set up the scripting environment by inserting the following immediately after the first line of the page, %@language=VBScript %:

```
<% Response.buffer = true
on error resume next %>
```

2. Create the remove_item function by inserting the following code in the body of the page:

```
<%
'*****************************************************************
'    function:     remove_item
'    Parameters:    prod_id
'    Purpose:     Remove item from shopping cart
'*****************************************************************
sub remove_item(prod_id)
    sqlText = "DELETE FROM mm_shopcart " &_
              "WHERE cust_id = " & session.SessionID & " " &_
              "AND prod_id = " & prod_id

    oConn.Execute sqlText

    if Err.number <> 0 then
        '**Handle Error**'
        Err.Clear
    end if
end sub
%>
```

3. Insert the following main script into the body of the page. This code sets up the db connection and calls the remove_item function. It then redirects the user to the shopcart.asp.

```
<%
set oConn = Server.CreateObject("ADODB.Connection")
oConn.Open Application("dbconn1_ConnectionString"), _
    Application("dbconn1_RunTimeUserName"), _
    Application("dbconn1_RunTimeUserPassword")
call remove_item(Request.QueryString("prod_id"), oconn)
oConn.Close
set oConn = nothing
Response.Redirect ("shopcart.asp")
%>
```

Save the current ASP as sc_delitem.asp.

Creating sc_clearall.asp

The last action page, sc_clearall.asp, removes all items from the user's shopcart and redirects him or her to the shopcart page. This page is implemented with some simple VBScript functions.

1. Set up the scripting environment by inserting the following immediately after the first line of the page, %@language=VBScript %:

```
<% Response.buffer = true
 on error resume next %>
```

2. Create the remove_all function by inserting the following in the body of the page. The remove_all function clears all the rows from the mm_shopcart table that match the current user and session information.

```
<%
'***************************************************************
'      function:     remove_all
'      Parameters:   none
'      Purpose:      Remove all items from shopping cart
'***************************************************************
sub remove_all()
    sqlText = "DELETE FROM mm_shopcart " &_
                    "WHERE( cust_id = " & session.SessionID & ");"

    oConn.Execute sqlText

    if Err.number <> 0 then
        '** Handle Error **'
        Err.Clear
    end if
end sub
%>
```

3. Insert the following main script into the body of the page. This code sets up the db connection and calls the remove_all function. It then redirects the user to the shop-cart.asp.

```
<%
set oConn = Server.CreateObject("ADODB.Connection")
    oConn.Open Application("dbconn1_ConnectionString"), _
Application("dbconn1_RunTimeUserName"), _
Application("dbconn1_RunTimeUserPassword")
call remove_all, oconn
    oConn.Close
set oConn = nothing
Response.Redirect ("shopcart.asp")
%>
```

Save the current ASP as sc_clearall.asp.

At this point, you've created the shopcart display page and three action pages. The customer can now add to the cart, remove a single item, clear the cart completely, and view the contents of the cart. The finished shopping cart will look something like Figure 24.5. You're ready to move on to the last piece of your e-commerce site, the checkout process.

FIGURE 24.5

The completed shopping cart.

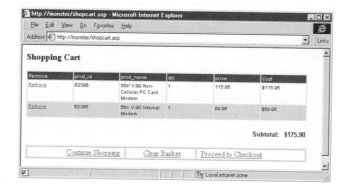

Implementing a Simple Checkout

After customers have filled their shopping cart, the next step is to place the order. You have to collect payment information, billing information, and shipping information. You then have to validate that information and create an order in your database.

This checkout process consist of two ASPs. The first, checkout_start.asp, handles the majority of the checkout functionality, including collecting the user information and creating the order in the database. The second page, checkout_confirmation, allows shoppers to review and print their final order information.

Creating checkout_start.asp

In the first step of the checkout, you complete several functions for the customers. First, you show them the contents of their cart and the totals for the order. Then you collect their personal information, including the billing information, shipping information, and credit card information. You will use a combination of functions and DTCs in this ASP. To make the building of this page easy, you divide the process into four tasks:

- Build the ability to see the contents of the shopping cart.
- Create the tables and fields that will collect the user information.
- Create the buttons and form actions.
- Insert the VBScript that will make up the remaining functions, including creating the order.

Showing the Contents of the Current Shopping Cart

To begin, you set up a number of RecordSets, a Grid DTC, and an HTML table to show customers the current contents of their cart.

1. Insert a RecordSet DTC with the following properties:
   - Name: rs_shopcart
   - SQL Text:

     `Select * from mm_shopcart where cust_id = ?`
   - Parameters: session.sessionid
   - CursorType: Static
   - LockType: Optimistic
   - Implementation: Automatically Open the Recordset

2. Insert a RecordSet DTC with the following properties:
   - Name: rs_orderheader
   - SQL Text:

     `Select * from mm_orderheader where cust_id = ?`
   - Parameters: session.sessionid
   - CursorType: Static
   - LockType: Optimistic
   - Implementation: *Uncheck* Automatically Open the Recordset.

3. Insert a RecordSet DTC with the following properties:
   - Name: rs_orderdetail
   - SQL Text: `Select * from mm_orderdetail where order_id = 1`
   - CursorType: Static
   - LockType: Optimistic
   - Implementation: *Uncheck* Automatically Open the Recordset.

4. Insert a RecordSet DTC with the following properties:
   - Name: rs_customer
   - SQL Text: `Select * from mm_customer where cust_id = ?`
   - Parameters: session.sessionid
   - CursorType: Static
   - LockType: Optimistic
   - Implementation: *Uncheck* Automatically Open the Recordset.

NOTE

You might have noticed that the Recordset objects that you are inserting here, with the exception of rs_shopcart, are not automatically opened. In many cases, they will fail to return any records. We included them anyway so that you could easily implement a look-me-up feature for returning customers.

5. Insert a Grid DTC with the following properties:
   - Name: grid_shopcart
   - Width: 600 pixels
   - Style: Basic Navy
   - Recordset: rs_shopcart
   - Available Fields: prod_id, prod_name, qty
   - Add Unbound Column: `=format_price([price])`
   - Add Unbound Column: `=calc_price([price],[qty])`
   - Navigation: *Uncheck* Enable Paging.

6. Insert an HTML table for displaying order pricing (tax, shipping, subtotal, and total). The table should have four rows and two columns.

7. Switch to Source view, and populate the HTML table with the following code. Note that you haven't yet defined these functions (you will, later in this section) but you can still put the calls in place now.
   - Row 1: Subtotal: `<%=calc_total_product%>`
   - Row 2: Shipping: `<%=calc_total_ship%>`
   - Row 3: Tax: `<%=calc_total_taxes%>`
   - Row 4: Total: `<%=calc_total_grand%>`

At this point, you've finished the first part of the checkout_start ASP, and users can see the contents of their cart. Figure 24.6 shows what this will look like when you're finished.

FIGURE 24.6

The first section of checkout_start. asp.

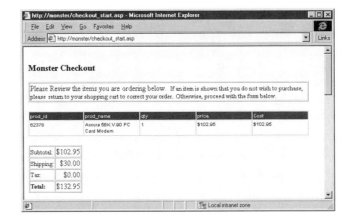

Collecting Customer Information

Now you must create four HTML tables and fill them with TextBox DTCs. These tables will collect the personal information, billing information, shipping information, and credit card information.

1. Insert an HTML table with two rows and two columns for collecting personal information. Populate the table with text and TextBox DTCs. The TextBox DTCs should reference the rs_order_header recordset and fields shown in Figure 24.7.

FIGURE 24.7

The Personal Information table.

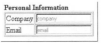

2. Insert an HTML table with eight rows and two columns for collecting billing information. Populate the table with text and TextBox DTCs. The TextBox DTCs should reference the rs_customer recordset and fields shown in Figure 24.8.

FIGURE 24.8

The Billing Information table.

3. Insert an HTML table with eight rows and two columns for collecting shipping information. Populate the table with text and TextBox DTCs. The TextBox DTCs should reference the rs_customer recordset and fields shown in Figure 24.9.

FIGURE 24.9

The Shipping Information table.

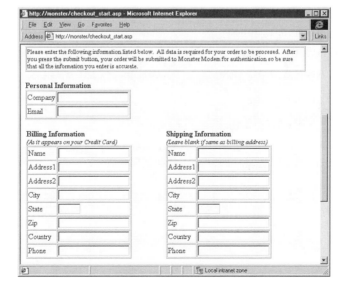

Shipping Information
(Leave blank if same as billing address)

Name	shipco
Address1	shipaddr1
Address2	shipaddr2
City	shipcity
State	shipstate
Zip	shipzip
Country	shipcountry
Phone	shipphone

4. Insert an HTML table with four rows and two columns for collecting credit card information. Populate the table with text and TextBox DTCs. The TextBox DTCs should reference the rs_customer recordset and fields shown in Figure 24.10.

FIGURE 24.10

The Credit Card Information table.

Credit Card Information

Credit Card Type	cc_ty
Card Number	cc_number
Expiration Month	cc_e
Expiration Year	cc_exp_

When you complete these steps, the second section of this ASP will be finished. Customers can enter their information onto the order. This section of the page will look something like Figure 24.11.

FIGURE 24.11

The second section of checkout_start. asp.

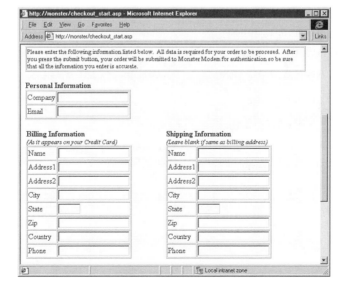

Setting Up Form Actions

Now that the customer has entered his or her information, you must create the form actions that result from pushing a button. You will do this using a FormManager and two buttons.

1. Insert a Button DTC for canceling an order.
   - Name: btn_cancel
   - Caption: Cancel Order

2. Insert a Button DTC for submitting an order.
   - Name: btn_submit
   - Caption: Submit Order

3. Insert a FormManager DTC.

4. Add a mode named `Default`.
   - Actions Performed: `btn_cancel` - `disabled` - `false`
   - Actions Performed: `btn_submit` - `disabled` - `false`

5. Add a mode named `Submit`.
   - Actions Performed: `thisPage` - `navigateURL` - (`"checkout_confirmation.asp"`)

6. Add a mode named `Cancel`.
   - Actions Performed: `thisPage` - `navigateURL` - (`shopcart.asp`)

7. Add actions for the FormManager.
   - Default - `btn_cancel` - `onclick` - `Cancel`
   - Transitions: None
   - Default - `btn_submit` - `onclick` - `Submit`
   - Transitions: `thisPage` - `execute.submit_order` - ()

8. Insert a PageObject DTC.
   - Add Execute Method: submit_order
   - Add Reference: checkout_confirmation.asp
   - *Uncheck* Client.
   - *Check* Server.

Writing VBScript Functions

The form actions for the page are now defined. To complete the page, you must write a series of 13 functions. The functions do a number of important jobs in this page, including

- Executing formatting and calculations on data in the database
- Inserting the order information and customer information into the database

> **NOTE**
>
> To keep the sample application simple, we've purposely written only those functions that are absolutely necessary. In a real application, you would want to insert additional functionality at this point, for example, validation of the input fields, a more complicated tax calculator, or a more sophisticated shipping calculator. You can easily add these functions by creating a VBScript that implements your specific piece of business logic and including it here as a function. You can then call the function from within the submit_order function defined in step 12.

1. Initialize the global variables that will be used throughout the page application, by inserting the following code in the `<HEAD>` section of the page:

   ```
   <%
       dim product, taxes, ship, grand, subtotal
       dim fields()
       dim values()
   %>
   ```

2. Insert the following code into the page body to create the format_price function. format_price is used by the grid to format the price into a currency format.

   ```
   <%
       function format_price(price)
           format_price = formatcurrency(price)
       end function
   %>
   ```

3. Insert the following code into the page body to create the calc_price function. This function multiplies the price of an item times the quantity in the basket.

   ```
   <%
       function calc_price(price, qty)
           product = product + (price * qty)
           calc_price = formatcurrency((price * qty))
       end function
   %>
   ```

4. Insert the following code into the page body to create the calc_total_product function. This function returns a formatted value for the total product cost.

```
<%
    function calc_total_product()
        calc_total_product = formatcurrency(product)
    end function
%>
```

5. Insert the following code into the page body to create the calc_total_taxes function. This function returns a formatted value for the total tax cost

```
<%
    function calc_total_taxes()
        taxes = 0.0      'Monster is covering the cost of tax if it
                         'applies to the buyer. Most out-of-state
                         'traffic will not have to pay tax. If your
                         'tax algorithm is more complicated, it goes here.
        calc_total_taxes = formatcurrency(taxes)
    end function
%>
```

6. Insert the following code into the page body to create the calc_total_ship function. This function returns the total cost of shipping for the order.

```
<%
    function calc_total_ship()
        'Monster has a simple shipping cost algorithm. You can
        'substitute a more complicated shipping routine here.
        if( product >= 10 and product < 50) then ship = 15
        if( product >= 50 and product < 100) then ship = 25
        if( product >=100) then ship = 30
        calc_total_ship = formatcurrency(ship)
    end function
%>
```

7. Insert the following code into the page body to create the calc_total_grand function. This function calculates and returns the total grand cost.

```
<%
    function calc_total_grand()
        grand = (ship + taxes + product)
        calc_total_grand = formatcurrency(grand)
    end function
%>
```

8. Insert the following code into the page body to create the add_detail function. This function adds the items from the shopping cart into mm_orderdetail as part of completing the order.

```
<%
    sub add_detail(order_id)
        redim fields(4)
        redim values(4)
```

```
        rs_orderdetail.open
        rs_shopcart.moveFirst
        do while not(rs_shopcart.EOF or rs_shopcart.BOF)
            fields(0) = "order_id"
            fields(1) = "prod_id"
            fields(2) = "qty"
            fields(3) = "price"
            fields(4) = "prod_name"
            values(0) = order_id
            values(1) = rs_shopcart.fields.getValue("prod_id")
            values(2) = rs_shopcart.fields.getValue("qty")
            values(3) = rs_shopcart.fields.getValue("price")
            values(4) = rs_shopcart.fields.getValue("prod_name")
            rs_orderdetail.addImmediate fields, values
            rs_shopcart.moveNext
        loop
        rs_orderdetail.close
    end sub
%>
```

9. Insert the following code into the page body to create the clear_shopcart function. This function deletes all the items from a user's shopping cart after he or she has "checked out."

```
<%
    sub clear_shopcart(byVal id, byRef oConn)
        sqlText = "DELETE from mm_shopcart WHERE cust_id = " & id
        oConn.Execute (sqlText)
    end sub
%>
```

10. Insert the following code into the page body to create the add_customer function. This function adds a customer into mm_customer as part of completing the order.

```
<%
    sub add_customer(byVal cust_id)
        redim fields(18)
        redim values(18)
        fields(0) = "cust_id"
        fields(1) = "fullname"
        fields(2) = "company"
        fields(3) = "email"
        fields(4) = "billaddr1"
        fields(5) = "billaddr2"
        fields(6) = "billcity"
        fields(7) = "billstate"
        fields(8) = "billzip"
        fields(9) = "billcountry"
        fields(10) = "billphone"
        fields(11) = "shipco"
        fields(12) = "shipaddr1"
        fields(13) = "shipaddr2"
```

```
            fields(14) = "shipcity"
            fields(15) = "shipstate"
            fields(16) = "shipzip"
            fields(17) = "shipcountry"
            fields(18) = "shipphone"
            values(0) = cust_id
            values(1) = fullname.value
            values(2) = company.value
            values(3) = email.value
            values(4) = billaddr1.value
            values(5) = billaddr2.value
            values(6) = billcity.value
            values(7) = billstate.value
            values(8) = billzip.value
            values(9) = billcountry.value
            values(10) = billphone.value
            values(11) = shipco.value
            values(12) = shipaddr1.value
            values(13) = shipaddr2.value
            values(14) = shipcity.value
            values(15) = shipstate.value
            values(16) = shipzip.value
            values(17) = shipcountry.value
            values(18) = shipphone.value
             rs_customer.open
             rs_customer.addImmediate fields, values
            rs_customer.close
        end sub
    %>
```

11. Insert the following code into the page body to create the add_orderheader function. This function adds the general order information into mm_orderheader as part of the order process.

```
    <%
        sub add_orderheader(byVal cust_id, byVal order_id)
            redim fields(12)
            redim values(12)
            fields(0) = "cust_id"
            fields(1) = "order_date"
            fields(2) = "ship_date"
            fields(3) = "cc_type"
            fields(4) = "cc_number"
            fields(5) = "cc_exp_mo"
            fields(6) = "cc_exp_yr"
            fields(7) = "status"
            fields(8) = "total_product"
            fields(9) = "total_ship"
            fields(10) = "total_taxes"
            fields(11) = "total_grand"
            fields(12) = "order_id"
```

```
                values(0) = cust_id
                values(1) = Now()
                values(2) = Now()
                values(3) = cc_type.value
                values(4) = cc_number.value
                values(5) = cc_exp_mo.value
                values(6) = cc_exp_yr.value
                values(7) = "0"
                values(8) = calc_total_product()
                values(9) = calc_total_ship()
                values(10) = calc_total_taxes()
                values(11) = calc_total_grand()
                values(12) = order_id
                rs_order_header.open
                rs_order_header.addImmediate fields, values
                rs_order_header.close
        end sub
    %>
```

12. Insert the following code into the page body to create the submit_order function.

    submit_order is the main procedure that controls the checkout process. It collects and processes the business rules for checking a customer out. Additionally, it is also the only page-level function defined in the checkout_start PageObject.

```
    <%
        sub submit_order()
            dim order_id, cust_id
            ' Open a global connection for record processing.
            set oConn = Server.CreateObject("ADODB.Connection")
    oConn.Open Application("dbconn1_ConnectionString"), _
        Application("dbconn1_RunTimeUserName"), _
        Application("dbconn1_RunTimePassword")
                    'Get a valid order_id
                    order_id = get_next_id("order_id", oConn)
                    'Get a valid customer_id if needed.
                    cust_id = get_next_id("cust_id", oConn)
                    'Add the order's header information into the database.
                    call add_orderheader(cust_id, order_id)
                    'Add the customer's information into the database
                    call add_customer(cust_id)
                    'Add the order detail information into the database.
                    call add_detail(order_id)
                    'Clear the shopping cart of a shopper's items.
                    call clear_shopcart(session.SessionID, oConn)
                    'Set session customer_id number for confirmation page.
                    checkout_confirmation.setcust_id(cust_id)
                    'Set session order_id number for confirmation page.
                    checkout_confirmation.setorder_id(order_id)
            oConn.Close()
        end sub
    %>
```

13. Insert the following code into the page body to create the get_next_id function. This is a generic function that simply looks up the next available id in mm_next_seed and returns that id. It can be used to return the next customer id, order id, or any other id that you want to track in mm_next_seed.

```
<%
    function get_next_id(field, oConn)
        sqlText = "select " & field & " from mm_next_seed;"
        insert = false
        set rs = oConn.Execute(sqlText)
        id = (clng(rs.Fields.Item(0).Value) + 1)
        set RS = nothing
        do while insert = false
            sqlInsertSeed = "UPDATE mm_next_seed SET " & field & " =
            ➥" & (id)
            oConn.Execute(sqlInsertSeed)
            If Err.number <> 0 then
                id = id + 1
                Err.Clear
            else
                insert = true
            end if
        loop
        get_next_id = id
    end function
%>
```

Creating checkout_confirmation.asp

Although checkout_start.asp handles most of the heavy lifting in the checkout process, this second ASP has one very important role to play. By displaying all information in the database that has an order_id and cust_id equal to that of the current shopper, it enables them to check their final order information and to print it for future reference.

Because this page is relatively simple, you will be able to create it by using design-time controls exclusively. Creating this page involves two tasks:

- Create the page object and recordsets.
- Display the order information to the customer.

Creating the Page Object and Recordsets

To begin, you set up a PageObject DTC to handle the incoming application variables being passed to the page from checkout_start. Then, you set up a few RecordSet DTCs to allow you access to the order information.

1. Create a new ASP in the Monster project: checkout_confirmation.asp.

2. Insert a PageObject DTC in the page.

3. Set the following properties in the PageObject DTC:

   - order_id - Session - none - Read/Write
   - cust_id - Session - none - Read/Write

4. Insert a RecordSet DTC in the page with the following properties:

   - Name: rs_orderlevel
   - SQL Text: `Select * from mm_orderheader, mm_customer where mm_orderheader.cust_id = mm_customer.cust_id and mm_orderheader.order_id = ? and mm_customer.cust_id = ?`
   - Parameter: `thisPage.getorder_id()`
   - Parameter: `thisPage.getcust_id()`
   - CursorType: Static
   - LockType: ReadOnly
   - Implementation: *Check* Automatically Open the Recordset.

5. Insert a RecordSet DTC in the page with the following properties:

   - Name: rs_itemlevel
   - SQL Text: `Select * from mm_orderdetail where order_id = ?`
   - Parameters: `thisPage.getorder_id()`
   - CursorType: Static
   - LockType: ReadOnly
   - Implementation: *Check* Automatically Open the Recordset.

Displaying Order Information

Now that you've set up the variable-handling and data access DTCs, you're ready to display the information to the customer.

You use Label DTCs to show each individual field in the order-level information and a Grid DTC to display the individual items from the order.

In the example, we didn't try to make this pretty at all, but you will want to take a little time playing with HTML to make this look good when printed.

1. Insert Label DTCs for each of the following fields in the rs_orderlevel recordset to display the order-level information:

- company
- email
- fullname
- billaddr1
- billaddr2
- billcity
- billstate
- billzip
- billcountry
- billphone
- shipco
- shipaddr1
- shipaddr2
- shipcity
- shipstate
- shipzip
- shipcountry
- shipphone

2. Insert a Grid DTC for displaying the item-level information by binding it to the rs_itemlevel Recordset.

   - Name: grid_items
   - Width: 600 pixels
   - Style: Basic Navy
   - Available Fields: prod_id, qty, prod_name
   - Navigation: *Uncheck* Enable Paging.

With these steps accomplished, you now have a very simple, but complete, e-commerce application that allows your customers to browse and select products, add them and remove them from a shopping cart, and place an order.

Other E-Commerce Features

Now that the basic functionality is in place, there are a number of advanced features you might want to consider implementing in your e-commerce application. Many of these are becoming de facto standards on the Internet, and customers expect to find this functionality on any shopping site.

Online Order Tracking

The most common support call received by online vendors is the question "Where is my order?" You can minimize these calls and provide a higher level of service to the customer by providing an order-tracking system.

The basic order-tracking system can look up an order for a customer, based on any combination of customer information. A good combination to start with is the customer's email address and order number.

When the order is found in the database, you can display it in a manner similar to the checkout_confirmation screen, although you might not want to show credit card information, for security reasons.

As you become more sophisticated, you might want to add a customer password to your e-commerce site. You can collect this password during the first checkout process and use it later to look up a customer. This way, you can show customers *all* their orders, rather than rely on just one order number.

Real-Time Credit Card Validation

Another feature now common on shopping sites is the validation of customers' credit cards during the checkout process. This feature is good for both customers and merchants. Customers can tell immediately whether they've mistyped some part of their credit card information. In some cases, they can be warned when they exceed a limit. The merchant is protected to some extent against fraud.

The simplest method of validating a credit card is called a Luhn-Mod-10 check. This algorithm, which is freely available on the Internet, can be written as a VBScript function and performed on a card number in the checkout_start asp. This validation simply checks to ensure that the card number is valid, which protects against typos and randomly entered numbers. A disadvantage of this is that there is no guarantee that the bank will consider the credit card valid. It is easy to generate a card number that will pass a Luhn-Mod-10 check.

Another option is to use a real-time credit card processor, such as CyberSource or CyberCash. These third parties supply an API that you can build in to your checkout process. The API encrypts the credit card information entered by the customer and transmits it to a processing center. Several tests can then be run on that information, including AVS (Address Verification Services), fraud checks, and limit checks.

Automated Cross-Selling

In a traditional retail environment, salespeople are motivated to add related, high-margin items to an order. On the Web, although you don't have a salesperson, you can still try to sell additional items on each order. For example, everyone who buys a laptop is going to need a case. The trick is to present a compelling offer to the consumer at the right moment in the purchase process.

Cross-selling can significantly affect an online business. Increasing the number of items on an order can result in higher margins, increased average order revenue, and more repeat business.

There are many ways to implement automated cross-selling. One simple model is to build a table of relationships: Product x is related to product y. When the customer puts product x in the shopping cart, you can then promote product y. The trick to this is populating the table of relationships. Effective methods include

- Expert intelligence—In product categories where there are clear relationships, such as computers, the best thing to do is to have an expert manually declare each relationship. For example, only one type of battery fits a given laptop: A computer product manager must hand-code that relationship.

- Collaborative filtering—In product categories where the relationship between products is more subjective, such as books and music, you can infer cross-selling relationships automatically by using collaborative filtering products such as NetPerceptions or LikeMinds. These products look at purchase patterns of large groups of people over time and infer relationships, based on this data. For example, assume that many people who buy a Beatles album also buy a Rolling Stones album. The next time a customer puts a Beatles album in his or her shopping cart, you can promote a Stones album.

Order/Product Data Exporting

The e-commerce application you built in this chapter doesn't address the actual fulfillment of the order. In many cases, fulfillment is handled by a separate inventory management system or by an outsource fulfillment company. In these cases, you might have to develop a system to export the order header and detail information in a flat file format. The information can then be transferred to the other system or service provider.

Another export need might be for product information. Pricing agents are becoming very common on the Internet. If you are selling in a category that is covered by these agents, you might be able to improve your positioning in these systems by providing them with a daily or weekly listing of your products and prices. In this case, you have to export certain fields from your product database to a flat file.

Summary

In this chapter, you learned how to build the key pieces of an e-commerce application, including

- A shopping cart that allows the user to add items, remove items, and clear the cart entirely
- A checkout process that shows the shopping cart, gathers the user's information, and creates the order in the database

You used a combination of design-time controls and VBScript functions to implement your application. As you add functionality to the example, you will find the design and debugging tools in Visual InterDev helpful.

In combination with the catalog application you built in Chapter 23, the functionality in this chapter is the core of any e-commerce application. When you become an expert at implementing shopping carts and checkout processes, you can improve the site even further by adding advanced features such as cross-selling, credit card validation, and export features.

Appendixes

PART V

IN THIS PART

APPENDIX A

HTML 4.0 Reference

by Lee Anne Phillips, Bob Correll, and Will Kelly

IN THIS APPENDIX

HTML 4.0 is a major upgrade to the HTML standard to meet the design and development needs of Web developers worldwide, both casual and professional. This appendix provides an extensive reference to the elements and attributes of the language as specified by the World Wide Web Consortium.

> **NOTE**
>
> This appendix is based on the information in the *HTML 4.0 Specification W3C Working Draft 17-Sep-1997*. The latest version of this document can be found at `http://www.w3.org/TR/WD-html40/`.

To make the information readily accessible, this appendix organizes HTML elements according to their function in the code you use to create your pages.

HTML Functionality

There are three basic types of elements: the "housekeeping" structure of each page, which doesn't actually alter the high-level rendering of the document directly; block-level tags that affect the layout of the document directly; and text-level tags that operate inline. In addition, there are mnemonic "entities" that allow you to access various characters commonly used in European languages and scientific works but not usually found on most keyboards. These entities are described in Appendix B, "VBScript 1.2 Language Reference," which also has information on browser differences. Because HTML is designed to display your page in a browser, we'll say a few words about them before we start.

Browsers and Platforms

Browsers are the power tools of the Web, and like all tools, they come in many different types and sizes to fit almost any pocketbook. No matter what you pay, or don't pay, none of them are perfect, none will display every tag exactly as you think it should, and some might have quirks that are annoying to live with. So you should look at several before you commit yourself. Appendix G, "Scripting Object Model Reference," has a small selection to choose from, but you should think about your intended purpose before you choose.

If you're on a tight budget, try one of the low-cost browsers that runs on a 386 or 486 with Windows, or an equivalent on the Mac Classic. The mainstream, heavily advertised browsers that everyone talks about will give little satisfaction on a machine like that, but

Opera or Mosaic will run like a top. Likewise, if you want to look at your second cousin's site in China or Saudi Arabia, you'll probably want to try Tango or Internet with an Accent to allow you to see the glyphs properly.

If you want to see all the latest Java goodies and multimedia razzmatazz, you should probably figure on a Pentium or newer Mac platform with either Netscape Navigator or Microsoft Internet Explorer. Support for Netscape on the Web is better, but either will perform well.

If you have special needs, like a requirement for an audio or Braille browser, Appendix G has the URLs of a few links that might help you choose the most appropriate platform and software for this complex decision.

The resources of this book will also help, both the tags as listed in this appendix and the many discussions of resources throughout. Browsers will be a while catching up to the full power of the new HTML 4.0 specification, and as a Web designer, you should know that are many people are happy with the browser they have and will never upgrade. Many Web developers have a collection of a dozen or more browsers on several platforms because they like to look at their work in all the many ways it will be displayed.

HTML 4.0 Philosophy and Practice

The World Wide Web is about communication. Like any medium of conversation, possibilities exist for misunderstanding and confusion. The new standards are designed to help make communication better and more inclusive for everyone. For a while, it was OK that the language of the Web was English by default, but that limitation restricted it to relatively few people worldwide. As you study the tags, you'll see how the additions have been carefully chosen to let more people in on the conversation and make it easier to allow for differences in the way people communicate and understand. It's really pretty cool.

> **NOTE**
>
> In the following list, some tags are placed for convenience with related tags and marked with an asterisk where they belong or are also appropriate. Some tags are placed where they do belong and are also referenced where many people might look for them, also for convenience.
>
> Some tags and attributes are deprecated, which means that they are not liked by the standards committee and should be avoided, if possible. Deprecated tags are marked with a little degree symbol (°).

HTML 4.0 tags are grouped in the following order in this appendix:

- Structural (Housekeeping) Elements

  Basic structural elements: BODY, HEAD, HTML

  Header elements: BASE, ISINDEX÷, LINK, META, NOSCRIPT, SCRIPT, STYLE, TITLE

  Frames: FRAMESET, FRAME, IFRAME, NOFRAMES

  SGML special tags: !-- (comment) --, !DOCTYPE

- Block-level Elements

  Basic block elements: ADDRESS, BLOCKQUOTE, CENTER÷, DIV, FIELDSET, H1–H6, HR, ISINDEX÷*, P, PRE

  Lists: DD, DIR÷, DL, DT, LI, MENU÷, OL, UL

  Forms: BUTTON, FIELDSET, FORM, INPUT, LABEL, LEGEND, OPTION, SELECT, TEXTAREA

  Tables: CAPTION, COL, COLGROUP, TABLE, TBODY, TD, TFOOT, TH, THEAD, TR

- Text-level Elements

  Text markup: B, BIG, I, S÷, SMALL, STRIKE÷, TT, U÷

  Phrase markup: ACRONYM, ADDRESS*, BLOCKQUOTE*, CITE, CODE, DEL, DFN, EM, INS, KBD, PRE*, SAMP, STRONG, VAR

  Special markup: A, APPLET÷, BASEFONT÷, BDO, BR, FONT÷, IFRAME*, IMG, NOSCRIPT*, OBJECT, Q, SCRIPT*, SPAN, SUB, SUP

  Client-side image maps: AREA, MAP

  Form control text: BUTTON*, INPUT*, LABEL*, SELECT*, TEXTAREA*

Within each section, the elements are listed alphabetically and the following information is given:

- The tag itself and its closing tag, if it has one. If a tag is optional, it's surrounded by square brackets, but the brackets themselves are never part of any tag.

- Usage: A general description of the element.

- Syntax: A simple example of how the tag is written on the page. Optional elements are surrounded by square brackets. Optional attributes are shown with a placeholder in italics—*attributes*—to show that the actual attributes listed later in the section go in that position.

- Start/End Tag: Indicates whether these tags are required, optional, or forbidden.

- Attributes: Lists the attributes of the element with a short description of their effect. If a default value exists, it's printed in **bold**.

- Intrinsics: Lists the intrinsic events that can be detected.

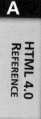

> **NOTE**
>
> HTML 4.0 introduces several new attributes and intrinsic events that apply to a large number of elements. They are called out by name at the end of the appropriate list but, because they always have exactly the same effect and description, please refer to the last section of this appendix, "Common Attributes and Intrinsic Events," for a more complete explanation.

- Empty: Indicates that the element must be empty.
- Notes: Relates any special considerations when using the element and indicates whether the element is new or deprecated.
- Introduced: The version of HTML that standardized the element.
- Browsers: Indicates which versions of the popular Web browsers—Netscape Navigator and Microsoft Internet Explorer—support the HTML element.
- Example: Gives a short code example that illustrates how the tag is used.
- Note: The element being highlighted appears in **bold**. For the purposes of illustration, deprecated elements and attributes are sometimes used in the example, but are rendered in *italics* to show that they're no longer recommended.

Structural (Housekeeping) Elements

HTML relies on several elements to give structure to a document (as opposed to structuring the text within the document) and supply information that's used by the browser or search engines.

Basic Structural Elements: BODY, HEAD, HTML

These are the basic tags on which all pages are founded. They are all unique in that they can almost always be inferred from the context, and many pages will work just fine without any of them. It's a very good habit to put them in, however, because they form a framework for your own thinking and help prevent mistakes that could cause some browsers to break your page.

[<BODY]...[</BODY>]

Usage: Contains the content of the document.

Syntax:	`<BODY [attributes]>the body of the HTML doc</BODY>`
Start/End Tag:	Optional/Optional
Attributes:	`background="..."` Deprecated. URL for the background image.
	`bgcolor="..."` Deprecated. Sets background color.
	`text="..."` Deprecated. Text color.
	`link="..."` Deprecated. Link color.
	`vlink="..."` Deprecated. Visited link color.
	`alink="..."` Deprecated. Active link color.
	`class=`, `id=`, `style=`, `title=`, `lang=`, `dir=` Common attributes.
Intrinsics:	`onload="..."` Intrinsic event
	`onunload="..."` Intrinsic event triggered when document unloads.
	`onclick=`, `ondblclick=`, `onmousedown=`, `onmouseup=`, `onmouseover=`, `onmousemove=`, `onmouseout=`, `onkeypress=`, `onkeydown=`, `onkeyup=` Common intrinsic events.
Empty:	No
Notes:	There can be only one BODY element and it must follow the HEAD. The BODY element can be replaced by a FRAMESET element. The presentational attributes are deprecated in favor of setting these values with style sheets.
Introduced:	HTML 1.0
Browsers:	Netscape Navigator 0.9, 1.*x*, 2.*x*, 3.*x*, 4.*x*; Microsoft Internet Explorer 1.*x*, 2.*x*, 3.*x*, 4.*x*.
Example:	`<BODY>`

```
    <P align=center>
      In Scarlet town, where I was born<BR>
      There was a fair maid dwellin',<BR>
      Made every youth cry <I>Well-a-way! </I><BR>
      Her name was Barbara Allen.
    </BODY>
```

[`<HEAD>`]...[`</HEAD>`]

Usage:	This is the document header; it contains other elements that provide information to users and search engines.
Syntax:	`[<HEAD [attributes]>]header information[</HEAD>]`
Start/End Tag:	Optional/Optional

Attributes:	`profile="..."` URL specifying the location of META data.
	`lang=`, `dir=` Common attributes.
Empty:	No
Notes:	There can be only one HEAD per document. It must follow the opening HTML tag and precede the BODY.
Introduced:	HTML 1.0>]
Browsers:	Netscape Navigator 0.9, 1.*x*,2.*x*, 3.*x*, 4.x; Microsoft Internet Explorer 2.*x*, 3.*x*, 4.*x*.
Example:	

```
<HTML>
<HEAD>
    <TITLE>This is the text that will appear in the
    ➠browser title bar</TITLE>
</HEAD>
<BODY>
    <P> The title element contains the title text
        that appears in the subject line of the
        ➠browser.
    <P>It should be accurate, descriptive, and give
    ➠readers
        a reference to what is included on the page.
        ➠Remember that
        most browsers place the title in the bookmark
        ➠if the user
        wants to save your site and come back later.
        ➠You can help
        her by making a snappy and distinctive title
        ➠that identifies
        the site and tell who you are in a very few
        ➠words.
    </BODY>
</HTML>>]
```

[<HTML]...[</HTML>]

Usage:	The HTML element contains the entire document.
Syntax:	`[<HTML [attributes]>]body and other HTML elements[</HTML>]`
Start/End Tag:	Optional/Optional
Attributes:	`version="..."` URL of the document type definition specifying the HTML version used to create the document.
	`lang=`, `dir=` Common attributes.
Empty:	No
Notes:	The version information is duplicated in the `<!DOCTYPE...>` declaration, so it's not essential. >]

Introduced:	HTML 1.0
Browsers:	Netscape Navigator 0.9, 1.*x*,2.*x*, 3.*x*, 4.*x*; Microsoft Internet Explorer 2.*x*, 3.*x*, 4.*x*.
Example:	

```
<HTML>
  <HEAD>
    <TITLE>The Gallery</TITLE>
  </HEAD>
  <BODY bgcolor="#FFFFFF">
    <H1 align="center">The Gallery</H1>
  </BODY>
</HTML>>]
```

Header Elements: BASE, ISINDEX÷, LINK, META, NOSCRIPT, SCRIPT, STYLE, TITLE

Header elements occur in the head of an HTML document and have little, if any, effect on the direct formatting of the document; however, in the case of SCRIPT and STYLE, they can dynamically alter the default formatting.

<BASE>

Usage:	All other URLs in the document are resolved against this location.
Syntax:	<BASE *[attributes]*>
Start/End Tag:	Required/Forbidden
Attributes:	href="..." The URL of the linked resource.
	target="..." Determines where the resource will be displayed (user-defined name, _blank, _parent, **_self**, _top).
Empty:	Yes, closing tag is forbidden.
Notes:	Located in the document HEAD.
Introduced:	HTML 2.0
Browsers:	Netscape Navigator 1.0, 2.x, 3.x, 4.x; Microsoft Internet Explorer 2.0, 3.0, 4.0. occur
Example:	

```
<HTML>
  <HEAD>
    <TITLE>Base Tag Anatomy</TITLE>
    <BASE href="http://www.example.com/anatomy/">
  </HEAD>
  ... >
```

`<ISINDEX>` ÷

Usage:	Creates a primitive form that prompts the user for input.
Syntax:	`<ISINDEX [attributes]>`
Start/End Tag:	Required/Forbidden
Attributes:	`prompt="..."` Deprecated. Provides a prompt string for the input field.
	`class=, id=, style=, title=, lang=, dir=` Common attributes.
Empty:	Yes, closing tag is forbidden.]
Notes:	Deprecated. Use the `INPUT` element in a `FORM` instead.
Introduced:	HTML 3.2 occur
Browsers:	Netscape Navigator 1.0, 2.*x*, 3.*x*, 4.*x*; Microsoft Internet Explorer 2.0, 3.0, 4.0.
Example:	

```
<HTML>
  <HEAD>
    <TITLE>Searchable Index</TITLE>
    <ISINDEX prompt="Enter your search string:">
  </HEAD>
  <BODY>
  ...
  </BODY>
</HTML> occur ]
```

`<LINK>`

Usage:	Defines the relationship between a link and a resource.
Syntax:	`<LINK [attributes]>`
Start/End Tag:	Required/Forbidden
Attributes:	`href="..."` The URL of the resource.
	`rel="..."` The forward link types.
	`rev="..."` The reverse link types.
	`type="..."` The Internet content type.
	`media="..."` Defines the destination medium (`screen`, `print`, `projection`, `Braille`, `speech`, `all`). occur
	`target="..."` Determines where the resource will be displayed (user-defined name, `_blank`, `_parent`, **`_self`**, `_top`).
	`class=, id=, style=, title=, lang=, dir=` Common attributes.

Intrinsics:	onclick=, ondblclick=, onmousedown=, onmouseup=, onmouseover=, onmousemove=, onmouseout=, onkeypress=, onkeydown=, onkeyup= Common intrinsic events. >
Link Types:	contents Link refers to a document serving as a table of contents.
	index Link refers to a document serving as an index for the current document.
	glossary Link refers to a document serving as a glossary for the current document.
	copyright Link refers to a copyright statement for the current document. occur
	next Link refers to a document that's next in an ordered series of documents.
	previous Link refers to the previous document in an ordered set of documents. >
	start Link refers to the first document in an ordered series of documents.
	help Link refers to a document that includes help information. occur
	bookmark≥Link refers to a bookmark included in a document.
Empty:	Yes, closing tag is forbidden.
Notes:	Located in the document HEAD. In theory, you could create quite sophisticated navigation systems with these attributes, including automatic language selection and other goodies. Unfortunately, most browsers don't actually do anything with the information.
Introduced:	HTML 2.0 occur
Browsers:	Netscape Navigator 1.0, 2.0, 3.*x*, 4.*x*; Microsoft Internet Explorer 2.0, 3.0, 4.0.
Example:	...

```
<HEAD>
  <LINK href="contents.html" rel="next"
  ➥rev="prev">
</HEAD>
... >
```

`<META>`

Usage:	Supplies information about the document.
Syntax:	`<META [attributes]>`
Start/End Tag:	Required/Forbidden
Attributes:	`http-equiv="..."` HTTP response header name.
	`name="..."` Name of the meta-information.
	`content="..."` Content of the meta-information.
	`scheme="..."` Assigns a scheme to interpret the metadata. occur
	`lang=`, `dir=` Common attributes.
Empty:	Yes, closing tag is forbidden.
Notes:	The content of the `<META>` element is used for indexing purposes by many spiders and Web search engines.
Introduced:	HTML 2.0
Browsers:	Netscape Navigator 1.0, 2.*x*, 3.*x*, 4.*x*; Microsoft Internet Explorer 2.0, 3.0, 4.0.
Example:	`<HTML>`

```
<HTML>
  <HEAD>
    <TITLE>Author, Author</title>
    <META name="author" content="Joe Sample">
    <META name="keywords" content="research
    ➥writing html">
  </HEAD>
  <BODY>
<H1>Example Page</H1>
<H2>by Joe Sample</H2>
...
  </BODY>
</HTML> occur
```

`<NOSCRIPT>...</NOSCRIPT>`

Usage:	The `NOSCRIPT` element provides alternative content for browsers unable to execute a script.
Syntax:	`<NOSCRIPT>alternative content</NOSCRIPT>`
Start/End Tag:	Required/Required

Attributes:	None
Empty:	No
Notes:	This is really an inline text element placed here for convenience so that both <SCRIPT> tags are together. occur
Introduced:	HTML 4.0
Browsers:	Netscape Navigator 3.0, 4.0; Microsoft Internet Explorer 4.0.
Example:	

```
<HTML>
   <HEAD>
     <TITLE>Noscript Demonstration</TITLE>
   </HEAD>
   <BODY>
     <SCRIPT type ="text/javascript">
     <!--
       document.write ("<B>Hello, world.</B>")
       /-->
     </SCRIPT>
     <NOSCRIPT>
       <P>Hello, world.
     </NOSCRIPT>
   </BODY>
</HTML> occur
```

<SCRIPT>...</SCRIPT>

Usage:	The SCRIPT element contains client-side command sequences that are executed by the browser.
Syntax:	<SCRIPT [attributes]>script commands</SCRIPT>
Start/End Tag:	Required/Required
Attributes:	type="..." Script language Internet content type.
	language="..." Deprecated. The scripting language, deprecated in favor of the type attribute.
	src="..." The URL for the external script.
Empty:	No
Notes:	You can set the default scripting language in the META element. occur
Introduced:	HTML 4.0
Browsers:	Netscape Navigator 1.0, 2.0, 3.x, 4.0; Microsoft Internet Explorer 3.x, 4.0.

Example: . . .

```
<SCRIPT type ="text/javascript">
<!--
  document.write ("<B>Hello, world.</B>")
/-->
</SCRIPT> occur
```
          . . .

<STYLE>...</STYLE>

Usage: Creates an internal style sheet.

Syntax: `<STYLE [attributes]>style sheet contents</STYLE>`

Start/End Tag: Required/Required

Attributes: `type="..."`   The Internet content type.

                    `media="..."`   Defines the destination medium (`screen`, `print`, `projection`, `braille`, `speech`, `all`).

                    `title="..."`   The title of the style.

                    `lang=`, `dir=`   Common attributes.

Empty: No occur

Notes: Located in the HEAD element. It's a good idea to escape the style sheet with a comment, although not strictly necessary because some browsers, on seeing any text in the header, assume that the body has been reached and start rendering.

Introduced: HTML 4.0

Browsers: Netscape Navigator 4.0; Microsoft Internet Explorer 3.*x*, 4.0.

Example:
```
<HTML>
  <HEAD>
    <TITLE>Intro to Style Sheets</title>
    <STYLE type="text\css">
      <!--
        /* make all paragraphs red */
        p: (color: red : font-style: bold)
        -->
    </STYLE>
  </HEAD>
</HTML> occur
```

<TITLE>...</TITLE>

Usage: This is the name you give your Web page. The TITLE element, located in the HEAD element, is displayed in the browser window title bar.

Syntax: `<TITLE [attributes]>title of the page</TITLE>`

Start/End Tag: Required/Required

Attributes: `lang, dir`

Empty: No

Notes: This tag is required in every document. Only one title allowed per document.

Introduced: HTML 1.0 occur

Browsers: Netscape Navigator 1.0, 2.*x*, 3.*x*, 4.*x*; Microsoft Internet Explorer 2.0, 3.0, 4.0.

Example:
```
...
<HEAD>
  <TITLE>The title appears in the browser title
  ➥bar</TITLE>
</HEAD>
... occur
```

Frames: FRAMESET, FRAME, IFRAME, NOFRAMES

Frames create separate "panels" in the Web browser window that are used to display content from different source documents.

<FRAME>

Usage: Defines a FRAME.

Syntax: `<FRAME [attributes]>`

Start/End Tag: Required/Forbidden

Attributes: `name="..."`   The name of a frame.

`src="..."`   The source to be displayed in a frame.

`frameborder="..."`   Toggles the border between frames (`0`, `1`).

`marginwidth="..."`   Sets the space between the frame border and content.

`marginheight="..."`   Sets the space between the frame border and content.

`noresize`   Disables sizing. `>`

`scrolling="..."`   Determines scrollbar presence (`auto`, `yes`, `no`).

Empty: Yes, closing tag is forbidden.

Notes: Frames first gained notice as one of the popular Netscape extensions released with Netscape Navigator 2.0. Netscape Communications Corporation then proposed it to the W3C to be part of the next HTML standard.

Introduced:	HTML 4.0
Browsers:	Netscape Navigator 2.0, 3.*x*, 4.*x*; Microsoft Internet Explorer 3.0, 4.0.
Example:	

```
<!DOCTYPE html public "-//IETF//DTD HTML//EN">
<HTML>
  <HEAD>
    <TITLE>Technical Writing</TITLE>
    <META name="FORMATTER" content="Microsoft FrontPage
    ➥2.0">
  </HEAD>
  <FRAMESET rows="12%,*,12%">
    <FRAME src="frtop.htm" name="top" noresize>
    <FRAMESET cols="35%,65%">
      <FRAME src="frconten.htm" name="contents">
      <FRAME src="frmain.htm" name="main">
    </FRAMESET>
    <FRAME src="frbottom.htm" name="bottom" noresize>
  <NOFRAMES>
    <BODY>
      <P>This Web page uses frames, but your browser
      ➥doesn't
      support them. Please go to my non-frames version
      ➥of
      <A href="tw_nonf.htm">Technical Writing
      ➥Resources</A>.
    </BODY>
  </NOFRAMES>
  </FRAMESET>
</HTML>>
```

<FRAMESET>...</FRAMESET>

Usage:	Defines the layout of FRAMES within a window.
Syntax:	<FRAMESET *[attributes]*>*contents of frame set*</FRAME-SET>
Start/End Tag:	Required/Required
Attributes:	rows="..." The number of rows.
	cols="..." The number of columns.
	onload="..." The intrinsic event triggered when the document loads.
	onunload="..." The intrinsic event triggered when the document unloads.
Empty:	No
Notes:	FRAMESETs can be nested.
Introduced:	HTML 4.0

Browsers: Netscape Navigator 2.0, 3.*x*, 4.*x*; Microsoft Internet Explorer 3.0, 4.0.

Example:

```
<HTML>
  <HEAD>
    <TITLE>Three Ages</TITLE>
  </HEAD>
  <FRAMESET rows="*,*,*">
    <FRAME src="childhood.htm">
    <FRAME src="maturity.htm">
    <FRAME src="oldage.htm">
  </FRAMESET>
  <NOFRAMES>
    <BODY>
      <P>
      This is the unframed version of the Three Ages
      ➥page<BR>
      Please choose one of the following
      ➥destinations:<BR>
      <A href="childhood.htm">Childhood</A><BR>
      <A href="maturity.htm">Maturity</A><BR>
      <A href="oldage.htm">Old Age</A><BR>
    </BODY>
  </NOFRAMES>
</HTML>
```

<IFRAME>...</IFRAME>

Usage: Creates an inline frame.

Syntax: `<IFRAME [attributes]>contents of inline frame</IFRAME>`

Start/End Tag: Required/Required

Attributes: `name="..."`   The name of the frame.

`src="..."`   The source to be displayed in a frame.

`frameborder="..."`   Toggles the border between frames (0, 1).

`marginwidth="..."`   Sets the space between the frame border and content.

`marginheight="..."`   Sets the space between the frame border and content.

`scrolling="..."`   Determines scrollbar presence (auto, yes, no).

`align="..."`   Deprecated. Controls alignment (**left**, center, right, justify).

`height="..."`   Height.

`width="..."`   Width.

Empty:	No
Notes:	IFRAME is really an inline element but is placed here for convenience.
Introduced:	HTML 4.0
Browsers:	Microsoft Internet Explorer 3.0, 4.0.
Example:	

```
<HTML>
  <HEAD>
    <TITLE>Three Ages</TITLE>
  </HEAD>
  <BODY>
    <P>These the three ages, childhood,
      <IFRAME src="childhood.htm">
      maturity,
      <IFRAME src="maturity.htm">
      and old age
      <IFRAME src="oldage.htm">.
  </BODY>
</HTML>
```

<NOFRAMES>...</NOFRAMES>

Usage:	Alternative content when frames are not supported.
Syntax:	<NOFRAMES>*contents displayed in browsers that don't support frames*</NOFRAMES>
Start/End Tag:	Required/Required
Attributes:	None
Empty:	No
Introduced:	HTML 4.0
Browsers:	Netscape Navigator 2.*x*, 3.*x*, 4.*x*; Microsoft Internet Explorer 3.0, 4.0.
Example:	

```
...
<NOFRAMES>
  <BODY>
    <P>This Web page uses frames, but your browser
    ➡doesn't
    support them. Please go to my non-frames version of
    ➡<A
    href="tw_nonf.htm">Technical Writing Resources</a>.
  </BODY>
</NOFRAMES>
...
```

SGML Special Tags: `!-- (comment) --`, `!DOCTYPE`

These tags are both special cases: SGML (Standard Generalized Markup Language) markup that's also part of HTML. SGML comments, in particular, are a source of anomalous behavior in browsers because many programmers are confused about exactly how they work. It might be best to avoid using `!DOCTYPE` because none of the mainstream browsers support it and it could cause your pages to fail validation checks by online or local HTML validators, most of which do support it.

`<!-- ... -->`

Usage:	SGML comment. Used to insert notes or scripts that aren't displayed by the browser.
Syntax:	`<![-- ... --]*>`
Start/End Tag:	N/A
Attributes:	None
Empty:	N/A
Notes:	Comments are a special case. The actual comment tags are two dashes (`--`) surrounding each comment, but the comment must be enclosed in an SGML command: `<! ... >`. The first two dashes must follow the `<!` with no intervening spaces, and there must be a space immediately after. Comment dashes must occur in pairs, so if there are multiple comments, there will be four dashes (`-- --`) between each. Many browsers don't handle comments correctly; the most common errors are not allowing multiline comments, exiting the comment on the second set of dashes, or exiting the comment at the first `>`. All these behaviors are errors, but should be taken into account both by the designer.
Introduced:	HTML 2.0
Browsers:	Netscape Navigator 1.0, 2.*x*, 3.*x*, 4.x; Microsoft Internet Explorer 1.*x*, 2.*x*, 3.*x*, 4.*x*.
Example:	

```
<HTML>
<!-- Nobody ever seems to read comments anymore.-->
<!-- The same holds true for multiple-line comments like
    the one you're reading right now.-->
<!-- This is a series of comments --
  -- although many browsers --
  -- don't interpret them correctly -->
<!-- This is a <P> tag in a comment, which many
    ➥browsers don't
    handle correctly.-->
</HTML> both
```

`<!DOCTYPE...>`

Usage:	Version information appears on the first line of an HTML document and is an SGML declaration rather than an element.
Syntax:	`<!doctype html public "[standard DTD name]">`
Start/End Tag:	Required/None
Attributes:	None
Empty:	N/A
Notes:	This tag may be omitted because few browsers actually support it. In fact, it might cause problems unless you have particular reasons to validate against a certain DTD because there's no way to say you're trying to cover all bases by including elements from several. both
Introduced:	HTML 1.0
Browsers:	Netscape Navigator 0.9, 1.x,2.x, 3.x, 4.x; Microsoft Internet Explorer 2.x, 3.x, 4.x.

Example:	`<!DOCTYPE html public "-//IETF//DTD HTML 4.0//EN">`
	`<HTML>`
	`... both`

Block-level Elements

Block-level elements cause a break in the flow of text and affect the formatting of the document.

Basic Block Elements: ADDRESS, BLOCKQUOTE, CENTER÷, DIV, FIELDSET, H1-H6, HR, ISINDEX÷*, NOSCRIPT*, P, PRE

Basic block elements alter the document's formatting and cause a break in the flow of text but are not part of, nor do they contain, other block elements.

`<ADDRESS>...</ADDRESS>`

Usage:	Provides a special format for author or contact information or allows automatic extraction of an address by a process.
Syntax:	`<ADDRESS [attributes]>address or contact information</ADDRESS>`
Start/End Tag:	Required/Required
Attributes:	`class=, id=, style=, title=, lang=, dir=` Common attributes.

Intrinsics:	`onclick=`, `ondblclick=`, `onmousedown=`, `onmouseup=`, `onmouseover=`, `onmousemove=`, `onmouseout=`, `onkeypress=`, `onkeydown=`, `onkeyup=` Common intrinsic events.
Empty:	No
Notes:	This element causes a break in the flow of text, so it's included here. The `BR` element is commonly used inside the `ADDRESS` element to break the lines of an address. Some browsers render the contents as italic text.
Introduced:	HTML 2.0
Browsers:	Netscape Navigator 1.0, 2.0, 3.x, 4.x; Microsoft Internet Explorer 2.0, 3.0, 4.0.
Example:	`<ADDRESS>`

```
author@example.com<BR>
123 Main Street<BR>
Anytown, IN<BR>
USA
</ADDRESS>
```

`<BLOCKQUOTE>...</BLOCKQUOTE>`

Usage:	Used to display long quotations.
Syntax:	`<BLOCKQUOTE [attributes]>text of blockquote</BLOCKQUOTE>`
Start/End Tag:	Required/Required
Attributes:	`cite="..."` The URL of the quoted text or the reason for the change.
	`class=`, `id=`, `style=`, `title=`, `lang=`, `dir=` Common Attributes
Intrinsics:	`onclick=`, `ondblclick=`, `onmousedown=`, `onmouseup=`, `onmouseover=`, `onmousemove=`, `onmouseout=`, `onkeypress=`, `onkeydown=`, `onkeyup=` Common intrinsic events.
Empty:	No
Notes:	Usually rendered with an offset from both margins. Related to but not the same as the `<Q>` tag, which marks an inline quote.
Introduced:	HTML 2.0
Browsers:	Netscape Navigator 1.0, 2.0, 3.x, 4.x; Microsoft Internet Explorer 2.0, 3.0, 4.0.

Example: . . .

```
<BLOCKQUOTE cite="http://www.teresaofavila.com/">
  I only wish that I could write with both hands, so as
  ➥not to forget
  one thing while I am saying another. &mdash; Teresa
  ➥of Avila
</BLOCKQUOTE>
```

`<CENTER>...</CENTER>` ÷

Usage: Used to center an HTML element.

Syntax: `<CENTER [attributes]>centered text or elements</CENTER>`

Start/End Tag: Required/Required

Attributes: `class=`, `id=`, `style=`, `title=`, `lang=`, `dir=`   Common attributes.

Intrinsics: `onclick=`, `ondblclick=`, `onmousedown=`, `onmouseup=`,
                `onmouseover=`, `onmousemove=`, `onmouseout=`, `onkeypress=`,
                `onkeydown=`, `onkeyup=`   Common intrinsic events.

Empty: No

Notes: Deprecated. Defined in HTML 4.0 as a synonym for `<DIV align="center">`, which should be used instead.

Introduced: HTML 2.0

Browsers: Netscape Navigator 1.1, 2.0, 3.x, 4.x; Microsoft Internet Explorer 2.0, 3.0, 4.0.

Example:
```
<CENTER>
  <A href="http://www.example.org/pancake/">Pancake
  ➥Breakfast!</A>
</CENTER>
```

`<DIV>...</DIV>`

Usage: The `DIVISION` element is used to add structure to a block of text.

Syntax: `<DIV [attributes]>structured text</DIV>`

Start/End Tag: Required/Required

Attributes: `align="..."`   Deprecated. Controls alignment (**left**, `center`, `right`, `justify`).

                `class=`, `id=`, `style=`, `title=`, `lang=`, `dir=`   Common attributes.

Intrinsics: `onclick=`, `ondblclick=`, `onmousedown=`, `onmouseup=`,
                `onmouseover=`, `onmousemove=`, `onmouseout=`, `onkeypress=`,
                `onkeydown=`, `onkeyup=`   Common intrinsic events.

Empty: No

Notes: Cannot be used in a P element. The align attribute is deprecated
               in favor of controlling alignment through style sheets.

Introduced: HTML 2.0

Browsers: Netscape Navigator 2.0, 3.*x*, 4.*x*; Microsoft Internet Explorer 2.*x*,
               3.*x*, 4.*x*.

Example:
```
<HTML>
  <DIV align="left">
    <P>...for as ye think I fear too much,
  </DIV>
  <DIV align="right">
    <P>be you well aware that you fear not as far too
    ➥little.
  </DIV>
  <DIV align="center">
    <P>- Elizabeth Grey
  </DIV>
</HTML>
```

`<H1>...</H1>` Through `<H6>...</H6>`

Usage: The six headings (H1 is the uppermost, or most important) are
               used in the BODY to structure information hierarchically.

Syntax: `<H1 [attributes]>heading text</H1>`

Start/End Tag: Required/Required

Attributes: align="..." Deprecated. Controls alignment (**left**, center,
               right, justify).

               class=, id=, style=, title=, lang=, dir= Common attributes.

Intrinsics: onclick=, ondblclick=, onmousedown=, onmouseup=,
               onmouseover=, onmousemove=, onmouseout=, onkeypress=,
               onkeydown=, onkeyup= Common intrinsic events.

Empty: No

Notes: Visual browsers display the size of the headings in relation to their
               importance, with H1 being the largest and H6 the smallest. For
               compatibility, headings should start at H1 and proceed sequentially
               down to the lowest value. The align attribute is deprecated in
               favor of controlling alignment through style sheets.

Introduced: HTML 1.0

Browsers: Netscape Navigator 1.0, 2.*x*, 3.*x*, 4.*x*; Microsoft Internet Explorer
               2.*x*, 3.*x*, 4.*x*.

Example:
```
<HTML>
  <HEAD>
    <TITLE>Heading examples</TITLE>
  </HEAD>
    <H1> This little piggy is heading style 1</H1>
    <H2> This little piggy is heading style 2</H2>
    <H3> This little piggy is heading style 3</H3>
    <H4> This little piggy is heading style 4</H4>
    <H5> This little piggy is heading style 5</H5>
    <H6> This little piggy is heading style 6</H6>
    <P> Header elements automatically create vertical
    ➥white space surrounding the header proportionally.
</HTML>
```

<HR>

Usage: Horizontal rules can be used to separate sections of a Web page.

Syntax: `<HR [attributes]>`

Start/End Tag: Required/Forbidden

Attributes: `align="..."`   Deprecated. Controls alignment (**left**, center, right, justify).

                `noshade="..."`   Displays the rule as a solid color.

                `size="..."`   Deprecated. Controls the size of the rule.

                `width="..."`   Deprecated. Controls the width of the rule.

                `class=, id=, style=, title=, lang=, dir=`   Common attributes.

Intrinsics: `onclick=, ondblclick=, onmousedown=, onmouseup=, onmouseover=, onmousemove=, onmouseout=, onkeypress=, onkeydown=, onkeyup=`   Common intrinsic events.

Empty: Yes, closing tag is forbidden.

Notes: There are many different schools of thought on using the `<HR>` tag, but some designers are straying away from this tag to make better use of white space to separate page elements.

Introduced: HTML 2.0

Browsers:	Netscape Navigator 0.9, 1.*x*,2.*x*, 3.*x*, 4.*x*; Microsoft Internet Explorer 2.*x*, 3.*x*, 4.*x*.
Example:	...

```
  <H2>Section One</H2>
...
<HR>
  <H2>Section Two</H2>
  ...
```

`<ISINDEX>...</ISINDEX>* ÷`

Notes:	Operates as a block-level element that creates a primitive form and discussed in the "Structural (Housekeeping) Elements" section as a header element. Deprecated. Use the `INPUT` element in a `FORM` instead.

`<P>`

Usage:	Defines a paragraph.
Syntax:	`<P [attributes]>`
Start/End Tag:	Required/Optional
Attributes:	`align="..."` Deprecated. Controls alignment (**left**, `center`, `right`, `justify`).
	`class=, id=, style=, title=, lang=, dir=` Common attributes.
Intrinsics:	`onclick=, ondblclick=, onmousedown=, onmouseup=, onmouseover=, onmousemove=, onmouseout=, onkeypress=, onkeydown=, onkeyup=` Common intrinsic events.
Empty:	No
Notes:	The closing tag is usually omitted.
Introduced:	HTML 1.0
Browser:	Netscape Navigator 1.0, 2.x, 3.x, 4.x; Microsoft Internet Explorer 2.0, 3.0, 4.0.
Example:	`<P align=center>HTML 4 is a major upgrade to the HTML`⮕`standard.`

`<PRE>...</PRE>`

Usage:	Displays preformatted text.
Syntax:	`<PRE [attributes]>formatted text</PRE>`
Start/End Tag:	Required/Required
Attributes:	`width="..."` The width of the formatted text.
	`class=, id=, style=, title=, lang=, dir=` Common attributes.

Intrinsics:	`onclick=`, `ondblclick=`, `onmousedown=`, `onmouseup=`, `onmouseover=`, `onmousemove=`, `onmouseout=`, `onkeypress=`, `onkeydown=`, `onkeyup=` Common intrinsic events.
Empty:	No
Note:	The `<PRE>` element is an excellent way to add already formatted text documents to a Web page because it preserves the document's original formatting.
Introduced:	HTML 2.0
Browsers:	Netscape Navigator 1.0, 2.0, 3.x, 4.x; Microsoft Internet Explorer 2.0, 3.0, 4.0.
Example:	

```
<PRE width ="80%">
Acquisitions Editors      Technical Editors      Editorial
➥Assistant
 Development Editors       Office Manager         Mailroom
➥Attendant
   Production Editors      Typist
            Copy Editors   Clerk                  Other
          ➥Workers
</PRE>
```

Lists: DD, DIR÷, DL, DT, LI, MENU÷, OL, UL

Like all block elements, list elements cause a break in the flow of the text, but they are special in that they can contain or be a part of other block elements. You can organize text into a more structured outline by creating lists, which can also be nested.

`<DD>...[</DD>]`

Usage:	The definition description used in a DL (definition list) element.
Syntax:	`<DD [attributes]>description of the word being defined[</DD>]`
Start/End Tag:	Required/Optional
Attributes:	`class=`, `id=`, `style=`, `title=`, `lang=`, `dir=` Common attributes.
Intrinsics:	`onclick=`, `ondblclick=`, `onmousedown=`, `onmouseup=`, `onmouseover=`, `onmousemove=`, `onmouseout=`, `onkeypress=`, `onkeydown=`, `onkeyup=` Common intrinsic events.
Empty:	No
Notes:	Can contain block-level content, such as the `<P>` element.

Introduced:	HTML 2.0
Browsers:	Netscape Navigator 1.0, 2.0, 3.x, 4.x; Microsoft Internet Explorer 2.0, 3.0, 4.0.
Example:	

```
<DL>
   <DT> Publications Manager
     <DD> The person in charge of coordinating all
          departmental activities.
   <DT> Technical Writer
     <DD> The person who writes a technical manual.
   <DT> Technical Editor
     <DD> The person who is responsible for the technical
          accuracy of the finished manual.
</DL>
```

`<DIR>...</DIR>` ÷

Usage:	Creates a multi-column directory list, in theory.
Syntax:	`<DIR [attributes]>directory list contents</DIR>`
Start/End Tag:	Required/Required
Attributes:	`compact` Deprecated. May display the list in a compact form.
	`class=, id=, style=, title=, lang=, dir=` Common attributes.
Intrinsics:	`onclick=, ondblclick=, onmousedown=, onmouseup=, onmouseover=, onmousemove=, onmouseout=, onkeypress=, onkeydown=, onkeyup=` Common intrinsic events.
Empty:	No
Notes:	Must contain at least one list item. This element is deprecated in favor of the UL (unordered list) element. Originally, this element was to be used for listing files.
Introduced:	HTML 2.0
Browsers:	Netscape Navigator 1.0, 2.0, 3.x, 4.x; Microsoft Internet Explorer 2.0, 3.0, 4.0.
Example:	

```
<DIR>
   <LI><CODE>README.</CODE>
   <LI><CODE>INSTALL</CODE>
   <LI><CODE>ERRATA</CODE>
</DIR>
```

`<DL>...</DL>`

Usage:	Creates a definition list.
Syntax:	`<DL [attributes]>contents of definition list</DL>`

Start/End Tag:	Required/Required
Attributes:	`compact` Deprecated. May display the list in a compact form.
	`class=`, `id=`, `style=`, `title=`, `lang=`, `dir=` Common attributes.
Intrinsics:	`onclick=`, `ondblclick=`, `onmousedown=`, `onmouseup=`, `onmouseover=`, `onmousemove=`, `onmouseout=`, `onkeypress=`, `onkeydown=`, `onkeyup=` Common intrinsic events.
Empty:	No
Notes:	Must contain at least one `<DT>` or `<DD>` element in any order.
Introduced:	HTML 2.0
Browsers:	Netscape Navigator 1.0, 2.0, 3.x, 4.x; Microsoft Internet Explorer 2.0, 3.0, 4.0.
Example:	`<DL>`

```
<DL>
    <DT> Publications Manager
      <DD> The person in charge of coordinating all
      ➥departmental activities.
    <DT> Technical Writer
      <DD> The person who writes a technical manual.
    <DT> Technical Editor
      <DD> The person who is responsible for the technical
      ➥accuracy of the finished manual.
</DL>
```

`<DT>...[</DT>]`

Usage:	The definition term (or label) used in a DL (definition list) element.
Syntax:	`<DT [attributes]>text of definition term[</DT>]`
Start/End Tag:	Required/Optional
Attributes:	`class=`, `id=`, `style=`, `title=`, `lang=`, `dir=` Common attributes.
Intrinsics:	`onclick=`, `ondblclick=`, `onmousedown=`, `onmouseup=`, `onmouseover=`, `onmousemove=`, `onmouseout=`, `onkeypress=`, `onkeydown=`, `onkeyup=` Common intrinsic events.
Empty:	No
Notes:	Must contain text (which can be modified by text markup elements).
Introduced:	HTML 2.0
Browsers:	Netscape Navigator 1.0, 2.0, 3.x, 4.x; Microsoft Internet Explorer 2.0, 3.0, 4.0.

Example: `<DL>`

    `<DT>``Publications Manager`
     `<DD>The person in charge of coordinating all`
        `departmental activities.`
    `<DT>``Technical Writer`
     `<DD>The person who writes a technical manual.`
    `<DT>``Technical Editor`
     `<DD>The person who is responsible for the`
        `technical accuracy of the finished manual.`
  `</DL>`

`<LI>...[</LI>]`

Usage:	Defines a list item within a list.
Syntax:	`<LI [attributes]>list item text[</LI>]`
Start/End Tag:	Required/Optional
Attributes:	`type="..."` Changes the numbering style (`1`, `a`, `A`, `i`, `I`) in ordered lists or bullet style (`disc`, `square`, `circle`) in unordered lists.
	`value="..."` Sets the numbering to the given integer, beginning with the current list item.
	`class=`, `id=`, `style=`, `title=`, `lang=`, `dir=` Common attributes.
Intrinsics:	`onclick=`, `ondblclick=`, `onmousedown=`, `onmouseup=`, `onmouseover=`, `onmousemove=`, `onmouseout=`, `onkeypress=`, `onkeydown=`, `onkeyup=` Common intrinsic events.
Empty:	No
Introduced:	HTML 2.0
Browsers:	Netscape Navigator 1.0, 2.0, 3.*x*, 4.*x*; Microsoft Internet Explorer 2.0, 3.0, 4.0.
Example:	`<UL>`

  `<LI>``Item 1`
  `<LI>``Item 2`
`</UL>`

`<MENU>...</MENU>` ÷

Usage:	Creates a single-column menu list.
Syntax:	`<MENU [attributes]>text of menu</MENU>`
Start/End Tag:	Required/Required
Attributes:	`compact` Deprecated. May display the list in a compact form.
	`class=`, `id=`, `style=`, `title=`, `lang=`, `dir=` Common attributes.

A

Intrinsics:	`onclick=`, `ondblclick=`, `onmousedown=`, `onmouseup=`, `onmouseover=`, `onmousemove=`, `onmouseout=`, `onkeypress=`, `onkeydown=`, `onkeyup=` Common intrinsic events.
Empty:	No
Notes:	Must contain at least one list item. This element is deprecated in favor of the `UL` (unordered list) element.
Introduced:	HTML 3.2
Browsers:	Netscape Navigator 1.0, 2.0, 3.*x*, 4.*x*; Microsoft Internet Explorer 2.0, 3.0, 4.0.
Example:	. . .

```
<MENU>
  <LI>Item 1
  <LI>Item 2
</MENU>
```

. . .

<OL>...</OL>

Usage:	Creates an ordered list.
Syntax:	`<OL [attributes]>text of ordered list</OL>`
Start/End Tag:	Required/Required
Attributes:	`type="..."` Sets the numbering style (`1`, `a`, `A`, `i`, `I`).
	`compact` Deprecated. May display the list in a compact form.
	`start="..."` Sets the starting number to the chosen integer.
	`class=`, `id=`, `style=`, `title=`, `lang=`, `dir=` Common attributes.
Intrinsics:	`onclick=`, `ondblclick=`, `onmousedown=`, `onmouseup=`, `onmouseover=`, `onmousemove=`, `onmouseout=`, `onkeypress=`, `onkeydown=`, `onkeyup=` Common intrinsic events.
Empty:	No
Notes:	Must contain at least one list item.
Introduced:	HTML 2.0

Browsers:	Netscape Navigator 1.0, 2.0, 3.*x*, 4.*x*; Microsoft Internet Explorer 2.0, 3.0, 4.0.
Example:	**<OL>**

```
<LI>Insert the CD-ROM into your CD-ROM drive.
<LI>From the Start menu, choose Run.
<LI>Enter <code>f:setup</code> to begin the
➥installation.
</OL>
```

<UL>...</UL>

Usage:	Creates an unordered list.
Syntax:	<UL *[attributes]*>text of unordered list</UL>
Start/End Tag:	Required/Required
Attributes:	type="..." Sets the bullet style (disc, square, circle).
	compact Deprecated. May display the list in a compact form.
	class=, id=, style=, title=, lang=, dir= Common attributes.
Intrinsics:	onclick=, ondblclick=, onmousedown=, onmouseup=, onmouseover=, onmousemove=, onmouseout=, onkeypress=, onkeydown=, onkeyup= Common intrinsic events.
Empty:	No
Notes:	Must contain at least one list item.
Introduced:	HTML 2.0
Browsers:	Netscape Navigator 1.0, 2.0, 3.*x*, 4.*x*; Microsoft Internet Explorer 2.0, 3.0, 4.0.
Example:	**<UL>**

```
<LI>Item 1
<LI>Item 2
<LI>Item 3
</UL>
```

Forms: BUTTON, FIELDSET, FORM, INPUT, ISINDEX*, LABEL, LEGEND, OPTION, SELECT, TEXTAREA

Like other block elements, forms cause a break in the flow of the text and formatting. Forms are a special case because they may contain, or be a part of, other block elements and create an interface for the user to select options and submit data back to the Web server.

`<BUTTON>...</BUTTON>`

Usage:	Creates a button.
Syntax:	`<BUTTON [attributes]>the button</BUTTON>`
Start/End Tag:	Required/Required
Attributes:	`name="..."` The button name.
	`value="..."` The value of the button.
	`type="..."` The button type (`button`, `submit`, `reset`).
	`disabled="..."` Sets the button state to disabled.
	`tabindex="..."` Sets the tabbing order between elements with a defined `tabindex`.
	`class=`, `id=`, `style=`, `title=`, `lang=`, `dir=` Common attributes.
Intrinsics:	`onfocus="..."` The event that occurs when the element receives focus.
	`onblur="..."` The event that occurs when the element loses focus. tag>>> tag>
	`onclick=`, `ondblclick=`, `onmousedown=`, `onmouseup=`, `onmouseover=`, `onmousemove=`, `onmouseout=`, `onkeypress=`, `onkeydown=`, `onkeyup=` Common intrinsic events.
Empty:	No
Introduced:	HTML 3.2
Browsers:	Netscape Navigator 3.x 4.x; Microsoft Internet Explorer 3.0, 4.0.
Example:	`<FORM action="..." method="...">`

```
  <INPUT type="radio" name= sex value="M"> Male
  <INPUT type="radio" name= sex value="F"> Female
  <BUTTON type="submit" name="submit" value="submit">
    <IMG src="/icons/submit.gif" alt="submit"></BUTTON>
</FORM>
```

`<FIELDSET>...</FIELDSET>`

Usage:	Groups related controls.
Syntax:	`<FIELDSET [attributes]>related controls</FIELDSET>`
Start/End Tag:	Required/Required
Attributes:	
Empty:	No

Introduced: HTML 3.2

Browsers: Netscape Navigator 3.*x*, 4.*x*; Microsoft Internet Explorer 3.0, 4.0.

Example:
```
<HTML>
  <HEAD>
    <TITLE>Fieldset Legend</TITLE>
  </HEAD>
  <BODY>
    <FORM action="http://www.example.com/cgi-
    ➥bin/testing.pl" method="post">
      <FIELDSET>
        <LEGEND align="top">Customer Name</LEGEND>
        Last Name: <INPUT name="lastname" type="text"
        ➥tabindex="1">
        First Name: <INPUT name="firstname" type="text"
        ➥tabindex="2">
      </FIELDSET>
      <FIELDSET>
        <LEGEND align="top">Interests</LEGEND>
        <INPUT name="surfing"
               type="checkbox"
               value="surfing" tabindex="3">Surfing
               ➥</INPUT>
        <INPUT name="hiking"
               type="checkbox"
               value="hiking" tabindex="4">Hiking
               ➥</INPUT>
      </FIELDSET>
    </FORM>
  </BODY>
</HTML>
```

`<FORM>...</FORM>`

Usage: Creates a form that holds controls for user input.

Syntax: `<FORM [attributes]>contents of the form</FORM>`

Start/End Tag: Required/Required

Attributes: `action="..."`   The URL for the server action.

`method="..."`   The HTTP method (GET, POST). GET is deprecated.

`enctype="..."`   Specifies the MIME (Internet media type).

`target="..."`   Determines where the resource will be displayed (user-defined name, _blank, _parent, _self, _top).

`accept-charset="..."`   The list of character encodings. Default value is ISO-8859-1.

`class=, id=, style=, title=, lang=, dir=`   Common attributes.

Intrinsics:	`onsubmit="..."` The intrinsic event that occurs when the form is submitted.
	`onreset="..."` The intrinsic event that occurs when the form is reset.
	`onclick=, ondblclick=, onmousedown=, onmouseup=, onmouseover=, onmousemove=, onmouseout=, onkeypress=, onkeydown=, onkeyup=` Common intrinsic events.
Empty:	No
Introduced:	HTML 2.0
Browsers:	Netscape Navigator q.0, 2.*x*, 3.*x*, 4.*x*; Microsoft Internet Explorer 2.0, 3.0, 4.0.

Example:	`<FORM action="http://www.example.com/cgibin/`
	`➥register.pl">`
	`    contents of form`
	`</FORM>`

`<INPUT>`

Usage:	Defines controls used in forms.
Syntax:	`<INPUT [attributes]>`
Start/End Tag:	Required/Forbidden
Attributes:	`type="..."` The type of input control (`text`, `password`, `checkbox`, `radio`, `submit`, `reset`, `file`, `hidden`, `image`, `button`).
	`accept="..."` File types allowed for upload.
	`name="..."` The name of the control (required except for `submit` and `reset`).
	`value="..."` The initial value of the control (required for radio buttons and checkboxes).
	`checked="..."` Sets the radio buttons to a checked state.
	`disabled="..."` Disables the control.
	`readonly="..."` For text password types.
	`size="..."` The width of the control in pixels except for text and password controls, which are specified in number of characters.
	`maxlength="..."` The maximum number of characters that can be entered.
	`src="..."` The URL to an image control type.
	`alt="..."` An alternative text description.
	`usemap="..."` The URL to a client-side image map.

align="..." Deprecated. Controls alignment (**left**, center, right, justify).

tabindex="..." Sets the tabbing order between elements with a defined tabindex.

class=, id=, style=, title=, lang=, dir= Common attributes.

Intrinsics: onfocus="..." The event that occurs when the element receives focus.

onblur="..." The event that occurs when the element loses focus.

onselect="..." Intrinsic event that occurs when the control is selected.

onchange="..." Intrinsic event that occurs when the control is changed.

onclick=, ondblclick=, onmousedown=, onmouseup=, onmouseover=, onmousemove=, onmouseout=, onkeypress=, onkeydown=, onkeyup= Common intrinsic events.

Empty: Yes, closing tag is forbidden.

Input Types: text Creates a single line text box.

password Similar to text, but the entered text is rendered in the field in a way that hides the actual alpha and numeric characters that were entered.

checkbox An on/off switch. When checked, it is "on"; when not checked, it's "off".

radio An on/off switch.

submit Creates a submit button for submitting text.

image Creates a graphical submit button.

reset Creates a reset button.

button Creates a button with no default behavior.

hidden Creates an element not rendered by the user agent.

file Prompts the user for a filename.

Introduced: HTML 2.0

Browsers: Netscape Navigator 1.0, 2.*x*, 3.*x*, 4.*x*; Microsoft Internet Explorer 2.0, 3.0, 4.0.

Example:
```
<FORM ...>
  <INPUT type="radio" name="sex" value="M"> Male
  <INPUT type="radio" name="sex" value="F"> Female
</FORM>
```

`<ISINDEX>* ÷`

Notes: Operates as a block-level element that creates a primitive form and discussed in the "Structural (Housekeeping) Elements" section as a header element. Deprecated. Use the `INPUT` element in a `FORM` instead.

`<LABEL>...</LABEL>`

Usage: Labels a control.

Syntax: `<LABEL [attributes]>labeled control</LABEL>`

Start/End Tag: Required/Required

Attributes: `for="..."` Associates a label with an identified control.

`disabled="..."` Disables a control.

`accesskey="..."` Assigns a hotkey to this element.

`class=`, `id=`, `style=`, `title=`, `lang=`, `dir=` Common attributes.

Intrinsics: `onfocus="..."` The event that occurs when the element receives focus.

`onblur="..."` The event that occurs when the element loses focus.

`onclick=`, `ondblclick=`, `onmousedown=`, `onmouseup=`, `onmouseover=`, `onmousemove=`, `onmouseout=`, `onkeypress=`, `onkeydown=`, `onkeyup=` Common intrinsic events.

Empty: No

Introduced: HTML 4.0

Browsers: Netscape Navigator 4.*x*; Microsoft Internet Explorer 4.0.

Example:
```
<HTML>
  <FORM action="..." method="post">
    <TABLE>
      <TR>
        <TD><LABEL for="first">First name</LABEL>
            <TD><INPUT type="text" name="firstname"
            ➥id="first">
        <TR>
          <TD><LABEL for="last">Last name</LABEL>
              <TD><INPUT type="text" name="lastname"
              ➥id="last">
   ...
      </TABLE>
    <form>
</HTML>
```

<LEGEND>...</LEGEND>

Usage:	Assigns a caption to a FIELDSET.
Syntax:	<LEGEND *[attributes]*>*fieldset caption*</LEGEND>
Start/End Tag:	Required/Required
Attributes:	class, id, style, title, lang, dir, onclick, ondblclick, onmousedown, onmouseup, onmouseover, onmousemove, onmouseout, onkeypress, onkeydown, onkeyup
	align="..." Deprecated. Controls alignment (**left**, center, right, justify).
	accesskey="..." Assigns a hotkey to this element.
Empty:	No
Introduced:	HTML 3.2
Browsers:	Netscape Navigator 3.*x*, 4.*x*; Microsoft Internet Explorer 3.0, 4.0.
Example:	

```
<HTML>
  <HEAD>
    <TITLE>Fieldset Legend</TITLE>
  </HEAD>
  <BODY>
    <FORM action="http://www.example.com/cgi-bin/
    ➥testing.pl" method="post">
      <FIELDSET>
        <LEGEND align="top">Customer Name</LEGEND>
        Last Name: <INPUT name="lastname" type="text"
        ➥tabindex="1">
        First Name: <INPUT name="firstname" type="text"
        ➥tabindex="2">
      </FIELDSET>
      <FIELDSET>
        <LEGEND align="top">Interests</LEGEND>
        <INPUT name="surfing"
                type="checkbox"
                value="surfing" tabindex="3">Surfing
                ➥</INPUT>
        <INPUT name="hiking"
                type="checkbox"
                value="hiking" tabindex="4">Hiking
                ➥</INPUT>
      </FIELDSET>
    </FORM>
  </BODY>
</HTML>
```

`<OPTION>...</OPTION>`

Usage:	Specifies choices in a SELECT element.
Syntax:	`<OPTION [attributes]>choices in a SELECT element</OPTION>`
Start/End Tag:	Required/Optional
Attributes:	`selected="..."` Specifies whether the option is selected.
	`disabled="..."` Disables control.
	`value="..."` The value submitted if a control is submitted.
	`class=, id=, style=, title=, lang=, dir=` Common attributes.
Intrinsics:	`onclick=, ondblclick=, onmousedown=, onmouseup=, onmouseover=, onmousemove=, onmouseout=, onkeypress=, onkeydown=, onkeyup=` Common intrinsic events.
Empty:	No
Introduced:	HTML 2.0
Browsers:	Netscape Navigator 1.0, 2.*x*, 3.*x*, 4.*x*; Microsoft Internet Explorer 2.0, 3.0, 4.0.
Example:	

```
<HTML>
    ...
    <FORM action="..." method="post">
        ...
        <SELECT name="order" size="1">
            <OPTION value="one"> One potato
            <OPTION value="two"> Two potato
            <OPTION value="three"> Three potato
        </SELECT>
        ...
    </FORM>
    ...
</HTML>
```

`<SELECT>...</SELECT>`

Usage:	Creates choices for the user to select.
Syntax:	`<SELECT [attributes]>choices</SELECT>`
Start/End Tag:	Required/Required
Attributes:	`name="..."` The name of the element.
	`size="..."` The width in number of rows.
	`multiple` Allows multiple selections.

	`disabled="..."`	Disables the control.
	`tabindex="..."`	Sets the tabbing order between elements with a defined `tabindex`.
	`class=, id=, style=, title=, lang=, dir=`	Common attributes.
Intrinsics:	`onfocus="..."`	The event that occurs when the element receives focus.
	`onblur="..."`	The event that occurs when the element loses focus.
	`onselect="..."`	Intrinsic event that occurs when the control is selected.
	`onchange="..."`	Intrinsic event that occurs when the control is changed.
	`onclick=, ondblclick=, onmousedown=, onmouseup=, onmouseover=, onmousemove=, onmouseout=, onkeypress=, onkeydown=, onkeyup=`	Common intrinsic events.

Empty: No

Introduced: HTML 3.2

Browsers: Netscape Navigator 1.0, 2.*x*, 3.*x*, 4.*x*; Microsoft Internet Explorer 3.0, 4.0.

Example:
```
<HTML>
    ...
    <FORM action="..." method="post">
        ...
        <SELECT name="choice" size="2">
            <OPTION value="one">One fish
            <OPTION value="two">Two fish
            <OPTION value="red">Red fish
            <OPTION value="blue">Blue fish
        </SELECT>
        ...
    </FORM>
    ...
</HTML>
```

`<TEXTAREA>`...`</TEXTAREA>`

Usage: Creates an area for user input with multiple lines.

Syntax: `<TEXTAREA [attributes]>area for user input</TEXTAREA>`

Start/End Tag: Required/Required

Attributes:	`name="..."`	The name of the control.
	`rows="..."`	The width in number of rows.
	`cols="..."`	The height in number of columns.
	`disabled="..."`	Disables the control.
	`readonly="..."`	Sets the displayed text to read-only status.
	`tabindex="..."`	Sets the tabbing order between elements with a defined `tabindex`.
	`class=`, `id=`, `style=`, `title=`, `lang=`, `dir=`	Common attributes.
Intrinsics:	`onfocus="..."`	The event that occurs when the element receives focus.
	`onblur="..."`	The event that occurs when the element loses focus.
	`onselect="..."`	Intrinsic event that occurs when the control is selected.
	`onchange="..."`	Intrinsic event that occurs when the control is changed.
	`onclick=`, `ondblclick=`, `onmousedown=`, `onmouseup=`, `onmouseover=`, `onmousemove=`, `onmouseout=`, `onkeypress=`, `onkeydown=`, `onkeyup=`	Common intrinsic events.
Empty:	No	
Notes:	Text to be displayed is placed within the start and end tags.	
Introduced:	HTML 3.2	
Browsers:	Netscape Navigator 1.0, 2.*x*, 3.*x*, 4.*x;* Microsoft Internet Explorer 3.0, 4.0.	
Example:		

```
<HTML>
  <HEAD>
    <TITLE>Form Demonstration</TITLE>
  </HEAD>
  <BODY>
    <FORM="http://www.example.com/sender" method="post">
      <TEXTAREA rows="30" cols="60">
        Text area preloaded content goes here
      </TEXTAREA>
  </BODY>
</HTML>
```

Tables: CAPTION, COL, COLGROUP, TABLE, TBODY, TD, TFOOT, TH, THEAD, TR

Tables are meant to display data in a tabular format. Before the introduction of HTML 4.0, tables were widely used for page layout purposes, but with the advent of style sheets, the W3C is discouraging that use.

<CAPTION>...</CAPTION>

Usage:	Displays a table caption.
Syntax:	`<CAPTION [attributes]>caption text</CAPTION>`
Start/End Tag:	Required/Required
Attributes:	`align="..."` Deprecated. Controls alignment (`left`, `center`, `right`, **top**, `bottom`).
	`class=`, `id=`, `style=`, `title=`, `lang=`, `dir=` Common attributes.
Intrinsics:	`onclick=`, `ondblclick=`, `onmousedown=`, `onmouseup=`, `onmouseover=`, `onmousemove=`, `onmouseout=`, `onkeypress=`, `onkeydown=`, `onkeyup=` Common intrinsic events.
Empty:	No
Notes:	Optional
Introduced:	HTML 3.2
Browsers:	Netscape Navigator 1.1, 2.0, 3.*x*, 4.*x*; Microsoft Internet Explorer 2.0, 3.0, 4.0.
Example:	`<TABLE cellspacing="2" cellpadding="5">`

```
<!-- Use IE valign= in addition to align= to achieve the
➥same --
   -- effect on the page in spite of IE non-standard
   ➥syntax -->
   <CAPTION align="bottom" valign="bottom">Holmes,
1997</CAPTION>
```

<COL>

Usage:	Groups columns within column groups in order to share attribute values.
Syntax:	`<COL [attributes]>`
Start/End Tag:	Required/Forbidden
Attributes:	`span="..."` The number of columns the group contains.
	`width="..."` The column width as a percentage, pixel value, or minimum value.

align="..." Horizontally aligns the contents of cells (**left**, center, right, justify, char).

char="..." Sets a character on which the column aligns. The default value is the decimal point character in the default language.

charoff="..." Offset to the first alignment character on a line.

valign="..." Vertically aligns the contents of a cell (top, middle, bottom, baseline).

class=, id=, style=, title=, lang=, dir= Common attributes.

Intrinsics: onclick=, ondblclick=, onmousedown=, onmouseup=, onmouseover=, onmousemove=, onmouseout=, onkeypress=, onkeydown=, onkeyup= Common intrinsic events.

Empty: Yes, closing tag is forbidden.

Introduced: HTML 4.0

Browsers: Netscape Navigator 3.*x*, 4.*x*; Microsoft Internet Explorer 2.0, 3.0, 4.0.

Example:
```
<TABLE cellspacing="2" cellpadding="5">
 <COLGROUP>
    <COL width="40">
    <COL width="0*">
    <COL width="2*">
 <COLGROUP align="center">
    <COL width="1*">
    <COL width="3*" align="char" char=":">
 <THEAD>
  <TR>
    ...
 </TABLE>
```

`<COLGROUP>...[</COLGROUP>]`

Usage: Defines a column group.

Syntax: `<COLGROUP [attributes]>columns group[</COLGROUP>]`

Start/End Tag: Required/Optional

Attributes: span="..." The number of columns in a group.

width="..." The width of the columns.

align="..." Horizontally aligns the contents of cells (**left**, center, right, justify, char).

char="..." Sets a character on which the column aligns. The default value is the decimal point character in the default language.

charoff="..." Offset to the first alignment character on a line.

`valign="..."`   Vertically aligns the contents of a cell (`top`, `middle`, `bottom`, `baseline`).

`cellpadding="..."`   Spacing in cells.

`class=, id=, style=, title=, lang=, dir=`   Common attributes.

Intrinsics: `onclick=, ondblclick=, onmousedown=, onmouseup=, onmouseover=, onmousemove=, onmouseout=, onkeypress=, onkeydown=, onkeyup=`   Common intrinsic events.

Empty: No

Introduced: HTML 3.2

Browsers: Netscape Navigator 3.*x*, 4.*x*; Microsoft Internet Explorer 2.0, 3.0, 4.0.

Example:
```
<TABLE >
<COLGROUP span="2" width="200">
  <TR>
     <TH>Microsoft
         <TH>Corel
  <TR>
     <TD>MS Word 97
         <TD>WordPerfect 8
</TABLE>
```

`<TABLE>...</TABLE>`

Usage   Defines a table.

Syntax   `[<TABLE [attributes]>]contents of table[</TABLE>]`

Start/End Tag   Required/Required

Attributes   `align="..."`   Horizontally aligns the contents of cells (**`left`**, `center`, `right`, `justify`, `char`).

`bgcolor="..."`   Deprecated. Sets the background color for the table.

`border="..."`   Width in pixels of the border surrounding the table.

`cellpadding="..."`   Defines the gutter surrounding each cell.

`cellspacing="..."`   Defines the gutter within each cell.

`cols="..."`   Defines the number of columns in the table.

`frame="..."`   Defines which sides of the table frame will be visible. (**`void`**, `above`, `below`, `hsides`, `lhs`, `rhs`, `vsides`, `box`, `border`)

`rules="..."`   Defines which interior rules will be visible. (**`none`**, `groups`, `rows`, `cols`, `all`)

`width="..."`   Defines the desired width of the table.

`class=, id=, style=, title=, lang=, dir=`   Common attributes.

A

Intrinsics:	`onclick=, ondblclick=, onmousedown=, onmouseup=,` `onmouseover=, onmousemove=, onmouseout=, onkeypress=,` `onkeydown=, onkeyup=` Common intrinsic events.
Empty	No
Introduced	HTML 3.2
Browsers	Netscape Navigator 3.*x*, 4.*x*; Microsoft Internet Explorer 2.0, 3.0, 4.0.
Example:	

```
<TABLE>
  <TR>
     <TH>Microsoft
        <TH>Corel
  <TR>
     <TD>MS Word 97
        <TD>WordPerfect 8
</TABLE>
```

[<TBODY>]...[</TBODY>]

Usage:	Defines the table body.
Syntax:	`[<TBODY [attributes]>]contents of table body[</TBODY>]`
Start/End Tag:	Optional/Optional
Attributes:	`align="..."` Horizontally aligns the contents of cells (**left**, `center, right, justify, char`).
	`char="..."` Sets a character on which the column aligns. The default value is the decimal point character in the default language.
	`charoff="..."` Offset to the first alignment character on a line.
	`valign="..."` Vertically aligns the contents of cells (`top`, `middle`, `bottom`, `baseline`).
	`class=, id=, style=, title=, lang=, dir=` Common attributes.
Intrinsics:	`onclick=, ondblclick=, onmousedown=, onmouseup=,` `onmouseover=, onmousemove=, onmouseout=, onkeypress=,` `onkeydown=, onkeyup=` Common intrinsic events.
Empty:	No
Introduced:	HTML 3.2
Browsers:	Netscape Navigator 3.*x*, 4.*x*; Microsoft Internet Explorer 2.0, 3.0, 4.0.
Example:	

```
<HTML>
<HEAD>
  <TITLE>Flange Manufacturing Statistics</TITLE>
</HEAD>
```

```
<BODY>
...
  <TABLE cellspacing="2" cellpadding="5">
    <CAPTION align="bottom" valign="bottom">Flange usage
            data from Holmes, 1997</CAPTION>
    <THEAD>
      <TR>
          <TH colspan="4" align="center">
              <B>Flange Market Share by Type</B>
      <TR>
          <TH>Closet
              <TH>Safety
                  <TH>Stanchion
                      <TH>Wheel
    <TBODY>
      <TR>
          <TD>21%
              <TD>48%
                  <TD>12%
                      <TD>73%
    <TFOOT>
      <TR>
          <TD colspan="4" align="center">
              <B>Note: These figures are entirely
              ➥fictional</B>
  </TABLE>
...
</BODY>
</HTML>
```

<TD>...[</TD>]

Usage:	Defines a cell's contents.
Syntax:	`<TD [attributes]>cell contents[</TD>]`
Start/End Tag:	Required/Optional
Attributes:	`axis="..."` Abbreviated name. The default value is the cell content.

`axes="..."`   One or more axis names identifying row and/or column headers pertaining to the cell and separated by commas.

`nowrap="..."`   Deprecated. Turns off text wrapping in a cell.

`bgcolor="..."`   Deprecated. Sets the background color.

`rowspan="..."`   The number of rows spanned by a cell.

`colspan="..."`   The number of columns spanned by a cell.

`align="..."`   Horizontally aligns the contents of cells (**left**, center, right, justify, char).

`char="..."`   Sets a character on which the column aligns. The default value is the decimal point character in the default language.

`charoff="..."`   Offset to the first alignment character on a line.

`valign="..."`   Vertically aligns the contents of cells (`top`, **`middle`**, `bottom`, `baseline`).

`class=, id=, style=, title=, lang=, dir=`   Common attributes.

Intrinsics:	`onclick=, ondblclick=, onmousedown=, onmouseup=,` `onmouseover=, onmousemove=, onmouseout=, onkeypress=,` `onkeydown=, onkeyup=` Common intrinsic events.
Empty:	No
Introduced:	HTML 2.0
Browsers:	Netscape Navigator 1.1, 2.0, 3.*x*, 4.*x*; Microsoft Internet Explorer 2.0, 3.0, 4.0.
Example:	`<TR>`

```
    <TD>MS Word 97
        <TD>FrameMaker
```

`<TFOOT>...[</TFOOT>]`

Usage:	Defines the table footer.
Syntax:	`<TFOOT [attributes]>contents of footer[</TFOOT>]`
Start/End Tag:	Required/Optional
Attributes:	`align="..."` Horizontally aligns the contents of cells (**`left`**, `center`, `right`, `justify`, `char`).

`char="..."`   Sets a character on which the column aligns. The default value is the decimal point character in the default language.

`charoff="..."`   Offset to the first alignment character on a line.

`valign="..."`   Vertically aligns the contents of cells (`top`, `middle`, `bottom`, `baseline`).

`class=, id=, style=, title=, lang=, dir=`   Common attributes.

Intrinsics:	`onclick=, ondblclick=, onmousedown=, onmouseup=,` `onmouseover=, onmousemove=, onmouseout=, onkeypress=,` `onkeydown=, onkeyup=` Common intrinsic events.
Empty:	No
Introduced:	HTML 2.0
Browsers:	Netscape Navigator 2.*x*, 3.*x*, 4.*x*; Microsoft Internet Explorer 2.0, 3.0, 4.0.

Example: **\<TFOOT\>**
                 \<TR\>
                  \<TD colspan="4"
                      align="center"\>Note: Data from Holmes, 1997

\<TH\>...[\</TH\>]

Usage: Defines the table header data cells.

Syntax: \<THEAD *[attributes]*\>*contents of table header*[\</TH\>]

Start/End Tag: Required/Optional

Attributes: axis="..."   Abbreviated name. The default value is the cell con-
                tent.

                axes="..."   One or more axis names identifying row and/or col-
                umn headers pertaining to the cell and separated by commas.

                nowrap="..."   Deprecated. Turns off text wrapping in a cell.

                bgcolor="..."   Deprecated. Sets the background color.

                rowspan="..."   The number of rows spanned by a cell.

                colspan="..."   The number of columns spanned by a cell.

                align="..."   Horizontally aligns the contents of cells (left,
                center, right, justify, char).

                char="..."   Sets a character on which the column aligns. The
                default value is the decimal point character in the default language.

                charoff="..."   Offset to the first alignment character on a line.

                valign="..."   Vertically aligns the contents of cells (top, **middle**,
                bottom, baseline).

                class=, id=, style=, title=, lang=, dir=   Common attributes.

Intrinsics: onclick=, ondblclick=, onmousedown=, onmouseup=,
                onmouseover=, onmousemove=, onmouseout=, onkeypress=,
                onkeydown=, onkeyup=   Common intrinsic events.

Empty: No

Notes: Browsers should at least center the text content and many also bold-
                face the header text.

Introduced: HTML 2.0

Browsers: Netscape Navigator 1.1, 2.0, 3.*x*, 4.*x*; Microsoft Internet Explorer
                2.0, 3.0, 4.0.

Example: ...
                \<TABLE\>
                 \<TR\>
                    \<TH\>MS Word 97
                      \<TH\>FrameMaker

```
        <TR>
            <TD>97
                <TD>102
        </TABLE>
        ...
```

`<THEAD>...[</THEAD>]`

Usage:	Defines the table header.
Syntax:	`<THEAD [attributes]>contents of table header[</THEAD>]`
Start/End Tag:	Required/Optional

Attributes: `align="..."`   Horizontally aligns the contents of cells (**left**, `center`, `right`, `justify`, `char`).

`char="..."`   Sets a character on which the column aligns. The default value is the decimal point character in the default language.

`charoff="..."`   Offset to the first alignment character on a line.

`valign="..."`   Vertically aligns the contents of cells (`top`, `middle`, `bottom`, `baseline`).

`class=`, `id=`, `style=`, `title=`, `lang=`, `dir=`   Common attributes.

Intrinsics: `onclick=`, `ondblclick=`, `onmousedown=`, `onmouseup=`, `onmouseover=`, `onmousemove=`, `onmouseout=`, `onkeypress=`, `onkeydown=`, `onkeyup=`   Common intrinsic events.

Empty:	No
Introduced:	HTML 2.0
Browsers:	Netscape Navigator 3.x, 4.x; Microsoft Internet Explorer 2.0, 3.0, 4.0

Example:

```
<HTML>
  <HEAD>
    <TITLE>Tables Demonstration</TITLE>
  </HEAD>
  <BODY>
    <TABLE>
      <CAPTION>This is a caption</CAPTION>
    <THEAD>
      <TR>
          <TH>Column One
              <TH>Column Two
    <TBODY>
      <TR>
          <TD>Sample A
              <TD>Sample B
    </TABLE>
  </BODY>
</HTML>
```

<TR>...[</TR>]

Usage:	Defines a row of table cells.
Syntax:	`<TR [attributes]>contents of table row[</TR>]`
Start/End Tag:	Required/Optional
Attributes:	`align="..."` Horizontally aligns the contents of cells (**left**, `center`, `right`, `justify`, `char`).
	`char="..."` Sets a character on which the column aligns. The default value is the decimal point character in the default language.
	`charoff="..."` Offset to the first alignment character on a line.
	`valign="..."` Vertically aligns the contents of cells (`top`, `middle`, `bottom`, `baseline`).
	`bgcolor="..."` Deprecated. Sets the background color.
	`class=, id=, style=, title=, lang=, dir=` Common attributes.
Intrinsics:	`onclick=, ondblclick=, onmousedown=, onmouseup=, onmouseover=, onmousemove=, onmouseout=, onkeypress=, onkeydown=, onkeyup=` Common intrinsic events.
Empty:	No
Introduced:	HTML 2.0
Browsers:	Netscape Navigator 1.1, 2.*x*, 3.*x*, 4.*x*; Microsoft Internet Explorer 2.0, 3.0, 4.0.
Example:	

```
<HTML>
  <HEAD>
    <TITLE>File Formats</TITLE>
  </HEAD>
  <BODY>
    <TABLE>
      <TR>
          <TH>Graphics Formats
              <TH>Doc Formats
      <TR>
          <TD>.gif
              <TD>.doc
      <TR>
          <TD>.jpg
              <TD>.fm
    </TABLE>
  </BODY>
</HTML>
```

Text-level Elements

Text-level elements flow like text and do not directly alter the layout or formatting of the document. Some of these tags affect the text's physical appearance; others are designed to mark text with lexical importance, meaning, or role. For example, both <I> and <EM> are usually rendered as italic type, but <EM> refers to emphasis, which might be available in languages that don't have any equivalent to italics.

Text Markup: B, BIG, I, S÷, SMALL, STRIKE÷, TT, U÷

Text characteristics, such as the size, weight, and style, can be directly modified by using these elements, but the HTML 4.0 specification encourages you to use style sheets instead. However, these text characteristics will probably have a long life to support the needs of Web users who choose not to use "mainstream" browsers like Netscape Communicator 4.0 or Microsoft Internet Explorer 4.0. Access for the disabled, for example, is primarily by means of text-mode browsers, and many non-European languages are not well served by the browser market in general. All these people require another sort of browser, and it's thoughtful to be sensitive to their needs when designing almost any Web site.

<B>...</B>

Usage: Bold text.

Syntax: `<B [attributes]>bolded text</B>`

Start/End Tag: Required/Required

Attributes: `class=, id=, style=, title=, lang=, dir=` Common attributes.

Intrinsics: `onclick=, ondblclick=, onmousedown=, onmouseup=, onmouseover=, onmousemove=, onmouseout=, onkeypress=, onkeydown=, onkeyup=` Common intrinsic events.

Empty:	No
Introduced:	HTML 1.0 flow
Browsers:	Netscape Navigator 1.0, 2.0, 3.*x*, 4.*x*; Microsoft Internet Explorer 2.0, 3.0, 4.0.
Example:	`<P>The <B>virtual server name</B> should be the same name as your Web server.`

`<BIG>...</BIG>>`

Usage:	Large text.
Syntax:	`<BIG [attributes]>large text</BIG>`
Start/End Tag:	Required/Required
Attributes:	`class=, id=, style=, title=, lang=, dir=` Common attributes.
Intrinsics:	`onclick=, ondblclick=, onmousedown=, onmouseup=, onmouseover=, onmousemove=, onmouseout=, onkeypress=, onkeydown=, onkeyup=` Common intrinsic events.
Empty:	No flow
Introduced:	HTML 3.2
Browsers:	Netscape Navigator 2.0, 3.*x*, 4.*x*; Microsoft Internet Explorer 2.0, 3.0, 4.0.
Example: >	`<P><BIG>HEY</BIG>, come over here!`

`<I>...</I>`

Usage:	Italicized text.
Syntax:	`<I [attributes]>italicized text</I>`
Start/End Tag:	Required/Required
Attributes:	`class=, id=, style=, title=, lang=, dir=` Common attributes
Intrinsics:	`onclick=, ondblclick=, onmousedown=, onmouseup=, onmouseover=, onmousemove=, onmouseout=, onkeypress=, onkeydown=, onkeyup=` Common intrinsic events.

Empty:	No flow
Introduced:	HTML 2.0
Browsers:	Netscape Navigator 1.0, 2.*x*, 3.*x*, 4.*x*; Microsoft Internet Explorer 2.0, 3.0, 4.0.
Example:	`<P><I>HTML 4 Unleashed, Professional Reference` `➥Edition</I>`
	`is available from Sams.net Publishing.`

`<S>...</S>` ÷

Usage:	Strikethrough text.
Syntax:	`<S [attributes]>strikethrough text</S>`
Start/End Tag:	Required/Required
Attributes:	`class=, id=, style=, title=, lang=, dir=` Common attributes.
Intrinsics:	`onclick=, ondblclick=, onmousedown=, onmouseup=,` `onmouseover=, onmousemove=, onmouseout=, onkeypress=,` `onkeydown=, onkeyup=` Common intrinsic events.
Empty:	No flow
Notes:	Deprecated. Use the `DEL` tag if possible.
Notes:	Same as the `STRIKE` element.
Introduced:	HTML 3.2
Browsers:	Netscape Navigator 3.0, 4.0; Microsoft Internet Explorer 3.0, 4.0.
Example:	`<P><S>The contract expires on October 7, 1997</S>`

`<SMALL>...</SMALL>`

Usage:	Small text.
Syntax:	`<SMALL [attributes]>small text</SMALL>`
Start/End Tag:	Required/Required
Attributes:	`class=, id=, style=, title=, lang=, dir=` Common attributes.
Intrinsics:	`onclick=, ondblclick=, onmousedown=, onmouseup=,` `onmouseover=, onmousemove=, onmouseout=, onkeypress=,` `onkeydown=, onkeyup=` Common intrinsic events.
Empty:	No flow

Notes:	Same tasks now performed by style sheets.
Introduced:	HTML 3.2
Browsers:	Netscape Navigator 2.0, 3.0, 4.0; Microsoft Internet Explorer 2.0, 3.0, 4.0.
Example:	`<P><SMALL>This is fine print.</SMALL>`

`<STRIKE>...</STRIKE>` ÷

Usage:	Strikethrough text.
Syntax:	`<STRIKE [attributes]>strikethrough text</STRIKE>`
Start/End Tag:	Required/Required
Attributes:	`class=, id=, style=, title=, lang=, dir=` Common attributes.
Intrinsics:	`onclick=, ondblclick=, onmousedown=, onmouseup=, onmouseover=, onmousemove=, onmouseout=, onkeypress=, onkeydown=, onkeyup=` Common intrinsic events.
Empty:	No flow
Notes:	Deprecated. Use the `DEL` tag if possible.
Introduced:	HTML 3.2
Browsers:	Netscape Navigator 3.0, 4.0; Microsoft Internet Explorer 2.0, 3.0, 4.0.
Example:	`<P><STRIKE>The contract expires on October 7,` ➥`1997</STRIKE>`

`<TT>...</TT>`

Usage:	Teletype (monospaced) text.
Syntax:	`<TT [attributes]>teletype text</TT>`
Start/End Tag:	Required/Required
Attributes:	`class=, id=, style=, title=, lang=, dir=` Common attributes.
Intrinsics:	`onclick=, ondblclick=, onmousedown=, onmouseup=, onmouseover=, onmousemove=, onmouseout=, onkeypress=, onkeydown=, onkeyup=` Common intrinsic events.
Empty:	No flow
Notes:	Often thought of nowadays as "typewriter text."
Introduced:	HTML 3.2
Browsers:	Netscape Navigator 1.0, 2.0, 3.x, 4.x; Microsoft Internet Explorer 2.0, 3.0, 4.0.

Example:
```
<P>The <TT>teletype element</TT> can be used to
➥represent many things
     like code, directory listings, and other elements
     ➥that need to stand out.
```

`<U>...</U>` ÷

Usage: Underlined text.

Syntax: `<U [attributes]>underlined text</U>`

Start/End Tag: Required/Required

Attributes: `class=, id=, style=, title=, lang=, dir=` Common attributes.

Intrinsics: `onclick=, ondblclick=, onmousedown=, onmouseup=, onmouseover=, onmousemove=, onmouseout=, onkeypress=, onkeydown=, onkeyup=` Common intrinsic events.

Empty: No flow

Notes: Deprecated.

Introduced: HTML 3.2

Browsers: Netscape Navigator 3.0, 4.0; Microsoft Internet Explorer 2.0, 3.0, 4.0.

Example:
```
<P><U>HTML 4 Unleashed, Professional Reference
Edition</U>
     is available from Sams.net Publishing.
```

Phrase Markup: ACRONYM, ADDRESS*, BLOCKQUOTE*, CITE, CODE, DEL, DFN, EM, INS, KBD, PRE*, SAMP, STRONG, VAR

Phrase markup focuses on the lexical meaning of a phrase or word, identifying it by its place in the structure of the sentence, instead of by a physical font characteristic. This identification method makes them easy to search for using automated methods and simplifies creating foreign language equivalents.

`<ACRONYM...</ACRONYMN>`

Usage: Used to define acronyms.

Syntax: `<ACRONYM [attributes]>acronym text</ACRONYM>`

Start/End Tag: Required/Required

Attributes: `class=, id=, style=, title=, lang=, dir=` Common attributes.

Intrinsics: `onclick=, ondblclick=, onmousedown=, onmouseup=, onmouseover=, onmousemove=, onmouseout=, onkeypress=, onkeydown=, onkeyup=` Common intrinsic events.

Empty:	No
Notes:	Use the `title` attribute to expand the acronym. This tag is particularly important for audio browsers because it tells the browser to spell out the acronym instead of trying to pronounce it. "Eff Bee Eye" is easier to hear and understand than "phbee."
Introduced:	HTML 4.0
Browsers:	Netscape Navigator 4.0; Microsoft Internet Explorer 3.0.
Example:	The `<ACRONYM title="Federal Bureau of ➥Investigation">FBI</ACRONYM>`

`<ADDRESS>...</ADDRESS>`*

Notes:	Operates as a block-level element and discussed in the "Block-level Elements" section as a basic block element.

`<BLOCKQUOTE>...</BLOCKQUOTE>`*

Notes:	Operates as a block-level element and discussed in the "Block-level Elements" section as a basic block element.

`<CITE>...</CITE>`

Usage:	Cites a reference.
Syntax:	`<CITE [attributes]>contents of the citation</CITE>`
Start/End Tag:	Required/Required
Attributes:	`class=`, `id=`, `style=`, `title=`, `lang=`, `dir=` Common attributes.
Intrinsics:	`onclick=`, `ondblclick=`, `onmousedown=`, `onmouseup=`, `onmouseover=`, `onmousemove=`, `onmouseout=`, `onkeypress=`, `onkeydown=`, `onkeyup=` Common intrinsic events.
Empty:	No
Introduced:	HTML 2.0
Browsers:	Netscape Navigator 1.0, 2.0, 3.*x*, 4.*x*; Microsoft Internet Explorer 2.0, 3.0, 4.0.

Example:	`<P>`
	`She drinks the honey of her vision.  <CITE>(Mira Bai, c.`
	`➥1530)</CITE>`

`<CODE>...</CODE>`

Usage:	Identifies a line or section of code for display.

Syntax:	`<CODE [attributes]>text in code format</CODE>`
Start/End Tag:	Required/Required
Attributes:	`class=, id=, style=, title=, lang=, dir=` Common attributes.
Intrinsics:	`onclick=, ondblclick=, onmousedown=, onmouseup=, onmouseover=, onmousemove=, onmouseout=, onkeypress=, onkeydown=, onkeyup=` Common intrinsic events.
Empty:	No
Introduced:	HTML 2.0
Browsers:	Netscape Navigator 1.0, 2.0, 3.*x*, 4.*x*; Microsoft Internet Explorer 2.0, 3.0, 4.0.
Example:	`<P> You need to save your files in the`
	`➥<CODE>c:\examples</CODE> directory.`

A

HTML 4.0
REFERENCE

`<DEL>...</DEL>`

Usage:	Shows text as having been deleted from the document since the last change.
Syntax:	`<DEL [attributes]>deleted text</DEL>`
Start/End Tag:	Required/Required
Attributes:	`class=, id=, style=, title=, lang=, dir=` Common attributes.
Intrinsics:	`onclick=, ondblclick=, onmousedown=, onmouseup=, onmouseover=, onmousemove=, onmouseout=, onkeypress=, onkeydown=, onkeyup=` Common intrinsic events.
	`cite="..."` The URL of the source document.
	`datetime="..."` Indicates the date and time of the change.
Empty:	No
Notes:	New element in HTML 4.0.
Introduced:	HTML 4.0
Browsers:	Netscape Navigator 4.0; Microsoft Internet Explorer 4.0.
Example:	

```
<HTML>
  <BODY>
    <P>Type in<DEL cite="revision.html"
        datetime="1997-10-31T23:15:30-
        ➥08:00">Enter</DEL>
        <KBD>red0202</KBD>
      as your password.
  </BODY>
</HTML>
```

`<DFN>...</DFN>`

Usage:	Defines an enclosed term.
Syntax:	`<DFN [attributes]>contents of the definition</DFN>`
Start/End Tag:	Required/Required
Attributes:	`class=, id=, style=, title=, lang=, dir=` Common attributes.
Intrinsics:	`onclick=, ondblclick=, onmousedown=, onmouseup=, onmouseover=, onmousemove=, onmouseout=, onkeypress=, onkeydown=, onkeyup=` Common intrinsic events.
Empty:	No
Introduced:	HTML 2.0
Browsers:	Netscape Navigator 3.*x*, 4.*x*; Microsoft Internet Explorer 2.0, 3.0, 4.0.
Example:	`<DFN>Security guard: An employee with responsibility for controlling access to an entryway or area</DFN>`

`<EM>...</EM>`

Usage:	Emphasized text.
Syntax:	`<EM [attributes]>emphasized text</EM>`
Start/End Tag:	Required/Required
Attributes:	`class=, id=, style=, title=, lang=, dir=` Common attributes.
Intrinsics:	`onclick=, ondblclick=, onmousedown=, onmouseup=, onmouseover=, onmousemove=, onmouseout=, onkeypress=, onkeydown=, onkeyup=` Common intrinsic events.
Empty:	No
Introduced:	HTML 3.2
Browsers:	Netscape Navigator 1.0, 2.0, 3.*x*, 4.*x*; Microsoft Internet Explorer 2.0, 3.0, 4.0.
Example:	`<P>This word is <EM>emphasized!</EM>`

`<INS>...</INS>`

Usage:	Shows text as having been inserted in the document since the last change.
Syntax:	`<INS [attributes]>inserted text</INS>`
Start/End Tag:	Required/Required
Attributes:	`cite="..."` The URL of the source document.
	`datetime="..."` Indicates the date and time of the change.
	`class=, id=, style=, title=, lang=, dir=` Common attributes.

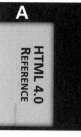

Intrinsics:	onclick=, ondblclick=, onmousedown=, onmouseup=, onmouseover=, onmousemove=, onmouseout=, onkeypress=, onkeydown=, onkeyup= Common intrinsic events.
Empty:	No
Notes:	New element in HTML 4.0.
Introduced:	HTML 4.0
Browsers:	Netscape Navigator 4.0; Microsoft Internet Explorer 4.0.
Example:	`<INS cite="revision.html"` `datetime="1997-10-31T23:15:30-08:00">Enter</INS>` `<KBD>red0202</KBD> as your password.`

`<KBD>...</KBD>`

Usage:	Indicates text a user would type.
Syntax:	`<KBD [attributes]>text to be typed</KBD>`
Start/End Tag:	Required/Required
Attributes:	class=, id=, style=, title=, lang=, dir= Common attributes.
Intrinsics:	onclick=, ondblclick=, onmousedown=, onmouseup=, onmouseover=, onmousemove=, onmouseout=, onkeypress=, onkeydown=, onkeyup= Common intrinsic events.
Empty:	No
Introduced:	HTML 2.0
Browsers:	Netscape Navigator 1.0, 2.0, 3.x, 4.x; Microsoft Internet Explorer 2.0, 3.0, 4.0.
Example:	`<P>Type in <KBD>red0202</KBD> as your password.`

`<PRE>...</PRE>*`

Notes:	Operates as a block-level element and discussed in the "Block-level Elements" section as a basic block element.

`<SAMP>...</SAMP>`

Usage:	Identifies sample output, as from a computer screen or printer.

Syntax: `<SAMP [attributes]>sample output</SAMP>`

Start/End Tag: Required/Required

Attributes: `class=, id=, style=, title=, lang=, dir=`   Common attributes.

Intrinsics: `onclick=, ondblclick=, onmousedown=, onmouseup=, onmouseover=, onmousemove=, onmouseout=, onkeypress=, onkeydown=, onkeyup=`   Common intrinsic events.

Empty: No

Introduced: HTML 3.2

Browsers: Netscape Navigator 1.0, 2.0, 3.*x*, 4.*x*; Microsoft Internet Explorer 2.0, 3.0, 4.0.

Example:
```
<P>The ticket printer will eject the completed sales
    receipt containing the date and amount of
➥purchase:<BR><BR>
<SAMP>Oct 31, 1997<BR>
        Purchase Amount: $32.56<BR>
        Thank you for shopping at XYZ Market
</SAMP>
```

`<STRONG>...</STRONG>`

Usage: Stronger emphasis.

Syntax: `<STRONG [attributes]>text with strong emphasis</STRONG>`

Start/End Tag: Required/Required

Attributes: `class=, id=, style=, title=, lang=, dir=`   Common attributes.

Intrinsics: `onclick=, ondblclick=, onmousedown=, onmouseup=, onmouseover=, onmousemove=, onmouseout=, onkeypress=, onkeydown=, onkeyup=`   Common intrinsic events.

Empty: No

Introduced: HTML 2.0

Browsers: Netscape Navigator 1.0, 2.0, 3.*x*, 4.*x*; Microsoft Internet Explorer 2.0, 3.0, 4.0.

Example:
```
...
<P><STRONG>Warning:</STRONG> Close cover before
striking match.
...
```

`<VAR>...</VAR>`

Usage: A variable.

Syntax: `<VAR [attributes]>variable</VAR>`

Start/End Tag: Required/Required

Attributes:	`class=`, `id=`, `style=`, `title=`, `lang=`, `dir=` Common attributes.
Intrinsics:	`onclick=`, `ondblclick=`, `onmousedown=`, `onmouseup=`, `onmouseover=`, `onmousemove=`, `onmouseout=`, `onkeypress=`, `onkeydown=`, `onkeyup=` Common intrinsic events.
Empty:	No
Introduced:	HTML 2.0
Browsers:	Netscape Navigator, 2.*x*, 3.*x*, 4.*x*; Microsoft Internet Explorer 2.*x*, 3.*x*, 4.*x*.
Example:	...

```
<P>The <VAR>virtual server name</VAR> should be the
    same name as your Web server.
...
```

Special Markup: A, APPLET÷, BASEFONT÷, BDO, BR, FONT÷, IFRAME*, IMG, NOSCRIPT*, OBJECT, Q, SCRIPT*, SPAN, SUB, SUP

`<A>...</A>`

Usage:	Used to define links and anchors.
Syntax:	`<A [attributes]>text of anchor</A>`
Start/End Tag:	Required/Required
Attributes:	`charset="..."` Character encoding of the resource. The default value is `ISO-8859-1`.
	`name="..."` Defines an anchor.
	`href="..."` The URL of the linked resource.
	`target="..."` Determines where the resource will be displayed (user-defined name, `_blank`, `_parent`, `_self`, `_top`).
	`rel="..."` Forward link types.
	`rev="..."` Reverse link types.
	`accesskey="..."` Assigns a hotkey to this element.
	`shape="..."` Allows you to define client-side image maps by using defined shapes (`default`, `rect`, `circle`, `poly`).
	`coords="..."` Sets the size of the shape using pixel or percentage lengths.
	`tabindex="..."` Sets the tabbing order between elements with a defined `tabindex`.
	`class=`, `id=`, `style=`, `title=`, `lang=`, `dir=` Common attributes.

Intrinsics:	`onclick=`, `ondblclick=`, `onmousedown=`, `onmouseup=`, `onmouseover=`, `onmousemove=`, `onmouseout=`, `onkeypress=`, `onkeydown=`, `onkeyup=` Common intrinsic events.
Empty:	No
Introduced:	HTML 1.0
Browsers:	Netscape Navigator 1.0, 1.1, 2.*x*, 3.*x*, 4.*x*; Microsoft Internet Explorer 2.0, 3.0, 4.0.

Example:

```
<HTML>
  <HEAD>
    <TITLE>Link Example</TITLE>
  </HEAD>
  <BODY>
    <P> Please reference: <A href="example.htm">
    ➥Example</A>.
  </BODY>
</HTML>
```

`<APPLET>...</APPLET>` ÷

Usage:	Includes a Java applet.
Syntax:	`<APPLET [attributes]>contents of the applet</APPLET>`
Start/End Tag:	Required/Required
Attributes:	`codebase="..."` The URL base for the applet.
	`archive="..."` Identifies the resources to be preloaded.
	`code="..."` The applet class file.
	`object="..."` The serialized applet file.
	`alt="..."` Displays text while loading.
	`name="..."` The name of the applet.
	`width="..."` The height of the displayed applet.
	`height="..."` The width of the displayed applet.
	`align="..."` Deprecated. Controls alignment (**left**, center, right, justify).
	`hspace="..."` The horizontal space separating the image from other content.
	`vspace="..."` The vertical space separating the image from other content.
Empty:	No

Notes:	Applet is deprecated in favor of the OBJECT element. It was originally one of the proprietary Netscape extensions introduced to support embedding Java applets in HTML pages.
Introduced:	HTML 3.2
Browsers:	Netscape Navigator 2.0, 3.x, 4.x; Microsoft Internet Explorer 2.0, 3.0, 4.0.
Example:	`<APPLET code="name.class" width="pixels" height=` ➡`"pixels"></APPLET>`

`<BASEFONT>` ÷

Usage:	Sets the base font size.
Syntax:	`<BASEFONT [attributes]>`
Start/End Tag:	Required/Forbidden
Attributes:	`size="..."` The font size (1 through 7, or relative, such as +3).
	`color="..."` The font color.
	`face="..."` The font type.
Empty:	Yes, closing tag is forbidden.
Notes:	Deprecated in favor of style sheets and because use of this element tends to cause huge problems for users who have non-European fonts loaded or disabled users who depend on certain font characteristics.
Introduced:	HTML 3.2
Browsers:	Netscape Navigator 1.0, 2.0, 3.x, 4.x; Microsoft Internet Explorer 2.0, 3.0, 4.0.
Example:	`<P><BASEFONT size ="2">` The `<B>`virtual server name`</B>` ➡should be the same name as your Web server.

`<BDO>...</BDO>`

Usage:	The BDO (bidirectional override) element is used to selectively alter the default text direction for inline text.
Syntax:	`<BDO [attributes]>content of BDO</BDO>`
Start/End Tag:	Required/Required
Attributes:	`lang="..."` The language of the document.
	`dir="..."` The text direction (`ltr`, `rtl`).
Empty:	No

Introduced:	HTML 4.0
Browsers:	Currently none.
Notes:	The dir attribute is mandatory. The BDO element is proposed as part of the enhancement to deal with the internationalization of HTML. It's needed for languages like Arabic and Hebrew, which are written from right to left but may have inline elements, such as included English words or numbers, which should read from left to right. This tag can also be used to include individual words in any language with a different writing order or to create a special effect.
Example:	`... <BDO dir="rtl">.rorrim a ni gnikool ton er'uoy ,` `➡siht daer nac uoy fI</BDO> ...`

`<BR>`

Usage:	Forces a line break.
Syntax:	`<BR [attributes]>`
Start/End Tag:	Required/Forbidden
Attributes:	`clear="..."` Sets the location where next line begins after a floating object (none, **left**, right, all).
	`class=, id=, style=, title=, lang=, dir=` Common attributes.
Intrinsics:	`onclick=, ondblclick=, onmousedown=, onmouseup=, onmouseover=, onmousemove=, onmouseout=, onkeypress=, onkeydown=, onkeyup=` Common intrinsic events.
Empty:	Yes, closing tag is forbidden.
Introduced:	HTML 1.0
Browsers:	Netscape Navigator 1.0, 2.0, 3.x, 4.x; Microsoft Internet Explorer 2.0, 3.0, 4.0.
Example:	`...`

```
<P>The &lt;BR&gt; tag is used to make a line break
   between each example.<BR>
   The &lt;BR&gt; tag is used to make a line break
   between each example.<BR>
   The &lt;BR&gt; tag is escaped in this code fragment
   so that it displays correctly on the page
   as well as being used to control line breaks.
   This technique is often valuable when creating
   tutorial pages that must display HTML without
   rendering it.
...
```

`<FONT>...</FONT> ÷`

Usage:	Changes the font size and color.
Syntax:	`<FONT [attributes]>text</FONT>`
Start/End Tag:	Required/Required
Attributes:	`size="..."` The font size (1 through 7, or relative, such as +3).
	`color="..."` The font color.
	`face="..."` The font type.
Empty	No
Notes:	Deprecated in favor of style sheets and because use of this element tends to cause huge problems for users who have non-European fonts loaded or disabled users who depend on certain font characteristics.
Introduced:	HTML 3.2
Browsers:	Netscape Navigator 1.1, 2.0, 3.*x*, 4.*x*; Microsoft Internet Explorer 2.0, 3.0, 4.0.
Example:	`<P><FONT face="Arial">This is an example of using the`
	`deprecated FONT element to designate Arial type`
	`➥</FONT>`

`<IFRAME>...</IFRAME>*`

Notes:	Operates as an inline element within the body of the document but discussed for convenience in the "Structural Elements" section as a frames element, where it's actually not permitted.

`<IMG>`

Usage:	Includes an image in the document.
Syntax:	`<IMG [attributes]>`
Start/End Tag:	Required/Forbidden
Attributes:	`src="..."` The URL of the image.
	`alt="..."` Alternative text to display.
	`align="..."` Deprecated. Controls alignment (**bottom**, middle, top, left, right,).
	`height="..."` The height of the image.
	`width="..."` The width of the image.
	`border="..."` Border width.
	`hspace="..."` The horizontal space separating the image from other content.

vspace="..." The vertical space separating the image from other content.

usemap="..." The URL to a client-side image map.

ismap Identifies a server-side image map.

class=, id=, style=, title=, lang=, dir= Common attributes.

Intrinsics: onclick=, ondblclick=, onmousedown=, onmouseup=, onmouseover=, onmousemove=, onmouseout=, onkeypress=, onkeydown=, onkeyup= Common intrinsic events.

Empty: Yes, closing tag is forbidden.

Introduced: HTML 2.0

Browsers: Netscape Navigator 1.0, 2.*x*, 3.*x*, 4.*x*; Microsoft Internet Explorer 2.0, 3.0, 4.0.

Example:
```
<HTML>
  <HEAD>
    <TITLE>Picture</TITLE>
  </HEAD>
  <BODY>
    <IMG src="picture1.jpg" alt="[Self-portrait]">
  </BODY>
</HTML>
```

<NOSCRIPT>...</NOSCRIPT>*

Notes: Operates as an inline element within the body of the document but discussed for convenience in the "Structural Elements" section as a head element, where it's actually not permitted.

<OBJECT>...</OBJECT>

Usage: Includes an object.

Syntax: <OBJECT *[attributes]*>contents of the object</OBJECT>

Start/End Tag: Required/Required

Attributes: declare A flag that declares but doesn't create an object.

classid="..." The URL of the object's location.

codebase="..." The URL for resolving URLs specified by other attributes.

data="..." The URL to the object's data.

type="..." The Internet content type for data.

codetype="..." The Internet content type for the code.

standby="..." Shows message while loading.

A

`align="..."` Deprecated. Controls alignment (`texttop`, `middle`, `textmiddle`, `baseline`, `textbottom`, `left`, `center`, `right`, `justify`).

`height="..."` The height of the object.

`width="..."` The width of the object.

`border="..."` Displays the border around an object.

`hspace="..."` The space between the sides of the object and other page content.

`vspace="..."` The space between the top and bottom of the object and other page content.

`usemap="..."` The URL to an image map.

`shapes=` Allows you to define areas to search for hyperlinks if the object is an image.

`name="..."` The URL to submit as part of a form.

`tabindex="..."` Sets the tabbing order between elements with a defined `tabindex`.

`class=`, `id=`, `style=`, `title=`, `lang=`, `dir=` Common attributes.

Intrinsics: `onclick=`, `ondblclick=`, `onmousedown=`, `onmouseup=`, `onmouseover=`, `onmousemove=`, `onmouseout=`, `onkeypress=`, `onkeydown=`, `onkeyup=` Common intrinsic events.

Empty: No

Notes: This element can be nested to any level, with the outermost level that the browser is capable of stopping recursion. The innermost level should be plain text to allow the widest possible number of browsers to provide meaningful content.

Introduced: HTML 4.0

Browsers: Netscape Navigator 3.*x*, 4.*x*; Microsoft Internet Explorer 2.0, 3.0, 4.0.

Example: `...`

```
<OBJECT title="Barking Dog"
  classid="Barking.py">
  <OBJECT data="Barking.mpeg" type="application/mpeg">
    <OBJECT src="Barking.gif">
      [Barking Dog Logo]
    </OBJECT>
  </OBJECT>
</OBJECT>
...
```

<PARAM>

Usage:	Initializes an object.
Syntax:	`<PARAM [attributes]>`
Start/End Tag:	Required/Forbidden
Attributes:	`name="..."` Defines the parameter name.
	`value="..."` The value of the object parameter.
	`valuetype="..."` Defines the value type (**data**, `ref`, `object`).
	`type="..."` The Internet media type.
Empty:	Yes, closing tag is forbidden.
Notes:	Must precede other object content. Used with `<OBJECT>` and depre-cated `<APPLET>` tags.
Introduced:	HTML 3.2
Browsers:	Netscape Navigator 1.0, 2.0, 3.*x*, 4.*x*; Microsoft Internet Explorer 2.0, 3.0, 4.0.
Example:	`<HTML>`

```
   <HEAD>
   </HEAD>
   <BODY>
     ...
     <APPLET code="tickertape.class" width="400"
     ➥height="40">
       <PARAM name="message" value="This is a test
       ➥message.">
       <PARAM name="speed" value="10">
       <PARAM name="textcolor" value="120,120,0">
     </APPLET>
     ...
   </BODY>
</HTML>
```

<Q>...</Q>

Usage:	Used to display short quotations that don't require paragraph breaks.
Syntax:	`<Q [attributes]>short quotation</Q>`
Start/End Tag:	Required/Required
Attributes:	`cite="..."` The URL of the quoted text.
	`class=, id=, style=, title=, lang=, dir=` Common attributes.
Intrinsics:	`onclick=, ondblclick=, onmousedown=, onmouseup=,` `onmouseover=, onmousemove=, onmouseout=, onkeypress=,` `onkeydown=, onkeyup=` Common intrinsic events.

Empty:	No
Notes:	Some browsers insert language-appropriate quotation marks around the inline quote. New element in HTML 4.0.
Introduced:	HTML 4.0
Browsers:	Netscape Navigator 4.0; Microsoft Internet Explorer 4.0.
Example:	`<Q cite="http://www.enheduanna.com">O lady of all` `➥truths...</Q>`

`<SCRIPT>...</SCRIPT>*`

Notes:	Operates as an inline element within the body of the document but discussed in the "Structural Elements" section as a head element, where it's also permitted.

`<SPAN>...</SPAN>`

Usage:	Organizes the document by defining an inline span of text.
Syntax:	`<SPAN [attributes]>defined span of text</SPAN>`
Start/End Tag:	Required/Required
Attributes:	`class=`, `id=`, `style=`, `title=`, `lang=`, `dir=` Common attributes.
Intrinsics:	`onclick=`, `ondblclick=`, `onmousedown=`, `onmouseup=`, `onmouseover=`, `onmousemove=`, `onmouseout=`, `onkeypress=`, `onkeydown=`, `onkeyup=` Common intrinsic events.
Empty:	No
Notes:	Equivalent to `<DIV>` but operates as an inline text element instead of forcing a break.
Introduced:	HTML 3.2
Browsers:	Netscape Navigator 3.0, 4.*x*; Microsoft Internet Explorer 2.0, 3.0, 4.0.

Example:	`<P>`
	`<DIV id="Books-HTML" class="Books">`
	`  Book Title: <SPAN class="Books-Title">HTML 4`
	`  ➥Unleashed,`
	`  Professional Reference Edition</SPAN>`
	`  ISBN: <SPAN class="Books-ISBN">1-57521-380-X</SPAN>`
	`</DIV>`

`<SUB>...</SUB>`

Usage:	Creates subscript.
Syntax:	`<SUB [attributes]>text in subscript</SUB>`
Start/End Tag:	Required/Required

Attributes:	class=, id=, style=, title=, lang=, dir= Common attributes.
Intrinsics:	onclick=, ondblclick=, onmousedown=, onmouseup=, onmouseover=, onmousemove=, onmouseout=, onkeypress=, onkeydown=, onkeyup= Common intrinsic events.
Empty:	No
Notes:	Used in scientific notations and some languages.
Introduced:	HTML 3.2
Browsers:	Netscape Navigator 2.0, 3.*x*, 4.*x*; Microsoft Internet Explorer 2.0, 3.0, 4.0.
Example:	`<P>The chemical formula for water is: H<SUB>2</SUB>O`

`<SUP>...</SUP>`

Usage:	Creates superscript.
Syntax:	`<SUP [attributes]>text in superscript</SUP>`
Start/End Tag:	Required/Required
Attributes:	class=, id=, style=, title=, lang=, dir= Common attributes.
Intrinsics:	onclick=, ondblclick=, onmousedown=, onmouseup=, onmouseover=, onmousemove=, onmouseout=, onkeypress=, onkeydown=, onkeyup= Common intrinsic events.
Empty:	No
Notes:	Used for superscript abbreviations, certain languages, and exponentiation.
Introduced:	HTML 3.2
Browsers:	Netscape Navigator 2.0, 3.*x*, 4.*x*; Microsoft Internet Explorer 2.*x*, 3.*x*, 4.*x*.
Example:	`<P>M<SUP>lle</SUP> Robards and W<SUP>m</SUP> Shakespeare met on 3<SUP>rd</SUP> Street` `<P>This is a simple equation: 3<SUP>3</SUP> = 27`

Client-Side Image Maps: AREA, MAP

`<AREA>`

Usage:	The AREA element is used to define links and anchors.
Syntax:	`<AREA [attributes]>`
Start/End Tag:	Required/Forbidden

Attributes: `shape="..."`   Allows you to define client-side image maps by using defined shapes (`default`, `rect`, `circle`, `poly`).

`coords="..."`   Sets the size of the shape using pixel or percentage lengths.

`href="..."`   The URL of the linked resource.

`target="..."`   Determines where the resource will be displayed (user-defined name, `_blank`, `_parent`, `_self`, `_top`).

`nohref="..."`   Indicates that the region has no action.

`alt="..."`   Displays alternative text.

`tabindex="..."`   Sets the tabbing order between elements with a defined `tabindex`.

Empty: Yes, closing tag is forbidden.

Notes: Only valid within a `MAP` container.

Introduced: HTML 3.2

Browsers: Netscape Navigator 1.0, 2.0, 3.*x*, 4.*x*; Microsoft Internet Explorer 2.0, 3.0, 4.0.

Example:
```
<HTML>

<MAP name="page1">
  <AREA shape="circle" coords="70,70,35">
  <AREA shape="rectangle" coords="65,65,80,80">
</MAP>
```

`<MAP>...</MAP>`

Usage: When used with the `AREA` element, creates a client-side image map.

Syntax: `<MAP [attributes]>contents of image map</MAP>`

Start/End Tag: Required/Required

Attributes: `name="..."`   The name of the image map to be created.

`class=`, `id=`, `style=`, `title=`   Common attributes.

Empty: No

Introduced: HTML 3.2

Browsers: Netscape Navigator 1.0, 2.*x*, 3.*x*, 4.*x*; Microsoft Internet Explorer 2.0, 3.0, 4.0.

Example:
```
<HTML>

<MAP name="page1">
<AREA shape="circle" coords=",70,70,35">
<AREA shape="rectangle" coords="65,65,80,80">
</MAP>
```

Form Control Text: BUTTON*, INPUT*, LABEL*, SELECT*, TEXTAREA*

<BUTTON>...</BUTTON>*

Notes: Operates as an inline element within the body of a form and discussed in the "Block-level Elements" section as a form element, where it is permitted.

<INPUT>...</INPUT>*

Notes: Operates as an inline element within the body of a form and discussed in the "Block-level Elements" section as a form element, where it is permitted.

<LABEL>...</LABEL>*

Notes: Operates as an inline element within the body of a form and discussed in the "Block-level Elements" section as a form element, where it is permitted.

<SELECT>...</SELECT>*

Notes: Operates as an inline element within the body of a form and discussed in the "Block-level Elements" section as a form element, where it is permitted.

<TEXTAREA>...</TEXTAREA>*

Notes: Operates as an inline element within the body of a form and discussed in the "Block-level Elements" section as a form element, where it is permitted.

Common Attributes and Intrinsic Events

Four core attributes apply to many elements:

- id="..."   A unique global identifier that allows the element to be individually acted on by a style sheet or other process.
- class="..."   A list of classes, non-unique identifiers separated by spaces, which allows the element to be acted on as a group by a style sheet or other process.

- `style="..."` Inline style information.
- `title="..."` Provides more information for a specific element, as opposed to the TITLE element, which creates a title for the entire Web page.

Two attributes for internationalization apply to many elements:

- `lang="..."` The ISO language identifier.
- `dir="..."` The text direction (**ltr**, `rtl`).

The following intrinsic events apply to many elements:

- `onclick="..."` A pointing device (such as a mouse) was single-clicked.
- `ondblclick="..."` A pointing device (such as a mouse) was double-clicked
- `onmousedown="..."` A mouse button was clicked and held down.
- `onmouseup="..."` A mouse button that was clicked and held down was released.
- `onmouseover="..."` A mouse moved the cursor over an object.
- `onmousemove="..."` The mouse was moved.
- `onmouseout="..."` A mouse moved the cursor off an object.
- `onkeypress="..."` A key was pressed and released.
- `onkeydown="..."` A key was pressed and held down.
- `onkeyup="..."` A key that was pressed has been released.

JavaScript 1.2
Language
Reference

IN THIS APPENDIX

How This Reference Is Organized

The first part of this reference is organized by object, with properties and methods listed by the object to which they apply. The second part covers independent functions in JavaScript not connected with a particular object, as well as operators in JavaScript.

A Note About JavaScript 1.2

JavaScript 1.2 is designed to interface seamlessly with Netscape Navigator 4.0. New features have been introduced in various areas of the language model, including but not limited to the following:

- Events
- Objects
- Properties
- Methods

Netscape Navigator 4.0 has been coded to support these new features, but earlier versions of Navigator have not. Backward compatibility is, therefore, an issue.

In this appendix, techniques that work only in Netscape Navigator 4.0 and later are clearly marked. At each heading, the words "Navigator 4.0 Only" will appear.

Finally, note that when developing, you should now clearly identify which version of JavaScript you're using. If you don't, your scripts might not work. You identify the version by using the LANGUAGE attribute in the <SCRIPT> tag. The following are some examples:

```
<Script Language = "JavaScript"> - Compatible with 2.0 and above

<Script Language = "JavaScript 1.1"> - Compatible with 3.0 and above

<Script Language = "JavaScript 1.2"> - Compatible with 4.0 and above
```

The following codes are used next to section headings to indicate where objects, methods, properties, and event handlers are implemented:

- C—Client JavaScript. (Server JavaScript is not covered in this appendix.)
- 2—Netscape Navigator 2.
- 3—Netscape Navigator 3.
- 4—Netscape Navigator 4 only. (That's not to say Navigator 4 works with these items only; Navigator 4 will handle all implementations.)
- I—Microsoft Internet Explorer 4.

The anchor Object [C|2|3|4|I]

The anchor object reflects an HTML anchor.

Properties

- name—A string value indicating the name of the anchor. (Not 2|3)

The applet Object [C|3]

The applet object reflects a Java applet included in a Web page with the <APPLET> tag.

Properties

- name—A string reflecting the NAME attribute of the <APPLET> tag.

The area Object [C|3]

The area object reflects a clickable area defined in an imagemap; area objects appear as entries in the links array of the document object.

Properties

- hash—A string value indicating an anchor name from the URL.
- host—A string value reflecting the host and domain name portion of the URL.
- hostname—A string value indicating the host, domain name, and port number from the URL.
- href—A string value reflecting the entire URL.
- pathname—A string value reflecting the path portion of the URL (excluding the host, domain name, port number, and protocol).
- port—A string value indicating the port number from the URL.
- protocol—A string value indicating the protocol portion of the URL, including the trailing colon.
- search—A string value specifying the query portion of the URL (after the question mark).
- target—A string value reflecting the TARGET attribute of the <AREA> tag.

Methods

- getSelection—Gets the current selection and returns this value as a string.

Event Handlers

- onDblClick—Specifies JavaScript code to execute when the user double-clicks the area. (Not implemented on Macintosh; Netscape Navigator 4.0 Only.) (4)

- onMouseOut—Specifies JavaScript code to execute when the mouse moves outside the area specified in the <AREA> tag.

New Properties with JavaScript 1.2

type	Indicates a MouseOut event.
target	Indicates the object to which the event was sent.
layer[n]	Where [n] represents X or Y, used (with page[n] and screen[n]) to describe the cursor location when the MouseOut event occurred.
page[n]	Where [n] represents X or Y, used (with layer[n] and screen[n]) to describe the cursor location when the MouseOut event occurred.
screen[n]	Where [n] represents X or Y, used (with layer[n] and page[n]) to describe the cursor location when the MouseOut event occurred.

- onMouseOver—Specifies JavaScript code to execute when the mouse enters the area specified in the <AREA> tag.

New Properties with JavaScript 1.2

type	Indicates a MouseOver event.
target	Indicates the object to which the event was sent.
layer[n]	Where [n] represents X or Y, used (with page[n] and screen[n]) to describe the cursor location when the MouseOver event occurred.

continues

B

JAVASCRIPT 1.2 LANGUAGE REFERENCE

New Properties with JavaScript 1.2

page[n]	Where [n] represents X or Y, used (with layer[n] and screen[n]) to describe the cursor location when the MouseOver event occurred.
screen[n]	Where [n] represents X or Y, used (with layer[n] and page[n]) to describe the cursor location when the MouseOver event occurred.

The array Object [C|3|I]

The array object provides a mechanism for creating arrays and working with them. New arrays are created with *arrayName* = new Array() or *arrayName* = new Array(*arrayLength*).

Properties

- length—An integer value reflecting the number of elements in an array.
- prototype—Used to add properties to an array object.

Methods

- concat(*arrayname*) —Combines elements of two arrays and returns a third, one level deep, without altering either of the derivative arrays. (Netscape Navigator 4.0 Only.)
- join(*string*)—Returns a string containing each element of the array separated by *string*. (Not I)
- reverse()—Reverses the order of an array. (Not I)
- slice(arrayName, beginSlice, endSlice)—Extracts a portion of some array and derives a new array from it. The beginSlice and endSlice parameters specify the target elements at which to begin and end the slice. (Netscape Navigator 4.0 Only.)
- sort(*function*)—Sorts an array based on function, which indicates a *function* defining the sort order. *function* can be omitted, in which case the sort defaults to dictionary order. Note: sort now works on all platforms.

The button Object [C|2|3|I]

The button object reflects a pushbutton from an HTML form in JavaScript.

Properties

- enabled—A Boolean value indicating whether the button is enabled. (Not 2|3)
- form—A reference to the form object containing the button. (Not 2|3)
- name—A string value containing the name of the button element.
- type—A string value reflecting the TYPE attribute of the <INPUT> tag. (Not 2|I)
- value—A string value containing the value of the button element.

Methods

- click()—Emulates the action of clicking the button.
- focus()—Gives focus to the button. (Not 2|3)

Event Handlers

- onMouseDown—Specifies JavaScript code to execute when a user presses a mouse button.
- onMouseUp—Specifies JavaScript code to execute when the user releases a mouse button.
- onClick—Specifies JavaScript code to execute when the button is clicked.
- onFocus—Specifies JavaScript code to execute when the button receives focus. (Not 2|3)

B

JAVASCRIPT 1.2
LANGUAGE
REFERENCE

The checkbox Object [c|2|3|I]

The checkbox object makes a check box in an HTML form available in JavaScript.

Properties

- checked—A Boolean value indicating whether the check box element is checked.
- defaultChecked—A Boolean value indicating whether the check box element was checked by default (that is, it reflects the CHECKED attribute).
- enabled—A Boolean value indicating whether the check box is enabled. (Not 2|3)
- form—A reference to the form object containing the check box. (Not 2|3)
- name—A string value containing the name of the check box element.
- type—A string value reflecting the TYPE attribute of the <INPUT> tag. (Not 2|I)
- value—A string value containing the value of the check box element.

Methods

- `click()`—Emulates the action of clicking the check box.
- `focus()`—Gives focus to the check box. (Not 2|3)

Event Handlers

- `onClick`—Specifies JavaScript code to execute when the check box is clicked.
- `onFocus`—Specifies JavaScript code to execute when the check box receives focus. (Not 2|3)

The combo Object [C|I]

The `combo` object reflects a combo field in JavaScript.

Properties

- `enabled`—A Boolean value indicating whether the combo box is enabled. (Not 2|3)
- `form`—A reference to the `form` object containing the combo box. (Not 2|3)
- `listCount`—An integer reflecting the number of elements in the list.
- `listIndex`—An integer reflecting the index of the selected element in the list.
- `multiSelect`—A Boolean value indicating whether the combo field is in multiselect mode.
- `name`—A string value reflecting the name of the combo field.
- `value`—A string containing the value of the combo field.

Methods

- `addItem(index)`—Adds an item to the combo field before the item at *index*.
- `click()`—Simulates a click on the combo field.
- `clear()`—Clears the contents of the combo field.
- `focus()`—Gives focus to the combo field.
- `removeItem(index)`—Removes the item at *index* from the combo field.

Event Handlers

- `onClick`—Specifies JavaScript code to execute when the mouse clicks the combo field.
- `onFocus`—Specifies JavaScript code to execute when the combo field receives focus.

The date Object [C|2|3|I]

The date object provides mechanisms for working with dates and times in JavaScript. Instances of the object can be created with the following syntax:

```
newObjectName = new Date(dateInfo)
```

Here, *dateInfo* is an optional specification of a particular date and can be one of the following:

```
"month day, year hours:minutes:seconds"
```

```
year, month, day
```

```
year, month, day, hours, minutes, seconds
```

The latter two options represent integer values.

If no *dateInfo* is specified, the new object represents the current date and time.

Properties

- `prototype`—Provides a mechanism for adding properties to a date object. (Not 2)

Methods

- `getDate()`—Returns the day of the month for the current date object as an integer from 1 to 31.

- `getDay()`—Returns the day of the week for the current date object as an integer from 0 to 6 (0 is Sunday, 1 is Monday, and so on).

- `getHours()`—Returns the hour from the time in the current date object as an integer from 0 to 23.

- `getMinutes()`—Returns the minutes from the time in the current date object as an integer from 0 to 59.

- `getMonth()`—Returns the month for the current date object as an integer from 0 to 11 (0 is January, 1 is February, and so on).

- `getSeconds()`—Returns the seconds from the time in the current date object as an integer from 0 to 59.

- `getTime()`—Returns the time of the current date object as an integer representing the number of milliseconds since January 1, 1970 at 00:00:00.

- `getTimezoneOffset()`—Returns the difference between the local time and GMT as an integer representing the number of minutes.

- `getYear()`—Returns the year for the current date object as a two-digit integer representing the year less 1900.

- parse(*dateString*)—Returns the number of milliseconds between January 1, 1970 at 00:00:00 and the date specified in *dateString*, which should take the following format: (Not I)

  Day, DD Mon YYYY HH:MM:SS TZN

  Mon DD, YYYY

- setDate(*dateValue*)—Sets the day of the month for the current date object. *dateValue* is an integer from 1 to 31.

- setHours(*hoursValue*)—Sets the hours for the time for the current date object. *hoursValue* is an integer from 0 to 23.

- setMinutes(*minutesValue*)—Sets the minutes for the time for the current date object. *minutesValue* is an integer from 0 to 59.

- setMonth(*monthValue*)—Sets the month for the current date object. *monthValue* is an integer from 0 to 11 (0 is January, 1 is February, and so on).

- setSeconds(*secondsValue*)—Sets the seconds for the time for the current date object. *secondsValue* is an integer from 0 to 59.

- setTime(*timeValue*)—Sets the value for the current date object. *timeValue* is an integer representing the number of milliseconds since January 1, 1970 at 00:00:00.

- setYear(*yearValue*)—Sets the year for the current date object. *yearValue* is an integer greater than 1900.

- toGMTString()—Returns the value of the current date object in GMT as a string using Internet conventions in the following form:

  Day, DD Mon YYYY HH:MM:SS GMT

- toLocaleString()—Returns the value of the current date object in the local time using local conventions.

- UTC(*yearValue, monthValue, dateValue, hoursValue, minutesValue, secondsValue*)—Returns the number of milliseconds since January 1, 1970 at 00:00:00 GMT. *yearValue* is an integer greater than 1900. *monthValue* is an integer from 0 to 11. *dateValue* is an integer from 1 to 31. *hoursValue* is an integer from 0 to 23. *minutesValue* and *secondsValue* are integers from 0 to 59. *hoursValue*, *minutesValue*, and *secondsValue* are optional. (Not I)

The document Object [C|2|3|I]

The document object reflects attributes of an HTML document in JavaScript.

Properties

- alinkColor—The color of active links as a string or a hexadecimal triplet.
- anchors—Array of anchor objects in the order they appear in the HTML document. Use anchors.length to get the number of anchors in a document.
- applets—Array of applet objects in the order they appear in the HTML document. Use applets.length to get the number of applets in a document. (Not 2)
- bgColor—The color of the document's background.
- cookie—A string value containing cookie values for the current document.
- embeds—Array of plugin objects in the order they appear in the HTML document. Use embeds.length to get the number of plug-ins in a document. (Not 2|I)
- fgColor—The color of the document's foreground.
- forms—Array of form objects in the order the forms appear in the HTML file. Use forms.length to get the number of forms in a document.
- images—Array of image objects in the order they appear in the HTML document. Use images.length to get the number of images in a document. (Not 2|I)
- lastModified—String value containing the last date of the document's modification.
- linkColor—The color of links as a string or a hexadecimal triplet.
- links—Array of link objects in the order the hypertext links appear in the HTML document. Use links.length to get the number of links in a document.
- location—A string containing the URL of the current document. Use document.URL instead of document.location. This property is expected to disappear in a future release.
- referrer—A string value containing the URL of the calling document when the user follows a link.
- title—A string containing the title of the current document.
- URL—A string reflecting the URL of the current document. Use instead of document.location. (Not I)
- vlinkColor—The color of followed links as a string or a hexadecimal triplet.

Event Handlers

- onMouseDown—Specifies JavaScript code to execute when a user presses a mouse button.
- onMouseUp—Specifies JavaScript code to execute when the user releases a mouse button.

B

JAVASCRIPT 1.2
LANGUAGE
REFERENCE

- onKeyUp—Specifies JavaScript code to execute when the user releases a specific key. (Netscape Navigator 4.0 Only.) (4)

- onKeyPress—Specifies JavaScript code to execute when the user holds down a specific key. (Netscape Navigator 4.0 Only.) (4)

- onKeyDown—Specifies JavaScript code to execute when the user presses a specific key. (Netscape Navigator 4.0 Only.) (4)

- onDblClick—Specifies JavaScript code to execute when the user double-clicks the area. (Not implemented on Macintosh; Netscape Navigator 4.0 Only.) (4)

Methods

- captureEvents()—Used in a window with frames (along with enableExternalCapture), it specifies that the window will capture all specified events. New in JavaScript 1.2.

- clear()—Clears the document window. (Not I)

- close()—Closes the current output stream.

- open(*mimeType*)—Opens a stream that allows write() and writeln() methods to write to the document window. *mimeType* is an optional string that specifies a document type supported by Navigator or a plug-in (for example, text/html or image/gif).

- releaseEvents(*eventType*)—Specifies that the current window must release events (as opposed to capture them) so that these events can be passed to other objects, perhaps further on in the event hierarchy. New in JavaScript 1.2.

- routeEvent(event)—Sends or routes an event through the normal event hierarchy.

- write()—Writes text and HTML to the specified document.

- writeln()—Writes text and HTML to the specified document followed by a new-line character.

The `fileUpload` Object [C|3]

Reflects a file upload element in an HTML form.

Properties

- name—A string value reflecting the name of the file upload element.

- value—A string value reflecting the file upload element's field.

The `form` Object [C|2|3|I]

The `form` object reflects an HTML form in JavaScript. Each HTML form in a document is reflected by a distinct instance of the `form` object.

Properties

- `action`—A string value specifying the URL to which the form data is submitted.
- `elements`—Array of objects for each form element in the order in which they appear in the form.
- `encoding`—String containing the MIME encoding of the form as specified in the `ENCTYPE` attribute.
- `method`—A string value containing the method of submission of form data to the server.
- `target`—A string value containing the name of the window to which responses to form submissions are directed.

Methods

- `reset()`—Resets the form. (Not 2|I)
- `submit()`—Submits the form.

Event Handlers

- `onReset`—Specifies JavaScript code to execute when the form is reset. (Not 2|I)
- `onSubmit`—Specifies JavaScript code to execute when the form is submitted. The code should return a `true` value to allow the form to be submitted. A `false` value prevents the form from being submitted.

The `frame` Object [C|2|3|I]

The `frame` object reflects a frame window in JavaScript.

Properties

- `frames`—An array of objects for each frame in a window. Frames appear in the array in the order in which they appear in the HTML source code.
- `onblur`—A string reflecting the `onBlur` event handler for the frame. New values can be assigned to this property to change the event handler. (Not 2)

- onfocus—A string reflecting the onFocus event handler for the frame. New values can be assigned to this property to change the event handler. (Not 2)

- parent—A string indicating the name of the window containing the frame set.

- self—An alternative for the name of the current window.

- top—An alternative for the name of the topmost window.

- window—An alternative for the name of the current window.

Methods

- alert(*message*)—Displays *message* in a dialog box.

- blur()—Removes focus from the frame. (Not 2)

- clearInterval(*intervalID*)—Cancels timeouts created with the setInterval method. New in JavaScript 1.2.

- close()—Closes the window.

- confirm(*message*)—Displays *message* in a dialog box with OK and Cancel buttons. Returns true or false based on the button clicked by the user.

- focus()—Gives focus to the frame. (Not 2)

- open(*url,name,features*)—Opens *url* in a window named *name*. If *name* doesn't exist, a new window is created with that name. *features* is an optional string argument containing a list of features for the new window. The feature list contains any of the following name-value pairs separated by commas and without additional spaces:

toolbar=[yes,no,1,0]	Indicates whether the window should have a toolbar
location=[yes,no,1,0]	Indicates whether the window should have a location field
directories=[yes,no,1,0]	Indicates whether the window should have directory buttons
status=[yes,no,1,0]	Indicates whether the window should have a status bar
menubar=[yes,no,1,0]	Indicates whether the window should have menus
scrollbars=[yes,no,1,0]	Indicates whether the window should have scrollbars

`resizable=[yes,no,1,0]`	Indicates whether the window should be resizable
`width=pixels`	Indicates the width of the window in pixels
`height=pixels`	Indicates the height of the window in pixels

- `print()`—Prints the contents of a frame or window. This is the equivalent of the user clicking the Print button in Netscape Navigator. New in JavaScript 1.2.

- `prompt(message,response)`—Displays *message* in a dialog box with a text entry field with the default value of *response*. The user's response in the text entry field is returned as a string.

- `setInterval(function, msec, [args])`—Repeatedly calls a function after the period specified by the `msec` parameter. New in JavaScript 1.2.

- `setInterval(expression, msec)`—Evaluates *expression* after the period specified by the `msec` parameter. New in JavaScript 1.2.

- `setTimeout(expression,time)`—Evaluates *expression* after *time*; *time* is a value in milliseconds. The timeout can be named with the following structure:

  `name = setTimeOut(expression,time)`

- `clearTimeout(name)`—Cancels the timeout with the name *name*.

Event Handlers

- `onBlur`—Specifies JavaScript code to execute when focus is removed from a frame. (Not 2)

- `onFocus`—Specifies JavaScript code to execute when focus is removed from a frame. (Not 2)

- `onMove`—Specifies JavaScript code to execute when the user moves a frame. (Netscape Navigator 4.0 Only.)

- `onResize`—Specifies JavaScript code to execute when a user resizes the frame. (Netscape Navigator 4.0 Only.)

The `function` Object [CI3]

The `function` object provides a mechanism for indicating JavaScript code to compile as a function. This is the syntax to use the `function` object:

`functionName = new Function(arg1, arg2, arg3, ..., functionCode)`

This is similar to the following:

```
function functionName(arg1, arg2, arg3, ...) {
    functionCode
}
```

In the former, *functionName* is a variable with a reference to the function, and the function is evaluated each time it's used instead of being compiled once.

Properties

- arguments—An integer reflecting the number of arguments in a function.
- prototype—Provides a mechanism for adding properties to a function object.

The hidden Object [C|2|3|I]

The hidden object reflects a hidden field from an HTML form in JavaScript.

Properties

- name—A string value containing the name of the hidden element.
- type—A string value reflecting the TYPE property of the <INPUT> tag. (Not 2|I)
- value—A string value containing the value of the hidden text element.

The history Object [C|2|3|I]

The history object allows a script to work with the Navigator browser's history list in JavaScript. For security and privacy reasons, the actual content of the list isn't reflected into JavaScript.

Properties

- length—An integer representing the number of items on the history list. (Not I)

Methods

- back()—Goes back to the previous document in the history list. (Not I)
- forward()—Goes forward to the next document in the history list. (Not I)
- go(*location*)—Goes to the document in the history list specified by *location*, which can be a string or integer value. If it's a string, it represents all or part of a URL in the history list. If it's an integer, *location* represents the relative position of the document on the history list. As an integer, *location* can be positive or negative. (Not I)

The `image` Object [C|3]

The `image` object reflects an image included in an HTML document.

Properties

- `border`—An integer value reflecting the width of the image's border in pixels.
- `complete`—A Boolean value indicating whether the image has finished loading.
- `height`—An integer value reflecting the height of an image in pixels.
- `hspace`—An integer value reflecting the HSPACE attribute of the `<IMG>` tag.
- `lowsrc`—A string value containing the URL of the low-resolution version of the image to load.
- `name`—A string value indicating the name of the `image` object.
- `prototype`—Provides a mechanism for adding properties as an `image` object.
- `src`—A string value indicating the URL of the image.
- `vspace`—An integer value reflecting the VSPACE attribute of the `<IMG>` tag.
- `width`—An integer value indicating the width of an image in pixels.

Event Handlers

- `onKeyUp`—Specifies JavaScript code to execute when the user releases a specific key. (Netscape Navigator 4.0 Only.) (4)
- `onKeyPress`—Specifies JavaScript code to execute when the user holds down a specific key. (Netscape Navigator 4.0 Only.) (4)
- `onKeyDown`—Specifies JavaScript code to execute when the user presses a specific key. (Netscape Navigator 4.0 Only.) (4)
- `onAbort`—Specifies JavaScript code to execute if the attempt to load the image is aborted. (Not 2)
- `onError`—Specifies JavaScript code to execute if there's an error while loading the image. Setting this event handler to `null` suppresses error messages if an error occurs while loading. (Not 2)
- `onLoad`—Specifies JavaScript code to execute when the image finishes loading. (Not 2)

The `layer` Object [4]

The `layer` object is used to embed layers of content within a page; they can be hidden or not. Either type is accessible through JavaScript code. The most common use for layers is in developing Dynamic HTML (DHTML). With layers, you can create animations or other dynamic content on a page by cycling through the layers you have defined.

Properties

- `above`—Places a layer on top of a newly created layer.
- `background`—Used to specify a tiled background image of the layer.
- `below`—Places a layer below a newly created layer.
- `bgColor`—Sets the background color of the layer.
- `clip(left, top, right, bottom)`—Specifies the visible boundaries of the layer.
- `height`—Specifies the height of the layer, expressed in pixels (integer) or by a percentage of the instant layer.
- `ID`—Previously called `NAME`. Used to name the layer so that it can be referred to by name and accessed by other JavaScript code.
- `left`—Specifies the horizontal positioning of the top-left corner of the layer. Used with the `Top` property.
- `page[n]`—Where `[n]` is x or y. Specifies the horizontal (x) or vertical (y) positioning of the top-left corner of the layer, in relation to the overall, enclosing document. (Note: This is different from the `Left` and `Top` properties.)
- `parentLayer`—Specifies the layer object that contains the present layer.
- `SRC`—Specifies HTML source to be displayed with the target layer. (This source can also include JavaScript.)
- `siblingAbove`—Specifies the layer object immediately above the present one.
- `siblingBelow`—Specifies the layer object immediately below the present one.
- `top`—Specifies the vertical positioning of the top-left corner of the layer. (Used with the `Left` property.)
- `visibility`—Specifies the visibility of the layer. There are three choices: `show` (visible), `hidden` (not visible), and `inherit` (layer inherits the properties of its parent).
- `width`—Specifies the width of the layer. Used for wrapping procedures; that is, the width denotes the boundary after which the contents wrap inside the layer.

• z-index—Specifies the z-order (or stacking order) of the layer. Used to set the layer's position within the overall rotational order of all layers. Expressed as an integer. (Used where there are many layers.)

Events

• onBlur—Specifies JavaScript code to execute when the layer loses focus.

• onFocus—Specifies JavaScript code to execute when the layer gains focus.

• onLoad—Specifies JavaScript code to execute when a layer is loaded.

• onMouseOut—Specifies JavaScript code to execute when the mouse cursor moves off the layer.

New Properties

type	Indicates a MouseOut event.
target	Indicates the object to which the event was sent
layer[n]	Where [n] represents x or y, used (with page[n] and screen[n]) to describe the cursor location when the MouseOut event occurred
page[n]	Where [n] represents x or y, used (with layer[n] and screen[n]) to describe the cursor location when the MouseOut event occurred
screen[n]	Where [n] represents x or y, used (with layer[n] and page[n]) to describe the cursor location when the MouseOut event occurred

• onMouseover—Specifies the JavaScript code to execute when the mouse cursor enters the layer.

New Properties with JavaScript 1.2

type	Indicates a MouseOver event
target	Indicates the object to which the event was sent
layer[n]	Where [n] represents x or y, used (with page[n] and screen[n]) to describe the cursor location when the MouseOver event occurred

continues

New Properties with JavaScript 1.2

page[n]	Where [n] represents x or y, used (with layer[n] and screen[n]) to describe the cursor location when the MouseOver event occurred
screen[n]	Where [n] represents x or y, used (with layer[n] and page[n]) to describe the cursor location when the MouseOver event occurred

Methods

- captureEvents()—Used in a window with frames (along with enableExternalCapture), it specifies that the window will capture all specified events. New in JavaScript 1.2.

- load(*source, width*)—Alters the source of the layer by replacing it with HTML (or JavaScript) from the file specified in *source*. Using this method, you can also pass a width value (in pixels) to accommodate the new content.

- moveAbove(*layer*)—Places the layer above *layer* in the stack.

- moveBelow(layer)—Places the layer below *layer* in the stack.

- moveBy(x,y)—Alters the position of the layer by the specified values, expressed in pixels.

- moveTo(x,y)—Alters the position of the layer (within the containing layer) to the specified coordinates, expressed in pixels.

- moveToAbsolute(x,y)—Alters the position of the layer (within the page) to the specified coordinates, expressed in pixels.

- releaseEvents(*eventType*)—Specifies that the current window should release events instead of capturing them so that these events can be passed to other objects, perhaps further on in the event hierarchy. New in JavaScript 1.2.

- resizeBy(*width,height*)—Resizes the layer by the specified values, expressed in pixels.

- resizeTo(*width,height*)—Resizes the layer to the specified height and size, expressed in pixels.

- routeEvent(event)—Sends or routes an event through the normal event hierarchy.

The `link` Object [C|2|3|I]

The `link` object reflects a hypertext link in the body of a document.

Properties

- `hash`—A string value containing the anchor name in the URL.

- `host`—A string value containing the host name and port number from the URL.

- `hostname`—A string value containing the domain name (or numerical IP address) from the URL.

- `href`—A string value containing the entire URL.

- `pathname`—A string value specifying the path portion of the URL.

- `port`—A string value containing the port number from the URL.

- `protocol`—A string value containing the protocol from the URL (including the colon, but not the slashes).

- `search`—A string value containing any information passed to a `GET` CGI-BIN call (such as any information after the question mark).

- `target`—A string value containing the name of the window or frame specified in the `TARGET` attribute.

Event Handlers

- `onMouseDown`—Specifies JavaScript code to execute when a user presses a mouse button. (JavaScript 1.2 and Netscape Navigator 4.0 Only.) (4)

- `onMouseOut`—Specifies JavaScript code to execute when the user moves the mouse cursor out of an object. (JavaScript 1.2 and Netscape Navigator 4.0 Only.) (4)

New Properties with JavaScript 1.2

`type`	Indicates a `MouseOut` event
`target`	Indicates the object to which the event was sent
`layer[n]`	Where `[n]` represents x or y, used (with `page[n]` and `screen[n]`) to describe the cursor location when the `MouseOut` event occurred

continues

New Properties with JavaScript 1.2

page[n]	Where [n] represents x or y, used (with layer[n] and screen[n]) to describe the cursor location when the MouseOut event occurred
screen[n]	Where [n] represents x or y, used (with layer[n] and page[n]) to describe the cursor location when the MouseOut event occurred

- onMouseUp—Specifies the JavaScript code to execute when the user releases a mouse button.
- onKeyUp—Specifies the JavaScript code to execute when the user releases a specific key. (Netscape Navigator 4.0 Only.) (4)
- onKeyPress—Specifies the JavaScript code to execute when the user holds down a specific key. (Netscape Navigator 4.0 Only.) (4)
- onKeyDown—Specifies the JavaScript code to execute when the user presses a specific key. (Netscape Navigator 4.0 Only.) (4)
- onDblClick—Specifies the JavaScript code to execute when the user double-clicks the area. (Not implemented on Macintosh; Netscape Navigator 4.0 Only.) (4)
- moveMouse—Specifies the JavaScript code to execute when the mouse pointer moves over the link. (Not 2|3)
- onClick—Specifies the JavaScript code to execute when the link is clicked.
- onMouseOver—Specifies the JavaScript code to execute when the mouse pointer moves over the hypertext link.

New Properties with JavaScript 1.2

type	Indicates a MouseOver event
target	Indicates the object to which the event was sent
layer[n]	Where [n] represents x or y, used (with page[n] and screen[n]) to describe the cursor location when the MouseOver event occurred
page[n]	Where [n] represents x or y, used (with layer[n] and screen[n]) to describe the cursor location when the MouseOver event occurred
screen[n]	Where [n] represents x or y, used (with layer[n] and page[n]) to describe the cursor location when the MouseOver event occurred

The `location` Object [C|2|3|I]

The `location` object reflects information about the current URL.

Properties

- `hash`—A string value containing the anchor name in the URL.
- `host`—A string value containing the host name and port number from the URL.
- `hostname`—A string value containing the domain name (or numerical IP address) from the URL.
- `href`—A string value containing the entire URL.
- `pathname`—A string value specifying the path portion of the URL.
- `port`—A string value containing the port number from the URL.
- `protocol`—A string value containing the protocol from the URL (including the colon, but not the slashes).
- `search`—A string value containing any information passed to a GET CGI-BIN call (such as information after the question mark).

Methods

- `reload()`—Reloads the current document. (Not 2|I)
- `replace(url)`—Loads *url* over the current entry in the history list, making it impossible to navigate back to the previous URL with the Back button. (Not 2|I)

The `math` Object [C|2|3|I]

The `math` object provides properties and methods for advanced mathematical calculations.

Properties

- `E`—The value of Euler's constant (roughly 2.718) used as the base for natural logarithms.
- `LN10`—The value of the natural logarithm of 10 (roughly 2.302).
- `LN2`—The value of the natural logarithm of 2 (roughly 0.693).
- `LOG10E`—The value of the base 10 logarithm of e (roughly 0.434).
- `LOG2E`—The value of the base 2 logarithm of e (roughly 1.442).
- `PI`—The value of π; used to calculate the circumference and area of circles (roughly 3.1415).

- SQRT1_2—The value of the square root of one-half (roughly 0.707).
- SQRT2—The value of the square root of two (roughly 1.414).

Methods

- abs(*number*)—Returns the absolute value of *number*. The absolute value is the value of a number with its sign ignored—for example, abs(4) and abs(-4) both return 4.
- acos(*number*)—Returns the arc cosine of *number* in radians.
- asin(*number*)—Returns the arc sine of *number* in radians.
- atan(*number*)—Returns the arc tangent of *number* in radians.
- atan2(*number1*,*number2*)—Returns the angle of the polar coordinate corresponding to the Cartesian coordinate (*number1*,*number2*). (Not I)
- ceil(*number*)—Returns the next integer greater than *number*; in other words, rounds up to the next integer.
- cos(*number*)—Returns the cosine of *number*, which represents an angle in radians.
- exp(*number*)—Returns the value of E to the power of *number*.
- floor(*number*)—Returns the next integer less than *number*; in other words, rounds down to the nearest integer.
- log(*number*)—Returns the natural logarithm of *number*.
- max(*number1*,*number2*)—Returns the greater of *number1* and *number2*.
- min(*number1*,*number2*)—Returns the smaller of *number1* and *number2*.
- pow(*number1*,*number2*)—Returns the value of *number1* to the power of *number2*.
- random()—Returns a random number between zero and 1 (at press time, this method was available only on UNIX versions of Navigator 2.0).
- round(*number*)—Returns the closest integer to *number*; in other words, rounds to the closest integer.
- sin(*number*)—Returns the sine of *number*, which represents an angle in radians.
- sqrt(*number*)—Returns the square root of *number*.
- tan(*number*)—Returns the tangent of *number*, which represents an angle in radians.

The mimeType Object [Cl3]

The mimeType object reflects a MIME type supported by the client browser.

Properties

- `type`—A string value reflecting the MIME type.

- `description`—A string containing a description of the MIME type.

- `enabledPlugin`—A reference to `plugin` object for the plug-in supporting the MIME type.

- `suffixes`—A string containing a comma-separated list of file suffixes for the MIME type.

The `navigator` Object [C|2|3|I]

The `navigator` object reflects information about the version of browser being used.

Properties

- `appCodeName`—A string value containing the code name of the client (for example, "Mozilla" for Netscape Navigator).

- `appName`—A string value containing the name of the client (for example, "Netscape" for Netscape Navigator).

- `appVersion`—A string value containing the version information for the client in the following form:

  versionNumber (platform; country)

  For example, Navigator 2.0, beta 6 for Windows 95 (international version) would have an `appVersion` property with the value `"2.0b6 (Win32; I)"`.

- `language`—Specifies the translation of Navigator. (A read-only property.) New in JavaScript 1.2.

- `mimeTypes`—An array of `mimeType` objects reflecting the MIME types supported by the client browser. (Not 2|I)

- `platform`—Specifies the platform for which Navigator was compiled. (For example, Win32, MacPPC, UNIX.) New in JavaScript 1.2.

- `plugins`—An array of `plugin` objects reflecting the plug-ins in a document in the order of their appearance in the HTML document. (Not 2|I)

- `userAgent`—A string containing the complete value of the user-agent header sent in the HTTP request. The following contains all the information in `appCodeName` and `appVersion`:

  Mozilla/2.0b6 (Win32; I)

Methods

- `javaEnabled()`—Returns a Boolean value indicating whether Java is enabled in the browser. (Not 2|I)

- `preference(preference.Name, setValue)`—In signed scripts, this method allows the developer to set certain browser preferences. Preferences available with this method are the following:

`general.always_load_images`	`true`/`false` value that sets whether images are automatically loaded.
`security.enable_java`	`true`/`false` value that sets whether Java is enabled.
`javascript.enabled`	`true`/`false` value that sets whether JavaScript is enabled.
`browser.enable_style_sheets`	`true`/`false` value that sets whether style sheets are enabled.
`autoupdate.enabled`	`true`/`false` value that sets whether autoinstall is enabled.
`network.cookie.cookieBehavior`	(0,1,2) value that sets the manner in which cookies are handled. There are three parameters. 0 accepts all cookies; 1 accepts only those that are forwarded to the originating server; 2 denies all cookies.
`network.cookie.warnAboutCookies`	`true`/`false` value that sets whether the browser will warn on accepting cookies.

The `option` Object [C|3]

The `option` object is used to create entries in a select list by using the following syntax:

`optionName = new Option(optionText, optionValue,`
`③defaultSelected, selected)`

Then the following line is used:

`selectName.options[index] = optionName`.

Properties

- `defaultSelected`—A Boolean value specifying whether the option is selected by default.
- `index`—An integer value specifying the option's index in the select list.
- `prototype`—Provides a mechanism to add properties to an `option` object.
- `selected`—A Boolean value indicating whether the option is currently selected.
- `text`—A string value reflecting the text displayed for the option.
- `value`—A string value indicating the value submitted to the server when the form is submitted.

The password Object [C|2|3||]

The `password` object reflects a password text field from an HTML form in JavaScript.

Properties

- `defaultValue`—A string value containing the default value of the password element (such as the value of the VALUE attribute).
- `enabled`—A Boolean value indicating whether the password field is enabled. (Not 2|3)
- `form`—A reference to the `form` object containing the password field. (Not 2|3)
- `name`—A string value containing the name of the password element.
- `value`—A string value containing the value of the password element.

Methods

- `focus()`—Emulates the action of focusing in the password field.
- `blur()`—Emulates the action of removing focus from the password field.
- `select()`—Emulates the action of selecting the text in the password field.

Event Handlers

- `onBlur`—Specifies JavaScript code to execute when the password field loses focus. (Not 2|3)
- `onFocus`—Specifies JavaScript code to execute when the password field receives focus. (Not 2|3)

B

JAVASCRIPT 1.2 LANGUAGE REFERENCE

The `plugin` Object

The `plugin` object reflects a plug-in supported by the browser.

Properties

- `name`—A string value reflecting the name of the plug-in.
- `filename`—A string value reflecting the filename of the plug-in on the system's disk.
- `description`—A string value containing the description supplied by the plug-in.

The `radio` Object [C|2|3|I]

The `radio` object reflects a set of radio buttons from an HTML form in JavaScript. To access individual radio buttons, use numeric indexes starting at zero. For example, individual buttons in a set of radio buttons named `testRadio` could be referenced by `testRadio[0]`, `testRadio[1]`, and so on.

Properties

- `checked`—A Boolean value indicating whether a specific radio button is checked. Can be used to select or deselect a button.
- `defaultChecked`—A Boolean value indicating whether a specific radio button was checked by default (that is, it reflects the CHECKED attribute). (Not I)
- `enabled`—A Boolean value indicating whether the radio button is enabled. (Not 2|3)
- `form`—A reference to the `form` object containing the radio button. (Not 2|3)
- `length`—An integer value indicating the number of radio buttons in the set. (Not I)
- `name`—A string value containing the name of the set of radio buttons.
- `value`—A string value containing the value of a specific radio button in a set (that is, it reflects the VALUE attribute).

Methods

- `click()`—Emulates the action of clicking a radio button.
- `focus()`—Gives focus to the radio button. (Not 2|3)

Event Handlers

- onClick—Specifies the JavaScript code to execute when a radio button is clicked.

- onFocus—Specifies the JavaScript code to execute when a radio button receives focus. (Not 2|3)

The regExp Object

The regExp object is relevant to searching for regular expressions. Its properties are set before or after a search is performed. They don't generally exercise control over the search itself, but instead articulate a series of values that can be accessed throughout the search.

Properties

- input—The string against which a regular expression is matched. New in JavaScript 1.2.

- multiline [true, false]—Sets whether the search continues beyond line breaks on multiple lines (true) or not (false). New in JavaScript 1.2.

- lastMatch—Indicates the characters last matched. New in JavaScript 1.2.

- lastParen—Indicates the last matched string that appeared in parentheses. New in JavaScript 1.2.

- leftContext—Indicates the string just before the most recently matched regular expression. New in JavaScript 1.2.

- rightContext—Indicates the remainder of the string, beyond the most recently matched regular expression. New in JavaScript 1.2.

- $1,..$9—Indicates the last nine substrings in a match; those substrings are enclosed in parentheses. New in JavaScript 1.2.

The Regular Expression Object

The Regular Expression object contains the pattern of a regular expression.

Parameters

- regexp—Specifies the name of the regular expression object. New in JavaScript 1.2.

- pattern—Specifies the text of the regular expression. New in JavaScript 1.2.

Flags

- i—Specifies that during the regular expression search, case is ignored (that is, the search is not case sensitive).

- g—Specifies that during the regular expression search, the match (and search) should be global.

- gi—Specifies that during the regular expression search, case is ignored and during the regular expression search, the match (and search) should be global.

Properties

- global [true,false]—Sets the g flag value in code, such as whether the search is global (true) or not (false). New in JavaScript 1.2.

- ignoreCase [true,false]—Sets the i flag value in code, such as whether the search is case sensitive (true) or not (false). New in JavaScript 1.2.

- lastIndex—(Integer value) Indicates the index position at which to start the next matching procedure (for example, lastIndex == 2). New in JavaScript 1.2.

- source—(Read-only) Contains the pattern's text. New in JavaScript 1.2.

Methods

- compile—Compiles the regular expression. This method is usually invoked at script startup, when the regular expression is already known and will remain constant. New in JavaScript 1.2.

- exec(str)—Executes a search for a regular expression within the specified string (str). New in JavaScript 1.2. Note: It uses the same properties as the RegExp object.

- test(str)—Executes a search for a regular expression and a specified string (str). New in JavaScript 1.2. Note: It uses the same properties as the RegExp object.

The reset Object [C|2|3|I]

The reset object reflects a reset button from an HTML form in JavaScript.

Properties

- enabled—A Boolean value indicating whether the reset button is enabled. (Not 2|3)

- form—A reference to the form object containing the reset button. (Not 2|3)
- name—A string value containing the name of the reset element.
- value—A string value containing the value of the reset element.

Methods

- click()—Emulates the action of clicking the reset button.
- focus()—Specifies the JavaScript code to execute when the reset button receives focus. (Not 2|3)

Event Handlers

- onClick—Specifies the JavaScript code to execute when the reset button is clicked.
- onFocus—Specifies the JavaScript code to execute when the reset button receives focus. (Not 2|3)

B

JavaScript 1.2
Language
Reference

The screen Object (New in JavaScript 1.2)

The screen object describes (or specifies) the characteristics of the current screen.

Properties

- availHeight—Specifies the height of the screen in pixels (minus static display constraints set forth by the operating system). New in JavaScript 1.2.
- availWidth—Specifies the width of the current screen in pixels (minus static display constraints set forth by the operating system). New in JavaScript 1.2.
- height—Specifies the height of the current screen in pixels. New in JavaScript 1.2.
- width—Specifies the width of the current screen in pixels. New in JavaScript 1.2.
- pixelDepth—Specifies the number of bits (per pixel) in the current screen. New in JavaScript 1.2.
- colorDepth—Specifies the number of possible colors to display in the current screen. New in JavaScript 1.2.

The select Object [C|2|3]

The select object reflects a selection list from an HTML form in JavaScript.

Properties

- length—An integer value containing the number of options in the selection list.
- name—A string value containing the name of the selection list.
- options—An array reflecting each of the options in the selection list in the order they appear. The options property has its own properties:

defaultSelected	A Boolean value indicating whether an option was selected by default (that is, it reflects the SELECTED attribute).
index	An integer value reflecting the index of an option.
length	An integer value reflecting the number of options in the selection list.
name	A string value containing the name of the selection list.
selected	A Boolean value indicating whether the option is selected. Can be used to select or deselect an option.
selectedIndex	An integer value containing the index of the currently selected option.
text	A string value containing the text displayed in the selection list for a particular option.
value	A string value indicating the value for the specified option (that is, reflects the VALUE attribute).

- selectedIndex—Reflects the index of the currently selected option in the selection list.

Methods

- blur()—Removes focus from the selection list. (Not 2|3)
- focus()—Gives focus to the selection list. (Not 2|3)

Event Handlers

- onBlur—Specifies the JavaScript code to execute when the selection list loses focus.

- onFocus—Specifies the JavaScript code to execute when focus is given to the selection list.

- onChange—Specifies the JavaScript code to execute when the selected option in the list changes.

The string Object [C|2|3|I]

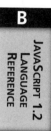

The string object provides properties and methods for working with string literals and variables.

Properties

- length—An integer value containing the length of the string expressed as the number of characters in the string.

- prototype—Provides a mechanism for adding properties to a string object. (Not 2)

Methods

- anchor(*name*)—Returns a string containing the value of the string object surrounded by an A container tag with the NAME attribute set to *name*.

- big()—Returns a string containing the value of the string object surrounded by a BIG container tag.

- blink()—Returns a string containing the value of the string object surrounded by a BLINK container tag.

- bold()—Returns a string containing the value of the string object surrounded by a B container tag.

- charAt(*index*)—Returns the character at the location specified by *index*.

- charCodeAt(*index*)—Returns a number representing an ISO-Latin-1 codeset value at the instant *index*. (Netscape Navigator 4.0 and Later Only.)

- concat(*string2*)—Combines two strings and derives a third, new string. (Netscape Navigator 4.0 and Later Only.)

- fixed()—Returns a string containing the value of the string object surrounded by a FIXED container tag.

- `fontColor(color)`—Returns a string containing the value of the string object surrounded by a FONT container tag with the COLOR attribute set to *color*, which is a color name or an RGB triplet. (Not I)

- `fontSize(size)`—Returns a string containing the value of the string object surrounded by a FONTSIZE container tag with the size set to *size*. (Not I)

- `fromCharCode(num1, num2, …)`—Returns a string constructed of ISO-Latin-1 characters. Those characters are specified by their codeset values, which are expressed as *num1*, *num2*, and so on.

- `indexOf(findString,startingIndex)`—Returns the index of the first occurrence of *findString*, starting the search at *startingIndex*, which is optional; if it's not provided, the search starts at the start of the string.

- `italics()`—Returns a string containing the value of the string object surrounded by an I container tag.

- `lastIndexOf(findString,startingIndex)`—Returns the index of the last occurrence of *findString*. This is done by searching backward from *startingIndex*. *startingIndex* is optional and is assumed to be the last character in the string if no value is provided.

- `link(href)`—Returns a string containing the value of the string object surrounded by an A container tag with the HREF attribute set to *href*.

- `match(regular_expression)`—Matches a regular expression to a string. The parameter *regular_expression* is the name of the regular expression, expressed either as a variable or a literal.

- `replace(regular_expression, newSubStr)`—Finds and replaces *regular_expression* with newSubStr.

- `search(regular_expression)`—Finds *regular_expression* and matches it to some string.

- `slice(beginSlice, [endSlice])`—Extracts a portion of a given string and derives a new string from that excerpt. *beginSlice* and *endSlice* are both zero-based indexes that can be used to grab the first, second, and third character, and so on.

- `small()`—Returns a string containing the value of the string object surrounded by a SMALL container tag.

- `split(separator)`—Returns an array of strings created by splitting the string at every occurrence of *separator*. (Not 2|I) split has additional functionality in JavaScript 1.2 and for Navigator 4.0 and later. That new functionality includes the following elements:

Regex and Fixed String Splitting	You can now split the `string` string by both regular expression argument and fixed string,
Limit Count	You can now add a limit count to prevent including empty elements within the string.
White Space Splitting	The capability to split on a white space (including any white space, such as space, tab, newline, and so forth).

- `strike()`—Returns a string containing the value of the `string` object surrounded by a `STRIKE` container tag.

- `sub()`—Returns a string containing the value of the `string` object surrounded by a `SUB` container tag.

- `substr(start, [length])`—Used to extract a set number (length) of characters within a string. Use `start` to specify the location at which to begin this extraction process. New in JavaScript 1.2.

- `substring(firstIndex,lastIndex)`—Returns a string equivalent to the substring beginning at *firstIndex* and ending at the character before *lastIndex*. If *firstIndex* is greater than *lastIndex*, the string starts at *lastIndex* and ends at the character before *firstIndex*. Note: In JavaScript 1.2, x and y are no longer swapped. To get this result, you must specify JavaScript 1.2 with the `language` attribute within the `<SCRIPT>` tag.

- `sup()`—Returns a string containing the value of the `string` object surrounded by a `SUP` container tag.

- `toLowerCase()`—Returns a string containing the value of the `string` object with all characters converted to lowercase.

- `toUpperCase()`—Returns a string containing the value of the `string` object with all characters converted to uppercase.

The `submit` Object [C|2|3|I]

The `submit` object reflects a submit button from an HTML form in JavaScript.

Properties

- enabled—A Boolean value indicating whether the submit button is enabled. (Not 2|3)
- form—A reference to the form object containing the submit button. (Not 2|3)
- name—A string value containing the name of the submit button element.
- type—A string value reflecting the TYPE attribute of the <INPUT> tag. (Not 2|I)
- value—A string value containing the value of the submit button element.

Methods

- click()—Emulates the action of clicking the submit button.
- focus()—Gives focus to the submit button. (Not 2|3)

Event Handlers

- onClick—Specifies the JavaScript code to execute when the submit button is clicked.
- onFocus—Specifies the JavaScript code to execute when the submit button receives focus. (Not 2|3)

The text Object [C|2|3|I]

The text object reflects a text field from an HTML form in JavaScript.

Properties

- defaultValue—A string value containing the default value of the text element (that is, the value of the VALUE attribute).
- enabled—A Boolean value indicating whether the text field is enabled. (Not 2|3)
- form—A reference to the form object containing the text field. (Not 2|3)
- name—A string value containing the name of the text element.
- type—A string value reflecting the TYPE attribute of the <INPUT> tag. (Not 2|I)
- value—A string value containing the value of the text element.

Methods

- focus()—Emulates the action of focusing in the text field.
- blur()—Emulates the action of removing focus from the text field.
- select()—Emulates the action of selecting the text in the text field.

Event Handlers

- onBlur—Specifies the JavaScript code to execute when focus is removed from the field.
- onChange—Specifies the JavaScript code to execute when the content of the field is changed.
- onFocus—Specifies the JavaScript code to execute when focus is given to the field.
- onSelect—Specifies the JavaScript code to execute when the user selects some or all of the text in the field.

The textarea Object [C|2|3|I]

The textarea object reflects a multiline text field from an HTML form in JavaScript.

Properties

- defaultValue—A string value containing the default value of the textarea element (that is, the value of the VALUE attribute).
- enabled—A Boolean value indicating whether the textarea field is enabled. (Not 2|3)
- form—A reference to the form object containing the textarea field. (Not 2|3)
- name—A string value containing the name of the textarea element.
- type—A string value reflecting the type of the textarea object. (Not 2|I)
- value—A string value containing the value of the textarea element.

Methods

- focus()—Emulates the action of focusing in the textarea field.
- blur()—Emulates the action of removing focus from the textarea field.
- select()—Emulates the action of selecting the text in the textarea field.

Event Handlers

- onKeyUp—Specifies the JavaScript code to execute when the user releases a specific key. (Netscape Navigator 4.0 Only.) (4)

- onKeyPress—Specifies the JavaScript code to execute when the user holds down a specific key. (Netscape Navigator 4.0 Only.) (4)

- onKeyDown—Specifies the JavaScript code to execute when the user presses a specific key. (Netscape Navigator 4.0 Only.) (4)

- onBlur—Specifies the JavaScript code to execute when focus is removed from the field.

- onChange—Specifies the JavaScript code to execute when the content of the field is changed.

- onFocus—Specifies the JavaScript code to execute when focus is given to the field.

- onSelect—Specifies the JavaScript code to execute when the user selects some or all of the text in the field.

The window Object [C|2|3|I]

The window object is the top-level object for each window or frame and the parent object for the document, location, and history objects.

Properties

- defaultStatus—A string value containing the default value displayed in the status bar.

- frames—An array of objects for each frame in a window. Frames appear in the array in the order in which they appear in the HTML source code.

- innerHeight()—Specifies the vertical size of the content area (in pixels). New in JavaScript 1.2.

- innerWidth()—Specifies the horizontal size of the content area (in pixels). New in JavaScript 1.2.

- length—An integer value indicating the number of frames in a parent window. (Not I)

- name—A string value containing the name of the window or frame.

- opener—A reference to the window object containing the open() method used to open the current window. (Not 2|I)

- `pageXOffset`—Specifies the current X position of the viewable window area (expressed in pixels). New in JavaScript 1.2.

- `pageYOffset`—Specifies the current Y position of the viewable window area (expressed in pixels). New in JavaScript 1.2.

- `parent`—A string indicating the name of the window containing the frameset.

- `personalbar [visible=true,false]`—Represents the Directories bar in Netscape Navigator and whether it's visible. New in JavaScript 1.2.

- `scrollbars [visible=true,false]`—Represents the scrollbars of the instant window and whether they are visible. New in JavaScript 1.2.

- `self`—A alternative for the name of the current window.

- `status`—Used to display a message in the status bar; it's done by assigning values to this property.

- `statusbar=[true,false,1,0]`—Specifies whether the status bar of the target window is visible.

- `toolbar=[true,false,1,0]`—Specifies whether the toolbar of the target window is visible.

- `top`—An alternative for the name of the topmost window.

- `window`—An alternative for the name of the current window.

Methods

- `alert(message)`—Displays *message* in a dialog box.

- `back()`—Sends the user back to the previous URL stored in the history list. (Simulates a user clicking the Back button in Navigator.) New in JavaScript 1.2.

- `blur()`—Removes focus from the window. On many systems, it sends the window to the background. (Not 2|I)

- `captureEvents()`—Used in a window with frames (along with `enableExternalCapture`), it specifies that the window will capture all specified events.

- `clearInterval(intervalID)`—Cancels timeouts created with the `setInterval` method. New in JavaScript 1.2.

- `close()`—Closes the window. (Not I)

- `confirm(message)`—Displays *message* in a dialog box with OK and Cancel buttons. Returns `true` or `false` based on the button clicked by the user.

- `disableExternalCapture()`—Prevents the instant window with frames from capturing events occurring in pages loaded from a different location. New in JavaScript 1.2.

- `enableExternalCapture()`—Allows the instant window (with frames) to capture events occurring in pages loaded from a different location. New in JavaScript 1.2.

- `find([string], [true, false], [true, false])`—Finds `string` in the target window. There are two true/false parameters: The first specifies the Boolean state of case sensitivity in the search; the second specifies whether the search is performed backward. New in JavaScript 1.2.

- `focus()`—Gives focus to the window. On many systems, it brings the window to the front. (Not 2|I)

- `forward()`—Sends the user to the next URL in the history list. (Simulates a user clicking the Forward button in Navigator.) New in JavaScript 1.2.

- `home()`—Sends the user to the user's Home Page URL. (For example, in a default configuration of Netscape Navigator, it sends the user to `http://home.netscape.com`.) New in JavaScript 1.2.

- `moveBy(horizontal, vertical)`—Moves the window according to the specified values `horizontal` and `vertical`. New in JavaScript 1.2.

- `moveTo(x, y)`—Moves the top-left corner of the window to the specified location; `x` and `y` are screen coordinates. New in JavaScript 1.2.

- `navigator(url)`—Loads `url` in the window. (Not 2|3)

- `open(url,name,features)`—Opens `url` in a window named *name*. If *name* doesn't exist, a new window is created with that name. *features* is an optional string argument containing a list of features for the new window. The feature list contains any of the following name-value pairs separated by commas and without additional spaces: (Not I)

`toolbar=[yes,no,1,0]`	Indicates whether the window should have a toolbar.
`location=[yes,no,1,0]`	Indicates whether the window should have a location field.
`directories=[yes,no,1,0]`	Indicates whether the window should have directory buttons.
`status=[yes,no,1,0]`	Indicates whether the window should have a status bar.

`menubar=[yes,no,1,0]`	Indicates whether the window should have menus.
`scrollbars=[yes,no,1,0]`	Indicates whether the window should have scrollbars.
`resizable=[yes,no,1,0]`	Indicates whether the window should be resizable.
`width=`*`pixels`*	Indicates the width of the window in pixels.
`alwaysLowered=[yes,no,1,2]`	Indicates (if true) that the window should remain below all other windows. (This feature has varying results on varying window systems.) New in JavaScript 1.2. Note: The script must be signed to use this feature.
`alwaysRaised=[yes,no,1,2]`	Indicates (if true) that the window should always remain the top-level window. (This feature has varying results on varying window systems.) New in JavaScript 1.2. Note: The script must be signed to use this feature.
`dependent[yes,no,1,2]`	Indicates that the current child window will die (or close) when the parent window does. New in JavaScript 1.2.
`hotkeys=[yes,no,1,2]`	Indicates (if true) that most hot keys are disabled within the instant window. New in JavaScript 1.2.
`innerWidth=pixels`	Indicates the width (in pixels) of the instant window's content area. New in JavaScript 1.2.
`innerHeight=pixels`	Indicates the height (in pixels) of the instant window's content area. New in JavaScript 1.2.

`outerWidth=pixels`	Indicates the instant window's horizontal outside width boundary. New in JavaScript 1.2.
`outerHeight=pixels`	Indicates the instant window's horizontal outside height boundary. New in JavaScript 1.2.
`screenX=pixels`	Indicates the distance that the new window is placed from the left side of the screen (horizontally). New in JavaScript 1.2.
`screenY=pixels`	Indicates the distance that the new window is placed from the top of the screen (vertically). New in JavaScript 1.2.
`z-lock=[yes,no,1,2]`	Indicates that the instant window does not move through the cycling of the z-order; that is, it doesn't rise above other windows, even if activated. New in JavaScript 1.2. Note: The script must be signed for this feature to work.
`height=pixels`	Indicates the height of the window in pixels.

- `print()`—Prints the contents of a frame or window. It's the equivalent of the user pressing the Print button in Netscape Navigator. New in JavaScript 1.2.

- `prompt(message,response)`—Displays *message* in a dialog box with a text entry field with the default value of *response*. The user's response in the text entry field is returned as a string.

- `releaseEvents(eventType)`—Specifies that the current window should release events instead of capturing them so that these events can be passed to other objects, perhaps further on in the event hierarchy. New in JavaScript 1.2.

- `resizeBy(horizontal, vertical)`—Resizes the window, moving from the bottom-right corner. New in JavaScript 1.2.

- `resizeTo(outerWidth, outerHeight)`—Resizes the window, using `outerWidth` and `outerHeight` properties. New in JavaScript 1.2.

- `routeEvent(event)`—Sends or routes an event through the normal event hierarchy. New in JavaScript 1.2.

- scrollBy(*horizontal, vertical*)—Scroll the viewing area of the current window by the specified amount. New in JavaScript 1.2.

- scrollTo(x, y)—Scrolls the current window to the specified position, calculated in x and y coordinates, starting at the top-left corner of the window. New in JavaScript 1.2.

- setInterval(*function*, msec, [args])—Repeatedly calls a function after the period specified by the msec parameter. New in JavaScript 1.2.

- setInterval(*expression*, msec)—Evaluates *expression* after the period specified by the msec parameter. New in JavaScript 1.2.

- setTimeout(*expression,time*)—Evaluates *expression* after *time*, which is a value in milliseconds. The timeout can be named with the following structure:

  name = setTimeOut(*expression,time*)

- scrollTo(*x,y*)—Scrolls the window to the coordinate *x,y*. (Not 2|I)

- stop()—Stops the current download. It's the equivalent of the user pressing the Stop button in Netscape Navigator.

- clearTimeout(*name*)—Cancels the timeout with the name *name*.

B

JAVASCRIPT 1.2
LANGUAGE
REFERENCE

Event Handlers

- onDragDrop—Specifies the JavaScript code to execute when the user drops an object onto the window. (Netscape Navigator 4.0 and Later Only.) (4.0)

- onBlur—Specifies the JavaScript code to execute when focus is removed from a window. (Not 2|I)

- onError—Specifies the JavaScript code to execute when a JavaScript error occurs while loading a document. It can be used to intercept JavaScript errors. Setting this event handler to null effectively prevents JavaScript errors from being displayed to the user. (Not 2|I)

- onFocus—Specifies the JavaScript code to execute when the window receives focus. (Not 2|I)

- onLoad—Specifies the JavaScript code to execute when the window or frame finishes loading.

- onMove—Specifies the JavaScript code to execute when the user moves a window. (Netscape Navigator 4.0 Only.)

- onResize—Specifies the JavaScript code to execute when a user resizes the window.

- onUnload—Specifies the JavaScript code to execute when the document in the window or frame is exited.

Independent Functions, Operators, Variables, and Literals

Independent Functions

- escape(*character*)—Returns a string containing the ASCII encoding of *character* in the form %xx; xx is the numeric encoding of the character. (Cl2l3lI)

- eval(*expression*)—Returns the result of evaluating *expression*, which is an arithmetic expression. (Cl2l3lI)

- isNaN(*value*)—Evaluates *value* to see if it's NaN. Returns a Boolean value. (Cl2l3lI) (On UNIX platforms, not 2.)

- parseFloat(*string*)—Converts *string* to a floating-point number and returns the value. It continues to convert until it hits a nonnumeric character and then returns the result. If the first character can't be converted to a number, the function returns NaN (zero on Windows platforms). (Cl2l3lI)

- parseInt(*string,base*)—Converts *string* to an integer of base *base* and returns the value. It continues to convert until it hits a nonnumeric character and then returns the result. If the first character can't be converted to a number, the function returns NaN (zero on Windows platforms). (Cl2l3lI)

- taint(*propertyName*)—Adds tainting to *propertyName*. (Cl3)

- toString()—This is a method of all objects. It returns the object as a string or returns "[object *type*]" if no string representation exists for the object. (Cl2l3) Note: In JavaScript 1.2, it converts objects and strings into literals.

- unescape(*string*)—Returns a character based on the ASCII encoding contained in *string*. The ASCII encoding should take the form "%integer" or "hexadecimalValue". (Cl2l3lI)

- untaint(*propertyName*)—Removes tainting from *propertyName*. (Cl3)

Statements

- break—Terminates a while or for loop and passes program control to the first statement following the loop. (2l3l4) Note: In JavaScript 1.2, break has the added functionality of being able to break out of labeled statements.

- comment—Used to add a comment within the script. This comment is ignored by Navigator. Comments in JavaScript work similarly to those in C. They are enclosed in a /* (start), */ (end) structure. (2l3l4)

- `continue`—Terminates execution of statements in a `while` or `for` loop and continues iteration of the loop. (2|3|4) Note: In JavaScript 1.2, `continue` has added functionality that allows you to continue within labeled statements.

- `do while`—Sets up a loop that continues to execute statements and code until the condition evaluates to `false`. New in JavaScript 1.2.

- `export`—Used with the `import` statement. In secure, signed scripts, it allows the developer to export all properties, functions, and variables to another script. New in JavaScript 1.2.

- `for([initial-expression]; [condition]; [incremental-expression];))`—Specifies the opening of a `for` loop. The arguments are these: initialize a variable (`initial-expression`), create a condition to test for (`condition`), and specify an incrementation scheme (`incremental-expression`). (2|3|4)

- `for...in`—Imposes a variable to all properties of an object and executes a block of code for each. (2|3|4)

- `function [name]()`—Declares a function so that it can be referred to or reached by event handlers (or other processes). (2|3|4)

- `if...else`—A structure used to test whether a certain condition is true. `If...else` blocks can contain nested statements and functions (and call them) if a condition is either true or false. (2|3|4)

- `import`—Used with the `export` statement. In secure, signed scripts, it allows the developer to import all properties, functions, and variables from another script. New in JavaScript 1.2.

- `label (labeled statements)`—Statement that creates a label or pointer to code elsewhere in the script. By calling this label, you redirect the script to the labeled statement.

- `new`—Creates an instance of a user-defined object. (It can also be used to create an instance of built-in objects, inherent to JavaScript, such as new `Date`.) (2|3|4)

- `return [value]`—Specifies a value to be returned by a given function. For example, `return` x returns the variable value associated with *x*. (2|3|4)

- `switch`—Evaluates an expression and attempts to match it to a `case` pattern or label. If the expression matches the `case`, trailing statements associated with that label are executed. New in JavaScript 1.2. (Operates similarly to the `switch` statement in C shell syntax.)

- `this`—A statement used to refer to a specific object, as shown in this example: [2|3|4]

```
onClick = 'javascript:my_function(this.form)'
```

B

JAVASCRIPT 1.2
LANGUAGE
REFERENCE

- `var [name]`—Declares a variable by name. (2|3|4)
- `while`—Statement that begins a `while` loop. `while` loops specify that as long as (while) a condition is true, execute some code. (2|3|4)
- `with`—Statement that sets the value for the default object; a method that's similar to creating a global variable with a function. (2|3|4)

Operators

- Assignment Operators—See Table B.1. (C|2|3|I)

TABLE B.1 ASSIGNMENT OPERATORS IN JAVASCRIPT

Operator	Description
=	Assigns the value of the right operand to the left operand
+=	Adds the left and right operands and assigns the result to the left operand
-=	Subtracts the right operand from the left operand and assigns the result to the left operand
*=	Multiplies the two operands and assigns the result to the left operand
/=	Divides the left operand by the right operand and assigns the value to the left operand
%=	Divides the left operand by the right operand and assigns the remainder to the left operand

- Arithmetic Operators—See Table B.2. (C|2|3|I)

TABLE B.2 ARITHMETIC OPERATORS IN JAVASCRIPT

Operator	Description
+	Adds the left and right operands
-	Subtracts the right operand from the left operand
*	Multiplies the two operands
/	Divides the left operand by the right operand
%	Divides the left operand by the right operand and evaluates to the remainder
++	Increments the operand by one (can be used before or after the operand)

Operator	Description
- -	Decreases the operand by one (can be used before or after the operand)
-	Changes the sign of the operand

- Bitwise Operators—Bitwise operators deal with their operands as binary numbers, but return JavaScript numerical value. (See Table B.3.) (C|2|3|I)

TABLE B.3 BITWISE OPERATORS IN JAVASCRIPT

Operator	Description
AND (or &)	Converts operands to integers with 32 bits, pairs the corresponding bits, and returns one for each pair of ones. Returns zero for any other combination.
OR (or ¦)	Converts operands to integers with 32 bits, pairs the corresponding bits, and returns one for each pair when one of the two bits is one. Returns zero if both bits are zero.
XOR (or ^)	Converts operands to integer with 32 bits, pairs the corresponding bits, and returns one for each pair when only one bit is one. Returns zero for any other combination.
<<	Converts the left operand to an integer with 32 bits and shifts bits to the left the number of bits indicated by the right operand. Bits shifted off to the left are discarded, and zeros are shifted in from the right.
>>>	Converts the left operand to an integer with 32 bits and shifts bits to the right the number of bits indicated by the right operand. Bits shifted off to the right are discarded, and zeros are shifted in from the left.
>>	Converts the left operand to an integer with 32 bits and shifts bits to the right the number of bits indicated by the right operand. Bits shifted off to the right are discarded, and copies of the leftmost bit are shifted in from the left.

- Logical Operators—See Table B.4. (C|2|3|I)

TABLE B.4 LOGICAL OPERATORS IN JAVASCRIPT

Operator	Description
&&	Logical "and." Returns `true` when both operands are true; otherwise, it returns `false`.
||	Logical "or." Returns `true` if either operand is true. It returns `false` only when both operands are false.
!	Logical "not." Returns `true` if the operand is false and `false` if the operand is true. This is a unary operator and precedes the operand.

- Comparison Operators—See Table B.5. [C|2|3|I]

TABLE B.5[EM]LOGICAL (COMPARISON) OPERATORS IN JAVASCRIPT

Operator	Description
==	Returns `true` if the operands are equal
!=	Returns `true` if the operands are not equal
>	Returns `true` if the left operand is greater than the right operand
<	Returns `true` if the left operand is less than the right operand
>=	Returns `true` if the left operand is greater than or equal to the right operand
<=	Returns `true` if the left operand is less than or equal to the right operand

- Conditional Operators—Conditional expressions take one form:

  `(condition) ? val1 : val2`

  If `condition` is true, the expression evaluates to `val1`; otherwise, it evaluates to `val2`. (C|2|3|I)

- String Operators—The concatenation operator (+) is one of two string operators. It evaluates to a string combining the left and right operands. The concatenation assignment operator (+=) is also available. (C|2|3|I)

- The `typeof` Operator—The `typeof` operator returns the type of its single operand. Possible types are `object`, `string`, `number`, `boolean`, `function`, and `undefined`. (C|3|I)

- The `void` Operator—The `void` operator takes an expression as an operand but returns no value. (C|3)

- Operator Precedence: JavaScript applies the rules of operator precedence as follows (from lowest to highest precedence):

  Comma (,)

  Assignment operators (=, +=, -=, *=, /=, %=)

  Conditional (? :)

  Logical OR (¦¦)

  Logical AND (&&)

  Bitwise OR (¦)

  Bitwise XOR (^)

  Bitwise AND (&)

  Equality (==, !=)

  Relational (<, <=, >, >=)

  Shift (<<, >>, >>>)

  Addition/subtraction (+, -)

  Multiply/divide/modulus (*, /, %)

  Negation/increment (!, -, ++, --)

  Call, member (( ), [ ])

VBScript 2.0 Reference

IN THIS APPENDIX

VBScript 2.0 is a lightweight scripting language that provides both server-side and client-side scripting functionality. VBScript is the default scripting language of the Internet Information Server, and is used to provide advanced server-side processing that extends the power and reach of your Web server. VBScript can be run on the Web server to process application logic and is used to generate the standard HTML. As a result of only delivering standard HTML to the clients, no browsers, user groups, or operating systems are restricted from receiving information from your Web site or Web-enabled applications.

Scripting Active Server Pages

Dynamically generating HTML based on server-side scripts is made possible by the Active Server scripting engine. The Internet Information Server provides native scripting support for VBScript and JScript. To ensure that the proper scripting engine interprets your script, specify the scripting language for the Active Server Page using the LANGUAGE directive. The LANGUAGE tag must be made on the first line of code on the Active Server Page, as shown below:

```
<%@ LANGUAGE="VBSCRIPT" %>
```

This example sets VBScript as the page scripting language responsible for interpreting the script nested within the inline ASP delimiters `<%  %>`. VBScript can be embedded within these delimiters and directly integrated within the HTML on a page, as shown in the following code:

```
<%@ LANGUAGE="VBSCRIPT" %>
<HTML>
<BODY>
    <% If session("NewUser") Then %>
<P>Hello, Welcome to the online community news letter</P>
<% Else %>
    <P>Welcome back, <% Session("UserName") %>! </P>
<% End If%>
</BODY>
</HTML>
```

VBScript procedures can be implemented in two ways on the Internet Information Server: either within the ASP delimiters, `<%` and `%>`, or by explicitly using the `<SCRIPT>` tag. To embed procedures within your ASP delimiters, define the subroutine or procedure as shown below:

```
<%
Sub CalcNewBalanceRef(ByRef Balance)
    Balance = (FormatCurrency(Balance+Balance*22.5/100/12))
    Response.Write Balance
End sub
%>
```

The previous code example creates a subroutine called CalcNewBalance and accepts an argument named Balance. The procedure can then be accessed from the script by using the Call statement, as shown in the following example:

```
<%@ LANGUAGE="VBSCRIPT" %>
<HTML>
<BODY>
<% '=== Begin Sub ===
Sub CalcNewBalanceRef(Balance)
     Balance = (FormatCurrency(Balance+Balance*22.5/100/12))
     Response.Write Balance
End Sub
%>
'==== Begin Body ===
Dim myAcctBalance
myAcctBalance = 3250
Call CalcNewBalanceRef(myAcctBalance)
%>
</BODY>
</HTML>
```

You can also create individual procedure calls with the <SCRIPT> tag. However, if this script is going to run on the server, you need to include the RUNAT attribute to specify where the script should be executed.

```
<SCRIPT RUNAT = Server LANGUAGE = "VBScript">
<!--
   Function TrapNull(vDBText)
      Dim Ret
      If ISNULL(vDBText) Then
          Ret = ""
      Else
          Ret = Trim(vDBText)
      End if
      TrapNull = Ret
End Function
-->
</SCRIPT>
```

In this example, a function called TrapNull removes Null characters by using the IsNull function. If the data is Null, a zero-length string is returned to the calling function. If the value is not null, the Trim function will eliminate any leading or trailing spaces from the string and return the value to the calling parent code. For example, the previous example could be called as shown in the following code:

```
<TR><TD Align = "Left"><% Response.Write TrapNull(tbl_user_name)
➡%></TD></TR>
```

You can also use multiple scripting languages within ASP, as shown below:

```
<%@ LANGUAGE="VBSCRIPT" %>
<HTML>
<SCRIPT LANGUAGE = "JScript" RUNAT = SERVER>
function WriteJavaScript(str){
     Response.Write(str);
     }
</SCRIPT>
<SCRIPT LANGUAGE="VBScript" RUNAT=SERVER>
Function WriteVBScript(str)
     Response.Write(str)
End Function
</SCRIPT>

<BODY>

<%
str = "Hello, Welcome to the online community news letter<BR>"
WriteJavaScript(str)
str = "Today's top news stories are:<BR>"
WriteVBScript(str)
%>

</BODY>
</HTML>
```

This previous example demonstrated using the LANGUAGE tag to assign the default script-ing languages that translate the script embedded between the <%   %> delimeter and also demostrates how to add VBScript and JavaScript functions to the same ASP page. This script will produce the following results:

```
Hello, Welcome to the online community news letter
Today's top news stories are:
```

VBScript can also be implemented as a client-side scripting vehicle, but only for the Internet Explorer browser. To use VBScript on the client, use the <SCRIPT> tag:

```
<SCRIPT LANGUAGE="VBScript">
<!--
Sub loadAbortRetryIgnor()
     dim strMsg, iButton, strTitle, indexid
     strMsg = "Could Not Access Database"
     '=== Set the message string
     iButton = vbAbortRetryIgnore + vbQuestion + vbDefaultButton2
     strTitle = "VBScript Abort, Ignore and Retry Message Box"
     '=== Set the title bar text
     indexid = MsgBox(strMsg, iButton, strTitle)
     '=== Trap the results
End Sub
-->
</SCRIPT>
```

VBScript only has one datatype: the Variant datatype. The Variant is used because of its flexibility with all datatypes. The Variant datatype is unique in the sense that the Variant actually changes behavior depending on the type of data it is storing. The Variant does use subtypes to help provide some optimization and datatype-specific functionality. The subtype information is shown in Table C.1.

TABLE C.1 THE VARIANT SUBTYPES

Subtype	Description
Empty	Variant is un-initialized.
Null	Variant intentionally contains no valid data.
Boolean	Contains either True or False.
Byte	Contains integer in the range 0 to 255.
Integer	Contains integer in the range –32,768 to 32,767.
Currency	–922,337,203,685,477.5808 to 922,337,203,685,477.5807.
Long	Contains integer in the range –2,147,483,648 to 2,147,483,647.
Single	Contains a single-precision, floating-point number in the range –3.402823E38 to –1.401298E-45 for negative values; 1.401298E-45 to 3.402823E38 for positive values.
Double	Contains a double-precision, floating-point number in the range –1.79769313486232E308 to –4.94065645841247E-324 for negative values; 4.94065645841247E-324 to 1.79769313486232E308 for positive values.
Date (Time)	Contains a number that represents a date between January 1, 100 to December 31, 9999.
String	Contains a variable-length string that can be up to approximately 2 billion characters in length.
Object	Contains an object.
Error	Contains an error number.

C

VBSCRIPT 2.0
REFERENCE

If the variant subtype is identified as Empty, the variable's value is 0 for numeric variables or a zero-length string ("") for string variables.

Operators

VBScript has a wide range of built-in operators that are user to manipulate, control, and compare variables. The VBScript operators are listed in Table C.2.

TABLE C.2 Operators

Name	Symbol	Description
Addition Operator	+	Sums two numbers.
And Operator	&	Performs a logical conjunction on two expressions.
Concatenation Operator	&	Forces string concatenation of two expressions.
Division Operator	/	Divides two numbers.
Eqv Operator	EQV	Performs a logical equivalence on two expressions.
Exponentiation Operator	^	Raises a number to the power of an exponent.
Imp Operator	IMP	Performs a logical implication on two expressions.
Integer Division Operator	\	Divides two numbers and returns an integer result.
Is Operator	IS	Compares two object reference variables.
Mod Operator	MOD	Divides two numbers and returns only the remainder.
Multiplication Operator	*	Multiplies two numbers.
Negation Operator	–	Finds the difference between two numbers or sets the negative value a number.
Not Operator	NOT	Performs logical negation on an expression.
Or Operator	OR	Performs a logical disjunction on two expressions.
Subtraction Operator	–	Finds the difference between two numbers or sets the negative value a number.
Xor Operator	XOR	Used to perform a logical exclusion on two expressions.

Statements and Conditional Statements

VBScript uses statements to define and help organize coding structures. Conditional statements are used to control application flow and program execution. Table C.3 displays the declaration statements and conditional statements found in VBScript 2.0.

TABLE C.3 STATEMENTS

Name	Description
Call	Transfers program execution to a subroutine or function.
Const	Declares a constant's value to use in place of literal values.
Dim	Declares variables and allocates storage space.
Do...Loop	Repeats a block of statements while a condition returns True.
Erase	De-allocates dynamic array storage space.
Exit	Exits a procedure or conditional statement.
For...Next	Repeats a group of code statements a specified number of times.
For Each...Next	Repeats a group of code statements for each element in an array or collection.
Function	Declares a function procedure.
If...Then...Else	Conditionally executes a group of statements.
On Error	Enables error-handling.
Option Explicit	Forces explicit declaration of all variables.
Private	Used to declare and allocate storage space for private variables.
Public	Used to declare and allocate storage space for public variables.
Randomize	Initializes the random-number generator.
ReDim	Declares dynamic array variables and allocates or reallocates storage space.
Rem	Used to add comments or remarks within the code.
Select Case	Executes one of several groups of statements, depending on the value of an expression.

continues

C

VBSCRIPT 2.0
REFERENCE

TABLE C.3   CONTINUED

Name	Description
Set	Assigns an object reference to a variable or property.
Sub	Declares subroutine procedure.
While...Wend	Executes a series of statements as long as a given condition is True.

Intrinsic Functions

VBScript provides access to compiled application logic built into the VBScript programming language by the use of functions. These functions usually accept information, process the information, and return the results of the function to the calling line of code. Table C.4 can be used to help identify a function name depending on its functionality.

TABLE C.4   VBSCRIPT 2.0 FUNCTION CATEGORIES

Category or Topic	Function Name
Array handling	Array, IsArray, Erase, LBound, UBound
Conversions	Abs, Asc, Chr, CBool, Cbyte, CCur, Cdate, CDbl, Cint, CLng, Sng, CStr, DateSerial, DateValue, Hex, Oct, Fix, Int, Sgn, TimeSerial, TimeValue
Dates/times	Date, Time, DateAdd, DateDiff, DatePart, DateSerial, DateValue, Day, Month, MonthName, Weekday, WeekdayName, Year, Hour, Minute, Second, Now, TimeSerial, TimeValue
Formatting Strings	FormatCurrency, FormatDateTime, FormatNumber, FormatPercent
Input/Output	InputBox, LoadPicture, MsgBox
Math	Atn, Cos, Sin, Tan, Exp, Log, Sqr, Rnd
Script engine ID	ScriptEngine, ScriptEngineBuildVersion, ScriptEngineMajorVersion, ScriptEngineMinorVersion
Strings processing	Asc, Chr, Filter, Instr, InstrRev, Join, Len, LCase, Ucase, Left, Mid, Right, Replace, Space, Split, StrComp, String, StrReverse, LTrim, RTrim, Trim
Variants processing	IsArray, IsDate, IsEmpty, IsNull, IsNumeric, IsObject, TypeName, VarType

For a complete alphabetical listing of VBScript functions and their descriptions, see
Table C.5.

TABLE C.5   ALPHABETICAL LISTING OF VBSCRIPT 2.0 FUNCTIONS

Function Name	*Description*
Abs	Returns the absolute value of a number.
Array	Returns a Variant containing an array.
Asc	Returns the ANSI character code of a string.
Atn	Returns the arctangent of a number.
CBool	Returns an expression that has been converted to a Boolean subtype.
CByte	Returns an expression that has been converted to a Byte subtype.
CCur	Returns an expression that has been converted to a Currency subtype.
CDate	Returns an expression that has been converted to a Date subtype.
CDbl	Returns an expression that has been converted to a Double subtype.
Chr	Returns the character associated with the specified ANSI character code.
CInt	Returns an expression that has been converted to an Integer subtype.
CLng	Returns an expression that has been converted to a Long subtype.
Cos	Returns the cosine of an angle.
CreateObject	Creates and returns a reference to an Automation object.
CSng	Returns an expression that has been converted to a Single subtype.
CStr	Returns an expression that has been converted to a String subtype.
Date	Returns the current system date.
DateAdd	Returns a date to which a specified time interval has been added.
DateDiff	Returns the number of intervals between two dates.
DatePart	Returns the specified part of a given date.
DateSerial	Returns a Variant of subtype Date for a specified year, month, and day.

C

VBSCRIPT 2.0
REFERENCE

continues

TABLE C.5   CONTINUED

Function Name	*Description*
DateValue	Returns a Variant of subtype Date.
Day	Returns a whole number between 1 and 31, inclusive, representing the day of the month.
Exp	Returns e (the base of natural logarithms) raised to a power.
Filter	Returns a zero-based array containing a subset of a string array.
Fix	Returns the integer portion of a number.
FormatCurrency	Returns an expression formatted as a currency value.
FormatDateTime	Returns an expression formatted as a date or time.
FormatNumber	Returns an expression formatted as a number.
FormatPercent	Returns an expression formatted as a percent value with a trailing percent (%) symbol.
Hex	Returns a string representing the hexadecimal value of a number.
Hour	Returns a whole number representing the hour of the day between 0 and 23.
InputBox	Displays a prompt for an input dialog box.
InStr	Returns the numeric position of the first occurrence of one string within another.
InStrRev	Returns the numeric position of one string within another string from the end of string.
Int	Returns the integer portion of a number.
IsArray	Returns a Boolean value indicating if a variable is an array.
IsDate	Returns a Boolean value indicating if an expression can be converted to a date.
IsEmpty	Returns a Boolean value indicating whether a variable has been initialized.
IsNull	Returns a Boolean value that indicates whether an expression contains no valid datatypes.
IsNumeric	Returns a Boolean value indicating whether an expression can be evaluated as a number.
IsObject	Returns a Boolean value indicating whether an expression refers to an Automation object.
Join	Returns a string created by joining strings stored in an array.
LBound	Returns the base index value for a dimension of an array.
LCase	Returns a string that has been converted to lowercase.

Function Name	Description
Left	Returns the specified number of characters from the left side of a string.
Len	Returns the number of characters in a string.
LoadPicture	Returns a reference to a picture object.
Log	Returns the natural logarithm of a number.
LTrim	Returns a copy of a string without leading spaces.
Mid	Returns a specified number of characters from a string.
Minute	Returns the amount of the minutes in the current system's time.
Month	Returns the month of the year.
MonthName	Returns a string identifying the specified month.
MsgBox	Displays a message in a dialog box.
Now	Returns the current system date and time.
Oct	Returns a string representing the octal value of a number.
Replace	Returns a string in which a specified sub-string has been replaced with another sub-string a specified number of times.
Right	Returns a specified number of characters from the right side of a string.
Rnd	Returns a random number.
Round	Returns a number rounded to a specified number of decimal places.
RTrim	Returns a copy of a string without trailing spaces.
ScriptEngine	Returns the scripting language in use.
ScriptEngineBuildVersion	Returns the build version number of the script engine in use.
ScriptEngineMajorVersion	Returns the major version number of the script engine in use.
ScriptEngineMinorVersion	Returns the minor version number of the scripting language in use.
Second	Returns the seconds value of the current system time.
Sgn	Returns an integer indicating whether a number is positive, negative or zero.
Sin	Returns the sine of an angle.
Space	Returns a string consisting of the specified number of spaces.
Split	Returns a zero-based, one-dimensional array containing a specified number of sub-strings.

C

VBSCRIPT 2.0
REFERENCE

continues

TABLE C.5 CONTINUED

Function Name	Description
Sqr	Returns the square root of a number.
StrComp	Returns a value indicating the result of a string comparison.
StrReverse	Returns a string in which the character order of a specified string is reversed.
String	Returns a repeating character string of the length specified.
Tan	Returns the tangent of an angle.
Time	Returns the current system time.
TimeSerial	Returns the time for a specific hour, minute, and second.
TimeValue	Returns the current time.
Trim	Returns a copy of a string without leading and trailing spaces.
TypeName	Returns subtype information about a variable.
UBound	Returns the largest available subscript for a dimension of an array.
UCase	Returns a string that has been converted to uppercase.
VarType	Returns the subtype of a variable.
Weekday	Returns a whole number representing the day of the week.
WeekdayName	Returns the specified day of the week.
Year	Returns the current year.

The following section demonstrates how to use each function by exposing the syntax of the VBScript 2.0 intrinsic functions.

The Abs() Function

Description: Returns the absolute value of a number.

Syntax: Abs(*number*)

Arguments: *number* is any numeric expression.

The Array() Function

Description: Returns a Variant containing an array.

Syntax: Array(*clist*)

Arguments: *clist* is a comma-delimited list of values to add to the array.

The Asc() Function

Description: Returns the ANSI character code of a string.

Syntax: Asc(*string*)

Arguments: *string* is any valid string expression.

The Atn() Function

Description: Returns the arctangent of a number.

Syntax: Atn(*number*)

Arguments: *number* is any valid numeric expression.

The CBool() Function

Description: Returns an expression that has been converted to a Boolean subtype.

Syntax: CBool(*expression*)

Arguments: *expression* is any valid expression.

The CByte() Function

Description: Returns an expression that has been converted to a Byte subtype.

Syntax: CByte(*expression*)

Arguments: *expression* is any valid expression.

C

VBSCRIPT 2.0
REFERENCE

The CCur() Function

Description: Returns an expression that has been converted to a Currency subtype.

Syntax: CCur(*expression*)

Arguments: *expression* is any valid expression.

The CDate() Function

Description: Returns an expression that has been converted to a Date subtype.

Syntax: Cdate(*expression*)

Arguments: *expression* is any valid date expression.

The CDbl() Function

Description: Returns an expression that has been converted to a Double subtype.

Syntax: CDbl(*expression*)

Arguments: *expression* is any valid expression.

The Chr() Function

Description: Returns the character specified by the ANSI character code.

Syntax: Chr(*ansicode*)

Arguments: *ansicode* is the ANSI character code.

The CInt() Function

Description: Returns an expression that has been converted to an Integer subtype.

Syntax: CInt(*expression*)

Arguments: *expression* is any valid expression.

The CLng() Function

Description: Returns an expression that has been converted to a Long subtype.

Syntax: CLng(*expression*)

Arguments: *expression* is any valid expression.

The Cos() Function

Description: Returns the cosine of an angle.

Syntax: Cos(*number*)

Arguments: *number* is any valid numeric expression.

The CreateObject() Function

Description: Creates and returns a reference to ActiveX Automation object.

Syntax: CreateObject(*objname*)

Arguments: *objname* is any valid ActiveX Automation object.

The CSng() Function

Description: Returns an expression that has been converted to a Variant of subtype Single.

Syntax: CSng(*expression*)

Arguments: *expression* is any valid expression.

The CStr() Function

Description: Returns an expression that has been converted to a Variant of subtype String.

Syntax: CSng(*expression*)

Arguments: *expression* is any valid expression.

The Date() Function

Description: Returns the current system date.

Syntax: Date()

Arguments: none

The DateAdd() Function

Description: Returns a date to which a specified time interval has been added.

Syntax: DateAdd(*timeinterval, number, date*)

Arguments: *timeinterval* is time interval to add (as specified in Table C.6), *number* is amount of time intervals to add, and *date* is starting date.

TABLE C.6 TIME INTERVALS

Setting	Description
YYYY	Year
Q	Quarter
M	Month
D	Day
W	Weekday
WW	Week
H	Hour

continues

Table C.6   CONTIUED

Setting	Description
M	Minute
S	Second

The `DateDiff()` Function

Description: Returns the number of intervals between two dates.

Syntax: DateDiff(*timeinterval*, *date1*, *date2* [,*firstdayofweek*[, *firstweekofyear*]])

Arguments: *timeinterval* is time interval to add (as specified in Table C.6); *date1* and *date2* are valid date expressions to be evaluated; and firstdayofweek and firstweekofyear are optional values to specify the first day of the week and first week of the year.

The `DatePart()` Function

Description: Returns the specified part of a given date.

Syntax: DatePart(*timeinterval*, *date*[, *firstdayofweek*[, *firstweekofyear*]])

Arguments: *timeinterval* is time interval to add (as specified in Table C.6); Date is a valid date expression; and firstdayofweek and firstweekofyear are optional values to specify the first day of the week and first week of the year.

The `DateSerial()` Function

Description: Returns a Date subtype for a specified year, month, and day.

Syntax: DateSerial(*year*, *month*, *day*)

Arguments: *year* is the numeric expression representing the year; *month* is the numeric expression representing the month; and *day* is the numeric expression representing the day.

The `DateValue()` Function

Description: Returns a Date subtype.

Syntax: DateValue(*date*)

Arguments: *date* is any valid date expression.

The `Day()` Function

Description: Returns a whole number representing the day of the month.

Syntax: `Day(date)`

Arguments: `date` is any valid date expression.

The `Exp()` Function

Description: Returns e, the base of natural logarithms, raised to a power.

Syntax: `Exp(number)`

Arguments: `number` is any valid numeric expression.

The `Filter()` Function

Description: Returns a zero-based array containing subset of a string array.

Syntax: `Filter(InputStrings, Value[, bInclude[, Compare]])`

Arguments: `InputStrings` is a one-dimension string array; `Value` is the value being searched; `bInclude` (optional), `True` or `False`. If set to `True`, the return array contains values found. `False` returns an array containing elements not matching the search. `Compare` is an optional value indicating comparison constant.

The `Fix()` Function

Description: Returns the first negative integer greater than or equal to *number.*

Syntax: `Fix(number)`

Arguments: `number` is any valid numeric expression.

The `FormatCurrency()` Function

Description: Returns an expression formatted as a currency value.

Syntax: `FormatCurrency(Expression[,iDigits [,bLeadingDigit [,bParen [,bGroupDigits]]]])`

Arguments: `Expression` is valid numeric expression; `iDigits` is an optional numeric value used to indicate number of digits to right of decimal point; `bLeadingDigit` is an optional tristatevalue used to display leading zero; `bParen` is an optional Tristate value used to display parenthesis around negative values; and `bGroupDigits` is an optional tristatevalue used to display number as specified in the group delimiter settings of the Control Panel's regional settings. The `Tristate` values are displayed in Table C.16

The `FormatDateTime()` Function

Description: Returns an expression formatted as a date or time.

Syntax: `FormatDateTime(Date[,NamedFormat])`

Arguments: `Date` is any valid date expression, and `NamedFormat` is an optional date/time constant in Table C.10

The `FormatNumber()` Function

Description: Returns an expression formatted as a number.

Syntax: `FormatNumber(Expression[,iDigits [,bLeadingDigit [,bParen [,bGroupDigits]]]])`

Arguments: `Expression` is valid numeric expression; `iDigits` is an optional numeric value used to indicate number of digits to right of decimal point; `bLeadingDigit` is an optional tristatevalue used to indicate to display leading zero; `bParen` is an optional tristatevalue used to display parenthesis around negative values; and `bGroupDigits` is an optional tristatevalue used to display number as specified in the regional settings of the Control Panel.

The `FormatPercent()` Function

Description: Returns an expression formatted as a percent value with a trailing percent (%) symbol.

Syntax: `FormatPercent(Expression[,iDigits [,bLeadingDigit [,bParen [,bGroupDigits]]]])`

Arguments: `Expression` is valid numeric expression; `iDigits` is an optional numeric value used to indicate number of digits to right of decimal point; `bLeadingDigit` is an optional tristatevalue used to indicate to display leading zero; `bParen` is an optional tristatevalue used to display parenthesis around negative values; and `bGroupDigits` is an optional tristatevalue used to display numbers as specified in the group delimiter settings of the Control Panel's regional settings.

The `Hex()` Function

Description: Returns a string representing the hexadecimal value of a number.

Syntax: `Hex(number)`

Arguments: `number` is any valid numeric expression.

The `Hour()` Function

Description: Returns a whole number representing the hour of the day between 0 and 23.

Syntax: Hour(*time*)

Arguments: *time* is any valid date/time expression.

The `InputBox()` Function

Description: Displays a prompt for an input dialog box.

Syntax: InputBox(*promptmsg*[, *title*][, *default*][, *xpos*][, *ypos*][, *helpfile*, *context*])

Arguments: *promptmsg* is the message string to be displayed in dialog box; *Title* (optional) is the string expression displayed in the title of the dialog box; *Default* (optional) is the string expression displayed in the text box of the dialog box; *Xpos* (optional) is number of twips from the left side of the dialog box to the left of the screen; *Ypos* (optional) is the number of twips from the top of the dialog box to the top of the screen; *Helpfile* (optional) specifies the location of a help file; and *Context* (optional) specifies the help context number in *helpfile*. Twips is a graphical constant used to set the `ScaleMode` property of an object

The `InStr()` Function

Description: Returns the numeric position of the first instance of one string within another.

Syntax: InStr([*start*,]*strSearchme*, *strsearchfor*[, *compare*])

Arguments: *start* (optional) is the numeric position to start the string search; *strSearchme* is the string expression to be searched; *strsearchfor* is the string expression search value; and *compare* (optional) is the value indicating comparison constant as described in Table C.8.

The `InStrRev()` Function

Description: Returns the numeric position of one string within another starting from the end of string.

Syntax: InStrRev(*strSearchme*, *strsearchfor* [, *start*[, *compare*]])

Arguments: *strSearchme* is the string expression to be searched; *strsearchfor* is the string expression search value; *start* (optional) is the numeric position to start the string search; and *compare* (optional) is the value indicating comparison constant as described in Table C.8.

The `Int()` Function

Description: Returns the integer portion of a number.

Syntax: Int(*number*)

Arguments: *number* is a valid numeric expression

The `IsArray()` Function

Description: Returns a Boolean value indicating whether a variable is an array.

Syntax: IsArray(*vName*)

Arguments: *vName* is the name of the variable to be determined.

The `IsDate()` Function

Description: Returns a Boolean value indicating whether the expression can be converted to a date.

Syntax: IsDate(*expression*)

Arguments: *expression* is any valid expression.

The `IsEmpty()` Function

Description: Returns a Boolean value indicating whether a variable has been initialized.

Syntax: IsEmpty(*expression*)

Arguments: *expression* is any valid expression.

The `IsNull()` Function

Description: Returns a Boolean value that indicates whether an expression contains no valid datatype.

Syntax: IsNull(*expression*)

Arguments: *expression* is any valid expression.

The `IsNumeric()` Function

Description: Returns a Boolean value indicating whether an expression can be evaluated as a number.

Syntax: `IsNumeric(expression)`

Arguments: *expression* is any valid expression.

The `IsObject()` Function

Description: Returns a Boolean value indicating whether an expression refers to an `Automation` object.

Syntax: `IsObject(expression)`

Arguments: *expression* is any valid expression.

The `Join()` Function

Description: Returns a string created by joining strings stored in an array.

Syntax: `Join(alist[, delimiter])`

Arguments: *aList* is the name of a one-dimensional array; and `delimiter` (optional) is the string delimiters used to separate the elements within the string, the default value is the space (" ") character.

The `LBound()` Function

Description: Returns the base index value for a dimension of an array.

Syntax: `LBound(arrayname[, dimension])`

Arguments: *arrayname* is the name of any array; and *dimension* (optional) is a number indicating the dimension to find the lower bound.

The `LCase()` Function

Description: Returns a string that has been converted into lowercase characters.

Syntax: `LCase(string)`

Arguments: *string* is any valid string expression.

The `Left()` Function

Description: Returns the number of characters from the left side of a string.

Syntax: Left(*string, length*)

Arguments: *string* is any valid string expression; and *length* is the amount of characters to return.

The `Len()` Function

Description: Returns the number of characters in a string or the number of bytes required to store a variable.

Syntax: Len(*string ¦ varname*)

Arguments: *string* is any valid string expression; or *varname* is any valid variable name.

The `LoadPicture()` Function

Description: Returns a reference to a picture object.

Syntax: LoadPicture(*picturename*)

Arguments: picturename is the name of the picture filename.

The `Log()` Function

Description: Returns the natural logarithm of a number.

Syntax: Log(*number*)

Arguments: *number* is any valid numeric expression greater than 0.

The `LTrim()` Function

Description: Returns a string without leading spaces.

Syntax: LTrim(*string*)

Arguments: *string* is any valid string expression.

The `Mid()` Function

Description: Returns a specified number of characters from a string.

Syntax: Mid(*string, start*[, *length*])

Arguments: *string* is any valid string expression; *start* is numeric character position to begin extraction from; and *length* (optional) is the number of characters to return.

The `Minute()` Function

Description: Returns the amount of the minutes in current systems time.

Syntax: `Minute(time)`

Arguments: *time* is any valid time expression.

The `Month()` Function

Description: Returns the number of the month of the year.

Syntax: `Month(date)`

Arguments: *date* is any valid date expression.

The `MonthName()` Function

Description: Returns a string identifying the specified month.

Syntax: `MonthName(month[, bAbbreviate])`

Arguments: *month* is the numeric representation for a given month; `bAbbreviate` (optional) is a Boolean value used to display month abbreviations. `True` will display the abbreviated month name, and `False` (default) will not show abbreviation.

The `MsgBox()` Function

Description: Displays a message in a dialog box.

Syntax: `MsgBox(prompt[, buttons][, title][, helpfile, context])`

Arguments: *prompt*; *buttons* is an optional numeric expression ndicating button style to display (see Table C.13 for `messagebox` constants); *title* (optional) is a string expression that is displayed in the title bar of the message box; *helpfile* (optional) specifies the location of the help file; and *context* (optional) specifies the help context number in the help file.

The `Now()` Function

Description: Returns the current system date and time.

Syntax: `Now()`

Arguments: none

The Oct() Function

Description: Returns a string representing the octal value of a number.

Syntax: Oct(*number*)

Arguments: *number* is any valid numeric expression.

The Replace() Function

Description: Returns a string in which a specified substring has been replaced with another substring a specified number of times.

Syntax: Replace(*strSearchMe*, *strSearchFor*, *strReplaceWith* [, *start*[, *count*[, *compare*]]])

Arguments: *strSearchMe* is a string expression containing a sub-string to be replaced; *StrSearchFor* is the string expression to search for within *strSearchMe*; *strReplaceWith* is the string expression to replace sub-string *strSearchFor*; *start* (optional) is the numeric character position to begin search; *count* (optional) is the numeric amount of time to replace values; and *compare* (optional) is a value indicating comparison constant.

The Right() Function

Description: Returns a specified number of characters from the right side of a string.

Syntax: Right(*string*, *length*)

Arguments: *string* is any valid string expression; and *length* is any valid number expression representing the number of characters to return.

The Rnd() Function

Description: Returns a random number.

Syntax: Rnd[(*number*)]

Arguments: *number* is any valid numeric expression.

The Round() Function

Description: Returns a number rounded to a specified number of decimal places.

Syntax: Round(*expression*[, *numRight*])

Arguments: *expression* is any valid numeric expression to be rounded; and *NumRight* (optional) is any numeric expression use to indicate the amount of digits to the right of the decimal point.

The RTrim() Function

Description: Returns a copy of a string without trailing spaces.

Syntax: RTrim(*string*)

Arguments: *string* is any valid string expression.

The ScriptEngine() Function

Description: Returns the scripting language in use.

Syntax: ScriptEngine()

Arguments: none

The ScriptEngineBuildVersion() Function

Description: Returns the build version number of the script engine in use.

Syntax: ScriptEngineBuildVersion()

Arguments: none

The ScriptEngineMajorVersion() Function

Description: Returns the major version number of the script engine in use.

Syntax: ScriptEngineMajorVersion()

Arguments: none

The ScriptEngineMinorVersion() Function

Description: Returns the minor version number the scripting language in use.

Syntax: ScriptEngineMinorVersion()

Arguments: none

The Second() Function

Description: Returns the current seconds value of the current system time.

Syntax: Second(*time*)

Arguments: *time* is any valid time expression.

The Sgn() Function

Description: Returns an integer indicating the sign of a number.

Syntax: Sgn(*number*)

Arguments: *number* is any valid numeric expression.

The Sin() Function

Description: Returns the sine of an angle.

Syntax: Sin(*number*)

Arguments: *number* is any valid numeric expression that can express an angle in radians.

The Space() Function

Description: Returns a string expression consisting of the number of defined spaces.

Syntax: Space(*number*)

Arguments: *number* is any valid numeric expression.

The Split() Function

Description: Returns a zero-based, one-dimensional array containing elements constructed from a string expression.

Syntax: Split(*expression*[, *delimiter*[, *count*[, *compare*]]])

Arguments: *expression* is a string expression to build the one-dimensional array; *delimiter* (optional) is the string delimiter used separate elements; *Count* (optional) is the number elements to return; and *compare* (optional) is the value indicating comparison constant, as described in Table C.8.

The Sqr() Function

Description: Returns the square root of a number.

Syntax: Sqr(*number*)

Arguments: *number* is any valid numeric expression greater than or equal to zero.

The StrComp() Function

Description: Returns a value indicating the result of a string comparison.

Syntax: StrComp(*string1, string2*[, *compare*])

Arguments: *string1* and *string2* are any valid string expression to be compared; and *compare* (optional) value indicating comparison constant as described in Table C.8.

The StrReverse() Function

Description: Returns a string where the character order has been reversed.

Syntax: StrReverse(*string*)

Arguments: *string* is any valid string expression.

The String() Function

Description: Returns a repeating character string of the length specified.

Syntax: String(*number, character*)

Arguments: *number* is any valid numeric expression greater than zero; and *character* is ANSI character code used to build the string.

The Tan() Function

Description: Returns the tangent of an angle.

Syntax: Tan(*number*)

Arguments: *number* is any valid numeric expression that can express an angle in radians.

The Time() Function

Description: Returns the current system time.

Syntax: Time()

Arguments: none

The TimeSerial() Function

Description: Returns the time for a specific hour, minute, and second.

Syntax: TimeSerial(*hour, minute, second*)

Arguments: *hour* is any numeric expression between 1 and 23; *minute* is any numeric expression; and *second* is any numeric expression.

The `TimeValue()` Function

Description: Returns the current time.

Syntax: `TimeValue(time)`

Arguments: *time* is any valid time expression.

The `Trim()` Function

Description: Returns a string without leading and trailing spaces.

Syntax: `Trim(string)`

Arguments: *string* is any valid string expression.

The `TypeName()` Function

Description: Returns subtype information about a variable.

Syntax: `TypeName(varName)`

Arguments: *varName* is the required variable name.

The `UBound()` Function

Description: Returns the largest available subscript for a dimension of an array.

Syntax: `UBound(arrayname[, dimension])`

Arguments: *arrayname* is the name of a valid array; and *dimension* (optional) number indicating the dimension to find the upper bound.

The `UCase()` Function

Description: Returns a string that has been converted to uppercase characters.

Syntax: `UCase(string)`

Arguments: *string* is any valid string expression.

The `VarType()` Function

Description: Returns the subtype of a variable.

Syntax: `VarType(varName)`

Arguments: *varName* is the required variable name.

The `Weekday()` Function

Description: Returns a whole number representing the day of the week.

Syntax: `Weekday(date, [firstdayofweek])`

Arguments: *date* is any valid date expression; and `Firstdayofweek` is an optional Date constant to assign first day of week, as seen in Table C.9.

The `WeekdayName()` Function

Description: Returns the specified day of the week.

Syntax: `WeekdayName(weekday, [abbreviate, [firstdayofweek]])`

Arguments: *weekday* is the numeric representation for the day of the week; `Abbreviate` is an optional Boolean value (if set to `True`, the weekday name will be abbreviated; if set to `False`, the full weekday name is displayed); and `Firstdayofweek` is an optional Date constant to assign first day of week, as seen in Table C.9.

The `Year()` Function

Description: Returns the current year.

Syntax: `Year(date)`

Arguments: *date* is any valid date expression.

Constants

VBScript gives developers the capability to use constants to replace unmemorable or difficult-to-read numeric or string values. These intrinsic constants can be referenced by either their names or by their values.

Color Constants

VBScript gives you the ability to use color constants within your scripts. These constants, as shown in Table C.7, can be referenced directly in your scripts.

TABLE C.7   COLOR CONSTANTS

Constant	Value	Description
vbBlack	&h00	Black
vbRed	&hFF	Red
vbGreen	&hFF00	Green
vbYellow	&hFFFF	Yellow
vbBlue	&hFF0000	Blue
vbMagenta	&hFF00FF	Magenta
vbCyan	&hFFFF00	Red
vbWhite	&hFFFFFF	White

Comparison Constants

Many intrinsic VBScript functions perform comparisons to complete a task. These give you the capability to explicitly define the comparison method by using the comparison constants shown in Table C.8.

TABLE C.8   COMPARISON CONSTANTS

Constant	Value	Description
VbBinaryCompare	0	Performs a binary comparison.
VbTextCompare	1	Performs a textual comparison.
VbDatabaseCompare	2	Performs a comparison based on information extracted in the database where the comparison is to be performed.

The Date/Time Constants

VBScript 2.0 provides new date/time functions that help speed scripting development and eliminate excessive coding that would otherwise have to be done by hand. Many of the new functions utilize the date/time constants to help customize the functions (see Table C.9).

TABLE C.9 DATE/TIME CONSTANTS

Constant	Value	Description
vbSunday	1	Sunday
vbMonday	2	Monday
vbTuesday	3	Tuesday
vbWednesday	4	Wednesday
vbThursday	5	Thursday
vbFriday	6	Friday
vbSaturday	7	Saturday
vbFirstJan1	1	Use the week in which January 1 occurs (default).
VbFirstFourDays	2	Uses the first week that has at least four days in the new year.
VbFirstFullWeek	3	Uses the first full week of the year.
VbUseSystem	0	Uses the date format contained in the regional settings on the host computer.
VbUseSystemDayOfWeek	0	Uses the day of the week specified in your system settings for the first day of the week.

Date Format Constants

In addition to the new date/time functionality, VBScript 2.0 also introduces new date format functions that can use the constants shown in Table C.10.

TABLE C.10 DATE FORMAT CONSTANTS

Constant	Value	Description
VbGeneralDate	0	Displays a date and/or time.
VbLongDate	1	Displays a date using the long date format.
VbShortDate	2	Displays a date using the short date format.
VbLongTime	3	Displays a time using the long time format.
VbShortTime	4	Displays a time using the short time format.

Notice that date and time settings are controlled within your regional settings found in the Control Panel. Consider the following script:

```
<%
Response.Write FormatDateTime(now,VbGeneralDate) &"<BR>"
Response.Write FormatDateTime(now,VbLongDate) &"<BR>"
Response.Write FormatDateTime(now,VbShortDate) &"<BR>"
Response.Write FormatDateTime(now,VbLongTime) &"<BR>"
Response.Write FormatDateTime(now,VbShortTime) &"<BR>"
%>
```

The previous script will produce the following results:

```
10/12/97 3:47:05 PM
Sunday, October 12, 1997
10/12/97
3:47:05 PM
15:47
```

File Input/Output Constants

The file input/output constants are used to tap into the functionality of the `FileSystemObject`. The `FileSystemObject` provides access to files on the server. The `FileSystemObject` can open a file with three different permission levels. The constants enabling read-only, write-new, and file-append modes are shown in Table C.11.

TABLE C.11 FILE INPUT/OUTPUT CONSTANTS

Constant	Value	Description
ForReading	1	Opens a file for read-only access.
ForWriting	2	Opens a file for write access. If the file exists, the previous content is overwritten.
ForAppending	8	Opens a file and appends the data stream to the end of the file.

Miscellaneous Constants

VBScript uses the constant shown in Table C.12 to represent an error returned from an ActiveX Automation object.

TABLE C.12 MISCELLANEOUS CONSTANTS

Constant	Value	Description
VbObjectError	&h80040000	Error message from an Automation Object

The MsgBox Constants

The message box uses two sets of constants, the display constants, as displayed in Table C.13, are used to create the look and feel of the message box. The message box result constants are used to determine the user response to the displayed message box.

TABLE C.13 MESSAGE BOX DISPLAY CONSTANTS

Constant	Value	Description
vbOKOnly	0	Displays OK button only.
vbOKCancel	1	Displays OK and Cancel buttons.
vbAbortRetryIgnore	2	Displays Abort, Retry, and Ignore buttons.
vbYesNoCancel	3	Displays Yes, No, and Cancel buttons.
vbYesNo	4	Displays Yes and No buttons.
vbRetryCancel	5	Displays Retry and Cancel buttons.
vbCritical	16	Displays Critical Message icon.
vbQuestion	32	Displays Warning Query icon.
vbExclamation	48	Displays Warning Message icon.
vbInformation	64	Displays Information Message icon.
vbDefaultButton1	0	First button is set as the default button.
vbDefaultButton2	256	Second button is set as the default button.
vbDefaultButton3	512	Third button is set as the default button.
vbDefaultButton4	768	Fourth button is set as the default button.
vbApplicationModal	0	The user must respond to the message box before continuing work in the current application.
VbSystemModal	4096	System modal. All applications are suspended until the user responds to the message box.

You can trap the user response by the return values of the message box. The constants shown in Table C.14 are used to identify which button the user selected in the message box.

TABLE C.14 MESSAGE BOX RESULTS CONSTANTS

Constant	Value	Description
vbOK	1	OK button was clicked.
vbCancel	2	Cancel button was clicked.
vbAbort	3	Abort button was clicked.
vbRetry	4	Retry button was clicked.
vbIgnore	5	Ignore button was clicked.
vbYes	6	Yes button was clicked.
vbNo	7	No button was clicked.

String Constants

VBScript can use string constants to help control output to the current page or file, as shown in Table C.15.

TABLE C.15 STRING CONSTANTS

Constant	Value	Description
vbCr	Chr(13)	Carriage return
vbCrLf	Chr(13) & Chr(10)	Carriage returnñline feed combination
vbFormFeed	Chr(12)	Form feed; not useful in Microsoft Windows
vbLf	Chr(10)	Line feed
vbNewLine	Chr(13) & Chr(10) Chr(10)	Platform- or specific newline character; whatever is appropriate for the platform
vbNullChar	Chr(0)	Character having the value 0
vbNullString	String having value 0	Not the same as a zero-length string (""); used for calling external procedures
vbTab	Chr(9)	Horizontal tab
vbVerticalTab	Chr(11)	Vertical tab; not useful in Microsoft Windows

Tristate Constants

VBScript combines Boolean functionality with the capability to use the default values of a function into one set of constants called *tristate constants*. The tristate constants are shown in Table C.16. Typically, the default settings are extracted from the computer's region settings as found in the Control Panel.

TABLE C.16 TRISTATE CONSTANTS

Constant	Value	Description
TristateTrue	-1	True
TristateFalse	0	False
TristateUseDefault	-2	Use default setting of calling function

VarType Constants

VBScript enables you to determine the Variant subtype a variable is stored as by using the Vartype function. The Vartype function returns the subtype values shown in Table C.17.

TABLE C.17 VARTYPE CONSTANTS

Constant	Value	Description
vbEmpty	0	Un-initialized (default)
vbNull	1	Contains no valid data
vbInteger	2	Integer subtype
vbLong	3	Long subtype
vbSingle	4	Single subtype
vbDouble	5	Double subtype
vbCurrency	6	Currency subtype
vbDate	7	Date subtype
vbString	8	String subtype
vbObject	9	Object
vbError	10	Error subtype
vbBoolean	11	Boolean subtype
vbVariant	12	Variant
vbDataObject	13	Data access object
vbDecimal	14	Decimal subtype
vbByte	17	Byte subtype
vbArray	8192	Array

VBScript Objects

VBScript provides access to four built-in objects (see Table C.18). These objects are used to encapsulate a specific area of code functionality. The objects use methods, shown in Table C.19, to perform an action, and have properties, shown in Table C.20, to describe the object.

TABLE C.18   VBSCRIPT OBJECTS

Name	Description
Dictionary	Object that stores data key, item pairs.
Err	Contains runtime error information.
FileSystemObject	Provides access to a computer's file system.
TextStream	Provides sequential file access.

VBScript Object Methods

VBScript uses methods to perform an action on or to control an object. Table C.19 provides a quick guide to the VBScript 2.0 methods.

TABLE C.19   VBSCRIPT 2.0 METHODS

Method	Description
Add	Adds a key and item pair to a Dictionary object.
Clear	Clears all settings of the Err object.
Close	Closes an open TextStream file.
CreateTextFile	Creates a specified filename and returns a TextStream object.
Exists	Returns whether a specified key exists in the Dictionary object.
Items	Returns an array containing all items in a Dictionary object.
Keys	Returns an array containing all existing keys in a Dictionary object.
OpenTextFile	Opens a specified file and returns a TextStream object.
Raise	Generates a runtime error.
Read	Reads characters from a TextStream file.
ReadAll	Reads an entire TextStream file.
ReadLine	Reads an entire line from a TextStream file.
Remove	Removes a specific key, item pair from a Dictionary object.

Method	Description
RemoveAll	Removes all key, item pairs from a Dictionary object.
Skip	Skips a specified number of characters when reading a TextStream file.
SkipLine	Skips the next line when reading a TextStream file.
Write	Writes a specified string to a TextStream file.
WriteBlankLines	Writes a specified number of newline characters to a TextStream file.
WriteLine	Writes a specified string and newline character to a TextStream file.

VBScript Object Properties

Properties of an object are used to describe specific information about an object. The properties of VBScript objects are shown in Table C.20.

TABLE C.20   PROPERTIES

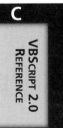

C

VBSCRIPT 2.0
REFERENCE

Name	Description
AtEndOfLine	Returns whether the file pointer is positioned immediately on the end-of-line marker in a TextStream file.
AtEndOfStream	Returns whether the file pointer is positioned the end of a TextStream file.
Column	Returns the column number of the character position in a TextStream file.
CompareMode	Sets and returns the comparison mode for comparing string keys in a Dictionary object.
Count	Returns the number of items in a Dictionary object.
Description	Returns or sets a descriptive string associated with an error.
HelpContext	Sets or returns a context ID for a topic in a help file.
HelpFile	Sets or returns a path to a Help File.
Item	Sets or returns an item for a specified key in a Dictionary object.
Key	Sets a key in a Dictionary object.
Line	Returns the current line number in a TextStream file.
Number	Sets or returns a numeric value specifying an error.
Source	Sets or returns the name of the object that generated the error.

Active Server Pages Object Reference

Active Server Pages derives its rich functionality from the use of six inherent objects. These six objects do have to be explicitly instantiated but are directly built into Active Server Pages. These objects have their own predefined roles and each has its own properties, methods, and events. These objects form the foundation of ASP development and consequently have their own chapters dedicated to fully describe them. The following provides a brief overview of each objects functionality.

Controlling the Application Object

The Application object is used to manage all information in the ASP application. The information can be accessed and passed between different users in the application. The Application object has two events, the Application_OnStart and Application_OnEnd events, as shown in Table D.1. The Application object is created by the Active Server to represent the instantiation of an Active Server application. The Application object is created when a user requests any page in the ASP application's virtual directory. Once the Application object is started, all subsequent users can reference its objects and variables.

TABLE D.1   THE Application OBJECT'S EVENTS

Event	Description
Application_OnStart	Initiated when the ASP application is first started.
Application_OnEnd	Initiated when the ASP application is terminated.

These individual application events are found in the GLOBAL.ASA file and are executed in a manner similar to any subroutine or function.

```
<SCRIPT LANGUAGE="VBScript" RUNAT = "Server">

Sub Application_OnStart
➥'=== Defines Application Object's OnStart Event
Application("strMessage")= "Welcome to Active Server Pages"
End Sub
Sub Application_OnEnd

End Sub


</SCRIPT>
```

However, if an event is called and no event procedure is defined, a runtime error will occur because a reference is being made to an event that does not exist.

Declaring Application-Level Variables

Application-level variables are accessible by all users of the application. Application-level variables can be defined as needed in any .ASP file, not just in the `Application_OnStart` and `Application_OnEnd` events of the `GLOBAL.ASA` file.

To declare an application variable, use the following syntax:

```
Application(varName)
```

Application_OnStart Event

The `Application_OnStart` event requires the following syntax within the `GLOBAL.ASA` file:

```
<SCRIPT LANGUAGE=ScriptLanguage RUNAT=Server>
Sub Application_OnStart
. . .
End Sub </SCRIPT>
```

The `Application_OnStart` event is executed before any user or session event is triggered. Any attempts to call a `Session`, `Response`, or `Request` object will generate a fatal runtime error because these objects have not been created at this point. However, you are able to reference the `Server` object.

Application_OnEnd Event

The `Application_OnEnd` event requires the following syntax within the `GLOBAL.ASA` file:

```
<SCRIPT LANGUAGE=ScriptLanguage RUNAT=Server>
Sub Application_OnEnd
    '=== Your Script Here
End Sub

</SCRIPT>
```

The `Application_OnEnd` event occurs when the Web server is shut down. As a result, the `Application` object is destroyed. The shutting down of the Web server can occur with the termination of the HTTP service or when the `GLOBAL.ASA` file needs to be recompiled and reloaded into memory.

D

ACTIVE SERVER
PAGES OBJECT
REFERENCE

Controlling Application-Level Variables with Methods

The Application object has two methods designed to control variable access: the Lock and UnLock methods. These methods help to prevent multiple users from changing application-level variables at the same time (see Table D.2).

TABLE D.2   THE Application OBJECT'S METHODS

Name	Description
Lock	Prevents other clients from changing Application object properties.
UnLock	Enables other clients to modify the Application object's properties.

Lock Method

The Lock method is to control the Application object's properties by preventing concurrent users from modifying the same application-level variable at the same time. The Lock method is implemented by using the following syntax:

```
Application.Lock
```

UnLock Method

The Application.UnLock method releases control of the application variables. The UnLock method is implemented using the following syntax:

```
Application.UnLock
```

The Application.UnLock method is implicitly called when the processing of a page is complete and the UnLock method has not been called or when the script processing times out. The default page-level script timeout value is 90 seconds.

Instantiating Application-Level Objects

You can create a reference to an application-level object's automation object by embedding the unique class identifier either by the ProgID or the ClassID within the object tag. The ProgID represents the registered name of the object. The ClassID refers to the registered class number of the object. To create a server-side object, use the following syntax:

```
<OBJECT RUNAT=Server SCOPE = Application ID=Identifier
➥{PROGID="progID"¦CLASSID="ClassID"}>
</OBJECT>
```

where *Scope* identifies the object's lifetime and *ID* identifies the object's instantiated name.

The <OBJECT> tag must be placed outside of the <SCRIPT> </SCRIPT> tags used to define the GLOBAL.ASA file. If an <OBJECT> tag or any other tag is found between the <SCRIPT> tags, the script interpreter will try to process the <OBJECT> tags and generate an error. This <SCRIPT> and <OBJECT> tag layout is illustrated in the following code:

```
<SCRIPT LANGUAGE="VBScript" RUNAT="Server">
Sub Application_OnStart
    '=== Application Level events and object placed here
End Sub

Application_OnStart
</SCRIPT>

<OBJECT RUNAT=Server SCOPE=Application ID=MyDataConn
➥PROGID="RemoteConn.DataConn">
</OBJECT>
```

The application-level object can now be accessed from any ASP file in the application by using the ID name of the object.

Controlling the Server Object

The Server object is an ASP object used to control administrative features of the IIS Web server and actions that deal with the HTTP service. The Server object represents a control interface to the HTTP service. The Server object is referenced using the following syntax:

```
Server.Method/Property
```

where Server is the Active Server object.

The Server object has four methods that are used to control various aspects of the Web server, as shown in Table D.3.

TABLE D.3 THE Server OBJECT'S METHODS

Method	Description
CreateObject	Creates a Server instance of an object.
HTMLEncode	Utilizes HTML encoding to deliver text to browser.
MapPath	Translates the virtual Web server path to the physical path on the server.
URLEncode	Utilizes URL encoding techniques.

The `CreateObject` Method

Perhaps one of the most exciting aspects of Active Server Pages is the capability to create an instance of an ActiveX object. This capability to tap into ActiveX objects provides a virtually endless number of ways to deliver information to any Web client that were once only available to propriety client software or dedicated network connections. The `Server` object acts as a translator between the in-house data and logic stores and virtually any HTML-compliant browser. The `CreateObject` method uses the following syntax:

```
Server.CreateObject(progID)
```

where *progID* is the class or type of object to be instantiated. The *progID* also requires the following special format:

```
appname.objecttype
```

where *appname* is the application name hosting the object and *objecttype* is the class or type of the object to create. All COM-based objects are required to have one class type per application name.

The `CreateObject` method only creates objects that have page-level scope. If you need to access the same component multiple times, in most situations you would benefit from using an application- or session-level object.

The `MapPath` Method

The `Server` object uses the `MapPath` method to track and manage path information on the server. The `MapPath` method requires the following syntax:

```
Server.MapPath( path )
```

where `Server` is the Active Server object and *path* is a physical or virtual directory. There are two basic rules to remember with the path variables.

- Path arguments that start with a backslash (\) or a forwardslash (/) are used to represent virtual directories.
- Path arguments that do not start with the backslash or forward slash represent relative directories.

The `ScriptTimeOut` Property

The `ScriptTimeOut` property is a property of the `Server` object that prevents a process from running endlessly. The `ScriptTimeOut` value requires the following syntax:

```
Server.ScriptTimeout = Seconds
```

where *Seconds* indicates the number of seconds allotted for page-level scripting to process. After this amount of time has been reached, the Server object terminates the process and writes an event to the event log.

Using Server Encoding Techniques

All Web technology is based on the transfer of simple text across the Internet or an intranet via the TCP/IP protocol and the translation of that text into content within the Web browser. Because the browser only interprets text, embedded non-ASCII characters get misinterpreted as text or simply are not available from the keyboard. The Server object uses the URLEncode and HTMLEncode methods to ensure the proper character translation between the Web server and browser.

The URLEncode Method

The URLEncode method of the Server object is used to deliver explicit information from the Web server to the client via the URL. To ensure that all the characters entered by the user are properly passed to the server, the characters must be scanned to ensure that only known characters are being sent. To use the URL encoding methods, use the following syntax:

```
Server.URLEncode(string)
```

where Server is the Server object and *string* is the string to apply the URL encoding rules.

The URLEncode method performs the following processes to the data:

- Spaces are transformed into plus (+) symbols.
- Fields are left unencoded.
- An unencoded equal sign assigns an unencoded field name with the data value.
- Non-ASCII characters are transformed into escape codes.

Using the HTMLEncode Method

The HTMLEncode method is used by the server to explicitly define the characters to be displayed on a page. To use the HTMLEncode feature, use the following syntax:

```
Server.HTMLEncode(string)
```

where Server is the Server object and *string* is the string to encode. The HTMLEncode method is important to ensure that the proper characters get displayed on the page and not processed by the server.

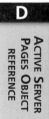

The `ObjectContext` Object: Interacting with the Transaction Server

With the Internet Information Server 4.0, Active Server Pages have a direct interface to controlling components in the Microsoft Transaction Server. This interface is made possible through the `ObjectContext` object. When the scripting engine processes this directive, the Active Server Page is executed as a transaction on the Transaction Server. To initiate the transaction processing of the `ObjectContext` object, use the following directive syntax:

```
<%@ Transaction = Required %>
```

`ObjectContext` uses two methods to control the objects managed by the Microsoft Transaction Server, as shown in Table D.4.

TABLE D.4 THE `ObjectContext` OBJECT'S METHODS

Method	*Description*
SetComplete	Sets the work of an object as a success and permanently accepts the changes to the resource.
SetAbort	Sets the work of an object as a failure and returns the resource to its original state, neglecting any changes made to the resource.

The `SetComplete` Method

The `SetComplete` method is used to commit an MTS object's transaction as a success. The changes made by the object method on a resource are permanently committed. To accept changes made by object, use the following syntax:

```
ObjectContext.SetComplete
```

After the `SetComplete` method is executed, the `OnTransactionCommit` event is triggered.

The `SetAbort` Method

The `SetAbort` method is used to roll back changes made by an object managed by the MTS. When the `SetAbort` method is called, the object has completed its work and is returned to its original state. To reject changes made by the MTS object, use the following syntax:

```
ObjectContext.SetAbort
```

After the `SetAbort` method is executed, the `OnTransactionAbort` event is triggered.

Trapping the `ObjectContext`'s Events

`ObjectContext` has two events that are triggered after the `ObjectContext`'s methods are executed, as shown in Table D.5.

TABLE D.5   THE `ObjectContext` EVENTS

Event	Description
OnTransactionCommit	Event triggered after the `ObjectContext.SetComplete` method is executed.
OnTransactionAbort	Event triggered after the `ObjectContext.SetAbort` method is executed.

The `OnTransactionCommit` Event

The `OnTransactionCommit` event is triggered by the `ObjectContext` object `SetComplete` method. When the `SetComplete` method is processed, the script will process the `OnTransactionCommit` subroutine.

```
Sub OnTransactionCommit()
    Response.Redirect "CreateVirutalReceipt.ASP"
End Sub
```

The relationship between `OnTransactionCommit` event and `ObjectContext.SetComplete` method is demonstrated in the following example:

```
<%@TRANSACTION = Required %>
<%
Sub OnTransactionCommit()
    Dim strMessage
    strMessage ="This was generated by executing the SetComplete method"
    strMessage = strMessage & "to trigger the OnTransactionCommit event"
    Response.Write strMessage
End Sub
```

```
%>
<HTML>
<HEAD>
<TITLE>Set Complete</TITLE>
</HEAD>
<BODY>

<%
ObjectContext.SetComplete
%>

</BODY>
</HTML>
```

The code example initiates transaction processing using the TRANSACTION = Required directive and executes the SetComplete method to trigger the OnTransactionCommit() event. In this example, the OnTransactionCommit subroutine, writes the following text to the page:

```
This text message was generated by executing the SetComplete
➥method to trigger the OnTransactionCommit event
```

OnTransactionAbort **Event**

Similar to its counterpart, the OnTransactionAbort event is triggered when the ObjectContext object SetAbort event is executed. When the SetAbort method is processed, the script will process the OnTransactionCommit event.

```
Sub OnTransactionAbort()
    Response.Redirect "InsufficientFunds.ASP"
End Sub
```

You can apply the same example shown in the OnTransactionCommit to OnTransactionAbort, as shown in the following example:

```
<%@TRANSACTION = Required %>
<%
Sub OnTransactionAbort()
    Dim strMessage
    strMessage ="This text message was generated by executing
    ➥the SetAbort method "
    strMessage = strMessage & "to trigger the OnTransactionAbort event"
    Response.Write strMessage
End Sub
%>
<HTML>
<HEAD>
<TITLE>Set Abort</TITLE>
</HEAD>
<BODY>
```

```
<%
ObjectContext.SetAbort
%>

</BODY>
</HTML>
```

The example initiates transaction processing using the `TRANSACTION = Required` directive and executes the `SetAbort` method to trigger the `OnTransactionAbort()` event. In this example, the `OnTransactionAbort` subroutine writes the following text to the page:

```
This text message was generated by executing the SetAbort method
➥to trigger the OnTransactionAbort event.
```

Communicating with Web Client: The Response Object

The Active Server uses the `Response` object to control and manage the data sent to the browser. The `Response` object is responsible for controlling the delivery of data, writing HTTP header information, writing text, HTML, scripting variables, and non-textual information, and controlling cookies on the client browser.

The Response Collection

The `Response` object uses the `Cookie` collection to manage and control both cookie files and the data stored within the cookies. The `Cookie` collection enables single or multiple variables to be stored and manipulated in temporary text files on the client's browser. The `Response` collection is shown in Table D.6.

TABLE D.6   THE `Response` COLLECTION

Collection Name	Description
Cookies	Sets cookies values.

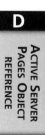

The Cookies Collection

The `Cookies` collection enables single or multiple variables to be stored and manipulated in temporary text files on the client's browser. The `Cookies` collection requires the following syntax:

```
Response.Cookies(Cookie)[(key)¦.attribute] = value
```

where `Response` is the built-in `Response` object, `Cookie` is the name of the cookie file, *key* identifies a dictionary element, *attribute* is a specific characteristic of the cookie, and *value* is the value being assigned to the cookie.

Notice that you do not have to manually trap and replace non-ANSCI characters, that is, encode the string data that will be transferred to the cookie. The encoding process automatically filters out any non-ANSCI characters.

The `Cookies` collection also uses attributes to help manage cookies on the browser. Table D.7 displays the cookie attributes that can be set by the `Response` collection.

TABLE D.7 THE ATTRIBUTES OF THE `Response` Cookie COLLECTION

Name	Description
Expires	Sets the date when the cookie will expire.
Domain	Specifies cookie delivery to only members specified by this domain.
Path	Determines the delivery path information.
Secure	Specifies whether the cookie is secure.
HasKey	Returns whether the cookie contains keys.

The Response Object's Properties

The `Response` object has various properties that can be used to set characteristics of information delivered by the server. Table D.8 illustrates the `Response` object's properties.

TABLE D.8 THE RESPONSE PROPERTIES

Property Name	Description
Buffer	Sets whether or not page output is buffered.
Charset	Appends the name of the character set to the content-type header.
Expires	Sets the amount of time before the page cached on the browser expires.
ExpiresAbsolute	Sets the date and time a page cached on a browser expires.
IsClientConnected	Determines whether the browser has disconnected from the server.

Property Name	Description
Status	Indicates the status line returned by the server.
PICS	Adds the value of a PICS label to the PICS-label field of the response header.

The Buffer Property

The Buffer property is used to control and regulate when information is sent to the requesting browser. The Web server can either stream information to the user as the server is processing the script, or it can wait to release all the data after the entire script is finished processing. The output buffering uses the following syntax:

```
Response.Buffer [= flag]
```

where Response is the Response object and *flag* can be set to either True or False. If True, the server buffering is cached until the entire ASP page has completed processing or until the Flush or End methods have been called. If the flag is set to False, server buffering is disabled.

The CacheControl Property

The Response object uses the CacheControl property to enable a proxy server to cache output from Active Server Pages. The CacheControl requires the following syntax:

```
Response.CacheControl [= True/False ]
```

The CharSet Property

The CharSet property of the Response object is used to set the character set of the ContentType to be displayed on the requesting browser. The CharSet property controls the ContentType by using the following syntax:

```
Response.Charset(CharSetName)
```

where *CharSetName* is the character set designated for a particular page.

The ContentType Property

The ContentType Response object property enables you to specifically control the HTTP content-type that is sent to the browser. The browser uses the content-type information to determine how it should interpret the information, such as treating the information as text, HTML, or as an image file. The ContentType functionality is implemented using the following syntax:

```
Response.ContentType [= ContentType ]
```

where *ContentType* is the browser specific MIME Content type.

The Expires Property

The Expires property is an interesting feature that enables you to specify the amount of time in minutes before the page is expired from the browser cache. The Expires property uses the following syntax:

```
Response.Expires [= number]
```

where *number* is the number of minutes the page will remain active in the cache. Once this time has expired, the browser will be forced to retrieve information from the hosting site.

The ExpiresAbsolute Property

ExpiresAbsolute is an extension of the Expires property. The ExpiresAbsolute property enables you to specify the exact time and date a page will expire in the browser's cache. The ExpiresAbsolute property requires the following syntax:

```
Response.ExpiresAbsolute [= [date] [time]]
```

where *date* is the date on which the page will expire and *time* indicates the time the page will expire. However, note the expiration date and time is converted to Greenwich Mean Time.

The PICS Property

The PICS property of the Response object enables you to control rating values of the PICS-label field in the response header. This functionality can be controlled by implementing the following syntax:

```
Response.PICS(Picslabel)
```

where *PicsLabel* is the formatted PICS label.

The Status Property

The Response object uses the Status property to control the status line returned by the Web server. The status line is used to determine the results of the Web server request and are specified by HTTP specifications. To implement this functionality, use the following syntax:

```
Response.Status = StatusDescription
```

where *StatusDescription* is the status code and status code description. The following is a list of common HTTP status lines that can be returned by the Web server.

400 Bad Request

410 Unauthorized - Login Failed

404 Not Found

406 Not Acceptable

412 Precondition Failed

414 Request-URL Too Long

500 Internal Server Error

501 Not Implemented

502 Bad Gateway

One of the most common uses of the `Status` property is to check or authenticate the rights of the requesting user. For example, to force user validation for a page, use the following code to prompt the user for a username and password dialog box, use the following code:

```
<% Response.Status = "401 Unauthorized" %>
```

The `IsClientConnected` Property

`IsClientConnected` tracks whether the requesting browser has disconnected from the server since the last time the server issued a `Response.Write` command. The `IsClientConnected` property requires the following syntax:

```
Response.IsClientConnected()
```

The `IsClientConnected` property provides an extension of the `Session.Timeout` capability by enabling the requesting browser to exceed the session timeout variable without losing server connection and is often implemented before processing script. The following example tests the `Response` object to see whether the connection is valid before calling a function to transfer data.

```
If Response.IsClientConnected Then
        vTransfer = TranferInfo("AcctRetail", "AcctWholeSale")
Else
        VTransfer = ReConnect("UserName", "Department")
End If
```

Sending Output to the Browser: The Response Methods

The `Response` methods are used to explicitly control information flow from the server to the browser. Table D.9 lists the available `Response` methods.

TABLE D.9 THE Response METHODS

Method Name	Description
Write	Writes a string to the current HTTP output.
BinaryWrite	Writes information to the current HTTP output without any character conversion.
Clear	Erases any buffered HTML output.
End	Stops the Web server from processing the script and returns the current result.
Flush	Bypasses buffering and sends output immediately to client.
Redirect	Attempts to automatically route the browser to a URL.
AddHeader	Writes a string to the HTML header.
AppendToLog	Writes a string to the end of the Web server log entry.

The Write Method

The `Write` method of the `Response` object is used to send output to the browser. The `Write` method requires the following syntax:

```
Response.Write variant
```

where *variant* is any `Variant` datatype supported by the Visual Basic scripting engine.

When using the `Response.Write` method, the `Variant` datatype to be delivered to the client cannot contain the string `%>`. This string is interpreted by the scripting engine as an end script delimiter. Instead, use the string `%\>` to write the closing script delimiter tag.

The `Write` method uses the `Variant` datatype to send information to the browser. The `Variant` datatype, although the most versatile of datatypes, does have it limitations. The `Variant` datatype itself can only contain 1,022 bytes of information. If you try to use a variable that is larger than 1,022 bytes, a runtime error will occur.

The `AddHeader` Method

The `AddHeader` method enables you to add header information to the existing HTTP header. To use the `AddHeader` method, use the following syntax:

```
Response.AddHeader name, value
```

where *name* is the name of the new header variable and *value* is the value assigned to the new header variable.

The `AddHeader` method must be called before any content is sent to the browser. Failure to do so will generate a runtime error because the HTTP protocol first sends header information to the browser.

The `AppendToLog` Method

The `AppendToLog` method of the `Response` object enables you to append information directly to the Web server log file. To use this functionality, use the following syntax:

```
Response.AppendToLog string
```

where `Response` is the built-in `Response` object and *string* is an 80-byte character string.

The `BinaryWrite` Method

The `BinaryWrite` method enables direct non-formatted output to be displayed to the requesting browser. This direct output is useful when displaying non-string information, such as various image formats. To use the `BinaryWrite` method, use the following syntax:

```
Response.BinaryWrite data
```

where *data* is information that will be sent to the browser without any character conversion.

D

ACTIVE SERVER
PAGES OBJECT
REFERENCE

The `Clear` Method

The `Clear` method is used to erase any HTML that has been buffered on the server. The `Clear` property uses the following syntax:

```
Response.Clear
```

where `Response` is the built-in `Response` object and `Clear` is the `Clear` method.

The `End` Method

The `End` method also is used to manage the buffered server output. The `End` method returns the current buffered output up to the point where the `End` method is called. To use the `End` method, use the following syntax:

```
Response.End
```

where `Response` is the built-in `Response` object and `End` activates the `End` method.

The `Flush` Method

The `Flush` method is used by the `Response` object to immediately send any buffered output to the browser. The syntax for the `Flush` method is as follows:

```
Response.Flush
```

where `Response` is the built-in `Response` object and `Flush` calls the `Flush` method. The `Flush` method can only be used if buffering has been activated.

The `Redirect` Method

The `Redirect` method is used to route the browser to another Web page. The `Redirect` method is implemented by using the following syntax:

```
Response.Redirect URL
```

where `Response` is the built-in `Response` object and `URL` is the Uniform Resource Locator that indicates where the browser is to be routed.

Retrieving Information Using the `Request` Object

The `Request` object is responsible for retrieving information from the Web browser. The `Request` object uses collections, properties, and methods to retrieve information from the user.

Accepting User Information Using the `Request` Collections

The `Request` object uses separate objects that can be grouped together to interface with the calling client (see Table D.10).

TABLE D.10   THE Request COLLECTION

Collection Name	Description
ClientCertificate	Retrieves the certification fields issued by the Web browser.
Cookies	Retrieves the values of the cookies sent in an HTTP request.
Form	Retrieves the values of form elements posted to the HTTP request.
QueryString	Retrieves the values of the variables in the HTTP query string.
ServerVariables	Retrieves the values of predetermined environment variables.

The ClientCertificate Collection

The Request object's ClientCertificate collection is used to provide proper security identification across unsecured environments. The ClientCertificate keys are shown in Table D.11.

TABLE D.11   THE ClientCertificate CERTIFICATION FIELDS

Key	Description
Subject	Returns a list of subfield values that contain information about the subject of the certificate.
Issuer	Contains a list of subfield values containing information about the issuer of the certificate.
ValidForm	Returns when the certificate becomes valid.
ValidUntil	Specifies when the certificate expires.
SerialNumber	Returns the certification serial number as an ASCII representation of hexadecimal bytes.
Certificate	Returns the binary stream of the entire certificate content in ASN.1 format.

The use of subfields enables specific information to be retrieved from the Subject and Issuer key fields mentioned above. Table D.12 presents the available subfields for the ClientCertificate collection.

TABLE D.12   THE ClientCertificate COLLECTION SUBFIELDS

Value	Description
C	Specifies the name of the country of origin.
O	Specifies the company or organization name.

continues

D

TABLE D.12   CONTINUED

Value	Description
OU	Specifies the name of the organizational unit.
CN	Specifies the common name of the user.
L	Specifies a locality.
S	Specifies a state or province.
T	Specifies the title of the person or organization.
GN	Specifies a given name.
I	Specifies a set of initials.

If no certificate is sent, the ClientCertificate collection returns EMPTY.

The Cookies Collection

The Cookies collection is used by the Request object to retrieve values stored in text files on the client's machine.

The Cookies collection requires the following syntax:

```
Request.Cookies(cookie)[(key)¦.attribute]
```

Its properties are summarized in Table D.13.

TABLE D.13   Cookies COLLECTION PROPERTIES

Property	Description
HasKeys	Returns if the cookie contains keys.

The Form Collection

The Form collection helps to extract data from information submitted via the HTTP Post method. The Forms collection requires the following syntax:

```
Request.Form(parameter)[(index)¦.Count]
```

where *parameter* is the name of the Form collection, *index* is the specific form element, and *Count* identifies the number of elements that exist on a form.

For example, the following creates an ASP variable name vUserName by extracting values entered in HTML forms fields named txtUserFirstName and txtUserLastName:

```
<%
vUserName = Request.Form("txtUserFirstName") & " "
```

```
⇒& Request.Form("txtUserLastName")
%>
```

The `QueryString` Collection

The `QueryString` collection is used by the `Request` object to extract variables from the HTTP query string. The query string is textual content that occurs after the question mark character (?) in the URL string.

```
Request.QueryString(variable)[(index)¦.Count]
```

where `Request` is the `Request` object, *variable* is the name of the variable name in the query string, *index* is the element index, and *Count* specifies the number of variables in the query string.

For example, to populate an ASP variable named `myDBDrilldown` from a `QueryString` variable named `myDatabaseStr`, use the following syntax:

```
<% myDBDrillDown = Request.QueryString("myDatabaseStr ") %>
```

If the URL `http:/ASPapp/loadDB.asp?myDatabaseStr=AcctNumber` was submitted to the server, the text `AcctNumber` would be assigned to the ASP variable.

The `ServerVariables` Collection

The `ServerVariables` collection is used to obtain server environmental variables. To use these features, the `ServerVariables` collection requires the following syntax:

```
Request.ServerVariables (ServerVariable)
```

where *ServerVariable* is name of the server variable. Table D.14 displays a list of common server variables.

TABLE D.14 THE SERVER VARIABLES

Variable Name	Description
*ALL_HTTP	Displays All HTTP headers sent by the client.
*ALL_RAW	Retrieves all headers as they are sent by the client.
*APPL_MD_PATH	Retrieves the metabase path for the ISAPI DLL.
*APPL_PHYSICAL_PATH	Retrieves the physical path corresponding to the Metabase.
AUTH_TYPE	Displays the authentication method used by the server.
*AUTH_USER	Retrieves the authenticated user name in Raw format.
AUTH_PASSWORD	Displays the value entered in the client's authentication dialog using Basic authentication security.

continues

TABLE D.14   CONTINUED

Variable Name	Description
*CERT_COOKIE	Returns the Unique ID for client certificate.
*CERT_FLAGS	Displays whether the client certificate is valid.
*CERT_ISSUER	Displays Issuer field of the client certificate.
CERT_KEYSIZE	Returns the number of bits in Secure Sockets Layer connection key size.
*CERT_SERIALNUMBER	Displays the client certificate Serial number field.
*CERT_SERVER_ISSUER	Displays the of the server certificate Issuer field.
*CERT_SERVER_SUBJECT	Displays the server certificate Subject field.
*CERT_SUBJECT	Displays the client certificate Subject field.
CONTENT_LENGTH	Returns the length of the content.
CONTENT_TYPE	Returns the data type of the content.
GATEWAY_INTERFACE	Returns the version of the CGI specifications used on the server.
HTTP_<HeaderName>	Returns the information in the *HeaderName*.
*HTTPS	Returns whether or not the request came in through secure channel (SSL).
*HTTPS_KEYSIZE	Returns the number of bits in Secure Sockets Layer connection key size.
*HTTPS_SECRETKEYSIZE	Returns the number of bits in server certificate private key.
*HTTPS_SERVER_ISSUER	Returns the server certificate Issuer field.
*HTTPS_SERVER_SUBJECT	Displays the server certificate Subject field.
*INSTANCE_ID	Returns the ID for the IIS instance.
*INSTANCE_META_PATH	Returns the metabase path for the instance of IIS that responds to the request.
LOGON_USER	Displays the NT login account the request is made from.
PATH_INFO	Displays the server path information.
PATH_TRANSLATED	Returns the translated version of the PATH_INFO.
QUERY_STRING	Returns the query string in the URL.
REMOTE_ADDR	Displays the IP address of the requesting machine.
REMOTE_HOST	Displays the name of the requesting host.
REQUEST_METHOD	Returns the method that initiated the request.
SCRIPT_NAME	Displays the virtual path to the executing script.
SERVER_NAME	Returns the server's host name, DNS alias, or IP address.

Variable Name	Description
SERVER_PORT	Returns the server port number the request is made on.
SERVER_PORT_SECURE	Returns a 1 if request is made on a secure port, 0 if unsecured.
SERVER_PROTOCOL	Returns the name and version of the requesting protocol.
SERVER_SOFTWARE	Returns the name and version of HTTP server.
URL	Returns the base portion of the URL.

*In the table, * indicate the new IIS 4.0 Server variables.*

The Request Properties and Methods

The Request object has one property and one method. The TotalBytes property dictates the total amount of bytes sent in the request. The BinaryRead method is use to accept and store data sent from a browser.

The TotalBytes Property

The TotalBytes property is used to return the number of bytes sent by the client, and requires the following syntax:

```
Request.TotalBytes
```

The BinaryRead Method

The BinaryRead method is used to read binary information that is sent to the server from a POST request. To use the BinaryRead method, use the following syntax:

```
myBinArray = Request.BinaryRead(count)
```

where count is the number of bytes to place into an array named myBinArray.

Managing the Session Object

The Session object is responsible for managing information for a specific user session. These variables are not accessible by other user sessions, but they can be passed from page to page within the ASP application. The Session object is created when a new user enters an application. The termination of the application or the application's timeout threshold destroys the Session object for the user.

The `Session` Object: A Cookie-Dependant System

The `Session` object is based on using cookies to store and transfer a unique user ID between the browser client and the Web server. This session ID is used to create and reference `Server` objects specific to a particular user. If cookies are not permitted on the client browser (because of firewall issues, browser incompatibility, or desktop/network security concerns), the `Session` object is rendered useless. If cookies are not permitted, ASP applications can still be developed and deployed. However, most of the state tracking will have to be done through more cumbersome methods, such as using HTML hidden fields and passing information via the URL.

When a user enters the application, the server first checks to see if the requesting user has a valid `SessionID`. If the `SessionID` is found in the HTTP header, the user is identified as an active user and is able to continue in the application. If no `SessionID` is found in the header, the server generates an identifier and sends it to the browser's cookie. This identifier is needed to create a unique `Session` object that represents the specific user session. The purpose of the identifier is to generate an exclusive identification to tie the actions of the browser client to corresponding objects on the Web server. Each time a browser request is made, this unique token is passed to identify the appropriate request.

> **CAUTION**
>
> `Session` objects are only supported on Web browsers that support cookies.

In a cookie-compliant browser world, the `Session` object greatly helps manage the user in the application. However, when dealing with a non-secure cookie-compliant browser, it is not possible to safely track user information via the `Session` object. Typically, this is of importance where client impersonation might occur. The counterfeiting of a user can occur in two situations. The first is if the session ID is captured while the data is in transit between the client and server. The second possible security violation occurs when the cookie file itself is copied from the user machine to another machine. With two valid session cookies, the user is able to temporary clone himself onto another machine.

Implementing `Session` Variables and Properties

The `Session` object is responsible for managing user information. The user can create and manipulate the `Session` object's methods and properties using the following syntax:

```
Session.property¦method
```

where Session is the Session object. The Session object has four properties, as listed in Table D.15.

TABLE D.15   THE Session OBJECT'S PROPERTIES

Property	Description
SessionID	Returns the unique user session identifier.
TimeOut	Returns or sets the user timeout value in minutes.
CodePage	Sets the language attribute for the deployed pages.
LCID	Sets the local identifier used to set local date, currency, and time formats.

Declaring Session Variables

To create or reference a session variable, use the Session object and the name of the variable using the following syntax:

```
ObjectLevel(varName)
```

where *ObjectLevel* is the Session object and *varName* is the name of the variable.

Notice that you do not have to use the Dim, Redim, Public, Private, or Const declared statements that are found in VBScript to create variables.

Because the session variables are only available to the specific user session, no Lock and UnLock methods are needed to prevent simultaneous updates to the same variable. However, great care should be taken to ensure the correct spelling of session- and application-level variables. If a session or application variable is misspelled, a new variable with that misspelling is created.

The SessionID Property

The Session object uses the SessionID to keep track of user information from page to page within the ASP application. The server generates the SessionID when a new session is started. The SessionID is available using the following syntax:

```
Session.SessionID
```

The TimeOut Property

The TimeOut property sets or returns the amount of time, in minutes, that the Session object can remain inactive before the user's Session object is destroyed. To set the TimeOut property, use the following syntax:

```
Session.Timeout [ = nMinutes]
```

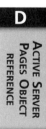

where `Session` is the `Session` object and *nMinutes* is the timeout value specified in minutes.

The `LCID` Property

The `LCID` property is used to set the local identifier properties for an ASP. The local identifier is used to control the display formatting that is specific to a localized location or region. The `LCID` property requires the following syntax:

```
Session.LCID(=LCIDcode)
```

where *LCIDcode* is the valid local identifier. The `LCID` is standard abbreviation that identifies localized formatting issues such as time, date and currency formats.

The `CodePage` Property

The `CodePage` property of the `Session` object is used to assign the system code page for an ASP. To implement this feature, use the following syntax:

```
Session.CodePage = CodePage
```

where *CodePage* is valid code page for the scripting engine.

Trapping Session Events

The `Session` object uses two events, shown in Table D.16 to help monitor when a user enters and exits the ASP application. A new `Session` object is created by the Active Server to represent when a new user has entered the ASP application. Once the `Session` object is started, information pertaining to that user's session can be stored on the Web server.

TABLE D.16 THE `Session` OBJECT'S EVENTS

Event	Description
Session_OnStart	Triggered when a new user enters ASP application.
Session_OnEnd	Initiated when the ASP Session Object is terminated.

The `Session_OnStart` Event

To trap the start of the `Session` object, you must use the `GLOBAL.ASA` file. The `Session_OnStart` event requires a layout similar to the following `GLOBAL.ASA` syntax:

```
<SCRIPT LANGUAGE = ScriptLanguage RUNAT=Server>
```

```
Sub Session_OnStart
    '=== The Code to be executed when a new user enters the app
End Sub

Session_OnStart          '=== Calls the procedure Session_OnStart

</SCRIPT>
```

Session events can reference any other ASP object in the `OnStart` and `OnEnd` events.

The `Session_OnEnd` Event

The `Session_OnEnd` event, which is located in the optional `GLOBAL.ASA` file, is triggered when the current `Session` objects are closed. The `Session_OnEnd` event requires the following syntax:

```
<SCRIPT LANGUAGE=ScriptLanguage RUNAT=Server>

Sub Session_OnEnd
    '=== Closing code here
End Sub

</SCRIPT>
```

where *ScriptLanguage* is any script-compliant language. The `Session_OnEnd` event is triggered when the `Session` object is abandoned or times out. During this pre-shutdown of the `Session` object, all interaction with the client browser is prohibited while the existing requests in the queue are processed.

Any ASP code requests to the `Response` or `Request` objects in the `Session_OnEnd` event will generate an error. References to all objects internal to the Web server, such as the `Server`, `Application`, or `Session` objects, are still valid. However, reference to the `Server.MapPath` method will cause a `type mismatch` error to occur. Table D.17 illustrates the valid object calls for the `Session_OnEnd` event.

TABLE D.17   Session_OnEnd OBJECT CALLS

Valid Objects	*Invalid Object Calls*
Server	Request
Session	Response
Application	

D

ACTIVE SERVER
PAGES OBJECT
REFERENCE

Controlling User Session Resources

The Abandon method is used to destroy and release the resources consumed by inactive Session objects. The termination of the Session object is called using the following syntax:

```
Session.Abandon
```

where Session is the current Session object. In most situations, the Abandon method will be executed implicitly when the Session.Timeout value has passed.

The Session.Abandon method has some special scoping characteristics that are important to remember. First, when the Session.Abandon method is called, the Web server continues to process the remaining ASP code on the page. This is unlike the Server.TimeOut event and the Response.Redirect method, where code execution on that page is instantly terminated.

The second scoping issue of the Session object is that all object properties that were created before the Session.Abandon method will be unavailable after the Abandon method is called. The Abandon method destroys the properties of the Session object without destroying the Session object itself.

Third, because the Session object is not yet destroyed, the Session object can be used to store user properties. Only after the page has completely finished processing is the current Session object placed in the queue for destruction.

Using Session-Level Objects

Session-level objects can be categorized into two classes based on how the item is declared, as shown in Table D.18. Objects can be declared with or without the <OBJECT> tag. If the session-level object is declared as an object using the <OBJECT> tag, the object is a managed by the StaticObject collection. If the object is not declared using the <OBJECT> tag, the session-level item is managed by the Contents collection.

TABLE D.18 THE Session COLLECTION

Name	Description
Contents	Contains all session-level items that have not been created with the <OBJECT> tag.
StaticObject	Contains all session-level objects declared with the <OBJECT> tag.

The Contents Collection

The Contents collection is used to contain all items that have been created during a session that have not been declared with the <OBJECT> tag. The Contents collection requires the following syntax:

```
Session.Contents( Key )
```

where *Key* is the name of the property to retrieve.

The StaticObject Collection

The StaticObject collection is similar to the Contents collection, but StaticObject is used to manage all session-level objects that have been declared with the <OBJECT> tag. The StaticObject collection uses the following syntax:

```
Session.StaticObjects( Key )
```

where *Key* is the property to retrieve. StaticCollection can also be used to reference a single session variable or multiple session variables.

ActiveX Data Objects Reference

The ActiveX Data Objects provide you with an interface to OLE DB data sources. Figure E.1 shows the entire ADO object model based on version 2.x. For the most up-to-date information, see Microsoft's ADO site: http://www.microsoft.com/data.ado.

FIGURE E.1.

The ActiveX Data Objects object model.

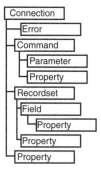

This appendix is designed as a reference to all the objects that are included in the ADO object model. The collections and objects are listed in alphabetical order with tables indicating and describing all the methods and properties available to each.

Command Object

The Command object contains the properties and methods necessary to execute SQL commands using ADO. Tables E.1 and E.2 summarize the methods and properties of the Command object.

TABLE E.1 Command OBJECT METHODS

Method	Description
Cancel	Cancels an asynchronously executing command
CreateParameter	Creates a new Parameter object
Execute	Executes the command

TABLE E.2 Command OBJECT PROPERTIES

Property	Description
ActiveConnection	Returns or sets the active Connection object
CommandText	Returns or sets the command text
CommandTimeout	Returns or sets the timeout in seconds
CommandType	Returns or sets the command type
Name	Returns the name of the object

Property	Description
Parameters	Returns the parameters for this command
Prepared	Returns or sets whether to compile this command before executing
Properties	Returns the dynamic properties of object
State	Returns the current state of the object

Connection Object

The `Connection` object manages a data provider connection in ADO. Table E.3 describes the `Connection` object events, Table E.4 summarizes the `Connection` object methods, and Table E.5 lists the `Connection` object properties.

TABLE E.3   Connection OBJECT EVENTS

Event	Description
BeginTransComplete	Fired after the `BeginTrans` method is completed
CommitTransComplete	Fired after the `CommitTrans` method is completed
ConnectComplete	Fired after the `Open` method is completed
Disconnect	Fired after the `Close` method is completed
ExecuteComplete	Fired after the `Execute` method is completed
InfoMessage	Fired when an information message comes from the data provider
RollbackTransComplete	Fired after the `RollbackTrans` method is complete
WillConnect	Fired before a connection is made
WillExecute	Fired before the `Execute` method is performed

TABLE E.4   Connection OBJECT METHODS

Method	Description
BeginTrans	Begins a transaction
Cancel	Cancels an asynchronous operation
Close	Closes an object
Execute	Executes a SQL statement or query
Open	Open the connection
OpenSchema	Returns a `Recordset` object filled with database information
RollbackTrans	Rolls back a transaction

E

ACTIVEX DATA OBJECTS REFERENCE

TABLE E.5 Connection OBJECT PROPERTIES

Property	Description
Attributes	Indicates characteristics of the object
CommandTimeout	Returns or sets the timeout for the Execute method
ConnectionString	Returns or sets the connection string
ConnectionTimeout	Returns or sets the timeout to establish a connection
CursorLocation	Returns or sets where the cursor is created
DefaultDatabase	Returns or sets the default database
Errors	Returns the collection of Error objects raised by data providers
IsolationLevel	Returns or set the level of isolation for transactions
Mode	Returns the available permissions for modifying data
Properties	Returns the dynamic properties for the object
Provider	Returns the name of the data provider
State	Returns the current state of the object
Version	Returns the ADO version number

Errors Collection, Error Object

The Errors collection and Error object manage the data provider generated errors for a Connection object. Tables E.6 and E.7 list the methods and properties for the Errors collection. Table E.8 lists the properties for the Error object.

TABLE E.6 ERRORS COLLECTION METHODS

Method	Description
Clear	Clears the collection
Refresh	Refreshes the items in the collection

TABLE E.7 ERRORS COLLECTION PROPERTIES

Property	Description
Count	Returns the number of items in the collection
Item	Returns the specified object from the collection

TABLE E.8   ERROR OBJECT PROPERTIES

Property	Description
Description	Returns the description of the error
HelpContext	Returns a Help Context Id if a HelpFile is available
HelpFile	Returns the name of a help file where help on the error is available
NativeError	Returns the error number reported by the underlying API or interface
Number	Returns the error number
Source	Returns the name of the source of the error
SQLState	Returns the five-character ANSI standard error

Fields Collection, Field Object

The `Fields` collection and `Field` object are the columns or fields returned in a `Recordset` object. Table E.9 summarizes the methods of the `Fields` collection. Table E.10 describes the properties of the `Fields` collection. Tables E.11 and E.12 lists the methods and properties of the `Field` object.

TABLE E.9   FIELDS COLLECTION METHODS

Method	Description
Append	Appends an object to the collection
Delete	Deletes an object from the collection
Refresh	Refreshes the items in the collection

TABLE E.10   FIELDS COLLECTION PROPERTIES

Property	Description
Count	Returns the number of items in the collection
Item	Returns the specified object from the collection

TABLE E.11   FIELD OBJECT METHODS

Method	Description
AppendChunk	Appends data to the object's value
GetChunk	Returns a portion of data from the object's value

TABLE E.12   FIELD OBJECT PROPERTIES

Property	Description
ActualSize	Returns the size of the field
Attributes	Indicates characteristics of the object
DataFormat	Returns or sets the stdDataFormat object
DefinedSize	The defined size of the field
Name	The name of the object
NumericScale values will be resolved	Returns or sets the number of decimal places to which numeric
OriginalValue opened	Returns the values of the field when the Recordset was first
Precision values	Returns or sets the maximum number of digits used to represent
Properties	Returns the dynamic properties for the object
Type	Returns the datatype
UnderlyingValue	Returns the object's current value in the database
Value	Returns the object's current value in the Recordset

Parameters Collection, Parameter Object

The Parameters collection and Parameter object are used with the Command object to execute stored procedures. Tables E.13 and E.14 list the methods and properties for the Parameters collection. Table E.15 lists the method for the Parameter object, and Table E.16 lists the properties of the Parameter object.

TABLE E.13   Parameters COLLECTION METHODS

Method	Description
Append	Appends an object to the collection
Delete	Deletes an object from the collection
Refresh	Refreshes the items in the collection

TABLE E.14   Parameters COLLECTION PROPERTIES

Property	Description
Count	Returns the number of items in the collection
Item	Returns the specified object from the collection

TABLE E.15   Parameter OBJECT METHOD

Method	Description
AppendChunk	Appends data to the object's value.

TABLE E.16   Parameter OBJECT PROPERTIES

Property	Description
Attributes	Indicates characteristics of the object
Direction	Returns or sets the direction of the parameter
Name	The name of the object
NumericScale	Returns or sets the number of decimal places to which numeric values will be resolved
Precision	Returns or sets the maximum digits used to represent values
Properties	Returns the dynamic properties for the object
Size	Returns the maximum size of the object
Type	Returns the datatype
Value	Returns the object's value

Properties Collection, Property Object

The Properties collection and the Property object manage dynamic characteristics for an ADO object. Tables E.17 and E.18 list the methods and properties of the Properties collection. Table E.19 lists the properties of the Property object.

TABLE E.17 Properties COLLECTION METHOD

Method	*Description*
Refresh	Refreshes the items in the collection

TABLE E.18 Properties COLLECTION PROPERTIES

Property	*Description*
Count	Returns the number of items in the collection
Item	Returns the specified object from the collection

TABLE E.19 Property OBJECT PROPERTIES

Property	*Description*
Attributes	Indicates characteristics of the object
Name	The name of the object
Type	Returns the datatype
Value	Returns the object's value

Recordset Object

The Recordset object handles the rows returned from an opened table or executed query. Tables E.20, E.21, and E.22 describe the events, methods, and properties of the Recordset object.

TABLE E.20   Recordset OBJECT EVENTS

Event	Description
EndOfRecordset	Fired when the end of the Recordset is reached
FetchComplete	Fired when the entire Recordset is fetched
FetchProgress	Fired to indicate the progress of the data fetch
FieldChangeComplete	Fired after a field is changed
MoveComplete	Fired after the Recordset moves to another record
RecordChangeComplete	Fired after a record is changed
RecordsetChangeComplete	Fired after the Recordset is changed
WillChangeField	Fired before a field's value is changed
WillChangeRecord	Fired before a record is changed.
WillChangeRecordset	Fired before the Recordset is changed.
WillMove	Fired before the Recordset moves to another record.

TABLE E.21   Recordset OBJECT METHODS

Method	Description
AddNew	Adds a new record to the object
Cancel	Cancels an asynchronously executing command
CancelBatch	Cancels changes before BatchUpdate has been called
CancelUpdate	Cancels changes before an Update has been called
Clone	Returns a duplicate Recordset
Close	Closes the object
CompareBookmarks	Compares two bookmarks
Delete	Deletes from the Recordset
Find	Finds a record in the Recordset
GetRows	Retrieves records into an array
GetString	Retrieves records into a string
Move	Moves the position of the current record
MoveFirst	Moves to the first record of the Recordset
MoveLast	Moves to the last record of the Recordset
MoveNext	Moves to the next record of the Recordset

continues

E

ACTIVE X DATA
OBJECTS
REFERENCE

TABLE E.21 CONTINUED

Method	Description
MovePrevious	Moves to the previous record of the `Recordset`
NextRecordset	Clears current `Recordset` and moves to the next `Recordset`
Open	Opens the object
Requery	Refreshes the `Recordset` by re-executing the underlying query
Resync	Refreshes the `Recordset` to the current database values
Save	Saves the `Recordset` to a file
Supports	Returns whether the object supports a particular function
Update	Saves the changes to the current row to the database
UpdateBatch	Saves the changes of the current batch to the database

TABLE E.22 Recordset OBJECT PROPERTIES

Property	Description
AbsolutePage	Returns or sets the page of the current record
AbsolutePosition	Returns or sets the current record position by ordinal
ActiveCommand	Returns the command object that created the `Recordset`
ActiveConnection	Returns the active connection used by the Recordset
BOF	Returns whether the current record position is before the beginning of the `Recordset`
Bookmark	Returns or sets a bookmark for the current record
CacheSize	Returns or sets the number records that will be cached in local memory
CursorLocation	Returns or sets where the cursor will be created
CursorType	Returns or sets the type of cursor
DataMember	Returns or sets the data member to retrieve from the object referenced by the datasource property
DataSource	Returns or sets the object containing data the `Recordset` represents
EditMode	Returns the editing status of the current record
EOF	Returns if the current record position is past the end of the `Recordset`
Fields	Returns the collection of `Field` object's in the `Recordset`
Filter	Returns or sets the filter for data

Property	Description
LockType	Returns or sets the locking strategy
MarshalOptions	Returns or sets how the `Recordset` should be marshaled using DCOM
MaxRecords	Returns or sets the maximum number of records to return
PageCount	Returns the number of pages the `Recordset` contains
PageSize	Returns or sets the size of the pages
Properties	Returns the dynamic properties for the object
RecordCount	Returns the number of records
Sort	Returns or sets the sort criteria
Source	Returns or sets the source of the data
State	Returns the current state of the object
Status	Returns the status with regards to batch updates
StayInSync	Returns or sets whether the parent row should change when underlying child rows change in a hierarchical `Recordset`

Transact-SQL Quick Reference

The focus for this chapter is to describe the elements in the Transact-SQL (T-SQL) language. I will go through most of the language constructs in T-SQL. This isn't intended to be a learning book for the general SQL language. There are several such books on the market from beginner's level to advanced level; some describe the standard ANSI SQL syntax and some specialize on T-SQL. Look for the *Sams Teach Yourself* line of books on SQL and Transact-SQL and *SQL Unleashed* and *SQL Server Programming Unleashed* from Sams Publishing for more specific information on each of these.

New in SQL Server 7.0

Transact-SQL is an evolving language. As with any new release of SQL Server, version 7 includes enhancements to the Transact-SQL dialect. Here follows a brief outline of some of the major enhancements.

Unicode Support

The character set chosen at installation time cannot be changed without transfer of data and rebuild of the installation. Because storage usage for each character is one byte, the maximum number of characters that can be represented is 256. Some of these characters are special characters, so the actual number of available characters is lower. Unicode uses two bytes storage area for each character, which means that 65,536 characters can be represented. Unicode is supported through three new datatypes: *nchar*, *nvarchar*, and *ntext*. Note, however, that twice as much storage area is needed for Unicode data than for the old *char*, *varchar*, and *text* data.

ALTER TABLE, ALTER PROCEDURE, ALTER TRIGGER, ALTER VIEW

It's now possible to change the definition for an object without having to drop and re-create the object. When re-creating an object, permissions have to be re-granted or re-revoked.

ALTER TABLE was restricted in earlier versions of SQL Server. Except for adding and dropping constraints, adding a column was all that could be done. This column had to allow NULL as well.

Many scripts have been written over the years to create an intermediate table with the desired table structure, copying over data and renaming the tables. Some tools, such as Visual Database Tools, found in Visual InterDev, could perform these operations behind the scenes.

With version 7, columns can be dropped from a table, datatypes can be altered, and a column with NOT NULL can be added if a default value or identity attribute is defined for that column.

T-SQL and ANSI/ISO SQL-92

T-SQL has evolved significantly over the years, and so have the ANSI standards for the SQL language. ANSI SQL-92 is a significantly larger standard than its predecessors. There are three levels defined in ANSI SQL-92: Entry, Intermediate, and Full.

SQL Server supports the Entry Level of ANSI SQL-92. Naturally, you will find a number of special statements and features in SQL Server, not defined by the ANSI standard. Examples of such features are as follows:

- Operating system–dependent statements, such as defining physical database storage.

- Legacy syntax and commands. Even if the current version supports the ANSI way of expressing a command, backward compatibly is a major issue.

- Extensions to the ANSI standards. All vendors strive at implementing competitive features. Microsoft is no exception.

So, version 7.0 is a superset of the Entry level of the ANSI SQL-92 standard. Although this was achieved in version 6.5, Microsoft continues to add support for the ANSI standard. This includes new language constructs as well as encouraging developers to express statements as defined by the ANSI standard.

Cursor Enhancements

You are now given the same expressive power when working with SQL cursors as you have with API cursors. Microsoft has introduced an alternative syntax to declaring a cursor in T-SQL. You can explicitly define whether the cursor should be STATIC, INSENSITIVE, or DYNAMIC.

If you don't declare the cursor as read-only, you can also define the level of concurrency with our cursor definition. You can define a cursor for READ_ONLY, SCROLL_LOCKS, or OPTIMISTIC concurrency.

In version 6, all cursor's scope was global; that is, a cursor ran out of scope when the connection was terminated. You now have the ability to define local cursors, which scope is within the creating batch.

You can also return a cursor variable from a stored procedure and process the cursor from the calling batch or stored procedure. This can improve re-use because you can define a generic cursor and call it from several stored procedures or batches.

Creating Database Objects

A database consists of a number of elements or objects. Information about a particular object is found in a system table. In Table F.1, you find the various object types and where information about the objects is stored.

TABLE F.1 OBJECTS AND SYSTEM TABLES IN SQL SERVER

Object Type	System Table
Table, View,	sysobjectsStoredProcedure,Trigger,Default, Rule
Constraints	sysconstraints, sysreferences
Index	sysindexes
Datatypes	systypes

To create a database object, CREATE permissions must be granted to the user. The creator of an object becomes the object owner (sometimes referred to as DBOO, or Database Object Owner). The database owner (dbo) can create an object with another username as the owner. The object will be created in the current database unless another database is specified. The following lists some examples:

```
CREATE TABLE customers
```

The customers table will be owned by the creator and created in the current database.

```
CREATE TABLE pubs..customer
```

The customers table will be created in the pubs database, if the login ID that executes the statement has a username in pubs.

```
CREATE TABLE steve.customer
```

This command can be executed by the dbo and creates a table, which will be owned by the username steve. The table will be created in the current database.

Tables

The table is the only type of information carrier in a relational database. The table has a structure containing a set of rows and a set of columns. Well, perhaps not a proper set. Column can be addressed not only by name but also by position when performing an

INSERT. Rows can contain duplicates. A debate has been going on for a rather lengthy time regarding these subjects, but I won't dive further into that debate here.

Each column (or rather, the data to be stored in the column) is based on a datatype, which limits the possible "values" that can be stored in the column and also defines behavior when adding, subtracting, and so on. The column can have further restrictions as well.

Restrictions can be defined at the table level as well; for instance, that a combination of two columns has to be unique within the table.

A table can be created using the CREATE TABLE statement. You can also use Enterprise Manager, which has been given a better and more powerful interface in version 7. Note that Enterprise Manager act as a graphical front-end which, in turn, generates the CREATE TABLE command.

This is the basic syntax for the CREATE TABLE command:

```
CREATE TABLE table_name
(column_name datatype {identity NOT NULL ¦ NULL}
[, ...])
```

TERMINOLOGY IN THE RELATIONAL MODEL

The relational model uses different terminology for tables, columns, and rows. A table is called a relation; a column is called attribute, and a row is called tuple. Note, however, that the current ANSI SQL standard doesn't use this terminology, nor is it widely used. The following example creates a customer table with three columns: customer ID, the customer's name, and a comment:

```
CREATE TABLE customers
(customer_id INT IDENTITY NOT NULL,
customer_name VARCHAR(100) NOT NULL,
customer_comments VARCHAR(5000) NULL)
```

SQL Server Object Names

All objects in SQL Server are named. Examples of objects are tables, views, stored procedures, and so on. Names for objects must be unique within the database, but remember that the object owner is a part of the name. So the table steve.customer isn't the same as john.customer.

Whether object names are case sensitive depends on the case sensitivity chosen at installation time of the SQL Server. Case sensitivity applies to object names as well as character data stored in tables.

Object names (or Identifiers) can be up to 128 characters, including letters, symbols (_, @, or #), and numbers. The first character must be an alphabetic (a–z or A–Z) character. Variables and temporary tables have special naming schemes. Note that an object name cannot include spaces. By using Quoted Identifiers, characters that otherwise would be illegal in object names can be used. However, avoid using Quoted Identifiers if possible. You might find a great utility application that doesn't support quoted identifiers. An example of this is SQLMAINT.EXE in SQL Server 6.5.

OBJECT OWNERSHIP

It is recommended that the dbo owns all objects in most cases. This simplifies administration and makes it easier for programmers and end-users when referring to the object. Handling permissions on Stored Procedures and Views is also easier if the same user owns all objects.

Column Properties

A column can have several properties. Some restrict what can be stored in the column, whereas others provide functionality (a counter for instance).

DETERMINING CASE SENSITIVITY

To determine case-sensitivity for a SQL Server installation, execute the stored procedure sp_helpsort.

NULL | NOT NULL

The NULL and NOT NULL keywords define whether a column can contain the null symbol. You cannot define NULL for a column that is to be used as the Primary Key or the Identity column. It is generally recommended to keep the columns that allow NULLs to a minimum because it is difficult to deal with missing information.

IDENTITY(seed, increment)

IDENTITY defines a counter. A new value will be generated for each row that is inserted into the table.

The identity property can only be defined for integer types of columns. This includes INT, SMALLINT, TINYINT, DECIMAL, and NUMERIC, provided that the last two have scales of 0.

ROWGUIDCOL

ROWGUIDCOL defines the column as a row global unique identifier. It can only be defined for columns of the datatype UNIQUEIDENTIFIER. The purpose of this property is to generate values that are unique across tables and SQL Servers. To generate the unique value, the function NEWID() is used, which returns a value that is useful only for the UNIQUEIDENTIFIER datatype.

<column_constraint>

Available constraints are Primary Key, Unique, Foreign Key, Check, and Default. A constraint does exactly what the name implies—constraint the possible values that can be used within the column. The feature is used to achieve as consistent data as possible within the database.

Example

You want to create an order table with the following columns:

- Order number. A globally unique ID. This column is defined as a primary key. For each value inserted, a new value is issued through a default constraint.

- Customer number. A customer number that is a foreign key to the customer table.

- Order Date. This can be automatically inserted through a default constraint. Note that the default constraint removes the time part of the value returned from GETDATE().

Listing F.1 is the CREATE TABLE statement for an orders table.

LISTING F.1   THE CREATE TABLE STATEMENT FOR THE ORDERS TABLE

```
1 CREATE TABLE orders
2 (order_id UNIQUEIDENTIFIER DEFAULT NEWID() PRIMARY KEY
  ➥ NOT NULL,
3 customer_id INT REFERENCES customers(customer_id),
4 order_date DATETIME DEFAULT CONVERT(CHAR(8),
  ➥ GETDATE(), 112))
```

Notes on Identity Columns

The identity functionality isn't designed, in all situations, to produce continuous values. If a row is deleted, that value won't be reused. If an insert is rolled back, the value won't be reused.

An explicit value cannot be inserted for the identity column unless SET
IDENTITY_INSERT <*table_name*> ON has been run. Only the table owner can explicitly
insert the identity value.

To reset the value to the current highest (or lowest) value, run DBCC
CHECKIDENT(<*table_name*>).

A Primary Key constraint (or Unique constraint) should always be defined for a column
if the column is a key. The identity feature isn't designed for uniqueness per se.
Duplicates can occur if IDENTITY_INSERT is used, or if SQL Server looses track of its
internal counter for the identity value and starts over again at the seed value. This behavior happened quite often in versions 6.0 and 6.5, especially if SQL Server was unexpect-
edly shut down.

Renaming Objects

An object can be renamed, using the sp_rename system stored procedure. The syntax for
renaming an object is

sp_rename {'*object_name*'} [, '*new_name*'] [, '*object_type*']

Where *object_type* can be COLUMN, DATABASE, INDEX, OBJECT,or USERDATATYPE.

Adding Columns to a Table

Sometimes a column has to be added to a table. This is generally because you find out
that there are more attributes that you want to store for the entity described by the table.
A column can be added with the ALTER TABLE command.

CHECK DEPENDENT OBJECTS

Make sure that the objects that depend on the renamed object are handled
(Views, Stored Procedures, and so on). SQL Server will give you a warning that
changing an object name may break script and stored procedures, which is
absolutely true.

I strongly encourage you to check which objects depends on the object, edit the
dependents' source code, and re-create them. The system stored procedure
sp_depends will give a repor of which objects depend on another object.

A column added to a table with earlier versions of SQL Server had to allow NULL. This was a bit annoying because you generally try to avoid NULL, if possible.

But what do you insert in the current rows for the new column? With version 7, you can define a default value, or the added column can be defined with the identity attribute.

Let's say that you want to add a column to the customer table. To increase customer service, an estimated shipping date must be given for each order. The estimated shipping date for existing orders will be set to 1900-01-01 to clearly mark the rows that were inserted before this column was added.

```
ALTER TABLE orders ADD estimated_shipping_date DATETIME
➡ NOT NULL DEFAULT '19000101'
```

The default value could later be removed or changed to something more meaningful.

Temporary Tables

A *temporary table* is a table that exists for the duration of the connection that created it. By using a hash sign (#) as the first letter in the table name, SQL Server makes the table a temporary table. A temporary table can be explicitly created with the use of the CREATE TABLE statement or implicitly with the use of SELECT INTO.

The temporary table is only available for the connection that created the table. All temporary tables are created in the tempdb database, but don't worry about name clashes. SQL Server will append a unique identifier on the table name, so even if another connection creates a temporary table with the same name, they will be named differently in the *tempdb* database.

So, why create temporary tables? If you have a complex query, it might be easier to solve it by breaking it up in steps. Or you might want to store some values so that you can do further calculations on them.

Global and Permanent Temporary Tables

A global temporary table is available for other connections. You create a global temporary table by preceding its name with two hash signs (##). This can be useful if an application uses several connections and you want the temporary table to be available for all connections. If a stored procedure creates a local temporary table, it will be removed when the procedure terminates. The procedure is considered a connection in this aspect. But a global temporary table will be available after the procedure executed.

You can also create a permanent temporary table. By explicitly creating the table in the tempdb database, it will be available after the connection that created it terminates. It will disappear when SQL Server restarts because tempdb is re-created at startup.

SIZING TEMPDB

The default size of the tempdb database is too small for almost all production installations. It is impossible to recommend a "right" size for tempdb offhand, but a good rule of thumb is to either make it as big as your biggest table in the system, or half the size of your biggest database.

The tempdb database is also used to store the internal worktables that SQL Server creates for some operations, for instance sorting, group by, and so on.

DROPPING TABLES FOR SPACE

It is always a good idea to drop the table when it isn't needed anymore. This will free up space in tempdb, which might become critical if your connections live for a long time.

SELECT, INSERT, UPDATE, and DELETE

These four basic statements enable us to retrieve and modify data in our tables. SELECT retrieves data from one or more tables, INSERT inserts rows into one table, UPDATE modifies rows in one table, and DELETE removes rows from one table.

You could easily fill a book with examples and explanations for these statements. This section covers the major parts of the syntax and shows some simple examples.

The SELECT Statement

The SELECT statement has the following basic syntax:

```
SELECT column1[, column2, ...]
 FROM table1[, table2, ...]
 WHERE search_conditions
```

You want to return all author's first and last names, living in Utah, from the authors table. You also want to rename the column heading in our result.

```
SELECT au_lname AS 'First', au_fname AS 'Last'
  FROM authors
 WHERE STATE = 'UT'
```

By default, SQL Server returns all rows that meet our search conditions. By specifying SELECT DISTINCT, duplicates are removed.

The column(s) that you base your search condition on don't have to be returned in the resultset. You can filter rows in several ways with the WHERE clause. The following predicates are available for the WHERE clause:

Operators: =, <> (not equals), <, >, >=, >=.

BETWEEN *expression1* AND *expression2*. Between is inclusive.

IN(*element1, element2, ...*). Returns all rows with values that are equal to the elements specified in the list.

LIKE *string_expression*. Used for pattern matching. Table F.2 lists the available wildcard characters.

TABLE F.2   WILDCARDS AND LIKE

Wildcard	Meaning
%	Any number of characters
_	Any single character
[]	Any character listed in the bracket

Logical OR and AND are used to connect multiple search arguments.

The ORDER BY clause sorts the resultset by the specified column or columns. Ascending sorting is default, ORDER BY column_name DESC can be used to specify descending ordering. You should always specify ORDER BY if you expect a certain order for your data. Rows in a table constitute a set, and a set isn't ordered.

Listing F.2 shows an example that exemplifies some of the clauses described.

LISTING F.2   USING WHERE AND ORDER BY

```
1 SELECT au_lname, au_fname, state
2   FROM authors
3  WHERE state IN('CA', 'KS')
4    AND au_lname LIKE 'S%'
5 ORDER BY au_lname
```

The TOP keyword can be used to restrict the number of rows returned. In Listing F.3, you want to retrieve the title and price for the five most expensive books.

LISTING F.3 USING TOP TO RESTRICT THE NUMBER OF ROWS RETURNED

```
1 SELECT TOP 5 price, title
2 FROM titles
3 ORDER BY price DESC
4 price               title
5 -------------------------------------------------------------
6 22.9500             But Is It User Friendly?
7 21.5900             Computer Phobic AND Non-Phobic Indi...
8 20.9500             Onions, Leeks, and Garlic: Cooking ...
9 20.0000             Secrets of Silicon Valley
10 19.9900            The Busy Executive's Database Guide
```

You can add WITH TIES, which might produce more than the requested rows. There are several books with the price of $19.99. In Listing F.4, add WITH TIES so all those books are returned.

LISTING F.4 USING TOP WITH TIES

```
1 SELECT TOP 5 WITH TIES price, title
2 FROM titles
3 ORDER BY price DESC
4 price               title
5 -------------------------------------------------------------
6 22.9500             But Is It User Friendly?
7 21.5900             Computer Phobic AND Non-Phobic Indi...
8 20.9500             Onions, Leeks, and Garlic: Cooking ...
9 20.0000             Secrets of Silicon Valley
10 19.9900            The Busy Executive's Database Guide
11 19.9900            Straight Talk About Computers
12 19.9900            Silicon Valley Gastronomic Treats
13 19.9900            Prolonged Data Deprivation: Four Ca...
```

REPLACING ROWCOUNT

The TOP keyword is new to version 7.0. To get the same functionality, SET ROWCOUNT *n* was often used in previous versions. TOP is used by the optimizer, though, so it will often result in better performance than using ROWCOUNT.

If you don't use ORDER BY with TOP, the actual rows returned will be chosen arbitrarily, based on the execution plan chosen by the optimizer. You can also specify TOP n PERCENT to restrict the number of rows based on a percentage value instead of an absolute value.

You can store the resultset in a table instead of retrieving it with the use of SELECT column(s) INTO table_name. The table specified will be created with the same structure as the resultset. A temporary table is created in tempdb if you precede the table name with one or two hash signs. If you want to create a permanent table with SELECT...INTO, you must set the database option select into/bulkcopy to TRUE.

With the UNION keyword, a logical union between two or more resultsets is returned. This query returns the city and state of each author and publisher as a single resultset:

```
SELECT city, state FROM authors
UNION ALL
SELECT city, state FROM publishers
```

By default, SQL Server removes all duplicates. You can add the keyword ALL if you don't want duplicates to be removed.

GROUP BY and HAVING

GROUP BY and HAVING are used with aggregated functions (which are described in the functions section of this chapter). GROUP BY enables us to calculate aggregates for groups within our tables. The following example calculates the average price for each book category in the titles table:

```
SELECT type, AVG(price)
FROM titles
GROUP BY type
```

```
business        13.7300
mod_cook        11.4900
popular_comp  21.4750
psychology      13.5040
trad_cook       15.9633
UNDECIDED       NULL
```

If a WHERE clause is used, it is applied before the grouping takes place. The following query calculates the average price per book category for books published by the publisher with ID 1389:

```
SELECT type, AVG(price)
FROM titles
WHERE pub_id = 1389
GROUP BY type
```

```
business     17.3100
popular_comp 21.4750
```

HAVING enables us to restrict the number of aggregations returned. The clause is applied after the grouping is applied. You want to return the average price for book categories, but only the categories with an average that is higher than $14:

```
SELECT type, AVG(price)
FROM titles
GROUP BY type
HAVING AVG(price) > $14
```

```
popular_comp 21.4750
trad_cook    15.9633
```

CUBE, ROLLUP, and the GROUPING Function

CUBE, ROLLUP, and GROUPING clauses are used in conjunction with GROUP BY.

When you use CUBE, you will get extra rows in the resultset. The extra rows are super aggregates. If you add CUBE to the query that returns the average price for book categories, you will get an extra row with the average price of all books, as shown in Listing F.5.

LISTING F.5   USING CUBE TO CALCULATE SUPER AGGREGATES

```
 1 SELECT type, AVG(price) AS average
 2 FROM titles
 3 GROUP BY type
 4 WITH CUBE
 5
 6 type             average
 7 ---------------------------
 8 business      13.7300
 9 mod_cook      11.4900
10 popular_comp  21.4750
11 psychology    13.5040
12 trad_cook     15.9633
13 UNDECIDED     NULL
14 NULL          14.7662
```

The book type is returned as NULL for the extra row. In Listing F.6, you use the grouping function to present the extra row in a more explicit manner:

LISTING F.6 USING THE GROUPING FUNCTION

```
1 SELECT type, AVG(price) AS average, GROUPING(type) AS
  ➥super
2 FROM titles
3 GROUP BY type
4 WITH CUBE
5
6 type          average                super
7 ------------------------------------------------
8 business      13.7300                0
9 mod_cook      11.4900                0
10 popular_comp 21.4750                 0
11 psychology   13.5040                 0
12 trad_cook    15.9633                 0
13 UNDECIDED    NULL                    0
14 NULL         14.7662                 1
```

The value 1 is returned for each super aggregate presented for the grouped column specified.

CUBE is more useful if you group over several columns. In Listing F.7, you want to return the average price grouped by book type and publisher.

LISTING F.7 GROUPING OVER SEVERAL COLUMNS

```
1 SELECT type, pub_id, AVG(price) AS average
2 FROM titles
3 GROUP BY type, pub_id
4
5 type          pub_id average
6 ------------------------------------------
7 business      0736   2.9900
8 psychology    0736   11.4825
9 mod_cook      0877   11.4900
10 psychology   0877   21.5900
11 trad_cook    0877   15.9633
12 UNDECIDED    0877   NULL
13 business     1389   17.3100
14 popular_comp 1389   21.4750
```

In Listing F.8, you add WITH CUBE. This gives you the total average, the average for each book type, and the average for each publisher.

LISTING F.8   GROUPING OVER SEVERAL COLUMNS WITH CUBE

```
1 SELECT type, pub_id, AVG(price) AS average
2 FROM titles
3 GROUP BY type, pub_id
4 WITH CUBE
5
6 type           pub_id average
7 ---------------------------------------
8 business       0736   2.9900
9 business       1389   17.3100
10 business       NULL   13.7300
11 mod_cook       0877   11.4900
12 mod_cook       NULL   11.4900
13 popular_comp 1389    21.4750
14 popular_comp NULL    21.4750
15 psychology     0736   11.4825
16 psychology     0877   21.5900
17 psychology     NULL   13.5040
18 trad_cook      0877   15.9633
19 trad_cook      NULL   15.9633
20 UNDECIDED      0877   NULL
21 UNDECIDED      NULL   NULL
22 NULL           NULL   14.7662
23 NULL           0736   9.7840
24 NULL           0877   15.4100
25 NULL           1389   18.9760
```

ROLLUP is similar to CUBE, but it produces a subset of the super aggregates. It is sensitive to the position of the column in the GROUP BY clause; it goes from right to left and produces super aggregates along the way. In Listing F.9, super aggregates are calculated for publishers and for all titles, but not for book types.

LISTING F.9   USING THE ROLLUP CLAUSE

```
1 SELECT type, pub_id, AVG(price) AS average
2 FROM titles
3 GROUP BY type, pub_id
4 WITH ROLLUP
5 type           pub_id average
6 ---------------------------------------
7 business       0736   2.9900
8 business       1389   17.3100
9 business       NULL   13.7300
10 mod_cook       0877   11.4900
11 mod_cook       NULL   11.4900
12 popular_comp 1389    21.4750
13 popular_comp NULL    21.4750
```

```
14 psychology    0736    11.4825
15 psychology    0877    21.5900
16 psychology    NULL    13.5040
17 trad_cook     0877    15.9633
18 trad_cook     NULL    15.9633
19 UNDECIDED     0877    NULL
20 UNDECIDED     NULL    NULL
21 NULL          NULL    14.7662
```

Joining Tables

You can also correlate two tables, performing a join. Generally, you "connect" the tables using a common column, which is most often a column for which a FOREIGN KEY - PRIMARY KEY relationship has been specified.

ANSI JOIN SYNTAX

The ANSI-92 join syntax (or ANSI JOIN for short) was introduced in version 6.5, and is now the preferred way of expressing joins.

One advantage with the ANSI JOIN syntax is that the actual join operation performed is easier to read because it is explicitly stated in the FROM clause. You can also assume that Microsoft is more eager to fix problems regarding ANSI JOINs than the older T-SQL join syntax.

There are two ways that you can specify a join:

- Specifying the join condition in the WHERE clause. This is an older way of specifying a join, but it is still supported. Those of you who have been using SQL for a while are probably more familiar to this method.

- Specifying the join condition in the FROM clause. This is compliant to the ANSI-92 standard.

The following example shows both ways of expressing a join. Both statements return the same resultset:

```
SELECT title, qty
 FROM titles t, sales s
 WHERE t.title_id = s.title_id

SELECT title, qty
 FROM titles t INNER JOIN sales s ON t.title_id = s.title_id
```

You also introduced a table alias in the example. You aliased the title table to the name t and sales to s. This is useful when you have to refer to a table in several places in the query; you don't have to type the whole table name each time.

The different types of joins are INNER, OUTER, and CROSS. An INNER join is based on equality between the column values. The OUTER join returns all rows from a controlling table (specified with LEFT OUTER or RIGHT OUTER) even if there is no match from the other table. Columns returned from that other table will have the NULL symbol for the returned rows. A CROSS join returns all possible combinations of rows, also called a *cartesian product*.

SUBQUERY OR JOIN?

You will often find that you can achieve the same result with a subquery or a join. A join is often more efficient that a subquery (with the exception of when you want to remove duplicates, where a subquery with EXISTS is more efficient).

With the ANSI syntax, you specify the join type explicitly in the FROM clause, whereas the join type in the older join syntax is specified in the WHERE clause.

Subqueries

You can use a subquery in place of an expression. Depending on the context, restrictions exist on the subquery. The query might only be allowed to return one column and even one row.

If the subquery only returns one row and one column, it can be used in place of any expression. This example returns all books published by "Binnet & Hardley":

```
SELECT title FROM titles
 WHERE pub_id =
 (SELECT pub_id FROM publishers
  WHERE pub_name = "Binnet & Hardley")
```

An error message is returned if the subquery would have returned several rows.

A subquery must always appear in parentheses.

You can use a subquery that returns one column and several rows with the IN predicate. The following example returns all publishers of business books:

```
SELECT pub_name FROM publishers
 WHERE pub_id IN
```

```
(SELECT pub_id FROM titles
  WHERE type = 'business')
```

A subquery that returns several rows and several columns (in fact, all columns) can be used with the EXISTS keyword. The following example returns the same resultset as the above example:

```
SELECT pub_name FROM publishers p WHERE EXISTS
  (SELECT * FROM titles t
  WHERE p.pub_id = t.pub_id
  AND type = 'business')
```

You return all columns from the subquery. And you don't have a column relationship between the queries. Your relationship is between the tables; the subquery is a *correlated subquery*. The inner query refers to the outer in the WHERE clause (WHERE p.pub_id = t.pub_id). SQL Server executes the inner query for each row in the outer query, testing for a match on pub_id.

Adding Rows with INSERT

You use the INSERT statement to add rows to a table. The following example adds one row to the authors table:

```
INSERT authors (au_id, au_lname, au_fname, phone, contract)
VALUES('123-65-7635', 'Johnson', 'Lisa', '408 342 7845', 1)
```

The number of values in the VALUES list must match the number in the column list. You can omit the column list, but I recommend strongly against it. That INSERT statement is dependent on the column ordering and would break if the table were re-created with another column ordering.

You can also omit columns from the table, but the column must allow NULL, have a default value, be of the timestamp datatype, or have the identity property defined for it.

To insert more than one row, you must use INSERT with a subquery. The following query inserts all authors from California into a table called authors_archive:

```
INSERT authors_archive
  (au_id, au_lname, au_fname, phone, city, state, zip)
SELECT au_id, au_lname, au_fname, phone, city, state, zip
FROM authors WHERE state = 'CA'
```

A useful feature is that you can EXECute any statement as the subquery, as long as it returns a resultset that is compatible with the table. Listing F.10 creates a table to hold information from DBCC SQLPERF(logspace) and inserts the resultset returned by that command into the table.

Listing F.10   Using INSERT with a Subquery That Isn't an Ordinary SELECT
Statement

```
1 CREATE TABLE log_space
2 (cap_date DATETIME DEFAULT GETDATE(),
3  db sysname,
4  log_size FLOAT,
5  space_used FLOAT,
6  status BIT)
7
8 INSERT log_space(db, log_size, space_used, status)
9 EXEC ('DBCC SQLPERF(logspace)')
```

Modifying Rows with UPDATE

The UPDATE statement is straightforward. You specify the table to be updated, and which column(s), new value(s), and rows should be updated. The following statement changes the royalty to 15% and price to $25 for title 1032.

```
UPDATE titles
 SET royalty = 15, price = $25
 WHERE title_id = 'BU1032'
```

If you omit the WHERE clause, all rows will be updated.

Removing Rows with DELETE

To remove rows from a table, use the DELETE statement. To remove the title BU1032:

```
DELETE titles WHERE title_id = 'BU1032'
```

If you omit the WHERE clause, all rows will be removed.

If you really want to remove all rows, it's much more efficient to use the TRUNCATE TABLE statement, which doesn't log each deleted row to the transaction log.

SQL Server Functions

Microsoft has added more then 30 functions in version 7, and this to an already quite large number of functions. Some of the functions are shortcuts to get information that could be retrieved in other ways. For instance, there is a function to get an object ID if you know the object's name, but looking it up in the sysobjects table also does this.

```
USE pubs
SELECT OBJECT_ID('authors')
SELECT id FROM sysobjects WHERE name = 'authors'
```

Other functions are more essential, like some of the mathematical functions (okay, it could be argued that you could calculate the square root, for instance, in T-SQL, but it wouldn't be very efficient).

Most functions have the structure

```
FUNCTION_NAME(parameter1, parameter2, ...)
```

The parameters might be an expression (like a column name), a constant, or a special code (for instance, a formatting code).

SPLITTING COLUMNS

Excessive use of string functions against a column might indicate that the column should be split up to several columns. For example, if you find yourself often parsing out first name and last name from a name column, perhaps you should split up the name into two columns.

A function returns a value. The datatype for the value depends on what function you are using. Let's have a look at available functions, grouped by category:

String Functions

The string functions enable you to perform concatenation, parsing manipulation, and so on of strings.

Table F.3 lists the available string functions. They can be used against any string expression.

TABLE F.3 STRING FUNCTIONS

Function Name	Returns	New in 7.0
ASCII(*char*)	The ASCII code for the leftmost character in *char*.	
CHAR(*int*)	A character for *int* (an ASCII code).	
CHARINDEX(*char_pattern*, *char*, [*int_start*])	Starting location of *char_patthern* within *char*; optionally, starting search at *int_start*.	

continues

TABLE F.3 CONTINUED

Function Name	Returns	New in 7.0
DIFFERENCE(char1, char2)	The difference between the two character expressions. Used for phonetic match.	
LEFT(char, int)	int characters from left of char.	
LEN(char)	Number of characters in char, excluding trailing blanks.	*
LOWER(char)	char in lowercase.	
LTRIM(char)	char without leading spaces.	
NCHAR(int)	The character for a given Unicode value.	*
PATINDEX(char_pattern,	Starting position of char) char_pattern in char, or 0 if the pattern is not found.	
REPLACE(char1, char2, char3)	Replaces all occurrences of char2 with char3 in char1.	*
QUOTENAME(char, [char_quote])	char as a valid quoted identifier. Adds the characters [and] (default, can be changed to ' or ", specified as char_quote) at beginning and end of char. Returns a Unicode string.	*
REPLICATE(char, int)	Repeats char, int times.	
REVERSE(char)	Reverses char.	
RIGHT(char, int)	int characters from right of char.	
RTRIM(char)	char without trailing spaces.	
SOUNDEX(char)	A four-character string, used for comparison of phonetic match.	
SPACE(int)	A string of int spaces.	
STR(float, [length, [decimal]])	float as a character string, with length of length and decimal numbers of decimals. Default length is 10 and default number of decimals is 0.	
STUFF(char1, start, length, char2)	Replaces length of characters from char1 with char2, starting at start.	

Function Name	Returns	New in 7.0
SUBSTRING(*char*, *start*, *length*)	Returns *length* number of characters from *char*, from *start* position.	
UNICODE(*char*)	Returns the Unicode code for the leftmost character in *char*.	*
UPPER(*char*)	Returns *char* in uppercase.	

The operator + can be used to concatenate strings.

The following example uses SUBSTRING and string concatenation to present each author's first letter in the first name and then the last name.

```
SELECT SUBSTRING(au_fname,1,1) + '. ' + au_lname FROM authors
```

Mathematical Functions

The mathematical functions listed in Table F.4 perform calculations based on the input values and return a numeric value. There are no new mathematical functions introduced in version 7.

TABLE F.4   MATHEMATICAL FUNCTIONS

Function Name	Returns
ABS(*numeric*)	The absolute (positive) value of *numeric*.
ACOS(*float*)	The arc cosine for *float*.
ASIN(float)	The arc sine for *float*.
ATAN(*float*)	The arc tangent for *float*.
ATAN2(*float1*, *float2*)	Returns the arc tangent whose tangent is between *float1* and *float2*.
CEILING(*numeric*)	The smallest integer value, which is higher than or equal *numeric*.
COS(*float*)	The trigonometric cosine of *float*.
COT(*float*)	The trigonometric cotangent of *float*.
DEGREES(*numeric*)	The number of degrees for a given angle, *numeric*, given in radians.
EXP(*float*)	The exponential value of *float*.
FLOOR(*numeric*)	The largest integer value, which is lower than or equal *numeric*.

continues

TABLE F.4   CONTINUED

Function Name	Returns
LOG(*float*)	The natural logarithm of *float*.
LOG10(float)	The base-10 logarithm of *float*.
PI()	The constant pi.
POWER(*numeric1, numeric2*)	The value of *numeric1* to the specified power, given in *numeric2*.
RADIANS(*numeric*)	Radians of *numeric*, given in degrees.
RAND([seed])	A random value between 0 and 1. Seed can be specified as the starting value.
ROUND(*numeric, length, func*)	Rounds the specified *numeric* to specified *length*. If *func* is specified and not 0, *numeric* is truncated to *length*.
SIGN(*numeric*)	1 if *numeric* is positive, 0 if *numeric* is 0 and –1 if *numeric* is negative.
SIN(*float*)	The trigonometric sine of *float*.
SQUARE(*float*)	The square of *float*.
SQRT(*float*)	The square root of *float*.
TAN(*float*)	The trigonometric tangent of *float*.

The operators +, -, *, /, and %(modulo) are also available for numeric expressions.

Date Functions

The date functions perform operations such as formatting and subtraction. The expression given is of a datetime datatype.

Some of the functions take a *datepart* as an argument. The *datepart* specifies what part of our datetime datatype you want to operate on. Table F.5 shows the elements of datepart that you can specify.

TABLE F.5   AVAILABLE CODES FOR DATEPART

Datepart	Abbreviation	Possible Values
year	yy	1753–9999
quarter	qq	1–4
month	mm	1–12
day of year	dy	1–366

Datepart	Abbreviation	Possible Values
day	dd	1–31
week	wk	1–53
weekday	dw	1–7
hour	hh	0–23
minute	mi	0–59
second	ss	0–59
millisecond	ms	0–999

The date- and time-related functions are listed in Table F.6.

TABLE F.6 DATE- AND TIME-RELATED FUNCTIONS

Function Name	Returns	New in 7.0
DATEADD(*datepart*, *int*, *date*)	Adds *int dateparts* to date.	
DATEDIFF(*datepart*, *date1*, *date2*)	The number of *dateparts* between *date1* and *date2*.	
DATENAME(*datepart*, *date*)	A character string with the *datepart* name of *date*.	
DATEPART(*datepart*, *date*)	The *datepart* of *date*.	
GETDATE()	The current date and time.	
DAY(*date*)	The day-of-month part as an integer.	*
MONTH(*date*)	The month as an integer.	*
YEAR(*date*)	The year as an integer.	*

The operators + and – can be used directly on datetime expressions in version 7.0. The implied datepart is days. Here is an example where you use the + operator to add one day to the current date.

```
SELECT GETDATE(), GETDATE() + 1

1998-03-28 16:08:33    1998-03-29 16:08:33
```

USING SYSTEM FUNCTION

It is better to use the system functions than directly query the system tables. If the system tables change in forthcoming releases of SQL Server (as they did with version 7.0), your applications and scripts will still work if you use the system functions. You can also use a new set of views in SQL Server 7 for retrieving system table–related information. The views are independent of the system tables and all have the object owner INFORMATION_SCHEMA.

System Functions

The system functions (shown in Table F.7) are useful for retrieving information such as column names, table names, and so on. Basically, many of them are shortcuts for querying the system tables.

TABLE F.7 SYSTEM FUNCTIONS

Function Name	Returns	New in 7.0
CAST(*expression* AS *datatype*)	The cast function is a synonym for the CONVERT function and converts *expression* to *datatype*.	*
COALESCE(*expr1*, [*expr2*,,,])	The first non-null expression.	
COL_LENGTH(*table*, *column*)	The length of *column* in *table*.	
COL_NAME(*table_id*, *column_id*)	The name of *column_id* in *table_id*.	
COLUMNPROPERTY(*id*, *column*, *property*)	Information about a *column* in a table, given the *id*. Or returns information for a parameter, given in *column*, for a stored procedure. The *property* parameter defines the type of information to be returned.	*
CONVERT(*datatype[(length)]*, *expression*, *style*)	Converts *expression* to *datatype*. For conversion of datetime or float expression, style defines formatting (see below).	

Function Name	Returns	New in 7.0
CURSOR_STATUS(*local*, *cursor_name* ¦ *global*, a*cursor_name* ¦ *variable*, *cursor_name*)	A code to the caller of stored procedure that indicates whether the procedure has returned a cursor and if the resultset contains any rows.	*
DATABASEPROPERTY (*database_name*, *property*)	Information, defined in *property*, for *database_name*.	*
DATALENGTH(*expression*)	The storage area of *expression*, including trailing blanks for character information.	
DB_ID([*db_name*])	The database id of *db_name* or the current database.	
DB_NAME([*db_id*])	The database name of *db_id* or the name of the current database.	
GETANSINULL([*db_name*])	The default nullability of *db_name* for the current database.	
GETCHECKSUM(*col_name*)	A checksum value for the values in *col_name*.	*
HOST_ID()	The process id of the client applications process.	
HOST_NAME()	The client's workstation name.	
IDENT_INCR(*table*)	The identity increment for the identity column in *table*.	
IDENT_SEED(*table*)	The identity seed for the identity column in *table*.	
INDEX_COL(*table*, *index_id*, *key_id*)	The column name for the specified *table*, *index_id*, and *key_id*.	
IS_MEMBER(*group* ¦ *role*]	1 if user is member of specified NT *group* or SQL Server *role*; otherwise 0.	*

continues

TABLE F.7 CONTINUED

Function Name	Returns	New in 7.0
IS_SRVROLEMEMBER role [, *login*])	1 if users login id is member of specified server *role*; otherwise 0. An explicit *login* name can be specified.	*
ISDATE(*char*)	1 if *char* is in a valid datetime format; otherwise 0.	
FILE_ID(*filename*)	The id for *filename*.	*
FILE_NAME(*file_id*)	The filename for *file_id*.	*
FILEGROUP_ID(*filegroupname*)	The id for *filegroupname*.	*
FILEGROUP_NAME(*filegroup_id*)	The filegroup name for *filegroup_id*.	*
ISNULL(*expression*, *value*)	*value* if *expression* is NULL.	
ISNUMERIC(*char*)	1 if *char* can be converted to a numeric value; otherwise 0.	
NEWID()	A generated global unique identifier.	*
NULLIF(*expr1*, *expr2*)	Null if *expr2* equals *expr2*.	
OBJECT_ID(*object_name*)	The ID for *object_name*.	
OBJECTPROPERTY(*object_id*, *property*)	Information of *object_id*. *property* defines type of information to be returned.	*
PARSENAME(*object_name*, *object_part*) *object_part* of *object_name*.		*
PERMISSIONS(*object_id*[, *column*])	A bitmap indicating permissions on *object_id* and optionally *column*.	*
STATS_DATE(*table_id*, *index_id*)	Date when the distribution page was updated for *index_id* on *table_id*.	
SUSER_ID(*login_name*)	The loginid of specified *login_name*. Included for backward compatibility, use SUSER_SID instead.	

Function Name	Returns	New in 7.0
SUSER_NAME([*login_id*])	The login name of *login_id*. Included for backward compatibility, use SUSER_NAME instead.	
SUSER_SID([*login*])	Security identification number (SID) for *login*.	*
SUSER_SNAME([*login_id*])	The login name of *login_id*.	*
TRIGGER_NESTLEVEL([*tr_object_id*])	Nesting level of specified or current trigger.	*
TYPEPROPERTY(*data_type*, property)	Information, defined in *property*, for *data_type*.	*
USER_ID([*user_name*])	The user id for *user_name*.	
USER_NAME([*user_id*])	The username for *user_id*.	

The following example returns the title ID and price for all books. If the price isn't set (NULL), you return a price of 0:

```
SELECT title_id, ISNULL(price, 0) FROM titles
```

NILADIC FUNCTIONS AS ALIASES

These are basically aliases to SQL Server system functions. If you use them for default values in tables and run sp_help for the table, edit the table, or script the table in Enterprise Manager, you will notice that they have been translated to the corresponding system function.

Let us expand the example a little bit. You want to display a string, 'Not Priced' for those who have NULL. You have to convert the price to a character value before replacing NULL with our text string:

```
SELECT title_id, ISNULL(CONVERT(CHAR(10),price),
➥'Not Priced') FROM titles
```

Niladic Functions

This group of functions is basically a set of system functions. The reason for grouping them separately is that they are used without parentheses after the function name. They are defined in the ANSI SQL-92 standard and shown in Table F.8.

You often find niladic functions used as defaults in CREATE TABLE and ALTER TABLE.

TABLE F.8   NILADIC FUNCTIONS

Function Name	Returns	Corresponding System Function
CURRENT_TIMESTAMP	Current date and time	GETDATE()
CURRENT_USER	The user's username	USER_NAME()
SESSION_USER	The user's username	USER_NAME()
SYSTEM_USER	The user's login name	SUSER_NAME()
USER	The user's username	USER_NAME()

In Listing F.11, you create a table with three columns, with defaults for the current date-time, the user's login name, and the username. The INSERT statement inserts default values for all columns and the SELECT statements retrieve the row inserted.

LISTING F.11   USING NILADIC FUNCTIONS WITH THE INSERT STATEMENT

```
 1 CREATE TABLE my_defaults
 2 (the_datetime DATETIME DEFAULT CURRENT_TIMESTAMP,
 3 users_login CHAR(20) DEFAULT SYSTEM_USER,
 4 users_name CHAR(20) DEFAULT CURRENT_USER,)
 5
 6 INSERT my_defaults DEFAULT VALUES
 7
 8 SELECT * FROM my_defaults
 9
10 1998-03-29 19:09:52.377      sa                      dbo
```

Aggregate Functions

The aggregate functions differ from the other groups. Aggregate functions perform an aggregation for a column over a set of rows.

Table F.9 lists the aggregate functions available in SQL Server.

TABLE F.9   AGGREGATE FUNCTIONS

Function Name	*Returns*	*New in 7.0*
AVG([ALL ¦ DISTINCT] *expression*)	The average of all values given in *expression*.	
COUNT([ALL ¦ DISTINCT] *expression* ¦ *)	The number of non-NULL values in *expression*. NULL are counted if * is specified.	
MAX([ALL ¦ DISTINCT] *expression*)	The maximum value in *expression*.	
VARP(*expression*)	The statistical variance for the population for all values in the given *expression*.	*
STDEVP(*expression*)	The statistical standard deviation for the population for all values in the given *expression*.	*
MIN([ALL ¦ DISTINCT] *expression*)	The minimum value in *expression*.	
SUM([ALL ¦ DISTINCT] *expression*)	The sum of all values in *expression*.	
VAR(*expression*)	The statistical variance of all values in the given *expression*.	*
STDEV(*expression*)	The statistical standard deviation of all values in the given *expression*.	*

By adding the keyword DISTINCT, only distinct values will be aggregated. The default is ALL. You should note that NULL values aren't included in the aggregates. The one exception to that is COUNT(*), which counts the number of rows returned from the relational expression.

Say that you want to count the number of rows, prices, and distinct prices in the title table:

```
SELECT COUNT(*) AS Total, COUNT(price) AS Prices,
➥ COUNT(DISTINCT price) AS "Distinct prices"
 FROM titles
```

```
Total       Prices      Distinct prices
18          16          11
```

Apparently, two books aren't priced yet or you don't know the price (NULL), and you have a total of 5 duplicate prices.

Now you want to perform some real aggregation over the prices:

```
SELECT MAX(price) AS 'Max', MIN(price) AS 'Min', AVG(price)
➥ AS 'Average' FROM titles
```

```
Max                 Min                 Average
22.9500             2.9900              14.7662
```

Note that even though NULL usually counts low, the minimum price is $2.99 because NULL is excluded from the aggregate.

Aggregate functions are often used in conjunction with GROUP BY. The following example retrieves the average price for each book category:

```
SELECT type, AVG(price) AS Average
 FROM titles
 GROUP BY type
```

```
type          Average
business      13.7300
mod_cook      11.4900
popular_comp  21.4750
psychology    13.5040
trad_cook     15.9633
UNDECIDED     NULL
```

Programming Constructs

The languages that interface with Database Management Systems are sometimes divided into three categories:

- DML (Data Manipulation). This includes the ability to read and manipulate the data, for instance, SELECT, INSERT, DELETE, and UPDATE.
- DDL (Data Definition Language). Creating and altering the storage structures like CREATE TABLE.
- DCL (Data Control Language). Defining permissions for data access, for instance, GRANT, REVOKE, and DENY.

T-SQL includes other statements that can be useful, for instance, to "tie together" the DML statements in a stored procedure.

The IF Statement

The IF statement uses the following syntax:

```
IF boolean_expression
    statement_block
ELSE
    statement_block
```

The IF statement takes one argument: boolean_expression, which is an expression that can evaluate to TRUE or FALSE. The code to be conditionally executed is a statement block. You define a statement block with the statements BEGIN and END. In Listing F.12, you have a script that checks for the existence of a table, prints a message if the table exists and, if so, drops the table.

LISTING F.12   USING THE IF STATEMENT TO PERFORM CONDITIONAL PROCESSING

```
1 IF OBJECTPROPERTY(OBJECT_ID('orders'), 'istable') = 1
2 BEGIN
3   PRINT "Dropping orders Table"
4   DROP TABLE orders
5 END
6 ELSE
7   PRINT "Table orders does not exist"
```

WHILE, BREAK, and CONTINUE

The WHILE statement enables you to loop while an expression evaluates to true. The syntax for WHILE is

```
WHILE boolean_expression
statement_block
BREAK
statement_block
CONTINUE
```

BREAK exits the WHILE loop and CONTINUE stops unconditionally and evaluates the boolean_expression again.

RETURN

RETURN is used to stop execution of the batch and thus, the stored procedure and trigger. When used in a stored procedure, RETURN can take an integer as an argument. The value zero indicates successful execution. Microsoft reserves the values –1 to –99 (currently –1 to –14 are in use), so you should use values outside that range.

GOTO

GOTO (yes, there is a goto statement in T-SQL) branches to a defined label. GOTO can be useful for error handling in stored procedures, for example. In Listing F.13, you have a fragment of a stored procedure where you check for errors after each statement and exit the procedure with a return code if an error occurred.

LISTING F.13 USE OF GOTO AND RETURN

```
1 BEGIN TRAN
2 INSERT orders(customer_number) VALUES(1)
3  IF @@ERROR <> 0 GOTO err_handle
4 RETURN 0
5 ...
6 err_handle:
7 RAISERROR ('An error occured in the stored procedure.
  ➥ The transaction has been rolled back', 12, 1)
8 ROLLBACK TRANSACTION
9 RETURN -101
```

WAITFOR

You can use WAITFOR to halt execution for a specified delay (WAITFOR DELAY) or until a specified time (WAITFOR TIME). In the following example, you want to generate a deadlock (for instance you might have defined an alert for the deadlock error and want to test it). You must be able to start execution of both batches more or less simultaneously for the deadlock to occur, so introduce a wait for 10 seconds.

Execute the two code blocks in Listing F.14 from two separate windows (connections) in the Query Analyzer.

LISTING F.14 USING WAITFOR TO INTRODUCE A DELAY OF 10 SECONDS

```
1 --Execute from one connection
2 BEGIN TRAN
3 UPDATE authors SET au_lname = au_lname
4 WAITFOR DELAY '00:00:10'
5 UPDATE titles SET title = title
6 ROLLBACK TRAN
7
8 --Execute from another connection
9 BEGIN TRAN
10 UPDATE titles SET title = title
11 UPDATE authors SET au_lname = au_lname
12 ROLLBACK TRAN
```

> **WORKAROUND FOR CHARACTER LIMITATIONS**
>
> If the string you want to execute is longer than 8000 characters (or 4000 if you use Unicode), you can concatenate the contents of two or more variables in the EXECUTE command:
>
> EXEC(@var1 + var2)
>
> This is a more useful trick if you are running version 6.x because the maximum length of a CHAR or VARCHAR is 255 characters on version 6 and previous versions.

EXECute

The EXEC (or EXECute) command is used as a keyword for executing stored procedures. Introduced in version 6, you also were given the ability to execute strings and variables containing strings. This can be very useful.

You want to perform UPDATE STATISTICS for all tables in the database. The UPDATE STATISTICS command doesn't accept a variable as its parameter. So you build the command in a variable and execute the contents of the variable:

```
DECLARE @tbl_name NVARCHAR(128)
SELECT @tbl_name = 'authors'
EXEC('UPDATE STATISTICS ' + @tbl_name)
```

This is powerful in conjunction with cursors, which you will have a look at further on.

Another example is if you want to write a stored procedure that will SELECT rows from a table name passed to it as an argument.

The following syntax will produce an error message:

```
SELECT * FROM @tbl_name
```

because SQL Server doesn't accept variables for table names, column names, and so on:

```
CREATE PROC general_select @tbl_name NVARCHAR(128) AS
 EXEC('SELECT * FROM ' + @tbl_name)
GO
EXEC general_select authors
```

Batches

A *batch* is quite simply a set of commands sent to SQL Server for execution. The batch term as used here is not to be confused with traditional batch processing, where mass modifications are being performed, often at low-activity periods.

Basically, SQL Server receives a string (hopefully containing T-SQL commands) from the client application. SQL Server parses this string as a unit, searching for keywords. If a syntax error is found, none of the statements in the batch are executed, and an error message is returned to the client application.

Avoid mixing T-SQL text on the same line as the GO command. You can do it if GO is the first command on the line, but the text is easier to read if GO is on its own row. If you have any other text before GO, the string "GO" is sent to SQL Server for parsing, and is not used to separate batches. This generally leads to syntax error.

In the Query Analyzer, ISQL, and OSQL, the string GO is used to separate batches. When the tool finds the string GO, it takes all text up to the previous GO and submits it to SQL Server for execution.

There are restrictions for batches, such as what commands can be combined with other commands within a batch. Some examples are

- You cannot combine any command within a batch. Most CREATE commands have to be executed in a single batch. The exceptions are CREATE TABLE, CREATE INDEX, and CREATE DATABASE.

- When calling a stored procedure, you must precede the procedure name with EXECute, if it's not the first string in a batch. If SQL Server doesn't recognize the first string in a batch, it quite simply assumes that it's a call to a stored procedure.

A related concept is the script. A *script* is quite simply a text file containing one or more batches. Scripts are often used with the Query Analyzer, ISQL, and OSQL. GO doesn't have to be specified after the last command in a script file; the tools will automatically generate an end of batch signal.

Listing F.15 creates a table and then a view. Note that the CREATE commands have been separated with GO.

LISTING F.15 CREATE A TABLE AND A VIEW THAT ONLY DISPLAY RECENT ORDERS

```
1 CREATE TABLE orders
2 (order_number UNIQUEIDENTIFIER DEFAULT NEWID()
  ➥ PRIMARY KEY NOT NULL,
3 customer_number INT REFERENCES
  ➥ customers(customer_number),
4 order_date DATETIME DEFAULT CONVERT(CHAR(8),
  ➥ GETDATE(), 112))
5 GO
6 CREATE VIEW recent_orders AS
7 SELECT order_number, customer_number, order_date
8 FROM orders
9 WHERE order_date > GETDATE() - 14
```

Comments

Everyone who has to review or change code knows the importance of comments. Even if it feels obvious during writing what the code does, it certainly won't be that obvious at a later time.

When SQL Server finds a comment, it doesn't execute anything until the end of the comment. The Query Analyzers syntax coloring indicates commented text with a green color by default. SQL Server supports two types of comment markers:

```
/* Comments */
```

These comment markers are useful when commenting several lines. None of the text between the comment markers is parsed, compiled, or executed.

```
-- Comments
```

SQL Server won't execute the text following the markers until end of the line. The -- comment markers are defined in ANSI SQL-92.

Both types of comments can be nested within a /*...*/ comment block. The end of batch (GO) separator can't be specified within a /*...*/ comment block.

Here is an example of a batch with a comment block first that describes what the batch performs and with a comment block further down that can be removed for debugging purposes.

```
/* Retrieves all orders that have been submitted the last
/* day.
The SELECT COUNT is only for debugging purposes */
SELECT order_number, customer_number, order_date
 FROM orders
 WHERE order_date > GETDATE() -1
--SELECT 'Number of orders returned':, @@ROWCOUNT
```

Local Variables

Local variables enable you to store values temporarily. The variable is always declared as a certain datatype. The datatype can either be system supplied or user-defined. The variable's name always begins with the @ sign and it is declared with the DECLARE statement.

The variable is assigned a value with the SELECT statement, or (new in version 7.0) the SET statement.

Listing F.16 prints out the number of distinct book types in the titles table. First you declare a local variable, then you assign it a value, and finally you print the contents of the variable.

LISTING F.16   ASSIGNING A VALUE TO A LOCAL VARIABLE AND PRINTING THE CONTENTS OF THAT VARIABLE

```
1 DECLARE @user_msg VARCHAR(255)
2 SELECT @user_msg = 'There are ' + CONVERT(VARCHAR(3),
3 (SELECT COUNT(DISTINCT type) FROM titles))
    ➥ + ' book types in the titles table.'
4 PRINT @user_msg
5
6 There are 6 book types in the titles table.
```

BATCHES AND VARIABLE LIFE SPAN

The life span of a local variable is a batch. After the batch has processed, the variable ceases to exist.

If you want to store a value to live between batches in T-SQL, you have to create a (temporary) table to store the value in.

Local variables are often used in stored procedures.

Functions That Were Called Global Variables in Earlier Releases

This set of functions was called Global Variables in earlier releases of SQL Server. The name Global was quite confusing because it implies that the scope of the variable is longer than a local variable. They were often mistaken for variables that a user can declare and that live across batches, which isn't the case. You can name a variable starting with two at signs (@@), but it will still behave just as a local variable.

These functions contain information that is maintained by SQL Server. They exist so that an application can check things like the error code for the last executed command, and so on. The functions are very useful because some of them contain information that cannot be found elsewhere, or would be hard to obtain with other means.

For *connection-specific* functions (see Table F.10), SQL Server maintains separate values for each connection.

TABLE F.10 CONNECTION-SPECIFIC FUNCTIONS

Variable Name	Description
@@CURSOR_ROWS	Number of rows populated in the last opened cursor.
@@DATEFIRST	Indicates the first day of week (7 is Sunday, 1 is Monday, and so on).
@@ERROR	The error number generated by the last executed command. This is very valuable for error checking in stored procedures, batches, and triggers.
@@FETCH_STATUS	Indicates whether a fetch operation from a cursor was successful or not.
@@IDENTITY	The identity value generated by the last insert statement. The @@IDENTITY value isn't affected by other connection inserts.
@@LOCK_TIMEOUT	The locking timeout value, in milliseconds.
@@LANGID	The connections language ID in use.
@@LANGUAGE	The connections language in use, acharacter string.
@@NESTLEVEL	The nesting level for stored procedures and triggers.
@@PROCID	The ID of the currently executing stored procedure.
@@ROWCOUNT	The number of rows affected (modified or read) by the last command.
@@SPID	The connection ID.
@@TEXTSIZE	The maximum number of bytes returned by a SELECT statement when reading text and image data. Note that this can be further limited by the client application.
@@TRANCOUNT	The transaction nesting level.
@@ERROR	Useful for error handling in stored procedures and triggers. In the Listing F.17, you check @@ERROR after each statement and branch into an error handling routine if an error occurred.

LISTING F.17 THE USE OF THE @@ERROR FUNCTION TO CHECK FOR ERRORS

```
1 BEGIN TRAN
2 INSERT orders(customer_number) VALUES(1)
3  IF @@ERROR <> 0 GOTO err_handle
4 RETURN 0
5 ...
6 err_handle:
7 RAISERROR ('An error occured in the stored procedure.
   ➥ The transaction has been rolled back', 12, 1)
8 ROLLBACK TRANSACTION
9 RETURN ñ101
```

In Listing F.18, you need to find out the identity value generated by our last insert, so you use the @@IDENTITY function. Note that you need to save the value returned from @@IDENTITY into a local variable if you need it after the next INSERT statement. All INSERT statements update @@IDENTITY, even those that insert into a table without an identity column. You don't have to worry about other connections inserts because @@IDENTITY is maintained per connection.

LISTING F.18   USING THE @@IDENTITY FUNCTION TO GET THE LATEST GENERATED IDENTITY VALUE

```
 1 CREATE TABLE customers
 2 (customer_id INT IDENTITY PRIMARY KEY NOT NULL,
 3 customer_name NVARCHAR(100) NOT NULL,
 4 customer_comments NVARCHAR(1000) NULL)
 5
 6 CREATE TABLE orders
 7 (order_number UNIQUEIDENTIFIER DEFAULT NEWID() PRIMARY
     ➥ KEY NOT NULL,
 8 customer_number INT REFERENCES customers(customer_id),
 9 order_date DATETIME DEFAULT CONVERT(CHAR(8),
     ➥ GETDATE(), 112))
10 GO
11
12 DECLARE @cust_id INT
13 INSERT customers (customer_name, customer_comments)
14 VALUES ("Hardware Suppliers AB", "Stephanie is contact.")
15 SELECT @cust_id = @@IDENTITY
16 INSERT orders (customer_number)
17 VALUES (@cust_id)
```

The monitoring-related functions are mostly listed here in Table F.11 for completeness. Typically, DBCC SQLPERF and SQL Performance Monitor gives similar information in a more useful fashion.

TABLE F.11   MONITORING-RELATED GLOBAL VARIABLES

Variable Name	Description
@@CONNECTIONS	The number of login attempts since the last restart of SQL Server.
@@CPU_BUSY	The number of time-ticks (currently 1/100 second) that the machine's CPU has been doing SQL Server work since the last restart of SQL Server.
@@IDLE	The number of time-ticks (currently 1/100 second) that the machine's SQL Server has been idle since the last restart of SQL Server.

Variable Name	Description
@@IO_BUSY	The number of time-ticks (currently 1/100 second) that SQL Server has been doing I/O operations since the last restart of SQL Server.
@@PACK_RECEIVED	The number of packets received by SQL Server since the last restart of SQL Server.
@@PACK_SENT	The number of packets sent by SQL Server since the last restart of SQL Server.
@@PACKET_ERRORS	The number of times that an error occurred while sending a packet since the last restart of SQL Server.
@@TOTAL_ERRORS	The number of times that an error occurred while reading or writing since the last restart of SQL Server.
@@TOTAL_READ	The total number of physical reads since the last restart of SQL Server.
@@TOTAL_WRITE	The total number of physical writes since the last restart of SQL Server.

The *general* functions (see Table F.12) are mostly useful for administration purposes. The most useful one is @@VERSION, which returns the version number, including the service pack level.

TABLE F.12   GENERAL GLOBAL VARIABLES

Variable Name	Description
@@DBTS	The current timestamp for the database.
@@MAX_CONNECTIONS	The maximum number of user connections that the installation can support. @@MAX_CONNECTIONS doesn't reflect the currently configured value of user connections.
@@MAX_PRECISION	The maximum precision value for decimal and numeric datatypes.
@@MICROSOFTVERSION	A Microsoft internal version number. This shouldn't be used for version checking and handling. Use @@VERSION instead.
@@SERVERNAME	The name of the SQL Server. This should match the machine name; if it doesn't, you might want to drop the old (wrong) name with sp_dropserver and add the new (correct) name with sp_addserver.

continues

TABLE F.12   CONTINUED

Variable Name	Description
@@SERVICENAME	The name of the service that executes SQL Server. This should be MSSQLServer if the service name isn't changed.
@@TIMETICKS	The number of microseconds per time-tick.
@@VERSION	The SQL Server version number.

Listing F.19 shows how you can use @@VERSION to check the version number of the SQL Server.

LISTING F.19   USING THE @@VERSION FUNCTION TO DETERMINE THE VERSION OF SQL SERVER

```
1 SELECT @@VERSION
2
3 SELECT
4 SUBSTRING(@@VERSION, (CHARINDEX('Server   ',
    ➥ @@VERSION) + 8), 1) AS Major,
5 SUBSTRING(@@VERSION, (CHARINDEX('Server   ',
    ➥ @@VERSION) + 10), 2) As Minor,
   SUBSTRING(@@VERSION, (CHARINDEX('Server   ',
    ➥ @@VERSION) + 20), 3) AS 'Service Pack'
6
7
8 Microsoft SQL Server  7.00 - 7.00.390 (Intel X86)
9 Dec 13 1997 03:16:48
10 Copyright  1988-1997 Microsoft Corporation
11
12 Major Minor Service Pack
13 7     00     390
```

RAISERROR

The RAISERROR command originates from the Db-Library programming API. A Db-Library application registers two callback functions. SQL Server executes a callback function when it sends a message or an error message to the client.

The *message handler* is called when messages are sent from SQL Server to the clients, such as messages generated from the PRINT command.

The *error handler* is called from SQL Server when an error occurs. You can generate an error message with the RAISERROR command.

An ODBC application cannot register callback functions, so a program can check for these messages and errors by the use of function calls. The same applies for OLE-DB applications, which can retrieve message and error information through the SQLOLEDB interfaces.

Managing SQL Server Errors

Most error messages are stored in the sysmessages table in the master database. An error message consists of the error number, a severity level, and a description. Table F.13 shows the details available in the sysmessages table.

TABLE F.13   COLUMNS IN THE sysmessages TABLE

Column Name	Description
Error	The error number. Every error message has a unique error number.
Severity	The severity level. Higher severity level (generally) indicates a more severe problem. SQL Server will terminate the connection and perform a rollback (if a transaction vas started) for severity levels over 19.
Description	The message string with placeholders.

Some error messages are stored in the sysservermessages table in the msdb database. Some of these are informational messages. One example of these messages is the message written to NT's Event log for each backup that SQL Server performs. The messages in the sysservermessages table have severity levels of 110, 120, and 130.

When a message is written to the Eventlog or sent to a client application, it also includes state. The state is an internal value, which can describe the error further. If you report a problem to Microsoft, you might be asked for the state, for example.

Microsoft has done a rough grouping of the severity levels. This isn't as consistent as you might wish it were. This is because the messages have evolved over a long time, and from two companies (Sybase and Microsoft). So take Table F.14 with a grain of salt.

Table F.14 Descriptions of Severity Levels

Severity Level	Description
0–10	Informational messages
11	Object not found
12	Not used
13	Transactional syntax errors
14	Insufficient permissions
15	Syntax errors in SQL
16	Miscellaneous
17	Insufficient resources
18	Internal Errors, non-fatal
19	Resource problems, fatal
20–25	Fatal errors
110	Server information
120	Server warnings
130	Server errors

You can also add your own error messages. This can be useful for centralizing error reporting from your application. Messages can also be managed with the stored procedures sp_addmessages, sp_dropmessage, and sp_altermessage. The error number has to be greater than 50000.

The RAISERROR and PRINT Commands

A message can be generated with the RAISERROR command. This is a good way to communicate that an error has occurred to a client application from triggers and stored procedures. The RAISERROR command has the following syntax:

```
RAISERROR([err_no]¦[err_string], severity, state,
➥ [argument1[, ...]] options
```

If you supply an err_string, the error number will be 50000. If you supply an error number, that error number has to be defined in the sysmessages table. Arguments are used to insert data (table names and so on) into the message string. If you want to use arguments, you have to define the error message with placeholders for the arguments.

The available options are

- LOG. The message will be sent to NT's Eventlog.

- NOWAIT. The message is sent directly to the client. This is useful for long running operations so that the application can display s status indicator, for instance.

- SETERROR. The global variable @@error will be set to 50000, even if severity is lower than 11.

Listing F.20 adds a user-defined message and calls it from T-SQL code.

LISTING F.20 ADDING AN ERROR MESSAGE TO SQL SERVER AND GENERATING THE ERROR

```
1 sp_addmessage 50001, 16, 'The row(s) from table %s could not
➥ be deleted. There are rows in table %s that
➥ refers to this row. Delete those rows first.'
2 RAISERROR (50001, 16, 1, 'Titles', 'Titleauthor')
3 Server: Msg 50001, Level 16, State 42000
4 The row(s) from table Titles could not be deleted.
➥ There are rows in table Titleauthor that
➥ refers to this row. Delete those rows first.
```

One situation where you might find the state parameter useful is if you execute a script using ISQL or OSQL. By executing the RAISERROR with a state of 127, the processing of the script file terminates. Let us say that you have a simple batch file, which executes as follows:

```
ISQL /Usa /P /iMyBatch.SQL /n
```

The script file (MyBatch.SQL) contains the code in Listing F.21.

LISTING F.21 USING STATE 127 TO TERMINATE A BATCH PROCESSED WITH ISQL OR OSQL

```
1 -- Exit if users connected to database.
2 IF (SELECT COUNT(*) FROM master..sysprocesses
3    WHERE dbid = DB_ID('pubs')) > 0
4 RAISERROR ('Cannot proceed with batch, users connected
➥ to database.', 16, 127)
5 GO
6 -- If not, continue with whatever you want to do
7 SELECT au_fname, au_lname FROM pubs..authors
```

If the IF statement evaluates to true, the RAISERROR statement will terminate the processing of the script file. This isn't the same as if you would have issued a RETURN statement. The return statement would have terminated the batch, but the following batch(es) would have been executed.

The PRINT command returns a string to the client application's message handler. This should not be considered an error. PRINT is quite commonly used for batch processing where you want to print information to the log about the processing. The print command takes one argument, a string expression. This can be a string constant, local variable, or global variable. In version 7, string expressions can be concatenated in the print command. The following example shows that feature to display the name of the current month:

```
PRINT 'The current month is ' + DATENAME(mm, GETDATE())
➥ + '.'
The current month is April.
```

SET Options

The SET command can be used to alter the connection's behavior. Options set with the SET command stay active until the connection terminates. Most SET commands take ON or OFF as arguments, while some take a specific value. Many of the SET statements don't take effect until the next batch. In the follows tables, the default behavior is displayed in a bold typeface.

The tuning-related SET parameters (shown in Table F.15) are generally used when analyzing and optimizing queries. They can give you information as to how a query is executed by SQL Server and also, to some extent, control how a query is executed.

TABLE F.15   TUNING-RELATED SET PARAMETERS

Parameter	Arguments	Description
FORCEPLAN	ON¦OFF *	Makes SQL Server process a JOIN in the same order as specified in the FROM clause.
NOEXEC	ON¦OFF *	SQL Server will optimize the query but not execute it. Used in conjunction with SHOWPLAN in earlier releases of SQL Server.
PARSEONLY	ON¦OFF *	SQL Server will parse the query but not optimize or execute it.

Parameter	Arguments	Description
SHOWPLAN_ALL	ON¦OFF *	Displays the query plan that SQL Server uses to execute the query, and doesn't execute the query. This is intended for programs that parse the output, like the Query Analyzer. For textual output, use SHOWPLAN_TEXT instead.
SHOWPLAN_TEXT	ON¦OFF *	Displays the query plan that SQL Server uses to execute the query, and doesn't execute the query.
STATISTICS_IO	ON¦OFF *	Displays information regarding I/O activity for each query.
STATISTICS_TIME	ON¦OFF *	Displays information regarding execution time for each query.

Default Options Are Noted by an Asterisk (*)

In Listing F.22, you turn on SHOWPLAN_TEXT so that the execution plan is returned to the client.

LISTING F.22   USE OF SHOWPLAN_TEXT

```
 1 SET SHOWPLAN_TEXT ON
 2 GO
 3 SELECT title, au_fname, au_lname
 4   FROM titles t
 5     JOIN titleauthor ta ON t.title_id = ta.title_id
 6     JOIN authors a ON ta.au_id = a.au_id
 7
 8 StmtText
 9 SELECT title, au_fname, au_lname
10   FROM titles t
11     JOIN titleauthor ta ON t.title_id = ta.title_id
12     JOIN authors a ON ta.au_id = a.au_id
13
14 StmtText
15 ¦--Nested Loops(Inner Join)
16         ¦--Nested Loops(Inner Join)
17         ¦      ¦--Index Scan(pubs..authors.aunmind)
18         ¦      ¦--Index Seek(pubs..titleauthor.UPKCL_taind,
   ➥ titleauthor.au_id=authors.au_id)
19         ¦--Index Seek(pubs..titles.UPKCL_titleidind,
   ➥ titles.title_id=titleauthor.title_id)
```

With the transaction handling–related SET parameters (see Table F.16) you can override SQL Server's default transaction-handling semantics. By default, one transaction (connection) cannot read or modify another transaction's modified data, but a transaction can both read and modify data that another transactions has read.

TABLE F.16   TRANSACTION HANDLING–RELATED SET PARAMETERS

Parameter	Arguments	Description
CURSOR_CLOSE_ON_COMMIT	ON¦OFF *	Controls whether cursors should be closed on commit.
IMPLICIT_TRANSACTIONS	ON¦OFF *	An implicit BEGIN TRANSACTION is triggered for most DML statements when turned ON.
REMOTE_PROC_TRANSACTIONS	ON¦OFF *	A distributed transaction is started when a remote procedure is executed from a local transaction when turned ON.
TRANSACTION_ISOLATION_LEVEL	READ_ COMMITTED * ¦READ_ UNCOMMITTED¦ REPEATABLE_ READ¦ SERIALIZABLE	Specifies the degree of isolation between concurrent transactions.
XACT_ABORT	ON¦OFF *	When turned on, SQL Server will roll back the current transaction if an error occurs.

Default Options Are Noted by an Asterisk (*)

In Listing F.23, you turn on IMPLICIT_TRANSACTIONS, issue two DELETE statements, print out the nesting level, and perform a ROLLBACK.

LISTING F.23   SETTING IMPLICIT_TRANSACTIONS TO GET IMPLICIT BEGIN TRANSACTION

```
1 SET IMPLICIT_TRANSACTIONS ON
2 GO
3 DELETE FROM titles WHERE title_id = 'BU1032'
4 DELETE FROM titleauthor WHERE title_id = 'BU1032'
5 SELECT 'Transaction nesting level is: ' +
  ➥ CAST(@@TRANCOUNT AS VARCHAR(5))
6 ROLLBACK TRAN
```

```
7 Server: Msg 547, Level 16, State 23000
8 DELETE statement conflicted with COLUMN REFERENCE
  ➥ constraint 'FK__sales__title_id__1CF15040'.
  ➥ The conflict occurred in database 'pubs',
  ➥ table 'titleauthor', column 'title_id'
9 Transaction nesting level is: 1
```

With the formatting-related SET parameters (see Table F.17) you can specify, for instance, the order for which day, month, and year part is specified when entering data.

TABLE F.17   SET PARAMETERS, WHICH CONTROL FORMATTING OF DATA

Parameter	Arguments	Description
DATEFIRST	\<number\>	Specifies which day is the last weekday. The default is 7 (Saturday).
DATEFORMAT	\<mdy\>	Specifies how SQL Server will interpret the date, month, and year part when inserting date-time data in numeric format.
FMTONLY	ON¦OFF *	SQL Server will only return meta-data to the client when turned ON.
IDENTITY_INSERT	\<tblname\> ON¦OFF *	Enables you to enter an explicit value for an identity column when turned on.
LANGUAGE	\<language_name\>	Controls in which language error messages should be returned. The language must be available on the server. It also controls the language used when returning name of weekday and month with the DATENAME function.
NOCOUNT	ON¦OFF *	Controls whether the number of rows affected by the last command should be returned to the client application. Even if turned off, the count is still available in the @@ROWCOUNT global variable.
OFFSETS	ON¦OFF *	Controls whether the offset for certain T-SQL keywords should be returned to DB-Library applications.
PROCID	ON¦OFF *	Controls whether the ID of a stored procedure should be returned to the calling DB-Library application.

continues

TABLE F.17   CONTINUED

Parameter	Arguments	Description
ROWCOUNT	\<number\>	Causes SQL Server to stop processing the query after a specified number of rows are processed. Note that this also applies to data modification statements. In version 7, use the TOP keyword if you want to control how many rows should be returned from a SELECT statement.
TEXTSIZE	\<number\>	Controls how many bytes a SELECT statement returns from text and ntext columns. Note that ntext uses two bytes per character.

The default specified applies for the US English language. Default options are noted by an asterisk (*).

In Listing F.24, you want to return the weekday and month that a book is published in the Swedish language. First the language is added with the call to sp_addlanguage. The call to sp_addlanguage is found in the script file instlang.sql.

LISTING F.24   USING sp_addlanguage TO ADD A LANGUAGE TO SQL SERVER

```
1 exec sp_addlanguage 'Svenska','Swedish',
2 'januari,februari,mars,april,maj,juni,juli,augusti,
  ➡ september,oktober,november,december',
3 'jan,feb,mar,apr,maj,jun,jul,aug,sep,okt,nov,dec',
4 'måndag,tisdag,onsdag,torsdag,fredag,lördag,söndag',
5 ymd,1
6 SET LANGUAGE swedish
7 GO
8 SELECT '"' + RTRIM(title) + '" is published on a '
  ➡ + DATENAME(dw, pubdate) + ' in ' +
  ➡ DATENAME(mm, pubdate) + '.'
10 FROM titles
11 WHERE title_id = 'PC1035'
12 "But Is It User Friendly?" is published on a söndag in juni.
```

Listing F.25 sets the date format for specifying datetime data. Note the SELECT statement shows the three available options to specify datetime data. SET DATEFORMAT only applies to the Numeric format.

LISTING F.25 USING SET DATEFORMAT TO SPECIFY DEFAULT DATE PART
INTERPRETATION FOR NUMERIC DATE FORMAT

```
1 SET DATEFORMAT ymd
2 GO
3 SELECT CONVERT(smalldatetime, '1999.12.31') as 'Numeric',
4   CONVERT(smalldatetime, '19991231') as 'Unseparated',
5   CONVERT(smalldatetime, 'Dec 1999 31') as 'Alphabetic'
6
7 Numeric              Unseparated            Alphabetic
8 1999-12-31 00:00:00  1999-12-31 00:00:00
  ➡ 1999-12-15 00:00:00
```

The ANSI-related and miscellaneous SET parameters (listed in Table F. 18) control behavior for comparison to NULL, division by 0, and so on.

TABLE F.18 ANSI AND MISCELLANEOUS SET PARAMETERS

Parameter	Arguments	Description
ARITHABORT	ON¦OFF *	Terminates a query if overflow or divide-by-zero occurs when turned on. Note that rows can be returned before the abort occurs.
ARITHIGNORE	ON¦OFF *	Returns NULL is overflow or divide-by-zero occurs if turned on. No warning message is sent to the client. Default behavior is that NULL and a warning message is returned.
NUMERIC_ROUNDABORT	ON¦OFF *	Controls level of reporting when loss of precision occurs.
ANSI_NULL_DFLT_OFF	ON¦OFF *	Set this to ON if you don't want a column to allow NULL when you create a table and don't specify NULL or NOT NULL.
ANSI_NULL_DFLT_ON	ON¦OFF *	Set this to ON if you want a column to allow NULL when you create a table and don't specify NULL or NOT NULL.
ANSI_NULLS	ON¦OFF *	Controls how comparison to NULL should be handled. By default, NULL = NULL equals true. SET ANSI_NULLS to ON changes evaluation to false.
ANSI_PADDING	ON¦OFF *	Specifies whether char, varchar, and varbinary columns should be padded with blanks and zeroes, respectively. Behavior is specified at CREATE time of the table.

continues

TABLE F.18   CONTINUED

Parameter	Arguments	Description
ANSI_WARNINGS	ON¦OFF *	Generates a warning if an aggregate function is applied over rows that contain NULL and if INSERT or UPDATE specifies data with length that exceeds the column definitions for character, Unicode, or binary data. A division by 0 or overflow will result in rollback of the statement if this option is set.
DEADLOCK_PRIORITY	NORMAL *¦LOW	If LOW, this connection will be the preferred victim if a deadlock occurs. If your application handles deadlock gracefully set, this to LOW, to increase the chance that an application that doesn't handle deadlock can continue processing in the event of a deadlock situation.
DISABLE_DEF_	ON¦OFF *	Set to ON if youCNST_CHK want SQL Server to halt execution immediately if a statement is performed that violates to a constraint. By default, SQL Server will continue processing and recheck at the end of the statement.
FIPS_FLAGGER	OFF *¦ENTRY¦	Specifies whether INTERMEDIATE¦FULLSQL Server will generate awarning if a statement doesn't comply with the specified level of the FIPS 127-2 standard.
QUOTED_IDENTIFIER	ON¦OFF *	Will not check for keyword violation for strings surrounded with double quotes.

Default options are noted by an asterisk (*).

In Listing F.26, you explore the differences when checking for the NULL symbol depending on how ANSI_NULLS is set. The preferred way of checking for the NULL symbol is by using IS NULL and IS NOT NULL, which is consistent regardless of how ANSI_NULLS is set.

LISTING F.26   CHECKING FOR NULL

```
1 SET ANSI_NULLS OFF
2 GO
3 SELECT title_id, price FROM titles WHERE price = NUL
4 SELECT title_id, price FROM titles WHERE price IS NULL
```

```
 5
 6 title_id price
 7 MC3026    NULL
 8 PC9999    NULL
 9 title_id price
10 MC3026    NULL
11 PC9999    NULL
12
13 -- Note that both statements return two tows.
14 SET ANSI_NULLS ON
15 GO
16 SELECT title_id, price FROM titles WHERE price = NULL
17 SELECT title_id, price FROM titles WHERE price IS NULL
18
19 title_id price
20 title_id price
21 MC3026    NULL
22        PC9999    NULL
23 Note that the first statement returns zero rows.
```

You can specify many of the SET parameters in the ODBC client configuration (the ODBC DSN). This feature introduced some problems. For instance, a stored procedure could have been written so that the parameters were assigned NULL as default, and a check for a value was done inside the procedure. This check was sometimes written as IF @parameter = NULL (which evaluates to false when ANSI_NULLS is ON).

Cursors

The SQL language is a set-based language, in contrast to most programming languages. This leads to an impedance mismatch between the languages. You need some way to interface between the two languages. Most programming interfaces to SQL Server are based on function calls: you specify a query to execute through one function call, and execute the query through another function call, and so on. But what do you do with the result?

If this were a data modification statement, you probably only check for the return code and give the user some feedback. If it were a SELECT statement, you probably want to read through the rows returned and display them or perform further processing for the rows (unless you only retrieve one row, and know that in advance).

So, you build some kind of loop to go through your resultset and perform some processing for each row. If you only want to display the rows, you can simply fetch them as they arrive to the client, reading from your input buffer. But what if you need to perform further processing for each row, for instance do some calculations and update the "current row"? This can be done though a cursor.

A cursor is a placeholder in a resultset from a query. You cannot navigate in a table because a table (or rather the contents in a table) is a set, but you can navigate through the result from a query.

Let's say that you have a leads table, and you want to predict the value of sales for the forthcoming three months. You find the leads table in Listing F.27.

LISTING F.27   THE LEADS TABLE

```
 1 CREATE TABLE leads
 2 (l_id INT IDENTITY,
 3 customer INT,
 4 est_sale FLOAT,
 5 close_date SMALLDATETIME DEFAULT DATEADD(dd, 30,
     ➡ GETDATE())),
 6 prob FLOAT DEFAULT 20,
 7 sales_person CHAR(8),
 8 category VARCHAR(30))
 9
10 SELECT * FROM leads
11
12 l_id customer est_sales close_date prob salesperson
     ➡ category
13 -- -- -- -- -- -- -- -- -- -- -- -- -- -- --
14 1    1     600    Apr 15 199 30    Steve      books
15 2    1     200    Apr 25 199 55    John       paper
16 3    5     400    May  1 199 40    Kelly      books
17 4    3     900    May 12 199 25    Lisa       misc
18 5    7     200    Jun  1 199 15    John       misc
19 6    6     700    May 10 199 50    Bob        paper
20 7    5     450    Apr 10 199 10    Richard    books
21 8    13    600    May 15 199 80    John       misc
22 9    5     1200   Apr 10 199 50    Ann        books
23 10   16    200    Jun 15 199 50    Andy       books
24 11   7     800    May 20 199 40    Bob        misc
25 12   9     600    Apr 20 199 30    Lisa       paper
26 13   3     900    Apr 15 199 60    John       paper
27 14   16    300    May 25 199 25    Kelly      misc
28 15   11    700    Jun 20 199 45    Lisa       books
```

You want to do a projection based on multiplying the estimated sale to the probability of a sale occurring, and them summarize the projections:

```
SELECT SUM(est_sale * probability/100) FROM leads
```

But what if you want to try to be a bit more precise? Based on experience

- Some salespeople are too optimistic, whereas others are conservative. Lisa's probability is usually 20% low and Steve's is usually 30% high.
- In June, you always have an additional 20% discount.
- The book projections are usually low, so you want to increase it by 15%.
- Customer 2 has a tendency to ask for a bid, but seldom buys. You want to lower the probability with 50% for customer 2.

Some Approaches

You certainly could retrieve all rows to the client computer and perform all aggregations in the client application. This would make a rather poor use of SQL Server's power. You would have to write a lot of code and retrieve many records to the client computer. You could imagine what amount of network bandwidth it would take if the table has tens of millions of rows.

So, you decide to use a cursor. You loop through each row, save relevant column information in variables, and perform your calculations.

CURSORS VS. SET-BASED OPERATIONS

You might think that you should use a set-based operation instead of a cursor. I agree, so hold on. I will get to that later.

Cursor Example and Some Syntax

In Listing F.28, you find the code for performing your projection. Have a look at it, and I will explain it in detail further on.

LISTING F.28   CALCULATING SALES PROJECTION USING A CURSOR

```
1 DECLARE lead_cur CURSOR FOR
2 SELECT customer, est_sale, close_date, prob,
   ➥ sales_person,
3        category
4  FROM leads
5 FOR READ ONLY
6
7 DECLARE
8 @sum_sales FLOAT,
```

continues

LISTING F.28 CONTINUED

```
 9 @customer INT,
10 @est_sale FLOAT,
11 @close_date SMALLDATETIME,
12 @prob FLOAT,
13 @sales_person CHAR(8),
14 @category VARCHAR(30)
15
16 SELECT @sum_sales = 0
17 OPEN lead_cur
18
19 FETCH lead_cur INTO
20 @customer, @est_sale, @close_date, @prob,
   ➥ @sales_person,
21 @category
22
23 WHILE @@FETCH_STATUS = 0
24   BEGIN
25 IF @sales_person = 'Lisa'   — Lisa usually
   ➥ projects low
26 SELECT @prob = @prob * 1.2
27 IF @sales_person = 'Steve' — Steve usually
28 ➥ projects high
29 SELECT @prob = @prob * 0.7
30 IF @customer = 2 — Customer 2 has a low buying rate
31 SELECT @prob = @prob * 0.5
32 IF DATEPART (mm, @close_date ) = 6 — Discount
   ➥June sales
33 SELECT @prob = @prob * 0.8
34 IF @category = 'Books' — Increase book projections
35 SELECT @est_sale = @est_sale * 1.15
36
37 SELECT @sum_sales = @sum_sales + @est_sale * @prob / 100
38 FETCH lead_cur INTO
39 @customer, @est_sale, @close_date, @prob,
   ➥ @sales_person,
40 @category
41 END
42
43 CLOSE lead_cur
44 SELECT @sum_sales AS "Estimated Sales"
45 DEALLOCATE lead_cur
```

Declaring Cursors

A cursor is declared for a SELECT statement. The ANSI defines the following syntax to declare a cursor:

```
DECLARE cursor_name [INSENSITIVE] [SCROLL] CURSOR
FOR select_statement
[FOR {READ ONLY ¦ UPDATE [OF column_list]}]
```

SQL AND API LEVEL CODE

The cursor types actually use the same code in SQL Server, so it is quite natural that you have the ability to use the same features at the SQL level as you have at the API level.

In version 7, an alternative way of declaring a cursor was introduced to give the cursor the same capabilities as the API-based cursor. I will discuss API Cursors further down.

The syntax for Transact-SQL cursors is the following:

```
DECLARE cursor_name CURSOR
[LOCAL ¦ GLOBAL]
[FORWARD_ONLY ¦ SCROLL]
[STATIC ¦ KEYSET ¦ DYNAMIC]
[READ_ONLY ¦ SCROLL_LOCKS ¦ OPTIMISTIC]
FOR select_statement
[FOR {READ ONLY ¦ UPDATE [OF column_list]}]
```

You cannot use COMPUTE, COMPUTE BY, FOR BROWSE, and INTO in the select_statement.

Let us use our example to discuss the DECLARE statement:

```
DECLARE lead_cur CURSOR FOR
SELECT customer, est_sale, close_date, probability,
➡ sales_person, product_category
 FROM leads
FOR READ ONLY
```

Our cursor declares a SELECT statement that reads from a single table. You don't want to update any data based on cursor position, so declare the cursor as READ ONLY.

As for all queries, it is a good idea to limit the number of rows that the cursor will process through a WHERE clause. And if SQL Server can use an index to find the rows, even better.

The cursor name must follow the general rules for identifiers.

Local and Global Cursors

A new feature in version 7 is that you can specify whether the cursor should be local or global.

If you have used cursors with version 6, you have used global cursors. The cursor is implicitly deallocated at termination of the connection.

A local cursor's scope is a batch (which implies stored procedure and trigger). The cursor is implicitly deallocated when the batch terminates, unless a reference to it is passed to calling stored procedure, batch, and so on. Then it will go out of scope when the last variable referring to it goes out of scope.

In Listing F.29, you write a general stored procedure that returns the name of all tables in a database. Then you can use that procedure for performing certain maintenance routines against our tables, like UPDATE STATISTICS, rebuilding indexes, and so on. Listing F.29 shows the stored procedure definition.

LISTING F.29 CREATING A STORED PROCEDURE THAT RETURNS A CURSOR THAT CAN BE USED TO OPERATE AGAINST EACH TABLE IN A DATABASE

```
1 CREATE PROC cur_tbl_names @tbl_cur CURSOR VARYING
  ➥ OUTPUT AS
2 SET @tbl_cur = CURSOR LOCAL FORWARD_ONLY FOR
3 SELECT TABLE_NAME FROM INFORMATION_SCHEMA.TABLES
4 WHERE TABLE_TYPE = 'BASE TABLE'
5 OPEN @tbl_cur
```

First, you can see that the parameter @tbl_cur is defined as CURSOR VARYING OUTPUT. This is needed if you want to return a "reference" to the cursor from the procedure.

The SELECT statement returns all table names in the database. It might look a bit strange for those of you who have worked with SQL Server's earlier versions. INFORMATION_SCHEMA.TABLES is one of the system table–independent views that are used for looking at catalog information. These views are defined in the ANSI standard, so I encourage you to use them when possible.

In Listing F.30, you have the code that calls the procedure.

LISTING F.30 CALLING THE PROCEDURE CREATED IN LISTING F.29

```
1 DECLARE @tbls CURSOR
2 DECLARE @table_name sysname
3 EXEC cur_tbl_names @tbl_cur = @tbls OUTPUT
4 FETCH NEXT FROM @tbls INTO @table_name
```

```
5 WHILE @@FETCH_STATUS = 0
6  BEGIN
7   EXEC('DBCC DBREINDEX( ' + @table_name + ')')
8   FETCH NEXT FROM @tbls INTO @table_name
9  END
```

You get a reference to the cursor, execute your stored procedure and then you have a standard loop for that cursor. Now you can write several batches (or stored procedures) that uses the same cursor, and if you want to exclude any tables, you only modify the code once—in the stored procedure.

You might wonder what sysname is. It is a built-in datatype, used for identifiers.

Declaring Variables

So how do you process values from the cursor?

You could quite simply display each row to the user, as a number of one-row resultsets. But that doesn't make much sense. It would be much simpler to issue an ordinary SELECT statement and display the rows to the user as you read the rows from the input buffer.

What you really want to do is store the value for some of the columns into local variables and perform some processing based on those values.

Note that I have chosen the same variable names as those returned from the SELECT statement. This makes it easier to remember the variable names when processing the cursor, and it makes it easier to maintain the code.

```
DECLARE
 @sum_sales FLOAT,
 @customer INT,
 @est_sale FLOAT,
 @close_date SMALLDATETIME,
 @probability FLOAT,
 @sales_person CHAR(8),
 @product_category VARCHAR(30)
```

You also need to initialize the summary variable:

```
SELECT @sum_sales = 0
```

Opening Cursors

When you open a cursor, the SELECT statement is executed and the cursor becomes populated. At that point in time, the cursor will be positioned above the first row:

```
OPEN lead_cur
```

You can check how many rows the resultset contains with the global variable @@CURSOR_ROWS. If the value is –1, the cursor is being populated asynchronously.

If you close a cursor and open it again, the SELECT statement is re-executed. Bear this in mind, so you don't re-execute your SELECT statement if you don't have to.

Fetching Rows

Now it's time to start reading rows from your cursor. This is done with the FETCH command.

```
FETCH lead_cur INTO
 @customer, @est_sale, @close_date, @probability,
 @sales_person, @product_category
```

The default for FETCH is to get the next row from the cursor. You will look at scrolling capabilities further on. If you specify too many or too few variables after INTO, you will get a runtime error. The same happens if you specify a variable type for which SQL Server cannot perform an implicit datatype conversion.

The Main Loop

This is where the real processing occurs. The loop looks like this:

```
WHILE @@FETCH_STATUS = 0
 BEGIN
  IF @sales_person = 'Lisa'  — Lisa usually projects low
     SELECT @probability = @probability * 1.2
  IF @sales_person = 'Steve' — Steve usually projects high
     SELECT @probability = @probability * 0.7
  IF @customer = 2 — Customer 2 has a low buying rate
     SELECT @probability = @probability * 0.5
  IF DATEPART (mm, @close_date ) = 6 — Discount June
  ➥ sales by 20%
     SELECT @probability = @probability * 0.8
  IF @product_category = 'Books' — Increase book
  ➥projections
     SELECT @est_sale = @est_sale * 1.15

 SELECT @sum_sales = @sum_sales + @est_sale *
 ➥@probability / 100
 FETCH lead_cur INTO
  @customer, @est_sale, @close_date, @probability,
  ➥@sales_person, @product_category
 END
```

You loop while @@FETCH_STATUS = 0. A value of –1 means that you have navigated outside the cursor. A value of –2 means that the row that you are trying to fetch has been deleted—all columns will contain the NULL symbol.

Closing the Cursor

You want to close the cursor as soon as you don't need it anymore. Open cursors hold locks on the underlying tables and use valuable resources.

You can re-open the cursor, which means that the statement is executed again and the cursor is repopulated:

```
CLOSE lead_cur
SELECT @sum_sales AS "Estimated Sales"
```

Deallocating Cursors

When you are finished with the cursor definition, you deallocate it. You cannot declare a cursor with the same name until you have deallocated the previous cursor.

```
DEALLOCATE lead_cur
```

It is a good idea to deallocate a cursor when you don't need it anymore. The query plan will be released from memory at that time, and it makes the structure of your code clearer.

Updating with Cursors

How can you update a cursor when the cursor is a resultset, and not the data itself? What you do is update based on the cursor position. The modification can be either an UPDATE or a DELETE.

Declaring a Cursor FOR UPDATE

To be able to update based on the cursor position, the cursor must be declared FOR UPDATE:

```
[FOR {READ ONLY ¦ UPDATE [OF column_list]}]
```

If you don't specify a column_list, all columns will be updateable.

If your SELECT statement is a join, you could update several tables through the same cursor. This doesn't probably have that much meaning for ANSI cursors, but it is possible.

Listing F.31 shown an example of an updateable cursor.

LISTING F.31 AN UPDATEABLE CURSOR

```
1 DECLARE upd_cur CURSOR FOR
2 SELECT title, au_lname, au_fname
3   FROM titles t
4   JOIN titleauthor ta ON t.title_id = ta.title_id
5   JOIN authors a ON ta.au_id = a.au_id
6   WHERE state = 'CA'
7   ORDER BY title
8 FOR UPDATE
```

Obviously, columns with computed values and aggregates cannot be updated.

Scrolling Capabilities

If you declare the cursor with the SCROLL keyword, you can navigate as you choose within the resultset. An example of the leads cursor declared with scroll capabilities would look like:

```
DECLARE lead_cur SCROLL CURSOR FOR
SELECT customer, est_sale, close_date, probability,
 sales_person, product_category FROM leads
FOR READ ONLY
```

For a scrollable cursor, you can use the FETCH statement to navigate in a more flexible way:

```
FETCH [NEXT ¦ PRIOR ¦ FIRST ¦ LAST ¦ ABSOLUTE n ¦ RELATIVE n]
```

If you omit the navigational argument, NEXT will be performed. You don't need a scrollable cursor in order to FETCH NEXT.

Scrollable cursors are most useful as API cursors, where a user, for instance can move up and down a list box and choose some entry based on a cursor value.

INSENSITIVE Cursors

A cursor declared as insensitive won't be affected by updates done through the table(s) that it is based on. SQL Server will quite simply make a copy of the cursor data and store it in the tempdb database.

An insensitive cursor is useful if you want to take a snapshot of the data and don't want to be disturbed by changes to the underlying data while you process the cursor data.

An insensitive cursor isn't updateable.

Cursors and Concurrency

You must be careful when using cursors so you don't block other users' access to the data. If the code executing isn't in the scope of a transaction, SQL Server will only apply shared locks for the duration of the fetch request. SQL Server will automatically implement optimistic concurrency. If you try to update a row through the cursor, and some other user updated it, SQL Server will issue an error message to the client application.

CURSORS IN A TRANSACTION

If a cursor is used inside a transaction, shared locks are held on all rows that are fetched until the end of transaction. This can lead to poor concurrency.

If you use the T-SQL extension to DECLARE CURSOR, you can control the cursor concurrency behavior:

```
[READ_ONLY ¦ SCROLL_LOCKS ¦ OPTIMISTIC]
```

- If you use READ_ONLY, you cannot update through the cursor and shared locks are only held during each fetch operation.
- When using SCROLL_LOCKS, SQL Server acquires scroll locks as you read data into the cursor. Subsequent updates based on the cursor are guaranteed to succeed.
- With OPTIMISTIC, you get optimistic concurrency as described in the preceding text.

API Cursors

So far, you have looked at how you can use cursors through T-SQL. The most common use of cursors, though, is through the application programming interface, API. Each API has calls or methods for defining cursor capabilities.

In fact, you can say that all results from SQL Server are returned through a cursor. The simplest case is that the client retrieves rows one at a time scrolling forward (reading from the input buffer) through the resultset. This is called a *default resultset*.

If you need more advanced scrolling capabilities, part of the resultset needs to be cached somewhere, so you can use, say, a key when searching for the previous row. This caching can be done at the client or at the server.

CURSOR MODELS AND PERFORMANCE

The cursor model chosen can have a severe impact at performance. See the section "Avoiding Cursors" for some examples.

Client cursors are implemented at the client side. ODBC or OLE-DB caches the necessary information. There are no cursor calls sent to SQL Server. Client cursors are useful if

- You have a slow network connection to the SQL Server.
- There are not too many rows in the resultset or you will navigate through a major part of the resultset.
- You will allow the user to interact rapidly through the cached resultset.

A Web-based application is a good example where client cursors can be valuable. For example, a SQL statement is sent to SQL Server to retrieve a number of customer names. This resultset is buffered at the client side. When the user chooses a customer, another SQL statement is executed and customer details are presented in the Web browser.

API Server Cursors are implemented through the API cursor support in SQL Server. SQL Server has a number of `sp_cursor` extended stored procedures used by ODBC and OLE-DB, which implement API Server Cursors.

By default, server-side cursors are used in the programming APIs, but the programmer can choose to use client cursors instead.

You can also choose how many rows are to be returned with each fetch operation sent to SQL Server (*fat* cursors). This isn't possible with Transact-SQL cursors; it wouldn't make any sense because all processing is done at the server.

Avoiding Cursors

I have encountered numerous situations where performance was slow due to improper use of cursors. You should always aim at letting SQL Server perform what it's good at: set-based operations. It makes little sense having advanced RDBMS and only using it for retrievals of one row at a time.

Your cursor example can be performed with one SELECT statement, as shown in Listing F.32.

LISTING F.32 THE LEADS CURSOR EXAMPLE PERFORMED WITH ONE SELECT STATEMENT

```
 1 SELECT "Sum of Sales" = SUM(
 2 est_sale * prob / 100
 3 *
 4 CASE category WHEN 'Books' THEN 1.15 ELSE 1 END
 5 *
 6 CASE DATEPART (mm, close_date ) WHEN 6 THEN 0.8
   ➥ ELSE 1 END
 7 *
 8 CASE sales_person WHEN 'Lisa' THEN 1.2 WHEN
   ➥ 'Steve' THEN 0.7 ELSE 1 END
 9 *
10 CASE WHEN customer = 2 THEN 0.5 ELSE 1 END)
```

The advantage with this approach is a significant performance improvement. The possible disadvantage is that you obviously need to know SQL.

As another example, imagine that you want to increase the discount for all customers who have bought for a certain amount of money.

You could retrieve all rows, check the amount bought, and if it is over that amount, update that customer's discount. This would require that you retrieve all rows, one network roundtrip for each customer, and one UPDATE statement for each row that you want to update.

Thinking set based, you could quite simply issue an UPDATE statement that raises the discount for all customers who meet the requirements (the WHERE clause). SQL Server can use an index to find the rows and all processing is done at the server. This update statement would be easier to construct than the procedural processing as well.

The performance implications are obvious. Okay, it is a simple example, but the same applies for more advanced operations.

On the companion CD, you find a Visual Basic application that demonstrates the differences. I performed some timing and the following table presents the results.

Let us have a look at some details first. My server was a Pentium 2, 333 MHz with 128MB of RAM. I used the Leads table with 50,000 rows. Several tests were performed:

- SQL-based cursors through RDO and ADO.
- A SELECT statement, using CASE through RDO and ADO.
- Performing all calculations at the client side, fetching all rows. Both the Default Resultset and fetching a number of rows at a time (executing an sp_cursor procedure at the server for each fetch) were used. I fetched 100 rows at a time with RDO and 1 row at a time with ADO.

The client I used was a Pentium 120 MHz with 72MB of RAM. The machines were connected through an isolated 10 Mb Ethernet. Table F.19 displays execution time in seconds both when running the Visual Basic program at the server and at the client.

TABLE F.19 PERFORMANCE COMPARISON BETWEEN DIFFERENT CASES OF CURSORS

Cursor	API	Server	Client
SQL	RDO	8.8	8.5
SQL	ADO	8.8	8.6
None	RDO	2.0	2.0
None	ADO	1.9	1.9
Default resultset	RDO	20	106
Server cursor	RDO	23	101
Default resultset	ADO	20	116
Server cursor	ADO	650	983

ADO AND RDO

Note the difference between ADO and RDO when using server cursor. Without any further investigation, you can safely assume that this is due to the difference in the number of rows retrieved with each fetch. SQL Server executes an sp_cursor procedure for each fetch. I used a block size of 100 for RDO and 1 for ADO.

There is quite a difference between 2 seconds and 983 seconds of execution time!

The numbers speak for themselves.

Scripting Object Model Reference

by Ken Cox

Objects in the Scripting Object Model

Button Object

The Button script object is familiar to anyone who has seen an HTML form. You click the button to initiate an event. However, the button may also take the form of an image. Table G.1 lists the properties, methods, and events available with the Button script object.

TABLE G.1   PROPERTIES, METHODS, AND EVENTS OF THE Button SCRIPT OBJECT

Name	Type
advise	Method
alt	Property
disabled	Property
display	Method
getStyle	Method
hide	Method
id	Property
isVisible	Method
maintainState	Property
name	Property
onclick	Event
setStyle	Method
show	Method
src	Property
unadvise	Method
value	Property

Checkbox Object

The Checkbox script object provides a way for users to make a yes or no choice on a Web page. The Scripting Object Model's Checkbox object can be bound to a data source, changed, and hidden with script. Table G.2 lists the properties, methods, and events available with the Checkbox script object.

TABLE G.2   PROPERTIES, METHODS, AND EVENTS OF THE Checkbox SCRIPT OBJECT

Name	Type
advise	Method
disabled	Property
display	Method
getCaption	Method
getChecked	Method
getDataField	Method
getDataSource	Method
hide	Method
id	Property
isVisible	Method
maintainState	Property
name	Property
onclick	Event
setCaption	Method
setChecked	Method
setDataField	Method
setDataSource	Method
show	Method
unadvise	Method
value	Property

G

SCRIPTING OBJECT
MODEL
REFERENCE

Grid Object

The Grid object presents a table that is bound to a database and includes buttons for navigating through a recordset. By using script, you can change the appearance of the buttons, bind the grid to a different recordset, and make the object appear and disappear. Table G.3 lists the methods available with the Grid script object.

TABLE G.3 METHODS OF THE Grid SCRIPT OBJECT

Name	*Type*
bindAllColumns	Method
getPagingNavbar	Method
getRecordsetNavbar	Method
hide	Method
isVisible	Method
show	Method

Label Object

The Label object places text on the HTML page, either as plain text or with full HTML markup. Using script, you can change the text and its attributes on-the-fly and bind the Label object to information in a database. Table G.4 lists the properties and methods of the Label script object.

TABLE G.4 PROPERTIES AND METHODS OF THE Label SCRIPT OBJECT

Name	*Type*
advise	Method
display	Method
getCaption	Method
getDataField	Method
getDataFormatAs	Method
getDataSource	Method
hide	Method
id	Property
isVisible	Method
maintainState	Property
name	Property
setCaption	Method
setDataField	Method
setDataFormatAs	Method
setDataSource	Method
show	Method
unadvise	Method

Listbox Object

The `Listbox` script object is a useful element for giving users a choice of an unknown number of items. With scripting, you can add and remove items, test the value of any item, or clear the entire display. Table G.5 lists the properties, methods, and events supported by the `Listbox` script object.

TABLE G.5   PROPERTIES, METHODS, AND EVENTS OF THE `Listbox` SCRIPT OBJECT

Name	Type
additem	Method
advise	Method
clear	Method
disabled	Property
display	Method
getCount	Method
getDataField	Method
getDataSource	Method
getRowSource	Method
getText	Method
getValue	Method
hide	Method
id	Property
isVisible	Method
maintainState	Property
name	Property
onchange	Event
removeItem	Method
selectByText	Method
selectByValue	Method
selectedIndex	Property
setDataField	Method
setDataSource	Method
setRowSource	Method
setText	Method
show	Method
size	Property
unadvise	Method

G

SCRIPTING OBJECT
MODEL
REFERENCE

OptionGroup Object

An `OptionGroup` script object lets users accept only one item from among the available choices. Using the Scripting Object Model (SOM), you can change the appearance of the `OptionGroup` object, update its text, add and remove items, and set or retrieve the value of an option. Table G.6 shows the properties, methods, and events supported by the `OptionGroup` script object.

TABLE G.6 PROPERTIES, METHODS, AND EVENTS OF THE `OptionGroup` SCRIPT OBJECT

Name	Type
addItem	Method
advise	Method
clear	Method
display	Method
getAlignment	Method
getBorder	Method
getButton	Method
getCaption	Method
getCount	Method
getDataField	Method
getDataSource	Method
getRowSource	Method
getSelectedIndex	Method
getValue	Method
hide	Method
id	Property
isVisible	Method
maintainState	Property
name	Property
onchange	Event
removeItem	Method
selectByCaption	Method
selectByIndex	Method
selectByValue	Method
setAlignment	Method

Name	Type
setBorder	Method
setCaption	Method
setDataField	Method
setDataSource	Method
setRowSource	Method
setValue	Method
show	Method
unadvise	Method

PageObject Object

The PageObject script object lets you define methods and properties that apply to a whole page. In effect, the page becomes an object that can interact with other page objects. Table G.7 lists the properties, methods, events, and objects of the PageObject script object.

TABLE G.7   PROPERTIES, METHODS, EVENTS, AND OBJECTS OF THE PageObject SCRIPT OBJECT

Name	Type
advise	Method
cancelEvent (client only)	Property
createDE (server only)	Method
endPageContent (server only)	Method
execute	Child object
firstEntered (server only)	Property
getState	Method
location	Property
navigate	Child object
navigateTarget (client only)	Property
navigateURL	Method
onbeforeserverevent (client only)	Event
onenter (server only)	Event

continues

TABLE G.7 CONTINUED

Name	Type
onexit (server only)	Event
setState	Method
startPageContent (server only)	Method
unadvise	Method

execute Child Object

The PageObject object includes the execute child object. With the execute object, you call scripted functions stored in other pages, but you remain on the same Web page. This ability to execute remote procedures is handy if you have many pages that require a calculation or a lookup. It is especially efficient in Web applications in which the formula is likely to change. In such a case, you have to update the code in only one page, not hundreds of pages.

To show execute in action, you start with the remote page stripspace.asp, which is handled as an object through its own PageObject script object, called myfunctions. Inside this remote page, you will find the following function, which accepts a string, strips out any spaces, and returns the result to the caller:

```
Function StripSpaces(thestring)
phraselength=len(thestring)
for counter=1 to phraselength
  if mid(thestring,counter,1) <> chr(32) then
    tempstr=tempstr & mid(thestring,counter,1)
  end if
next
StripSpaces=tempstr
Textbox1.value=StripSpaces
end function
```

Next, you set up the current page—the one that calls on the remote page.

Before you can use the execute object, you have to prepare the references to the script object that you will be calling. You do this with the PageObject's design-time control. In effect, you use the DTC to embed in your current page the location and filename of the remote page, as well as the functions or methods on the remote page that you want to execute. Figure G.1 shows the settings used in execute.asp on the CD-ROM.

FIGURE G.1

Use the References tab of the PageObject *DTC to establish the page object and method you are executing.*

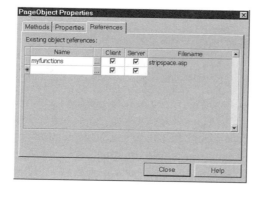

When you have created a remote script and references to it, the current page (execute.asp) can call the remote procedure. In the following code snippet, a click of Button1 passes the text in Textbox2 to the StripSpaces function in stripspaces.asp (also known as the PageObject myfunctions). The returned value goes into Textbox1 on the current page.

```
function Button1_onclick() {
callobject= myfunctions.execute.StripSpaces(Textbox2.value);
Textbox1.value=callobject.return_value
}
```

The complete source code for these examples is on the CD-ROM. Keep in mind that you might have to update the PageObject references to reflect your server's name and your Web.

navigate Child Object

The PageObject object includes the navigate child object. With the navigate object, you call scripted functions stored in other pages and navigate to those remote pages. This is different from the execute child object, which stays on the current page while calling remote procedures.

To show navigate in action, you start with the remote page stripspace.asp, which is handled as an object through its own PageObject script object, called myfunctions. Inside this remote page, you will find the following function, which accepts a string, strips out any spaces, and returns the result:

```
Function StripSpaces(thestring)
phraselength=len(thestring)
for counter=1 to phraselength
  if mid(thestring,counter,1) <> chr(32) then
    tempstr=tempstr & mid(thestring,counter,1)
  end if
```

```
next
StripSpaces=tempstr
Textbox1.value=StripSpaces
end function
```

Next, you set up the current page (navigate.asp), the one that calls on the remote page.

Before you can use the `navigate` object, you have to prepare the references that you will be making. You do this with the `PageObject`'s design-time control. In effect, you use the DTC to embed in your current page the location and filename of the remote page and the functions or methods on the remote page that you want to execute. Figure G.2, later in this appendix, shows the settings used in navigate.asp on the CD-ROM.

Having created a remote script and references to it, the current page (navigate.asp) can call the remote procedure. In the following code snippet, a click of `Button1` passes the text in `Textbox2` to the `StripSpaces` function in stripspaces.asp (also known as the `PageObject` myfunctions). Because you are navigating rather than executing, the returned value appears in `Textbox1` on the remote page (stripspaces.asp).

```
function Button1_onclick() {
myfunctions.navigate.StripSpaces(Textbox2.value);
}
```

The complete source code for these examples is on the CD-ROM. Keep in mind that you might have to update the `PageObject` references to reflect your server name and Web.

Recordset Object

The SOM provides the `Recordset` object that lets you connect to and retrieve records from a database. Using the methods supported by the `Recordset` object, you can open, close, query, add, remove, update, and navigate through the recordset. Table G.8 lists the properties, methods, events, and objects of the `Recordset` script object.

TABLE G.8 PROPERTIES, METHODS, EVENTS, AND OBJECTS OF THE Recordset SCRIPT OBJECT

Name	Type
absolutePosition	Property
addImmediate	Method
addRecord	Method
advise	Method
BOF	Property
cancelUpdate	Method

Name	Type
close	Method
deleteRecord	Method
EOF	Property
fields	Child object
(getCount)	Method
(getName)	Method
(getValue)	Method
(setValue)	Method
getBookmark	Method
getConnectString	Method
getCount	Method
getDHTMLDataSourceID	Method
getParameter	Method
getRecordSource	Method
getSQLText	Method
id	Property
isOpen	Method
maintainState	Property
move	Method
moveAbsolute	Method
moveFirst	Method
moveLast	Method
moveNext	Method
name	Property
onafterupdate	Event
onbeforeopen	Event
onbeforeupdate	Event
ondatasetchanged	Event
ondatasetcomplete	Event
onrowenter	Event
onrowexit	Event
open	Method

continues

TABLE G.8 CONTINUED

Name	Type
requery	Method
setBookmark	Method
setParameter	Method
setRecordSource	Method
setSQLText	Method
unadvise	Method
updateRecord	Method

RecordsetNavbar Object

The RecordsetNavbar script object is a set of buttons that let you navigate through a recordset. You can use script to change the appearance of the buttons, their layout, and the number of records moved per click. Table G.9 lists the properties, methods, and events of the RecordsetNavbar script object.

TABLE G.9 PROPERTIES, METHODS, AND EVENTS OF THE RecordsetNavbar

Name	Type
advise	Method
cancelOperation	Method
display	Method
getAlignment	Method
getButton	Method
getButtonStyles	Method
getDataSource	Method
hide	Method
id	Property
isOperationCancelled	Method
isVisible	Method
maintainState	Property
name	Property
onfirstclick	Event
onlastclick	Event

Name	Type
onnextclick	Event
onpreviousclick	Event
pageSize	Property
setAlignment	Method
setButton	Method
setButtonStyles	Method
setDataSource	Method
show	Method
unadvise	Method
updateOnMove	Property

Textbox Object

The Textbox script object is a familiar HTML text input device. Using the SOM, you can receive an event notification when the contents of the text box have changed. You can change the size of the control, hide it, or set the number of characters that it will accept. Table G.10 lists the properties, methods, and events of the Textbox script object.

TABLE G.10 PROPERTIES, METHODS, AND EVENTS OF THE Textbox SCRIPT OBJECT

Name	Type
advise	Method
disabled	Property
display	Method
getColumnCount	Method
getDataField	Method
getDataSource	Method
getMaxLength	Method
getRowCount	Method
getStyle	Method
hide	Method
id	Property
isVisible	Method

continues

TABLE G.10 CONTINUED

Name	Type
maintainState	Property
name	Property
onchange	Event
setColumnCount	Method
setDataField	Method
setDataSource	Method
setMaxLength	Method
setRowCount	Method
setStyle	Method
show	Method
unadvise	Method
value	Property

Properties of the Scripting Object Model

Properties are a set of characteristics of an object. For instance, a `Button` object can be disabled and show a given text string. This section contains all the properties for all the script objects in the SOM. For each property, there is a snippet of code to demonstrates how it is used. On the CD-ROM, you will find a file (with the property name) that demonstrates the use of the property.

absolutePosition Property

The absolutePosition property is the 1-based index of the absolute position of the current record within the recordset. For example, the following code fills the text box with the position of the current record. You will find a complete working example on the CD-ROM in the file absolutePosition.asp.

```
Textbox3.value=Recordset1.absolutePosition
```

alt Property

This is the alternative text on a button object that appears in the browser when you declare an image for a button, but the image file is not available. You might also see this

Scripting Object Model Reference

APPENDIX G

983

G

SCRIPTING OBJECT
MODEL
REFERENCE

text on the screen as a type of ToolTip when you hover the mouse over the image. The following JavaScript function changes the `alt` text for `Button1` when you click the button. Run the file alt.asp on the CD-ROM to see the effect.

```
function mybutton_onclick() {
mybutton.alt='Replaced!';
}
```

BOF Property

The `BOF` (Beginning of File) property, which belongs to the `Recordset` object, returns True while the cursor is before the first record of the recordset. In the following code snippet, assume that the cursor is already at the first record. Clicking the button attempts to move the cursor to the preceding record. At this point, the cursor is before the first record, and the code puts a message on the HTML page. The file bof.asp shows the `BOF` property in action.

```
<%
sub button1_onclick()
Recordset1.movePrevious
if Recordset1.BOF=true then
    Response.Write "Hit beginning of file"
end if
end sub
%>
```

cancelEvent Property

The `cancelEvent` property, part of the `PageObject` script object, determines whether to pass a client-side event to the server for processing.

In the following code example, the `onbeforeserverevent` event traps the click of the Delete button. If the user confirms the deletion in the client-side Alert box, the `onclick` event is passed to the server. If the user doesn't confirm the action, the script sets the `cancelEvent` property to True. When `cancelEvent` is True, the click of the Delete button never reaches the server. The complete script is on the CD-ROM in the file cancelEvent.asp.

```
<SCRIPT language="VBscript" runat=server>
sub btnDelete_onclick()
Recordset1.deleteRecord
end sub
</SCRIPT>

<SCRIPT LANGUAGE="Javascript">
function thisPage_onbeforeserverevent( myobj, myevent ){
if (myobj=="btnDelete"){
```

```
if(myevent=="onclick"){
    if (confirm("Confirm Deletion?")){
        alert("Deleted.");
    }
    else {
        alert("Setting cancelEvent to true.");
        thisPage.cancelEvent = true;
    }
}
}
}
```

disabled Property

When the script object's `disabled` property is True, the object can't receive the focus and is left out of the tab order. The `disabled` property applies to the `Checkbox`, `Listbox`, and `Textbox` script objects. In the following JavaScript function, a click of the button disables the objects called `mycheckbox` and `mytextbox`. When you run the code in disabled.asp on the CD-ROM, you will notice that the text box displays characters, but you can't change the text.

```
function mybutton_onclick() {
mycheckbox.disabled=true;
mytextbox.value='These controls are disabled.';
mytextbox.disabled=true;
```

EOF Property

The `EOF` (End of File) property, which belongs to the `Recordset` object, returns True while the cursor is after the last record of the recordset. In the following code snippet, assume that the cursor is already at the last record. Clicking the button attempts to move the cursor to the next record. At that point, the cursor is after the last record, and the code puts a message on the HTML page. The file eof.asp on the CD-ROM shows the `EOF` property in action.

```
<%
sub button1_onclick()
Recordset1.moveNext
if Recordset1.EOF=true then
    Response.Write "Hit end of file"
end if
end sub
%>
```

firstEntered Property

The `firstEntered` `PageObject` property is useful for determining whether a form has already been submitted. The `firstEntered` property returns True if the page has not yet posted any data by way of a form to this same page. If there has been a POST, firstEntered returns False. In the following code snippet, the first time the page appears, the user sees a colorful button image. Subsequent refreshes of the page show only a regular button. The complete source code is on the file firstEntered.asp on the CD-ROM.

```
Sub thisPage_onenter()
if thisPage.firstEntered=true then
  Button1.src="welcome.gif"
  Button1.setStyle 1
else
  Button1.value="Sorry, no fanfare the second time."
  Button1.setStyle 0
end if
End Sub
```

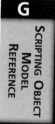

id Property

The id property, like the name property, is a character string that identifies a control. In the following JavaScript function, a click of the button changes the button's id to notmybuttonnow. The full source code is on the CD-ROM in the file id.asp.

You should be careful when changing the id property on-the-fly. Doing so can complicate or even crash your code because previous references to the object might no longer be valid.

```
function mybutton_onclick() {
mybutton.id='notmybuttonnow';
}
```

The id property applies to the Button, Checkbox, Label, Listbox, OptionGroup, Recordset, RecordsetNavbar, and Textbox script objects.

maintainState Property

The maintainState property determines whether the script object's state is maintained during trips to the server. In the following example, clicking Button1 sets maintainState to False for Textbox1:

```
Sub Button1_onclick()
Textbox1.maintainState=false
Textbox1.value=Textbox1.maintainState
End Sub
```

Look for the full example in the file maintainState.asp on the CD-ROM. The maintainState property applies to the Button, Checkbox, Label, Listbox, OptionGroup, Recordset, RecordsetNavbar, and Textbox script objects.

name Property

The name property, like the id property, is a character string that identifies a script object. In the following JavaScript function, a click of the button changes the button's name to notmybuttonnow. The full source code is on the CD-ROM in the file name.asp.

```
function mybutton_onclick() {
mybutton.name='notmybuttonnow';
}
```

The name property applies to the Button, Checkbox, Label, Listbox, OptionGroup, Recordset, RecordsetNavbar, and Textbox script objects.

navigateTarget Property

You can use the PageObject's navigateTarget property with the navigate method to force navigation into a different frame.

> **CAUTION**
>
> Make sure that the frameset object and frame names that you supply to the navigateTarget property exist. If not, you will get nasty script errors.

The following code is from toc.asp, which fills the left frame in the frameset created by navigateTarget.asp. Before calling the navigateURL method, the script sets the target frame (tmain) in which the HTML page will appear. By clicking a button, in the left frame, you make a different page appear in the right frame.

```
<SCRIPT language=JavaScript>
function Button1_onclick() {
thisPage.navigateTarget=window.parent.frames.tmain;
thisPage.navigateURL("main2.htm");
}
function Button2_onclick() {
thisPage.navigateTarget=window.parent.frames.tmain;
thisPage.navigateURL("main3.htm");
}
</SCRIPT>
```

pageSize Property

The pageSize property of the RecordsetNavBar script object determines how many records to move for each click of the button. By default, the Next and Previous buttons on the `RecordsetNavBar` object move one record at a time. You can change the number of records by setting the `pageSize` property to an integer greater than 1. In the following code snippet, the navigation buttons Previous (`RecordsetNavbar1.getButton(1)`) and Next (`RecordsetNavbar1.getButton(2)`) move three records instead of one on each click. The file eof.asp on the CD-ROM shows the `EOF` property in action.

```
function _initRecordsetNavbar1()
{
    RecordsetNavbar1.pageSize=3;
    RecordsetNavbar1.setAlignment(1);
    RecordsetNavbar1.setButtonStyles(170);
    RecordsetNavbar1.updateOnMove = false;
    RecordsetNavbar1.setDataSource(Recordset1);
    RecordsetNavbar1.getButton(0).value = ' ¦< ';
    RecordsetNavbar1.getButton(1).value = '  <  ';
    RecordsetNavbar1.getButton(2).value = '  >  ';
    RecordsetNavbar1.getButton(3).value = ' >¦ ';
}
```

selectedIndex Property

Used in a `Listbox` script object, the `selectedIndex` property sets or returns the index of a selected entry. This property enables you to preset an item as a choice within a list box. The `selectedIndex` is a *zero-based integer*, meaning the first item in the list box has an index of zero.

In the following example, the `selectedIndex` property of `Listbox1` is set to 3, meaning the fourth item (`Yellow`) is highlighted. The full working code is on the CD-ROM in the file selectedIndex.asp.

```
<%
Listbox1.selectedIndex = 3
Listbox1.addItem "Green",1
Listbox1.addItem "Blue",2
Listbox1.addItem "Red",3
Listbox1.addItem "Yellow",4
Response.Write Listbox1.selectedIndex & "<BR>"
Listbox1.display
%>
```

size Property

The `size` property of the `Listbox` script object sets or returns the number of items that appear in a list box display, not the number that the list box actually contains. For instance, if you set the `size` property to 3, as shown in the following code, the list box is tall enough to display three of the five choices. You have to scroll to see the remainder of the entries. Look for the file size.asp on the CD-ROM for the full source code.

```
<%
Listbox1.size = 3
Listbox1.addItem "Green",1
Listbox1.addItem "Blue",2
Listbox1.addItem "Red",3
Listbox1.addItem "Yellow",4
Listbox1.addItem "White",5
Listbox1.display
%>
```

src Property

The src property applies to the Button script object when the button is displayed as an image. This property is a handy way to change the appearance of a button on-the-fly by changing the image file to which the button refers.

For instance, in the following code snippet, the script object Button1 starts life as the image "push.gif", but the script tests a certain session variable and, based on the results, changes the src property to "done.gif", which is a different image. To see the effect, run the full source code in the file src.asp on the CD-ROM.

```
<%
session("state")= not session("state")
if session("state") then
  Button1.src="done.gif"
else
  Button1.src="push.gif"
end if
%>
<P>
<!--#INCLUDE FILE="_ScriptLibrary/Button.ASP"-->
<SCRIPT LANGUAGE=JavaScript RUNAT=Server>
function _initButton1()
{
    Button1.src = 'push.gif';
    Button1.alt = 'Push this button';
    Button1.setStyle(1);
}
function _Button1_ctor()
{
    CreateButton('Button1', _initButton1, null);
}
</script>
<% Button1.display %>
<%response.write "<P>Button1.src=" & Button1.src%>
```

updateOnMove Property

The updateOnMove property applies to the RecordsetNavbar script object. When set to True, the recordset is updated each time the user clicks a button on the RecordsetNavbar object. When False, you, as programmer, have to provide a means to update the data in the recordset, using the updateRecord method.

In the following code snippet, the updateOnMove property of the myNavbar RecordsetNavbar is set to False. If the user changes information in a bound field, the change is lost when he or she clicks the navigation buttons, because there's no automatic update. For a full example of the updateOnMove property, look on the CD-ROM in the file updateOnMove.asp.

```
function _initmyNavbar()
{
    myNavbar.setAlignment(1);
    myNavbar.setButtonStyles(170);
    myNavbar.updateOnMove = false;
    myNavbar.setDataSource(myRecordset);
    myNavbar.getButton(0).value = ' |< ';
    myNavbar.getButton(1).value = ' < ';
    myNavbar.getButton(2).value = ' > ';
    myNavbar.getButton(3).value = ' >| ';
}
```

value

The value property sets or retrieves the value attribute of the Button and Textbox script objects. The following code snippet, found in the file value.asp on the CD-ROM, uses the onclick event of the Button object to change the button's text and the contents of the text box.

The value property is often used in a Textbox script object to capture user responses. Other code can subsequently validate or reformat the text and even re-insert the corrected text for the user.

Because the value property of a button sets the button text, you can reuse the same button object by updating the value with script.

```
<%
sub button1_onclick()
Button1.value="Don't click"
Textbox1.value="This is the value I provided"
end sub
%>
```

G

Methods of the Scripting Object Model

Methods are functions of an object that perform some action. The SOM in Visual InterDev 6 (VI 6) offers a wide variety of methods for its objects, ranging from adding and deleting records to changing text and making the script object disappear from the screen.

This section contains all the methods for all the script objects in the SOM. For each method, there is a snippet of code to demonstrate how it is used. On the CD-ROM, you will find a file bearing the method name that shows the method in action.

addImmediate Method

The `addImmediate` method of the `Recordset` script object adds a record, including its field values, all in one step.

> **NOTE**
>
> Microsoft has reported a bug that affects the `addImmediate` method in VI 6: "Inserting a New Record with `addImmediate` May Fail." Check Knowledge Base article Q190591 for more information and the current status.

To use `addImmediate`, include the field names as an array and the corresponding values as another array and pass both to the method, the `fields` array first. The syntax is shown in this code snippet. The complete working code is on the CD-ROM in the file addImmediate.asp.

```
<%
sub Button1_onclick()
Dim flds(1)
Dim vals(1)
flds(0) = "IPAddress"
flds(1) = "EventTime"
vals(0) = Request.ServerVariables("REMOTE_ADDR")
vals(1) = now()
Recordset1.open
Recordset1.addImmediate flds, vals
end sub
%>
```

addItem Method

The `addItem` method, used by the `Listbox` and `OptionGroup` script objects, adds an item to the available items. When calling `addItem`, you should pass the name of the item, its value, and its index. In the following subroutine, each click of the mouse inserts another month name, month number, and index value into a list box and option group. On the CD-ROM, look for the file addItem.asp, which contains the full source code for the `addItem` example.

```
<%
sub Button1_onclick()
x=session("x")+1
Listbox1.addItem MonthName(x,0),x,x
OptionGroup1.addItem MonthName(x,0),x,x
session("x")=x
if session("x")>11 then session("x")=11
end sub
%>
```

addRecord Method

The `addRecord` method, which belongs to the `Recordset` script object, creates a new record in the current recordset. To write data into the newly created record, you have to use the `updateRecord` method.

> **NOTE**
>
> Microsoft has reported a bug in the `addRecord` method in an article titled "Inserting a New Record with `addImmediate` May Fail." The article warns that "if you are using `addRecord()` and `updateRecord()` to insert new records, you could run into this bug if you call `updateRecord()` and then `addRecord()` on the same round-trip." Check Knowledge Base article Q190591 for more information and the current status.

Because of problems with adding a record and updating it during the same trip to the server, the following code sample uses a two-trip method. A click of `Button2` adds a record, disables `Button2`, and enables `Button1`. After the record has been added, you can click Button1 to update the record. The full source code is included on the CD-ROM in the file addRecord.asp.

```
Sub Button1_onclick()
Recordset1.updateRecord
Button2.disabled=false
Button1.disabled=true
End Sub

Sub Button2_onclick()
Button1.disabled=false
Recordset1.addRecord
Button2.disabled=true
End Sub
```

`advise` Method

Use the `advise` method to extend the SOM beyond the built-in events. As the example here shows, you can add an event that you wouldn't normally find in a server-side script.

The `advise` method registers an object to be notified when an event fires, and it indicates what function to call when that event occurs. In the following code sample, the `advise` method in the first subroutine "advises" the Web page that when `Button3` fires an onmouseover event, the server should run the script function called `Button3_onmouseover()`:

```
Sub thisPage_onenter()
myhandle=Button3.advise("onmouseover",
 ➥"Button3_onmouseover()")
End Sub
```

For its part, the `Button3_onmouseover()` routine writes a string and the time to `Label1`, as shown in the following snippet:

```
Sub Button3_onmouseover()
Label1.setCaption "Mouseover event at " & time()
end sub
```

In this case you've created a server-side onmouseover event, even though the SOM doesn't support this event directly.

Note that you can cancel the registration by calling the `unadvise` method. However, if you are using `unadvise`, make sure that you get a handle from the `advise` method. For another example of the `advise` method, see the `unadvise` method later in this appendix.

The advise method is available in the `Button`, `Checkbox`, `Listbox`, `OptionGroup`, `PageObject`, `Recordset`, `RecordsetNavbar`, and `Textbox` script objects.

See the files advise.asp and unadvise.asp on the CD-ROM for examples of the advise method in action.

bindAllColumns Method

The bindAllColumns method of the Grid script object makes all columns visible in the grid. This is a handy shortcut way of getting all your data from a table onto the grid with very little code. The following example is from bindAllColumns.asp on the CD-ROM. This code snippet shows how the bindAllColumns method avoids having to include columns one by one when you want to include them all:

```
<SCRIPT LANGUAGE=JavaScript RUNAT=Server>
function _initGrid1()
{
Grid1.pageSize = 20;
Grid1.setDataSource(Recordset1);
Grid1.bindAllColumns();
Grid1.hasPageNumber = true;
}
function _Grid1_ctor()
{
   CreateDataGrid('Grid1',_initGrid1);
}
</SCRIPT>

<% Grid1.display %>
```

cancelOperation Method

The cancelOperation method of the RecordsetNavbar script object cancels a click or move from the navigation bar. This method prevents the moveFirst, movePrevious, moveNext, and moveLast methods from navigating through the recordset. For example, in the following code snippet, the user can move to the last record only once. At that point, the moveLast button on RecordsetNavbar1 displays the text End, and further clicks trigger the button's cancelOperation method. You will find the full working example on the CD-ROM in the file cancelOperation.asp.

```
Sub RecordsetNavbar1_onlastclick()
RecordsetNavbar1.getButton(0).value = " |< "
if RecordsetNavbar1.getButton(3).value = " >| " then
  RecordsetNavbar1.getButton(3).value = "End"
end if
if RecordsetNavbar1.getButton(3).value = "End" then
  RecordsetNavbar1.cancelOperation
  RecordsetNavbar1.getButton(0).value = " |< "
end if
End Sub
```

cancelUpdate Method

The `cancelUpdate` method of the `Recordset` script object cancels the changes that are about to be made to the current record. In the following code snippet, the Save button's `onclick` event checks the IP address of the computer and, if necessary, calls the recordset's `cancelUpdate` method to prevent the save from happening:

```
Sub Save_onclick()
if Request.ServerVariables("REMOTE_ADDR") =
    ➥"111.111.111.115" then
Response.Write "You can't save from address
    ➥111.111.111.115"
Recordset1.cancelUpdate
end if
End Sub
```

Look in the file cancelUpdate.asp on the CD-ROM for a complete example of this method.

clear Method

Use the `clear` method with the `Listbox` and `OptionGroup` script objects to remove all items from the object.

In the following code snippet, a click of `Button1` calls the `clear` method to remove all items from `Listbox1`. The routine adds a generic item to the list box as a placeholder. The complete source code that demonstrates the `clear` method is on the CD-ROM in the file clear.asp.

```
Sub Button1_onclick()
ListBox1.clear()
Listbox1.addItem("--None--")
OptionGroup1.clear()
OptionGroup1.addItem("--None--")
Button1.value="Cleared"
End Sub
```

close Method

The `close` method of the `Recordset` script object closes the recordset object. This method is often useful when you are changing a SQL query on-the-fly. In that case, you have to close the recordset before opening it with the new results.

The following code snippet, from close.asp on the CD-ROM, shows how clicking one button opens the recordset and clicking the other button closes the recordset:

```
Sub Button1_onclick()
Recordset1.open()
End Sub

Sub Button2_onclick()
Recordset1.close()
End Sub
```

createDE Method

The `PageObject` object's `createDE` method creates a data environment named `DE`, which you can use to reference command objects and connections. The VI environment creates a data environment automatically when you add a data command to your project. The following example, an excerpt from createDE.asp on the CD-ROM, shows the creation of the data environment `DE`:

```
thisPage.createDE();
var rsTmp = DE.Recordsets('Command2');
Recordset1.setRecordSource(rsTmp);
Recordset1.open();
```

deleteRecord Method

The `deleteRecord` method, which belongs to the `Recordset` script object, removes the current record from the recordset.

In the following code snippet, the `onclick` event of `Button1` gets a record number from `Textbox1`. The routine calls the `moveAbsolute` method to move to the record and then calls `deleteRecord` to remove the record. Notice that you should use the `requery` method after deleting a record. The complete working example of the `deleteRecord` method is in the deleteRecord.asp file on the CD-ROM.

```
Sub Button1_onclick()
if Textbox1.value <> "" then
   Recordset1.moveAbsolute cint(Textbox1.value)
   Recordset1.deleteRecord
end if
Textbox1.value =1
Recordset1.requery
End Sub
```

display Method

The `display` method inserts the script object into the HTML stream. That is, the text that supports the object is sent to the browser. Use the `show` and `hide` methods to make the object visible or invisible on the screen. The `display` method is supported by the `Button`, `Checkbox`, `Listbox`, `OptionGroup`, `Label`, `RecordsetNavbar`, and `Textbox` script objects.

In the following code snippet, a click of `Button2` displays `Button1` using the `display` method and makes `Button2` disappear from the screen by calling the button's `hide` method. The complete example is on the CD-ROM in the file display.asp.

```
Sub Button2_onclick()
Button1.display
Button2.hide
End Sub
```

endPageContent Method

Use the `PageObject`'s `endPageContent` method to mark the end of text to insert into the HTML stream. Text that appears after the `endPageContent` is not passed to the Response object and therefore does not appear in the browser.

You can use this method to create conditional text on the HTML page. In the following excerpt from endPageContent.asp on the CD-ROM, the script checks whether the person is a member and, based on the result, starts and stops the output of text:

```
<%
if thisPage.getmember()=true then
thisPage.startPageContent()
%>
Welcome member!</FONT></H2>
<% end if%>

<%if thisPage.getmember()=true then
thisPage.endPageContent()
end if
%>

<%if thisPage.getmember()=false then%>
If you'd like to join, click the button!</FONT></H2>
<H3>
<!--#INCLUDE FILE="_ScriptLibrary/Button.ASP"-->
<SCRIPT LANGUAGE=JavaScript RUNAT=Server>
function _initButton1()
{
  Button1.value = 'Join';
  Button1.setStyle(0);
}
```

```
function _Button1_ctor()
{
  CreateButton('Button1', _initButton1, null);
}
</script>
<% Button1.display %>

<%end if
%>
```

getAlignment Method

The getAlignment method retrieves the alignment of the OptionGroup and RecordsetNavbar script objects. If the object's buttons are displayed horizontally, getAlignment returns a value of 0. A value of 1 indicates that the buttons are aligned vertically.

In the following example from getAlignment.asp on the CD-ROM, a click of Button1 toggles the alignment of two sets of buttons. The subroutine fetches the current alignment with the getAlignment method and sets the new alignment with the setAlignment method.

```
Sub Button1_onclick()
dim align
align=OptionGroup1.getAlignment()
if align=1 then
    align=0
else
    align=1
end if
OptionGroup1.setAlignment(align)
RecordsetNavbar1.setAlignment(align)
End Sub
```

getBookmark Method

The getBookmark method belongs to the Recordset script object. Calling getBookmark while on a record is like marking the record for reference later. You can return to the marked record with setBookmark.

> **NOTE**
>
> The names of getBookMark and setBookMark sound as though they should be reversed. It is easier to keep them straight if you consider that getBookMark is getting the bookmark information from the record and that setBookMark is setting the current record to the record that matches the bookmark you provide.

In the following code snippet, a click of Button2 fetches the bookmark information from a record. After clicking Button3 to navigate to another record, you can click Button1 to return to the bookmarked record. Button1 calls the setBookMark method and passes it the bookmark information.

```
Sub Button2_onclick()
session("bmkmrk")= Recordset1.getBookMark()
Textbox1.value=Textbox2.value
End Sub

Sub Button1_onclick()
Recordset1.Open()
Recordset1.setBookMark(session("bmkmrk"))
End Sub

Sub Button3_onclick()
Recordset1.moveNext()
End Sub
```

getBorder Method

Use the getBorder method of the OptionGroup script object to determine whether there's a border around an option box. The getBorder method returns 0 if there is no border and 1 if there is a border.

The following code, from getBorder.asp on the CD-ROM, shows how to use getBorder and setBorder and a button's onclick event to toggle a border around OptionGroup1:

```
Sub Button1_onclick()
border=OptionGroup1.getBorder()
if border = 0 then
   OptionGroup1.setBorder(1)
   Button1.value="Remove Border"
else
   OptionGroup1.setBorder(0)
   Button1.value="Add Border"
end if
End Sub
```

getButton Method

The getButton method returns a reference to one of the Button objects that is part of the OptionGroup or RecordsetNavbar script objects. The sample code that follows shows how you can use the getSelectedIndex method to determine which button is selected and, with that value, get a reference to the button itself. After you have the reference, you can retrieve the button's `value` or other property. The complete code for the sample is on the CD-ROM in the file getButton.asp.

```
Sub Button1_onclick()
sel=OptionGroup1.getSelectedIndex()
val=OptionGroup1.getButton(sel).value
Response.Write "The option you selected returned a
➥ value of  " & val
End Sub
```

getButtonStyles Method

The `getButtonStyles` method returns a byte whose value depends on whether individual buttons in the `RecordsetNavbar` script object are set as text or as images. For instance, if all the buttons are images, the binary value is 01010101 bin or 85 decimal. If all the buttons are text, the binary value is 10101010 or 170 decimal. By reading individual bits, you can determine the status of any and all buttons within the group.

The following excerpt from getButtonStyles.asp displays the decimal value returned by the `getButtonStyles` method:

```
Sub Button1_onclick()
myval = RecordsetNavbar2.getButtonStyles()
Response.Write "getButtonStyles() returns " & myval
End Sub
```

See the code in setButtonStyles.asp for a utility that calculates the values that set any or all the buttons as text or images within a `RecordsetNavbar` object.

getCaption Method

The getCaption Method returns the text of a `Label` script object, and the caption portion of `OptionGroup` and `Checkbox` script objects.

If you get text such as this `function _LBL_getCaption()` instead of the text you expected, you probably forgot to put brackets on the method in VBScript.

The following snippet from getCaption.asp on the CD-ROM fetches the text from a `Label` script object and displays the text in a text box:

```
<%
mytext=Label1.getCaption()
Textbox1.value=mytext
%>
```

getChecked Method

The getChecked method returns True if the Checkbox scripting object is checked; otherwise, it returns False. In the code snippet that follows, the subroutine determines whether the check box is checked and reports the results by setting the caption of a Label script object. The complete code is in getChecked.asp on the CD-ROM.

```
Sub Button1_onclick()
chkvalue=Checkbox1.getChecked()
if chkvalue = false then
  Label1.setCaption("The checkbox is not checked.")
else
  Label1.setCaption("The checkbox is checked..")
end if
End Sub
```

getColumnCount Method

The getColumnCount method returns the number of columns of a Textbox script object. The code that follows retrieves the number of columns in Textbox1 and reports the results to the screen by setting the caption of the Label1 object. You will find the complete code on the CD-ROM in getColumnCount.asp.

```
Sub Button1_onclick()
col=Textbox1.getColumnCount()
Textbox1.value=space(col-1) & "x"
Label1.setCaption("The textbox is " & col & " columns wide.")
End Sub
```

getConnectString Method

The getConnectString method, available from the Recordset script object, returns the connection string that is being used by the recordset. The following code calls getConnectString to retrieve the connection string for Recordset1. The full source code is available on the CD-ROM in the file getConnectString.asp.

```
<%
conn=Recordset1.getConnectString()
Label1.setCaption(conn)
%>
```

getCount Method

Use the getCount method with the Listbox, OptionGroup, and Recordset script objects and the fields child object to return the number of items in the object. The following code snippet writes the number of fields in `Recordset1`. See getCount.asp on the CD-ROM for complete examples of using `getCount` with all the objects that support it.

```
<%Response.Write "The number of Recordset1 fields items: "
 ➥& Recordset1.fields.getCount()%>
```

getDataField Method

The `getDataField` method returns the name of the recordset data field to which the object is bound. You can use this method with the `Checkbox`, `Label`, `Listbox`, `OptionGroup`, and `Textbox` script objects.

The following code snippet uses `getDataField` to retrieve the name of the recordset data field to which `Textbox1` is bound. Look for the file getDataField.asp on the CD-ROM for the full source code.

```
<%Label1.setCaption("The textbox is bound to: " &
 ➥Textbox1.getDataField())%>
```

getDataFormatAs Method

Use the `getDataFormatAs` to determine whether the `Label` scripting object is rendering HTML code as HTML or as regular text. This method returns `html` if the object renders HTML markup. If not, it returns `text`. The following code snippet displays the data format that `Label1` is using. For the complete code, see getDataFormatAs.asp on the CD-ROM. For further information, see the `setDataFormatAs` method.

```
<%
Response.Write "Label1's format is: " &
➥Label1.getDataFormatas() & "<P>"
%>
```

getDataSource Method

The `getDataSource` method returns the `Recordset` script object to which the scripting object is bound. You can use this method with the `Checkbox`, `Label`, `Listbox`, `OptionGroup`, `RecordsetNavbar`, and `Textbox` script objects.

The following code snippet displays the name of the data source to which `RecordsetNavbar1` is bound. The complete source code is on the CD-ROM in the file getDataSource.asp. See also the `setDataSource` method.

```
<%
Response.write "The navbar is bound to: " &
➥RecordsetNavbar1.getDataSource().name
%>
```

getDHTMLDataSourceID Method

The getDHTMLDataSourceID method returns the data source for the Recordset script object. This method is used in client-side script only.

In the following code snippet, Label1 displays the data source ID after all the data has been received by the client. For the full source code, refer to getDHTMLDataSourceID.htm on the accompanying CD-ROM.

```
function Recordset1_ondatasetcomplete() {
Label1.setCaption(Recordset1.getDHTMLDataSourceID());
}
```

getMaxLength Method

The getMaxLength method returns the maximum number of characters that the Textbox script object accepts. Notice that this value does not necessarily correspond to the physical width of the text box on the screen.

In the following code snippet, Textbox1 displays the maximum number of characters that it will accept. For the full source code, see getMaxLength.asp on the CD-ROM. Also, see the setMaxLength method.

```
<%Textbox1.value="Max chars.=" & Textbox1.getMaxLength()%>
```

getName Method

The getName method of the fields child object returns the name of the field. The field name corresponds to the zero-based index value that you pass to this method. For example, in the following excerpt from getName.asp on the CD-ROM, the code displays the name of the first field in Recordset1:

```
<%
Response.Write Recordset1.fields.getName(0)
%>
```

getPagingNavbar Method

The getPagingNavbar method creates a reference to the navigation object of the Grid script object. Use this method to set paging and navigation options.

> **NOTE**
>
> Microsoft has reported a bug related to this method in "getRecordsetNavbar and getPagingNavbar Methods Do Not Work." The article reports this workaround: Make sure that you put parentheses at the end of each of the Grid's methods. Instead of `Grid.getRecordsetNavbar.updateOnMove`, type `Grid.getRecordsetNavbar().updateOnMove`.

In the following excerpt from `getPagingNavbar.asp`, the `Button1 onclick` routine creates a reference to `Grid1`'s navigation bar object. When it has the reference, the code displays the name of the navigation bar (`Grid1_PageNavbar`) in the browser.

```
Sub Button1_onclick()
set objPageNavbar = Grid1.getPagingNavbar()
Response.write objPageNavbar.name
End Sub
```

getParameter Method

The `getParameter` method, which belongs to the `Recordset` script object, returns the parameter that was passed to a stored procedure or parameterized query. As shown in the following sample code, when you call `getParameter`, you have to pass the index value of the parameter in question. Look for a working example on the CD-ROM in getParameter.asp.

```
<%Response.Write Recordset2.getParameter(1)%>
```

get*property* Method

The get*property* method (where *property* is a user-defined name) returns the value of *property*. This method belongs to the `PageObject` script object.

You create the property name on the `PageObject` property sheet. As shown in Figure G.2, you type the name of the user-defined property on the `Properties` tab.

The following code snippet sets the value of the user-defined property `kprop` to `"myvalue"` and then retrieves and displays the value, using `getkprop()`:

```
<%
thisPage.setkprop("myvalue")
Response.write thisPage.getkprop()
%>
```

With this method, the PageObject script object gives you easy access to page, session, and application variables that you create. The complete source code is on the CD-ROM in the file getproperty.asp. See also the set*property* method.

FIGURE G.2

Define your own properties in the PageObject's property sheet.

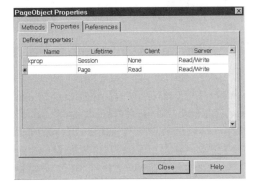

getRecordsetNavbar Method

The getRecordsetNavbar method returns a reference to the recordset navigation object contained in the Grid script object. After you create the reference to the recordset navigation bar, you can manipulate its properties.

> **NOTE**
>
> Microsoft has reported a bug related to this method in "getRecordsetNavbar and getPagingNavbar Methods Do Not Work." The article reports this workaround: Make sure that you put parentheses at the end of each of the Grid's methods. Instead of Grid.getRecordsetNavbar.updateOnMove, type Grid.getRecordsetNavbar().updateOnMove.

The following code snippet uses the navigation bar reference to change the third button into an image button. The button then uses bike.gif as its source image. See the complete source code in the file getRecordsetNavbar.asp on the CD-ROM.

```
Sub Button1_onclick()
set objrsNavbar = Grid1.getRecordsetNavbar()
objrsNavbar.getButton(2).src="bike.gif"
objrsNavbar.getButton(2).setStyle 1
Button1.disabled=true
End Sub
```

getRecordSource Method

The `getRecordSource` method of the `Recordset` script object returns an ADO recordset object. This lets you use properties and methods that aren't supported in the `Recordset` script object itself.

The following sample code gets a reference to `Recordset1` (`myRS`) and uses that reference to set properties such as `CacheSize`. Check the complete source code on the CD-ROM in the file getRecordSource.asp.

```
<%
set myRS=Recordset1.getRecordSource()
Response.write "CursorType: " &  myRS.CursorType & "<BR>"
Response.Write "CacheSize: " & myRS.CacheSize & "<BR>"
Response.write "CursorLocation: " &
➥myRS.CursorLocation & "<BR>"
Response.Write "LockType: " & myRS.LockType & "<BR>"
%>
```

getRowCount Method

The `getRowCount` method returns the number of rows (lines) of a `Textbox` script object.

In the following code, a click of `Button1` causes `Textbox1` to display the number of rows it allows. For the full source code, see getRowCount.asp on the CD-ROM. See also the `setRowCount` method.

```
Sub Button1_onclick()
Textbox1.value= Textbox1.getRowCount()
End Sub
```

getRowSource Method

The `getRowSource` method returns a reference to the `Recordset` script object to which the `Listbox` or `OptionGroup` lookup is bound.

The following sample code shows how to get the name of the recordset to which `Listbox1` is bound. See getRowSource.asp on the CD-ROM for the complete code. Also, see the `setRowSource` method.

```
Sub Button1_onclick()
Textbox1.value=Listbox1.getRowSource().name
End Sub
```

getSelectedIndex Method

The `getSelectedIndex` method returns the zero-based index of the selected radio button in the `OptionGroup` script object.

In the following code snippet, a click of the button fills Textbox1 with the index value of the selected item in OptionGroup1. See getSelectedIndex.asp on the CD-ROM for the complete source code.

```
Sub Button1_onclick()
Textbox1.value=OptionGroup1.getSelectedIndex()
End Sub
```

getSQLText Method

The getSQLText method returns the SQL text that was used to return the recordset for the Recordset script object.

The following code inserts the SQL text from Recordset1 into Textbox1. For the complete source code, see getSQLText.asp on the CD-ROM. See also the setSQLText method.

```
Sub Button1_onclick()
Textbox1.value=Recordset1.getSQLText()
End Sub
```

getState Method

The getState method, which belongs to the PageObject script object, returns a user-defined variable that was defined using setState().

In the following example, Textbox1 is filled with the value of the variable kenval. For the complete source code, see getState.asp on the CD-ROM.

```
Sub Button2_onclick()
Textbox1.value=thisPage.getState(kenval)
End Sub
```

getStyle Method

For the Button and Textbox script objects, the getStyle method retrieves a value for the current object style, such as whether it is a text area or password box, or an image or text button. The following example shows the meanings of the returned values. For a demonstration of the getStyle method, see getStyle.asp on the CD-ROM.

```
Sub Button1_onclick()
select case Textbox1.getStyle()
  case 0
  Textbox1.value="0=Textbox"
  case 1
  Textbox1.value="1=Textarea"
  case 2
  Textbox1.value="2=Password"
end select
```

```
select case Button1.getStyle()
  case 0
  Textbox2.value="0=Text"
  case 1
  Textbox2.value="1=Image"
end select
End Sub
```

getText Method

The getText method retrieves the text (not the item's value) from the selected item in the Listbox script object.

In the following example, each time you select an item, the text appears in Textbox1. See getText.asp on the CD-ROM for the source code.

```
Sub Listbox1_onchange()
Textbox1.value=Listbox1.getText()
End Sub
```

getValue Method

The getValue method returns the value of a selected item from a Listbox or OptionGroup script object, or the name field of the fields script object.

The following code sample retrieves the value from a list box, formats it, and displays it as the caption of Label1. See getValue.asp on the CD-ROM for the source code and its colorful effect.

```
Sub Listbox1_onchange()
thevalue=Listbox1.getvalue(Listbox1.selectedIndex)
Label1.setDataFormatAs "html"
Label1.setCaption "<font color=#" & thevalue & ">" &
➥thevalue & "</font>"
End Sub
```

hide Method

The Button, Checkbox, Grid, Label, Listbox, OptionGroup, RecordsetNavbar, and Textbox script objects support the hide method. As shown in the sample code that follows, this method makes the script object invisible. See also the show method. The source code is available on the CD-ROM in the file hide.asp.

```
Sub Checkbox2_onclick()
if Checkbox2.getChecked() then
   Button1.show()
else
   Button1.hide()
end if
End Sub
```

isOpen Method

The isOpen method returns True if the Recordset script object is open, False if it is not open.

The following code sample tests Recordset1 each time it opens and closes the recordset. The complete working example of the isOpen method is in the isOpen.asp file on the CD-ROM.

```
Sub Button1_onclick()
if Recordset1.isOpen() then
  Recordset1.close()
  Button1.value="Open recordset"
else
  Recordset1.open()
  Button1.value="Close recordset"
end if
Label1.setCaption Recordset1.isOpen()
End Sub
```

isOperationCancelled Method

The isOperationCancelled method, which belongs to the Recordset script object, returns True when a move method was cancelled. The following excerpt from isOperationCancelled.asp shows the use of this method.

```
if  RecordsetNavbar1.isOperationCancelled() then
    Label1.setCaption "An operation was cancelled."
  else
    Label1.setCaption ""
  end if
```

isVisible Method

The isVisible method returns True if the Button, Checkbox, Grid, Label, Listbox, OptionGroup, RecordsetNavbar, or Textbox script object is visible. This method returns False if the object is not visible.

In the following example, the code checks whether the Label1 object is visible and hides or shows it, depending on the result. Look for a full example on the use of the isVisible method on the CD-ROM in the file isVisible.asp.

```
Sub Button1_onclick()
if Label1.isVisible() then
  Button1.value="Click to show message"
  Label1.hide()
else
```

```
    Label1.show()
    Button1.value="Click to hide message"
end if
End Sub
```

move Method

When passed a positive integer, the move method moves the recordset cursor the stated number of records toward the end of the recordset. A negative integer moves toward the beginning of the recordset. All moves are relative to the current cursor position.

The following example accepts an integer from Textbox3 and moves that number of records within the recordset. See the full source code in move.asp on the CD-ROM.

```
Sub Button1_onclick()
if Textbox3.value <> "" then
result=Recordset1.move(cint(Textbox3.value))
end if
End Sub
```

moveAbsolute Method

The moveAbsolute method, which belongs to the Recordset script object, positions the cursor at the record number that is passed to the method.

In the following example, the script accepts a value in Textbox3 and moves to that record number in Recordset1. See the full source code in moveAbsolute.asp on the CD-ROM.

```
Sub Button1_onclick()
if Textbox3.value <> "" then
  theval= cint(Textbox3.value)
  Recordset1.moveAbsolute(theval)
end if
End Sub
```

moveFirst Method

The moveFirst method moves the cursor to the first record in the Recordset script object.

The following code demonstrates the use of this method. See the CD-ROM file moveFirst.asp for the complete source code.

```
Sub Button1_onclick()
Recordset1.moveFirst()
End Sub
```

moveLast Method

The `moveLast` method moves the cursor to the last record in the `Recordset` script object.

The following code demonstrates the use of this method. See the CD-ROM file moveLast.asp for the complete source code.

```
Sub Button1_onclick()
Recordset1.moveLast()
End Sub
```

moveNext Method

The `moveNext` method moves the cursor one record toward the end of the `Recordset` script object.

The following code demonstrates the use of this method. See the CD-ROM file moveNext.asp for the complete source code.

```
Sub Button1_onclick()
Recordset1.moveNext()
End Sub
```

movePrevious Method

The `movePrevious` method moves the cursor one record toward the beginning of the `Recordset` script object.

The following code demonstrates the use of this method. See the CD-ROM file movePrevious.asp for the complete source code.

```
Sub Button1_onclick()
Recordset1.movePrevious()
End Sub
```

navigateURL Method

The `navigateURL` method loads into the browser the page name that is passed to the method. This method requires the `PageObject` script object.

> **NOTE**
>
> Microsoft has acknowledged a bug in this method, under the title "Using Page Object to Navigate URL with Spaces Causes Error." The workaround is to replace spaces in the URL with the characters %20. Check Knowledge Base article ID Q193999 for updates or fixes.

In the following example, the browser displays the page (URL) that the user has typed into Textbox1. The complete source code is on the CD-ROM in the file navigateURL.asp.

```
Sub Button1_onclick()
thisPage.navigateURL(Textbox1.value)
End Sub
```

open Method

The open method opens a Recordset. It belongs to the Recordset script object.

In some circumstances, you will get an error if you try to open a recordset that is already open. Use the isOpen() method to check the recordset's status.

In the following code snippet, taken from open.asp on the CD-ROM, a click of Button1 opens Recordset1:

```
Sub Button1_onclick()
Recordset1.open()
End Sub
```

removeItem Method

The removeItem method, which belongs to the Listbox and OptionGroup script objects, removes the item number passed to the method.

The following code removes an item from Listbox1 and OptionGroup1 on each mouse click. When there are no more items to remove, the button is disabled. See the file removeItem.asp on the CD-ROM for the complete code for this example.

```
Sub Button1_onclick()
if not (Listbox1.removeItem(0) AND
  ➡OptionGroup1.removeItem(0)) then
  Button1.value="Done"
  Button1.disabled=true
end if
End Sub
```

requery Method

The requery method, which belongs to the Recordset script object, returns a new set of records from the open Recordset script object. You usually have to call the requery method after adding a record.

In the following example, the code adds a record to `Recordset1` and requeries the recordset. Then it reports the number of records and the SQL string that created the recordset. For the full source code, see requery.asp on the CD-ROM.

```
Sub Button1_onclick()
Dim flds(1)
Dim vals(1)
flds(0) = "IPAddress"
flds(1) = "EventTime"
vals(0) = Request.ServerVariables("REMOTE_ADDR")
vals(1) = now()
Recordset1.addImmediate flds, vals
Recordset1.requery()
Label1.setCaption Recordset1.getCount()
Label2.setCaption Recordset1.getSQLText()
End Sub
```

selectByCaption Method

When passed a text value, the `selectByCaption` method selects the matching item in the `OptionGroup` script object.

In the following example, the value of `Button1` (`"Tiger"`) is passed to the `selectByCaption` method that selects the Tiger option in the option group. See the file selectByCaption.asp on the CD-ROM for the complete code for this example.

```
Sub Button1_onclick()
OptionGroup1.selectByCaption(Button1.value)
Button1.value="Tiger"
End Sub
```

selectByIndex Method

When passed an index value, the `selectByIndex` method selects the matching item in the `OptionGroup` script object.

The following script passes a random index value to the `selectByIndex` method. The method selects the button of the item that has that index value. See the file selectByIndex.asp on the CD-ROM for the complete code for this example.

```
Sub Button1_onclick()
Randomize
indx=cint((3) * Rnd )
OptionGroup1.selectByIndex(indx)
End Sub
```

selectByText Method

When passed a text string, the selectByText method selects the item that matches the text in the Listbox script object.

In the following example from selectByText.asp, the click of Button1 selects the item whose text is LP in Listbox1. See the file selectByText.asp on the CD-ROM for the complete code for this example.

```
Sub Button1_onclick()
Listbox1.selectByText("LP")
End Sub
```

selectByValue Method

When passed a value, the selectByValue method selects the item that matches the value in the Listbox script object.

In the following example from selectByValue.asp, the click of Button1 passes the value of 2 to Listbox1. Doing so selects the item whose value is 2, which in this case is the item whose text is 45.

```
Sub Button1_onclick()
Listbox1.selectByValue(2)
End Sub
```

See the file selectByValue.asp on the CD-ROM for the complete code for this example.

setAlignment Method

When set to 0, the setAlignment method aligns OptionGroup and RecordsetNavbar script object buttons vertically. Use 1 to align the buttons horizontally.

The following code from setAlignment.asp on the CD-ROM toggles the alignment of the option group and navigation bar buttons:

```
Sub Button1_onclick()
dim align
align=OptionGroup1.getAlignment()
if align=1 then
  align=0
else
  align=1
end if
OptionGroup1.setAlignment(align)
RecordsetNavbar1.setAlignment(align)
End Sub
```

setBookmark Method

The setBookmark method moves to the previously bookmarked record in the Recordset script object. In the following sample code, the previous bookmark is established with the getBookmark method. No matter where you navigate in the recordset, clicking Button2 returns you to the bookmarked record by calling setBookmark. See the CD-ROM file setBookmark.asp for the complete source code.

```
Sub Button2_onclick()
session("bmkmrk")= Recordset1.getBookMark()
Textbox1.value=Textbox2.value
End Sub

Sub Button1_onclick()
Recordset1.Open()
Recordset1.setBookMark(session("bmkmrk"))
End Sub

Sub Button3_onclick()
Recordset1.moveNext()
End Sub
```

setBorder Method

When passed a value of 0, the setBorder method removes the border around the OptionGroup object. Use 1 if you want a border.

The following example toggles the border around OptionGroup1. See the CD-ROM file setBorder.asp for the complete source code.

```
Sub Button1_onclick()
border=OptionGroup1.getBorder()
if border = 0 then
   OptionGroup1.setBorder(1)
   Button1.value="Remove Border"
else
   OptionGroup1.setBorder(0)
   Button1.value="Add Border"
end if
End Sub
```

setButtonStyles Method

The setButtonStyles method sets whether the push buttons on the RecordsetNavbar are text-style buttons or images. Passing the value 170 makes all the buttons appear as regular buttons. A value of 85 sets all the buttons as images.

The following code is from setButtonStyles.asp, a utility that calculates the values for various combinations of button styles:

```
Sub Button1_onclick()
totalval=0
c8=2
c7=8
c6=32
c5=128
if Checkbox8.getChecked() then
  c8=1
end if
if Checkbox7.getChecked() then
  c7=4
end if
if Checkbox6.getChecked() then
  c6=16
end if
if Checkbox5.getChecked() then
  c5=64
end if
totalval=c8 + c7 + c6 + c5
Textbox1.value=totalval
RecordsetNavbar1.setButtonStyles totalval
RecordsetNavbar1.getButton(0).value = " |< "
RecordsetNavbar1.getButton(1).value = "  <  "
RecordsetNavbar1.getButton(2).value = "  >  "
RecordsetNavbar1.getButton(3).value = " >| "
RecordsetNavbar1.getButton(0).src = "start.gif"
RecordsetNavbar1.getButton(1).src = "prev.gif"
RecordsetNavbar1.getButton(2).src = "next.gif"
RecordsetNavbar1.getButton(3).src = "end.gif"
End Sub
```

setCaption Method

The setCaption method sets the text of a Label script object, and the caption portion of OptionGroup and Checkbox script objects.

In the following snippet from setCaption.asp, a click of Button1 takes the text from Textbox1 and sets it as the text for Label1:

```
Sub Button1_onclick()
mytext=Textbox1.value
Label1.setCaption(mytext)
End Sub
```

setChecked Method

The setChecked method sets the state of the Checkbox script object. When passed the value True, the method makes the check box checked. The value False clears the check box.

In the following excerpt from setChecked.asp, a click of Button1 toggles the checked status of Checkbox1:

```
Sub Button1_onclick()
Checkbox1.setChecked(not Checkbox1.getChecked())
End Sub
```

setColumnCount Method

Use the setColumnCount method to set the width of the Textbox script object in columns.

In the code that follows, each click of Button1 doubles the width of Textbox1. See the CD-ROM file setColumnCount.asp for the complete source code.

```
Sub Button1_onclick()
Textbox1.setColumnCount(Textbox1.getColumnCount()*2)
col=Textbox1.getColumnCount()
Textbox1.value=col
Label1.setCaption("The textbox is now " & col & " columns wide.")
End Sub
```

setDataField Method

Use the setDataField method to set the recordset field to which a Checkbox, Listbox, OptionGroup, Textbox, or Label script object is bound.

In this example from setDataField.asp, the user can choose the data field from an option box. The setDataField method binds Textbox1 to the chosen field.

```
Sub Button2_onclick()
Textbox1.setDataField(OptionGroup1.getValue())
Label1.setCaption Textbox1.getDataField()
End Sub

Sub Button1_onclick()
Recordset1.moveNext()
Button2_onclick()
End Sub
```

setDataFormatAs Method

When passed the value `"text"`, the `setDataFormatAs` method specifies that the caption text of the `Label` script object should be rendered as plain text. When passed the value `"html"`, the caption text should be rendered as HTML markup.

The following example demonstrates the difference between the rendering of `Label1`, depending on whether the data format is `"text"` or `"html"`. See the CD-ROM file setDataFormatAs.asp for the complete source code and to see the effect of each value.

```
Sub Button1_onclick()
Label1.setDataFormatAs "text"
Label1.setCaption "<FONT color=red>Check the rendering.</FONT>"
End Sub

Sub Button2_onclick()
Label1.setDataFormatAs "html"
Label1.setCaption "<FONT color=red>Check the rendering.</FONT>"
End Sub
```

setDataSource Method

Use the `setDataSource` method to designate the `Recordset` script object to which the `Checkbox`, `Listbox`, `OptionGroup`, `RecordsetNavbar`, `Textbox`, or `Label` script object should bind for its data. This method enables you to programmatically establish or switch recordsets.

> **NOTE**
>
> Microsoft has reported a bug in VI 6 that pertains to this method: "RecordsetNavbar's Datasource Does Not Persist." Check Knowledge Base article ID Q190946 for updated information or fixes.

The following code, from setDataSource.asp on the CD-ROM, changes the data source for `Textbox1`, depending on which button is clicked. Notice in `setDataSource` that the original code created by the design-time control has been converted to text and altered to allow the switching of recordsets.

```
Sub Button1_onclick()
Textbox1.setDataSource Recordset1
Textbox1.setDataField "CompanyName"
End Sub

Sub Button2_onclick()
Textbox1.setDataSource Recordset2
Textbox1.setDataField "EventTime"
End Sub
```

G

SCRIPTING OBJECT MODEL REFERENCE

setMaxLength Method

The setMaxLength method sets the maximum number of characters that a Textbox script object can accept, regardless of the width of the text box on the page.

The following code sets the maximum number of characters of Textbox1 to 9, even though there appears to be space for more text. See the CD-ROM file setMaxLength.asp for the complete source code.

```
Sub Button1_onclick()
Textbox1.setMaxLength(9)
End Sub
```

setParameter Method

The setParameter method of the Recordset script object passes a parameter to a stored procedure or parameterized query. The first value is an integer representing the index of the parameter. The second value passed to setParameter is the value being passed to the stored procedure or query.

> **NOTE**
>
> Microsoft Knowledge Base article ID Q191149 reports this bug in VI 6:
> "setParameter Does Not Work in Client Scripting Platform."

The following code snippet passes the value of 50 to the stored procedure called byroyalty that is part of the SQL Server pubs database. For the complete code, see the file setParameter.asp on the CD-ROM.

```
Sub Recordset2_onbeforeopen()
Recordset2.setParameter 1, 50
End Sub
```

set*property* Method

Use the set*property* method to assign values to user-defined properties. In this method, *property* is the name of the property that you previously defined with the PageObject DTC.

In the following example, the property kprop is set to "myvalue" using the setkprop method and then read back using the getkprop method. These methods require the PageObject script object. See the CD-ROM file set*property*.asp for the source code.

```
<%
thisPage.setkprop("myvalue")
Response.write thisPage.getkprop()
%>
```

setRecordSource Method

The setRecordSource method sets the connection properties that are required when opening a Recordset script object. If you pass one parameter to this method, it is an ADODB recordset object. If you pass two parameters, they are the connection string and the SQL statement.

The following code snippet from setRecordSource.asp shows the use of the setRecordSource method when passing an ADODB recordset object. For the complete source code, see setRecordSource.asp on the CD-ROM.

```
var cmdTmp = Server.CreateObject('ADODB.Command');
var rsTmp = Server.CreateObject('ADODB.Recordset');
cmdTmp.ActiveConnection = DBConn;
rsTmp.Source = cmdTmp;
cmdTmp.CommandType = 2;
cmdTmp.CommandTimeout = 10;
cmdTmp.CommandText = '`Products`';
rsTmp.CacheSize = 10;
rsTmp.CursorType = 3;
rsTmp.CursorLocation = 3;
rsTmp.LockType = 3;
Recordset1.setRecordSource(rsTmp);
Recordset1.open();
```

setRowCount Method

The setRowCount method sets the number of rows (lines) of a Textbox script object.

In the following example, clicking Button2 sets the number of rows of Textbox1 to 10, expanding the height of the text box. To see the effect, run setRowCount.asp on the CD-ROM.

```
Sub Button1_onclick()
Textbox1.value= Textbox1.getRowCount()
End Sub

Sub Button2_onclick()
Textbox1.setRowCount(10)
Textbox1.value= Textbox1.getRowCount()
End Sub
```

setRowSource Method

The setRowSource method designates the Recordset script object, the field that is the source of the data, and the bound field for a Listbox or OptionGroup script object.

> **TIP**
>
> If you plan to set the source programmatically, take care when creating the Listbox or OptionGroup with the design-time controls. Leave the Recordset and Field boxes blank in the DTC.

In the following code snippet from setRowSource.asp, Listbox1's recordset source is set to Recordset1. The object draws its field data from the ContactFirstName field, and it is bound to the ContactFirstName field.

```
Sub Button1_onclick()
Listbox1.setRowSource Recordset1,"ContactFirstName",
    ➡"ContactFirstName"
End Sub
```

setSQLText Method

This is an important method for changing recordsets on-the-fly or based on user input. The setSQLText method sets the SQL statement that the Recordset script object uses to query the database.

> **NOTE**
>
> Microsoft has reported a bug in VI 6 that relates to this method: "ADO Error 800a0cc1 Using SetSQLText Or SetRecordSource." Check Microsoft Knowledge Base article ID Q190589 for updates or fixes.
>
> To get satisfactory results, you might have to close the recordset before using setSQLText. You should call setSQLText and then open the recordset.

The following code snippet shows the setSQLText method in action. For the source code, see the file setSQLText.asp on the CD-ROM.

```
Sub Button1_onclick()
Recordset1.close
```

```
Recordset1.setSQLText "select * from `Orders` where
  ➥EmployeeID=2"
Recordset1.open
End Sub
```

setState Method

The setState method, which belongs to the PageObject script object, sets the value of a user-defined property. You can reference this user-defined property from one page to another or within the same page. The first value that you pass to the setState method is the property name, and the second is the value you want to assign to the property.

In the following example, a click of Button1 assigns the current date and time to the property called kenval. You will find the complete working code in setState.asp on the CD-ROM.

```
Sub Button1_onclick()
thisPage.setState kenval,now()
Textbox1.value="thisPage.setState kenval,now()"
Button2.disabled=false
End Sub
```

G

SCRIPTING OBJECT MODEL REFERENCE

setStyle Method

By passing various values to the setStyle method, you set the style of the Button and Textbox script objects. A Button script object can appear as a normal button or as an image button. A Textbox script object can appear as a text box, text area control, or a password box.

The following sample code shows the meanings of the valid values for each object. For the full working code, see setStyle.asp on the CD-ROM.

```
Sub Button1_onclick()
select case Textbox1.getStyle()
  case 0
  Textbox1.value="0=Textbox"
  case 1
  Textbox1.value="1=Textarea"
  case 2
  Textbox1.value="2=Password"
end select
select case Button1.getStyle()
  case 0
  Textbox2.value="0=Text"
  case 1
  Textbox2.value="1=Image"
```

```
end select
End Sub

Sub Button2_onclick()
Textbox1.setStyle(1)
Button1.src="getstyle.gif"
Button1.setStyle(1)
Button1_onclick()
End Sub
```

setText Method

The setText method sets the text of the selected item in a Listbox script object.

In the following code snippet from setText.asp, a click of Button1 replaces the selected item in Listbox1 with the text found in Textbox1:

```
Sub Button1_onclick()
Listbox1.setText Textbox1.value,Listbox1.selectedIndex
End Sub
```

setValue Method

The setValue method sets the value of a Listbox, OptionGroup, or fields script object. This method requires two parameters. The first is the value that you want to set, and the second is the zero-based index value of the item to set.

In the following example, a click of the button sets the value of the first item in Listbox1 to 25. The complete source code is available on the CD-ROM in the file setValue.asp.

```
Sub Button1_onclick()
Listbox1.setValue 25, 0
End Sub
```

show Method

Use the show method to make a Button, Checkbox, Grid, Label, Listbox, OptionGroup, RecordsetNavbar, or Textbox script object visible in the browser.

In the following sample code, checking or clearing Checkbox5 makes the recordset navigation bar (RecordsetNavbar1) appear or disappear, respectively. For the complete source code, see show.asp on the CD-ROM.

```
Sub Checkbox5_onclick()
if Checkbox5.getChecked() then
   RecordsetNavbar1.show()
else
```

```
    RecordsetNavbar1.hide()
end if
End Sub
```

startPageContent Method

The `startPageContent` method marks the beginning of text that you are passing to the `Response` object for insertion into the HTML stream. You can use this `PageObject` script object method to send (or not send) text to the browser, based on conditions such as whether the person is a registered user of the Web site.

The following code illustrates the use of the `startPageContent` method. The full source code is on the CD-ROM in the file startPageContent.asp.

```
<%
if thisPage.getmember()=true then
thisPage.startPageContent()
%>
Welcome member!</FONT></H2>
<% end if%>

<%if thisPage.getmember()=true then
thisPage.endPageContent()
end if
%>
```

unadvise Method

The `unadvise` method cancels notifications that were set by the `advise` method. The first parameter describes the event to ignore, and the second parameter is the identifier that was returned when the `advise` method was called. You can use `unadvise` with the `Button`, `Checkbox`, `Listbox`, `OptionGroup`, `PageObject`, `Recordset`, `RecordsetNavbar`, and `Textbox` script objects.

In the next snippet, the `advise` method is called in the `window_onload` event. This method starts watching for an `onblur` event that is fired from `Textbox1`. Note that `onblur` is not supported directly by the SOM. When the `onblur` event fires, the method "advises" the subroutine `Textbox2_onfocus()` of the fact so that it can spring into action. In this case, `Textbox2_onfocus()` grabs the text from the top text box and duplicates it in the bottom text box. The `unadvise` method enters the picture when the user clicks `Button1`. The `onclick` event calls `unadvise` and tells the page to stop watching for the `onblur` event that is identified by the value stored in the variable `myhandle`. As a result, new text inserted into the top text box is no longer duplicated during the `onblur` event. The complete source code is on the CD-ROM in the file unadvise.asp.

```
<SCRIPT ID=serverEventHandlersVBS LANGUAGE=vbscript>
Dim myhandle
Sub window_onload
myhandle=Textbox1.advise("onblur","Textbox2_onfocus()")
End Sub

sub Textbox2_onfocus()
Textbox2.value=Textbox1.value
end sub

Sub Button1_onclick()
Textbox1.unadvise "onblur", myhandle
End Sub

</SCRIPT>
```

Because your code is likely to be contained in subroutines, make sure that you make the variable that holds the handle for the advise event a global variable. Otherwise, your attempt to use unadvise will fail because the handle variable is private to the sub.

updateRecord Method

Use the updateRecord method to write the latest data into the current record of the Recordset script object. The recordset must be open when updateRecord is called.

In the following excerpt from updateRecord.asp, a click of Button1 updates the current record:

```
Sub Button1_onclick()
Recordset1.updateRecord
End Sub
```

Events of the Scripting Object Model

An *event* is any action that is recognized by one of the SOM objects. The most obvious events are the click of a mouse (onclick) or a change in the contents of a text box (onchange). However, the SOM includes more sophisticated events, such as one that fires just before a form is posted to the Web server (onbeforeserverevent).

This section includes all the events that are supported by the objects in the Visual InterDev 6 SOM. For each event are an explanation and a code snippet showing how it is used. On the CD-ROM, you will find a file for each event that demonstrates its function.

Keep in mind that if an event is not supported directly in the SOM, you might be able to create support for the event by using the `advise` method.

onafterupdate Event

The `onafterupdate` event of the `Recordset` script object fires after the `updateRecord` method is complete.

In the following example, the text on `Label1` changes to indicate that the `onafterupdate` event has fired. The full source code is on the CD-ROM in the file onafterupdate.asp.

```
Sub Button1_onclick()
Recordset1.updateRecord
End Sub

Sub Recordset1_onafterupdate()
Label1.setCaption "The record was updated."
End Sub
```

onbeforeopen Event

The `onbeforeopen` event fires just before the `Recordset` script object opens. This provides the opportunity to insert changes to the SQL statement (and thus the recordset contents) by using the `setSQLText` method.

For example, in the following code snippet, the first time the page appears, `Recordset1` is sorted with the newest entries first. On subsequent refreshes, the SQL statement changes the sort order to show the oldest entries first. For the complete source code, see onbeforeopen.asp on the CD-ROM.

```
Sub Recordset1_onbeforeopen()
if thisPage.firstEntered then
  Recordset1.setSQLText "select * from TimeIP
➥ORDER BY EventTime DESC"
else
  Recordset1.setSQLText "select * from TimeIP
➥ORDER BY EventTime ASC"
end if
End Sub
```

onbeforeserverevent Event

The `onbeforeserverevent` fires before a form is posted to the server. This event works only in client script and requires the `PageObject` script object.

In the following example, the `onbeforeserverevent` receives the name of the object that has initiated the server event (`mySubmit`) and the type of event (`onclick`). Using the object and event information, the script determines whether the user really wants to navigate to a new page. The complete code is on the CD-ROM in onbeforeserverevent.asp.

```
<SCRIPT ID=clientEventHandlersJS LANGUAGE=javascript>
<!--
function thisPage_onbeforeserverevent( obj, event){
  if (obj=="mySubmit"){
    if(event=="onclick"){
      if (confirm("Do you really want to go there today?")){
        alert("Okay, here we go!");
      }
      else {
        alert("Staying put!");
        thisPage.cancelEvent = true;
      }
    }
  }
}
//-->
</SCRIPT>
```

onbeforeupdate Event

The onbeforeupdate event fires before an update of the Recordset script object. This event gives you a chance to validate the data and cancel the update if something is amiss.

In the following example, a click of Button1 starts the update of the current record of Recordset1. However, before the update takes place, the onbeforeupdate event intervenes. The script checks whether the user is trying to insert a loopback IP address. If that's the case, it cancels the update of the record. The file onbeforeupdate.asp on the CD-ROM shows the onbeforeupdate event in action.

```
Sub Button1_onclick()
Recordset1.updateRecord
End Sub

Sub Recordset1_onbeforeupdate()
if left(Recordset1.fields.getValue("IPAddress"),3) = "127"
➥then
   Label1.setCaption("Oops! You cannot use the
➥loopback/localhost address.")
   Recordset1.CancelUpdate()
end if
End Sub
```

onchange Event

The onchange event fires when you change the contents or a setting in a Listbox, OptionGroup, or Textbox script object. Note that you might have to move the focus to trigger the event.

In the following excerpt from onchange.asp, a change in Listbox1 updates the text of Label1:

```
Sub Listbox1_onchange()
Label1.setCaption "Listbox1 is " & Listbox1.getText() &
➥"=" & Listbox1.getValue()
End Sub
```

onclick Event

The onclick event fires when you click a Button or Checkbox script object. In the following example from onclick.asp, a click of Button1 sets the text of Label1 to the button's name and value properties:

```
Sub Button1_onclick()
Label1.setCaption "Button1 is " & Button1.name & "=" &
➥Button1.value
End Sub
```

ondatasetchanged Event

The ondatasetchanged event fires when there's a change to a dataset or when a new dataset is requested.

In the following example, any change to the dataset (apart from the initial display) changes the text on Label1. The complete source code is in ondatasetchanged.asp on the CD-ROM.

```
Sub Recordset1_ondatasetchanged()
if thisPage.firstEntered=false then
  Label1.setCaption "There's been a change to the dataset!"
end if
End Sub
```

ondatasetcomplete Event

The ondatasetcomplete event fires when the download of the recordset from the server is complete. In the following sample code, the effect of ondatasetcomplete is most noticeable on a slow connection. The text of Label1 changes after all the data is ready on the client. The file ondatasetcomplete.htm on the CD-ROM shows the `ondatasetcom-plete` event in action.

```
function Recordset1_ondatasetcomplete() {
Label1.setCaption("All the data for Recordset1 is in.");
}
```

> **NOTE**
>
> Microsoft reports a bug that affects this event: "Error Calling Some Methods from `OnDatasetComplete`." For more information and the status of the bug, check Knowledge Base article ID Q190768.

onenter Event

The `onenter` event fires at the beginning of Active Server Pages page processing. By combining the `onenter` event with the `PageObject`'s `firstEntered` property, you can change the page content based on whether the user has seen the page before. The following code sample from onenter.asp demonstrates this technique by changing the appearance of the button:

```
Sub thisPage_onenter()
if thisPage.firstEntered=true then
  Button1.src="welcome.gif"
  Button1.setStyle 1
else
  Button1.value="Sorry, no fanfare the second time."
  Button1.setStyle 0
end if
End Sub
```

onexit Event

The `onexit` event fires when the Active Server Pages page finishes processing. This event requires the `PageObject` script object. You can use this event to call cleanup procedures or to log information to a file, as in the following example. When the page finishes processing, the script writes the date and time to a file on the `c:` drive. Check the full source code for this event on the CD-ROM in the file onexit.asp.

```
Sub thisPage_onexit()
Set fs = CreateObject("Scripting.FileSystemObject")
Set a = fs.CreateTextFile("c:\onexitfile.txt", true)
```

```
a.WriteLine("Onexit fired at " & now())
a.Close
set fs=nothing
set a=nothing
End Sub

Sub Button1_onclick()
thisPage.navigateURL "onenter.asp"
End Sub
```

onfirstclick Event

The onfirstclick event fires when you click the first (far left) button of the RecordsetNavbar script object.

In the following example, clicking the first button of RecordsetNavbar1 launches an alert box. See the CD-ROM file onfirstclick.htm for the complete source code.

```
function RecordsetNavbar1_onfirstclick() {
alert("Yes, this is the first on the left");
}
```

onlastclick Event

The onlastclick event fires when you click the last (far right) button of the RecordsetNavbar script object.

In the following example, clicking the last button of RecordsetNavbar1 launches an alert box. See the CD-ROM file onlastclick.htm for the complete source code.

```
function RecordsetNavbar1_onlastclick() {
alert("Yes, this is the last on the right.");
}
```

onnextclick Event

The onnextclick event fires when you click the second button from the right of the RecordsetNavbar script object.

In the following example, clicking the second button from the right of RecordsetNavbar1 launches an alert box. See the CD-ROM file onnextclick.htm for the complete source code.

```
function RecordsetNavbar1_onnextclick() {
alert("Yep, the Next button!");
}
```

onpreviousclick Event

The onpreviousclick event fires when you click the second button from the left of the RecordsetNavbar script object.

In the following example, clicking the second button from the left of RecordsetNavbar1 launches an alert box:

```
function RecordsetNavbar1_onpreviousclick() {
alert("Yep, the Previous button!");
}
```

For a working example of the onpreviousclick event, see the file onpreviousclick.htm on the CD-ROM.

onrowenter Event

The onrowenter event fires when the cursor moves to a record in the Recordset script object.

In the following excerpt from onrowenter.asp, each click of Button1 moves the recordset cursor. When the onrowenter event fires, the script updates the total number of onrowenter events.

```
Sub Recordset1_onrowenter()
session("rowtotal")=session("rowtotal") + 1
End Sub
Sub Button1_onclick()
Recordset1.moveFirst()
End Sub
```

onrowexit Event

The onrowexit event fires when the cursor leaves a record in the Recordset script object.

In the following example from onrowexit.asp, a click of Button1 moves the cursor to the first record. Each time the cursor leaves a record, the code tracks the total number of events.

```
Sub Recordset1_onrowexit()
session("rowextotal")=session("rowextotal") + 1
End Sub
Sub Button1_onclick()
Recordset1.moveFirst()
End Sub
```

INDEX

Other Related Titles

Programming Windows 98/NT Unleashed
0672313537
Viktor Toth
$49.99 USA /
$71.95 CAN

Charlie Calvert's Delphi 4 Unleashed
0-672-31285-9
Charlie Calvert
$49.99 USA /
$71.95 CAN

Oracle8 Server Unleashed
0-672-31207-7
Joe Greene, et al.
$49.99 USA /
$71.95 CAN

Visual C++ 5 Unleashed, Second Edition
0672310139
Viktor Toth
$49.99 USA / 0 CAN

Programming Windows NT 4 Unleashed
0-672-30905-X
Dave Hamilton and Mickey Williams
$59.99 USA /
$84.95 CAN

C++ Unleashed
0672312395
Jesse Liberty
$39.99 USA / 0 CAN

Sams Teach Yourself Visual InterDev 6 in 21 Days
0-672-31251-4
L. Michael Van Hoozer, Jr.
$34.99 USA /
$49.95 CAN

Sams Teach Yourself Database Programming with Visual C++ 6 in 21 Days
0-672-31350-2
Lyn Robison
$34.99 USA /
$49.95 CAN

Building Enterprise Solutions with Visual Studio 6
0672314894
G.A. SULLIVAN
$49.99 USA /
$71.95 CAN

Visual Basic 6 Unleashed
067231309X
ROB THAYER
$39.99 USA / 0 CAN

SAMS

www.samspublishing.com

All prices are subject to change.

Get **FREE** books and more...when you register this book online for our Personal Bookshelf Program

http://register.samspublishing.com/

SAMS

Register online and you can sign up for our *FREE Personal Bookshelf Program...*unlimited access to the electronic version of more than 200 complete computer books — immediately! That means you'll have 100,000 pages of valuable information onscreen, at your fingertips!

Plus, you can access product support, including complimentary downloads, technical support files, book-focused links, companion Web sites, author sites, and more!

And, don't miss out on the opportunity to sign up for a *FREE subscription to a weekly e-mail newsletter* to help you stay current with news, announcements, sample book chapters and special events including sweepstakes, contests, and various product giveaways.

We value your comments! Best of all, the entire registration process takes only a few minutes to complete...so go online and get the greatest value going—absolutely FREE!

Don't Miss Out On This Great Opportunity!

SAMS is a product of Macmillan Computer Publishing USA—for more information, visit: *ww.mcp.com*

What's on the CD

The companion CD-ROM contains the source code used in the book as well as the following shareware products:

- WebTools for Active Server Objects by Hunt Interactive
- Defroster by IntraActive Software Corporation
- Active Form by IntraActive Software Corporation
- SA-FileUp by Software Artisans
- RuleZero by Vertigo Software
- Font Velocity by Vertigo Software
- Mega Pack 2 by Mabry Software, Inc.
- Adventia Chat Server by Adventia
- Visual InterCept by Raleigh Group International
- Bug Trapper by Mutek Solutions
- ActiveX Component Suite by Protoview

Windows 95 Installation Instructions

1. Insert the CD-ROM disc into your CD-ROM drive.
2. From the Windows 95 desktop, double-click the My Computer icon.
3. Double-click the icon representing your CD-ROM drive.
4. Double-click the icon titled START.EXE to run the CD-ROM interface.

NOTE

If Windows 95 is installed on your computer, and you have the AutoPlay feature enabled, the START.EXE program starts automatically whenever you insert the disc into your CD-ROM drive.

Windows NT Installation Instructions

1. Insert the CD-ROM disc into your CD-ROM drive.
2. From File Manager or Program Manager, choose Run from the File menu.
3. Type *<drive>*\START.EXE and press Enter, where *<drive>* corresponds to the drive letter of your CD-ROM. For example, if your CD-ROM is drive D:, type D:\START.EXE and press Enter. This will run the CD-ROM interface.

By opening this package, you are agreeing to be bound by the following agreement:

You may not copy or redistribute the entire CD-ROM as a whole. Copying and redistribution of individual software programs on the CD-ROM is governed by terms set by individual copyright holders.

The installer and code from the author(s) are copyrighted by the publisher and the author(s).

This software is sold as-is, without warranty of any kind, either expressed or implied, including but not limited to the implied warranties of merchantability and fitness for a particular purpose. Neither the publisher nor its dealers or distributors assumes any liability for any alleged or actual damages arising from the use of this program. (Some states do not allow for the exclusion of implied warranties, so the exclusion may not apply to you.)

NOTE: This CD-ROM uses long and mixed-case filenames requiring the use of a protected-mode CD-ROM Driver.